Secretarial Office Procedures

Ninth Edition

Mary Ellen Oliverio
Formerly Professor of Education
Teachers College
Columbia University

William R. Pasewark
Professor
Texas Tech University

Published by

K33 **SOUTH-WESTERN PUBLISHING CO.**

CINCINNATI   WEST CHICAGO, ILL.   DALLAS   PELHAM MANOR, N.Y.
PALO ALTO. CALIF.   BRIGHTON, ENGLAND

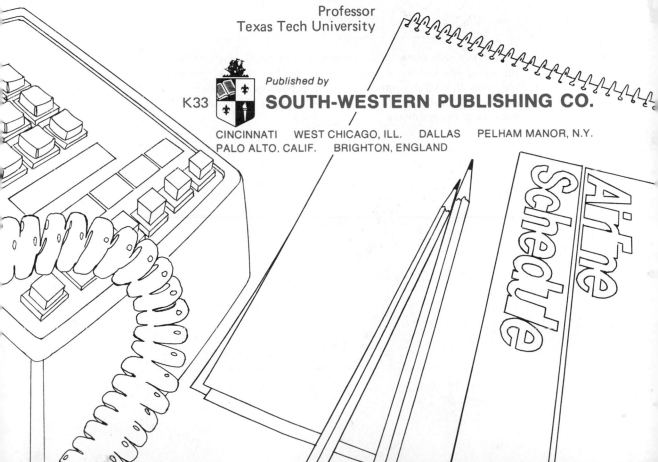

ISBN: 0-538-11330-8

Library of Congress Catalog Card Number: 76-7132

4 5 6 7 K 2 1 0

Printed in the United States of America

Preface

Office workers in today's business world need a thorough understanding of office procedures in order to accomplish their tasks with confidence and efficiency. SECRETARIAL OFFICE PROCEDURES, Ninth Edition, gives students the critical learnings necessary for the development of competencies for the office. Throughout the experience provided in this text, students use business skills acquired in earlier courses and are introduced to tasks that extend measurably their preparation for entry-level office work. Students are also given a comprehensive view of the modern office that will be valuable for progress in their careers and for further study in any field of business.

American offices are changing. The content of this Ninth Edition reflects technological changes that are gaining widespread acceptance. For example, students will become acquainted with *word processing, micrographics,* and *reprographics*. They will learn about the concern for productivity, economic use of resources, flow of work, and the interrelatedness of business functions.

The content of this edition also reflects the social changes evident in the office. These changes are the result of continuing progress in recognizing that sex, race, religion, and nationality are not relevant to the selection and promotion of personnel in today's work world. Illustrations and descriptions throughout this text reflect improving job opportunities for all Americans.

The entire textbook has been revised to aid the student in meeting these primary objectives:

1. To develop a comprehensive, realistic understanding of major responsibilities and tasks of the secretarial position.
2. To develop problem-solving skills within a framework of the varied functions in the office.
3. To develop skillful procedures for doing common office tasks with ease and assurance.
4. To develop a sensitivity to sound human relationships in the work environment.

5. To develop an awareness of career opportunities based on a foundation of secretarial skills and knowledge.
6. To develop insight for assessing one's own career goals as well as evaluating opportunities in the world of work.

The content has been updated and organized into Units that provide a combination of factual, explanatory, and realistic material to help students achieve the foregoing objectives. The Units are designed so that they may be interchanged, allowing the teacher to present them in any sequence. Additionally, there is a variety of exercises and problems at the conclusion of each Part of every Unit. Sections included are:

REVIEWING: Questions to check understanding of the content of each Part.

MAKING JUDGMENTS: Questions and problems which require decisions in realistic job situations.

WORKING WITH OTHERS: Cases that depict commonly encountered problems in human relationships in the office.

REFRESHING LANGUAGE SKILLS: Exercises that focus on points of English that are common weaknesses among beginning office workers.

PERFORMING SECRETARIAL TASKS: Activities that are typical of actual office duties and responsibilities.

IMPROVING SECRETARIAL SKILLS (Optional): Additional Projects and assignments that involve more complex secretarial tasks. (At the end of each Unit only.)

Available with SECRETARIAL OFFICE PROCEDURES, Ninth Edition, are a *Supplies Inventory* for students, a series of Simulated Office Activities (contained in the *Supplies Inventory*), and tests, one for each Unit as well as two comprehensive tests.

The *Teacher's Manual* has been extensively revised to provide more general suggestions as well as specific suggestions for teaching each Unit. New features include dictation keyed to each Unit to improve skills in taking and transcribing dictation, and transparency masters that focus on critical procedures and concepts.

This edition reflects the cooperation and assistance of many persons. We extend our appreciation to the secretarial workers, executives, teachers, and former students who graciously provided us with suggestions, insights, and information about the latest developments in equipment and procedures as well as with illustrations and examples.

Mary Ellen Oliverio
William R. Pasewark

To the Student

You are beginning a valuable educational experience in your preparation for work in today's office.

Today's office is an alive, vibrant place. Indeed, some are talking of an office revolution. The application of the latest technological advancements to business functions has resulted in a revolution in speed and effectiveness. As procedures have become more streamlined, office work has become more interesting and more challenging. Social changes are creating equal opportunities for all persons regardless of sex, race, religion, or nationality.

To help you prepare for a position in the exciting world of business, this text includes detailed instruction in office skills, specific information about office procedures, as well as explanations of critical concepts in secretarial work. You will be introduced to the usefulness of what you are studying in each Unit through case illustrations that depict realistic business situations. Then, to assure that you understand the material well, you will participate in end-of-part activities that pose questions, present cases and problems, and ask you to complete secretarial tasks. All activities are based on what actually takes place in modern offices in all types of organizations today. Finally, the Simulated Office Activities for SECRETARIAL OFFICE PROCEDURES will provide you with the opportunity to perform secretarial work in a realistic setting — specifically, as a secretary for *Travel Tours International*.

Although technology has affected the way in which the work in modern offices is done, the demand for competent secretarial workers continues. You will find that your achievement and advancement are limited only by your industriousness and your aspirations. SECRETARIAL OFFICE PROCEDURES will help you prepare for entry into the office, for further study in the field of business, and for future career opportunities.

We think you will be challenged by the tasks before you and the opportunities ahead of you.

Mary Ellen Oliverio
William R. Pasewark

Contents

The Secretary

Part 1

You and a Secretarial Position

Miss Karen Larsen has been secretary to Mr. Frederick Bolgard, personnel director of a large manufacturing company with headquarters in Chicago, for slightly more than one year. She began working as a clerk-typist when she graduated from high school four years earlier. Her first job was in a large insurance company. After about a year with the insurance company, where she had been promoted to a junior secretarial position, she was offered a job with the company for which she now works. The company is growing rapidly, because the demand for its innovative products is worldwide.

As secretary to the personnel director, Miss Larsen feels she is at the center of what is happening in the company. New developments always involve the staff, and her employer is constantly in the midst of fascinating projects. Miss Larsen maintains Mr. Bolgard's schedule, which is filled with appointments, meetings, and conferences not only in the home office, but in offices of the company throughout the United States and in twenty-five foreign countries.

Mr. Bolgard has delegated to Miss Larsen many tasks in conjunction with the home office staff. For example, Miss Larsen scans a number of professional magazines each month to note articles that are likely to be of interest to one or more of the personnel staff. Various reports involving applicants, beginning workers, and retiring workers are prepared by Miss Larsen.

Miss Larsen is a professional secretary; she has learned the work of the personnel department in relation to the total company thoroughly and accurately. She takes dictation, transcribes letters that Mr. Bolgard regularly signs without rereading, and handles all details for on-site meetings. Miss Larsen has been recommended for promotion to Administrative Assistant, and it appears that her promotion will be confirmed.

Miss Larsen is one of over fifteen million workers who are included in the United States Bureau of Census category of "clerical and kindred workers." The subcategory "secretary" indicates that approximately 3,200,000 are in it.

Job titles for many positions in the United States are not the same from one situation to another. The position of secretary is very difficult to describe accurately, because what a secretary does in one organization may differ a great deal from what a secretary does in another organization.

The National Secretaries Association defines the secretary as "an executive assistant who possesses a mastery of office skills, who demonstrates the ability to assume responsibility without direct supervision, who exercises **initiative** and judgment, and who makes decisions within the scope of assigned authority."

initiative:
ability to observe what needs to be done and do it

If you think about this definition, you realize that it does not tell you exactly what a particular secretary is likely to do. However, a key aspect of the secretarial position is clearly identified in the definition: the secretary is an executive assistant. Basically, this means that the secretary assumes responsibility for certain tasks, thus making the executive more effective. Executives, in general, establish policies, determine broad **priorities**, and specify particular courses of action. Their tasks are not manageable by themselves alone. Executives need assistants. The secretary is a key assistant.

priorities:
establishing the order for doing a given set of tasks

Illus. 1-1

The secretary is a key assistant to the executive.

Professional workers of many types need assistants. For example, nuclear physicists have research assistants; dentists have dental hygienists; doctors have medical technicians; accountants have junior accountants; and teachers have teaching assistants. In each instance, the assistants are given a variety of tasks to do. Some tasks are handled **independently**; others are directly related to immediate requests of employers. Increasingly, positions of assistance in the American work world are gaining professional status.

independently:
working alone

The Changing Secretarial Image

Until recently there was a common pattern of thinking of many positions as appropriate for men *or* women. When one thought, for example, of an engineer, nuclear physicist, accountant, or telephone repairer, many Americans thought of a man; at the same time, an elementary school teacher, nurse, librarian, or secretary was thought of as a woman.

Illus. 1-2

Today more opportunities exist for male secretaries and female managers.

Wilson Jones Company
A Division of Swingline, Inc.

However, in thinking about the **potential** of people, Americans became aware that human talent was not being developed as well as it might because of the restrictions based on sex. People began to ask, "Why can't a man be a librarian; why can't a woman be an engineer?" Today the United States is in the midst of changing attitudes. Young people in high school and college are encouraged to consider their interests without feeling restricted to particular "sex roles" in the labor market.

potential: that which can be developed

And, therefore, the secretary is no longer associated solely with the female worker. Of course, there have always been some male secretaries, but the percentage has been so small that the **predominant** impression has been that *all* secretaries were female. Today, however, more opportunities exist for male secretaries. At the same time, the executive is no longer thought of as solely male. Increasing opportunities are available for women who wish to serve in the ranks of management.

predominant: most noticeable

Such changes don't occur overnight; secretarial positions in the United States are still filled primarily by women, and most executive positions are filled by men. However, this book will reflect the changing attitude; and you will find both males and females depicted in both secretarial and executive positions.

There is an interesting historical note about the secretarial role. Did you know that there were *only* male secretaries a hundred years ago? There was a time when the office was considered "off bounds" for females. When a few women ventured forth in the 1870s to gain employment in the office, they were considered of questionable respectability. The American office remained **dominated** by male secretaries until the 1910s. Thereafter, the position of secretary became more and more associated with the female until it was for a period almost exclusively female.

dominated: controlled

The Secretary Among Office Workers

In business organizations there are typists, file clerks, clerk-typists, stenographers, secretaries, and administrative assistants. You may wonder what the differences are among all these titles. What makes a secretary a secretary and not a stenographer or a typist?

This question can be answered only *in general*, because titles are used differently from company to company. Illus. 1-3 on page 7 shows the differences in several common office positions.

As you can see, typists have a limited range of tasks. This means that they are spending most of their working day at the typewriter. However, the typing that is done may vary considerably each day. For example, on one day a group of typists in a large office in Chicago typed form letters, rough drafts of manuscripts, stencils, statistical tables, and forms. The stenographer's tasks are more varied than those of a typist but not as varied as those of a secretary. Stenographers generally work for a number of executives and spend much of their day taking dictation and transcribing it. Along with these principal duties they may handle telephone calls and maintain records.

Beginning Office Workers

Beginning office workers are generally assigned to positions where the tasks are not highly varied, so that you will find beginners holding positions as typists, file clerks, clerk-typists, and stenographers. All these positions require skills. Beginners are not expected to understand the functions of the company in which they find employment. Their first positions provide a means for them to gain understanding of the work of the company and thus become qualified for higher level positions. In any job where you handle some part of the paper work of the organization, you can learn much about the company that will aid you in developing the understanding necessary to assume more responsibility.

The Secretary

The secretary is seldom a beginning worker. Usually the secretary has had a more limited position in the company. From time to time, however, a secretary who has experience with another company is employed. With job experience in another company, a secretary will learn about the new company in very little time. A secretary does, at one time or another, all the tasks that typists, file clerks, clerk-typists, and stenographers do; but there are other responsibilities. A secretary works for one executive and sometimes for two. An executive expects a secretary to take messages by telephone and to place calls, to compose some letters, to do research and prepare materials for reports, and to act as a representative in dealing with the public and the staff in the company. Secretaries make appointments, prepare travel schedules, keep office files, and in-

forthcoming: form their employers of **forthcoming** conferences and appointments.
approaching

Promotions

Many companies follow the policy of promoting from within the company when they are filling secretarial positions. A personnel manager commented:

OFFICE POSITIONS		
Position	Primary Requirements	Primary Tasks
Typist	Typewriting, basic office procedures	Typing letters, filling in forms
File Clerk	Knowledge of filing, typewriting	Filing materials, finding materials, typing, rearranging files
Clerk—Typist	Typewriting, knowledge of filing, skill in use of calculating machines, basic office procedures	Typing, maintaining records, computing, handling mail
Stenographer	Stenography, typewriting, basic office procedures	Taking dictation, transcribing
Secretary	Stenography, typewriting, knowledge of work of office and company, human relations skills, knowledge of files, systems of work	Handling correspondence, including taking dictation and transcribing; managing paper work; handling telephone and callers; handling some tasks independently.
Administrative Assistant	Thorough knowledge of work of office and company, high level office skills, knowledge of office management, human relations skills	Organizing work of the office and carrying through with little direction, supervising other office workers, establishing priorities

Illus. 1-3

Secretaries are important persons in our company. To be effective in their jobs, they must not only know the office in which they work, but they must also understand the purpose of our total organization. We find that some of those who have stayed with our company have become familiar with our business. We want to take advantage of what they have learned, so that when we need to fill a vacancy in a secretarial position, we look to our office staff to discover who has good office skills and has developed an understanding of our company's business. One of these will be appointed to the secretarial job.

Through your study of secretarial office procedures you will become familiar with the wide range of tasks that secretaries perform.

Basic Skills of the Secretary

A study of secretarial workers includes the finding that there are almost nine hundred different duties carried out by secretaries! It would be a long discussion if we were to include all of these. Some, as you already know, are more important than others. Among the basic skills are those discussed in the following paragraphs.

Taking Dictation and Transcribing

The twin skills of taking dictation and transcribing are important communication responsibilities. Executives value the skill of secretaries who can take their messages quickly and accurately and prepare transcripts that need only signatures. Secretaries know how to use dictating-transcribing equipment, and they know the word processing services available in their companies.

Typewriting

While secretaries do not sit at their typewriters all day as typists do, they make use of typewriting skill frequently. What kinds of jobs do secretaries type? Let's list some of the tasks of a group of secretaries on just one day: A secretary to the public relations director of a chemical company typed a news release concerning a new product; a secretary to the editor of a monthly magazine typed a rough draft of an editorial which the editor had written out; a secretary to a university professor of history typed stencils of a new reading list for a course; a secretary to a lawyer typed a contract; a secretary to a doctor typed a case history.

Handling Communications

Many executives think of their offices as the center of a network of communications, and the secretary plays a key role in maintaining this network effectively. Secretaries answer the telephone, talk with visitors, and write memorandums and letters on their own. All these tasks require skill in the use of both oral and written English. Secretaries who score high in handling communications have these important skills:

1. Ability to spell, including the checking of words in a dictionary when in doubt.
2. Ability to meet people and talk with them pleasantly and with a command of the English language.
3. Ability to write briefly and to the point.
4. Ability to understand the meaning of messages.

An executive, talking about a secretary, said:

> I am always getting compliments about the manner in which Miss Almy handles telephone calls and visitors. Our customers remark about her poise, her excellent use of language, and the quickness with which she grasps the message and follows through with an answer. After struggling with a secretary who never understood messages and who left them on my desk in meaningless form, you can understand my enthusiasm for Miss Almy. She keeps communications flowing smoothly and pleasantly.

Illus. 1-4

Answering the telephone is an important duty of the secretary.

Bearings, Inc.

Operating Calculating Machines

There are many machines in the modern office that make tasks easier. For example, electronic calculators simplify computational tasks. Betty, a secretary to an architect, finds the electronic calculator an aid when she is determining the total cost of a new project from notes which her employer provides her. Lynn uses an adding machine to check the figures on invoices in a central buying office of a chain of department stores. Using calculating machines properly and fully can cut off minutes from many tasks.

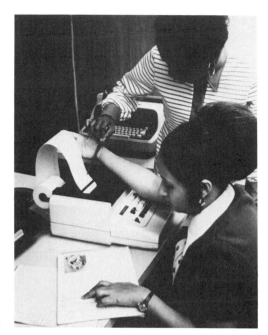

Illus. 1-5

Using a calculator to verify and check figures simplifies the work of a secretary.

Xerox

Copying and Duplicating

multiple:
more than one

Secretaries are often given tasks that require making **multiple** copies. They need to know the advantages of each of the methods available to them and the cost of each method. Modern businesses often have equipment for making copies directly as well as for reproducing copies from various kinds of masters and stencils.

Maintaining Records

Well-organized records and an orderly procedure for using them indicate an efficient secretary. Frequently a secretary is called on for information that is needed immediately. Linda, a secretary to a physician who is frequently invited to address meetings in all parts of the world, comments:

> I have to be able to find needed materials immediately, for it is not uncommon for Dr. Barnes to be on the telephone talking with a doctor in Stockholm when she will call me and say, "What is the title of the talk I am giving in London in late May?" And, as you would guess, I have to be able to put my hand on the file with the details of the London visit in seconds!

Secretaries are expected to maintain their records and to keep track of those that are removed temporarily. Unfiled stacks of material are a sign of poor attention to this important office task.

Handling Travel Arrangements

Most executives spend much time traveling, and their secretaries must become skillful travel agents if trips are to be well planned. Secretaries need to know the preferences of their employers when traveling and the travel possibilities. Making arrangements also requires a thorough understanding of the executive's schedule.

When all the details for a trip have been worked out, the secretary is expected to prepare an itinerary. An *itinerary* is an outline of the trip which includes the date and the exact time of departure and arrival for each part of the trip, the means of transportation to be used, the accommodations for which reservations have been made, appointments to be kept, and any other details that provide a full account of the trip.

Illus. 1-6

When all the details of a trip have been worked out, the secretary prepares an itinerary.

Preparation

Now that you have an overview of some of the key responsibilities of secretaries, you may be asking yourself: How do I prepare to enter such a professional position? There are three steps in the process of becoming a fully prepared secretary:

1. Acquire the basic skills and develop them so that you can use them in a wide variety of situations. Also, acquire a general understanding of the business world as well as procedures common in offices. Courses in high schools, business colleges,

community colleges, and four-year colleges are possibly the most valuable sources for this basic preparation.

2. As soon as you begin to work, even in a part-time position, study the tasks you handle in relation to the total work of the company. No matter what the nature of the work is, there are opportunities to gain further **insight** into the way businesses function.

3. Develop the attitude of the professional worker — that is, maintain a continuing interest in what you do and how you do it. Learn to evaluate what you do; set high standards for your own performance. Be generous and cooperative as you work with others in volunteer activities as well as in those for which you receive payment.

insight:
understanding

Rewards

When secretaries are asked about the rewards of their positions, their comments reflect varying sources of satisfaction.

Varied Opportunities

Persons with secretarial skills are employed in a wide variety of organizations, both public and private. They work in giant companies and in small professional offices; they are located in the great metropolitan centers of the world and in the small towns and suburban centers; they are employed by organizations involved with automobiles, steel, rubber, chemicals, paper, glass, stocks, farm equipment, finance, communications, banks, education, and law.

In spite of the development of more and more office technology, the work of the office still requires the secretarial employee. Projections of labor demands continue to show a steady, **persistent** need for secretarial workers, as well as general office workers.

persistent:
continuing without
letup

One young woman took advantage of the varied opportunities. Here is part of her own story:

> I love travel, new places — and I knew this when I was very young. As a high school student I studied secretarial courses which I found very interesting; I've also always loved music, so I majored in music in college. Then I went to New York City where I worked in the office of a music book company and spent my free time listening to music all over the city and doing some practicing myself. Then I moved to London, where I found a job immediately with a television company. I got acquainted with Covent Gardens and the fine music there. After two years, I thought I should get acquainted with Italy, so here I am in Milan where I work as a secretary to a producer and go to the opera at La Scala and Piccola Scala as often as possible!

Interesting Work

Rosanna works for the program director of a national television company. She comments:

> This office is exciting; we are always in the midst of creative, intense effort to design programs that Americans will find a pleasure to watch. My employer searches the world — really — for ideas. I like being in the midst of such activity.

Eliza is secretary to the director of an institute in molecular biology. She states:

> Some of the most important research in the basic behavior of cells is taking place here in our institute. Just think, this staff may find the causes of mysterious diseases. My work is never dull; I find it really fascinating.

Bob is secretary to the director of a major government department that is responsible for agricultural research in the United States. He says:

> My employer is involved in very important work. Our ability to provide all the food we need in our own country, as well as helping developing countries feed their increasing populations, depends to a great extent on the agricultural research underway now in various parts of the country. Since I grew up on a farm, I find this job very, very interesting and worthwhile.

Economic Returns

Salaries and an **array** of fringe benefits are provided secretaries. Salaries are competitive; that is, they are sufficiently attractive to encourage well-qualified persons to apply for such jobs. Salaries vary somewhat across the United States, but beginners can expect reasonable salaries that are based on their skills and their potential contributions. In most companies, there is a **systematic** evaluation of office workers for the purpose of determining salary **increments** and promotions.

array:
range

systematic:
organized, regular

increments:
increases

Working Conditions

Most offices are attractive places with modern furniture and tastefully designed decorations. In fact, secretaries find their offices pleasant places in which to work. Offices are often air-conditioned and scientifically lighted so that fatigue is minimized.

Secretaries tend to work approximately 35 hours a week, five days a week. Almost all firms pay secretaries for any overtime that they must

Illus. 1-7

Secretaries have attractive and pleasant working areas.

Colle & McVoy

work, and paid vacations are a standard fringe benefit for most workers who have been on their jobs for a minimum of six months.

REVIEWING

1. What do you believe are the primary differences between the position of stenographer and that of secretary?
2. In general, what are the responsibilities of the persons for whom secretaries work?
3. Are only female secretaries found in the modern office? Discuss.
4. Why is there concern that jobs in the American society be considered open to both male and female applicants?
5. What does a policy of promotion from within mean?
6. Identify four basic skills that secretaries should possess.
7. How would you describe the *professional attitude*?
8. Where can you acquire the skills and understandings needed for secretarial positions?
9. Where are secretaries needed in the modern society?
10. What do secretaries consider to be rewards of their work?

MAKING JUDGMENTS

1. Harriet has completed her junior year of high school and wants to work during the summer. She has taken several business courses, including typewriting and shorthand, and she felt that she could handle a secretarial assignment. She talked with the personnel director of a company in her home town and was offered a job as a clerk-typist for the summer. She declined, because she felt she was prepared to do a "higher level job." What do you think of Harriet's judgment?

2. Elena was an intelligent young woman who thought she would like very much to be a secretary to a top executive in an exciting organization. She studied a number of general business courses and found them interesting. She took typewriting and shorthand, but felt these were routine skills which would not be too valuable in a secretarial position. She thought that as a secretary, she would have a typist and stenographer assigned to her, and these two could handle the routines of typewriting and dictation. She would be free to organize the office, talk with visitors, arrange for conferences, plan trips, and do the tasks that she believed were central to the secretarial assignment. What do you think of Elena's idea of the secretarial position?

WORKING WITH OTHERS

Terri is a conscientious office worker. Her first job after graduation from high school was as a clerk-typist in a local company. After working in this job for about three months, the head of the department, Ms. Garcia, asked her to assume a secretarial assignment temporarily. One of the secretaries had been granted a leave of absence of three months to go with her husband on assignment to Lima, Peru. Although Terri didn't feel she was qualified to handle a secretarial job, she decided she would try it for such a short time.

Shortly before the secretary on leave was to return, Ms. Garcia talked with Terri. Mr. Vincent, the executive for whom Terri had been working, liked the manner in which Terri did her job and wanted her to stay in the position. He felt that the secretary on leave could be assigned to another office. Ms. Garcia told Terri that there were several openings from which the secretary on leave could choose where she would work. She also told Terri that when a person took a leave of absence, there was never assurance that the person would return to the position left. There was just the assurance that a job of the same rank and salary would be available.

What do you think Terri should do?

REFRESHING LANGUAGE SKILLS

A noun is: Examples:

a name of a person   Joseph, Ruth, Basil
                                            waiter, executive, typist
a name of a place   Lima, Caribbean Sea, Times
                                            Square
                                            town, village, street
a name of a thing   eraser, cabinet, desk, pic-
                                            ture
a name of a condition, state, or relation   initiative, democracy,
                                            alertness, responsibility

Type or write the sentences below, underscoring all the nouns.

Example: The <u>analysis</u> of all the <u>tables</u> will take at least one <u>month</u>.

1. The bank will consider the proposal of the citizens' committee, but there is no assurance that the response will be positive.
2. The secretary knows the references that are most helpful.
3. The details of the itinerary must be resolved before Mr. Healler returns to the office.
4. You will find all the postal regulations in the mailroom.
5. The executives want to improve communications with the public.
6. Secretarial procedures have application in many types of work.
7. The orientation for new workers is carefully planned.
8. The modern office is a comfortable, attractive environment.
9. Office workers are evaluated for promotions every six months.
10. Typewriting and shorthand are considered basic skills for the secretary.

PERFORMING SECRETARIAL TASKS

1. For one of the following topics type on plain paper a brief summary in which you express your own opinion on:
   a. The general nature of the secretarial position.
   b. The beginning jobs in business that are good preparation for an aspiring secretary.
   c. The preparation that is appropriate for a secretary.
2. In this Part you were introduced to the seven key tasks that you are likely to find in a secretarial position. You will have much opportunity during this course to develop skills and understandings in relation to these tasks. It is likely, though, that you already have some skills and understandings.

   Prepare an outline with the key tasks as major headings. Under each task list the skills and understandings you have at this point; then list the skills and understandings you hope to develop during the year. Type the outline on plain paper.

Part 2
Qualities for Job Success

Miss Denise Burns is secretary to Mr. William Kelly, a busy vice-president in one of the largest local banks. Mr. Kelly believes he could not handle the work of his office if he didn't have the cooperation of Miss Burns. Mr. Kelly is often away at meetings in various parts of the state. During such times, the work of the office must continue. He knows that Miss Burns will not only handle all the situations that arise, but that she will also work conscientiously and carefully. She is dependable and responsible. Mr. Kelly is grateful for such a fine secretary. Miss Burns says that it is very pleasant to work for someone who appreciates what she is endeavoring to do.

If you were to enter a roomful of secretaries and talk with them, you would soon realize that not all secretaries are alike! You would find that some are friendly, others are reserved. You would see some who are poised, others less so. You would notice that some are self-confident, others are shy and seemingly lack self-confidence. You would find that you could not describe the typical "secretarial personality." Secretaries are not alike. Of course, we would come to the same conclusion if we were with a group of scientists, baseball players, or television stars! Therefore, we must not simplify secretarial **traits** by talking about the "secretarial personality." However, studies have been made that have tried to identify secretarial traits that are prized by employers and fellow workers. Yet, even here it is not possible to identify traits that assure success and others that hasten failure. There are merely hunches about what appears to be valuable in achieving success. Some of the commonly identified traits will be discussed in this Part.

traits: characteristics

Personal Qualities

Business executives like their activities to be orderly and systematic. With a goal of efficiency, organizations choose office workers who reflect

Illus. 1-8

A secretary with a pleasant appearance and efficient manner will project a favorable image of the organization.

Courtesy of American Telephone & Telegraph

orderliness. The personal appearance of secretaries is, therefore, of concern to a company.

Personal Care

An attractive appearance begins with perfect personal care, and the secretary has to learn that attention to basic grooming needs can never be neglected. Some rules that should never be broken are:

1. Take a bath or shower at least once each day.
2. Use an antiperspirant or deodorant daily.
3. Brush your teeth at least twice each day.
4. Clean and wash your face thoroughly twice each day.
5. Manicure your nails regularly.
6. Wash your hair regularly.

Appropriate Appearance

Young men and women entering the business office will find that there are varying opinions about what is considered appropriate appearance. The office of today is far less formal than was the office of several decades ago. In an earlier period, there was general agreement on what were the right clothing and hairstyles for the office worker. Although proper appearance is not as definite now, young office workers must develop an awareness of what is appropriate for the offices in which they choose to work. In some companies there are recommendations for clothing and hairstyles; in others, there is an **assumption** that new workers will make good judgments on their own as to what is expected of them.

The nature of the organization for which you work will give you some guidance as to what is appropriate. Furthermore, if you observe people at work, noticing those who seem most attractively dressed for their work, you will develop some basis for making decisions about what you should wear.

Generally the clothing that the people of your community choose for going to work in business offices will be comfortable, but not as casual as the clothing chosen for leisure hours or vacation time or for doing chores at home. Clothes that call exaggerated attention to oneself are inappropriate for the office. One personnel assistant who interviews many beginning office workers commented:

> While we certainly don't expect our office workers to wear a uniform, we do care about how they look. They are meeting customers as well as the general public, and we think the office workers should present a neat, orderly, yet attractive appearance. I notice what young people wear when they come to the office for interviews. I expect to see them well groomed and in the type of clothing they could wear for an ordinary working day. If a young man comes in wearing sandals and open shirt, or a young woman appears wearing a peasant dress and shoes that are difficult to keep on her feet, for example, I gain the impression that they don't understand well the demands of the modern office. Such applicants are not likely to get a good rating.

Health

Respect for oneself begins with attention to basic health needs. Sufficient sleep, proper foods, and a reasonable amount of exercise are *absolutely* necessary if you are to be healthy.

Proper food provides the nutrients needed to maintain a healthy body with all the energy that you demand for the many activities in which you participate. While nutrition experts tell us about the importance of a good breakfast, many people fail to heed the advice. You should begin the day with a good breakfast which you eat in an unhurried fashion. Properly selected foods for lunch and dinner deserve attention, too.

To function well the body requires exercise. Plan your leisure hours to include activities that provide relaxation and a chance to use muscles that get little use in your regular work. Walking, bicycling, and sports, such as tennis, bowling, and swimming, will help you keep your body in fine form.

Although Charles enjoys his office work very much, he knows that to be in good form he must get some outdoor exercise regularly. He swims and plays a great deal of tennis during the summer and skis and ice skates during the winter months in the northern city where he works.

Christine lives and works in the center of a large city where it would be very easy to forego all kinds of physical activity. However, she plans her week carefully to include some type of relaxing activity. She rides her bicycle in the city parks, she plays tennis at the public courts, and as long as there is pleasant weather, she and friends frequently take a bus to a mountain community where they take hikes and ride horses.

Illus. 1-9

A secretary with poise and good posture conveys emotional stability and self-confidence.

Posture and Poise

An outstanding feature of a successful actor, actress, or model is posture and poise — the gracefulness of movements and the sense of well-being reflected. You, too, can develop such gracefulness and ease of movement by paying attention to your behavior. Are you aware of how you walk? Of how you sit? Of how you move across a room? Take time to be conscious of your movements and of your responses to people.

While posture is a significant part of conveying a sense of poise, there is more to the concept of *poise*. Poise is difficult to define. One definition is that it is the ability to remain gracious under all circumstances. The dictionary gives several definitions for this term. The one that is most appropriate for our discussion is "balance, equilibrium, stability." When we say that a person is poised we usually have observed that the person seems to know how to behave appropriately in a situation. A poised person maintains a sense of balance. Now we mean "sense of balance" in more than a physical sense. It is true that a person who drops and breaks a cup and saucer when extending a hand for a handshake would appear unusually awkward and not poised. But beyond the physical awkwardness there likely may be communicated a sense of emotional awkwardness — the person was not quite able to cope with the prospect of being introduced to someone. An employer discussed a young woman who failed to win a promotion by saying:

> Patricia is a valuable worker. Her skills are excellent; she is one of the best workers in the word processing center. When I was looking for a secretary, I interviewed Patricia. Then I realized that Patricia is far too shy, too uncomfortable in talking with others, to be effective in my office. She likes her quiet corner in the Center. I've talked with the Center supervisor, who will talk with Patricia. We think she should try to overcome her shyness; she should develop this aspect of her personality. Then, if she continues to want to stay where she is, that's fine; we just don't think she should stay because of a deficiency that a young woman with her talent should be able to overcome.

conveying: expressing

Voice and Language Usage

The quality of your voice and the skill with which you use language are important in a secretarial position. A pleasant, clear voice is attractive. A loud, demanding voice is unattractive; a very low, retiring voice makes communication difficult.

Secretaries should use a vocabulary that demonstrates wise and precise use of the language. The slang expressions of teenage talk sessions are out of place in the modern business office. "Isn't this groovy?" is just not the most appropriate reaction to a personnel bulletin announcing a new fringe benefit for all office workers!

General Work Qualities

To be an asset to the company a secretary must possess some general work qualities.

Cooperation

Secretaries work with others. In some instances they work closely with one executive; in other instances they work with several executives as well as with a number of other office workers. To be effective co-workers, secretaries must be aware of the needs of others and be willing to provide information and assistance when they are needed. Good secretaries enjoy helping others and maintaining an awareness of where help is needed throughout the day.

Involvement

Have you ever heard the comment, "He couldn't do a good job because his heart wasn't in it"? Do you know what this statement means? Good secretaries know what it means. They know that much of their success depends on their being fully involved in the work of the company. Their interest in what is going on is genuine and lasts through easy days as well as demanding days. The secretary to a dedicated executive commented:

> I'm so involved in this job I never know what time it is; I would hate to be a clock watcher. Mr. McMann is a very creative director of this quasi-public agency; you never know what his next project will be, except that you know it will be something that no one has tried previously. He has to convince men and women, and so there are always meetings here. These meetings are frequently after regular hours, and we always have refreshments. We have lovely, convenient facilities for meetings and good assistance from a local caterer, so I am able to organize everything easily. I always stay for evening meetings, because I want to be sure everything goes as planned — and, I must confess, I find the meetings fascinating as well as informative. The next day's dictation has more meaning.

significance: meaning

This secretary has captured the **significance** of behaving professionally and has gained much joy and satisfaction from the work.

You will want to think about the type of environment in which you will be able to become fully involved in your work. Do you like a busy, active place where you must give attention to several matters at the same time and must be able to meet deadlines that arise regularly? Or would you prefer to be in a carefully organized, smoothly functioning office where all that must be done is known long ahead of time and can be scheduled so that there are no last-minute rushes? Do you prefer to work with others in cooperative activity? Or would you rather have a set of tasks that are only slightly related to the work of others so that you can work alone? There are many variations in offices; you will want to get to know yourself so that you can make a wise choice.

Orderliness and Neatness

It is not clear if people are born orderly or if they acquire the trait in school. We do observe differences in the way in which people keep their notebooks, their desks, and their personal possessions. Regardless of the origin of an orderly nature, to be successful, secretaries *must be* orderly. **Chaos** develops quickly if a secretary just shoves papers in the desk drawers or lets them pile up on file cabinets. A work station must be well organized to avoid wasting time in finding room to work and in locating the supplies needed.

chaos:
great confusion

Neatness is indeed a companion trait to orderliness. Possibly, there is no more important illustration of the need for neatness than in your handwriting. A neat handwriting is clear and legible. Such a handwriting means that notes left for others in the office will be read with ease. As a secretary you will have many occasions to write messages, record figures, and fill in forms.

Illus. 1-10

Clear, legible handwriting is necessary for readable records.

Did you ever receive a note you could not read? Have you ever had difficulty reading your own handwriting? Then you can imagine how aggravating poor handwriting is to an employer, especially when a mistake in a figure or date, or the **illegibility** of a name or number, can mean a loss of time, money, and goodwill.

illegibility:
unreadability

In many cases your writing speed has an influence upon the quality of your writing. If you write at too fast a rate, your letters and numbers will be carelessly formed; and, if you write too slowly, the lines will waver. If you write with excessive speed, it will affect the exactness, alignment, and evenness of your strokes. Remember, if you are writing longhand, write it to be read. Keep your writing speed at the rate at which you can write letters and numbers that are readable.

Like all other skills, good handwriting cannot be retained long without conscientious practice. At one time you probably had training in penmanship, but you may have become careless and lost some of this valuable business skill. If you are to keep readable records, you must have clear, legible handwriting.

Orderliness and neatness reflect your caring about the details of your work and your consideration of others who work with you.

Trustworthiness

Executives frequently comment on their appreciation of a secretary whom they can trust. When one executive was asked to describe the behavior of a secretary who is trustworthy, she said:

> My present secretary is a perfect model. I can depend on her to continue to work when I am out of town or at a conference. She is careful about being on time regardless of my schedule. In other words, she doesn't need to be "checked in" each morning or at lunch time in order to be on time.
>
> I like a secretary I can trust, because otherwise I must do so much checking that the effectiveness of the work of our office is undermined. My work involves being away for a full day or often for a week. I never have to give any thought to what is happening back in my office. I know the secretary is arriving on time and is following through with all tasks that must be completed. I never have to ask when I get back if certain tasks have been done. I find my desk organized, and there is always a listing of what I had asked to be done with each item accounted for.

A secretary that an executive can trust adds many hours to the time that can be devoted to other jobs. The employer who has to check on the secretary isn't getting real work from that secretary. If the checking-up time is subtracted from the time spent on the job, the secretary's contribution to the work load may be very small.

Secretaries are in positions of confidence. They perform tasks involving highly confidential information about what is going on in an organization. They know about new developments before they become public announcements. To reveal such developments can seriously change the position of a company in relation to the public or in relation to competitive firms. You will need to cultivate the attitude that the business of your employer is not to be communicated to *anyone*.

Initiative

Anticipating what needs to be done is a valuable trait. Being able to take action on one's own increases the helpfulness of a secretary. Initiative, which is the ability to identify accurately what needs to be done and then follow through with the correct action, is a key characteristic of good secretaries. Most executives are grateful to secretaries who show initative in their jobs. One executive said:

anticipating:
looking forward to

> Mrs. Fenner makes my work so very, very easy, for she knows so well what must be done that I never need to spend time explaining details to her. When I dictate a letter inviting several people to our company for a meeting, she, without a word from me, will arrange for the conference room, coffee, and the materials necessary for the sessions.
>
> A secretary without initative needs such detailed directions for each day's work that I would find it difficult to do what I must get done. In fact, I would not tolerate for more than a brief period a secretary without this trait; that may sound harsh, but my style of work demands a self-motivated secretary.

Loyalty

To be *loyal* means that you are faithful to your employer. To be loyal implies that the secretary is *genuinely* helpful and concerned and has not merely learned how to *act* in the presence of the employer. Rather, the secretary can continue to be faithful when the employer is away. When talking with others, the loyal secretary has no wish to engage in office gossip.

The Environment In Which You Work

A secretary's conduct is influenced by the behavior exhibited in the work surroundings. Human beings are responsive to their environments and often encounter difficulty in living up to the standards that they have set for themselves. The qualities that have been described in this part are those that are desirable in workers. Actually many workers, including executives, secretaries, and other office personnel, do not measure up to the highest score on each of the desired traits or characteristics. Nonetheless, many people strive to improve the quality of their behavior. You must respect the efforts of those around you to improve their behavior in much the same fashion that you want others to respect your efforts.

You, as a future secretary, want to develop your own ideas of the kind of person you wish to become. Become aware of your own conduct and judge it against your own standards. Environments differ. In some it will be easy to measure up, while in others you will have to think through carefully what you should do. Each environment will offer some challenge to you to grow into a more mature personality. Sandra described a situation in this fashion:

> When I first met Mr. Langston, I wondered if I could work for him for more than a day. He seemed in such a hurry, and he gave me instructions for five different jobs at the same moment. There was no preliminary discussion of the general routine of the office. My reaction was: Here is a truly thoughtless man! That day was about six months ago! I must confess that the first two days were hectic — and I made a few mistakes. However, I soon realized that Mr. Langston was seriously interested in the company and in doing his job well. He gives his full attention to his work. He assumes that a secretary is *just* as interested as he is. I began to feel more confident. Then I realized that I liked his attitude toward a secretary, and I have grown to have respect for Mr. Langston. I find it very easy to be loyal to him and to do my work in a fully professional manner.

Illus. 1-11

Your success in the business world depends upon your goals and your desire to succeed.

Pitney-Bowes, Inc.

Whether or not you become a good secretary depends a good deal upon yourself. Your goals reflect your assessment of yourself and your own desire to succeed. As you are introduced to the responsibilities of secretarial work, you will not only want to assess your technical skills in handling such work, but you will also want to think about the personal qualities that are closely related to doing the work in a professional manner.

REVIEWING

1. Is there just one "secretarial personality?" Discuss.
2. What are some basic rules for good personal care?
3. How would you determine what is appropriate clothing for the office in which you find employment?
4. What factors must you consider as you endeavor to maintain good health?
5. How would you describe a person with poise?
6. Describe briefly some characteristics of a person without poise.
7. Why is cooperation considered important in the office?
8. Why is involvement considered important for a secretary?
9. How does a trustworthy person behave in the office?
10. How may a secretary demonstrate initiative in the office?

MAKING JUDGMENTS

1. Bette feels that all the attention to good health habits doesn't apply to her, because she feels she should live as she wants to live. She loves sweets, as she says, and she can't help it that she is considered overweight by her family and her close friends who try to tell her the truth! She thinks sports are too strenuous; she much prefers to watch television or "just sit" on the terrace when she arrives home after a day's work. What do you think of Bette's judgment?
2. Bob wants to work in an office, but hopes he will be able to get a job where not too much is expected of him. He doesn't want to get too involved in his work. He thinks if he works hard all day, he will be too tired to enjoy his leisure hours. Bob thinks life is primarily to be enjoyed, and he doesn't see how there could be much enjoyment in working all day. What are your reactions to Bob's thoughts?

WORKING WITH OTHERS

Nancy attended a liberal high school where she was able to dress as she liked. When she applied for an office job, she dressed as her secretarial studies teacher suggested one should dress for an interview. However, while Nancy talked with the personnel interviewer, she asked: "Is it necessary for me to dress as I am now dressed to work in your company? Would you mind, really, how I dress for work?"

What do you think the interviewer said to Nancy? What do you think of Nancy's question?

REFRESHING LANGUAGE SKILLS

Pronouns are words that serve as substitutes for nouns. They must agree with their antecedents (nouns for which they stand) in person, number, and gender.

> **Example:** The typewriter *that* Sally is currently using was lent to *her* by Tom in the accounting office because *he* doesn't need *it* for a week or more. (*typewriter* is the antecedent of *that*; *Sally* of *her*; *Tom* of *he*; and *typewriter* of *it*)

Type or write the following sentences, indicating the correct pronouns.

1. The filing cabinet (who, that) is against the left wall is full of inactive correspondence and (it, they) should be transferred.
2. Neither Jack nor Jim feels that (his, their) project is ready for discussion at this time.
3. (They, them), along with a group from another company, will be attending the seminar in Chicago.
4. All office workers need dictionaries available to (them, they).
5. The committee has promised to have (its, their) findings ready for review early next week.
6. Integrity is a quality that employers evaluate when interviewing candidates for positions in (its, their) company.
7. The secretary, as well as the stenographers, was uncertain as to what (she, they) should do at such a moment.
8. The group wants (its, their) decision announced at the opening session this morning at eleven.
9. The calculator (who, that) Mary is using was taken from Mina's office.
10. Alice and Marie finished (her, their) work early.

PERFORMING SECRETARIAL TASKS

1. Write or type a brief paragraph indicating how important each of the personal qualities discussed in this Part are for you and your fellow students as you prepare to enter the business world.
2. Imagine that you are responsible for observing beginning office workers in an organization that evaluates workers every six months.

What would you expect to observe in order to give a particular worker a "high score" on each of these factors:

a. Cooperation
b. Involvement
c. Orderliness
d. Trustworthiness
e. Initiative
f. Loyalty

You may want to respond in outline form, recording very specific, concrete observations (even though, at this point, such observations are merely imaginative).

3. Assume that you have the task of recording the following messages from telephone conversations. Use the forms in the *Supplies Inventory* if available. If forms are not available, use separate sheets of paper for each message. After you have written the three messages, reread them noticing the clarity of your handwriting. If you think your handwriting is not easy to read, rewrite the three messages.

Message 1:   To: T. W. Groves   9:30 a.m.
          From: Clifton Travel Services
          Flights on Thursday to Chicago:
          TWA 356, leaves Pittsburgh 11:15;
                      arrives Chicago 11:30
          Am 41   leaves Pittsburgh 12:10;
                      arrives Chicago 12:25
          Bra 643 leaves Pittsburgh 12:30;
                      arrives Chicago 12:45

Message 2:   To: T. W. Groves   11:15 a.m.
          From: W. E. Stone
          Disbursements through August 31:

Wages and Fees	$5,645.20
Computer Services	889.90
Supplies	231.00
Travel	347.75

Message 3:   To: T. W. Groves   11:30 a.m.
          From: L. W. Garlock of Stinson 651-4322
          The following prospective members should be invited to the meeting next week:
               Ms. Lynn Sterns
               1571 Castle Drive
               Penn Hills, PA 15235

               Mr. Wallace Howells
               561 Burton Road
               Churchill, PA 15235

3
General Responsibilities

Yvonne found herself thinking early one morning about the basic difference between her present position and her first position in the company. For one month she has been secretary to Mrs. T. R. Quinn, one of the vice-presidents. Three years earlier she was a clerk-typist, which was her first position after graduation from high school. She realized that possibly the most important difference between her present job and her first job is that she now has some responsibilities that are actually her own; Mrs. Quinn delegated these to her and now pays no further attention to them. In her first job she had a supervisor who gave her specific tasks to do and checked these tasks when they were finished. She now has considerable independence, for example, in organizing her office, in establishing work priorities, and in identifying what the office needs in order to function more efficiently.

Organizing and Maintaining the Work Station

Organizing the office and maintaining supplies and equipment are important responsibilities of the secretary.

The Work Station

work station:
place assigned for doing tasks

The secretary has general responsibility for maintaining the **work station** in good working order. Work stations for secretaries differ from company to company, but usually effort is made to provide both a comfortable and efficient work station. In some offices care is taken to furnish offices in a manner that is **aesthetically** attractive as well as **functionally** appropriate. In some organizations secretaries have private offices; in others, they have partially partitioned work stations; and in still others they work in reception areas.

aesthetically:
artistically

functionally:
suited for the tasks to be done

As a secretary, you should carefully look at your work station to determine if it is adequate. There may be minor **modifications** that you yourself might make that would allow you to work more efficiently. One new secretary commented about her office in these words:

modifications:
changes

> When I was shown my new office, I felt very fortunate. The office was attractive with coordinated furniture and file cabinets, the lighting was good, and the chair was very comfortable. However, as I began to work, I realized that the telephone was too far from the typewriter for me to answer it without getting up. Furthermore, I had no space for keeping paper supplies nearby. As I thought about other arrangements, I saw that with slight shifts, I could have the telephone closer to the typewriter and the file cabinets could be close enough to refer to them without getting up. I also found that a set of drawers could easily be attached to my modern table to give me space for supplies.

Equipment

The basic equipment that you are likely to find at a secretarial work station includes the following:

a. A desk
b. A typewriter
c. A telephone
d. File cabinets and some type of file for your desk
e. A desk lamp, if overhead lighting is considered inadequate
f. Desk trays for incoming and outgoing mail
g. A stapler
h. A desk calendar
i. A transcribing machine, possibly

The secretary assumes responsibility for maintaining all equipment in good working order. Needed repairs should be reported immediately so that the work of the office is not interrupted because of the **malfunctioning** of a typewriter or telephone, for example. Organizations generally have established procedures for reporting repairs. You will become acquainted with such procedures through reading the office manual or during the orientation period of your first days on the job. There may be forms to be completed for requesting maintenance service. You should keep a small supply of such forms on hand so that repairs can be quickly communicated to the office that takes care of them. You should be able to describe **precisely** the problem so that the repair task is easy to handle.

malfunctioning:
not operating properly

precisely:
exactly

Supplies

The secretary has need of many supplies that are available in a central stockroom in a large company. In a small organization, however, a

replenishing:
replacing

secretary may be responsible for maintaining the inventory of office supplies and **replenishing** them as necessary. In such instances the executive in charge of the office will discuss with the secretary the office supply companies from which the organization gets its supplies.

As you become acquainted with the nature of your work, you will be able to establish your supply needs and arrange to have on hand sufficient supplies to **minimize** the need for constantly returning to the stockroom for additional materials. The space you have available for supplies will to some degree determine how many supplies you keep on hand. Supplies for three to four weeks are generally considered adequate. Some supplies, such as stencils and cleaning fluids, **deteriorate** if they are not maintained in the proper environment, so a large supply is never a good idea.

minimize:
reduce to a limited number

deteriorate:
lessen in quality

If you are in a large company, your office stockroom may have a catalogue of all the items they regularly have in stock, so it is simple to place an order. If you should need some supplies that are not available through the stockroom, you will want to discuss with your employer how you should proceed. Sometimes the office manual will indicate the procedure to be used, but approval of the employer is commonly required.

If you are in a small office and the maintenance of office supplies is your responsibility, you will want to discuss the general task with your employer and establish what stock levels are to be maintained and what procedures you are to follow. If the former secretary has not developed this procedure in writing, you may want to do so when you have some free time. You should, of course, let your employer read your rough draft to be sure your procedures are correct and complete.

Decorations

There are varying possibilities for secretaries to decorate their work stations. In some companies where professional decorators have been hired to design, furnish, and decorate the total premises, individual employees, whether they are executives or secretaries, are asked not to make changes or additions. This may mean that a secretary is not to hang a favorite calendar at the work station or place a plant on a window ledge. In other places the attention to overall design and decoration is not so uniform, and a secretary may add something to the work station. It is a good idea to be sure what you want to do is appropriate. It may be wise to seek permission before following through on your own ideas. A business office is not the place for an unorganized display of one's favorite poems, cartoons, or postcards. One personnel director commented about the problem she faced and how she handled it:

While we had no policy about decorating offices because we are in an old building and there is no coordinated design, we do like our offices to be orderly and businesslike. We found that beginning workers were transforming their work stations. We began to see blown-up cartoons, postcards from vacationing friends, and even brightly colored pillows. The general appearance was not one of a clean, pleasant working environment. I knew that I had to do something.

I decided to have a meeting and take groups of ten beginning workers on a tour of these "decorated" areas. I told them ahead of time that I wanted them to view the offices with a critical eye, pretending that they were business people from outside on a first visit to our offices.

The experience worked quite well. They knew what I had in mind, and they saw how childish and inappropriate the decorations were. They were good sports and their decorations disappeared.

General Maintenance and Cleaning

There is some general maintenance that you should not overlook as a secretary. Cleaning your typewriter regularly, rearranging slightly disorganized files and book shelves, and cleaning the pencil shavings in the pencil sharpener should be a part of your weekly routines if such service is not provided by regular cleaning personnel.

In small offices the secretary may need some cleaning supplies in order to dust regularly, for there may not be daily cleaning services. In large organizations there is generally frequent cleaning service, and the secretary would need to do such tasks only when the regular cleaning staff were temporarily away because of illness or vacation.

The secretary should be familiar with the schedule for more extensive cleaning of windows, walls, woodwork, and bookshelves so that certain tasks can be organized to **facilitate** the work of the cleaning staff at such times.

facilitate: make easier

Establishing Priorities

Secretaries generally work without direct supervision and, therefore, assume responsibility for deciding the order in which they will do the tasks before them. The *establishing of priorities*, which means putting the tasks in one, two, three order, cannot be done unless secretaries have a thorough understanding of the work of their offices.

Planning the Day's Work

Many times secretaries talk with executives to determine what the important tasks are. However, unexpected events change plans, and

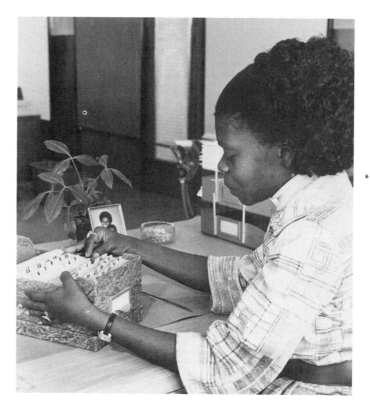

Illus. 1-12

Using a tickler file is one way for the secretary to stay on schedule.

Ohio National Life Insurance Company

secretaries must know how to revise work schedules to take account of changing situations.

The desk calendar, the executive's calendar, and the *tickler*, or follow-up, file all serve to keep a secretary on schedule. Secretaries know how to use these scheduling devices so that they are faithful aids to memory. One secretary commented on her failure to note the events of the day:

> At three yesterday afternoon Mr. Hallen came to my office and asked for the short report he had dictated earlier in the day. He said he wanted to review it before his meeting at 3:30. I hadn't transcribed it! I had completely overlooked the fact that the report was related to his afternoon meeting. I should have transcribed it immediately after returning to my desk yesterday morning so that he would have had ample time to review the report. I was certainly careless and hadn't considered the day's work very thoughtfully. Never again!

Organizing a Calendar

As you become acquainted with the work of your office, you will realize that some tasks are daily, others are weekly, still others are

Illus. 1-13

Planning ahead helps the secretary to meet deadlines.

monthly, and a few are **annual**. You may find it extremely helpful to set up a calendar for a year, noting those tasks that must be handled each month of the year. Weekly and daily tasks are usually not listed on such a calendar.

annual: yearly

You may find that a former secretary has left such a record and you may merely need to bring it up to date. As time goes by, some tasks are dropped and others added to the work of a particular office. Such a record of the year's activities may be maintained in a loose-leaf notebook so that changes may be made easily.

Reviewing Your Pattern of Work

In addition to gaining a year's **perspective** on the work that you must handle, there is another aspect of establishing priorities that you will not want to overlook. You should review how you use your time in relation to what must be done. As a secretary, you don't want to feel anxious because you aren't able to accomplish all that you think must be accomplished. You may find yourself feeling somewhat "behind" with your work and distressed by having insufficient time. Such a situation should

perspective: overview

serve to warn you that possibly you need to reconsider your priorities. You have failed to do what is most important first and, thus, you face deadlines that seem more and more unreasonable to you. Here are the reflections of one secretary in such a moment:

> I just didn't know what was wrong, but I was always behind. Why, I asked myself, am I not able to get my work done without all this last minute rushing and panic-stricken feeling? Well, I looked at myself honestly. I saw rather clearly what I had been doing. Mr. Stone is frequently out of the office and during such periods, I have the feeling that there isn't much for me to do, so I often begin working on some project that I've wanted to get to earlier — cleaning out old files, rearranging the books and periodicals, rearranging the manual I'm developing. At such times I just put aside the regular jobs that are in my "work-to-be-done" tray. Then I realize that Mr. Stone will be back in the office the next morning and there are all those jobs to be done. I usually work late into the night to complete them.
>
> I realize I must do the work that is urgent first, and if I work steadily while Mr. Stone is away, it is likely that I will have some time to get at my small projects. I shall try this plan; this is my promise to myself!

Being Alert to Company Developments

reinforce:
clarify; repeat

Companies often **reinforce** the written information sent to beginning employees by scheduling meetings from time to time where the information is explained and discussed. Such meetings give new employees information about what is going on in the company, such as changes in working conditions, work procedures, or employee benefits. However, as employees move into more responsible jobs, the company assumes that the employees will be able to keep informed by reading the bulletins, reports, and announcements that are sent to them. Therefore, secretaries are expected to read such material forwarded to their offices and note the implications for their work.

As a secretary, you will want to read carefully the material sent to you. You will want to keep informed of developments so that you better understand your own tasks, your rights and privileges, as well as the tasks you handle for your employer. You will also gain a more **compre-**

comprehensive:
complete;
thorough

hensive understanding of the goals of your organization and will be able to establish your own work goals more realistically.

Being aware of what is happening in your company will make it possible for you to participate more intelligently in the life of the organization. Companies encourage and appreciate participation. For example, there are frequently suggestion systems to seek the ideas of employees in improving work procedures as well as the organization of work.

Illus. 1-14

Reading the company's bulletin board is one way of obtaining information on what is going on in the company.

Ohio National Life Insurance Company

Increasing Productivity

Organizations strive to minimize costs. Most organizations are in business to make a profit. This means they strive to provide their goods or services so efficiently that after all costs have been taken care of there will be money which can be distributed to the owners of the business as a return on their investment. There are other organizations that are considered non-profit. Such organizations include schools, colleges, hospitals, and agencies that are supported by funds from local, state, and federal governments and by private contributions. While such organizations do not seek to make a profit in a business sense, they are cost conscious for they are interested in supporting as many activities as possible with the funds available. They, in the same way as profit-oriented businesses, strive to perform all tasks in an efficient manner so that there is little or no unnecessary expense.

All organizations are concerned with productivity — what personnel can accomplish during the course of the work day. Failing to work when there is work to do is one of the primary unnecessary costs in modern business. Such failure reduces the productivity of an office immeasurably. A responsible office worker strives to work systematically and regularly during the work day. This does not mean that the same tempo is maintained for the entire day. In fact, there are intervals of rest — commonly called coffee breaks — in most offices. Office workers should adhere to the schedule for such breaks. If, for example, there are 100 office workers in a company and they return from their coffee breaks 15 minutes late each morning and afternoon, there will be a loss of 50 hours of work each day. If the average worker in this group is earning $4 per hour, the cost for unproductive labor amounts to $200 per day! But, there are additional costs. During the 15 minutes when workers were not at their desks, there were telephone calls that were not answered, letters that were not transcribed, and visitors who were unattended. All these failures may lead to dissatisfied customers and loss of sales.

You should be aware of ways in which you can become more efficient in your job and maintain a high level of productivity. Do not hesitate to make suggestions to your employer for improving the way in which your work is done. Look for ways, for example, of simplifying repetitious tasks. One stenographer in a central word processing center recounted her observations and suggested:

> As I took instructions for jobs, I began to realize that the same instructions were given again and again. However, each time I was writing them down in my notebook. I began to keep a record of the separate instructions and after about three weeks, I compiled a listing — in alphabetical order — and I typed up an instruction sheet with all these common instructions on it. I showed it to the manager who liked it very much. Copies were made for all of us — and we all use it with pleasure!

Although efforts are constantly made to use the most efficient procedures, you should always realize that there may still be room for improvement in the way tasks are done. Thoughtful, imaginative observation of what you do and how you do it can lead to better ways of work. Better ways of work are often more pleasurable ways, too.

REVIEWING

1. What kind of work station does a secretary have?
2. Should a secretary assume that the work station is organized in the most efficient manner? Discuss.
3. What items are generally found at a secretarial work station?
4. Can a secretary expect a maintenance person to check on the functioning of all equipment? Discuss.
5. In a large company how does a secretary get needed supplies?
6. Is it a good idea for a secretary to maintain a year's supply of materials at the work station? Discuss.
7. Secretaries are generally free to decorate their work stations as they please. React to this statement.
8. What does it mean to establish priorities?
9. Why should secretaries read bulletins and reports about the company in which they are employed?

10. Why would companies want employees to offer suggestions for the improvement of the work of the company?

MAKING JUDGMENTS

1. When Charlotte began working for Mr. Lambertson, she was given a small office in an area of the building that had not been used for many months. The work station seemed adequate and there appeared to be sufficient equipment and supplies. However, as she began the tasks of the first day, she saw she didn't have a stapler and that the ribbon on the typewriter was so worn it was hardly possible to read the copy. She found some stationery, but the name of the company was slightly different from the present name. At this moment Charlotte can't do her work satisfactorily. What do you think she should do?

2. Stephen was appointed secretary to the purchasing director of a large electronic manufacturing company. He realized that one of his jobs was maintaining an up-to-date file of catalogs. He found a partially developed listing of the catalogs with an indication of the publishing date for each. He realized that the listing was out of date. There were catalogs on the shelves that had not been numbered; there were some that were two to three years old. The listing was typed on loose-leaf sheets. It seemed to be in no particular order. When someone came for a catalog, Stephen found that much time was spent trying to figure out if there was such a catalog among the shelves and where it might be. What do you believe Stephen should plan to do about the catalogs?

WORKING WITH OTHERS

Joyce works in a beautiful new building that is furnished with modern furniture. Her large office is very attractive and has a lovely view of a lake; she finds it a pleasant place in which to work and she tries to keep it clean and orderly. However, while she is out to lunch, a group of clerks use her office as a lunchroom. They don't ask her if they can; they just use it. They leave empty and half-empty paper cups, sandwich wrappings, etc., scattered on her work table. Joyce thinks she knows who the members of the group are.

What do you think Joyce should do about this problem?

REFRESHING LANGUAGE SKILLS

New developments invariably bring new words into the vocabulary. Thus, there are new words constantly being used in the work of the ever-changing business office. Below is a list of relatively new words, and after each word is a page reference where you will find some information about the new terms. Study each page; note the spelling of the term. Then write a sentence or two using the term appropriately.

1. Mailgram (p. 352)
2. Magnetic-media machine (p. 76)
3. Optical Character Reader (p.265)
4. Reprographics (p. 358)
5. Microfilm (p. 483)
6. Word processing (p. 42)
7. Lateral file (p. 427)
8. Retrieval (p. 486)
9. Shuttle flight (p. 498)
10. Infrared copier (p. 360)
11. Card dialer (p. 339)
12. Conference call (p. 345)
13. Administrative management (p. 610)
14. WATS (p. 345)
15. Teleprinter (p. 350)

PERFORMING SECRETARIAL TASKS

If possible, visit an office where a secretary is at work and observe the following:

a. The nature of the secretarial work station.
b. The equipment that the secretary has available.
c. The arrangement of the furniture and equipment.
d. The decorations in the office.

Based on your observations, write or type a brief essay evaluating the office in relation to the question: How adequate is the office for working efficiently? Be sure to describe precisely what you observed prior to making an evaluative statement.

If it is not possible to observe an office, write or type a brief essay in which you describe the working conditions under which you believe a secretary is able to function efficiently.

IMPROVING SECRETARIAL SKILLS (Optional)

Assume that you are secretary to the director of the personnel department and it is from this office that all staff bulletins are prepared and sent to all members of the company. You are expected to maintain a record of all the bulletins, for there are frequent references to them. Some of the bulletins go to all employees of the company; others go only to executives or office personnel or factory personnel.

You find that the former secretary had no system for keeping track of the bulletins; they were not numbered and they seemed to have been placed at random in a file folder. It is not always clear to which group a bulletin is directed.

Design what you think would be appropriate headings for the different bulletins and indicate what you might do to identify them easily. Also, describe the system you would use to keep track of the bulletins, which may number from 100 to 120 each year.

The Secretary and Word Processing

Part 1

Recording Dictation

Miss Jane Savio is secretary to Logan R. Grenz, vice-president in charge of programming for a national television company. Mr. Grenz corresponds with people around the world, and Miss Savio's primary task is taking dictation and transcribing. Mr. Grenz is a careful, well-organized executive; each morning he spends from one to two hours dictating messages to Miss Savio. She finds the dictation very fascinating and the topics are interestingly presented.

initiate:
introduce; begin

Communications provide the information which is basic to modern business. Millions of executives **initiate** a seemingly endless flow of messages. Over the years the procedures for handling messages have been refined so that efficiency continues to improve.

converting:
changing

Word processing is an important attempt to improve the efficiency of communication. Word processing may be considered simply as **converting** the spoken word into type. In today's office, word processing may be closely associated with sophisticated equipment that records dictation, edits and corrects it, and types it in a suitable form. In some companies, word processing centers combine a mechanical means of recording dictation with varying types of sophisticated machines.

editors:
those who read and correct written material

Although there are many ways of communicating messages, there continues to be dictation to a stenographer or secretary in many offices. Some executives prefer to give dictation to secretaries because they believe secretaries are **editors** of what they say and how they say it. Other executives, though, find it more efficient to use dictating machines or written notes. Here are comments of two business executives, both of whom have much correspondence to handle each week:

Possibly, I've grown too accustomed to a secretary who takes dictation, but I just don't see how I could handle my extensive correspondence without a top-flight secretary who has a thorough understanding of my work. I dictate three or four mornings a week for several hours;

Illus. 2-1

Word processing may involve sophisticated equipment.

IBM Corporation

my dictation varies considerably. During the course of dictation, I discuss troublesome situations with my secretary. I appreciate my secretary's comments, and as we talk together, I begin to see solutions that are feasible. It then takes only a moment to dictate either the full response or enough details for the secretary who will prepare the message. To me, dictation is not a one-way process; the secretary is an important partner.

I seldom ask my secretary to take dictation. I like a dictating machine which is always available. I organize my thoughts as I read a letter for the first time. At the same time, I merely have to switch on the machine and dictate an answer. I like to dictate every detail; I know exactly what I want to say. My secretary finds typing from the tapes very easy. If she is too busy to type them, they go to the word processing center for transcription.

Because of the **variations** in the style of work of business people, it is difficult to determine **absolutely** the best manner for handling many tasks, including those of dictation and transcription. The advantages and disadvantages continue to be discussed, argued, and defended. In general, though, as costs of office services mount, the pressure to find more economical methods increases.

variations:
differences

absolutely:
without question

Basic Stenographic Skills

You probably already possess the basic stenographic skills of writing shorthand and transcribing your notes. During your studies of SECRETARIAL OFFICE PROCEDURES, you will have many opportunities to further develop your skills in an office-like situation. For the application of your skills, you will need the ability to write shorthand at a faster-than-average rate, to maintain alertness to what is being said, and to write unfamiliar shorthand outlines.

Writing at Varying Rates

Stenographers and secretaries on the job find that they must have reserve skill if they are to handle dictation with ease. For example, while it may be true that an executive dictates *on the average* at approximately 80 words a minute, it is likely that there are moments when the dictation is much faster — possibly as fast as 150 words a minute — and other times when it is much slower. If secretaries are not able to write rapidly for brief periods, it is unlikely that they will record the total message.

Also, if a secretary must take a message on an unfamiliar topic, even though the individual words are familiar, a slightly faster-than-average rate may seem very fast. In your experience with office-style dictation, you will gain practice in variable rates and thus develop the skill to manage such dictation easily.

variable: changeable

Maintaining Alertness

exceptional: not ordinary

While there are some exceptional secretaries who can record messages in a seemingly mechanical, non-thinking manner, most secretaries feel the need to pay close attention to the task. Executives often interrupt dictation to give instructions or to discuss a matter that has come to mind that must be handled by the secretary.

From time to time, dictation is interrupted by a telephone call or by a caller who must talk briefly with the secretary or executive. After such interruptions the secretary can be helpful in returning to the dictation by quickly reading the final sentence or two so the executive can continue the dictation. Executives, especially if they are dictating long letters or reports, may need to reconsider an earlier portion of the dictation. They may ask that such a portion be read back by the secretary. The secretary must be following the dictation carefully to locate the portion requested by the dictator.

Writing Unfamiliar Words

Even if a secretary has a large vocabulary, from time to time new words will be encountered in taking dictation. The skill to record *sounds* and to construct readable shorthand outlines is a critical one. Without experience in writing unfamiliar outlines, secretaries are likely to stop in surprise at the sound of a new word — surprise that **precludes** mentally remembering the new word and hearing some of the words that follow. Thus, neither the new word nor several words after will be recorded. If the secretary records what is heard, an occasional strange word can be understood from the **context** when the secretary rereads the notes. As you have practice in taking dictation, note your response to unfamiliar words and try to record them without hesitation.

precludes:
does not allow

context:
part before and after

Learning the Work of the Executive

Secretaries find that recording dictation is a pleasurable activity when they are familiar with the work of their offices. You will want to develop a thorough knowledge of the subject matter of the correspondence. Such development is continuous, but within a short period secretaries usually have enough understanding to cope with the dictation task. Commonly used ways of becoming familiar with the work of an office are discussed briefly in the following paragraphs.

First, become acquainted with the correspondence that the executive handles. As you open the mail, sort it, and attach related correspondence. Give attention to content, to vocabulary, and to **significance** of the matter. If there is time, you may want to read some of the active files. Read for the purpose of gaining an understanding of your employer's work and its relationship to the company.

significance:
importance

Second, recognize that many activities that you perform in the office are **interrelated**. Telephone calls, for example, may concern the same topics that are discussed in letters and memorandums. Note how the topics are interrelated; mentally develop the full view of the work for which you provide valuable secretarial services.

interrelated:
dealing with the same matter

Third, scan professional and trade journals, reports, and conference proceedings that your executive receives. These often deal with the same matters that are discussed in the executive's dictation. Read or scan such materials to see the meaningfulness of them to the work of your office. One secretary commented:

> When I began working for Mr. Fraser, who is production manager in a chemical manufacturing company, I didn't know very much about the business. The world of *high purity, conductivity, alloy plating*, and *flatbed finishing machines* was foreign to me. I read letters, reports,

and journals in which I found the technical vocabulary which was caus-
ing me difficulty when taking dictation. A visit to one of our plants, a
thoughtful employer, and some at-home reading all helped to give me a
new vocabulary and some understanding of our field of specialization. I
find such learning a challenge — and I like it.

Taking Dictation

There is no "typical" manner in which employers handle their dictation. Indeed, there are many differences in dictation styles. Some employers set aside a certain time each day for dictation; others dictate from
time to time during the day. Some employers make notes as they read
their correspondence which aid them in dictating smoothly and quickly;
others seemingly think through their responses while in the process of
dictating. Some employers dictate slowly and clearly; others dictate rapidly and, at times, almost **indistinctly**. Some employers expect their
secretaries to sit by quietly with no reaction whatsoever during dictation; others like their secretaries to help them think through the messages they want to send.

indistinctly:
not clearly

Most executives try to handle their dictation in a manner that is efficient, and a new secretary must generally accept the executive's style. However, as a secretary becomes better acquainted with the work and the goals of the executive, there may be opportunity to offer some suggestions that would improve this office activity. Sometimes executives are very talented in a specialized field, but have had little experience in managing office functions. One secretary discussed her experience:

> Although I had been working for Mr. Hartford for only a short time, I realized that he didn't think about his dictation. He answered letters one at a time, at just any time during the day. I would be called to his office for a letter that he was initiating and after a few sentences, he would say: "Do you think you could get me the report? I'd better look at it before I finish this letter. . . ." He often began letters before he had thoroughly studied all the information necessary. Of course, this kind of situation is likely to happen from time to time, but with Mr. Hartford it was happening many times a day! Finally, I suggested to him that we could both get more done if he would give me a list of the materials he wanted to read before he began dictation and if we would set aside one time during the day for the major portion of his dictation. Do you know, he thought I was a very good observer — he is a scientist — and complimented me on my suggestions. He learned quickly.

Dictation Readiness

Whether the employer dictates only once each day or at different times throughout the day, the secretary is expected to be prepared to take dictation.

Illus. 2-3

A secretary must always be prepared to take dictation. Circumstances often require dictation readiness at a moment's notice.

acknowledge:
respond to

You should have on your desk, within easy reach, a notebook and pen and pencils. As soon as you **acknowledge** the executive's call you should take your notebook and writing tools for dictation and go into the executive's office. Sometimes the call will not be for dictation, but for other instructions. You will find it helpful to make notes of any instructions that your employer may wish to give you.

There are times when the executive's call interrupts an important task. Your first responsibility is to answer the call. If you are in the process of doing a task that must be completed shortly, you can tactfully mention this to your employer so that priorities may be established.

When you leave your desk, you must remember to take care of any confidential information that may be on your desk. It takes only a few seconds to turn over such material or insert it in a folder. If there is something in your typewriter that should not be read by others, you should quickly roll the platen back so that the copy cannot be seen by anyone passing your desk.

Dictation Tools

Your notebook and pen or pencils should be readily available. You will want to place a paper clip or a rubber band around the used portion

Illus. 2-4

A shorthand notebook
ready for dictation

of your notebook so that you can open it easily to a clean sheet where you can begin to take your notes. Also, you should date your notebooks so that if you must refer to your notes at a later date, you will find it easy to locate the desired message. Many secretaries follow the practice of writing the date in the bottom right-hand corner of the first page of the dictation. This corner reference makes it easy to flip through a notebook when searching for a particular day's dictation.

Dictation Procedures

You will want to be sure to mark clearly the beginning of each letter or report that is dictated. If there are special instructions that will be important and helpful to you when you begin transcribing, these should be written in sufficient detail to be understandable when you get back to your desk. Many secretaries use only the left column of the shorthand pad for taking dictation so that the right column is free for recording instructions as well as corrections that the executive may make during dictation.

Many executives hand the letter or report to which they have dictated a reply to the secretary as they complete the response. The material which the secretary has been given may be numbered with the same number as the response in the notebook. If it is turned face down, the letters in the notebook will be in the same order as the correspondence that is related to those letters.

When the dictator pauses to think, or is interrupted by the telephone or someone stopping by the office, the secretary should read notes, insert necessary punctuation marks, correct poor outlines, make longhand

Illus. 2-5

When the dictator pauses to think, the secretary makes any necessary changes in shorthand notes.

notes where necessary, or insert symbols to show words which must be checked for meaning or spelling. Some executives are sensitive to a secretary who seems to have nothing to do while they are thinking.

Henry James, a noted American novelist, was always concerned about what his secretary would do during his long pauses. His first secretaries were male (he wrote during the ending decades of the last century and the early years of this century); they smoked while they waited. When he interviewed the first young lady whom he felt could handle his job, he and she talked together about what she would do during the inevitable waiting periods; finally they found a solution which Mr. James liked very much; the young lady would crochet![1]

When changes are to be made in the notes you have taken, you will want to be sure that you make them carefully so that there will be no confusion when you begin to transcribe. If the dictator decides that what has just been dictated is to be taken out of the letter, you should draw a single line through the notes and begin the correction immediately after the part that was removed. If additions are made after the letter has been dictated, you should place a circled *A* at the point in your notes where the addition is to be typed when a transcript is prepared. Another circled *A* should appear at the beginning of the addition, wherever it appears, and double diagonal lines at the end of the addition. For a second addition, a circled *B* can be used, and so on.

If questions arise in your mind as you are taking dictation, you may want to make notes so that you can ask about them when the dictation is completed. Some secretaries keep separate notebooks for use in jotting down such questions. Others have a small pad on which they quickly note questions; still others use small cards. You will want to be sure that you have all the information needed to complete the transcription of the material dictated.

Kinds of Dictation

While much of the dictation that a secretary handles consists of letters, there may be interoffice memorandums, telegrams, reports, and instructions. Each type of dictation requires careful attention to details.

When a letter is dictated, the dictator will often begin with the salutation and expect the secretary to locate the address of the person or business to whom the letter is written. Generally the dictator will pass on to the secretary the letter just answered, and on it the secretary will find the information for the address. It is very important that the name of the

[1]Leon Edel, *The Master* (New York: J. P. Lippincott Co., 1972), p. 92.

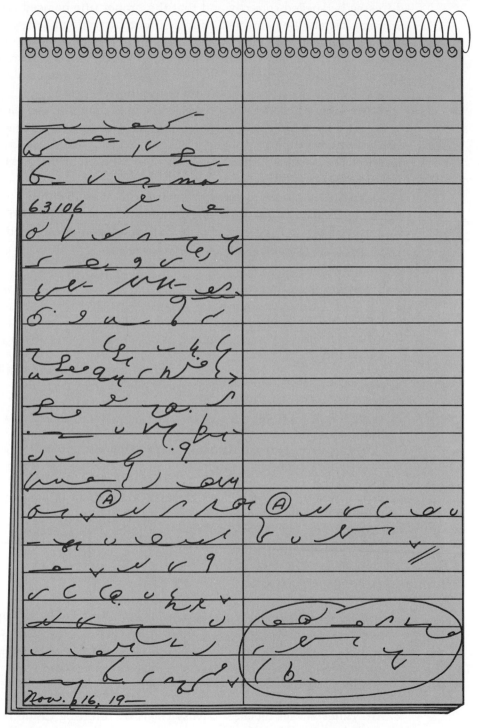

Illus. 2-6

addressee be spelled correctly and that the proper title be used. The dictator may dictate the name and address if not answering a letter. In such instances, the secretary may want to write the proper names in longhand to be sure that the name is spelled correctly. Many names that sound the same have different spellings, such as Brown and Browne or Burns and Byrnes. The secretary must be certain of the correct spelling.

When taking dictation for a telegram or mailgram, the secretary must be exceptionally careful to understand the message. The message is usually written in highly abbreviated form, so each word has great significance. The secretary must also know the urgency of the message for the kind of service to be used.

Reports are seldom dictated in final form. It is likely that the first draft is to be transcribed as a rough draft and returned for review and changes. A final draft may be dictated or typed from a corrected earlier draft.

REVIEWING

1. What is the basic meaning of *word processing*?
2. What are the two most common ways in which executives handle dictation?
3. Why is it necessary for a secretary to have reserve dictation skill?
4. How does a secretary reflect alertness when taking dictation?
5. How should a secretary record an unfamiliar word?
6. What might a secretary do to become acquainted with the work of the executive?
7. Why is it a good idea to date the pages of a shorthand notebook?
8. How may a secretary remember questions that arise while taking dictation?
9. Why may it be a good idea to use only one column of the shorthand notebook while taking dictation?
10. How do you handle an addition to a letter that is made after the letter was dictated?

MAKING JUDGMENTS

1. Helena finds that her employer uses terms that are unfamiliar to her. She is able to write something down for each unfamiliar word and she quickly circles it — her employer dictates rather slowly — and when the letter is finished, she asks the executive to tell her the meaning of the circled words. What do you think of Helena's action?
2. Mr. Hines always dictates to Miss Lewis by referring to the letter to be answered. When he has finished a letter, he just puts it on the

desk. When all the dictation is over, Miss Lewis gathers up the letters and reports on the desk. When she gets back to her desk, she takes time to put them in order. At this point she must read through her notes to determine which is first, second, etc. How would you improve this procedure?

3. Felice loves to take dictation, but she believes that *every word* must be in shorthand; she likes the way her notebook looks with no words in longhand. Would you follow Felice's practice? Explain.

WORKING WITH OTHERS

Carolyn is an excellent secretary. Her teachers recognized her talents while she was in high school. She took dictation rapidly, prepared perfect transcripts, and followed up on all matters.

As a junior secretary, shortly after graduation, she began working for Dr. Ullman, a scientist who was serving as an administrator. Dr. Ullman was internationally known; he had high standards for his own work. He dictated carefully and he appreciated the beautiful transcripts that Carolyn prepared. However, he was always, or so it seemed, searching for the *best* word, the *perfect* sentence, to express a particular thought. This meant that often one of Carolyn's perfectly typed transcripts would be returned because Dr. Ullman had changed his mind — Carolyn had transcribed what he said and what he said was actually adequate. Dr. Ullman knew he was responsible for the changes; in fact, he would say to Carolyn: "I'm terribly sorry, but I do like this new way of saying this. . . ."

Carolyn felt that Dr. Ullman was unduly particular and she felt he was wasting both his time and hers to revise and refine his messages.

What do you think of Carolyn's attitude? What would be your attitude in such a situation?

REFRESHING LANGUAGE SKILLS

Adjectives act as aids to nouns and pronouns by describing or limiting them. Adjectives answer such questions as: *What kind? Which one? Whose? How many?* On a separate sheet of paper, list the adjectives in the following sentences and indicate the question each adjective answers. (Articles, such as *a, an, the,* are considered adjectives, but you may disregard them for this exercise.)

Example: The secretary reads incoming mail and attaches related correspondence to some letters.

incoming	which?
related	what kind?
some	how many?

1. An efficient secretary uses techniques that simplify the many tasks done each day.
2. Fewer lines of a shorthand notebook are needed if one writes small outlines.
3. There is no typical style of dictation in the modern office.
4. An extensive vocabulary is a valuable asset for a secretary.
5. Monthly periodicals, annual reports, and conference proceedings all provide helpful information for learning about the work of the office.
6. There were six clerk-typists responsible for the special report.
7. When dictation is underway, the alert secretary gives full attention to what is being said.
8. Two stenographers were needed to handle the extensive dictation for the visiting vice-president.
9. Shorthand notebooks are numbered for easy reference.
10. The secretary's letter was carefully typed on a letterhead.

PERFORMING SECRETARIAL TASKS

1. Assume that you have been asked to talk to a group of beginning students in a stenography class on the topic "Office-Style Dictation." Write an outline of your key points on each of these subtopics:
   a. Recording dictation at varying speeds.
   b. Recording unfamiliar words.
   c. Interrupting the dictator when one fails to hear what was said.
   d. Recording corrections and additions.
2. Your instructor will dictate a letter to you (or you will record it from a machine) in office style. Use the suggestions discussed in this Part to indicate the changes and additions in your notes.

Part 2

Transcribing Dictation

As a junior secretary, Barbara Dearhammer found the tasks of dictation and transcription the most critical of her daily work. She realized that she must transcribe quickly and accurately, because her employer liked to have the morning's dictation ready for the afternoon's outgoing mail. She followed what she had learned in school — the need to organize her work, to write notes carefully, to read notes thoughtfully, to proofread attentively — and she found that she could accomplish her tasks calmly and competently.

Organizing for Transcribing

You will probably have a time schedule for your day's activities. Generally transcription is a daily activity. Executives like to have their dictation ready for signature on the same day the correspondence was given to the secretary, except, of course, for letters dictated at the end of the day.

You will find that an organized working area will **contribute** to your efficiency when transcribing. It is a good practice to keep your desk in good order at all times, so that if there is **urgency** in preparing a transcript, you can begin immediately upon your return to your desk.

contribute:
add to

urgency:
need to do a task
immediately

A desk in good order has the working surface free of papers, files, and books. Completed work, work in process, and work to be done should be in well-identified places. Supplies, including letterheads, carbon sheets, second sheets, envelopes, and erasers should be in appropriate places in desk drawers or specially designed places near the desk for easy access.

It is helpful to have at hand references such as a dictionary, company manual, and an English guide. You should also have available all the supplies needed to prepare transcripts. One beginning junior secretary said:

> While I knew that it was important to have your desk in order, I always thought it took too much time to get organized. Then, one day

Illus. 2-7

Efficient organization of desk contents

when I had a few minutes to think, I began to observe myself! I kept track of my own interruptions — how often I had to leave my desk to check on a word, to get a letterhead or an eraser, to go to the files for a full name. All of a sudden, I saw that my task was unnecessarily difficult. My productivity was very low because I wasn't organized. Well, I did organize my desk, and the ease with which I work now is amazing — and very pleasant.

The Transcribing Process

As soon as you return to your desk after dictation you may need to transcribe the rush items that were dictated. You should have marked such items so that they are easy to locate.

After taking care of the rush jobs, the other items are generally completed. You will usually want to go over your notes before you begin transcribing. This involves looking for words that must be checked in the dictionary, proper names that need to be checked in files, points of grammar that must be checked in a reference book, and facts that are missing.

Handling such details before transcribing will permit you to give full attention to the typewriting and, therefore, work with few interruptions.

Typing Letters and Reports

You will want your typewriter in good condition so that your transcription will be attractive and easy to read. You should report any needed repairs to the person responsible for maintenance of equipment. Using a typewriter in poor condition will lower your efficiency.

Your typewriter should be clean. You should clean your machine, particularly the type face, on a regular basis.

With a typewriter that is operating properly, you should be able to work at your best speed. You will want to be sure to set the margin stops and tabulator stops so that the material you are to type will be attractively centered on the page.

Handling Carbon Copies. Seldom will you make only an original of the material you are transcribing; copies are commonly required. There is a skill to handling multiple copies quickly.

To insert the original, separate carbon sheets, and separate copy sheets requires skill. You must remember to place the carbonized side of the carbon paper next to the copy sheet. Often it is necessary to release the paper release lever and slip the sheets into the machine **manually**, for it may not be possible to twirl the several sheets successfully. You may find the flap of a legal size envelope helpful in inserting several sheets. If you place the top edges of the sheets against the fold of the flap, you can twirl the sheets into the machine keeping all sheets in place. Another method for inserting carbon sheets is:

manually:
by hand

1. Arrange letterhead and second sheets and slip them behind the platen. Be sure they are firmly anchored.
2. Flip the pack forward over the front of the typewriter.
3. Turn the last sheet, which is the letterhead, back and insert a piece of carbon, shiny side upward, repeating this until all carbons have been inserted.
4. Turn the platen knob, bringing all the papers into typing position.

Carbon packs which are **preassembled** are the simplest to handle, because the single-time carbon is attached to the copy sheet in an easy-to-separate form. Because both the carbon paper and the copy sheets of such packs are very thin, it is generally simple to insert them together with the original sheet, unless you are making an unusually large number of carbon copies.

preassembled:
put together earlier

You should be careful to prepare easy-to-read and attractive carbon copies, because often these carbon copies are forwarded to others outside the organization or to other divisions of the same organization. The file copy, too, should be **legible**, not only because reference must be made at some future time, but also because it may be necessary to make photocopies of it. Secretaries find that if they give attention to the following points, they are able to use carbon paper successfully.

legible:
easy to read

1. Never squeeze the assembled sheets together. A thumb print or fingernail scratch on a sheet of carbon paper may spoil the appearance of the carbon copy.

2. Handle the carbon paper carefully so that the carbon is not transferred to the fingers. Keep your fingers free of carbon so that carbon smudges will not be transferred to the original and the carbon copies.

3. If the typewriter feed rolls make marks on the copy sheets, adjust the feed rolls and turn the paper up more slowly, or use carbon paper with a harder finish.

4. To make a large number of carbon copies, use lightweight carbon paper and lightweight paper; otherwise the last several carbon copies may be blurred, smudgy, and illegible.

5. Never use a wrinkled sheet of carbon paper, for it will cause a carbon smudge to appear on the copy.

6. Always keep carbon paper in a flat folder or box away from dust, moisture, and heat.

7. When several sheets of paper and carbon paper are being used in an assembly, clip the sheets of paper and carbon paper together at the top after they have been inserted in the machine. This prevents the copies, especially the last ones, from being wound around the platen of the typewriter.

8. By inserting the carbon paper after inserting the letterhead and onionskin or manifold, you can easily remove all the sheets of carbon paper from the pack without smudging by holding the top of the letterhead and onionskin (no carbon paper reaches the very top line of the pack) while you pull out all the carbon sheets by the small amount that sticks out from the bottom of the pack.

Illus. 2-8

Learning how to assemble a carbon pack quickly will improve your production rate when transcribing.

Making Corrections. Careful secretaries make corrections skillfully. Poor corrections and strikeovers give your work an untidy, careless appearance. Corrections can be made with one of the following:

1. *Correction tape or paper.* Small rolls or slips of paper with a white, transferable surface can be used to block out the incorrect letter or letters. To block out the incorrect letters it is necessary to type them once again with the white surface of the correction tape against the incorrect letters. It is then a simple procedure to backspace and insert the correct letters.
2. *Correction fluid.* A white fluid can be used to block out the incorrect letter or letters. You must be careful to use the minimum quantity of correction fluid possible because you don't want a **residue** of fluid to detract from the attractiveness of your page.
3. *Eraser.* There are several styles of erasers for use in making corrections of typed copy. Personal preference determines the choice of eraser. Here is a commonly used procedure for making corrections with an eraser:

   a. Move the carriage (carrier) to the right or left to prevent erasure particles from clogging the mechanism.
   b. Insert a solid metal or plastic shield or a 5" by 3" card directly behind the error in the original. Make certain that it is placed between the original and the first sheet of carbon paper. This protects the carbon copies from smudges.
   c. Place a plastic or metal shield with cutouts over the material to be erased. Use of the cutout shield will enable you to erase a single letter of single-spaced copy without smearing other letters or lines. Erase in a circular movement for more than one letter; use up and down motions for one letter.
   d. Move the solid shield to behind the first carbon copy and erase that copy, using the cutout shield.
   e. Continue erasing *all* carbon copies in the pack, moving from front to back of the pack.
   f. Check the alignment to be sure you will be typing on the same line as before.
   g. Strike the correct key or keys lightly, repeating the stroking until the desired shading is achieved.

residue: a remaining portion

There are times when the correction of an error requires that an extra letter or a word be inserted. A letter may be added if the letters are typed in such a way that each one occupies less space than it did before. On some machines, this is done by striking the first letter, then holding the backspacer down slightly and striking the second letter, and continuing in this manner until the complete word has been typed. You may want to practice this skill, called *squeezing*, if you have not as yet perfected it.

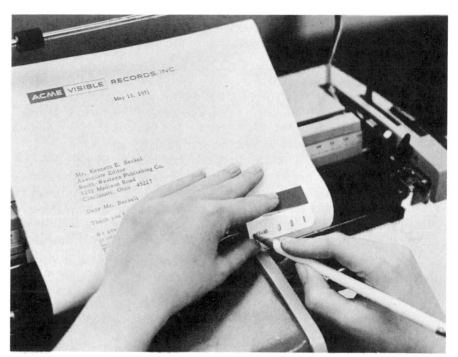

Illus. 2-9

Move the carriage to the side before erasing so that filings do not fall into the mechanism. Use a shield to protect copy that is not to be erased.

At other times the correction of an error requires that a letter be omitted. A letter may be omitted without spoiling the appearance of the page if the remaining letters are typed in such a way that each one occupies more space than it did before. This is done by striking the first letter, striking the space bar, then depressing the backspacer slightly and holding it in that position while striking the second letter, and continuing this operation until the complete word has been typed. This is called *spreading*.

If you are using an electric typewriter, you may have to use slightly different procedures for spreading and squeezing. On some electric typewriters, you will have to hold the carriage by hand while you type the letters in the correct places. On other electric machines, you will find a half-space key that will aid you in proper placement.

Preparing Blind Carbon Copies. There are times when a carbon copy is to be sent "blind." This means that the original copy is not to indicate the name of the person to whom the carbon is to be sent. After you have completed a letter that includes a blind carbon copy, the simplest procedure is to do the following:

1. Release the paper release lever and remove the original only from your typewriter.

2. Turn the remaining sheets and carbons back to the normal position for carbon copy notations.
3. Type flush with the left-hand margin: bcc: Mr. T. F. Smith.

This notation will then appear on the carbon copy for Mr. Smith and on the file copy. If several carbon copies are made and some are being sent in the regular manner, then the *bcc* reference will be on the copy that is designated blind and the file copy only.

Proofreading

Proofreading requires attention and a mental attitude that there *could* be errors in the copy you have just completed. Basically, you must take an unfamiliar view of what you have just typed. This means that you read the copy as though you have not seen it before. The common mental pattern is merely to repeat what you thought earlier, even though the earlier thought was incorrect. A secretary explained what she had to do when proofreading:

> I had to very deliberately read what I had typed, for I found that I didn't see the errors in my copy. For example, once I typed "letters" instead of "letter" (*When we received your letters. . . .*) However, in my mind, I knew that it was "letter," and I just didn't *see* the "s" on the word. Only by extreme attention that led to practically saying the words did I catch my errors. The type of concentration needed for proofreading can be developed, but you have to figure out a system to match your own mental processes.

The manner of proofreading is determined by the nature of your material and your understanding of it.

Regular Correspondence with Familiar Content. Generally, merely reading the copy in the typewriter is sufficient to proofread it adequately. Reading the copy means more, though, then reading *each* word; it means reading for understanding. You realize, of course, that if you were reading words only, you would assume the words "This think is . . ." are correct when they should have been "This thing is. . . ."

Unfamiliar Content. If you are proofreading copy that is not fully familiar to you, you will want to check each sentence against your shorthand notes, for you want to be assured that every word of the dictation has been transcribed correctly. When material is not familiar, it is easy to skip a word, a phrase, or a sentence and not realize that the message is incomplete.

Technical Material and Numbers. If there is considerable detail in tabulated form in a letter or report or table, you may find it wise to get the help of a co-worker to proofread your work carefully. Ask your co-worker to follow the copy while you read from the original notes or earlier draft. You will find the following suggestions for reading and checking numbers helpful:

1. Read 2948 as *two nine four eight*.
2. Read 0 (the number) as *oh*.
3. Read decimal point as *point*.
4. Read .0032 as *point oh oh three two*.
5. Read down columns, not up or across.
6. Verify totals by addition. This is a double check on the original and on the copy.

Completing the Transcribing Process

After you have carefully proofread your letter and made any necessary corrections, you should remove the letter and copies from your typewriter. At this point, you should prepare the envelopes necessary for the original and any carbon copies that are to be sent out. The envelope

Illus. 2-10

Ask a co-worker to help you proofread work that contains technical material or numbers.

should be placed face up with the flap over the top of the letter and enclosures.

If there are urgent items among those to be transcribed, you should prepare such items first and take them immediately to the executive for signing. Then you should see that they are forwarded for mailing as soon as possible.

The other general correspondence and reports should be kept together and taken to the dictator when the entire day's transcription has been completed. If you have more dictation than can be transcribed before the end of the day, you should give the completed items to your employer before the day is over so that the portion of the dictation that is transcribed can be mailed on that day.

Carbon copies of letters may be separated from the letters before they are taken to the dictator for signature, or they may be kept with the letters until the dictator has signed the letters. The latter procedure is simpler if the employer is likely to make changes in letters before signing them, for corrections can be made on all copies with no delay. Changes must be made on all copies, and you will want to be as careful about the way that corrections look on carbon copies as you are about the appearance of the original after the correction. If there are many changes, you will want to retype the letter.

If carbon copies are to be sent to others, you should prepare envelopes for such copies and give them to your employer if the practice is to sign or initial such copies. If the copies are to go out without signature, you will hold such copies aside until the executive has signed the original and it is ready for mailing.

Improving Your Transcribing Skill

You will find that your transcribing skill improves as you gain experience. Take advantage of your experience to become a superior transcriber. Below are some suggestions:

1. Double-check the spelling of the addressee's name when there is any doubt.
2. Check questions of grammar which come up during transcription in a good reference book.
3. Question your spelling and word division of all words for which you are not *absolutely* certain. With a dictionary at hand, it is a simple task to verify a correct spelling. Make a list of the words that cause you to hestitate and review the list to improve your spelling.

Illus. 2-11

Check questions of grammar in a good reference book when they come up during transcription.

4. Get in the habit of circling in your notebook the last word typed whenever an interruption occurs. A glance at the page will be all that is necessary to resume transcribing at the correct point. If this is not done, you may see an outline similar to the last word typed and begin transcribing at that point only to find that a part of the letter has been omitted.

5. Proofread carefully every letter you transcribe.

6. Use good judgment in correcting dictation given. If you feel major changes are necessary, it is generally wiser to check with the dictator than to assume the responsibility. Since a dictator may think you overly cautious if you check minor details, you should develop the ability to handle such checking on your own.

7. Note the reasons transcripts are returned to you for corrections or retyping. Note the errors you made in writing or reading your shorthand notes, in failing to observe a grammatical error, or in overlooking a typing error. Strive to reduce your errors in transcription to the point where they are extremely **infrequent** and where, if they do occur, they are due to very special problems and not merely carelessness on your part.

infrequent:
not often

Illus. 2-12

Be certain that your letters are free of errors before presenting them to the dictator for signing.

REVIEWING

1. Describe a desk maintained in good order.
2. How do you determine the order in which you transcribe your shorthand notes?
3. In what way may an envelope be helpful when inserting a number of sheets of paper and carbon sheets in your typewriter?
4. Why should you avoid using a wrinkled piece of carbon paper?
5. When is it necessary to use lightweight carbon paper?
6. How does spreading differ from squeezing in the correcting process?
7. Why would you prepare a blind carbon copy?
8. What technique would you use to proofread tabulated technical material?
9. At what point do you type the envelopes needed for the correspondence you are transcribing?
10. How may you indicate the last word typed from your shorthand notes at the time of an interruption during transcribing?

MAKING JUDGMENTS

1. Lila's typewriter isn't functioning correctly because the tabular mechanism seems broken. Lila, however, has grown accustomed to using the space bar to move the machine to the proper position. She thinks she now has very good skill on her broken machine and believes it would be a waste of money to get a repairer to come in. She likes to save money for her company. What do you think of Lila's judgment?

2. Bette was instructed to send a blind carbon copy of a letter to Mr. T. Sawyer. Therefore, when she had finished transcribing the letter, she removed all the sheets from the typewriter. Then she reinserted one carbon copy on which she typed: *bcc: Mr. T. Sawyer.* Would you have followed this procedure for the blind carbon copy notation? Explain.

3. Rob is an accurate typist, and he is confident that he senses every time he makes an error. Therefore, he believes proofreading the page before he removes it from the typewriter is a waste of time. Would you follow this technique? Explain.

WORKING WITH OTHERS

Penny transcribed a long, technical letter. As she was proofreading her second page against her shorthand notes, she saw that she had omitted an entire sentence from the first paragraph. She read the entire paragraph and decided that the letter sounded fine without the omitted sentence. She wondered if she should discuss the matter of the sentence with the executive or say nothing about the matter and merely hope that the executive would think nothing was missing from the letter. What do you think Penny should do?

REFRESHING LANGUAGE SKILLS

Verbs express action or state of being. They are closely related to their subjects so they must agree with their subjects in person and in number. Write or type the following sentences on a separate sheet of paper, choosing the correct verbs.

Example: The secretaries (proofread, proofreads) each transcript page before they (remove, removes) it from the typewriter.

The secretaries proofread each transcript page before they remove it from the typewriter.

1. Secretaries (take, takes) dictation at varying times during the day.
2. The secretary (should had, should have) supplies in order that he or she (is, was) ready to transcribe without delay.
3. A secretary's notes (reveal, reveals) command of stenography.

4. The speed and accuracy with which the secretary completes transcription (reflect, reflects) basic skills.
5. Punctuation marks needed in a letter (are, is) sometimes (dictated, dictates) by the executive.
6. The secretary (is, are) able to make many copies with the use of carbon paper.
7. After the secretary has (complete, completed) the letter and has (proofread, proofreads) it carefully, the letter may be (remove, removed) from the typewriter.
8. The carbon copies of a letter (is, are) separated from the letter.
9. Uncorrected errors in a transcript (is, are) inexcusable.
10. The secretary (avoid, avoids) dividing words at the end of two or more consecutive lines.

PERFORMING SECRETARIAL TASKS

1. Write in shorthand a brief listing of the procedures you would follow in transcribing. Type your outline.
2. What would you record in your shorthand notebook for each of the following instructions?
   a. Send blind copies of this letter to J. T. Howells and W. R. Olm.
   b. Check Brown's name; I am not sure how it is spelled.
   c. Set up the copy correctly; I want to review it before you type it on a master.

   What would you do about each of these instructions when you were back at your desk? Be prepared to discuss your actions.
3. You have been asked to type a copy of the comparative inventory report shown below. Set up the copy attractively on plain paper. After typing the report, ask a fellow student to help you proofread your copy. You should read from the copy given below while your fellow student checks your typewritten copy.

Kuhnert & Booser Corp. Inventories Dec. 31, 19--	Year	
	Current	Preceding
Finished Products	17 6 8 66 00	$13 5 54 1 00
Work in Process	2 6 9 71 00	2 53 1 6 00
Raw Materials	8 6 0 49 00	5 39 8 7 00
Supplies	2 9 7 73 00	2 4 5 21 00
Inventories at Cost	$31 9 6 59 00	$23 9 3 65 00

Part 3
Word Processing Equipment

Annamarie is a junior secretary in a large international manufacturing company in Boston. The flow of communications is important to the work of this world organization. Annamarie not only takes dictation from the assistant to the director of the budget, but she also transcribes tapes which the director prepares during the lunch hour, late at night, and on weekends. The volume of work in the office sometimes requires the use of the central word processing center, where a large number of transcribers prepare professional-looking copies in twenty-four hours or less.

Types of Equipment

transmit:
send

Modern companies increasingly provide a variety of ways of recording the messages their executives want to **transmit**. While the secretary in many offices continues to record dictation in shorthand, that same secretary may from time to time have the task of transcribing notes recorded on a dictating machine. The extent to which executives use machines for dictation depends on the nature of their work, the time at which they choose to dictate, and their **preference** for the way in which their dictation is to be recorded. The use of dictating machines continues to increase. The fact that you can work on another secretarial task while your employer is dictating on a machine means that the cost of dictating each letter is less. A secretary's time is far more costly than that of the machine. Furthermore, you will generally work regular hours. Executives often work after hours, and it is convenient to have equipment available for recording drafts of reports and letters. Executives also spend much time traveling; and, to continue to handle their communications, they frequently use dictating machines to prepare discs, tapes, or belts that can be easily mailed to the office for transcription.

preference:
choice

accommodate:
provide for

To **accommodate** these varied uses, equipment is available in portable units, in standard units, and in remote control network systems.

Portable Units

The small transistorized units provide an executive with the equipment to dictate in comfort at home, in a car, or on a trip. In fact, several airlines provide portable machines for business people who desire to dictate while on a flight. There is also a service that provides a dictating machine at the departure point of a flight or at a hotel. The discs on which the executive has dictated can be transcribed by a local branch office of the company or can be mailed back to the home office secretary.

Illus. 2-13

Small portable dictating equipment enables the executive to dictate anywhere, anytime.

Dictaphone Corporation

Standard Units

Separate machines for dictation or transcription are available with a variety of features and with different types of recording devices. The executive has one machine for dictating, and the secretary has a different machine for transcribing. Combination units are also available and are popular in offices where limited use is made of such equipment. A combination unit is used both for dictating and transcribing. Because only one person can use such a unit at one time, the work must be carefully

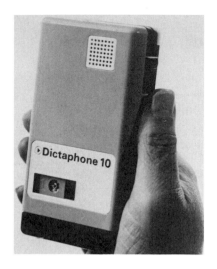

Standard dictating unit

Dictaphone Corporation

Portable dictating unit

Illus. 2-14

planned so that a secretary will not need to postpone transcription because the machine is requested once again by the executive.

Remote Control Systems

Networks of equipment provide a way for executives throughout a company to use the services of a word processing center. An executive may have only to push a simple fingertip control to begin dictation. In other instances, the executive dials a special number on the regular telephone and is connected to a machine that is ready for recording. There are many variations of networks available. For example, it is possible to have connections at several locations so that an executive at a branch office is able to call to the home office in another city and dictate on a machine. Furthermore, there are systems that allow the use of a regular outside telephone to call into a company where the dictating machines are available.

In a company where a word processing center has been installed, executives tend to use the service as a **supplement** to that provided by their secretaries. When their secretaries have unusually heavy workloads, the executives use the word processing center so that their secretaries need not transcribe the dictation. Word processors in the word processing center prepare the transcription and return it to the executives' offices for signing.

supplement:
something additional

WORD PROCESSING STEP BY STEP

Word processing – the transformation of ideas into printed form – refers to the complete sequence of dictating and transcribing operations involved in the production of typewritten materials in a business office.

Executive assembles materials for dictation and dictates by machine to word processing unit.

Dictation is routed to word processing unit which is composed of several transcribing secretaries.

Word processing manager decides priority of tasks and distributes work to transcribers.

Secretary transcribes dictation into finished typewritten product.

SECRETARIAL FUNCTIONS

Secretary or unit coordinator proofreads transcript.

Transcript (letter, report, memo, etc.) is submitted to executive for approval and signature.

EXECUTIVE FUNCTIONS

Illus. 2-15

The Secretary's Responsibility

Your executive's dictating and transcribing units should always be ready for use; therefore, from time to time you will want to check the machines to see that they are working properly. To continue to use a machine that is in need of repair is to work inefficiently. You must also see that there is an adequate supply of belts, discs, tapes, or cassettes on hand.

Dictating Skill Needed

As a secretary you may not be called upon to dictate. However, as your competence and responsibilities increase, you may be required to dictate messages that will be transcribed by other stenographers. Some techniques for machine dictation are discussed.

A hand microphone is usually used to record dictation on a machine in the office, or an instrument resembling a telephone is used to record dictation in a word processing center. The operation of the hand microphone varies slightly with the different models. Dictation machines all follow a basic pattern of providing a bar for starting and stopping the dictation. There are usually labeled keys or buttons for repeating a few words of the dictation, for indicating corrections, and for showing the length of each dictated letter.

To begin dictating, set the tape (disc, belt) in motion by a slight pressure on the starter bar. Hold the microphone just a few inches from your lips. Keep the tape (disc, belt) in motion only when you are actually dictating. If you are interrupted or if you need time to think, stop the machine.

Some manufacturers furnish desk microphones which may be used in place of the hand mouthpiece. The use of the hand mouthpiece is better when the machine is to be used in open offices or in places that are somewhat noisy or not too private. The desk microphone is used in private and quiet offices. The desk microphone is available with either hand or foot control for starting or stopping the machine. The foot control on the desk microphone frees both hands for making notes or for handling papers needed to dictate the reply.

The dictating unit will not only record but will also play back the dictation that has been completed. Thus, you may have the machine repeat your dictation for you at any point.

Special instructions to the transcriber may be dictated along with the regular dictation. Greater efficiency can be developed, however, by using a system of marks covering some of the routine instructions, including stating the number of carbon copies desired or indicating a rush letter. These marks may be made on a strip of scaled paper called an *indicator slip*, which is placed in a special holder attached to most dictating models. The marks referring to a particular letter are written or cut into the part of the indicator slip that is directly in front of the dictating machine. The beginning and the ending of a letter are also marked on this indicator slip in order to give the transcriber the opportunity to judge the length of the letter and to plan its placement on the letterhead. When either the dictation is finished or the record is filled, the tape or disc and its accompanying indicator slip are removed from the machine. The recording medium and the indicator slip, along with the files, are then delivered or sent to the person who is to transcribe the dictation.

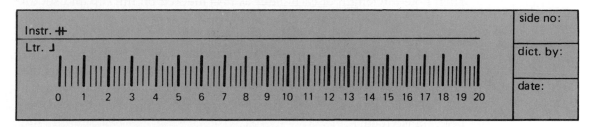

Illus. 2-16   Indicator slip

Dictating Suggestions

Efficient machine transcription depends to a large extent upon the quality of the dictation. The following five hints for improving machine dictation were prepared by Gray Dictation Systems:

1. Relax — be natural — you're talking to another person.
2. Hold the microphone two or three inches from your lips and speak directly into it.
3. Until it is a habit, be careful in the use of the dictate control so that you don't lose the first or last part of your dictation.
4. Have a mental outline of what you want to say, and say it clearly in a conversational tone at normal speed.
5. To help the transcriber, indicate the number of copies before you dictate a letter, identify paragraphs, and pronounce unusual names with special care or spell them out.

Transcribing

If your secretarial duties include machine transcription, you have many of the same problems that are encountered in transcribing from shorthand notes. The chief difference is that, in machine transcription, you type from listening rather than from shorthand notes.

Most transcribing machines are equipped with ear pieces or headsets that either fit into the ears or rest gently against the ears. You place the recording medium on the transcribing machine, then place the indicator slip in the slot provided for it, and proceed to transcribe.

For ease in the operation of the transcribing machine, adjust the controls to suit your particular needs. The speed control, the volume control, and the tone control are all adjustable.

The indicator slip which accompanies each recording should serve as a guide for efficient transcription. You should listen to the corrections and special instructions before beginning to type from the recording. Then note the length of each letter as it is marked on the slip and set the margin stops and the vertical spacing on the typewriter for the correct placement of the letter on the letterhead.

At first, transcription is usually performed by starting the machine, listening for a few words, a phrase, or a sentence, stopping the machine, typewriting the words, starting the machine again, listening for a few more words, and so on until each letter (or other material dictated) has been transcribed.

Illus. 2-17

Knowing how to use dictating equipment will free both you and your employer for other duties.

IBM Corporation

As skill increases, you should be able to type without interruption. It is then unnecessary to stop the transcribing machine to backspace to relisten to the dictation. You will be able to stop and start the transcribing machine without pausing in your typing.

The rate of machine transcription can be increased and the number of time-consuming errors can be reduced if the following suggestions of experienced transcribers are adopted:

1. Listen to the corrections and special instructions *before* transcribing any of the dictated material.
2. Use the indicator slip as a guide for the proper placement of material to be transcribed.
3. Be sure that you understand the meaning of the dictation before typing so that you will avoid
   (a) errors in grammar
   (b) errors in punctuation
   (c) errors in spelling
   (d) confusion of homonyms, such as *bare* for *bear*
4. Develop the power to carry dictation in your mind in order to avoid the overuse of the repeat key.
5. Develop the skill of an expert — keep the typewriter moving, but stop the transcribing unit. Listen to one phrase ahead of your typewriting.
6. Use the parts of the typewriter to advantage, especially the tabulator and the variable line spacer.

Other Word Processing Equipment

Because of the increasing amounts of paper work in the modern office, new methods are being sought to transform the spoken word into the written word more economically. One promising innovation is the highly sophisticated "power" typing equipment found in many word processing centers. Correspondence specialists in these centers transcribe many letters, memorandums, reports, manuscripts, and tables from machine dictation on automated typing equipment.

Power Typing Equipment

Magnetic or paper-tape media typewriters are used in some offices for correspondence and other routine office typewriting. These electronic typewriters are known as power typewriters because of the speed with which they can produce error-free copy. They are of two basic types: magnetic-media machines such as the IBM MT/ST (Magnetic Tape Selectric Typewriter) and the MC/ST (Magnetic Card Selectric Typewriter) and the paper-tape media machines such as the Edityper and Quin-typer.

Magnetic-Media Machines. This equipment consists of a standard keyboard Selectric typewriter attached to a magnetic tape or magnetic card reading-and-playback unit. As the operator types, the recording unit

Illus. 2-18

This typewriter is capable of automatically producing error-free copy at a speed of approximately 150 words per minute.

IBM Corporation

records the copy on magnetic tape or card. Errors are easily corrected directly on the tape or card. After the typing has been completed and all corrections made, the typist inserts a letterhead or sheet and any desired number of carbons in the machine. The machine retypes automatically, completely error-free at rates of 150 to 175 words a minute.

Paper-Tape-Media Machines. Paper-tape-media machines are very much like the magnetic tape machines except the copy is punched on paper tape.

The use of power typewriting equipment also allows duplication of a series of form letters rapidly. The operator inserts the letterhead; types

Courtesy of American Telephone & Telegraph Company

Illus. 2-19 Punched tape

the date, inside address, and salutation; identifies the code number of the form paragraphs or letter for the memory tape; and activates the machine. The machine then types the remainder of the letter automatically, error-free.

A skilled operator can run several machines at once, producing several hundred form letters a day.

REVIEWING

1. If a company has an excellent staff of secretaries, there would be no need to consider dictating-transcribing systems. What is your reaction to this statement?
2. Under what circumstances would a portable dictating unit be considered a good purchase?
3. What responsibilities concerning the dictating machine in the executive's office should the secretary assume?
4. At what point should you listen for instructions and corrections for a particular letter on a transcribing machine?
5. What is a combination dictating-transcribing unit? Under what conditions would one be recommended for an office?
6. What is the value of a dictation system that allows an executive outside the office to telephone directly to the word processing center where dictation can be immediately recorded?
7. Should the dictator keep the tape (disc, belt) constantly in motion once dictation has begun?

8. What skill do you need to keep your typewriter moving smoothly as you type from a transcribing machine?
9. What is a power typewriter?
10. What are two types of power typewriters?

MAKING JUDGMENTS

1. Alice regularly finds that the final words of the dictator are inaudible on the tapes she must transcribe. What would you do about this problem?
2. Mr. Bartlett never remembers to prepare an indicator slip. Therefore, Miss Wilson always makes a rough draft of a complete tape without listening to anything ahead of time. Afterwards she cuts apart her rough drafts, puts instructions with the items, as well as the corrections, and types final copies. Would you have handled this problem as she did? Explain.
3. Kristen feels that typewriting from listening to tapes is a totally different skill from typewriting from her own shorthand notes or from longhand. Therefore, when her employer asked her to transcribe a tape he had prepared at home on a portable dictating machine, she told him that although she had had a brief introduction to machine transcription while in high school, she didn't think she had had enough practice to be able to transcribe his work in a satisfactory manner. Would you have handled the request in the way Kristen did? Explain.

WORKING WITH OTHERS

Miss Nancy Silbers is secretary to Mr. Lee J. Wright, who is a very busy vice-president in a large bank. Miss Silbers prides herself on her excellent shorthand skills, and she likes taking dictation more than any other activity she must do each day.

One day Mr. Wright tells Miss Silber he has ordered a dictating machine as well as a transcribing unit. He told her that often he wants to dictate after working hours when he stays in the office or early in the morning.

He didn't ask Miss Silbers for her judgment about the purchase. Miss Silbers made no comment when he informed her about the new equipment. She was stunned, though, and her personal thought was: "Here I am with my good skill, and now I'll lose my shorthand speed. Oh, why did Mr. Wright do this to me?"

What do you think of Miss Silbers' attitude conveyed in her unexpressed thought?

REFRESHING LANGUAGE SKILLS

Type each of the following sentences using the correct verb.

1. The transcribers in a word processing center (prepare, prepares) copies that (are, is) returned to the executives for their signatures.
2. Theoretically, a good typist (produce, produces) a thousand lines of copy in a 7½ hour day.
3. There (are, is) various definitions of word processing.
4. There are numerous factors to take into account in deciding which kind of equipment (is, are) best suited to a particular office.
5. One of the advantages of tapes (are, is) that they can be fed into a computer.
6. The cost savings (suggest, suggests) that the equipment will be used in many firms.
7. The board of directors' meeting (are, is) recorded by a secretary.
8. Dictating and transcribing machines (is, are) used extensively to record and transcribe dictation in business offices where there (is, are) a heavy volume of correspondence.
9. The handling of correspondence (is, are) aided by the use of dictating and transcribing machines.
10. Either you are to use the dictating machine or I (am, are).

PERFORMING SECRETARIAL TASKS

If a dictating machine is available, dictate the following letter and then transcribe from your own recording, noting the clarity with which you dictated. If a dictating machine is not available, prepare a transcript of the copy. Use the letterhead provided in the *Supplies Inventory* if available; if not available, use plain paper.

This letter is to go to Mr. T. Y. Singer, Vice-President, T I W Hotel Associates, 1579 Avenue of the Americas, New York, NY 10032. I am surprised at the letters I'm receiving since that short presentation I made in Houston two weeks ago. I now realize that many companies are having problems in finding "quiet time" for executives. (¶) Our plan is really as simple as I stated it was: We have an official quiet time from 7:30 to 10 every morning. No meetings are held, conversations are discouraged, and the paging system is silenced. Secretaries screen incoming telephone calls and only the most essential ones are put through. In checking, we find that no more than two calls get through to our staff of 200 executives! (¶) Yes, we feel that communications are at the center of our business, but we realized our managers didn't have time to plan their day, to think through the significance of what they had to do. So, when we instituted the four-day work week, we felt we could use the first two and a half hours of a nine-hour day for organization, planning, and thinking. (¶) We realized that to consider only quantity in relation to communications was to underestimate the powerful value of quality. Much communication was worthless, because it was initiated somewhat thoughtlessly. (¶) We plan to prepare a somewhat detailed story of our experience, and when this is available, we shall send you a copy. Sincerely yours, Richard T. King, Sales manager

IMPROVING SECRETARIAL SKILLS (Optional)

Your instructor will dictate letters (or you will be able to listen to them from a recorded medium) that you are to transcribe on plain paper. Note the ease with which you are able to understand the corrections made by the dictator. Also, note the manner in which you made each correction. Proofread carefully.

3

Preparing
Mailable Letters

Part 1. Letter Placement and Styles
Part 2. Parts of the Letter
Part 3. Office Stationery

Part 1

Letter Placement and Styles

After graduating from high school, Ray Wilson joined the more than fifteen million office workers in the business world. A major part of his first job was typing letters. Ray felt this job was not very important until he talked with his supervisor, Mr. Hart, who explained that without well-produced written correspondence, the company could not carry on business. Mr. Hart said, "All letters should be typed so that their appearance attracts the attention of their recipients. Because the cost of a business letter has risen to almost $4, efforts should be made to help cut the cost of producing a letter." He reminded Ray that each letter requires time on the part of the dictator and the secretary. In addition, office costs, such as space, equipment, and lighting, must be added to the cost of the letter. And finally, the cost of the paper, envelopes, and other supplies used to produce attractive letters must be added to the cost. Ray realized that his job carried a great deal of responsibility, and he promised himself that he would produce letters which would be an asset to his company.

The First Impression

recipient:
receiver

The **recipient** of a letter sees the total letter on the sheet of paper and forms an impression before the message is read. A well-placed letter with clean, even type will make a very good first impression. Such a letter will encourage the recipient to read the letter with the care that your company would like it to receive. A poorly typewritten, carelessly placed letter may fail to get the attention it deserves. It is your responsibility as the secretary to judge each letter you typewrite with this question in mind: How will this letter look to the receiver?

A letter gives a good first impression if:

1. Margins, indentations, and spacing are pleasing to the eye.
2. Parts of the letter are correctly placed according to the style selected.

3. There are no obvious erasures and no strikeovers.
4. It is clean — has no smudges or fingerprints.
5. Type is even and clear.

Letter Styles

You will be told the letter style to use in the office where you work. Many companies use a standard style throughout their offices; in other companies, the person dictating the letters will decide the style to be used. There are three popular letter styles used in business offices today.

Modified Block Style

With the modified block style of letter (Letters A and B on page 84 and the model letter on page 84), the date is typed beginning at the horizontal center of the page. The inside address is blocked at the left margin. The first lines of the paragraphs may be indented (Letter A), or they may be blocked (Letter B). The complimentary close begins at the horizontal center of the page. Businesses use the modified block style more than any other style.

horizontal:
left to right rather than up and down

Block Style

In the block style (Letter C on page 84) all lines of the letter begin at the left margin. Because the letter can be typed without using tabular stops, it is easy to type. It is a modern style and is gaining popularity in many offices.

Simplified Style

The simplified style (Letter D on page 84) eliminates the salutation and the complimentary close. All lines begin at the left margin. This style, which is the easiest to type, was introduced and is promoted by the Administrative Management Society. This organization reports that this style saves 10.7 percent of the cost of preparing a letter.

eliminates:
gets rid of

Letter Punctuation

The most commonly used styles of punctuation are open and mixed. The open style, which is gaining in popularity, leaves out punctuation marks at the ends of the salutation and complimentary close (Letters B and C). In the mixed style of punctuation, a colon is typed after the salutation and a comma after the complimentary close (Letter A).

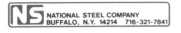

NATIONAL STEEL COMPANY
BUFFALO, N.Y. 14214   716-321-7841

November 18, 19--

Mr. Lloyd Fischer
Standard Steel Products
132 Keller Ave.
Reno, NV 89503

Dear Mr. Fischer:

    Thank you for your order for 12 steel racks of
commercial heavy weight, size 12" x 36 " x 75". We
are pleased to have this order from you

    A large shipment of these racks is on its way
from our factory. It should reach us within a few
days. We are, therefore, holding your order until
our shipment arrives. Unless we hear from you to
the contrary, we shall assume that this action is
satisfactory. We shall ship the racks as soon as
they arrive.

    The enclosed booklet on steel shelving may be
of interest to you. Let us know if we can serve
you further.

        Sincerely yours,

        George P. Burns

        George P. Burns, Manager
        Order Department

ra

Enclosure

Letter A
Modified block style, mixed
punctuation, indented paragraphs

Office of Samuel H. Hall
Attorney at Law
663 BLUE ASH TOWER   CINCINNATI, OHIO 45222   513-261-3883

January 28, 19--

Miss Jane Porter
President, Business Club
Kenton High School
Cincinnati, Ohio 45224

Dear Jane

I am glad to accept your invitation to meet with the
Thomas Jefferson High School Business Club. Thank
you very much for giving me a choice of three dates.
I would prefer to be with you on March 20 at 2:30 p.m.

I understand from what you told me over the telephone
that you would like me to speak on office procedures
and practices. I shall be very happy to do so. Within
the next week or ten days I shall send you the exact
title of my remarks so that you will be able to include
that item of information in your program.

May I suggest that I talk for approximately twenty
minutes so that about half of the time will be available
for the question and answer period that you would like
to have.

It will be good to return to the school where I
received my own training. I am looking forward with
pleasure to your meeting of March 20.

    Very truly yours

    Samuel H. Hall

    Samuel H. Hall

da

Letter B
Modified block style, open
punctuation, blocked paragraphs

AMERICAN METALS PRODUCTS, INC.
5223 Riley Avenue   Portland, OR 97202   503-333-6419

May 26, 19--

King & King, Inc.
225 Lucerne Avenue
Nashville, TN 37215

Ladies and Gentlemen

This letter will confirm our telephone conversation
of yesterday afternoon. We shall appreciate your
sending us information on surplus raw materials for
electronics that you have available for sale.

We are particularly interested right now in cold
rolled steel and pretinned nickel and silver. We are
interested, also, in coils of extra tough hard copper.

Keep us in mind when additional lots of materials
for electronics become available. We are suppliers
for South American outlets and are in constant need
of all types of electronic materials.

Yours very truly

Stanley Cooper

Stanley Cooper, Manager
Purchasing Department

jm

Letter C
Block style, open punctuation

Administrative
Management
Society
8221 Sydney Avenue   Kansas City, MO 64131
816-922-0984

September 20, 19--

Mr. Scott Chambers
Arrow Collection Services
243 Euclid Avenue
Tampa, FL 33609

AMS SIMPLIFIED LETTER

This letter is written in the style recommended by
the Administrative Management Society. The formal
salutation and complimentary close are omitted. These
are not the only changes that have been made, however.
Other improvements are given below:

1. The extreme left block format is used.

2. A subject heading is used and should be typed
   in capitals a triple space below the address.

3. Paragraphs are blocked (no indentations).

4. The writer's name and title are typed in capitals at the left margin at least three blank
   lines below the body of the letter.

5. The initials of the typist are typed at the
   left a double space below the writer's name.

Please show this letter to the correspondents in your
company. You will find that its use reduces your
letter-writing costs.

David S. Henry

DAVID S. HENRY, PRESIDENT

tm

Letter D
Simplified style

Illus. 3-1   Four business letter styles

Margins and Spacing

Placement of a letter on a sheet of letterhead paper is an ability that the good secretary develops with experience. With practice you will be able to balance properly each letter you type and you will not need to retype letters because the placement is not balanced. You will develop the skill needed to judge whether a letter is short, average, or long from the amount of space you used in taking your shorthand notes or from the indicator slip if the dictation was recorded on a machine.

Usually the best arrangement is achieved when the side margins are even and the bottom margin is slightly wider than the side margins. In some business offices, however, a standard length for the typewritten line is used for all business letters. The secretary then varies the spacing between the letterhead or top edge of the paper and the dateline according to the length of the letter. See the model letter on page 96 if you need to review the parts of a letter.

A letter placement table such as that shown below will help you **estimate** the spacing for letters. This placement table is for letters typed on 8½″ × 11″ paper and is easy to follow.

estimate: judge

LETTER PLACEMENT TABLE			
(1) Actual Words in Body of Letter*	(2) Letter Length	(3) Width of Side Margins	(4) Type Date on Line**
Up to 100	Short	2″	20
101–150	Medium	1½″	18
151–200	Medium	1½″	16
201–250	Medium	1½″	14
251–300	Medium	1½″	12
301–350	Long	1″	12
More than 350	Two-Page	1″	12

*Actual Words in Body of Letter represents the complete words — not the average five-stroke words used to measure typing speed.
**Count lines from top edge of paper.

Illus. 3-2

To judge letter placement from shorthand notes:

1. Estimate the number of words in the letter.
   (a) Estimate the number of shorthand outlines you write on each line: for example, six outlines on each line of your notebook.

(b) Count the number of lines of shorthand notes for the letter: for example, 31 lines in your notebook.

(c) Multiply the number of lines of shorthand notes by the number of outlines on each line: for example, 31 × 6 = 186.

2. Determine the width of the side margins from the Letter Placement Table: for example, 186 words (Column 1 of the Letter Placement Table) means the letter is of medium length (Column 2) and the side margins (Column 3) should be 1½" wide.

3. Determine the dateline from the Letter Placement Table; for example, the date for a letter with 186 words should be typed on Line 16 (Column 4).

As you become experienced and gain confidence, you will be able to estimate the correct placement for letters by merely glancing at your notes and judging the length visually.

Simplifying the Typewriting of Letters

Many office managers attempt to reduce the cost of letters in one or more of these ways:

1. Using open punctuation. Eliminating marks of punctuation after the salutation and complimentary close is a timesaving feature of open punctuation.

omitting:
leaving out

2. **Omitting** names that appear in the letterhead. For example, there is no need to typewrite the name of the company below the complimentary close if it appears in the letterhead. Also, the typewritten name and title of the dictator need not appear in the closing lines if they are in the letterhead.

3. Typewriting letters in block or simplified style. These letters can be typed faster than other letter styles because every line is started at the left margin and the tabular key is not used. In addition, in the simplified letter the salutation and complimentary close are omitted.

4. Using a standard line length for all letters. When the length of letters varies, a secretary can save time by establishing a standard line length and varying the distance between the letterhead and the date and between the complimentary close and the reference initials. Some offices use a six-inch line for all letters, and the skillful secretary can make each letter attractive

standardization:
established procedure

with this **standardization**.

Unit 3 • *Preparing Mailable Letters*

Interoffice Memorandums

In the office in which you will be employed, you may type many short business notes or reports on forms called interoffice memorandums. These memorandums remain within the organization itself. They are brief and to the point because their only purpose is to communicate with other members of the organization quickly and clearly. The chief advantage of these forms is that they can be typed quickly. Titles (*Mr.*, *Mrs.*, *Ms.*, *Dr.*, etc.), the salutation, the complimentary close, and the formal signature are usually omitted.

The forms, with the heading *Interoffice Memorandum*, may be printed on half sheets or whole sheets of paper, generally on less expensive paper than the company letterhead. The printed words *To, From, Date*, and *Subject*, with enough writing space after each of them, may be included in the heading of the form. Usually the company name also appears on the interoffice memorandum.

ACME CORPORATION   Interoffice Memorandum

    TO: Robert Turner   DATE: October 21, 19--

FROM: Wayne Mims   SUBJECT: Interoffice Memos

Start the interoffice memo two blank lines below the typewritten heading material and block it at the left margin.

Since the writer's name is in the heading there is no need to type it at the end of the message. The typist's initials are placed a double space below the message. All end-of-letter notations such as the typist's initials and carbon copy information are typed as they are in letters.

cm

cc Joan Wilson

Illus. 3-3

```
THE PRUETT COMPANY          INTEROFFICE MEMORANDUM


    TO:  Sam Conrad              DATE:  September 12, 19--
         Melvin Stuart
         Joe Conley           SUBJECT:  Departmental Meeting

  FROM:  Ralph Sanders

Because of recent large increases in the cost of almost all
office supplies, a meeting of department heads is called for
this Friday, September 16, at 3 p.m., in the Board Room.

Will you please come to this meeting prepared with suggestions
we can use to conserve office supplies.


  h
```

Illus. 3-4

You should leave two blank lines after the last line of the heading and the first line of the message. Short messages of not more than five lines may be double spaced; longer messages should be single spaced. Reference initials should be typed at the left margin one blank line below the last line of the message. When enclosures are sent with a memorandum, the enclosure notation should be typed one blank line below the reference initials.

An interoffice memorandum is often sent to a number of people within the organization. In such cases carbon copies or photocopies may be used. The names of all who are to receive copies, however, should be listed on the original and on all copies as shown above. Another practice is to type the original and one carbon file copy with the names of the recipients. The original, with any special enclosures, is sent to the first person on the list. When the first person is finished with it, a line is drawn through that person's name and the memorandum is sent along to the next person on the list. This is repeated until all the interested persons have seen it. This practice is most satisfactory when there is an enclosure or an attachment with the interoffice memorandum that is either too long or too difficult to reproduce.

REVIEWING

1. What will the recipient notice first about a letter?
2. Describe a letter which will give a good first impression.
3. Why is the simplified style of letter the easiest to type?
4. What are the features of the modified block style of letter?
5. How does mixed punctuation differ from open punctuation?
6. What is the best arrangement for margins on a typewritten letter?
7. When a standard length for the typewritten line is used to decide letter placement, how do you allow for the varying lengths of letters?
8. How do you determine letter placement from shorthand notes?
9. How would you determine the placement of a letter that has 135 words?
10. What features of an interoffice memorandum make it fast and easy to type?

MAKING JUDGMENTS

At 4:30 one afternoon, Mrs. Jean Clayton, supervisor of the two stenographers and one file clerk of Brown's Clutch and Transmission Company, realized that she would not have time to complete several important items which needed to be finished before the office closed. She decided to ask Ms. Conn, a new stenographer, to type a very important letter which would be sent to Mr. Fisher, one of the company's best customers. Because the letter had to reach Mr. Fisher by Monday, Mrs. Clayton intended to drop the letter off at the post office when she left work. At 4:55 Ms. Conn handed Mrs. Clayton the letter for her signature. In proofreading the letter, Mrs. Clayton found two very poor corrections and an uneven right margin. It is closing time and the letter must be mailed today. What do you think Mrs. Clayton should do?

WORKING WITH OTHERS

Miss Lois Cummings had just been hired as secretary to Ms. Durham. She has been typing her letters in modified block style with indented paragraphs and mixed punctuation because the previous secretary told Miss Cummings this is the way Ms. Durham seemed to prefer her letters. Miss Cummings believes that the simplified style of letter would be much faster and more economical to type and just as attractive as the modified block style. What should she do?

REFRESHING LANGUAGE SKILLS

An adverb is a word that modifies a verb, an adjective, or another adverb. An adverb answers the questions *how? when? where? how much? how little? to what degree? in what manner?*

Examples: She types *rapidly*. (Modifies verb *types*)

Recently she passed the C.P.S. examination. (Modifies verb *passed*)

He typed the letters and placed them *there*. (Modifies verb *placed*)

She worked *too rapidly* to be accurate. (*Too* modifies adverb *rapidly*; rapidly modifies verb *worked*)

List the adverbs in the following sentences. In a second column list the words they modify.

1. The report was nearly completed.
2. Recently the staff held its annual office party.
3. His employer never left the office before closing time.
4. The accountant studied the statement carefully.
5. Quietly and efficiently she worked on the reports until she completed them.
6. They found the report there.
7. Henry proofreads more accurately than Alice.
8. The longest line in the report was five inches wide.
9. The reports were very long.
10. The receptionist had too much to do.

PERFORMING SECRETARIAL TASKS

1. Assume that you are a secretary who writes approximately five characters to a shorthand line. You have taken three letters from your employer. The lengths of the letters are indicated below. For each letter decide the side margins you would use and on what line you would type the date.
   a. Letter No. 1 is 10 shorthand lines in length.
   b. Letter No. 2 is 25 shorthand lines in length.
   c. Letter No. 3 is 45 shorthand lines in length.

2. Using plain paper, type the thank you letter on the next page in the following ways:
   a. Block style, open punctuation.
   b. Modified block style, mixed punctuation, indented paragraphs.

Mr. Earl Imhoff
Darby Employment Service
4020 Princeton Avenue
Tampa, FL 33606

Dear Mr. Imhoff

Thank you for taking the time to discuss employment opportunities at Darby Employment Service with me last Wednesday afternoon. The suggestions you made during the interview will help me qualify for the office position I really want. (¶) I plan to take office education courses at Dutchess Community College next semester. They will be offered during evening hours in the Continuing Education Program. I have already found part-time employment as a clerk-typist in the Placement Office of the College. The day-to-day work in the Placement Office should give me valuable office experience. (¶) After I have completed the courses in the program and have acquired the office experience you consider essential, I hope you will grant me another interview.

Sincerely yours

Dora Steward

Part **2**

Parts of the Letter

When Miss Maria Mitchell first came to work for the Personnel Department of Steinle Electronics, she was eager to make a good impression. One of the first things she decided to do was to become familiar with her company's letter styles and preferences. Maria knew that her copy of the office manual would show her exactly how her company handled its written correspondence. In the section on letters, Maria found that her company made use of practically every letter part. The manual stressed that each letter has a specific purpose and that all letters should present clear and precise messages to recipients. Maria decided to master the different letter parts so that she could type them properly. She would then be able to concentrate on the content of her letters and become a more valuable secretary to her employer.

Parts of the Letter

To understand the business letter, you should know the parts of a letter and why each part is needed. You will not use all parts of a letter on every letter you type. However, some parts, such as the date and signature, are always included in a letter. You will need to use your judgment and the preference of your employer to decide which parts should be included in each letter. The parts of a letter listed below are illustrated on page 96.

1. Printed letterhead
2. Date
3. Mailing notation
4. Inside address
5. Attention line
6. Salutation
7. Subject line
8. Body
9. Complimentary close

10. Signature
11. Typed name
12. Title
13. Reference initials
14. Enclosure notation
15. Separate cover notation
16. Carbon copy notation
17. Postscript

The Letterhead

The letterhead (Item 1, page 96) is important because it gives the first impression that a company wishes to make on the recipient of the letter. For example, notice the industrial, "big business" impression of the National Steel Company letterhead, which is Letter A on page 84, in comparison with the individual, personal impression of letter B, the lawyer's letterhead, on the same page.

The letterhead may **influence** the placement of letters on the page for balance. A letterhead should be easy to read, attractive, and representative of the company that sends it.

influence:
affect

Date

The date on a letter (Item 2, page 96) is very important because it tells the sender and the recipient when the letter was typed. It helps the sender and the recipient identify a particular letter if several letters have been written by the sender to the same person. You must date every letter you typewrite. The dateline contains the name of the month written in full, the date, and the year. Abbreviated forms of the date, such as 11/13/–– or 11-13-––, should never be used in letters.

Type the date anywhere from 12 to 20 blank lines from the top of the page. The exact line on which to type the date is determined by the length of the letter as described in column 4 of the Letter Placement Table on page 85.

In the modified block style letter the date is typed at the horizontal center of the page (Letter A, page 84), and for the block style the date is typed starting at the left margin (Letter C, page 84).

Mailing Notation

When a special postal service such as registered mail or special delivery is to be used, a mailing notation to that effect may be typed in all capital letters even with the left margin and one blank line below the dateline (Item 3, page 96).

Inside Address

The inside address (Item 4, page 96) is typed three blank lines below the date at the left margin. If a mailing notation is used, the inside address is typed three blank lines below it. The inside address is a complete reference for filing the carbon copy in the sender's office. It also gives complete information as to whom the letter is directed at the recipient company, since often the envelope with the address on it is thrown away when the letter is opened. The inside address should contain the name, title (when appropriate), and the complete address of the person or the company to whom the letter is to be sent.

sparingly: infrequently

Abbreviations should be used **sparingly** because they give a somewhat careless appearance to the letter and because they can increase the difficulty of reading.

Name and Company Lines. The name of the person and the company should be typed to conform exactly with the style used by the person and the company receiving the letter. For example, if you were typing a letter to a man who writes his name *Edward R. Voiers*, you would not type his name *E. R. Voiers*. If an incoming letter does not show whether a woman is to be addressed by *Miss* or *Mrs.*, the modern trend is to use the title *Ms*.

Official Titles. When a person's official title is included in the address, it may be placed on either the first or second line (see example at the top of page 95). If the title is placed on the first line, it is separated from the person's name by a comma. Since either placement is correct, you should choose the one that will give better balance to the length of the lines in the address.

inclusive: including

Street Address Line. When the name of the street is a number from one to ten **inclusive**, the street name is spelled out (367 Second Avenue or 381 Tenth Street); figures are used for street names that are numbers above ten. When a street is identified by figures, the house number is separated from the street number by a hyphen with a space on either side, 157 – 179 Street. If the street number is preceded by *East, West, North,* or *South,* however, the hyphen is not necessary; for example, 589 South 117 Street.

City, State, and ZIP Code Line. The name of the city is separated from the name of the state by a comma.

The United States Postal Service has designated two-letter abbreviations for states to be used with the ZIP (Zone Improvement Plan) Code. A list of two-letter state abbreviations can be found on page 656 in

Appendix D. These approved abbreviations are written in all capital letters and without periods. Use of the ZIP Code reduces mailing costs and speeds mail deliveries by using automated equipment.

The Zip Code number should be typed on the same line as the city and state with one or two spaces after the state and with no mark of punctuation between the state and ZIP Code number.

Forms for addresses are:

```
Mr. Randolph G. Ludin, President
The American Duplicating Company
4646 Broad Street
Philadelphia, PA  19140

Ms. Jane A. Steinfeld
President, Investors Consultants
465 Avenue of the Americas
New York, NY  10011
```

Attention Line

The attention line (Item 5, page 96) directs a letter to a **specific** person or department for action even though the letter is addressed to the company. Some feel there is little value in an attention line, and that if attention should be given by a particular person, that person should be named in the address. However, most companies hesitate to open letters in a central office if they are addressed to an individual. If that person is not available at the time, the letter may remain unopened or unattended to until that person returns to the office. An attention line allows a letter to be opened in a central office and then directed to a specific person or department for action. If the person named in the attention line is not available, the letter can be directed to someone else for action.

specific: particular

An attention line is typed one blank line below the inside address. When an attention line is used and the inside address contains a company name, the salutation for the message is *Ladies and Gentlemen*, *Dear Sir or Madam*, or any other salutation appropriate for a corporation or business firm.

With Attention Line *Directed to a Person*	*With Attention Line* *Directed to a Position*
Acme Paper Company 4116 San Ramon Way Sacramento, CA 95825	Acme Paper Company 4116 San Ramon Way Sacramento, CA 95825
Attention Mr. B. A. Smith	Attention Sales Manager
Ladies and Gentlemen	Dear Sir or Madam

(1) Printed Letterhead	(1) **Barkers Publishing Company**
	Home Office 2854 Woodmere Avenue Chicago, IL 62521
	312-482-2870
(2) Date	(2) May 12, 19-- ← 1 Blank Line
(3) Mailing Notation	(3) SPECIAL DELIVERY ← 1 Blank Line
(4) Inside Address	(4) The Smythe Corporation
	3120 University Drive
	Seattle, WA 98105
(5) Attention Line	(5) Attention Office Manager ← 1 Blank Line
(6) Salutation	(6) Dear Sir or Madam
(7) Subject Line	(7) Letter Writing for the Executive ← 1 Blank Line
	In another envelope you will receive your copy of LETTER
	WRITING FOR THE EXECUTIVE. ← 1 Blank Line
	We know all office managers will be interested in this
	book because it tells how to write attractive and
	convincing letters with a minimum of expense. The most
(8) Body	(8) widely accepted letter styles and pointers on how to
	economize your letter writing process are explained. ← 1 Blank Line
	As you know, we have many other books dealing with
	different aspects of the business world. A list of
	these books and an order form are enclosed. We hope
	you will order other books to expand your business
	library. ← 1 Blank Line
	(9) Sincerely
(9) Complimentary Close	
(10) Signature	(10) *Kenneth H. Rhodes* ← 3 Blank Lines
(11) Typed Name	(11) Kenneth H. Rhodes
(12) Title	(12) Advertising Manager
(13) Reference Initials	(13) ht
(14) Enclosure Notation	(14) Enclosures
(15) Separate Cover Notation	(15) Separate Cover--Book ← 1 Blank Line
(16) Carbon Copy Notation	(16) cc Mr. Robert Nexton
(17) Post Script	(17) If you order as many as three books this month, you will
	receive a 10% discount on your purchase!

Model Letter, Modified Block Style, Open Punctuation, Block Paragraphs

Illus. 3-5

With No Attention Line

```
Acme Paper Company
4116 San Ramon Way
Sacramento, CA  95825

Ladies and Gentlemen
```

Salutation

The salutation (Item 6, page 96) is a greeting to the addressee, the person to whom the letter is written. It is typed one blank line below the address or attention line. The body of the letter begins one blank line below the salutation. A salutation may be as informal as *Dear Joe* or as formal as *Sir*.

The salutations shown below are arranged from the least formal to the most formal. Notice the capitalization used in each.

For Men	*For Women*
Dear Ken	Dear Sharon
My dear Ken	My dear Sharon
Dear Mr. Washington	Dear Miss (Mrs., Ms.) Simon
My dear Mr. Washington	My dear Miss (Mrs., Ms.) Simon
Dear Sir	Dear Madam
Sir	Madam

Subject Line

The writer of a letter may wish to use a subject line (Item 7, page 96) as a way of headlining or **emphasizing** the key topic of the letter. When a subject line is used, type it one blank line below the salutation. Leave one blank line after the subject line. The topic may be preceded by the word *Subject*, although there is a trend away from this. The subject line may be typed even with the left margin or centered on the page.

emphasizing: giving importance to

Body

One blank line follows the salutation before you begin the body of the letter (Item 8, page 96). Single spacing is always used for the body of the letter except for very short messages. Be sure to paragraph the body of the letter so that it will be easy to read. Leave one blank line between paragraphs to give the letter a more attractive appearance.

Keep the right margin as even as possible and about as wide as the left margin. You can do this by setting the right margin stop from five to eight spaces beyond the point where you want the line to end, so that the bell will ring just before the space where the line ends. You will still have space to complete a short word or add a hyphen for a word that must be hyphenated before the carriage is stopped by the right margin.

The Second Page

On letters of more than one page, each page except the first is numbered. The heading for the second and following pages should include (1) the name of the addressee as it appears on page one, (2) the page number, and (3) the date. Two styles of headings are the block form and the spread form; however, the block form is easier to type, since there is no need for centering or backspacing.

One of the following forms may be used at the top of the second and succeeding pages:

Block Form

```
Mr. Alan C. Mitchell
Page 2
June 16, 19--
```

Spread Form

```
Mr. Alan C. Mitchell    2    June 16, 19--
```

The space between the top of the second sheet and the heading should be about an inch (6 line spaces). Two blank lines should be left between the second-page heading and the body of the letter. Type at least two lines of the paragraph at the bottom of the first page, and carry over at least two lines of a paragraph to the top of the second page.

For the second page use plain bond paper of the same quality and color as the first-page letterhead.

Complimentary Close

The complimentary close (Item 9, page 96), which is typed one blank line below the body of the letter, is the *good-bye* of the letter. The complimentary close and the date start at the same horizontal point on the page. In the block style (See Letter C, page 84), the date and complimentary close begin at the left margin. In the modified block style (See Letter A, page 84), they begin at the horizontal center of the page. Only the first word of the complimentary close is capitalized. Some complimentary closings are shown below.

Business Letters

Yours truly	Yours sincerely
Yours very truly	Sincerely yours
Very truly yours	Very sincerely yours

Formal Letters

Respectfully yours   Yours respectfully

Friendly Letters

Cordially yours	Yours sincerely
Yours cordially	Sincerely yours

Signature, Typed Name, and Title

The letter is signed (Item 10, page 96) between the complimentary close and the typed name (Item 11, page 96). The typed name overcomes problems caused by a poorly written signature. The dictator's name is typed three to five blank lines below the complimentary close.

Yours truly

D. R. Dunlap

D. R. Dunlap, Vice-President

Sometimes the name of the company is typed as part of the signature. There is little **justification** for this practice if the company name is in the letterhead. If the company name is used, it is typed in all capital letters one blank line below the complimentary close. The name of the dictator is typed three to five blank lines below the company name. When the dictator's name and official title (Item 12, page 96) are used, the title may be typed on the same line as the typed name or on the line below the typed name.

justification:
good reason

Very truly yours

NORTHEASTERN SHIPPING ENTERPRISE

Marshall P. Barrington

Marshall P. Barrington
Purchasing Agent

A man's personal title, such as *Mr.* or *Dr.*, should not be shown before the signature or typed name. A woman's personal title, such as *Miss, Mrs.*, or *Ms.*, may be shown before either the signature or the typed name. If it is shown before the signature, the title should be enclosed in parentheses. If it is shown before the typed name, the title is not enclosed in parentheses. A married woman should show her legal name — her own first name, middle initial, and married last name if she uses her husband's surname in business.

Signature of an Unmarried Woman

Yours sincerely

Ann Bagley

Miss Ann Bagley

Yours sincerely

(Miss) Ann Bagley

Ann Bagley

Signature of a Married Woman or Widow

Yours sincerely

Jane L. Hart

Mrs. Jane L. Hart

Yours sincerely

(Mrs.) Jane L. Hart

Jane L. Hart

Some women, whether married or unmarried, prefer to use Ms. as their title.

*Signature of a Married or
Unmarried Woman*

Yours sincerely

Carolyn Rackler

Ms. Carolyn Rackler

If a woman wants to be known by her married name by using her husband's first name and middle initial (for example, Mrs. John B. Williamson), she can sign her legal name and place her married name below in parentheses.

Signature of a Married Woman

Very truly yours

*Alma A. Williamson
(Mrs. John B. Williamson)*

Mrs. Alma A. Williamson

Your employer may not be available to sign a letter that must be mailed. You may be asked to sign your employer's name and mail the letter. If you are requested to do this, be sure to initial the signature.

Very truly yours,

Robert E. Bailey
mh

Robert E. Bailey

You may write a letter over your own signature for your employer dealing with such routine matters as making a reservation or an appointment, canceling a reservation or an appointment, sending regrets that your employer is out of town and unable to attend a meeting scheduled before your employer returns to the office.

Very truly yours

Sandra Twill

Secretary to Angelo Quintuo

You must be sure that each letter is signed, either by your employer or yourself, before you fold it and insert it in an envelope for mailing.

Reference Initials

To indicate who typed the letter, place your initials (Item 13, page 96) in lowercase letters one blank line below the typed name even with the left margin. Sometimes you will see the initials of the dictator before the secretary's initials; but this is unnecessary work, since everyone knows who dictated the letter from the typed name below the signature.

Enclosure Notations

An enclosure is anything placed in the envelope with the letter. Any enclosure you send should be noted at the end of the letter. This is a reminder to you to be sure to include the enclosure. It is also a service to the addressee who can quickly check to see if the material is included in the envelope. The enclosure notation (Item 14, page 96) should be typed at the left margin one blank line below the reference initials. One enclosure is indicated by the word *Enclosure*. More than one enclosure may also be indicated by the word *Enclosures* typed on one line, followed by a list of the enclosures, each enclosure being listed on a separate line and indented five spaces from the left margin. Typical enclosure notations follow.

```
                  Enclosure
                  Enclosures 2
                  Enclosures
                          Price List
                          Circular
                          Sample X-14
```

Separate Cover Notations

When the letter refers to items sent under separate cover — that is, in another envelope or package and not included with the letter — you should type the proper notation at the left margin one blank line below the last enclosure line, or one blank line below the reference initial line if there are no enclosures. One item sent under separate cover is indicated by the words *Separate Cover*. Two or more separate cover items are usually indicated by the correct figure typed after the words *Separate Cover*. In some offices the means of transportation used for sending the separate cover material is indicated. If it is desired, the nature of the item or items may be indicated in the same manner as enclosure items. Frequently used separate cover notations are:

```
              Separate Cover
              Separate Cover 2
              Separate Cover--Express
              Separate Cover--Mail
                      Price List
```

Carbon Copy Notations

When you prepare a carbon copy for the information of a person other than the addressee of the letter, the notation *cc* (Item 16, page 96), followed by the name of that person, is typed at the left margin one blank line below the last line of typing. If it is not desirable for the addressee to know that a carbon copy has been sent to someone else, the reference notation *bc* (blind copy or *bcc* (blind carbon copy) should be typed with the name of the recipient on all carbon copies, but not on the original letter. Blind copy notations are typed in the usual position for noting carbon copy distribution. To save time the notation may be typed before the letter is removed from the machine by placing a card or piece of paper over the notation position on the original copy.

Postscript

Sometimes your employer will dictate a postscript to a letter. A postscript (Item 17, page 96) is a short message that is typed on the second line below all other notations. It may be **preceded** by the abbreviation

preceded:
come before

PS, but the modern trend is to type it in the same form as any paragraph in the letter without adding PS.

The postscript is sometimes used to take care of a detail omitted from the letter by mistake. It is often used, however, to emphasize a special point by setting it apart from the rest of the letter.

Addressing the Envelope

If the letter is to be handled efficiently by the postal clerks, it is very important that the address on the envelope be accurate and easily read.

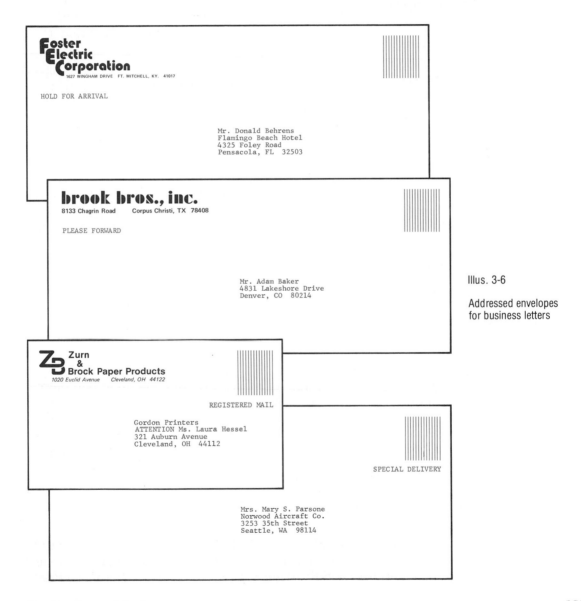

Illus. 3-6

Addressed envelopes for business letters

Note the illustration of typed envelopes on the preceding page. Type the address single spaced on the envelope exactly the same as the inside address of the letter.

An attention line should be typed immediately below the name of the company in the address. Special address notations, such as HOLD FOR ARRIVAL and PLEASE FORWARD, are typed in all capital letters two blank lines below the return address. Mailing notations, such as REGISTERED MAIL and SPECIAL DELIVERY, are typed in capital letters below the stamp.

REVIEWING

1. Why is the address of the recipient typed in a letter?
2. Why is the date on a letter important?
3. Where are the two places the title of the recipient may be typed in the address?
4. What does ZIP mean, and why is it used?
5. What salutation is used for a corporation?
6. Where does the subject line appear in a letter?
7. What kind of paper should be used for the second page of a two-page letter?
8. What is the difference between an enclosure notation and a separate cover notation?
9. Where are mailing notations such as SPECIAL DELIVERY and REGISTERED MAIL typed on the envelope?
10. Where are addressee notations such as HOLD FOR ARRIVAL, PLEASE FORWARD, and PERSONAL typed on the envelope?

MAKING JUDGMENTS

Mr. O'Neal has given his secretary, Mr. Sherman Thurman, permission to open his mail. One day when Mr. O'Neal is out of the office, Mr. Thurman opens a letter from a local furniture store, for which Mr. O'Neal has been anxiously waiting. There is an enclosure notation at the end of the letter. However, Mr. Thurman does not find any enclosure. What should he do about the missing enclosure?

WORKING WITH OTHERS

Mr. Pruitt, an executive in his early 60's, received a letter from Mr. Jackson of the Global Company. The salutation read, "Dear Lloyd." Just after Mr. Pruitt had read the letter, Mr. Payne, an associate of Mr. Pruitt, came into Mr. Pruitt's office. Mr. Pruitt asked Mr. Payne if he knew Mr. Jackson. Mr. Payne replied, "Yes, as you remember, he is the young salesman we met at lunch several weeks ago. I see him on the golf course quite often also. The impression I get from him is that he is trying to climb the ladder of success too fast. Why do you ask about him?" Mr. Pruitt replied, "Oh, I was just wondering if Mr. Jackson knew me well enough to call me by my first name." What do you think of Mr. Jackson's choice of salutation? Why?

REFRESHING LANGUAGE SKILLS

A preposition is a connecting word which shows the relation of a noun or pronoun to some other word in the sentence.

Type each sentence below, choosing the preposition which you believe is correct.

Example: Be conscious (of, with) economy when selecting stationery for the office.
Be conscious of economy when selecting stationery for the office.

1. The address of the envelope should be (like, as) the inside address in the letter.
2. (Inside, Inside of) the office the temperature was 80 degrees.
3. This report is different (from, than) the report that was prepared earlier today.
4. His new desk was identical (with, to) the one he had chosen from the catalog.
5. The executive went (in, into) the mail room to see if a letter she needed had been received.
6. A good secretary does not become angry (with, at) the employer.
7. The secretary should be careful (and, to) type all parts of the letter correctly.
8. Keep (off, off of) the grass.
9. The decision to use that style of letter was reached (between, among) the five secretaries.
10. The secretary must choose (between, among) two positions for the subject line of a letter.

PERFORMING SECRETARIAL TASKS

1. Read the letter on the following page carefully, observing the errors made in the placement of letter parts. Retype the letter on a letterhead in the *Supplies Inventory* or on plain paper in correct form, using the block style with open punctuation.

SPECIAL DELIVERY
June 3, 19 --
Mr. Leroy Birch
432 North Star
Tulsa, OK 93809

Dear Mr. Birch

Thank you for writing us about land in the Colorado mountains. We have many beautiful sites available in the $30,000 price bracket. Some of our sites are far from the beaten path, while others are situated in the heart of tourist country. We are enclosing some brochures, which we feel will help you select the most appropriate lot for you. Please feel free to call us any time.

Sincerely

Advertising Director

Eddie Conrad

ht

Enclosure

2. Type the following letters on letterheads from the *Supplies Inventory* or on plain paper. Prepare one carbon copy and address envelopes if the necessary supplies are available. If envelopes are typed, attach them to the letters in the manner described on page 63.
   a. Letter in *Block Style* — Type the letter in the illustration on page 96 in block style with open punctuation.
   b. *Two-Page Letter* — Type the following letter in modified block style with blocked paragraphs and open punctuation. The sign (¶) means paragraph.

August 17, 19 --, Mr. William R. Fritz, Manager, Whiteside Manufacturing Company, 928 Harrison Building, 1258 Columbus Drive, Los Angeles, California 90012.
Dear Mr. Fritz Irritated customers . . . lost orders . . . tied-up lines . . . delays and misunderstandings . . . garbled messages . . . excessive phone bills . . . wasted sales effort. These are some of the costly results of the poor telephone practices so common today in business. (¶) But they don't have to be common in *your* business. You can make sure *all* your calls — incoming and outgoing — are handled courteously, efficiently, and economically by using our unique training program, BETTER BUSINESS BY TELEPHONE. (¶) And right now, as a new subscriber, you will

receive a free bonus portfolio of past issues describing correct telephone techniques such as

— The 15 rules of telephone courtesy that *everyone* in business should follow.
— Why no secretary should *ever* have to use the blunt question "Who's calling?"
— How to build sales and goodwill when taking telephone orders.
— What to say — and what *not* to say — in handling complaint calls.
— Why so many executives now make and take their own telephone calls.
— The six ways to save time — and money — on all telephone calls.
— Why *new employees* need telephone training — and how to give it.
— How to handle the caller who doesn't want to give his or her name.
— *Why* and *how* to use the telephone to collect on past due accounts.
— How to turn more of your telephone *inquiries* into actual *sales.*

(¶) BETTER BUSINESS BY TELEPHONE has already helped more than 16,000 companies, of every size and type, make more effective use of their telephones. Included are small businesses — and such companies as Du Pont, American Airlines, Ford, Sears Roebuck, General Electric, *The Wall Street Journal*, etc. (¶) BETTER BUSINESS BY TELEPHONE will help you with every phase of your telephone operation, from handling routine calls to planning a complete telephone sales campaign. (¶) Regular twice monthly bulletins bring you the latest in tested telephone techniques . . . case histories showing how other progressive companies are solving telephone problems and making the most of telephone opportunities . . . hints on time- and money-saving procedures . . . ideas that spark your own thinking on how you can make your company's telephone contacts a sales and public relations *asset* rather than a liability. (¶) Along with the bulletins for management, you get regular twice monthly *Fone-Talks* for employees . . . all *Special Reports* and *Supplements* as issued . . . easy access to all past issues that may help you . . . and unlimited use of our *free mail consultation service* on your individual telephone problems. And your subscription starts with a "Telephone

Improvement Kit" which shows you exactly how to make the best possible use of our material. (¶) As a BETTER BUSINESS BY TELE-PHONE subscriber, you'll have everything you need to make your company's handling of the telephone as good as that of any company in the country . . . and to *keep* it that way. And you'll quickly see why we receive such comments as this from Helen C. Wood, President, H. C. Wood, Inc., Lansdowne, Pa.: "I have a warm feeling toward your organization because I feel you are rendering a splendid service to those business people who want to use the telephone effectively and efficiently." (¶) You'll find full information on rates on the enclosed order form. Just tell us how many copies of each bulletin you will need to cover your department heads and key employees. We'll do the rest. Sincerely yours, Arthur Dell, Manager, Customer Service.

Part 3
Office Stationery

During Karl's first week with the DeLeon Corporation, he was taken on a tour of all the departments in the company. The tour included a visit to the stockroom, where all the company's stationery and supplies were kept. Karl was surprised to see so many different kinds of letterhead stationery. He noticed that the stationery for the president's office was on a crisp, heavyweight paper with a very dignified letterhead, while the letterhead stationery used by the shipping department was on a lightweight paper of lesser quality. The supplies manager explained that the quality of the paper and the style of letterhead used differed among the departments, depending upon the nature of the department's work.

Using Office Stationery

Different types of office stationery can affect the quality of the typing on the paper.

1. *Quality:* High quality papers are easier to correct and have less **tendency** to leave erasure marks than is the case with low quality papers.

2. *Weight:* Very lightweight or thin paper will wrinkle and tear easily, while very heavy paper may be difficult to fold.

3. *Color:* While white is a satisfactory and appropriate color and is always in good taste, the use of a color appropriate to the nature of the business can sometimes be used very effectively. It is usually more difficult to erase on colored paper than it is to erase on white paper.

tendency:
a natural disposition to act in a certain way

Type of Paper Commonly Used

Bond paper, which was originally used for printing bonds, is most frequently used for business letters because it takes a typed impression clearly. It is firm and strong so that erasing is relatively easy. It is quite attractive in appearance, and it is more permanent than many types of paper. Bond paper may be purchased in various qualities ranging from inexpensive sulphite bond (wood content) to bond of 100 percent rag content. The best qualities are usually watermarked with a company's name or trademark. Each watermarked sheet has a right side for typing. When your paper is in typing position, the watermark should read across the sheet in the same direction as the typing.

Paper comes in a number of weights such as 9, 13, 16, 20, and 24 pounds. The paper most widely used is the 20-pound weight. The weight of bond paper is based on the weight of a ream (500 sheets) measuring 17" × 22" — four times the size of a standard letterhead. When the paper is cut into four equal parts, a ream of 20-pound paper in 8½" × 11" letterheads weighs five pounds.

Illus. 3-7

Business correspondence is always typed on the company's letterhead stationery.

It is generally considered false economy to use a poor quality letterhead paper. The difference in cost between poor quality paper and good quality paper is not great.

detract:
take away

Furthermore, a poor quality paper may **detract** so much from the attractiveness of a letter or may make erasing so difficult that it defeats the purpose of a letter that is otherwise in excellent form.

The second and succeeding pages of a letter are typed on paper without a letterhead but of the same quality and size as that on which the letterhead is printed.

Size of Paper

Letter paper may be obtained in a variety of sizes, but the following are most commonly used:

8½″ × 11″	Business or Regular
8″ × 10½″	Government
7¼″ × 10½″	Executive or Monarch
5½″ × 8½″	Baronial

The business or regular size, 8½″ × 11″, is the most widely used size for ordinary business correspondence. Legal size paper, which is 8½″ × 13″, is used for summaries, reports, briefs, and other legal papers but not for ordinary business correspondence. The executive or monarch size is used almost exclusively by executives and professional people who have their individual stationery for business or personal use.

The baronial size may be used for very short business letters; however, since there is a tendency to misplace or misfile it, the use of baronial paper is limited in most business firms.

The Letterhead

Quite commonly the printed letterhead includes the name of the firm, the mailing address, the telephone number, and, if it is not indicated in the name of the firm, the nature of the business. The branch or department, the name and the title of the official using the stationery, the address of the main office of the company, the location of branch offices, and the cable address are sometimes included. Usually the simpler the letterhead the more **dignified** is the appearance.

dignified: having formality of style

The return address on the envelope should harmonize with the letterhead. It is placed in the upper left corner of the envelope.

Paper for Carbon Copies

Paper for carbon copies, usually known as onionskin, manifold, or second sheets, is ordinarily much thinner than letterhead paper. The thin paper is best because you can type several carbon copies. A suitable paper for carbon copies is one that is thin but strong with a smooth surface so that the carbon impression will be clear.

Some firms use several different colors of paper for carbon copies to facilitate the identification of different types of letters in the files. For example, the carbon copies for ordinary correspondence may be on yellow paper, those for acknowledgment of orders may be on white

Illus. 3-8

Typical letterheads

paper, and those for collection letters may be on blue paper. Also, different colors of carbon copies are made when it is customary to prepare two or more copies for separate filing. For example, if a branch office makes two carbon copies — one for its own files and one for the home office files — the distribution of the copies may be easier if different colors are used.

For a two-page letter, both sides of the copy sheet may be used. This method reduces the amount of paper and avoids crowding files. When this is done, the first page of the carbon copy is reversed and turned upside down so that the second page heading is directly behind the last lines of the first page. Although a letter written on two sides of a thin sheet is not quite as readable as it would be if separate sheets were used, it is usually readable enough for a file copy. A carbon copy of the reply is sometimes typed directly on the back of a letter to keep related correspondence together and to save filing space.

Envelopes

The efficient secretary needs to know about the many types of business envelopes used in offices.

Standard Envelopes

There are two sizes of standard envelopes that are used more often than others: large (9½″ × 4⅛″), also called No. 10, or legal; and small 6½″ × 3⅝″), also called No. 6¾, or commercial.

The large envelope is used for one- and two-page letters and for letters with enclosures. The small envelope is always used with small letterheads and sometimes with one-page letters. Other sizes of envelopes may be used for special purposes, but a firm tries to avoid having a large supply of odd-size envelopes.

Envelopes should match the letterhead sheet in weight, finish, and color. If the envelopes and the letterheads are purchased at the same time and from the same company, differences in paper stock are avoided.

In addition to standard envelopes, there are three other types designed for special purposes: window, business reply, and interoffice envelopes.

Window Envelopes

Window envelopes are used in business to eliminate the need to address envelopes. The address on the letter, invoice, or other message, shows through the window. Window envelopes not only save time but prevent letters from being put into wrong envelopes.

The address must be written so that it can be seen through the window after the letter or bill is folded. Some businesses may have a mark printed on their stationery that shows the location for the address. The

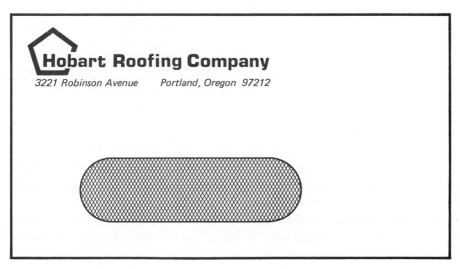

Illus. 3-9

Window envelope

first few letters should be checked to see whether they are correctly folded to show through the window. The method of folding the letter or bill for the window envelope is different from the method of folding used for an ordinary envelope. Methods of folding letters are described in Unit 7, Part 2, under "Handling Outgoing Mail."

Business Reply Envelopes and Cards

Your company can get a business reply permit from the post office. This lets you enclose a special business reply envelope or card that the addressee may return without paying postage. The post office collects postage from your company when it receives the returned envelopes and cards.

prospective:
likely to be

Such envelopes and cards are frequently used when a firm is sending out correspondence to which replies are invited such as sales literature inviting inquiries from prospective customers. The amount collected for a business reply envelope or card is more than the ordinary postage. A business reply envelope that is enclosed in a No. 6¾ envelope should be of slightly smaller size, such as No. 6¼. Likewise, a No. 9 business reply envelope should be used for an enclosure in a No. 10 envelope.

Illus. 3-10

Business reply card

Interoffice Envelopes

economical:
avoiding waste; thrifty

When mail is sent within the company, a business may use interoffice envelopes. These envelopes are economical since they can be used from about 20 to 48 times. By reusing envelopes, a company can save money. Time is also saved by handwriting the addressee's name on the envelope instead of taking time to place the envelope in the typewriter and typing the addressee's name.

INTEROFFICE CORRESPONDENCE

TO		DEPT.	TO		DEPT.	TO		DEPT.
	●			●			●	
	●			●			●	

Illus. 3-11   Interoffice envelope

REVIEWING

1. Why is bond paper most frequently used for business letters?
2. What should you consider when office stationery is to be selected?
3. Why is it considered false economy to use poor quality letterhead paper?
4. What information is generally part of the letterhead?
5. Why is a thin paper generally chosen for carbon copies?
6. Why would a firm use several different colors of paper for carbon copies?
7. Why would you use both sides of the copy sheet when typing a two-page letter?
8. How do you decide whether to use a small or a large envelope?
9. Why are window envelopes sometimes used?
10. When is postage for business reply cards and envelopes collected?

MAKING JUDGMENTS

Since Barbara is the only secretary in a small insurance office, she has many varied responsibilities, including ordering supplies for herself and for the two sales representatives. One morning when Barbara arrives at work, she finds a message on her desk which reads, "Barbara, Mr. Clark and I will be out of the office until late this afternoon. I have a rough draft of a two-page letter which needs to be typed and ready for my signature when I return." As Barbara is typing the letter, she reaches for a second sheet to complete the letter and finds that she is out of second sheets. She remembers placing an order for letterheads and second sheets about a week ago at the stationery store down the street. She was told that the order would be ready in about a week. Barbara knows that the second page of a two-page letter should be typed on paper of the same quality as the letterhead. However, the letterhead she is using is on cream colored stationery and the only other paper available in the office is white stationery. What would you suggest that Barbara do about finishing the letter?

WORKING WITH OTHERS

Mr. Juan Gomez has been asked to fill in as secretary to Mr. Rice while his regular secretary, Miss Mary Wilson, is on a leave of absence. During his first day of work for Mr. Rice, Juan discovers that he is almost out of letterhead paper. When he tells Mr. Rice about the situation, Mr. Rice remarks that he has always left the ordering of stationery and supplies up to Miss Wilson. He asks Juan to handle this matter. Juan notices that the stationery which Miss Wilson usually orders is very poor quality. Any correction of a typing error leaves a mark which detracts from the letter's appearance and makes it look messy. Juan knows that good quality paper is essential for neat and attractive letters. What should he do about ordering letterhead paper?

REFRESHING LANGUAGE SKILLS

A conjunction is a word that connects other words, phrases, or clauses. Conjunctions can be *coordinate* or *subordinate*. In this part, coordinate conjunctions are presented. In Unit 9, Part 4, we will present subordinate conjunctions. A coordinate conjunction connects equal elements in a sentence. Some coordinate conjunctions are *and, but,* and *for.*

Example: Her employer left instructions for her, *and* she completed the work quickly.
And is a coordinate conjunction connecting the independent clauses, *Her employer left instructions for her* and *she completed the work quickly.*

On a separate sheet of paper list the coordinate conjunctions in the following sentences.

1. Slowly and distinctly the secretary repeated the message.
2. She hurried to her desk and picked up the ringing telephone.

3. She and Maryanne were working on the annual report.
4. With much anxiety but with a smile, she walked toward the employer's office to discuss the raise.
5. She neither types well nor does she take dictation.

PERFORMING SECRETARIAL TASKS

1. Your employer has asked you to estimate how much stationery you use during a month. You know that you type about ten letters a day and that you make at least one carbon copy for each letter. Half of the letters require one extra carbon copy. Of course, you type an envelope for each letter. You estimate that you have to retype one letter and one envelope a day. You use about five sheets of carbon paper a week. Figure the total number of sheets of letterhead paper, copy paper, carbon paper, and envelopes you use in a month (four weeks, working five days a week).
2. Using a letterhead from the *Supplies Inventory* or plain paper, type the following letter in modified block style with mixed punctuation. Make one carbon copy.

October 10, 19—Dr. Phillip Strange, 410 Grant Street White Plains, NY 10604.

Dear Dr. Strange Subject: Location for Medical Office Thank you for your inquiry about a possible location for a medical office in Knoxville, Tennessee. We are glad to be able to tell you that we are soon going to start the construction of eight apartment houses that will provide for 124 families. These apartments will be located on Chestnut Street, just outside the main business district. Any one of the first floor apartments in these buildings would be admirably suited for a physician's office. The rents are reasonable, and the floor plans are unusually well designed. (¶) We have already rented some of the apartments and expect that by the time construction is completed practically all apartments will be rented. Since many of these families will move to Knoxville from other communities, they will undoubtedly wish to use the professional services of a physician. (¶) We are enclosing a floor plan of one of the apartments that we believe could be particularly adapted to your purposes. We should be glad to discuss this with you whenever it is convenient. Will you come to our office and talk this matter over; or may we ask our Mr. Williams, who is in charge of renting this property, to call on you sometime soon? Very truly yours Hawkins, Smith, & Adams Norman C. Hawkins, President Enclosure

IMPROVING SECRETARIAL SKILLS (Optional)

You are the secretary for a small, but rapidly growing company. When your company first began operations, there were only two executives to work for and it was no problem to type their correspondence according to their individual preferences. Now, after two years, there are four executives, and you find it difficult to keep up with their different preferences for letter styles. You have decided to suggest at the next staff meeting that the company select one letter style to use exclusively. You believe the block style letter to be the best one for this company. So that you will have a model letter to display at the staff meeting, compose and type a letter on plain white paper in the block style with open punctuation. In the letter explain the advantages of this letter style and why you believe it is the best one for your company. After you have typed the letter, label the various parts.

Letter Writing

Part 1. Basic Understandings
Part 2. Letter Composition

Part 1

Basic Understandings

Miss Valeria Porterfield is secretary to Ms. Frances Cantor, director of consumer affairs for a large manufacturer of household appliances. One of Miss Porterfield's primary tasks is handling the extensive correspondence which is received in the office. Ms. Cantor has delegated much of the basic correspondence to Miss Porterfield because she knows she understands the work of the office thoroughly. In addition, Miss Porterfield is able to write letters for Ms. Cantor after receiving a minimum of instruction. Ms. Cantor might say: "Miss Porterfield, will you please take these notes that I made at the meeting this morning, summarize them, and write a letter, enclosing the notes, to the four who were present," or "Of course, I will want to accept this invitation to participate in the session in San Francisco, but I need to know who the other participants are, how long I should plan to talk, whether I will be able to use visuals, and what the relation of this session is to the other sessions of the conference." Miss Porterfield records such comments in her shorthand notebook and later composes letters for Ms. Cantor's signature.

The modern business office is a communications center for the organization it serves. Secretaries are often given writing tasks ranging from answering routine request letters to preparing detailed reports after collecting the needed information. To complete such tasks successfully you must have command of basic writing skills as well as possess a **thorough** understanding of the company for which you work. In addition, there are some general rules that will aid you in preparing accurate, complete messages.

thorough: complete

Knowledge of English Grammar

From your study of English, you have developed basic skills in using the language appropriately. You may feel that a review would be helpful, and you will find such review in Appendix A. Also, you will continue to have the opportunity to recall your knowledge of language usage through the exercises included at the end of each part of this book.

Vocabulary of Business Correspondence

There are certain words that are frequently used in business. During your studies you have developed an understanding of many of these commonly used business terms. Think about their meanings and their proper use in correspondence. You will find a listing of often used business words in books such as *Word Division Manual: The Fifteen Thousand Most Used Words in Business Communication*.[1] Check your dictionary when you find a word that is unfamiliar to you.

The selection of words for their precise meanings is an important consideration in business messages. Using words that say exactly what you mean will make your message clear to the reader. Misunderstandings can cause delays in completing transactions. A line of poetry may convey a wide range of meanings to various readers. Inasmuch as poetry is an art form, such varied meanings are indeed acceptable. The goal of business writing, though, is to have each sentence mean the same thing to all who read it.

Words that add nothing to understanding and **trite** expressions reduce the effectiveness of business writing. Such expressions conceal the message from the reader who must read through excess words and mentally cancel them out to learn the intended message. Useless words and phrases are often found in business writing. However, the careful secretary avoids their use. Some common illustrations follow.

trite: meaningless from overuse

Common, but not the best	All that is necessary
end result	result
true facts	facts
integral part	part
grave emergency	emergency
inaugurate a change	begin
finalize	end or complete
Because of circumstances beyond our control, . . .	We have not . . .
At an early date . . .	Soon (or provide a specific date)
Attached hereto you will find	Attached is

[1]J. E. Silverthorn and Devern J. Perry (2d ed.; Cincinnati: South-Western Publishing Co., 1970).

Common, but not the best	All that is necessary
Enclosed please find	The (clipping) is enclosed
It affords us great pleasure to . . .	It is a pleasure
Thank you in advance	We shall appreciate
Would you kindly send . . .	Please send . . .

excerpt:
passage

Secretaries who are skillful in the use of language are invaluable in maintaining high quality written communications. Here is an **excerpt** from a letter received by a secretary:

We did not believe that 561 instances in a total of 2,500 were sufficient to demand high priority; but we believe, nevertheless, that that problem is of prime importance.

What does the writer wish to say? Will the reader be left confused? Will the reader wonder how important the problem is to the writer? If something does not demand high priority, how can it be of prime importance? What does *prime* mean if it doesn't mean *first*?

Planning Your Message

You will need to know the purpose of the message. If you are uncertain, it is unlikely that the recipient will get an understandable letter or report. Keeping the following questions in mind will help you handle your writing assignments properly.

Is Your Understanding of the Letter Correct?

You must understand thoroughly what the message is to say. If you are answering a letter, you will want to read the letter you received with attention to those details that you must include in your response. A question to keep in mind while you read the letter is: What does the writer want to know? You may wish to write brief notes of the points that require a response. Checking your understanding assures you that you will cover all the details in your message.

If you are writing a letter or report that was requested by your employer, be sure that you know clearly the reason for the message and what it is to convey. If, for example, your employer says, "Please draft a brief report on sales for the Western Region for the last year," you will need to know answers to questions such as:

Are the sales to be shown weekly? semimonthly? monthly?
Are the sales representatives to be indicated?
Are there to be analyses of shifts in percentages of sales?
For what period are the sales to be recorded? the calendar year?
the fiscal year?

Is Your Information Accurate and Current?

You should not assume that the information you had for an earlier piece of correspondence is accurate for the present. Prices change, policies shift, and circumstances are modified.

Illus. 4-1

An accurate business report or letter requires that information be checked carefully.

Most written communications require specific details. You should not *assume* that you know those details. You should always check the most reliable sources for information. Failure to get the most recent information may make it necessary to write further letters of explanation and often create embarrassing situations for a company. For example, a secretary who includes in a letter a price for a product, assuming that the last price was the correct one, may learn later that there has been a price increase. In the meantime the recipient of the letter may have placed an order based on the price the secretary quoted. The company may decide that it will honor the price quoted inasmuch as the customer was responding to recently received information. This means that the payment is less than it should be. However, to have informed the customer that the price quoted was inaccurate may have led to ill will between the company and the customer.

Is Your Language Appropriate and Clear?

The rules of language usage with which you have become acquainted in your English classes are very important to you as you compose letters. Be aware of the words and phrases you select. You want them to be sensible and helpful in conveying your message to the reader. Words chosen should be natural for the occasion. If the writer and the reader know each other well, the tone of the letter may be informal. However, if the writer knows a third person will read the letter, the tone of the letter should be more formal. In many, if not most, of the messages you will write you should assume a somewhat neutral role; the letter should convey the needed information in a straightforward fashion. The recipient of the letter gets no impression of the personality of the writer. For example, if you are responding to a request for a new bulletin, you may write the following:

The bulletin which you requested is enclosed. We hope that you will find it of interest. If we can provide additional details, please write to us.

You should not write:

Gee, does it make us happy to know that you want our bulletin, which is enclosed. We think it is a dandy, and we know you will feel the same. Read it quickly and completely and then if you find that you have some unanswered questions, drop us a line!

What words or phrases in this illustration do you feel are inappropriate for a business letter? You will want to be careful that your written language conveys the tone that is appropriate for your letters. There are many so-called everyday expressions that are satisfactory for use in speaking, but do not convey meaning accurately if used in writing.

Simple words should be chosen when they accurately convey your meaning. Long, pompous-sounding words can detract from the clarity of your message. For example:

use simple, direct words: *a careful review was made*
not pompous words: *a studious analysis was undertaken*

use simple, direct words: *another house was found*
not pompous words: *a substitute abode was uncovered*

Is Your Message Courteous?

In person-to-person meetings it is possible to convey courtesy in several ways — in your manner of looking at the person, in your tone of voice, in your general responsiveness. Letters have only words and these must be chosen skillfully if the recipient is to feel the response is gracious and courteous. You will want to read your letter while thinking of the response to it by the recipient. Authorities on letter writing underscore the need for the *you* approach in writing good letters. The *you* approach merely means that the letter writer has an understanding of the reader's possible responses to the message.

Not a courteous statement:	You promised to send us the material by the 15th; it is the 16th and we have not yet received it. You have broken your promise.
A courteous statement:	We have not yet received the material that you promised to send us by the 15th. Is it enroute? If it is not, can you let us know when we may expect to receive it?

Is Your Message Complete?

This step is a two-sided consideration. A letter must contain all information requested; at the same time a letter should contain no unnecessary information. Recipients ordinarily do not enjoy reading paragraph after paragraph of material that is of no interest to them. Two questions to guide you in checking completeness are:

Have all the writer's questions been clearly answered?
Is there any information here that is not *necessary* to the *purpose* of the message?

The Structure of the Message

The message reflects a structure from the first sentence to the last. There are many variations in structure, but all messages should answer *yes* to these questions:

Is Your Opening Appropriate?

Written communications must capture the reader's attention. The opening sentence should tell the reader why you are writing. In general, the point of the message should be clear very early in the first paragraph. However, there are times when there must be some background material presented before the point of the message will make sense to the reader. In such cases it is important that the opening sentence be of sufficient interest to hold the attention of the recipient until the reason for the letter is apparent.

Is Your Message Divided by Paragraphs?

Rules for paragraphing are flexible. Paragraphing provides a means of subdividing your message into meaningful units that aid the recipient in reading the message and in grasping the various points. The first sentence in a paragraph is a signal of the content of the paragraph, or it provides a **transition** from the message of the preceding paragraph.

transition:
means of linking one part to another

Is Your Message Presented Logically?

To insure a clear understanding of the letter, the information should be presented logically. To write a paragraph that cannot be understood until a later paragraph is read is to be thoughtless of the reader. Your message should unfold; it should provide the information in such a way that the reader will understand your message without rereading it. For example, to begin a letter *I will be happy to meet you in San Francisco on May 15* can be confusing if the letter being answered requested a meeting in Salt Lake City on April 14. The recipient immediately wonders: What about my request for a meeting on April 14? Wasn't my letter received? The recipient may find in a later paragraph a reference to the writer's inability to be in Salt Lake City on April 14.

Organizing Your Writing Tasks

You will want to develop an efficient procedure for handling your writing tasks so that you are efficient. Assume that you have read the mail and have set aside the letters that you will take care of yourself. The following steps may aid you in writing the answers quickly:

1. Read each of the letters, making notes for your response on the letter itself or in your shorthand notebook.
2. Make a list of all the information and enclosures you will need. As you gather the information you need, check each item off your list. Make a note of any items you cannot find.
3. Begin to write your answers. At first you may need to compose each letter in your shorthand notebook (preferably in

shorthand) and edit it before you type it. After you have gained some experience you will find that you will be able to compose your letters directly at the typewriter by merely reading the letter to be answered and looking at the brief notes you have made.

4. Read each letter before you remove it from your typewriter to be sure that it is complete as well as typed accurately.

5. Sign the letters on your own or for your employer, or leave them for your employer's signature. If you sign your employer's name, you should add your initials immediately below the signature. You will learn from your employer which letters you are to answer with your signature, which you are to answer and sign your employer's signature, and which you are to answer but leave on your employer's desk for signing. The pattern that your employer uses is a personal choice and you will learn what it is.

Illus. 4-2

Making notes from incoming letters aids you in writing your responses efficiently and accurately.

Employers differ in how they assign the task of handling correspondence. Some like a secretary to do much of the writing, but they want to see all the letters and sign them so that they are fully aware of the nature and extent of correspondence. Others merely want to know which correspondence the secretary has handled so that they have a general idea of what is happening. They feel no need for the detailed information that reading each letter would provide.

REVIEWING

1. How is a line of poetry likely to differ from a well-written sentence in a business letter?
2. Why should a secretary know the precise meaning of a business word?
3. What is objectionable about the use of the phrases "true facts" or "integral part"?
4. Why does the secretary need an understanding of the contents of the letter to be answered?
5. Why is up-to-date information important when answering a letter?
6. What is meant by a *neutral role* for a secretary writing for an employer?
7. What is the purpose of paragraphing?
8. How does a secretary determine if a letter is complete?
9. Why should a message be presented in logical order?
10. How does the secretary sign a letter written for the employer that is to be signed for the employer by the secretary?

MAKING JUDGMENTS

1. If beginning secretaries want to improve their business writing vocabulary, what would you suggest they do?
2. How might secretaries become acquainted with the writing style of employers to whom they were assigned?
3. What is the advantage to the secretary of setting aside time to handle all correspondence for the day?

WORKING WITH OTHERS

Mrs. Wilma Townsend returned from a Trade Fair very enthusiastic about the interest shown in the new machines of the International Electronics Company. Her enthusiasm was justified, for a steady flow of inquiries for additional information began to arrive in the office. Mr. Arnold Butler, secretary to Mrs. Townsend, didn't know what he should do. Mrs. Townsend was very busy with her continuing responsibilities and had given no attention to the mounting inquiries.

Mr. Butler decided that he would organize the inquiries according to types of questions asked. Then, he went to the Technical Division in the Company to secure the literature available for responding to such questions. Finally, he composed short, direct letters for each of the four categories in which he had placed the letters. During a pause in the dictation Mrs. Townsend was giving him, Mr. Butler outlined his proposal for handling the inquiries. What, do you believe, was Mrs. Townsend's reply to the suggestion presented to her by Mr. Butler?

REFRESHING LANGUAGE SKILLS

The apostrophe is used (1) to show the possessive case of nouns, (2) to show omission or contraction, (3) to form some plurals. Type the sentences below and insert apostrophes where needed.

Example: Arent the 2s and 3s on Caroles typewritten copy too light for photocopying?

Correct: Aren't the 2's and 3's on Carole's typewritten copy too light for photocopying?

1. Its not clear what should be done about Ms. Orrs leave of absence.
2. All the 4s, 5s, and 6s on these three pages are to be in boldface type.
3. Franks work in the printing office is praiseworthy.
4. Before a promotion, there must be a careful review of the worker by the workers supervisor.
5. All the mens clubs in this city have opened their memberships to women.
6. Jones and Williams print shop does all the work for our Department.
7. The Companys profits will be higher this year because of Mr. Clarks leadership.
8. When *thes* and *ands* are used in a title, they are not capitalized.
9. New York Citys mayor has a press conference at least once a month.
10. Before were able to do this job, we must obtain Miss Almonds permission.

PERFORMING SECRETARIAL TASKS

1. Each of the following letter portions include one or more of the faults discussed in this Part. Evaluate each portion carefully; then rewrite it in a manner you consider appropriate.

   a. In regard to the motors these are being shipped today and have somebody there to receive the order because it must be signed for and will you be good enough to acknowledge same by letter to me.
   b. In reply to your letter of February 10, we wish to advise you that an examination of our records shows that your life insurance policy is still in force. You should have realized this yourself, we believe.
   c. If you would specify more carefully on your orders that you want the latest models, it would save us lots of trouble and much expense.

d. If you will send me a big order right away, it will help me win a prize in the contest that our company is conducting and you will receive the best merchandise in the industry at the best prices ever.

2. Bring to class an actual business letter that you consider inadequate. Evaluate the letter and make a list of your specific criticisms. Be prepared to make an oral report in class.

3. Bring to class an actual business letter that you consider satisfactory. Make a list of the effective features of the letter. Be prepared to make an oral report in class.

Part 2
Letter Composition

Mr. Marvin Kaufman enjoys the responsibility of letter writing that his employer, Ms. Sarah Caldwell, has given him. Ms. Caldwell is vice-president for employee relations in a large bank in Dallas, Texas. After Mr. Kaufman had been working for approximately six months, Ms. Caldwell asked if he would be willing to assume some writing tasks. Mr. Kaufman quickly said, "Yes!" Ms. Caldwell, using carbon copies of letters for the preceding two weeks, reviewed with Mr. Kaufman the types of letters he would handle in the future. Mr. Kaufman finds this additional responsibility challenging and enjoyable.

Letters of Acknowledgment

Many executives follow the practice of responding to letters as soon as they are received. When your executive is away from the office, you may be expected to reply to letters. You should make no commitment in such responses. A letter of acknowledgment need say only that the letter has been received and that it will be called to the executive's attention. You may want to include the date of expected response.

A typical letter of acknowledgment signed by the secretary is:

Dear Mr. Warner

Mrs. Lang is out of town but is scheduled to return to the office on February 17. Your letter inviting her to participate in your fall conference will receive attention immediately upon her return.

I hope this delay in a response to your invitation will not be a problem for you.

Sincerely yours

Lyle T. Tunge

Lyle T. Tunge
Secretary to Mrs. Lang

Letters of Appointment

Frequent trips to other cities involve planning for appointments with people whom your executive would like to see. Your executive will often give you the facts and expect you to compose a gracious request for an appointment. Appointment letters should give the purpose as well as the time, date, and place of the appointment. The person granting the appointment frequently sets the time. Sometimes, however, an appointment may be set at the convenience of the individual seeking the appointment.

Here is an illustration of an appointment letter:

Dear Mr. Malloy

    While Mr. Polk is attending the National Dairy Show in Chicago during the week of April 15, he would like an opportunity to talk with you about your new equipment.

    Will it be possible for you to meet him in his suite at 4 p.m. on Tuesday, April 16? He will be staying at the Palmer House in downtown Chicago.

               Sincerely yours

               Kathleen Otto

               Mrs. Kathleen Otto
               Secretary to Mr. Polk

You may frequently write a letter confirming an appointment after you have checked the date and time with your employer.

An example of a confirmation letter follows:

Dear Mr. Polk

    It will be a pleasure for Mr. Malloy to meet you at 4 p.m. on April 16 in your suite at the Palmer House in Chicago. At that time he will have more information about our new equipment.

               Sincerely yours

               Martin Flaks

               Martin Flaks
               Secretary to Mr. Malloy

Illus. 4-3.

A secretary should always obtain the employer's approval of a schedule before confirming an appointment.

Letters Making Reservations

While most reservations are made by telephone, some are still made by letter. A request for a reservation should include the name and business **affiliation** of your employer, the accommodations desired, and the time of departure if a travel reservation, or the time of arrival if a hotel reservation.

affiliation: organization associated with

For a travel reservation:

> Ladies and Gentlemen
>
>   Please reserve a drawing room on your train, <u>The Limited</u>, leaving Denver for Salt Lake City at 10 a.m. on Sunday, December 12, for Mr. James E. Hoffman, General Sales Manager of the Empire Tape Recording Corporation. We will plan to call for the tickets on December 6.
>
>   Please confirm this reservation.
>
>   Yours very truly
>
>   *Arnold T. Garrison*
>
>   Arnold T. Garrison
>   Secretary to Mr. Hoffman

For a hotel reservation:

Ladies and Gentlemen

    Please reserve a single room for Sidney
Solari, President of the National Dairy
Association, for the night of November 13.
He plans to arrive at your hotel about 9 p.m.
He will be checking out at noon on November 14.

    We shall appreciate your confirmation of
this reservation.

                 Yours very truly

                 Gayle N. Larson

                 Miss Gayle N. Larson
                 Secretary to Mr. Solari

Letters Regarding Meetings

    Often you will be given full responsibility for writing to members of committees, of which your employer serves as chairperson, informing them of forthcoming meetings.

    An illustration of such a notice follows:

Dear Mrs. Landers

    The first meeting of the Finance Committee
of the Girl Scouts of the U.S.A. will be held
on Tuesday evening, October 13, at 7:30 in Room
1203A in the National Headquarters Offices here
in New York.

    Within a few days Miss Arnett will be sending
you a copy of the proposed budget. She is looking
forward to seeing you on the 13th.

                 Sincerely yours

                 Joyce T. Steer

                 Mrs. Joyce T. Steer
                 Secretary to Miss Arnett

    You will sometimes assume responsibility for acknowledging a letter concerning a meeting. You should first check the matter with your employer, who may have some personal or business appointments that are unknown to you, so that you can inform the person who has sent the notice whether your employer will be present. Such a letter follows:

Dear Miss Arnett

    Mrs. Landers regrets that she will be unable to attend the first meeting of the Finance Committee. She will be in Los Angeles on the day of your meeting. However, she plans to send you shortly a memorandum of her reactions to the proposed budget.

                Yours sincerely

Grace C. Birmingham

Ms. Grace C. Birmingham
Secretary to Mrs. Landers

Letters of Transmittal

From time to time your executive will ask you to send materials to other persons. As secretary to a lawyer, for example, you would routinely mail contracts, deeds, mortgages, and other legal documents. If you were the secretary to an executive who appears before public groups you might be asked to send copies of speeches, which have been reprinted, to those who request them. When you are asked to send such items, you should send a brief letter of transmittal. A carbon copy of the letter is then kept in the files as a permanent record of the mailing of the enclosures requested.

Illustrations of such letters that you may write are as follows:

Dear Professor Hockenberger

    Two copies of the address Ms. Bostick delivered before the Association for the Advancement of Management are enclosed.

    We are happy to send these to you. If you should need additional copies for classroom use, please let us know.

                Sincerely yours

Roland Galen

Roland Galen
Secretary to Ms. Bostick

Enclosures

Dear Mr. Alvarez

The contracts have been completed and are enclosed. There are small red checks at all points where your clients' signatures should appear.

Mr. Ladd will look forward to receiving these contracts within a week.

Sincerely yours

Norma Roselli

Ms. Norma Roselli
Secretary to Mr. Ladd

Enclosures

Illus. 4-4

When sending materials for the executive, a letter of transmittal is enclosed.

Follow-up Letters

Your employer may ask you to send a letter concerning a matter that has not yet been taken care of. You will find most of the details needed for the follow-up letter in the carbon copy of the first letter that was sent.

The date of the first letter is given, and most of the contents are restated. You may enclose a copy of the original letter.

Dear Ms. Cline

    On May 3 we asked you to submit an estimate of the cost of modernizing the lighting in our new offices on Third Avenue which we expect to occupy on February 1. We have not received the estimate, and we cannot go ahead with the other work until we hear from you.

    If you are still interested in the contract, will you please submit your estimate before December 12.

                Sincerely yours

                Thomas M. Joseph

                Thomas M. Joseph

Dear Mr. Pace

    On October 14 we sent you a letter in which we asked if you might be able to meet with our sales representatives from the Eastern Region to discuss the topic, "Helping a Customer Become Acquainted with a New Product."

    As of today we have not heard from you. Our program will go to press shortly, and we should like to list all participants on it. A copy of our earlier letter giving all the details of the meeting is enclosed.

    We hope that we shall have the pleasure of hearing from you by return mail.

                Sincerely yours

                Edward F. McKiernan

                Edward F. McKiernan

Enclosure

Thank You Letters

    You may be expected to handle thank you letters that are sent some-what regularly on receipt of certain publications or information. Thank you letters should express your appreciation sincerely and simply.

Dear Mr. Oatway

   Your contribution to last week's seminar of our junior executive group was greatly appreciated by all the participants. Discussion among the group continues to include points you raised in your opening remarks.

   The participants and I are most grateful for your generous and helpful cooperation. We thank you.

                        Yours sincerely

                        M. T. Mayberry

                        M. T. Mayberry

Remittance Letters

Many remittances, especially checks (frequently voucher checks), are self-explanatory and require no letter of remittance. This is especially true when payment is for an invoice or monthly bill. When a remittance is for an unusual payment, a remittance letter should be sent. The letter should indicate the purpose of the payment, the amount, and the form in which it is sent: check, draft, or money order. It should also include any necessary explanation. A remittance letter should include an enclosure notation. The notation is typed one blank line below the reference initials.

An illustration of a remittance letter follows:

Ladies and Gentlemen

   Our check for $1,290.49, in payment of Invoice 2913, is enclosed. We have deducted $129.50 from the original amount of the invoice to cover the cost of goods we returned to you.

                        Yours very truly

                        Dale S. Conley

                        Dale S. Conley

ve

Enclosure
   Check 219 for $1,290.49

Letters of Inquiry

A letter of inquiry seeks information. Since specific information is desired, the letter must be worded clearly. Questions must be asked in such a way that their meaning cannot be misunderstood. If it is necessary to get data on a complex subject or problem, a series of numbered questions should be asked. Follow this plan when you are composing a detailed letter of inquiry:

1. Give the subject of your inquiry at the beginning of the letter.
2. Give the reason for your inquiry and explain why the letter was addressed to the reader.
3. Add explanatory material that may be of help to the reader, such as specific details, definitions, dates, and descriptions.
4. End the letter courteously. Avoid stock phrases, such as, *Thanking you in advance* . . . or *Awaiting your reply, we remain*. . . . Instead, use *Any assistance you may give us will be greatly appreciated* or *We shall appreciate any assistance you give us.*

When the answer to a letter of inquiry will be a favor to you, enclose a stamped self-addressed envelope of convenient size.

A brief paragraph on a business letterhead and the signature may be all that is necessary for a good letter of inquiry.

Ladies and Gentlemen

    Some time ago you published a booklet entitled <u>An Office Manager's Guide for the Selection of New Office Equipment.</u> This booklet should be helpful in selecting equipment for our new branch office in Omaha. If it is still available, will you please send us a copy. Thank you.

Very truly yours

Daniel T. Levin

Daniel T. Levin

The answer to a letter of inquiry should be brief, adequate in covering all the questions asked, and courteous.

You should answer a letter of inquiry promptly. Promptness is a matter of courtesy and affords a real opportunity to build goodwill. A reply that leaves the business office the day the inquiry is received is certain to gain respect for the company. An illustration of a reply to a letter of inquiry follows:

Dear Mr. Levin

The booklet you requested, <u>An Office Manager's Guide for the Selection of New Office Equipment</u>, has just been reprinted. A copy is being mailed to you with our compliments.

Your interest in this booklet is appreciated. We hope it will prove helpful to you in selecting office equipment for your new branch office in Omaha.

Yours sincerely

L. T. Wynn

L. T. Wynn
Marketing Department

Letters Ordering Goods or Services

A letter written to purchase goods or services is an order letter. The order should be clear, specific, and complete. Misunderstanding means delay and inconvenience to both firms.

Usually every order for goods will show the following information: quantity, price, catalog number (if there is one), destination of shipment, method of shipment, desired delivery date (this determines the method of shipment to some degree), and the method of payment.

Order blanks are often distributed to regular customers by the seller. It is common practice, however, for business firms to print their own order forms. The use of these forms reduces the chances of making mistakes or omitting required information in ordering goods and does away with the need for writing order letters.

An illustration of a letter ordering goods is shown at the top of the next page.

Form Letters

In many offices some kinds of letters are written over and over again and it is, therefore, economical to compose letters that can be used in response to similar requests. Secretaries often build their own files of form letters and organize a coding system so that they can quickly locate an appropriate letter. Often form letters are written with **alternative** paragraphs so that the secretary can select the paragraph that is most appropriate for a particular recipient.

alternative:
offering a choice

Ladies and Gentlemen

We would like to place an order for the following item:

One 2' x 3' visual magnetic control board in dark green, MCB-279-70-DG, at $69.95

Our check 293 is enclosed. We would appreciate your sending us a copy of your latest brochure that provides information on letter styles.

Your prompt handling of this order will be appreciated.

Very truly yours

Jerome D. Skelly

Jerome D. Skelly
Office Manager

Enclosure

Letters acknowledging orders, sending out requested information, requesting references for prospective employees, and thanking companies or individuals for references are just a few of the instances where form letters are likely to be useful. Illustrations of form letter paragraph inserts follow.

Prospective Customer

1.   It was a pleasure to talk with you when you visited our booth at the recent _____ Convention. The material that we promised to mail you is enclosed.

2.   Mr. _____, our sales representative in your city, is ready to help you. He will be calling you to arrange an appointment at your convenience.

3.   Would you like additional information? Our representative in your area is _____ at _____, telephone _____. Your questions will receive prompt attention.

Requesting Reference

_____ has applied for
a position with our company and has given your
name as a reference. We would appreciate your
completing the attached form and returning it
in the enclosed self-addressed stamped envelope. There is space for any additional comments you may wish to make.

Thank you for your courtesy in responding to
this request.

Form letters are prepared in several ways. Sometimes each form letter is typed with an inside address and a salutation so it appears exactly as a personal letter. There are other times when form letters are prepared in quantity and the specific details for a particular recipient are added on the typewriter. It is generally obvious to the recipient that the letter is a form letter, for copying processes are not able to duplicate exactly the nature of typed copy. Increasingly, form letters and form paragraphs are prepared on a master tape, which is used on an automatic typewriter that provides a personal-looking letter very quickly.

REVIEWING

1. When is it necessary for a secretary to write a letter acknowledging receipt of a letter?
2. What information should be included in a letter requesting an appointment?
3. Does a letter confirming your employer's appointment contain any details? Explain.
4. What information must the secretary have from an employer before a letter of reservation for a hotel room can be written?
5. For what purpose is a letter of transmittal written?
6. In what way does a carbon copy of a letter prove to be useful when the matter of the original letter has not been taken care of by the recipient?
7. What is the purpose of a thank you letter?
8. Does every remittance require an accompanying letter? Explain.
9. Describe briefly the nature of a letter of inquiry.
10. Why should a company answer letters of inquiry quickly?

MAKING JUDGMENTS

1. Discuss the meaning of this recommendation: "The secretary should be noncommittal in a letter of acknowledgment."
2. "Every letter from an organization is an advertisement for that organization." What is your reaction to this claim?
3. Since the same letter is sent to many people, a secretary decided to make duplicate copies of the body on a stencil duplicating machine and add the date, inside address, and salutation at the typewriter or in longhand at the time a letter was to be sent. Evaluate the secretary's decision.
4. A secretary's letter requesting information closes with the sentence: "We appreciate and expect your prompt and full cooperation in this matter." Comment on the tone of this closing sentence.

WORKING WITH OTHERS

While Ms. Rachel T. Trafford was out of town, she received a letter asking her to make a presentation at a conference in London. Her secretary, Miss Denise Langworth, recalled that she had talked about the conference in London and thought she would go. In fact, when she checked her calendar, she found she had a note about the conference, but there was also a question mark. Miss Langworth felt that her hesitation would be resolved; she would definitely attend the conference, for now she had an opportunity to make an important presentation. Since there was an urgent tone to the letter of invitation, although the conference was eight months away, Miss Langworth decided to write the program chairperson to say that she was accepting for Ms. Trafford, who was out of town, but she was very sure — actually positive — that she would be thrilled to participate.

What do you think about the manner in which Miss Langworth handled this letter during her employer's absence?

REFRESHING LANGUAGE SKILLS

On a separate sheet of paper, type each of the following sentences, inserting the needed punctuation.

1. Felice has developed form letters for acknowledgment of purchase notice of premium due and acknowledgment of premium paid.
2. Many secretaries write letters of acknowledgment letters of appointment and letters of reservation.
3. When a remittance requires some special explanation a letter of remittance is written.

4. Many business forms such as checks and money orders are self-explanatory and they require no letter of remittance.
5. A series of form paragraphs as well as form letters can be helpful in saving time in handling recurring requests.
6. The personnel director will want to order copies of the new book on business communications *Concise Correct Complete Communications for Modern Business.*
7. The sales conference therefore must have a much broader more relevant theme than it had formerly.
8. An order letter should be clear specific and of course complete.
9. Mr. Thomas Jones will arrive in Denver during the early afternoon Wednesday September 14.
10. We wonder however if it is possible to order larger quantities at lower prices.

PERFORMING SECRETARIAL TASKS

1. While your employer, Mr. Winston F. Chase, is out of the country for a month, a letter is received from Mr. Quentin G. Haskins, program chairman for the annual convention of dairy equipment manufacturers. Mr. Haskins' address is: Department of Marketing Research, Trans American Farm Equipment, Inc., 571 Grain Road, Wichita, KS 67200. Mr. Haskins is inviting Mr. Chase to deliver a keynote address at the forthcoming convention. Do you believe you should respond to this letter? If your response is "yes," write a letter to Mr. Haskins. Use the letterhead provided in the *Supplies Inventory* or use plain paper.

2. During dictation one morning, your employer, Mr. Roy T. Edwards, says to you: "I've decided I need a portable dictating machine because I am going to be traveling a great deal during this next year. Would you please try to get some information on portable dictating machines for me?" Write a letter to a dictating machine equipment company, National Dictating Machines Company, 5713 Michigan Avenue, Chicago, IL 60622, seeking what you believe would be complete information for Mr. Edwards. Use the letterhead provided in the *Supplies Inventory* or use plain paper.

3. You are a secretary in the National Association of Accountants, an association which publishes a variety of books and pamphlets for its members. You have received an order letter from a member asking for "two copies of Preferred Practices Study." Unfortunately, you're not sure what the member wants. The member asked to be billed for the books, so there is no clue from the amount enclosed. There are two volumes of this Study. Volume I covers the summary of the data with major interpretations. Volume II covers examples of the

variations found in the data. The volumes are available in hard-bound ($9.50) or paperbound ($5.50), postage included. Write a letter seeking clarification, assuming that you can include an order form to simplify the member's response. The member is Mr. Wallace T. Rowe, 36 Tunellton Drive, Nashville, Tennessee 37203. Type the letter on the letterhead that is provided in the *Supplies Inventory* or use plain paper.

4. Your employer, Ms. Ruth Walker, has asked you to write to the Mountaintop Hotel, 3571 Greenview Avenue, San Francisco, CA 94132. Ms. Walker would like a room for the nights of December 4 and 5. She will be arriving at noon and will leave in the late afternoon. She wants a single room. Compose the letter you would send to the hotel over the name of your employer. Type the letter on the letterhead provided in the *Supplies Inventory* or on plain paper.

5. Assume that you are employed by Ms. Martha Morss, Executive Vice-President of the Sheldon Manufacturing Company, 216 Bolten Avenue, Seattle, WA 98121. Using the letterhead provided in the *Supplies Inventory*:

   a. Type a letter to the Franklin Paper Company, 50 Yesler Way, Seattle, WA 98101, asking them to quote prices and terms on 250 reams of bond paper and to submit samples. Your letter should specify weight, size, color, and finish you desire. (If you are in doubt about these items, refer to Part 3 of Unit 3.) Make two carbon copies of the letter.

   b. Type a letter to the Tacoma Equipment Manufacturing Corporation, 140 Columbia Street, Tacoma, WA 98422, ordering the following merchandise:

   6 quires Mimeograph Stencils
   #960, 8½" × 18",
   blue, $3.75 each

   6 boxes Ditto Master Units
   #24-1011, 8½" × 11",
   $6.40 each

   20 cans Spirit Fluid, #24-2010,
   1 gallon, $2.70 each

Make two carbon copies.

IMPROVING SECRETARIAL SKILLS (Optional)

Your employer comes from a meeting from downtown with a group of people who will participate in a panel discussion, for which your employer will serve as moderator. Your employer says to you: "Here is a copy of the preliminary program for the conference in Pittsburgh in early March. Please make copies of this program and send a copy with a covering letter to each of the five participants on my panel. Remind each of them that the meeting will be at 2 p.m. on the 4th and that I would like to meet with the group ten minutes before the scheduled meeting so we can make arrangements for our meeting. The meeting will be in the Jefferson Room on the 1st floor of the Convention Hotel. Many thanks." Compose the covering letter that you would send to each of the participants. Using plain paper, compose this letter directly at the typewriter, if possible. Then, read your letter, noting corrections in pencil or pen. Do you believe you should send an individually typed letter to each of the five persons? If so, why? Could you use a memorandum form? Under what circumstances would the memorandum form be sufficient?

UNIT

5

Typewriting Reports

Part 1. **Preparing Business Reports**
Part 2. **Parts of the Business Report**
Part 3. **Financial Statements and Reports**
Part 4. **Legal Papers, Minutes, and Resolutions**

Part 1

Preparing Business Reports

Mr. Alvin Ross is research director for the Bentley Manufacturing Company. Mr. Ross spends much of his time analyzing data and preparing business reports. Some of his reports are used only by his department, while others are sent to branch offices across the nation. One busy afternoon, Mr. Ross called his secretary, Mr. Terry Singleton, into his office and said, "Mr. Singleton, could you have our bimonthly products report ready for me this Friday instead of next Tuesday? I plan to go out of town next week for a managers' meeting." "I think I can," Mr. Singleton responded, "I already have the data compiled, and I can ask Sandra and Pam to help me with the typing." "Fine," Mr. Ross replied, "If you can get them to type the report, maybe you can get some information I need for a special report I'm preparing for my San Francisco trip." Mr. Singleton knows that by planning ahead for those reports which are due periodically, he can easily arrange his schedule to help his employer with other important matters. He also realizes that he can be even more valuable to Mr. Ross if he knows the various sources that can be used for the different types of information needed in his reports.

Importance of Reports

As a business becomes larger with more employees working apart from each other, it is more and more difficult to communicate with employees in person and have face-to-face discussions. Business reports make it possible to present much information to others in the company. As a secretary, you will probably type many reports; and, as you gain experience, your employer may ask you to help gather information to be used in reports.

A business report may be only one page, or a long, formal report of more than fifty pages. Some reports are sent to personnel within the company and others to people outside the company.

Illus. 5-1

Gathering information for a business report is often a secretarial responsibility.

Ohio National Life
Insurance Company

Steps in Report Writing

There is no *one* standard way to write a report; there are many ways. However, in drafting and revising a business report you and the preparer of the report, sometimes called the "originator," will usually take these steps:

1. The originator develops a broad idea of the problem to be covered in the report.
2. The originator prepares either a sketchy or a detailed outline of the contents.
3. The originator composes the first draft. The entire draft may be written in longhand, may be recorded on a dictating machine, or may be dictated directly to you.
4. You type the first draft in rough draft form.
5. The originator reorganizes and edits the first draft for content, wording, and sentence structure (usually with your help).
6. You type a second draft of the report.

7. The originator edits the second draft to insure the best presentation of the contents.
8. You type the report in its final form.
9. You double-check each page for accuracy, particularly accuracy of numbers.
10. You **collate** pages of the report.

The Outline

After the problem to be covered in the report has been determined, your employer prepares an outline.

An outline may be written in complete sentence form or in topical form. *Topical form* means that the topics or headings of the parts of the report are listed. Parallel construction should be used; that is, if one part of the outline is in sentence form, the next part should be a sentence, too. This makes it easier for the reader to understand the outline. Words, phrases, and sentences should not be mixed throughout the outline. No main heading or subheading should stand alone. For every Roman numeral "I," there should be a Roman numeral "II"; for every letter "A," a letter "B"; for every Arabic "1," an Arabic "2."

In the outline illustrated on page 151, each identifying number or letter is followed by a period and two spaces and begins just below the first word of the previous line.

The Rough Draft

A rough draft is your employer's first attempt to get important thoughts down on paper where they can be edited and improved. The draft may be revised and retyped many times; therefore, you will find the following ten suggestions helpful:

1. Use typing paper strong enough to withstand erasing easily. Do not use manifold paper or expensive letterhead paper.
2. Type double spacing so that the changes can be clearly marked and easily seen and followed.
3. Allow margins of 1½ inches at the top, bottom, and on both sides of each page to provide enough room for corrections.
4. X out typing errors and **deletions** in the first draft instead of taking time to erase them.
5. A carbon copy or photocopy should be made in case the original is misplaced. You may also wish to have an extra copy to cut up and paste when reorganizing the material.
6. Number each page in the draft in its proper sequence. Also assign a number to each **successive** revision of a draft and type the date on it.

deletions:
items to be taken out

successive:
following without
interruption

```
                    ANALYSIS OF OFFICE OPERATIONS

      I.  Introduction

          A.  Purpose of analysis

          B.  Summary

     II.  Proposed changes

          A.  Personnel
              1.  Designate an Administrative Manager
              2.  Standardize hiring procedure
              3.  Develop positive attitudes about office work
              4.  Improve morale
              5.  Provide inservice education for staff and partners
              6.  Evaluate and reward staff

          B.  Procedures
              1.  Standardize some office procedures
              2.  Delegate more office work to staff
              3.  Improve communication
              4.  Adopt an organizational chart
              5.  Adopt a work allocation chart
              6.  Develop a follow-up system
              7.  Improve reception and telephone services
              8.  Utilize automatic typewriters
              9.  Adopt an office manual

    III.  Prognosis for improvement

     IV.  Plan of action

      V.  Financial implications

     VI.  Conclusions and recommendations

    VII.  Appendices
```

Illus. 5-2 A topical outline of a report

7. Type a long insertion on a separate sheet of paper and give it a corresponding page number and letter. For example, the first insertion to be included on page 8 should be numbered "8A" and clearly marked "Insert 8A" at the point where it is to be inserted.
8. Type quoted matter of four lines or more single spaced and indent it in the same form as it will appear in the final draft.

9. Type footnotes single spaced at the bottom of the page, on a separate sheet, or, preferably, insert them in this manner immediately after the reference in the text but separated from the text by solid lines:

[1]Mary Ellen Oliverio and William R. Pasewark, _Secretarial Office Procedures_ (9th ed.; Cincinnati: South-Western Publishing Co., 1977), p. 152.

10. Keep all rough drafts in a file folder until the final draft has been approved. Your employer may decide to include words, phrases, and sentences deleted from previous drafts in the final draft of the report.

Illus. 5-3

Technical projects often require preliminary work prior to making a report.

IBM Corporation

Proofreaders' Marks

Proofreaders' marks are used to indicate corrections and revisions in rough drafts of business reports because they are clearly understood and easily followed. Their use greatly reduces the chance of error in the retyping of a draft. Standard proofreaders' marks, as they are indicated in a rough draft and corrected in the text, are shown on page 153. You will need to know their meanings to type from rough drafts of business documents efficiently.

PROOFREADERS' MARKS

Mark in Margin	Meaning of Mark	Correction or Change Marked in Text	Corrected or Changed Copy
∧	caret; indicates insertion is to be made	If you are interested ∧ we	If you are interested, we
◡	close up	on the pay‿roll	on the payroll
≡ or *caps*	capitalize	Mutual life of New York	Mutual Life of New York
¶	new paragraph	two or more lines. ¶ One caution	two or more lines. One caution
⌐	move to right	centered over the ⌐columns and then typed	centered over the columns and then typed
⌐	move to left	cc: Joseph H. Morrow ⌐Gerald A. Porter Allen A. Smith	cc: Joseph H. Morrow Gerald A. Porter Allen A. Smith
tr or ∿	transpose	monthly be(ne)fits	monthly benefits
ℐ	take out; delete	We wished you	We wish you
stet	leave it as it was originally	*commencing* ~~starting~~ next month	starting next month

Illus. 5-4 Proofreaders' marks

Typing the Report

The final draft of a business report should be typed on white bond paper (8½″ × 11″ in size) of good quality, preferably of 20-pound substance. The body of the report, except for footnotes and long quotations, should be double-spaced. The report should be typed so that it is attractive and easy to read. The typing line should be 6 to 6½ inches long: 60–65 pica spaces or 72–78 elite type spaces.

MARGINS FOR TYPING BUSINESS REPORTS

Margins	Unbound	Side Bound	Top Bound
Top margin			
First page	2 inches	2 inches	2½ inches
All other pages	1 inch	1 inch	1½ inches
Side margins			
Left	1 inch	1½ inches	1 inch
Right	1 inch	1 inch	1 inch
Bottom margin	1 inch	1 inch	1 inch

Illus. 5-5

The margins for typed reports are determined by the binding. If the preceding table of margins for unbound, side-bound, and top-bound reports is carefully followed, the report will be attractive.

Illus. 5-6

Rough draft report with proofreaders' marks

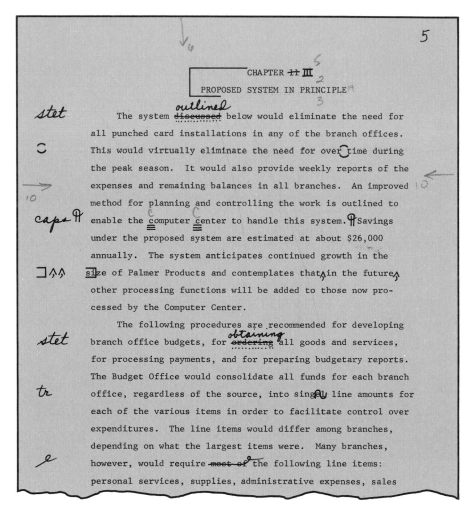

A light pencil mark about 1½" from the bottom edge of the page will alert you that you have but one line left to type at the bottom of the page. Be sure to erase this pencil mark when you are proofreading your final copy.

You may want to use a guide sheet like the one illustrated opposite. On a plain sheet of paper, make rulings with very dark ink to show the left and right margins. Numbering the horizontal lines of the right edge of the page is useful in allowing space for footnotes. The guide sheet is placed behind the original copy in the typewriter and followed for proper placement.

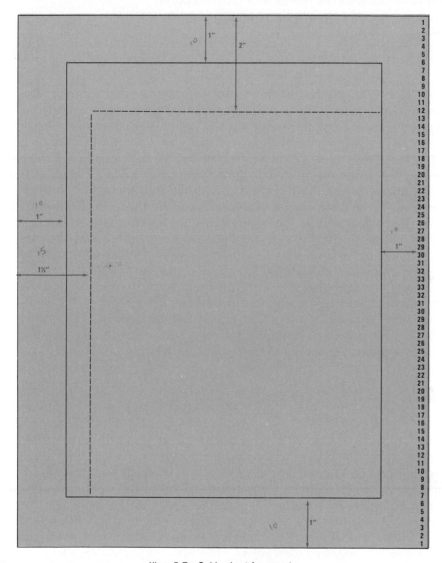

Illus. 5-7 Guide sheet for reports

REVIEWING

1. Why do businesses use reports?
2. What is the difference between preparing an outline in sentence form and preparing one in topical form?

3. What are the advantages of using proofreaders' marks to show corrections in reports and manuscripts?
4. What kind of paper should be used for the final draft of a report?
5. What determines the margins of typed reports?
6. How can a guide sheet help you in typing a report?

MAKING JUDGMENTS

Mr. Ralph Connally has been secretary to Mrs. Francis Kimball, district sales manager for a large furniture manufacturing corporation, for almost two years. During this time, Mr. Connally has gained much experience in report writing. Sometimes he types two or three drafts of a report before he and Mrs. Kimball are satisfied with its content. Earlier this week, Mr. Connally and Mrs. Kimball together edited the second draft of a quarterly report which must be turned into the national office on Monday. There were only a few changes to be made in the report, and Mr. Connally noted the changes on the second draft. Mrs. Kimball left town that same day, and since she would not be back before the report needed to be mailed, she left instructions for Mr. Connally to retype the report carefully, make the minor changes, and mail it. Mr. Connally has just spent two frantic hours looking for the second draft so he can retype it, but he cannot find it anywhere. He thinks he can remember all of the changes that were made on the second draft and is considering using the first draft and relying on his memory to make the proper corrections. What do you think Mr. Connally should do?

WORKING WITH OTHERS

Your employer, Mrs. Irwin, knows she can depend on you to help her prepare accurate and attractive business reports. For the past three weeks you have been collecting data for a report which Mrs. Irwin must present at the Board of Directors meeting. Two days before the meeting you read an article in a business magazine about a new aspect of the subject covered in Mrs. Irwin's report. Should you mention the article to Mrs. Irwin, knowing that it might mean revising the report for the meeting which is only two days away?

REFRESHING LANGUAGE SKILLS

Only one word in each line on the next page is spelled correctly. Type the correct spelling for each word. Then check the words in a dictionary and correct those you have misspelled.

acknowlege	acknoledge	acknowledge
advertising	advertizing	adverticing
cancellation	cancillation	cancelation
conveneint	convenient	conveniant
commision	commition	commission
finist	finiest	finest
immidiate	immideate	immediate
officail	official	officiel
personnel	personell	personall
reccommendation	recommendation	recomendation

PERFORMING SECRETARIAL TASKS

1. Type a final draft of the rough draft on page 154.
2. The following material contains 22 errors. Type the material exactly as shown in rough draft form. Remove the rough draft from the typewriter and use proofreaders' marks to indicate what changes are needed. Don't forget to divide the material into meaningful paragraphs. Type a final draft which includes all your corrections.

THE SECRETARYS' RESPONSIBILITIES FOR
BUSINESS REPORTS

The secertary has many responsibilities in preparing business reports. Once the executive has deceided on the subject of the report, the secretary aids in gathering facts. In order to gather all the neccessary information the secretary must know how use the library. Some sources to be checked is newspapers, periodicles, and books on that particular subject. After the employer has developed the first draft of the report the secretary edits it carefully. This cannot be done without a dictionery. When the final draft is ready to be typed the secretary should gather all of the necessary supplys. A high quality paper is needed for the original and a lower quality paper for any carbon copies. The carbon paper used will depemd on the typewriter and the number of copeis to be made. Great care must be taken with the typewriter to be sure that the keys are clean and that it has a new ribbon. Careful erasing is esssential. Noone should be able to tell that a corection has been made. If the carbon copies are to be sent outside the office corrections on them should also be made with care. The completed report should be proofraed with care. No uncorrected errors can be permited in the finished report. This may mean retyping different pages or even the entire report but the effort will be worthwhile. The completed report must be a work of which both the secretary and the executive can be proud.

Parts of the Business Report

As vice-president in charge of sales, Carla Holder works closely with her secretary, Mr. Collin Nunnelly, when preparing business reports. Ms. Holder likes the way Mr. Nunnelly combines his excellent office skills with a keen understanding of the purpose of each report. She knows that she can rely on him to present the data in an attractive form. Mr. Nunnelly knows that each part of a report has a specific purpose and is designed to make the material easy to read and understand. He also realizes that if a business report is to be effective, the information must be gathered carefully, it must be presented logically, and it must be typed accurately and attractively.

Parts of a Report

A long and detailed business report may contain many specific parts which are classified under three main headings: the introductory parts, the body of the report, and the supplementary parts. Before binding, they are arranged in this order:

A. Introductory Parts
   1. Cover
   2. Title page
   3. Preface or letter of transmittal
   4. Table of contents
   5. List of tables, charts, and illustrations
   6. Summary

B. Body of the Report
   1. Introduction
   2. Main body or text
   3. Conclusions and recommendations

C. Supplementary Parts
   1. Appendix
   2. Bibliography
   3. Index

The body of the report must be developed first; so it is usually typed first. Then the supplementary parts and the introductory parts of the report are typed.

The Cover

The cover should contain this information: the title of the report, the name of the person submitting it, and the date it was submitted.

The Title Page

The items of information that usually appear on the title page are the title of the report, the name of the author, the date, and the place of preparation. Sometimes reports include the name of the person (with **appropriate** title) for whom the report was prepared. (See Illustration 5-8 on page 160.)

appropriate: suitable; proper

Numbering Pages

Small Roman numerals (ii, iii, iv, etc.) are used to number the pages of the introductory parts of the report. The title page is considered as page "i" but no number is typed on it. The numbers are centered and typed one-half inch from the bottom of the page, and they are not followed by periods or any other punctuation.

Arabic numerals, without punctuation, are used to number the pages in the rest of the report. They begin with "1" and run **consecutively** throughout the report. The number on the first page of each section is centered and typed one-half inch from the bottom of the page. The pages that follow are numbered one-half inch from the top and even with the right margin. If the report is to be top bound, all page numbers are placed at the bottom of the page.

consecutively: one after the other in order

It is wise to number all pages at the same time after the entire report has been typed. If you type the numbers on the pages as you type the report and a rather long change has to be made, you will then have to renumber all pages following the change. Before page numbers are typed, they can be written in pencil on the first carbon copy, which will assist you in keeping the pages in numerical order.

```
                    ANALYSIS OF OFFICE OPERATIONS
                    ASSOCIATED INSURANCE CORPORATION




                                 For

                        Richard L. Lindell, President
                        Associated Insurance Corporation








                                 By

                           Charles R. Bruner
                      Office Management Consultants
                          2380 Peachtree Street
                           Atlanta, GA  48812
                             404-638-2291




                              July 2, 19--
```

Headings

You will choose from several types of headings to improve the appearance of the typed matter and to indicate the relationship of its parts. Headings make a report easier to read and understand. If the material is well organized, the headings and subheadings will serve as a basic outline for the report.

Main Headings. Main headings are usually centered on the page and typed in all capital letters. A main heading is normally followed by two blank lines.

Subheadings. There are two kinds of subheadings — side headings and paragraph headings.

Side Headings. Side headings are used to **indicate** major divisions of the main topic. They are typed even with the left margin with the main words starting with a capital letter. Side headings are followed by one blank line. They may also be underlined.

indicate: show

Paragraph Headings. If the text needs to be divided further, paragraph headings may be used. Paragraph headings are indented and underlined. Usually the main words of the heading are capitalized, and the heading is followed by a period.

CHAPTER II

PROPOSED CHANGES

A comprehensive analysis of Associated Insurance (AI) operations resulted in obvious changes to proposals that will increase office productivity. These changes are in the major categories of Personnel and Procedures.

Personnel

Some suggested changes in personnel are as follows:

Appoint an Administrative Manager. The most important priority for AI is to appoint an Administrative Manager who will be responsible for all office operations. Other possible names for this position could be Office Manager or Office Administrator.

The justifications for this new position are:

1. Partners would not have to spend so much time in the office and could devote more of their time and attention to outside selling that produces income.

2. The Administrative Manager will be responsible for the continuous improvement of present office procedures and the introduction of new procedures as AI grows.

3. Improved office procedures will permit us to serve our clients better which will improve our image and encourage additional business.

4. The present size of five partners and nine office staff and the complexity of AI's organization warrants an Administrative Manager.

5. The nature of the partner's major function of selling, requires them to be out of the office. Someone must be in the office at all times and be responsible for its operation.

6. Partners are well educated about selling insurance but none of the present personnel is educated to "back up the sales" in the office. Some of AI's selling strengths can be diluted by ineffective servicing of the policies we sell.

Illus. 5-9

A typed page of a report with headings and subheadings

Preface or Letter of Transmittal

The purpose of the preface or letter of transmittal, illustrated on page 162, is to interest the reader enough to read the entire report. The preface or letter of transmittal is written in a less formal and more personal style than the body of the report.

Table of Contents

OMC Office Management Consultants

2380 Peachtree Street   Atlanta, GA 44812   404-658-2291

July 3, 19--

Mr. Richard L. Lindell, President
Associated Insurance Corporation
2243 Sixteenth Street, N.W.
Washington DC 20134

ANALYSIS OF OFFICE OPERATIONS

Here is the report, ANALYSIS OF OFFICE OPERATIONS, covering our study of Associated Insurance Corporation.

On page 2 is a summary of priority items to implement for the Associated Insurance Corporation. The first course of action should be to designate an Administrative Manager who would be responsible for all of your office operations. A suggested procedure for hiring this person is described on page 3 of the report.

Associated Insurance already has an excellent foundation on which to develop efficient office systems. Your organization is success oriented, morale is high, and both partners and staff seem receptive to changes in your offices. We believe the aims of the analysis, to increase profits and to make office work more pleasant, can be obtained by adopting the recommendations in the report.

Everyone we worked with at Associated Insurance was helpful to the study and I wish you would express appreciation to each of them. We are ready to discuss the implementation of the report after you have had a chance to review it.

Charles Bruner
Office Systems Analyst

bb

Letter of Transmittal

Illus. 5-10

The preface or letter of transmittal usually will contain the following information:

1. The name of the person or organization that asked that the report be prepared.
2. The main purpose of the report.
3. The scope, or extent of coverage, of the report.
4. Acknowledgments of assistance in the preparation of the report.

If a separate summary is not included in the report, it is usually included in the letter.

Tables of Contents

The table of contents, shown on page 162, gives an overview of the material covered in the report by listing the main topics or chapter titles with their page numbers. The heading, *Table of Contents*, should be centered two inches from the top of the page and typed entirely in capital letters. Double spacing is used before the titles of chapters or main topics, and single spacing in all other instances. All important words in the chapter or main topic title should be capitalized. Each chapter should be preceded by its number which is typed in Roman numerals and followed by a period and two spaces. The Roman numerals should be lined up with the periods directly beneath each other. Leaders (periods and spaces **alternated**) should extend across the page from each title to guide the reader in finding the page number at the right.

alternated: first one and then the other

The periods in the leaders should also be in vertical **alignment**. This can be done easily by typing all periods at even numbers on the typewriter line scale. Before the final copy is typed, the table of contents should be checked against the text for correctness of titles and accuracy of page numbers.

alignment: positioning of points in relation to each other

List of Tables

The heading *List of Tables*, like all other main headings, is centered two inches from the top of the page and typed entirely in capital letters. The table numbers are typed in Arabic numerals followed by a period and two blank spaces. The first letter of every important word in the title of a table is typed with a capital letter. Leaders extend from the title to the Arabic page numbers at the right. Lists of charts and other illustrations are typed in the same form as the *List of Tables*.

Summary

The summary of the report is written after the entire report is completed. It gives the reader a quick overview that saves time and makes it easier to understand the detailed statements contained in the body of the report.

Body of the Report

The division headings in the body of the report should be the same as the titles that appear in the table of contents. Each division should begin on a new page with the word *Chapter* or *Section* centered two inches from the top of the page. It should be typed entirely in capital letters and followed by a chapter or section number typed in large Roman numerals. The title of the chapter or section is centered one blank line below and also typed in capital letters. A very long title should be broken into two or more lines and divided at the point where the thought in the title changes. With a long title the inverted pyramid style may be used — the top line longer than the second, and the second line longer than the third. Two blank lines should be left between the title and the first paragraph of the report.

inverted:
turned inside out or upside down

Quoted Material

Material from other sources is frequently quoted in business reports. All direct quotations should be typed exactly as they are written in the quoted source — in wording, spelling, punctuation, and paragraphing.

1. A brief quotation of fewer than four lines is typed in the text and enclosed with quotation marks.
2. A quotation of four lines or more is started on a new line and typed on shorter, single-spaced lines — indented from both the left and right margins. No quotation marks are used.
3. A quotation of several paragraphs need not be indented, but a quotation mark should precede each paragraph and should follow the final word of the last quoted paragraph.
4. A quotation within a quotation (an inside quotation) is enclosed with single quotation marks. The apostrophe is used as a single quotation in typed material.
5. Omissions in a quotation are shown by typing an ellipsis — three spaced periods for an omission within a sentence or between sentences, four periods for an omission at the end of a sentence.

Permission should be obtained to quote copyrighted material if it is to be widely distributed in duplicated reports or printed manuscripts. Material may be quoted from government publications without obtaining permission.

Footnotes

Footnotes refer the reader to information outside the text of a report. They are inserted to acknowledge and identify the source of the quoted information, to support points made by the author, to provide additional

7

Developing positive attitudes about office work is probably the most important challenge for Associated Insurance to increase office productivity. Office work is more difficult to measure and control than work on the farm and in the factory. AI must be sure to hire competent employees, then keep morale high so that all employees are working at their capacity. The result, hopefully, will be that while we cannot measure each employee's work accurately, we can, with reasonable assurance, expect that our office productivity is comparatively high.

Each partner must be convinced that while selling insurance policies is the first step toward a successful, profit-oriented business, servicing the customers' policies in the office is a necessary and important phase of the business. The time and effort of a partner to sell an insurance policy will be wasted if we lose the customer because the processing of the policy in the office was slow or inaccurate. The staff must be convinced of the importance of their work and the need to decrease the time, effort, and material to improve efficiency, reduce costs, and increase profits.[1] The partners and the office staff should be convinced of the vital role of the office at AI after they read the Conclusions and Recommendations, Chapter II, of this report.

[1]Charles J. Howard, Controlling Office Costs (3d ed.; Detroit: National Publishing Co., 1977), p. 61.

Illus. 5-11   A typed page of a report

material for the reader, or to **elaborate** on the meaning within the text. The Arabic number of a footnote is typed in the text just after the statement to be documented but slightly above the line of writing. For raised numbers, the platen is turned toward the typist a half space before the number is typed. The footnote itself, if it is the first reference to a particular work, should identify the author and the title of the work referred to, give facts about the publication of the work and the copyright date, and **cite** a specific page reference. (See Illustration 5-11.)

Later references to the same source need not repeat all these details; only *ibid.*, the abbreviation for *ibidem* (meaning in the same place), and the page number are used when references to the same work follow each other. The author's name, *op. cit.*, the abbreviation for *opere citato* (meaning in the work cited), and the page number are used when a previous reference has been made to the same source but other references are between. The author's name and *loc. cit.*, the abbreviation for *loco citato* (meaning in the same place), are used to refer to the same passage in a reference previously cited.

The footnotes below show the use of *ibid.*, *op. cit.*, and *loc. cit.*

_____

    [1]H. Webster Johnson, <u>How to Use the Bus-</u> <u>iness Library</u> (4th ed., Cincinnati: South-Western Publishing Co., 1972), p. 148.

    [2]Paul S. Burtness and Robert R. Aurner, <u>Effective English for Colleges</u> (5th ed., Cincinnati: South-Western Publishing Co., 1975), pp. 217-243.

    [3]<u>Ibid.</u>, p. 399.

    [4]Johnson, <u>op. cit.</u>, pp. 142-146.

    [5]Burtness and Aurner, <u>loc. cit.</u>

Footnotes should be typed according to the following guides:

1. They are separated from the text by a short, solid horizontal line of 15 pica or 18 elite spaces typed with the underscore key one line below the last line of the text.
2. The first line of the first footnote is typed one blank line below the short horizontal line. It is indented the same number of spaces as the paragraphs in the report. The **succeeding** lines of the footnote begin at the left margin.

3. The reference number, which corresponds with the footnote number in the text, is also typed slightly above the line of writing. It is typed without punctuation or a space between it and the first word of the footnote.

4. All footnotes are typed single space. A blank line is left between footnotes.
5. Footnotes are usually numbered in sequence from the first to the last page of a report or manuscript.

sequence:
in order of occurrence

Conclusions and Recommendations

The conclusions are the results of what has been presented in the report. The recommendations contain the writer's suggestions about action that should be taken as a result of the conclusions.

Appendix

The text of a long report may be followed by an appendix; it is omitted in a short report. It usually contains extra reference material not easily included in the text. It may also include tables containing complete original data, general reference tables, and other materials which will help to interpret and to add interest in the report.

Bibliography

All documentary sources (written material) referred to in a business report — books, articles, and periodicals — should be included in the bibliography. It should also include all the references consulted which had worthwhile information related to the report. The references listed in the bibliography should be arranged in alphabetical order by authors, by editors, or by titles if the authors' names are not available. Examples of references in a bibliography are given on page 168.

Gathering Information

Your employer may not have all the information that is needed to complete either the footnotes or the bibliography. Only a little information may be given you such as, "I think the title of the book is *Business Organization and Management* and the author is Tyler, but I'm not sure." Of course, your employer may not remember the author's first name or even how to spell the name. As for a newspaper article referred to, all your employer may remember is that it was in the *Times* last week. The rest is up to you.

There is even more to it than that. Very often in quoting material your employer may not correctly remember each word and may not have the exact statistics, nor the dates. This, too, is your responsibility. After checking the original sources, you make the changes that are necessary without annoying your employer with such details.

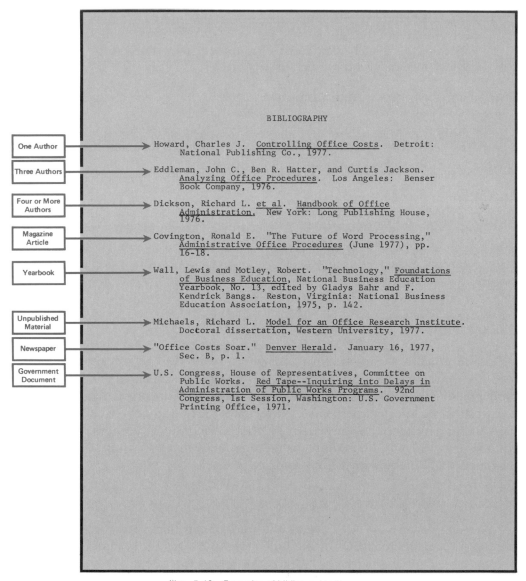

BIBLIOGRAPHY

One Author → Howard, Charles J. *Controlling Office Costs*. Detroit: National Publishing Co., 1977.

Three Authors → Eddleman, John C., Ben R. Hatter, and Curtis Jackson. *Analyzing Office Procedures*. Los Angeles: Benser Book Company, 1976.

Four or More Authors → Dickson, Richard L. *et al*. *Handbook of Office Administration*. New York: Long Publishing House, 1976.

Magazine Article → Covington, Ronald E. "The Future of Word Processing," *Administrative Office Procedures* (June 1977), pp. 16-18.

Yearbook → Wall, Lewis and Motley, Robert. "Technology," *Foundations of Business Education*, National Business Education Yearbook, No. 13, edited by Gladys Bahr and F. Kendrick Bangs. Reston, Virginia: National Business Education Association, 1975, p. 142.

Unpublished Material → Michaels, Richard L. *Model for an Office Research Institute*. Doctoral dissertation, Western University, 1977.

Newspaper → "Office Costs Soar." *Denver Herald*. January 16, 1977, Sec. B, p. 1.

Government Document → U.S. Congress, House of Representatives, Committee on Public Works., *Red Tape--Inquiring into Delays in Administration of Public Works Programs*. 92nd Congress, 1st Session, Washington: U.S. Government Printing Office, 1971.

Illus. 5-12   Examples of bibliographic forms

You may have to check reference books such as the *Reader's Guide to Periodical Literature, The New York Times Index,* and *The World Almanac.* In compiling reports or writing manuscripts, you will need to know what to look for, where to look, and how to get the information rapidly and correctly. Company purchased reference books, public libraries, trade journals, and business and local newspapers will be your best sources of information. Appendix H, page 678, contains a list of reference books which should also be of assistance to you.

Proofreading

All typewritten reports and manuscripts should be proofread before they are duplicated or printed. The text can be checked most effectively, particularly if it contains statistics, by having one of your co-workers assist you. (See Unit II, page 62, for suggestions on proofreading numbers.)

REVIEWING

1. What are the three main parts of a business report?
2. List the items of information usually given on the title page of a report.
3. Why is it wise to number all pages of a report at the same time after the entire report has been typed?
4. What is the purpose of side headings in a report?
5. What is the purpose of a letter of transmittal?
6. Why is the summary of a report placed after the table of contents and before the body of the report?
7. What should an author do before using copyrighted material which is to be widely distributed in duplicated or in printed form?
8. What information is contained in a footnote?
9. What is the purpose of an appendix?
10. What is a good procedure for checking the text of a report, particularly if it contains statistical material?

MAKING JUDGMENTS

Mrs. Betty Maxwell has just completed two very detailed reports which her employer will use in making presentations at a national food brokers convention. Mrs. Maxwell has proofread the reports once herself, but she would like two others in the office to proofread the reports also. One of the reports is very technical in nature and the other report contains many statistics and numerical data. Mrs. Maxwell decides to let Cynthia, her best proofreader, proofread the report containing the statistics, and to let Margaret, a less accurate proofreader, proofread the technical report. What do you think about Mrs. Maxwell's judgment in assigning the two reports to Cynthia and Margaret for proofreading? Do you believe she made the right assignments? Why or why not?

WORKING WITH OTHERS

Robert and Teresa are stenographers in the security services department of the Lawson Manufacturing Corporation. At 1:00 p.m., Robert rushed to Teresa's desk and said, "Teresa, I'm in a real bind to finish proofreading a report for Mr. Bailey. He needs it before a two o'clock staff meeting, so I wondered if you would help me proofread?" Teresa had all of her essential work for the day completed, and she was working on some filing. "I'm awfully sorry," Teresa replied, "but I really wanted to catch up on this filing." Robert was somewhat disturbed with Teresa's answer, but he returned to his desk and finished the proofreading alone. Two days later, Teresa's boss gave her a report and told her he had to have the report by five o'clock, because he needed to take it with him on a business trip. Teresa knew that she would need help to finish the report, and because it was a top priority item, she would need to ask someone who was familiar with that kind of report. Robert was the only other stenographer in the office who was familiar with the report, but Teresa was hesitant about asking him. Teresa remembered how she had responded to Robert when he needed help, and she began to wonder whether she had behaved properly. Do you think Teresa was right in refusing Robert? What do you think Teresa should do about the situation she is faced with now?

REFRESHING LANGUAGE SKILLS

Four easy rules must be kept in mind if you are to use question marks correctly.

A. A question mark follows a direct question — a period follows an indirect question, usually introduced by *whether* or *if*.

Examples: Is the Table of Contents typed?
He asked if the table of Contents had been typed.

B. In a series, if emphasis is desired, a question mark may follow each question.

Example: Where is the Preface? the Table of Contents? the List of Tables? the Appendix?

C. A question mark may be used inside parentheses to indicate doubt.

Example: The report will be sent to the president, the treasurer, the secretary(?), four sales representatives.

D. A question mark is placed inside or outside the second quotation mark, depending on content.

Examples: The employer asked, "Who typed the material on research and development?"
Who typed "Research and Development"?

Type the following sentences on a separate sheet of paper, inserting question marks and any other necessary punctuation.

1. If Mr. Lions doesn't return today, Vicki asked "who will help me prepare the report?"
2. Did you check the files, your desk, the wastebasket?
3. She asked if she could proofread the report tomorrow afternoon.

4. Who typed the title page for "The Annual Stockholders' Report."

5. Did I type the appendix correctly Nancy asked her supervisor.

6. The sales manager reported that 1971, 1972, 1973, and 1874 had been the company's best years.

7. Who proofread the Summary the Conclusion the Bibliography.

8. Does the Table of Contents come before or after the Summary.

9. The executive asked where did you obtain that data.

10. The author asked the company if he could quote material from their magazine.

PERFORMING SECRETARIAL TASKS

1. Using plain paper, type the following five items of information in the form of a title page for a report:

   a. Title: RESEARCH REPORT ON CONTROLLING OFFICE COSTS

   b. For: William C. Danberry, President of the Corbin Manufacturing Corporation

   c. By: Scott T. Milton, Director of Research and Development

   d. At: San Diego, California

   e. On: October 13, 19--

2. Using plain paper, type the following TABLE OF CONTENTS with appropriate margins on a single page:

	Page
Letter of Transmittal	ii
Table of Contents	iii
List of Tables	iv
List of Charts	v

Chapter

I. Report of the Chairman	1
Operations	1
Research and Development	3
Manufacture and Supply	5
Conduct of the Business	7
II. Directors and Officers	8
III. Consolidated Financial Statements	9
Statement of Earnings	9
Balance Sheet	11
Comparative Balance Sheets	13
IV. Auditor's Report	15
V. Property, Plant, and Equipment	17
VI. Inventories and Investments	18

3. Using a letterhead from the *Supplies Inventory* or plain paper, type the letter of transmittal on the following page in block form with open punctuation (current date).

13 ½ late Sept. = 1983

1" = 10

Dear Mr. Carleton

The

13

15 90

Mr. Thomas B. Carleton President Smith Paper Company Chester, PA 12055 Dear Mr. Carleton (¶1) The report which accompanies this letter covers the research on new products and the development of new markets for the Smith Paper Company. (¶2) Our employees made dramatic progress last year in developing new products and new markets which will contribute importantly to the Company's future growth. Some of the new products are shown elsewhere in this report; still others — not yet ready for the market — are in various stages of development. Our research and development expenses for last year were almost 25 percent greater than the previous year. After very careful study of the long-range opportunities open to us through research in the physical sciences and in marketing, we think it is safe to say that our total budgets for these important activities will probably be increased by as much as 50 percent over the next three years. (¶3) Smith employees at all levels are committed to a policy of improving the quality of our products and continuing the war against waste and inefficiency in every form. The credit for what we consider to be a truly remarkable achievement in research and development by the Smith Paper Company belongs not only to the Research Division but to all the men and women employed by the Company. Sincerely yours Walter A. Starr Director of Research and Development

4. Using plain paper, type the following page from an annual report to the stockholders with double spacing and margins set for binding at the side. The heading is *Research and Development*.

The Corporation's long-standing emphasis on research and development continues to be directed to new, improved products and to more economical processes and equipment. These activities, located at Yorktown Heights, New York, are conducted to assure the future success of the Corporation. The organization is composed of separate groups with personnel well trained in scientific fields such as chemistry, physics, engineering, and textile technology. Each group has adequate up-to-date facilities and equipment to do modern research in fields of expanding technology. (¶) The combination of the various technical talents at one location enables groups to conduct coordinated research on new fibers and packaging films — and basic or exploratory research directed toward the discovery of new products. Through research the competitive position of fiberglass tires has been improved by developing a method of processing fiberglass so that it is flexible and strong. As a result of this development, passenger car tires have been made even more durable under difficult road conditions.

Financial Statements and Reports

Miss Joyce Nickels has enjoyed her work in the Accounting Services Department of CTO Products. Her supervisor, Mrs. Clara Weavers, noticed that Miss Nickels was doing an excellent job on the statistical material she had been given and decided to give her another challenging task. One morning, Mrs. Weavers said, "Miss Nickels, you have been doing such fine work that I would like you to begin preparing financial statements and reports." To make sure that Miss Nickels understood the importance of her new responsibility, Mrs. Weavers added, "The financial reports which we prepare are essential to give our company officers and employees the information we need to operate our company efficiently. Many managerial decisions will be based upon information contained in our financial statements and reports. That is why it is so important for each report to be completely accurate. If you take your time and study the statements and reports we have on file, I think you will be able to do a good job." Miss Nickels returned to her work area knowing that her new responsibility would require a great deal of concentration, but she was glad for the opportunity to grow in her job.

Understanding Financial Statements

A business, like a person, at times, needs a checkup. The family doctor provides a check on the physical condition of a person. The doctor analyzes the findings and locates the cause of any physical problem the patient may have. The doctor is then able to prescribe medication for the problem.

Those who manage a business can discover the financial health of a business by studying reports called *financial statements*. The two reports, common to all types of business, which furnish the information necessary for management to determine the financial health of a business are the *balance sheet* and the *income statement*.

Balance Sheet

analysis:
careful study

A balance sheet, like a physical examination, reveals whether a business is healthy on a particular date. **Analysis** of the main parts shown in the balance sheet on page 178 enables management to tell whether, on a specific date, the business is healthy or sick. These parts are (1) *assets* (what the business owns), (2) *liabilities* (what the business owes) and *capital* or — the owners' share of the business.

On every balance sheet, the total assets always equal the total liabilities plus capital ($A = L + C$). The form of the balance sheet should make this basic bookkeeping **equation** obvious to the reader. Double lines typed beneath the figure representing *Total Assets* and beneath the figure representing *Total Liabilities and Capital* attract the reader's attention so it is **obvious** at a glance that the figures are equal.

equation:
a mathematical
statement that shows
equality

obvious:
easily seen

Income Statement

The income statement shows the financial progress of the business. It shows how successful, or unsuccessful, a business has been during the period stated in the heading of the report: for example, "For the Year Ended December 31, 19—." Success is measured in terms of net income, or net profit. A *net profit* results when the income is greater than the expenses. A *net loss* occurs when the opposite happens.

convenient:
suitable

Below the heading, the income statement shows in **convenient** form the income of the business, the cost of merchandise sold, the expenses, and the net income, or net loss, that resulted from the operation of the business during the fiscal period. The *fiscal period* is the time covered by the financial statement.

The double lines beneath the last dollar amounts listed on page 179 make the Net Income $470,133 immediately noticeable to the reader. Since this is the most important number on the income statement, the **emphasis** is justified. By studying the remaining numbers in the same column, the reader can understand why and how the net income occurred. For more detailed information, study the remaining columns on the report.

emphasis:
special attention

Producing Typewritten Financial Statements

You will have several major responsibilities in producing final copies of the financial statements. If the statements are to be correct and pleasing in appearance, careful study and planning are necessary before you begin to type.

Study Previous Reports

Before you type any financial statements for your employer, it is a good idea to examine earlier copies of income statements and balance sheets in the company files. Because executives compare new financial statements with previous ones, they usually prefer that the same general form be followed year after year.

Check Accuracy of Calculations

With a calculating machine, check to make sure that the addition and subtraction shown on the rough draft submitted for typing are correct. It is also wise to verify, by machine, the accuracy of the addition and subtraction of the figures typed on the final typewritten product. This checks the typing accuracy of numbers.

Illus. 5-13

Careful study and planning are necessary to produce correct and attractive financial statements.

C. Brewer and Company, Limited

Type the Financial Statements

A look at the financial reports of several companies would show many similarities and some minor differences in style. Points of similarity might include the following:

1. *Use of descriptive titles to introduce groups of similar accounts.* For example, in the balance sheet on page 178, assets which, during the normal course of business operations, will be converted to cash are listed under the title Current Assets. Notice that the first letter of the first word and important words in these introductory titles is capitalized.
2. *Indentations from the left to indicate subdivisions of larger units of information.* In the income statement on page 179, the depth of the horizontal indentations before Federal income taxes and State income taxes indicates that both types of expenses are of equal importance; also that both are subdivisions of a larger grouping labeled Operating Taxes. The additional depth of indentation before Current Taxes shows that it is a subdivision of Federal income taxes.
3. *Use of commas in the amount columns to separate each three digits, beginning to the left of the decimal point.* For example, in the income statement on page 179, the Local service figure for 1978 is $1,351,364.
4. *Vertical alignment of the decimal point in a column of figures.* Also, when one or more of the items in the amount columns indicate cents, every entry in any column should contain a decimal. For example:

$2,550.42
350.00
1,670.90
80.00

5. *A single line extending the width of the longest item in the column, typed beneath the last figure, to indicate addition or subtraction.*
6. *Double lines typed beneath figures at the bottom of the column to identify the final figure in a column.*
7. *Use of leaders (a line of either spaced or unspaced periods) to guide the reader's eye from the explanation column to the first column of amounts.* Leaders are especially necessary when the items in the explanation column vary widely in the amount of horizontal space used or when, on single spaced copy, there is so much space between the explanation column and the first amount column that it may be difficult to read across the page. Leaders should be aligned vertically on either even or odd spaces on the typewriter scale and should end at the same horizontal point.
8. *Information given in the heading of the financial statement.* Answers to each of the questions, who? what? when?, should be given on separate lines in that order. The balance sheet should

answer the question, When?, with a specific date; the income statement will answer it with a phrase which identifies the fiscal period covered.

9. *Use of the dollar sign with the first figure listed vertically in each amount column.* In the balance sheet on page 178, notice that in the first column the In service figure ($8,456,037) includes a dollar sign. Be sure to use a dollar sign with every figure which has double lines typed directly beneath it.

The important guideline to apply for minor points of style is to *be consistent.* Apply the test of consistency when making decisions related to the following points:

1. *Vertical spacing.* When deciding whether to single-space or double-space within a financial statement, consider:

   (a) Length of statement relative to the amount of vertical space available. The common practice is to avoid, if possible, two-page financial statements.

   (b) Ease of reading. Those who analyze financial statements are normally top-management people who have many demands on their time, attention, and efforts. Blank vertical lines scattered among single-space copy attract attention; therefore, use them for emphasizing especially important figures.

2. *Capitalization.*

   (a) In the heading. Some executives prefer that the entire heading of financial statements be typed in all capitals; others require all capitals for only the name of the business. The current trend seems to be away from the practice of using all capitals for every word in the heading of a financial statement.

   (b) In the explanation column. A common practice is to capitalize the first letter of the first word and each important word included in the explanation column. However, some executives prefer that only the first character of an account title be capitalized. (This practice is followed in both the income statement on page 179 and the balance sheet on page 178.)

3. *Colon.* A colon following a title is used to introduce like accounts (for example, on the income statement a colon following Operating Revenues). The colon indicates that a listing follows.

4. *Indentations.* The depth of the indentations depends on the amount of horizontal space available in relation to the number

CENTENNIAL UTILITIES
Balance Sheet
December 31, 1978

Assets

	December 31, 1977	December 31, 1978
Plant:		
In service..........................	$8,456,037	$7,774,099
Under construction...................	344,383	296,399
Other (held for future use).........	4,874	3,914
	8,805,294	8,074,412
Less: Accumulated depreciation...	1,770,614	1,673,448
	7,034,680	6,400,964
Current Assets:		
Cash.................................	32,234	34,237
Receivables..........................	399,870	355,382
Material and supplies................	41,289	30,329
Prepaid expenses.....................	38,840	37,497
	512,233	457,445
Deferred Charges.......................	85,908	69,224
Total Assets...........................	$7,632,821	$6,927,633

Liabilities and Capital

	December 31, 1977	December 31, 1978
Equity:		
Common shares--par value $13 1/7 per share..............................	$2,408,399	$2,408,399
Preferred shares--par value $100 per share, 7% cumulative..............	82,000	82,000
Capital in excess of par value......	336,566	336,566
Reinvested earnings.................	553,289	476,159
	3,380,254	3,303,124
Long and Intermediate Term Debt........	3,197,000	2,647,000
Interim Debt...........................	128,481	246,050
Other Current Liabilities:		
Accounts payable....................	248,410	214,385
Advanced billing and customers' deposits...........................	58,041	50,949
Dividends payable...................	51,806	51,806
Interest accrued....................	48,494	42,772
Taxes accrued.......................	32,766	38,148
	439,517	398,020
Deferred Credits:		
Accumulated deferred income taxes...	339,021	209,996
Unamortized investment tax credits..	139,184	114,691
Other...............................	9,364	8,752
	487,569	333,439
Total Liabilities and Capital.........	$7,632,821	$6,927,633

Illus. 5-14   A balance sheet

CENTENNIAL UTILITIES
Income Statement
For Year Ended December 31, 1978

	Year 1978	Year 1977
Operating Revenues:		
Local service......................	$1,351,364	$1,213,285
Foreign service....................	1,500,990	1,365,028
Advertising........................	138,147	128,773
Less: Provision for uncollectibles.	31,061	25,738
Total operating revenues.......	2,959,440	2,681,348
Operating Expenses:		
Maintenance........................	657,404	610,182
Depreciation.......................	417,452	386,628
Customer services..................	500,491	452,303
Pensions and other employee benefits	234,907	210,797
Services received under License		
Contract........................	30,308	25,216
Other operating expenses...........	173,786	154,811
Total operating expenses......	2,014,348	1,839,937
Net operating revenues........	945,092	841,411
Operating Taxes:		
Federal income taxes:		
Current.........................	70,916	77,647
Deferred........................	116,832	84,412
Investments tax credits.........	24,493	22,513
State income taxes:		
Current.........................	23,482	20,607
Deferred........................	12,193	5,812
Property, social security, and		
other taxes.....................	227,043	217,304
Total operating taxes........	474,959	428,295
Net income..................	$ 470,133	$ 413,116

Illus. 5-15   An income statement

of horizontal spaces needed to type the necessary columns across the page. The important thing to remember is that units of equal importance (such as Maintenance and Depreciation on the income statement on page 179) should be indented the same number of spaces.

Proofread the Final Product

Proofreading is easier, faster, and more accurate if the person reading the final typewritten product does not have to glance back and forth from the original to the copy being proofread. Either (1) ask another worker in the office to help — choose one who is particularly good at noticing details, or (2) dictate from the original copy onto a dictating machine and then check the final draft as you listen carefully to the recording.

The oral reader should be careful to indicate all capitalization, punctuation, use of dollar signs in figure columns, underscores, blank vertical spacing, and depth of indentations. Unless emphasized orally, these details are likely to be overlooked by the proofreader.

A common technique for proofreading columns of dollar amounts is to read down the columns, rather than across the columns.

File Carbon Copy of Final Draft

Before filing, on the copy write the name of the person responsible for the original preparation of the financial statement. Some executives require that the rough draft original submitted to a typist be filed along with the carbon copy of the final typewritten product.

Annual Reports of Corporations

creditors:
those to whom money is owed

As a means of informing interested persons such as investors, **creditors**, prospective investors and creditors, and large corporations, at the end of each fiscal year, well-illustrated complete reports about business activities are prepared for distribution. An annual report usually contains a letter to the shareholders from the president of the corporation accompanied by a statistical report of the highlights of the year, a description of newly developed products and recently acquired markets, and a number of financial reports with supporting information in the form of tables and graphs. Ordinarily the financial statements include a statement of income and a balance sheet.

Illus. 5-16

Portion of a tabular report

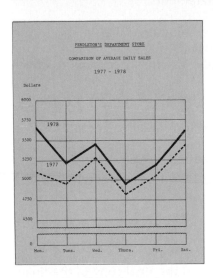

.Illus. 5-17   Line graph

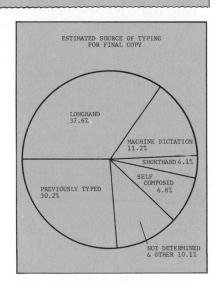

Illus. 5-18   Circle graph

Probably the most widely read table in the annual report is the one which shows a comparison of important figures for the present year with those of the previous year. The table labeled "Highlights of the Year," on this page, is such a **comparative** table. Topics included in this illustration are usually found in other comparative reports.

comparative: that which shows comparisons

Part 3 • Financial Statements and Reports

Much of the supporting information, such as a report on the amount of sales in the different territories, is presented in **columnar** form. Other information, such as the distribution of the sales dollar or the increase or decrease in annual sales, is often better presented by graphs.

Two of the most common types of graphs may include typewritten information: the line graph and the circle graph (see page 181). Two details relative to typing on a graph are especially important:

1. Center titles of graphs over the diagram and type it in all capital letters.
2. Center horizontally and vertically any typewritten material within the boundaries of the space to which the typewritten material applies. (See "Previously Typed" inside the large part of the circle graph in Illus. 5-18.)

REVIEWING

1. What two financial statements help a business determine its financial situation?
2. Name three kinds of information contained in a balance sheet.
3. What is the purpose of the income statement?
4. What is *net profit*?
5. What major responsibilities might a secretary have in producing final copies of the financial statements?
6. What is the fastest and most accurate way for a secretary to check the figures in a financial statement?
7. What questions are answered by the heading of a balance sheet and income statement?
8. What is the most important guideline to remember when making a decision on typing style?
9. How can a secretary speed up the proofreading process?
10. What information does the annual report of a corporation usually contain?

MAKING JUDGMENTS

1. Some believe that the person who typed the final copy of the financial statement should proofread while a second person reads orally from the original. Others believe that the person who typed the final copy should be the oral reader and a second person, one unfamiliar with the task, should do the proofreading on the final copy. Which is your choice and why?
2. Miss Owens had the task of typing an important financial report that had to be completed before closing time that day. Because she was

such a careful typist and because the time was short, she decided it was not necessary to proofread the report. What do you think of her decision?

WORKING WITH OTHERS

Because you are a fast and efficient proofreader, Mr. Helms often asks you to proofread the financial reports prepared by others in the office. While proofreading an annual report being compiled for the company's stockholders, you discover a wrong figure. You immediately call Diana, the typist who typed the report, into your office to point out the error. Diana listens to you, but doesn't really seem concerned about her mistake. What could you say to emphasize the importance of complete accuracy in preparing financial reports?

REFRESHING LANGUAGE SKILLS

A few of the more important comma usages follow:

A. To set off a nonrestrictive phrase or subordinate clause. (A phrase or clause is nonrestrictive if the main clause in the sentence expresses a complete thought when the nonrestrictive phrase or clause is taken out.)
B. To set off phrases or expressions at the beginning of a sentence when they are loosely connected with the rest of the sentence.
C. To set off parenthetical words, clauses, or phrases.
D. To set off words and phrases used in apposition.
E. To separate two or more adjectives if they both precede or follow the noun they modify, provided each adjective modifies the noun alone.

On a separate sheet of paper type the following sentences and insert commas where needed.

1. Unless there are any changes the annual report will be mailed to our stockholders next week.
2. Mr. Loomis needed last month's balance sheet which was filed two weeks ago.
3. After all the company did make a profit last year.
4. You must however get permission to leave early.
5. Mr. Nix the president of our company is visiting the Chicago office today.
6. Generally speaking preparing an income statement takes less time than preparing a balance sheet.
7. Neat accurate financial statements however difficult to type are worth the effort.
8. You will therefore want to make several copies of that financial statement.

9. Current assets and fixed assets current liabilities and longterm liabilities capital stock and retained earnings are terms you will find on a balance sheet.
10. The accountant Sam Breadlove talked with his assistant before taking the summary to the department manager Roy Marlowe.

PERFORMING SECRETARIAL TASKS

1. From the following data prepare a balance sheet for Fulton Enterprises as of December 31, 1978. Using plain paper, type the balance sheet in the same form as the illustration on page 178. (The first set of figures in each category represents 1977 figures; the second set, 1978.)

Assets:

Plant: In service $6,574,099 $7,256,027
Under construction $96,399 $44,383
Other (held for future use) $13,914 $14,874
(total): $6,684,412 $7,315,284
Less: Accumulated depreciation $673,448
$770,614
(total): $6,010,964 $6,544,670
Current Assets: Cash $16,237 $162,234
Receivables $455,382 $499,870
Material and supplies $20,329 $31,289
Prepaid expenses $27,497 $28,840
(total): $519,445 $722,233
Deferred Charges: $169,224 $185,908
Total Assets: $6,699,633 $7,452,811

Liabilities and Capital:

Equity: Common shares — par value 13^{1/7}$ per share
$2,308,399 $2,308,399
Preferred shares — par value $100 per share, 7%
cumulative $72,000 $72,000
Capital in excess of par value $236,566
$236,566
Reinvested earnings $576,159 $653,289
(total) $3,193,124 $3,270,254
Long and Intermediate Term Debt: $2,529,000
$3,147,000
Interim Debt: $546,050 $428,481
Other Current Liabilities: Accounts payable $14,385
$48,410

Advanced billing and customers' deposits $60,949
$68,041
Dividends payable $41,806 $41,806
Interest accrued $32,732 $38,494
Taxes accrued $48,148 $42,766
(total) $198,020 $239,517
Deferred Credits: Accumulated deferred income taxes
$109,996 $239,011
Unamortized investment tax credits $104,691
$109,184
Other $18,752 $19,364
(total) $233,439 $367,559
Total Liabilities and Capital: $6,699,633 $7,452,811

2. From the following data prepare an income statement for Fulton Enterprises for the year ending December 31, 1978. Using plain paper, type the income statement in the same form as the illustration on page 179. (The first set of figures in each category represents 1978 figures; the second, 1977.)

Operating Revenues: Local service $1,451,364 $1,313,285
Foreign service $500,990 $365,028
Advertising $138,147 $128,773
Less: Provision for uncollectibles $71,061 $65,738
Total operating revenues $2,019,440 $1,741,348

Operating Expenses: Maintenance $607,404 $560,182
Depreciation $317,452 $186,628
Customer services $50,491 $52,303
Pensions and other employee benefits $434,907
$310,797
Services received under License Contract $50,308
$85,216
Other operating expenses $273,786 $254,811
Total operating expenses $1,734,348 $1,449,937
Net operating revenues $285,092 $291,411

Operating Taxes: Federal income taxes: Current $90,916 $97,647
Deferred $16,832 $24,412
Investments tax credits $24,493 $22,513
State income taxes: Current $3,482 $2,607
Deferred $2,193 $2,812
Property, social security, and other taxes $27,043
$37,304
Total operating taxes $164,959 $187,295

Net income $120,133 $104,116

Part **4**

Legal Papers, Minutes, and Resolutions

After completing a two-year program for legal secretaries at a junior college, Loren Moyer went to work for the legal firm of Thompson, Barker, and Ashbrook. For a year, Loren worked with other typists in the word processing center. He became familiar with the terminology and procedures used by the attorneys as he typed legal documents from a transcribing machine. Now, as secretary to Mr. Ashbrook, Loren assists in preparing many legal documents. He realizes that he is responsible not only for making sure that the final drafts are free of errors, but also for keeping the information that is contained in all documents completely confidential.

Legal Papers

documents:
official papers

There are various kinds of legal papers, or **documents** — contracts, wills, deeds, leases, affidavits, powers of attorney. Some may be typewritten by the secretary; others are printed and merely require filling in various blanks to complete them. Some require the services of a notary public; others require witnesses only. At some time or other, you will probably be called upon to type or complete a legal document.

Typewritten Legal Papers

Legal documents may be typed on standard 8½" × 11" paper; however, most are typed on legal size paper which is 8½ inches wide and may vary from 13 to 15 inches in length. This paper may have printed left and right margin lines. The left margin rule is usually a double line; the right margin, a single line. In typing material on legal paper with printed margin rules, you should set the margin stops on your typewriter so that the margins of the typewritten material will be at least two spaces within the printed margin lines. If paper without printed margin rules is used for typing a legal paper, you should allow a 1½-inch left margin and a ½-inch right margin. Minimum margins of 2 inches at the top and 1 inch at the bottom are usually allowed. You should prepare enough carbon copies of all legal papers so that each person interested in the paper will have a copy, including at least one copy for the lawyer and one for the court record. An example of a typewritten legal document is shown on page 193. Note particularly the space between the printed margin lines and the left and right margins of the typewritten material, the spacing (triple spacing between the title and the first line, double spacing thereafter), the use of all capitals for certain words in the contract, the punctuation, and the arrangement of the closing lines.

Spacing. Typewritten legal documents are usually double-spaced, but you may single-space some of them, including wills and affidavits (a sworn statement in writing made under oath).

A type of legal paper may be purchased with consecutive numbers printed down the page at the left of the printed left margin line. The number "1" is approximately two inches from the top edge and indicates the position of the typewritten title. The other numbers indicate the positions of the typewritten lines of material and make possible easy reference to any particular part of the legal paper when its contents are being discussed. If the legal paper used does not contain these printed numbers, and if your employer wants to have such numbers on the completed document, it will be a simple matter for you to type them as you type the document.

Erasures. Because a legal paper states the rights or privileges and duties or obligations of the parties who sign it, and later may be submitted in a court of law as evidence, you should prepare each paper accurately and proofread it carefully. You may erase and correct some errors in typing legal papers; others may not be corrected. If the error and erasure affect only one or two letters in a relatively unimportant word, you may erase and make the correction. If, on the other hand, the error you make involves a word which might be important to the meaning of the part of the contract — substituting the word *may* for *must*, for example — or, if an error involves an amount of money, name, or date, the erasure should not be made but the complete paper should be retyped. In some cases, however, such corrections may be made if the corrected paper is initialed by all parties. If you are in doubt, you should ask your employer if it is necessary to retype the legal paper or if it is permissible to erase and correct the error.

Numbers, Dates, and Titles. Quantities in legal documents are usually written in both words and figures, as follows:

A scholarship of one thousand dollars ($1,000)
Under the terms of the will he will receive five thousand (5,000)
   dollars
A twenty- (20) year mortgage
Fifty (50) shares of Woolworth common stock
Five (5) percent interest

Dates are written in several forms. No one form, however, is more legal than another; therefore, there is no reason why you should not type a date in a legal form as you would type it in a letter. Variations are:

On this, the third day of November, 19—
This 16th day of June in the year 19—
This sixteenth day of June, in the year of our Lord, one thousand
   nine hundred and **seventy-seven**

Personal titles — Miss, Mr., Mrs. Ms. — are not used with names in legal documents. Professional titles — Dr., Prof. — are not ordinarily used either.

Printed Legal Forms

Legal documents may be prepared by typing the necessary information on a printed legal form. Standard forms for bills of sale, deeds, leases, mortgages, and wills may be purchased in stationery stores. However, important legal documents, even though they are on a printed form, should be checked by a lawyer.

When typing on printed legal forms, if the item of information that is filled in is important, such as a sum of money, the space that remains on either side of the item after it is typed should be filled in with hyphens. This eliminates the possibility of figures, letters, or words being added later to change the meaning of the typewritten insertion.

The same margins used for the printed matter should be used for the typewritten matter. When carbon copies are prepared, the position of the printed matter on each copy must be checked carefully so that the typewritten additions will appear in the proper places on all copies. Unless this check is made, the typewritten matter on a carbon copy may be written over some of the printed matter, and the copy may be illegible.

Notarized Legal Papers

authorized:
given right or power

Many legal documents are notarized. This means a signed statement is added by a notary public (a public official **authorized** by the state) to show that the paper has been signed in the notary's presence and that the signers have sworn that they are the same persons referred to in the document. The statement by the notary public usually is shown at the bottom of the same paper on which the legal document is typed. It may be shown on a separate page, however, if there is no room for it on the page that contains the legal material.

SINGLE ACKNOWLEDGEMENT

THE STATE OF TEXAS,

COUNTY OF ...*Bexar*..............)   BEFORE ME, the undersigned authority,

in and for said County, Texas, on this day personally appeared ...*Don Knight and*...................

...*Nancy Knight*...

....

known to me to be the person..*S*..whose name..*S*.......subscribed to the foregoing instrument, and acknowledged to me

that ..*T*..he*y*.executed the same for the purposes and consideration therein expressed.

GIVEN UNDER MY HAND AND SEAL OF OFFICE, This..*7th*....day of..*Friday*.......................,A.D. 19.--.

(L.S.)   ...*Vicky Raines*...............................

Notary Public.............*Bexar*............,County, Texas

My Commission Expires June 1, 19...............

Illus. 5-19   Statement of a notary public

Do not be surprised if your employer wishes you to become a notary public. In large offices one of the secretaries usually acts in this **capacity**. In an office building containing a number of small offices, a secretary employed in one of them may act as a notary public for all offices in the building.

capacity: position to carry out a duty

The laws for becoming a notary public differ in the various states. In many states an application accompanied by statements that show that the applicant is a citizen and a resident of the state, of the required age, and good character is submitted to the governor's office. If the application is granted, the notary public secures a notary's seal, which is a metal, hand-operated instrument that **embosses** on a legal paper the design of a seal containing the name of the notary. A notary's commission is for a limited period of time, usually for two years, but it may be renewed.

embosses: imprints by raising the surface of the paper

Typical Legal Documents

A discussion of a simple contract, a will, a deed, a lease, an affidavit, and a power of attorney — legal papers that are frequently prepared in a business office — will explain how to type legal papers.

Simple Contract. A *contract* is an agreement that can be enforced at law. It creates legal rights and responsibilities. It may be either oral or written; however, some contracts, such as those for the purchase of real estate, must be in writing. Before you type a contract, you should check to see that it includes the following essential information:

1. The date and the place of the agreement
2. The names of the parties entering into the agreement
3. The purpose of the contract
4. The duties of each party
5. The money, services, or goods given in consideration of the contract
6. The time period
7. The signatures of all the parties

The illustration on page 193 shows parts of a simple contract prepared on legal paper with printed margin lines.

Will. A *will* is a legal document which provides for the distribution of a person's property after death. The person who makes the will is the *testator* (man) or *testatrix* (woman). The testator or testatrix may designate an *executor* (man) or *executrix* (woman) to probate the will; that is, prove its validity to the court for the purpose of carrying out its provisions. Making a will is a technical matter and should be entrusted only to a qualified attorney. Illustration 5–21 on page 192 shows a properly prepared and correctly typed will.

validity:
having legal force

Deed. A *deed* is a formal written instrument by which title to real property is transferred from one person to another. All the details of the transaction should be approved by a lawyer before the deed is registered with the proper government agency.

Lease. A *lease* is a contract by which one party gives to another the use of real or personal property for a fixed price. This relationship exists when one person, the *lessee*, under an express or implied agreement, is given possession and control of the property of another, the *lessor*. The amount given by the lessee is called *rent* (for real property) or *consideration* (for personal property).

The lease shown on page 191 illustrates the typing problems involved in completing a printed form for a legal document. Observe where typewritten material has been inserted, the method of indicating the amount in words and figures, and the completion of certain words by adding letters that keep the sentences containing those words consistently in plural form.

This Lease Witnesseth:

THAT Bruce D. Damson and Denise L. Damson, husband and wife,
HEREBY LEASE TO Charles L. Burroughs
the premises situate in the City *of* Miami *in the County of*
Dade *and State of* Florida *described as follows:*

Building to be used as a restaurant located at 4531 Collins
Avenue, Pensacola, Florida

with the appurtenances thereto, for the term of ten (10) years *commencing*
June 1, *19 __ at a rental of* Seven hundred fifty (750)
dollars per month *, payable* monthly.

SAID LESSEE AGREES *to pay said rent, unless said premises shall be destroyed or rendered untenantable by fire or other unavoidable accident; to not commit or suffer waste; to not use said premises for any unlawful purpose; to not assign this lease, or underlet said premises, or any part thereof, or permit the sale of* his *interest herein by legal process, without the written consent of said lessor* S*; to not use said premises or any part thereof in violation of any law relating to intoxicating liquors; and at the expiration of this lease, to surrender said premises in as good condition as they now are, or may be put by said lessor* S*, reasonable wear and unavoidable casualties, condemnation or appropriation excepted. Upon nonpayment of any of said rent for* thirty *days, after it shall become due, and without demand made therefor; or if said lessee or any assignee of this lease shall make an assignment for the benefit of his creditors; or if proceedings in bankruptcy shall be instituted by or against lessee or any assignee; or if a receiver or trustee be appointed for the property of the lessee or any assignee; or if this lease by operation of law pass to any person or persons; or if said lessee or any assignee shall fail to keep any of the other covenants of this lease, it shall be lawful for said lessor* s, their *heirs or assigns, into said premises to reenter, and the same to have again, repossess and enjoy, as in* their *first and former estate; and thereupon this lease and everything herein contained on the said lessor* s '*behalf to be done and performed, shall cease, determine, and be utterly void*

SAID LESSORS AGREE *(said lessee having performed* his *obligations under this lease) that said lessee shall quietly hold and occupy said premises during said term without any hindrance or molestation by said lessor* s, their *heir or any person lawfully claiming under them.*

Signed this first *day of* May *A. D. 19 __*

IN THE PRESENCE OF:

Mark Patterson

Richard Markay

Bruce D. Damson

Denise L. Damson

Eugene R. Hooper

Illus. 5-20

Lease

Two-inch top margin for all pages

LAST WILL AND TESTAMENT OF CARL THOMAS RIEDEL

Testator's name in all capital letters

I, CARL THOMAS RIEDEL, of the County of Harris, State of Texas, being of sound and disposing mind and memory, and above the age of eighteen (18) years and lawfully married to THELMA JOYCE RIEDEL, do make, declare and publish this my Last Will and Testament revoking all Wills and Codicils previously made by me.

Double spacing

Copy typed within marginal rules

First: I direct that all of my just debts and funeral expenses be paid out of my estate as soon as they can be conveniently done without the unnecessary sacrifice of any properties of my estate by my Executrix or Executor, as the case may be, hereinafter appointed.

IN WITNESS WHEREOF I have hereunto set my hand at Houston, Texas, hereby declaring this to be my Last Will and Testament, on this the 13th day of September, A D., 19--.

Carl Thomas Riedel
Carl Thomas Riedel
Testator

The above instrument was now here published as his Last Will, and signed and subscribed by CARL THOMAS RIEDEL, the Testator, in our presence and we, at his request, in his presence, and the presence of each other, sign and subscribe our names thereto as attesting witnesses.

Paul F. Vetter
Witness

Nancy Klosterman
Witness

SUBSCRIBED and ACKNOWLEDGED before me by the said CARL THOMAS RIEDEL, Testator and subscribed and sworn to before me by the said witnesses, this the 13th day of September, A.D., 19--.

Margaret Neeld
Notary Public, Harris County, Texas

One-inch bottom margin

First page not numbered

Illus. 5-21 The format of a will

Affidavit. An *affidavit* is a written statement made under oath that the facts set forth are sworn to be true and correct. It must be sworn to before a proper official, such as a judge, justice of the peace, or a notary.

Power of Attorney. A *power of attorney* is a legal document authorizing one person to act as the attorney or agent of the grantor. The power of

AGENCY CONTRACT

　　　　This agreement, made and entered into on this, the tenth day of May, 19--, by and between TRAMMEL TRADE COMPANY, a corporation of Toledo, Ohio, the party of the first part, and Marvin Partain, of Enid, Oklahoma, the party of the second part,

　　　　WITNESSETH: That, whereas, the party of the first part is about to open a branch office to be located in Dallas, Texas, for the sale of its products, the said party of the first part hereby engages the services of Marvin Partain, the party of the second part, as manager of that office.

　　　　The party of the first part hereby agrees to pay the

first part from time to time.

　　　　IN WITNESS WHEREOF, The parties have hereunto affixed their hands and seals on the day and in the year first above written.

　　　　　　　　　　TRAMMEL TRADE COMPANY

Witnesses:

Barbara Davis　　　　　　　　　*Julian Hooper*　(Seal)
　　　　　　　　　　　　　　　　　　President
　　　　　　　　　　　　　　　　Party of the First Part

Paul Forest

　　　　　　　　　　　　　　　　Marvin Partain　(Seal)
　　　　　　　　　　　　　　　　Party of the Second Part

Illus. 5-22

Parts of a legal document typed on legal paper

attorney may be given to an experienced secretary by the employer. This power enables the secretary to act for the employer. It may authorize the secretary to sign checks and other legal documents for the employer. The power of attorney specifies the acts which the agent is authorized to perform for the principal. It may be granted for an indefinite period, for a specific period, or for a specific purpose only. It must be signed by the principal and should be notarized.

specifies:
names

Minutes

In our busy business world, with an executive's responsibility covering a wide range of activities, with the need for interchange of ideas, for mutual understandings, for decision-making based not on one person's point of view but on many, meetings are frequent and necessary. What you do in planning and in taking minutes can improve the effectiveness of a meeting. If you are called upon to take and transcribe minutes regularly, a knowledge of parliamentary procedure will be most helpful. This can be acquired by reading either *Robert's Rules of Order*, the standard guide for presiding officers and parliamentarians, or *Standard Code for Parliamentary Procedure*, by Sturgis.

parliamentary procedure:
the rules governing proceedings of a formal assembly

Minutes are the official records of meetings and show the action taken in them. The minutes of a meeting should be a clear, concise presentation of factual information, properly arranged. Since minutes are frequently used for reference, every detail included in them should be complete and accurate.

Illus. 5-23

When taking minutes at a meeting, the secretary records points of interest and importance.

The planning for a committee meeting, conference, or official meeting is usually done by the chairperson's secretary. If you are the chairperson's secretary, you will be expected to reserve the meeting room and to notify the members well in advance of each meeting. In addition, you may be responsible for getting paper and pencils for each member of the committee, getting material from the files which might be needed in the meeting, having water and glasses available, and providing for any coffee or refreshments which might be served.

Each member should receive an *agenda* which is a schedule of business to be covered at the meeting. You will also be expected to take and transcribe the minutes of many of the meetings called by your employer. As a general rule, the minutes are edited for omissions and corrections by the chairperson before they are distributed to the members.

Gathering Information for Minutes

If you are asked to take the minutes of a meeting, you should have the following information before the meeting starts: the name of the organization, the place, the date, the time of the meeting, and the agenda. You should know, or obtain, the names of those who should attend the meeting. With such a list you can quickly check attendance, and thereby know the names of those present and absent.

You should have available at the meeting the minutes of the previous meetings, particularly those of the last meeting, and any figures, letters, bulletins, reports, and legal papers that might be referred to during the meeting. This foresight on your part will help to keep the meeting running smoothly. The presiding officer or committee chairperson may suggest to you the data that should be available at the meeting. You should not leave the meeting to obtain information unless the chairperson asks you to do so.

As the meeting progresses, you should take down in shorthand the points that you think are of importance and interest, and, insofar as possible, you should identify the discussion with the names of those who **participate**. The names of those who make and second each motion should be recorded. Motions and resolutions, whether passed or not, should be taken and transcribed word for word because future proceedings are often governed by the interpretation placed on the wording.

participate: take part in

Typing the Minutes

The completeness of the typed minutes depends upon the formality of the meeting. The minutes of an informal meeting are brief and cover

```
                        MINUTES
                    BOARD OF DIRECTORS
                        UNITED WAY

Time and         The regular monthly meeting of the Board of Directors was
Place of         held on Wednesday, February 26, 19--, in the conference
Meeting          room of the United Way Building.  The meeting was called
                 to order at 4:00 p.m. by the President, Joseph Glover.

Attendance       Present were Joseph Glover, Keith Irwin, Michael Jobe,
                 David R. Knox, Anne Marshall, Charles M. Nichols, Nancy
                 Springer, Jack Tollcy, Beth Webb, and Ernest Wynne.

Approval of      The minutes of the January 29 meeting, which had been
Minutes          mailed to all the members of the Board, were approved.

Treasurer's      The Treasurer, Ernest Wynne, presented the attached list
Report           of pledges determined to be uncollectible.  The motion
                 was passed unanimously to charge these pledges to the
                 reserve established for that purpose.

Report of        Charles Nichols, reporting for the Planning Committee,
Standing         announced that Nancy Springer has been elected
Committee        Chairperson of the Planning Committee.

Report of        Beth Webb, Chairperson of the Well Baby Clinic Facilities
Special          Ad Hoc Committee, reported that funds for remodeling
Committee        the Well Baby Clinic are included in the $5.3 million
                 redevelopment recommendations sent by the City Council
                 to HUD.

Unfinished       Joseph Glover presented the recommendation of the
Business         Executive Committee that an additional $177 be allocated
                 to pay the plane fare of the auditor to attend a con-
                 ference on the new accounting system for United Way.
                 The motion was passed.

New Business     Joseph Glover explained the attached report and letter
                 sent to the local Boys Clubs.  Jack Mason presented the
                 attached Proposal for opening the John T. Henderson
                 Boys Club.  About 500 boys a day are expected to use the
                 facilities.  It is anticipated that transportation costs
                 can be absorbed in the present budget.

Date of          The next meeting of the Board will be held on Wednesday,
Next Meeting     March 19, in the conference room of the United Way Building.

Adjournment      The meeting adjourned at 5:05 p.m.


                                        Anne Marshall
                                        Secretary
```

Illus. 5-24   Minutes of a meeting

only the essential points; the minutes of a formal meeting are typed in detail according to a routine pattern. In most sets of minutes, the following points are covered:

1. Name of the group, committee, organization, or business.
2. Time, date, and place of the meeting, and whether it is a regular meeting or a special meeting.
3. Names of the presiding officer, secretary, and those present (also those absent if that can be determined). In the case of a meeting of a large organization, only the number of members present need be recorded to indicate that there was a *quorum* (the minimum number of members necessary for conducting the business of the group).
4. Reading of the minutes of the previous meeting, and the approval, amendment, or correction of those minutes.
5. Reports of the committees or persons who previously were assigned special duties: for example, the Treasurer's report, the reports of standing committees, and the reports of special committees.
6. Unfinished business and the action taken on it.
7. New business, the discussion, and the action taken.
8. Time, date, and place of the next meeting.
9. Time of adjournment.
10. Signature of the secretary or one responsible for the minutes.

Correcting the Minutes

Before the minutes are typed, they should be corrected, even rewritten if necessary, to be certain that they are as nearly perfect as possible when they are read at the next meeting. At the meeting it is sometimes necessary to make corrections in the minutes. If only a few words are affected, lines may be drawn through the incorrect words and the proper insertions made above them. If more than a few words are affected, lines may be drawn through the sentences or paragraphs to be corrected and the corrections written on a new page. The page number of the corrections should be indicated on the original minutes. The minutes should not be rewritten after they have been read and approved at the meeting.

Resolutions

During a meeting, you may be given the responsibility of preparing a resolution. Resolutions are written to express appreciation, to do honor, to indicate action, to express regret, to offer congratulations, to commemorate, or to present a program of action.

WHEREAS and *RESOLVED*, which are characteristic introductory terms in formal resolutions, are typed in capital letters. The first word after *WHEREAS* is not capitalized unless it is a proper name. No comma follows *WHEREAS* unless one is necessary to make the sentence clear. *RESOLVED* or *RESOLVED further* is usually followed by a comma and the first word after it is capitalized.

Some resolutions are less formal. In an informal resolution the terms *WHEREAS, RESOLVED,* and *Therefore be it* are eliminated, and the facts or events leading up to the resolution are stated simply and directly. For example, "The following resolution was unanimously adopted:

The Trustees of Martin College accept with thanks the sum of $25,000 representing a gift from the friends and colleagues of the late Harriet Simons for the establishment of the *Harriet Simons Scholarship Fund*. The income from the invested principal is to be used to assist able and needy high school graduates who have selected Martin College for their undergraduate studies. The Fund is to be administered by the Dean of Students."

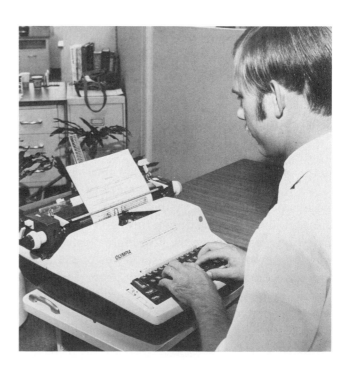

Illus. 5-25

Above average accuracy is required in typing legal documents and minutes.

REVIEWING

1. In what ways does legal paper differ from paper used for letters in business?

2. What are the minimum margins usually allowed on typewritten legal paper?
3. How many carbon copies of a legal document should a secretary make?
4. What is the advantage of using legal paper on which the lines are numbered?
5. What is the type of error that may be erased and corrected in a legal document?
6. How are quantities usually written in legal documents?
7. How should words be filled in on a printed legal form?
8. What is meant by the term *notarized*?
9. What is an *affidavit*?
10. What is an agenda, and when is it used?
11. What responsibilities might a secretary have in preparing for a committee meeting?
12. What information should the secretary have before the meeting starts?
13. What should the secretary bring to the meeting?
14. When should the minutes not be rewritten or changed?
15. What is the purpose of a resolution?

MAKING JUDGMENTS

1. Is a typing error in a legal paper more serious than a similar error in an important business letter?
2. If your employer asked you to compose a resolution of appreciation for a company official, where might you go to find information to include in the resolution?
3. When a secretary is taking minutes at a conference, what should be done about having the telephone at the secretary's desk answered? Why?

WORKING WITH OTHERS

As a legal secretary, Miss Stephens types contracts, wills, and other documents which contain a great deal of confidential information. She understands the importance of secrecy about such information and never discusses such matters with anyone else. While having lunch with Miss Phillips, a new member of the law firm's stenographic pool, Miss Stephens is surprised when Miss Phillips casually comments about the terms of a contract drawn up by the firm. What is Miss Stephens' responsibility in this situation?

REFRESHING LANGUAGE SKILLS

Three more uses of the comma are:

A. To separate long coordinate clauses that are joined by the conjunctions *and, but, for neither, nor,* and *or.* The comma is placed before the conjunction.
B. To set off a subordinate clause preceding a main clause.
C. To separate words, phrases, or clauses in a series. A comma precedes the last item in the series.

Type the following sentences on a separate sheet of paper and insert commas where necessary.

1. While the jury was out the lawyer talked with his client.
2. After the meeting she typed the minutes according to the rules of the committee.
3. Neither the attorney, nor her client agreed with the decision but the jury considered the will valid.
4. After he dictated the will the lease and the deed the attorney left for court.
5. The secretary proofread the will carefully for one mistake could invalidate the whole will.
6. Mr. Pelter wanted to revise his will but his lawyer was out of town.
7. Before the conference began the secretary handed each member an agenda.
8. Once the minutes had been signed the secretary could not make any changes.
9. Although there was not much evidence the jury decided in favor of the defendant.
10. Law firms use printed legal forms whenever possible for this saves much secretarial typing.

PERFORMING SECRETARIAL TASKS

1. Your task is to compose and type the minutes for the Stanford City-Council Child Welfare Board from the following brief notes (page 201) you took at the meeting.
   a. Use plain paper, 8½ × 11 inches.
   b. Make a rough draft to edit.
   c. Type a final copy using the format on page 196.
2. Type the lease beginning on page 202 on legal paper, making one carbon copy. Use the current date. If ruled legal paper is not available, rule in ink the necessary vertical lines on regular 8½" × 11" paper. Use a one-inch top margin.

Conference Room, Child Welfare Board Office

Regular meeting May 15, 19--, 11:45 a.m.

All members present - Staff present: Lynda Mullins, Beth Stevens

Minutes of April 14 approved

April 30 financial report accepted

Finance Committee presented next year's budget - motion passed to insert word "health" before the word "insurance" line 10 of budget. Judge Shaw requested budget by June 10.

Jane Dawson, Chairperson, Ad Hoc Nominations Committee, nominated Jim Weaver, Boys Club Director, for vacant Board position. West will recommend his name to County Commissioners Court.

Ken West read letter from Carolyn Mackey, caseworker, regarding John Reese, foster child at Heritage Hall - Letter stated John making good progress.

Letter read from J. K. Ferguson, County Auditor, approving Board's request to increase travel and foster care retroactive to January 1, 19-- for foster care, to February 1, 19-- for travel.

Next meeting June 19, 11:45 a.m., Conference Room, Child Welfare Board Office
Adjourned 12:50 p.m.

LEASE AGREEMENT

This agreement of lease, entered into this _____ day of
_____, 19--, by and between George Cain hereinafter called Lessor, and Mr. and Mrs. Tom Irwin hereinafter called Lessee,

WITNESSETH:

Lessor does hereby rent and lease unto Lessee that certain furnished/unfurnished apartment designated as Apartment A, within an Apartment House known as Cedar Lake Apartments, located at 3920 Harmony in Randall County, Texas for the term of six months commencing December 8, 19--, and ending May 8, 19--, to be used by lessee as a private residence and not otherwise, Lessee paying therefore the sum of eighteen hundred dollars ($1,800), payable three hundred dollars ($300) per month in advance on the first day of each month, as the same shall fall due to Lessor at 6739 Salem, Amarillo, Randall County, Texas.

The rental from the date of execution of this contract to the first day of the following month is three hundred dollars ($300) payable upon tenants taking possession. This includes all utilities.

At the end or other expiration of the terms, Lessee shall deliver up the demised premises in good order and condition, reasonable deterioration, damage by fire, tornado, or other casualty and the elements only excepted.

Lessee agrees to give access to Lessor or his agent within reasonable hours in order to show said premises for rent, sale, repair or inspection, as well as access to repairers for the purpose of maintaining said property. WITNESS, THE SIGNATURE OF THE PARTIES HERETO IN DUPLICATE, THIS _____ DAY OF _____, 19--.

Lessee: _____   Lessor: _____ _____

3. Type one original and one carbon copy of this will following the form on page 192. If ruled legal paper is not available, rule in ink the necessary vertical lines on regular 8½" × 11" paper.

LAST WILL AND TESTAMENT OF ROBERT LEWIS JONES

I, ROBERT LEWIS JONES, of Ada County, Idaho, do make, publish and declare this to be my Last Will and Testament, hereby revoking all Wills and Codicils previously made by me.

I hereby give, devise and bequeath my entire estate of every kind and character as follows: (a) To my wife, Linda Jones, my entire estate, if she survives. (b) If my wife shall not survive me, my entire estate shall be distributed, subject to the provisions of paragraph 2, to my then surviving issue, per stirpes. At the present time, my issue consists of my son, Ted R. Jones; my daughter, Lisa J. Jones; and my daughter, Jeanie A. Jones.

In the event that any share of my estate, or any share of a trust created under this Will shall otherwise be distributed at my death or upon the termination of such trust to a beneficiary who has not attained the age of twenty-three (23) years, such share shall be held by the Trustee as a separate and distinct trust for such persons until such person attains the age of twenty-three (23) years, at which time that trust shall terminate and the trust estate shall be distributed outright to such person, but if such person shall die prior to attaining the age of twenty-three (23) years, upon such person's death such trust shall terminate and the trust estate shall be distributed to such person's issue, but if none of such person's issue is then living to such person's then surviving brothers and sisters in equal shares, if none, to my then surviving issue, per stirpes.

In any event, and anything to the contrary notwithstanding, any trust created herein shall terminate upon the expiration of twenty-one (21) years after the death of the last to die of my wife and such of my issue as are living at the date of my death. Upon such termination the trust estate shall be distributed, free and clear of trust, to the beneficiary who is entitled to such trust estate.

No Trustee shall be liable for decreases in value or other losses, save and except only those which occur by reason of the Trustee's intentional misconduct, fraud, or gross negligence.

No part of any trust estate, under any circumstances, shall ever be liable for or charged with any of the debts, liabilities or obligations of the beneficiary or subject to seizure by any claimant or creditor of the beneficiary. The beneficiary, under any circumstances, shall not have the power to assign, convey, pledge, charge or otherwise encumber or in any manner anticipate or dispose of his or her interest in any trust estate until the same shall have been actually transferred, conveyed or paid over to him or her, free and clear of such trust.

I direct that all my just debts, funeral expenses and expenses in connection with my estate be paid as soon as practicable after my death.

The revenues, receipts, proceeds, disbursements, expenses, deductions, accruals or losses of each trust shall be allocated or apportioned between corpus and income in the discretion of the Trustee, and the determination of the Trustee need not necessarily be in accordance with the provisions of the Idaho Trust Act, which shall control only if such discretion is not exercised by the Trustee.

The Trustee herein provided for shall have and is hereby granted the powers and authority vested in Trustees under the Idaho Trust Act as the same now exists, or as it shall hereinafter be amended. In addition thereto, but not by way of limitation, my Trustee shall hold, manage, control, use, invest and reinvest, sell, exchange, encumber and lease the trust estate in the sole discretion of the Trustee in all things and under all circumstances, and to the same extent as if the Trustee was the owner thereof in fee simple, and all rights and privileges and powers given the Trustee may be exercised without application to any Court.

I hereby appoint my wife, Linda Jones, Independent Executrix under this Will and of my estate. In the event my wife should fail or cease to act, for any reason, I hereby appoint my sister, Lynn Smiley, as Independent Executrix under this Will and of my estate, and Trustee of all trusts created herein. In the event Lynn Smiley shall fail or cease to act, for any reason, I hereby appoint my brother, Leonard Donald Jones, as Independent Executor under this Will and of my estate, and Trustee of all trusts created herein. In the event Leonard Donald Jones shall fail or cease to act, for any reason, I hereby appoint my cousin, Joyce Fields, as Independent Executrix under this Will and of my estate, and Trustee of all trusts created herein. In the event Joyce Fields shall fail or cease to act, for any reason, I hereby appoint NORTHWESTERN NATIONAL BANK of Boise, Idaho, as Independent Executor under this Will and of my estate and Trustee of all trusts created herein, provided however, that any of the individuals appointed above, while acting as Trustee, may appoint another bank to act as successor Trustee in place of the NORTHWESTERN BANK of Boise, Idaho. No bond or other security shall be required of any Executor or Trustee and the Executor shall be independent of the supervision and direction of the Probate Court to the full extent permitted by law. I direct that no action shall be had in any court of probate jurisdiction in connection with this Will and the administration and settlement of my estate other than the probating and recording of this Will and the return of an inventory, appraisement and list of claims as provided by law. All references to Executor in this Will shall refer also to the Executrix then acting under the terms of this Will. In addition to having all the powers of an Independent Executor under the law of Idaho, the Executor shall have all the powers given the Trustee herein.

In the event my wife predeceases me or in the event of a common disaster, I hereby appoint my sister, Lynn Smiley, as guardian of the person of each of my surviving minor children. In the event that my sister fails or ceases to act, I appoint my brother, Leonard Donald Jones, as guardian of the persons of each of my minor children. In the event that both my sister and brother fail or cease to act as guardian, I appoint my cousin, Joyce Fields, as guardian of the person of each of my minor children. I direct that no bond be required of any of the above named guardians.

I hereby bequeath and donate my body to the WESTERN UNIVERSITY SCHOOL OF MEDICINE for the advancement of medical science and/or any parts of my body as replacements to aid living persons.

IN TESTIMONY WHEREOF, I have signed my name to this my Last Will and Testament at Boise, Idaho, on this the _____ day of _____, 19--.

_____

Robert Lewis Jones

The above instrument was now here published as his Last Will, and signed and subscribed by ROBERT LEWIS JONES, the Testator, in our presence and we, at his request, in his presence, and the presence of each other, sign and subscribe our names thereto as attesting witnesses.

_____

Witness

_____

Witness

SUBSCRIBED and ACKNOWLEDGED before me by the said ROBERT LEWIS JONES, Testator and subscribed and sworn to before me by the said witnesses, this the _____ day of _____, 19--.

_____

Notary Public, Ada County, Idaho

IMPROVING SECRETARIAL SKILLS (Optional)

Using plain paper, type the following report with footnotes as page 4 of a side-bound report.

where to look for information.[1] Communicating information in a report is not an easy task because of the vast amount of information that is usually covered. An effective report has no unnecessary words or sentences. If you simplify your writing so that your reader will have a clear understanding of all the terms you use, your report will be much more meaningful. Choosing just the right words to express your thoughts is imperative in conveying a clear message.[2]

In composing reports, you should try to use everyday language. Visualize yourself talking face-to-face with your reader, and try to use the actual words you would employ in normal conversation. Use the simplest words you know which will convey the thought clearly.[3]

Give your reports personality by using words which are strong and vigorous. However, avoid using many adjectives and adverbs because they take the reader's attention away from the important nouns and verbs. Avoid words which are fuzzy and have vague meanings. Stick to concrete words, which are usually short, familiar words.[4]

Since verbs are the strongest parts of speech, make frequent use of active-voice verbs in your report writing. Use your words economically in composing sentences which are concise.[5]

[1]Gilbert C. Stone, *Using Business Reference Books* (3rd ed., Seattle: Western Publishing Co., 1977), p. 15.

[2]Robert D. Maxwell and Arthur M. Woodward, *Report Writing* (4th ed., Seattle: Western Publishing Co., 1977), pp. 221–222.

[3]*Ibid.*, p. 238.

[4]Stone, *op. cit.*, pp. 42–45.

[5]Maxwell and Woodward, *loc. cit.*

The Secretary and Data Processing

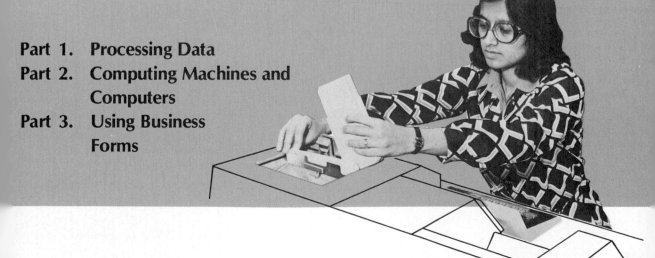

Part 1. Processing Data
Part 2. Computing Machines and Computers
Part 3. Using Business Forms

Part 1

Processing Data

Jim Herrera has been working for a large accounting firm for several months. He has been successful in this job because of his desire to learn all he can about the different departments in the firm. At lunch one day he told a friend that he had difficulty understanding data processing and would like to know more about that department. His friend suggested attending a course offered by American Data Processing Systems. The course is designed to help secretaries understand the principles of data processing. Immediately after lunch Jim called American Data Processing Systems to inquire about the course.

The Secretary Processes Data

The increasing use of electronic data processing (often abbreviated EDP) equipment in the modern office has changed office procedures and office work. The secretary's work has been changed in many instances also. Some of the **routine** tasks usually performed by a secretary are now performed by machines. For example, many companies now have their monthly financial statements prepared through the use of equipment. This frees the secretary to perform more of the **administrative** duties of an office.

As a secretary today, you must be familiar with the **vocabulary** of data processing. You may be directly involved with the data processing department and you must be familiar with the most common words used by the people who work in the data processing department.

You probably will not actually operate electronic data processing computers, although you may operate small electronic calculators. Your job may involve getting the data to be processed and using the information after it has been processed. This means you must know the many uses of the records and reports that are provided by the data processing department.

routine:
regular

administrative:
executive

vocabulary:
words and phrases

As a secretary you may also determine what information is necessary and what is not necessary for your employer to read. This will mean using your own judgment not only to determine *what* information your employer should receive but also to decide *how* it should be presented, so that it will take the least amount of time for your employer to read and understand. The use of data processing equipment can make your job more important by freeing you from routine tasks and allowing you to perform more challenging duties.

Illus. 6-1

Data processing plays an important role in decision making by providing useful information about business transactions.

What is Business Data Processing?

Data simply means the words (invoice, balances), numbers (382, 4½), and symbols (#, %) that businesses use in order to make decisions. *Processing* means arranging the data in a series of steps in an organized manner. When the words, numbers, and symbols are organized so that they have meaning, the result is called *information. Data processing*, therefore, is arranging words, numbers, and symbols to provide information. *Business data processing* means arranging words, numbers, and symbols about business **transactions** to provide useful information.

transactions: dealings

Whether you realize it or not, you are constantly processing data mentally. Consider the following situation:

Nan asked Roberta to go to the movie. Before she could decide, Roberta had to consider the following facts:

1. The cost of the movie
2. The length of the movie
3. The distance from home to the theater
4. The subject of the movie
5. What she might do instead of going to the movie

After analyzing each of the factors, Roberta decided she would go with Nan.

In deciding whether she would or would not go, Roberta was processing data. Although business decisions usually involve other types of matters, the procedures used are similar.

Data by itself is often meaningless. For example, if twenty sales invoices arrived in your office, it would be difficult to know the total dollar amount of sales by simply looking at the twenty separate invoices. The data must be added together to arrive at a total. This adding of numbers is processing data. The report which results from the processing can be useful to your employer in making many very important decisions about the business.

Data about business transactions is collected, processed, and reported to provide information. The data needed by a business will depend upon many factors, such as the size and type of business. The information needed by the owner of a small service station would not be the same as that needed by the executive of a large steel corporation. The more complex the operation of a firm the more different types of information it needs. The method for processing data will depend on such factors as the amount and kind of data and the time and money available for processing the data.

Some people think that data processing is a recent development. The term *data processing* is new, but the activity is not new. The processing of numbers, words, and symbols has progressed from manual methods through several stages to **sophisticated** electronic computers.

sophisticated:
complex; complicated

The Need for Processed Data

Data is needed for internal use (within the company) and external use (outside the company). Information is used internally to perform the daily activities of the business and to plan the future of the business.

External information is provided to stockholders (owners of the business), government agencies, unions, customers, suppliers, and creditors.

Some information serves several purposes. Payroll records, for example, give internal information for payment of salaries and also external information for financial reports to the government and unions.

Methods of Processing Data

Data may be processed by manual, mechanical, electronic unit record, or electronic computer means. There are **similarities** among these methods as well as differences.

similarities: likenesses

Processing Data Manually

The human mind was the earliest means of processing data. When a person hears or sees data, it becomes information to be stored in the brain. The brain is the processor which performs the operations upon the data. The information that results can take the form of the written or spoken word, or both.

Let's say you are asked to process an order. With the manual method of processing data, you would write a sales slip giving data, such as date, customer's name, customer's address, terms, quantity, and other vital information. Other records such as the invoice, journal entry, ledger, and customer's statement would be copied in handwriting.

It is easy to make errors in routine work, such as copying data from one form to another. The speed and accuracy with which the data is manually processed is **comparatively** low; and, for large volumes of work, the cost to process each document is relatively high.

comparatively: estimated or judged by comparing

Illus. 6-2

Manual means of processing data

Processing Data Mechanically

When the intelligence of the secretary is combined with the speed and accuracy of machines, an efficient system can be formed. Office equipment such as calculating machines, typewriters, and bookkeeping machines (see Part 2 of this Unit) are combined to perform operations more quickly than they could be performed manually.

If you were processing a sale using mechanical means of processing data, you would probably handwrite the sales slip but you would perform the calculations with an adding machine. By using a bookkeeping machine, the journal and ledger entries could be posted and the customer's statement prepared. Thus, you would combine your intelligence with the speed and accuracy of machines to form a mechanical data processing system.

Illus. 6-3

The adding machine is one means of processing data mechanically.

Processing Data Electronically

In recent years many mechanical data processing machines are being replaced by electronic machines which cost very little more to purchase and are more efficient than mechanical machines. For example, electronic calculators multiply and divide automatically, compute rapidly, and many calculator models can store data in memory registers.

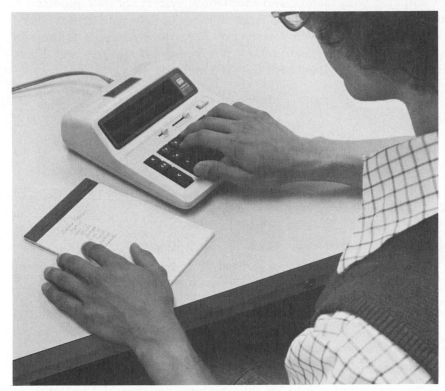

Illus. 6-4

Electronic calculators are more efficient than mechanical machines.

Processing Data by Unit Record

In the *unit record* system each individual or unit of record is kept on one punched card. Sometimes it is called a *punched card* system. Sometimes it is called a *tabulating system* because one of the important machines in the system is a tabulator.

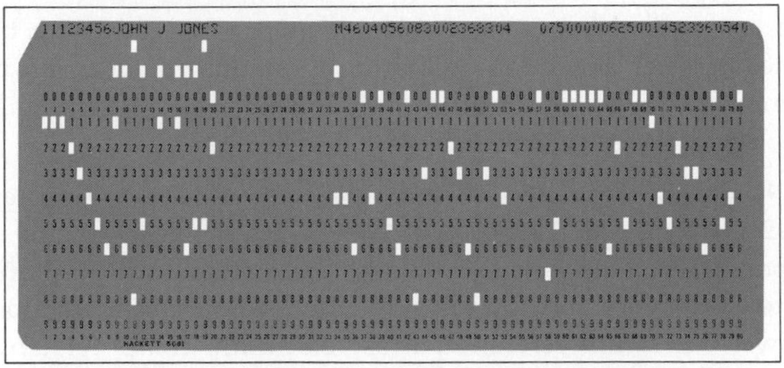

Illus. 6-5   Punched card

Compared with manual and mechanical systems of data processing, unit record equipment handles large volumes of data with greater speed and accuracy at a relatively lower cost. The system consists of the *card punch, verifier, sorter, collator, interpreter, reproducer,* and *tabulator*. Some of these machines are illustrated in Part 2 of this Unit.

Illus. 6-6

Tabulating means of processing data

Ohio National Life Insurance Company

If you processed a sale by this method, you would handwrite or typewrite the sales slip. It would provide the information needed to process the data by the unit record method. The sales slip data would be punched into a punched card and *verified*, or checked, for accuracy. The punched holes give the information in the form of a code that can be understood by the card punch machines. The punched cards would be processed by machine to produce the journal, ledger, and statement.

Processing Data by an Electronic Computer System

The computer plays a vital role in our lives today. The business world needs faster and more accurate information for decision-making. The computer can supply this information because of three main features — speed, accuracy, and storage.

Speed. If you were asked to multiply two 10-digit numbers, say 3,575,212,134 by 2,456,754,137, it would be a difficult task with a pencil and paper. This would be an impossible task if you tried to perform the calculations mentally and to remember the original numbers along with the answer for future reference. Most electronic computers, however, could do this calculation along with storing the results in a few *nanoseconds* (a nanosecond is equal to one billionth of a second).

Accuracy. Accuracy is very important in all businesses. When large numbers of items are processed, it is easy to make errors. In using computers, however, errors can be reduced because the information is *verified* before it is put into the computer. The computer then follows the same instructions each time without getting tired or bored. Often, human beings become tired and bored when doing **repetitious** work and, as a result, make errors.

Storage. Many different types of data can be stored in a computer until they are needed. Usually the data to be processed and the instructions for processing the data are stored in the computer by using magnetic drums, tapes, or disks. The computer is able to find this data very quickly when it is needed.

Let's say that you are asked to supply a sales slip to process a sale using electronic data processing equipment. You may either handwrite or type this sales slip. Information from the sales slip is then placed into the computer by entering it into punched cards or a terminal machine connected to the computer. The processing, or manipulation, of the data is performed by a list of instructions to the computer called a *program*. The computer can prepare the invoice, journal entry, ledger entry, and statement for the customer. Also, the computer will retain the information for future reference.

Illus. 6-7

The electronic computer is a highly sophisticated means of processing data.

Courtesy of American Telephone & Telegraph Company

The human mind is an adaptable but very **unreliable** processor of information. Human beings, however, are needed to handle situations where judgment is required. EDP combines the talents of people who are slow, inaccurate, and intelligent with computers which are fast, accurate, and not intelligent. Combining the advantages of the human mind and the electronic computer gives business an efficient system of providing information for decision making.

The Data Processing Cycle

Before a final report is prepared, the data to be used in the report must follow a series of steps called the data processing cycle. Regardless of the method used, the steps in the data processing cycle are (1) origin, (2) input, (3) processing, and (4) output.

Step 1 — Origin of Data

Origin means the beginning or start of something. In business the information to be processed originates in a variety of business papers. The business papers used to record data for the first time are called *source documents*. For example, when you go to a store to buy a stereo on a charge account, the sales clerk fills out a sales slip with your name and address, telephone number, description of the item you bought, and the price. This information written on the sales slip is the origin of data about your purchase of the stereo. The sales slip is the source document. Other source documents may include invoices, time cards, or checks.

Step 2 — Input of Data

The data recorded for processing is called *input*. The input of the data from the source document is recorded in such form that it can be easily **manipulated**, or processed. If the information is to be processed manually, this step may involve putting the information about the sale in a Sales Journal so that the store can get a total sales figure for the month. If the information is to be processed **automatically** by electronic equipment, this step will involve recording the data from the source document onto cards or tapes so that it can be processed on electronic equipment.

Step 3 — Processing of Data

The next step is to actually process the data. This may involve classifying, calculating, or summarizing the data. When you purchased your stereo, the information concerning the sale was written on a sales slip.

The information on the sales slip is processed (added, subtracted, multiplied, divided, or summarized) to prepare a monthly bill for you and to provide reports, such as the Monthly Sales Report, that are needed to run the business **efficiently**. The different machines used to process the data will be discussed in Part 2 of this Unit.

efficiently:
without waste of time
or effort

Step 4 — Output of Data

The final step in the data processing cycle provides the output of data. In this step the information that has been processed is organized and arranged in a usable form. The output document may take a variety of forms. Quite often it is a statement, an invoice, or a report. The output from your purchase of a stereo may include a monthly bill to you and a sales report for the store. When data is processed electronically, the output is often another punched card rather than a written report. You are familiar with the monthly utility bill you receive at your home; it is usually in the form of a punched card. This punched card can be processed automatically when it is returned to the company with payment.

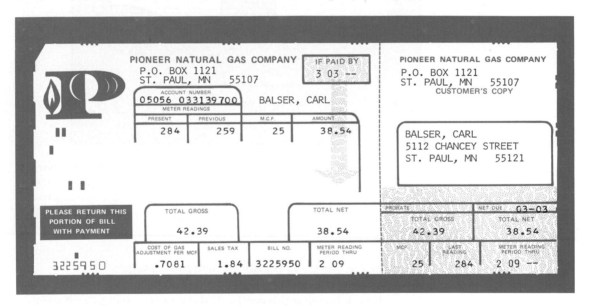

Illus. 6-8. Utility bill in the form of a punched card

Flow Chart Symbols

The steps in the data processing cycle can also be shown using a flow chart, which is a diagram of how something moves or flows in a business. Some of the symbols and their meanings in a flow chart follow.

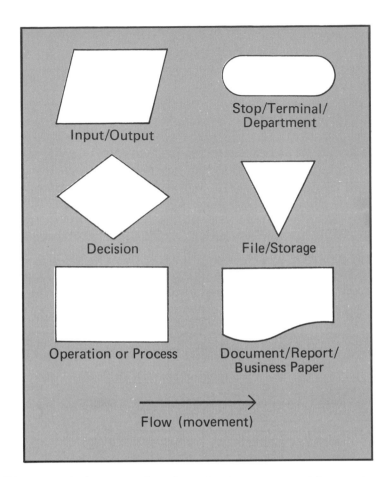

Input/Output

Stop/Terminal/
Department

Decision

File/Storage

Operation or Process

Document/Report/
Business Paper

Flow (movement)

These symbols are used to describe the process without using words. Using flow chart symbols, the process of filing a business paper is shown on the next page.

REVIEWING

1. What must a secretary know about data processing?
2. Define business data processing.
3. What factors determine the method of data processing to be used?
4. Distinguish between internal and external uses of information.
5. What are the disadvantages of processing data manually?
6. Name the five methods of processing data and briefly explain each.
7. What are the three main features of the computer when the data is processed by the electronic system?
8. Briefly discuss the four basic steps in the data processing cycle.
9. Draw the symbols used in a simple data processing diagram.
10. What is the advantage of using flow chart symbols?

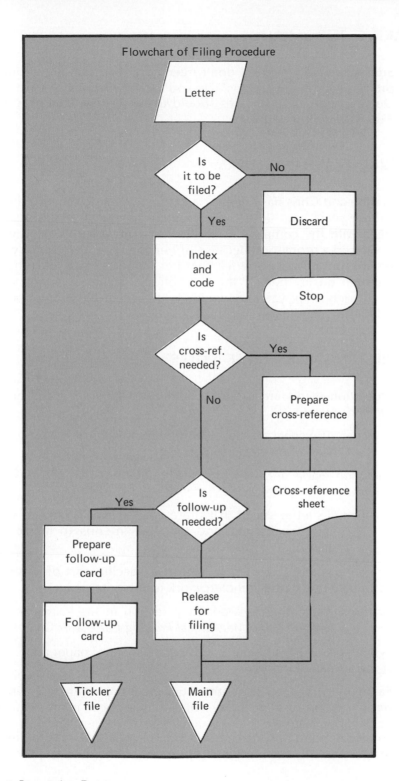

Flowchart of Filing Procedure

Letter

Is it to be filed? — No → Discard → Stop

Yes ↓

Index and code

Is cross-ref. needed? — Yes → Prepare cross-reference → Cross-reference sheet

No ↓

Is follow-up needed? — Yes → Prepare follow-up card → Follow-up card → Tickler file

No ↓

Release for filing → Main file

Illus. 6-10

MAKING JUDGMENTS

1. Sue, a secretary said, "I don't need to know anything about data processing. I'm a secretary." Do you agree with Sue?
2. Do you think all businesses should use electronic data processing? Explain why or why not.

WORKING WITH OTHERS

Maxine and Chris have been friends since Maxine came to the company three years ago. Both are competent keypunch operators. Chris has been with the company for eight years; however, Maxine was recently offered a promotion because of her ability to learn quickly. Chris resents Maxine because she felt that her longer service with the company should qualify her for the promotion. Maxine does not want to end their friendship, yet, she would like to accept the promotion. How should Maxine handle the situation?

REFRESHING LANGUAGE SKILLS

A. Quotation marks are used to enclose the beginning and end of a *direct* quotation.

   Example: The speaker said, "People entering business must understand how data is processed."

B. Quotation marks are used to set off quotations that are *built into* a sentence.

   Example: His letter stated that there are "several languages used in data processing" and that he "intends to master all of them."

C. Quotation marks are used to set off a specific part of a complete work. (The title of the complete work is put in italics.)

   Example: "Estimating Answers" is a section in the instruction book *Electronic and Mechanical Printing Calculator Course.*

Type the sentences below on a separate sheet of paper and correctly insert the quotation marks.

1. Earlier in the chapter the author states that copies made on an offset duplicator are of a much finer quality than those made on a stencil or fluid duplicator.
2. Since ball point pens have no carbon in their ink, said the teacher, images made by them will not reproduce by the thermal process.

3. Constant Division is the title of a section in the *Electronic Display Calculator Course* book.
4. The teacher told the students that they should always clear the machine before starting the solution to a problem.
5. Under the section Types of Copiers it states that the flatbed copier permits you to copy the pages inside of a bound book by placing the page of the book face down on the glass.

PERFORMING SECRETARIAL TASKS

1. Visit a local company that uses electronic data processing and write a report on your visit. Include in your report the advantages and disadvantages of electronic data processing to the firm and your reaction to the employee's acceptance of the system.
2. The following letter was received from a customer complaining about an error made by a computer on the customer's monthly statement.

Ladies and Gentlemen:

Again, I am returning this statement to you because it is incorrect. As I wrote you last month, I did not purchase the clock-radio charged to me August 5; yet it has not been subtracted from my account.

Will you please straighten out your computer? I will pay my bill as soon as this correction is made.

Sincerely yours,

Herman Jackson

Herman Jackson

You check the records and discover that an error was made by the sales clerk when writing the account number on the sales slip so the computer charged the clock-radio to the wrong account.

a. Using a letterhead from the *Supplies Inventory* or plain paper, write a letter explaining the situation to Mr. Jackson at 1011 Hudson Avenue, Cheyenne, WY 82001.
b. Was the error the computer's fault?
c. How does an error like this affect customer relations?
d. What can be done to prevent errors like this from happening again?

Part 2
Computing Machines and Computers

While Mr. Wilson was working in the payroll department, two of the latest data processing machines available were installed. The machines came with manuals to help each person learn to operate them correctly. The sales representative, however, suggested that one person in the department be taught everything about the machines. Mr. Wilson was chosen to receive instructions. After three days he had learned proper operation and care of the data processing machines. He was also given some valuable timesaving hints for efficient use of the machines.

You may have to check columns of figures, discounts, or percentages for a report or a letter that your employer has dictated. It may also be your responsibility, in a small office, to handle payrolls for several departments, sales analyses, financial statements, and expense reports. These business records contain many calculations that can be easily and accurately produced with the aid of an office machine. Computing and recording machines have been installed in modern business offices to handle the ever-increasing volume of paper work. You will frequently work with processed records when you are employed as a secretary, and you should have a clear understanding of the operation of the major data processing machines.

Calculating Machines

There is a variety of calculating machines that you may use as a secretary. The amount of work you do on a calculator will depend on the business in which you are working. Some of the duties you may perform using a calculator are checking a report containing computations, figuring the payroll, preparing financial statements, and verifying budget and expense reports. You need to be aware of the types of calculators available and the uses of each.

Electronic Calculators

The electronic calculator is the most modern of all the calculators and is replacing many other types of calculating machines. Models are **available** that will perform every kind of computation that is needed in a business office.

They compute very rapidly because numbers are entered on a keyboard with a touch system, and calculations are made electronically. They multiply and divide automatically; and, because of their computing speed, they are very efficient for multiplication and division problems. Some models can store amounts in separate memory registers until needed later in the calculations.

There are two types of electronic calculators — printing and display. Computations are done electronically on these calculators, but on most machines the printing is mechanical; that is, a wheel or bars strike the paper tape to print answers. Computations of electronic printing calculators are shown on a paper tape so that they can be checked for accuracy against the original document.

NCR Corporation

Illus. 6-11   Electronic printing calculator

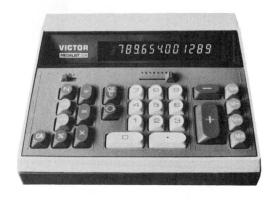

Victor Business Products Group

Illus. 6-12   Electronic display calculator

Computations for electronic display calculators are shown by lighted figures in a window directly above the keyboard. They are used when a printed record of the calculations on a tape is not needed. Display calculators have no moving parts and are completely silent. Portable, battery-operated models that can be held in one hand are available.

Ten-Key Listing Machines

As the name implies, a ten-key machine has only ten figure keys on the keyboard. Ten-key listing machines are used for addition and subtraction. Amounts are entered on the keyboard and printed on the paper tape in the order in which they are read. Each figure key, including the 0, or cipher key, is struck separately. For example, to list $50.60 you would strike the 5, 0, 6, and 0 keys and then strike the motor bar.

Illus. 6-13

Ten-key listing machine

Because the machine has only ten figure keys, all within easy reach, you will be able to enter amounts on the keyboard without looking at the keys after a few hours of instruction. Touch operation will increase your production rate and greatly reduce your chances of omitting amounts or transposing figures in an amount.

transposing: changing the position or order

Mechanical Printing Calculators

Mechanical printing calculators are still found in some offices, but in time they will be replaced with electronic printing calculators. Mechanical printing calculators have ten-figure keyboards and like the other ten-key machines can be operated by touch.

Calculations printed on the tapes can be checked against source documents from which the computations are made. They are all-purpose machines with automatic multiplication and division. Some models have memory storage.

Full-Keyboard Listing Machine

A full-keyboard listing machine (also known as a *full-bank adding machine*) has from five to twenty columns of keys ranging in ascending order from 1 to 9. There are no 0 keys on the keyboard; zeros are printed automatically. The full-keyboard listing machine is used primarily for addition and subtraction.

Some listing machines have movable carriages which hold statements and ledger cards. If you work in a small company, you will be able to do your billing work on the listing machine itself.

Bookkeeping Machines

Bookkeeping machines are also known as *billing* machines. The main advantages of bookkeeping machines are their ability to tabulate from one position to another and to print at high speeds. Reports such as statements, invoices, and checks can be prepared on a bookkeeping machine much more rapidly and accurately than they can be handwritten. Bookkeeping machines can perform addition; subtraction; and, with a special attachment, multiplication and division. They are particularly valuable in preparing repetitious data related to customer billing.

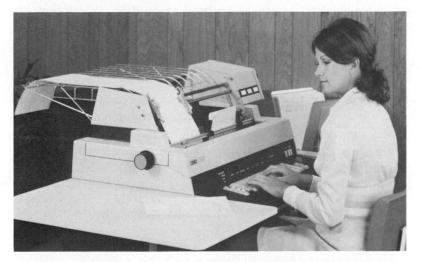

Illus. 6-14

Bookkeeping machine

NCR Corporation

Accounting Machines

These machines work faster and more automatically than bookkeeping machines. They are not, however, as efficient as computers. This machine has a *central processing unit* (sometimes called a *CPU*) that programs the work for the machine to do. The program is stored on paper tape in cabinets beside the machine. The operator sends data into the system using a keyboard similar to a typewriter but with additional keys.

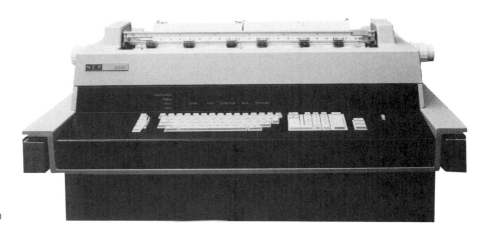

Unit Record System

As was mentioned in Part 1 of this Unit, the unit record method of processing data is also called the punched card system because data is recorded by punching holes in a card. The five machines used in the unit record system are illustrated here, and a brief description of how they are operated is given.

Card Punch Machine

The purpose of the card punch machine is to transfer data into a card by means of a punched code. The card punch operator reads the source document and depresses keys that punch holes in the cards. The holes represent numbers, letters, and symbols. The machine automatically feeds, positions, and ejects each card. The operator must strike the proper keys in the correct sequence.

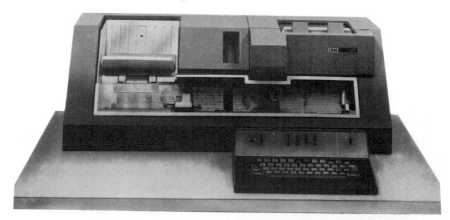

Verifier

Since accuracy is so **essential**, card verifying is necessary to check **original** card punching. A different operator usually verifies the original punching by striking the keys of a verifier while reading from the same source of information used to punch the cards. The verifying machine compares the key struck with the hole already punched in the column on the card. A difference causes the machine to stop, indicating a difference between the two operations.

essential:
very important

original:
the first

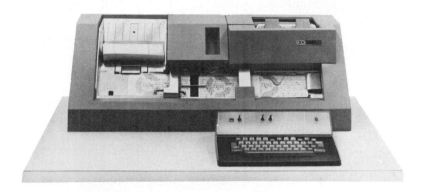

Illus. 6-17

Card verifier

IBM Corporation

Sorter

Imagine sorting from 800 to 1,000 cards a minute with complete accuracy! This is one of the outstanding advantages of the punched card system. After the punched cards have been verified, they are sorted into numeric or alphabetic order according to the information that has been punched in them. Payroll cards, for example, may be sorted alphabetically according to the last and first names of the employees or numerically according to their time card numbers.

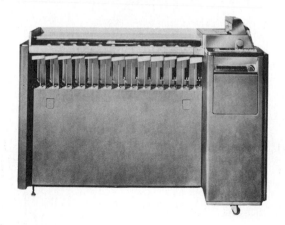

Illus. 6-18

Sorter

IBM Corporation

Tabulator

After the cards have been sorted, they are fed through a tabulator to transcribe and print automatically the information punched in the cards. The tabulator will print names and other descriptive information from a group of cards, add or subtract punched amounts, and print totals and grand totals only, without listing either the descriptive information or the separate amounts punched into the individual cards. Tabulating machines operate at speeds ranging from 100 to 150 cards a minute depending upon the type of machine used.

IBM Corporation

Illus. 6-19   Tabulator

Collator

merged:
combined; united; blended

Sometimes information is required from two or more card files. The cards from the files must be brought together and **merged** or matched before further processing is possible. A collator is used for this purpose.

IBM Corporation

Illus. 6-20   Collator

A collator can (1) merge two decks of punched cards in numeric sequence, (2) match the cards from two files having the same numeric data punched in them in a particular field, (3) select from a deck of cards only those cards having a certain number or a series of numbers in a specified field, or (4) check a file of cards to make sure that they are in **sequential** order.

sequential:
following in a series

Computers

Computers are associated with the term *electronic data processing* — the processing of records electronically. A typical electronic data processing system uses three groups of linked devices or machines to perform steps in an operation.

Input Unit

The input devices are used to enter instructions and data into the storage section of the system. The information to be placed in the computer may be recorded on punched cards, paper tape, or magnetic tape.

Central Processing Unit

The central processing unit includes:

1. The *storage section* which stores data, instructions, final results, historical data, master records, and any other information that can be **advantageously** stored within the computer.

advantageously:
favorably

Illus. 6-21

The central
processing unit

NCR Corporation

2. The *process section* which manipulates the data. Computing — addition, subtraction, multiplication, and division — is performed here.
3. The *control section* which could be called the nerve center of the data processing system. It receives each instruction of the program and analyzes it to determine the operation to be performed. The movement of data into or out of storage is supervised by the control section. It controls the actual execution of the operation. It **monitors** and supervises the flow of data within the system. It notifies the operator when attention is required.

monitors:
checks

Output Unit

The output devices are used to take the results of the processing out of the system. Output information can be on a continuous form, called a print-out; on up-dated magnetic tapes or disks, punched paper tape or cards; or displayed on a television-like screen at a terminal unit.

Visual display units are connected directly with a computer close by or many miles away. For example, a branch office in Tucson may not keep a complete set of records on its customers. The sales representative may want to know the type of merchandise that a specific customer ordered during the last three months, and this information is stored in the home office computer in Denver.

The operator types on the terminal unit requesting information from the computer. In a few seconds the computer will cause the information to appear on the screen of the terminal unit.

Illus. 6-22

Computer terminal unit

Courtesy of American Telephone
& Telegraph Company

By having a knowledge of the ways data can be processed, you are better prepared to perform your job in a modern office whether you work with computer **software** or printed documents such as payrolls, ledgers, and statements.

software: computer programs

REVIEWING

1. Under what circumstances might the secretary use calculating machines?
2. What feature distinguishes the electronic display calculator from the ten-key listing machine and the mechanical printing calculators?
3. What is one of the chief advantages of a ten-key listing machine?
4. What is the value of a paper tape on a listing machine?
5. What are the main advantages of bookkeeping machines?
6. What do punched holes on data cards represent?
7. What purpose does the verifier serve?
8. What is the function of an input device?
9. What are the three sections in a CPU?
10. What is the function of an output device?

MAKING JUDGMENTS

Mr. Thaxton has been an efficient secretary with the Bankacharge Credit Card Company for six years. At 4:45 p.m., Mr. Matthews, his employer, asked him to record a small amount of data on punched cards by closing time at 5 p.m. Mr. Thaxton was positive of his accuracy and by not using the verifier machine he was able to punch the cards for Mr. Matthews by 5 p.m. Mr. Thaxton was proud that he finished the task on time.

What do you think about his decision not to use the verifier?

WORKING WITH OTHERS

You have recently been employed by the National Building Suppliers. There are four other secretaries in the office. Elaine, the secretary with the most seniority, has been asked to assist you in learning how to operate an electronic calculator. Elaine resents having to spend her time teaching you and, as a result, often speaks sharply to you. What can you do to help decrease the tension in this situation? Is a willingness to help others a necessary trait for a good secretary?

REFRESHING LANGUAGE SKILLS

Using the suffixes *able* or *ible*, convert the following words into adjectives. Type both the root word and the adjective.

Examples: *Root Word*   *Adjective*
       predict   predictable
       defense   defensible

1. present
2. knowledge
3. convert
4. verify
5. consider
6. accept
7. conceive
8. force
9. manage
10. recognize

PERFORMING SECRETARIAL TASKS

1. Visit one or more offices in your community and do the following:
   a. Find out what adding and calculating machines are being used.
   b. Determine what particular kinds of jobs are being done on the various machines.
   c. Request some of the business forms that are used in connection with these jobs.

   Prepare a typewritten report on your visit and attach the forms collected.
2. Write to one or more manufacturers of adding and calculating machines asking for literature on their machines. Use this material for a bulletin board display.
3. If calculating machines are available to you, use one of the machines to do the following problem. If calculating machines are not available, do the problem manually.

   You purchase the following items from the Hopkins Office Supply Company:

		Total Due
15 boxes	Fluid Masters @ $3.51	$52.65
7 reams	Duplicating Paper @ $3.19	22.37
3 boxes	Carbon Paper @ $2.72	8.16
4 boxes	Envelopes @ $2.38	9.52
25	Pens @ $.25	6.50
6	Typewriter Ribbons @ $2.20	13.01
		$92.21

   a. Carefully check each item to make sure all extensions and totals are correct. On a separate sheet of paper indicate any corrections and the correct total.
   b. Hopkins Office Supply Company gives you a 2 percent discount if you pay your bill within ten days. What would be the total amount you should pay Hopkins Office Supply Company if you paid the bill within the ten days?

Part 3
Using Business Forms

Mr. John Graham has been secretary for three years to Mr. Hugh Clarke, Chief Engineer of the Prince Manufacturing Company. When he was first employed, Mr. Clarke liked to handle all purchase requisitions. He supplied Mr. Graham with all the information needed to type the forms. After checking each form, he would sign it. Now, Mr. Clarke has given John the full responsibility of seeing that the office has the necessary supplies. When someone in the department runs out of any office supplies, they report it to Mr. Graham. He fills out the requisition form, signs it himself, and sends it to the purchasing department.

Almost every operation in a business depends upon some type of business form on which data is processed. You and all office employees will work with business forms. Each of these forms should have a specific name and a specific purpose. When merchandise is bought, a purchase order is made out; when a sale is made, many forms are made out to record the complete transaction. When an automobile is produced, numerous forms are used along every step of its manufacture and sale. Forms are needed to record, process, and transmit the information and instructions required for business transactions in all kinds of businesses — from small, local establishments to large, national corporations.

What part will you, the secretary, have in handling business forms? Of course, how much or how little you use business forms will depend on the size of the office and the type of work in which your employer is engaged. As a secretarial office worker, you may fill out a handwritten form occasionally, but you will probably spend much more time preparing typewritten forms. You may also use a calculating machine along with the typewriter to complete forms containing computations. You may copy information and compile statistical data from business forms, and you will surely be expected to check, sort, and file forms.

Purpose of Business Forms

A business form is a printed sheet of paper on which information can be recorded. Many business forms are used as source documents for the data processing cycle.

The purpose of a business form is to make the processing of data more efficient by arranging information on a sheet of paper to reduce the time, effort, and material needed to prepare and to read the information.

The printed information on a form — for example, the firm name, address, telephone number, and column headings — eliminates the need for recopying this information on every document.

Another way to reduce the need for recopying data is to make multiple copies. When the data is needed by several people, the use of carbon paper saves time, reduces cost, and increases accuracy. Multicopy forms and carbonless paper are also used to make several copies of a business form.

Each section of a business form should serve a specific purpose. The heading shows that the form is an official document issued by a business firm. An invoice, for example, should be prepared on a firm's form to show that it is **authentic** (Illustration 6-23, page 236). The printed name of the form will indicate its purpose: an invoice (bill of sale); a purchase order (authority to buy); and a statement (a request for payment).

authentic:
genuine

The column headings will indicate what is to be typed in the column.

Form Design

You may not only work with business forms but may also be requested to make suggestions for the design of a new form. If a form that you are typing in business is difficult to complete because it is designed poorly, you might redesign the form for your employer and suggest that the next time it is printed that the new design be used. For efficient handling, the most important information on the form, whether it be the name of the form, invoice number, or due date, should be printed where it can be read easily and filed accurately.

To minimize the number of tabular stops, align typewritten information as much as possible with other typewritten information on the form. Arrows at the top of the form indicate where to set the left margin stop and tabular stops on your typewriter.

Insofar as possible, horizontal lines should not be printed on business forms that are generally typewritten, especially lines for names and addresses. A **vertical** line to separate dollars and cents in the amount

vertical:
up and down

columns should not be used. These lines merely add to the time spent in setting up the proper tab stops or in typing on lines. The name and address are usually typed within a specific area on the form to permit the use of a window envelope.

Business forms to be filled in on typewriters and other office machines should be designed to take advantage of the spacing and tabular **mechanisms** of the machines. For example, if a form is to be filled in on a typewriter, the horizontal spacing lines should be one sixth or one third of an inch apart to permit continuous single or double spaced typewriting and to make it unnecessary to use the variable line spacer.

mechanisms: devices

Ample space should be allowed at the top, bottom, and sides of the forms to permit binding, perforating, and stapling.

ample: enough

When business forms are used as source documents for transferring data to punched cards, the information that must be punched on the cards should appear in the same order on the business form. This will speed up the card punching process because the card punch operator can read and punch the information in sequence.

Forms for Selling

Recording the data about the sale of merchandise of services is one of the key operations of any business. The forms on which the sales data is recorded vary with the size and type of business, but all firms use a sales order form. Department stores and other retail stores also use "layaway" order forms, installment order forms, and sales books.

As a secretary, you should understand the sales procedures followed by modern business firms and the purpose of each of the standard sales forms because much of your dictation may deal with sales. If you are employed in a sales department or by a small firm, you may be expected to prepare and process sales forms.

Sales Invoice

When your company sells goods, information about the sale is recorded on a form called an *invoice*. You would call your company's copy of the invoice a *sales invoice* (Illustration 6-23, page 236). A copy of the same invoice would be called a *purchase invoice* by the buyer (Illustration 6-28, page 242).

The salesperson records (usually in handwriting) information about the sales on a *sales order* (or sales slip) form. The form provides space for the name and address of the customer, the customer's order number, the seller's invoice number, the shipping instructions, the terms of the payment, the number of items, a description of each item, and the unit price. The sales order usually lists any special instructions or conditions and the trade discounts allowed.

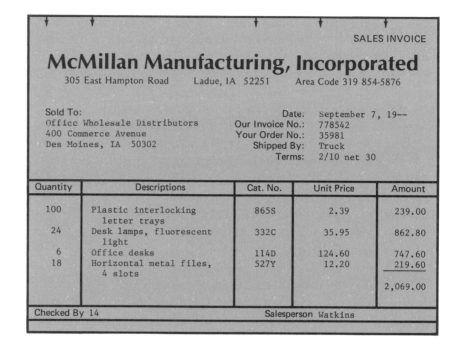

Illus. 6-23

Sales invoice

SALES INVOICE

McMillan Manufacturing, Incorporated
305 East Hampton Road   Ladue, IA 52251   Area Code 319 854-5876

Sold To:
Office Wholesale Distributors
400 Commerce Avenue
Des Moines, IA 50302

Date: September 7, 19—
Our Invoice No.: 778542
Your Order No.: 35981
Shipped By: Truck
Terms: 2/10 net 30

Quantity	Descriptions	Cat. No.	Unit Price	Amount
100	Plastic interlocking letter trays	865S	2.39	239.00
24	Desk lamps, fluorescent light	332C	35.95	862.80
6	Office desks	114D	124.60	747.60
18	Horizontal metal files, 4 slots	527Y	12.20	219.60
				2,069.00

Checked By 14   Salesperson Watkins

Credit Memorandum

merchandise: goods bought and sold in business

Some customers will return **merchandise** for one reason or another. Your firm, too, may return merchandise delivered too late to be of value; merchandise of the wrong kind, style, or color; or merchandise received in a damaged condition. In most instances, after the customer informs the seller about the situation, the customer will be instructed to return the merchandise. In some cases, such as with damaged goods, it may be more advantageous to make a special allowance to the customer to cover the loss if the merchandise is kept rather than returned.

When merchandise is returned or when an allowance is granted to a customer, a *credit memorandum* is issued. This credit memorandum is very much like an invoice and lists about the same information that appears on an invoice. At least two copies are made — one for the customer to whom the credit memorandum is issued and the other for the accounting department to be used in crediting the customer's account for the amount of the returned goods or of the allowance.

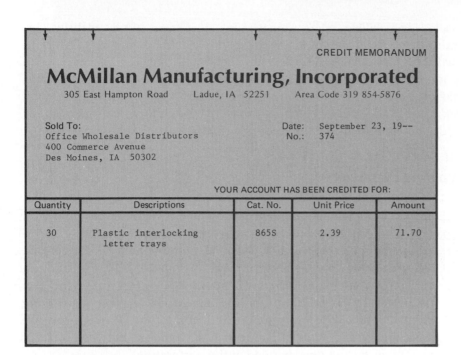

CREDIT MEMORANDUM

McMillan Manufacturing, Incorporated

305 East Hampton Road   Ladue, IA 52251   Area Code 319 854-5876

Sold To:
Office Wholesale Distributors
400 Commerce Avenue
Des Moines, IA 50302

Date: September 23, 19--
No.: 374

YOUR ACCOUNT HAS BEEN CREDITED FOR:

Quantity	Descriptions	Cat. No.	Unit Price	Amount
30	Plastic interlocking letter trays	865S	2.39	71.70

Illus. 6-24.

Credit memorandum

Credit Approval

When the purchase order is received without an accompanying payment in full, it must be approved by the seller's credit department before the merchandise is packed and shipped. The credit department may approve the shipment of the goods on the terms your firm suggests; but, for a firm with a poor credit reputation, it may decide that the goods should be shipped COD (Collect on Delivery). When the latter procedure is recommended, and the terms are different from the credit terms suggested by the buyer, it may be necessary to inform the customer tactfully in writing of the situation and ask whether the goods should be shipped under the **vendor's** terms. This is another duty sometimes performed by the secretary.

vendor:
seller

Billing

When the order is shipped by your firm, the bill or invoice is mailed. This **vital** operation of a business enterprise is commonly known as *billing*, but in some firms is called *invoicing*.

Your firm may not receive all bills at the end of the month. Some companies may bill at different times during the month. This **procedure**

vital:
important

procedure:
series of steps
followed to
accomplish something

public utilities:
government regulated
companies serving the
public

is called *cycle billing*. Many department stores and **public utilities**, including telephone companies and gas and electric companies, have divided their lists of customers and now send out bills on different dates in the month, rather than send out all bills at the end of the month. This makes it possible for the billing departments to work steadily, to avoid peak loads, and to send out bills promptly. For billing, companies may divide customer lists alphabetically, by districts, or by sales territories.

Preparing the Invoice

Every well-organized business establishes a definite procedure for preparing invoices. This procedure may differ with the number of invoices prepared by each concern. A small number of invoices may be prepared on typewriters, a large number on special billing machines, and a very large volume of invoices with data processing equipment.

perforations:
lines of small holes

Most invoices prepared on billing machines or data processing equipment are typed on continuous multiple forms. These forms are printed on continuous strips of paper with **perforations** between each set of forms. The forms can be separated at the perforation.

Calculating and Checking Invoices

All invoices should be checked for accuracy before they are mailed to the customers. The checking should be done by someone other than the person who actually prepared the invoice. The extensions can be checked with a desk calculator or by checking the items against precomputed tables. A *precomputed table* is one that lists the items that might be sold and in other columns the prices charged for the various units, such as a dozen, a gross, or a case.

Statements

At regular intervals, usually monthly, a *statement* of account is sent to each customer. The statement shows the amount owed at the beginning of the month, the charges and payments made during the month, and the balance owed at the end of the month.

Statements are usually prepared on bookkeeping machines, punched card tabulating machines, and other data processing equipment, depending upon the size of the business. However, in a small business the secretary may prepare the statement.

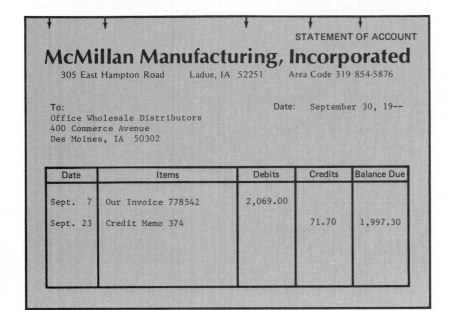

STATEMENT OF ACCOUNT

McMillan Manufacturing, Incorporated

305 East Hampton Road   Ladue, IA 52251   Area Code 319 854-5876

To: Date: September 30, 19--
Office Wholesale Distributors
400 Commerce Avenue
Des Moines, IA 50302

Date	Items	Debits	Credits	Balance Due
Sept. 7	Our Invoice 778542	2,069.00		
Sept. 23	Credit Memo 374		71.70	1,997.30

Illus. 6-25

Statement of account

Your knowledge and understanding of these key operations of purchasing and selling will enable you to be a more capable assistant and partner to the executive in any business.

Forms for Purchasing

The purchasing and receiving of goods are important operations in any business. In large organizations these operations are handled by separate departments; in small organizations they are handled by purchasing and receiving clerks and sometimes by secretaries. For example, secretaries are often given the responsibility for purchasing office supplies. Whether the buying is done through a department head, a purchasing agent, a purchasing clerk, or a secretary, the aim is the same — to secure for the firm the needed material and equipment of the desired quality at the most **reasonable** price. The **reputation** of the seller for honest dealing and prompt delivery is an important factor to be considered in deciding where major purchases should be made.

reasonable: fair

reputation: character

The purchasing procedure is a well-planned office routine in which each step is determined by the work that precedes it. The purchasing procedure follows this sequence: (1) requesting the goods needed; (2) obtaining quotations on the cost of the goods needed; (3) preparing a purchase order; (4) checking the incoming shipment; and (5) adjusting any damage or claim.

Purchase Requisition

Most of the work of the purchasing department involves the purchasing of goods and services for a firm. The *purchase requisition* is used to inform the purchasing agent or some other authorized buyer for the firm what specific items should be purchased. For example, if you are working for a large business and need bond paper for your office, you will prepare a purchase requisition and present it to the purchasing department. The purchasing department will then get the paper you need.

You will find that the purchase requisition requires such information as the current date, the date the goods are needed, and a detailed description of the goods requested which includes the trade name, catalog number, quantity to be ordered, and the price of each item, if it is known. It may also indicate the name and address of a firm from which the goods may be purchased. You must get all this information before completing this form.

Illus. 6-26

Purchase requisition

PURCHASE REQUISITION

Office Wholesale Distributors
400 Commerce Avenue   Des Moines, IA 50302   Area Code 515 376-9872

		Deliver To.:	Display Room
Requisition No.:	21101	Location:	1 Floor
Date Issued:	August 28, 19--	Job No.:	432-17
Date Required:	September 30, 19--	Approved By:	B.E.L.

Quantity	Description	Unit Price	Amount
100	Plastic interlocking letter trays #865S	2.39	239.00
24	Desk lamps, fluorescent light #332C	35.95	862.80
6	Office desks #114D	124.60	747.60
18	Horizontal metal files, 4 slots #527Y	12.20	219.60
			2,069.00

J. W. Hopkins
Department Supervisor

duplicate:
copy

You usually should prepare two copies of a purchase requisition. You send the original (after it has been signed by your employer) to the purchasing agent and keep the **duplicate** in your files If you are employed by a large organization, you may be required to prepare additional copies of each purchase requisition so that they may be available for the auditing department or other departments.

Purchase Order

The goods you requisitioned may be ordered in a number of ways: by writing an order letter, by sending a telegram, by making a telephone call, by giving an order to a salesperson, by filling out and mailing an order blank that is included as part of a catalog, or by filling out a *purchase order* that has been especially designed for the purpose. Most firms prefer to use purchase orders which they mail to the business from which they order goods (the vendors) because the purchase order is a written record for future references. If the goods are urgently needed by an executive, you can order them by telephone or telegraph; but a confirming purchase order to cover the transaction is prepared and mailed to the vendor later.

Illus. 6-27

Purchase order

PURCHASE ORDER

Office Wholesale Distributors
400 Commerce Avenue   Des Moines, IA 50302   Area Code 515 376-9872

To: McMillan Manufacturing, Inc.
     305 East Hampton Road
     Ladue, IA 52251

Date: August 29, 19--

Order No.:   06138

Ship By: Truck

Terms: 2/10 net 30

Quantity	Descriptions	Cat. No.	Unit Price	Amount
100	Plastic interlocking letter trays	865S	2.39	239.00
24	Desk lamps, fluorescent light	332C	35.95	862.80
6	Office desks	114D	124.60	747.60
18	Horizontal metal files, 4 slots	527Y	12.20	219.60
				2,069.00

By *S. L. Brooks*

You will usually prepare four or more copies of printed purchase orders because several departments in the firm will need a copy of each purchase order.

Purchase Invoice

When the vendor ships the merchandise you ordered, an invoice is usually sent to your firm on the same day. The invoice is known to the vendor as a *sales invoice* and to the buyer, your firm, as a *purchase invoice*.

PURCHASE INVOICE

McMillan Manufacturing, Incorporated

305 East Hampton Road   Ladue, IA 52251   Area Code 319 854-5876

Sold To:
Office Wholesale Distributors
400 Commerce Avenue
Des Moines, IA 50302

Date: September 7, 19--
Our Invoice No.:   778542
Your Order No.:   35981
Shipped By: Truck
Terms: 2/10 net 30

Quantity	Descriptions	Cat. No.	Unit Price	Amount
100	Plastic interlocking letter trays	865S	2.39	239.00
24	Desk lamps, fluorescent light	332C	35.95	862.80
6	Office desks	114D	124.60	747.60
18	Horizontal metal files, 4 slots	527Y	12.20	219.60
				2,069.00

Checked By 14	Salesperson Watkins

In a large firm incoming purchase invoices are usually handled by the purchasing department. As a rule only one copy is received, although some firms request additional copies. If you work in a small firm, you may be responsible for checking the purchase invoices against the terms and conditions of the purchase order to be sure that they agree.

REVIEWING

1. What is the difference between a purchase order, an invoice, and a statement?
2. Why is form design so important to the office worker? How is it related to the use of the typewriter?
3. What is the purpose of a sales order form?
4. When is a credit memorandum issued?
5. What action must be taken when the credit terms of the buyer and seller are different?
6. What is the advantage of cycle billing?
7. What is the purpose of a precomputed table?
8. What information is shown on a statement?
9. What are the steps in the purchasing procedure?
10. What is the purpose of a purchase order?

MAKING JUDGMENTS

As a secretary in a small electronics business, Mr. Paxton's job includes handling the company's purchases. During the day, employees tell him on the phone and in person about items to purchase. Mr. Paxton hurriedly writes down these orders on a handy piece of scrap paper. When he thinks it's time to place an order, he gathers up the pieces of paper on his desk and prepares a purchase order. How would you improve Mr. Paxton's purchasing procedure?

WORKING WITH OTHERS

Your job is to prepare purchase orders from purchase requisitions received from all other departments in the company. Ms. Jeter prepares purchase requisitions for the Accounts Receivable Department. Apparently she does not keep up with her work, because the date that goods are required on the purchase requisition is too close to the date the purchase requisition is issued. She brings purchase requisitions to you at the last minute and asks that you type her purchase orders ahead of orders from other departments that are submitted on time.

You have mentioned to Ms. Jeter several times that it is not fair to type her purchase orders before those you already have received. Ms. Jeter is now standing before you asking you to type her purchase order again before others. What do you say to her?

REFRESHING LANGUAGE SKILLS

Several of the words listed below are misspelled. Type the entire list giving the correct spelling for each word.

1. appreciation	14. procedure
2. prominant	15. schedulled
3. industral	16. recommendation
4. guarantee	17. suggestions
5. judment	18. provisions
6. necexxary	19. summarise
7. quantities	20. announcment
8. statement	21. acheive
9. specefications	22. license
10. memorandum	23. posess
11. recieve	24. possable
12. submitted	25. misspell
13. seqence	26. accurate

PERFORMING SECRETARIAL TASKS

1. If blank business forms are not available for the following problems, use plain paper and type the information that is ordinarily printed on such forms as shown in the illustrations in this part.

   Type invoices in duplicate for the following sales made by the Fancy Fragrances Manufacturing Company, 1505 North Berry Road, Bloomingdale, PA 18911, on February 2, 19—, shipped by truck, terms 2/10 net 30 days. The quantities and retail unit prices are given; you are to make all extensions and calculate the totals.

   a. Leiker's Department Store, 1200 Tanner Blvd., Greensboro, VI 22943:
      - 60 One-ounce bottles, "Love's Sparkle" Perfume, #3512, Price: $2.89 each
      - 25 Four-ounce boxes, "Wildflower" Dusting Powder, #1546, Price: $3.50 each
      - 200 Three-ounce bars, "Herbal Scented Soap Bars," #7911, Price: $.49 each
      - 50 Two-ounce bottles, "Red Roses" Bath Oil, #8134, Price: $3.60 each

   b. Callie Rogers, Inc., 233 S. E. Second Street, Davenport, VI 24239:
      - 75 Two-ounce jars, "Hearts-a-Flutter" Creme Sachet, #2157, Price: $2.15 each
      - 100 Disposable pocket size, "Confidence" Refreshers, #8777, Price: $.75 each
      - 30 One-ounce bottles, "Happy Times" Cologne, #2479, Price: $2.35 each

2. Type the following purchase requisition in duplicate for the Howell & Associates, Glenville, WI 54013

   a. Requisition No. 308 from the Purchasing Department for the Travel Department, 3 Floor; Date issued: May 6, 19—; Date Required: May 26, 19—; Approved by Frank Williams.
      - 1 Executive Desk, 78″ × 38″, Style 47765, Custom Finish. Price: $250.40.
      - 1 Executive Chair, Style T-9931, Top Grain Leather. Price: $85.95.

   b. Requisition No. 455 from the Purchasing Department for the Accounting Department, 2 Floor; Date Issued: July 15, 19—; Date Required: August 1, 19—; Approved by Harry Mitchell.
      - 2 Display Calculators, Model ST-099. Price $188.95 each.
      - 2 Calculating Machine Desks, 60″ × 30″, Style 4832-H. Metal Gray and Olive Green Finish. Price: $213.65 each.

3. Type monthly statements of account in duplicate to be sent to the following customers of Terrell's Luggage Shop, Canton, 868 Apple Avenue, DE 19935, October 1, 19--:

a. Paula M. Gainer, 4554 Highland Avenue, Canton, DE 19935:

Date	Code	Division	Charges	Credits
Sept. 1	C-98	339	98.79	
9	C-98	339	235.45	
20	R-70	251		98.79
29	R-70	251		30.79
30	C-98	339	500.00	

b. Susan A. Horton, 3901 Maplewood Avenue, Caplin, NJ 08212:

Date	Code	Division	Charges	Credits
Sept. 3	C-45	652	17.95	
10	C-45	652	341.55	
26	R-50	119		56.60

4. Your employer gives you this rough draft, handwritten form. Prepare a typewritten form on plain paper to be sent to the printer. Refer to the principles of form design on pages 234–235 if necessary.

Russell Stationery & Printing   SALES INVOICE

5362 Briley Parkway, San Francisco, CA 90235 Area Code 415 532-6701

Sold To:

Date:
Our Invoice No.:
Your Order No.:
Shipped By:
Terms:

Quantity	Descriptions	Cat. No.	Unit Price	Amount

Checked By   Salesperson

IMPROVING SECRETARIAL SKILLS (Optional)

Visit three local businesses and ask if you may have one of their purchase requisition forms. Try to visit businesses that are not alike such as a bank, a restaurant, and a retail store. Be prepared to answer the following questions either by giving an oral report in class, or by attractively displaying the forms and your answers on a poster.

a. How are the forms alike?
b. How are the forms different?
c. Which form do you think is best? Why?
d. How would you improve each form? Why?

UNIT 7

Using Mail and Shipping Services

Part 1
Handling Incoming Mail

One of Miss Valdez' responsibilities each morning is to take care of the mail for her employer, Mrs. Murray. Today the mail included three requests for information, a personal letter for her employer, two magazines, six business letters, and an advertisement for office furniture. Miss Valdez was able to handle the request letters herself, so she set them aside. She carefully read the business letters, making necessary notes in the margins and pulling needed folders from the files. Because of the small volume of mail, she was able to compose and type responses to the request letters quickly. Then she arranged all of the correspondence in proper sequence — the personal letter, business letters, request letters, advertisement, and magazines — and placed them on Mrs. Murray's desk.

The United States Postal Service presently handles about 90 billion pieces of mail every year. One of your first and most interesting duties as a secretary will be to assist your employer in handling mail. You can be of great help if you process the mail efficiently as it arrives and arrange it systematically before giving it to your employer.

The procedure for handling the mail will depend upon the size and type of business in which you are employed. In a large office the incoming mail is opened, sorted, and distributed by the mail department. In a small office, you will be expected to open, read, and sort all the incoming mail.

Opening the Mail

When the volume of incoming mail is very large, the letters are opened in the mail department with an electric mail opener. It trims a narrow strip off one edge of each envelope. The amount taken off is so small that there is little risk that the contents of the envelope will be damaged. To reduce the chances of cutting the contents, the envelopes may be jogged on the table before they are placed in the opener so that the contents will fall away from the edge that is to be trimmed.

Illus. 7-1

Electrically operated letter openers

Pitney Bowes

In the mail room the mail is sorted by departments. A sorting tray, with a separate compartment for each department, is used for this purpose. After the mail has been sorted, it is delivered by a mail clerk or a messenger. Usually mail is delivered several times a day, the first mail of the day being the heaviest.

When the mail reaches your employer's office, you should put aside the letters that can be answered or handled by you when you have some free time. This type of mail includes the communications that can be answered by sending the requester a form letter, circular, advertisement, or routine report. Requests for catalogs or price lists, for example, can be handled in this manner. Your employer may wish to see even these in order to be aware of all **inquiries** that are received before turning them over to you for handling. You request the mail department (usually by filling in a company form for that purpose) to send the catalog or price list immediately and note on the letter that it has been mailed. Your handling the routine items will make it much easier for your employer to answer the mail that requires a personal response.

inquiries: questions

If you open the mail in your office, use a letter opener or a paper knife. If you should cut a letter or an enclosure as you are opening an envelope, use transparent mending tape to repair it.

After you have opened the envelopes, remove the letters and other enclosures carefully. Look at each letter and its enclosures as soon as they are removed and attach the enclosures to the letter. If an enclosure is missing, you should note the **omission** in the margin of the letter. You may be expected to make up a special memorandum and keep it on file if the missing enclosure is a check, a money order, cash, or stamps.

Keep the envelopes until you have examined each letter for the signature and the address. If either is missing on the letter, attach the envelope to the letter. Sometimes a check is received with no other means of identification except the envelope in which it was mailed. If the date of the letter is different from the postmark, keep the envelope. Sometimes the envelope of an important document is stapled to the document because the date of mailing may prove to be of some importance. If, after you have thrown away the envelope, you notice that the return address is not printed or typed on a letter, you may be able to find the address in a telephone directory, a city directory, or in the correspondence files.

Mail marked *personal* should be delivered to the executive's desk unopened. If, by error you open a letter marked "personal" or "confidential," place the letter back in the envelope and write on the outside "Sorry — opened by mistake," and add your initials. Note each letter carefully before you open it so you don't make this error often.

Dating the Mail

After you have checked the incoming mail for enclosures, return addresses, and signatures, mark it with the date and time. You can do this with a pen or pencil, a rubber stamp, or a time stamp machine.

Illus. 7-2

A time stamp machine records time, date and identifying mark on letters, telegrams, and other documents.

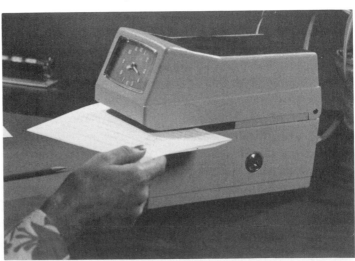

Cincinnati Time
Recorder Company

The date and time on the incoming mail may be important in correspondence about contracts, insurance, and some financial documents. The receiving date also reminds the recipient when the correspondence was received and may encourage a prompt reply.

Underlining and Annotating

If your employer prefers, you may further assist in handling correspondence by underlining and **annotating**. Good judgment is necessary here, however, since a letter that has too many markings may annoy an executive.

First of all, as you read, underline the key words and phrases in the letter. This will help an executive get a clear understanding of the letter rapidly. It will also give you a complete understanding of the contents of each letter.

Secondly, as you read, find out the answers to questions and problems that your employer will need to know before answering a particular letter. Write the answers and comments in the margins of the letter in clearly worded, legible handwriting. For example, if an order is received, check with the credit department and the shipping department to see if and when the order can be shipped. Then write the information on the letter so that your employer will have it when dictating the acknowledgment of the order. The notation can simply be: *Credit satisfactory, stock on hand for immediate shipment*.

A request for payment is an important piece of incoming mail that you must handle carefully. Make sure that the bill has not already been paid and then check the accuracy of every item and every amount before placing it on your employer's desk for payment. Your employer will have a great deal of confidence in you, knowing that the figures in incoming mail are accurate or that you have noted any errors.

A letter containing a check should also be handled with extreme care. You should immediately compare the amount of the enclosed check with the amount mentioned in the letter. If no letter, statement, or invoice comes with the check, verify the amount with the file copy of the bill. If it is the policy of your firm to turn all checks received over to the cashier immediately, write the amount of the check and the date it was received in the margin before giving the letter to your employer.

Another problem that you will **encounter** is the rerouting of letters addressed to your employer but actually related to someone else's work. In this case, just write the correct name above that of your employer. Include these with your employer's mail in the event that a covering note is necessary for the proper person or department.

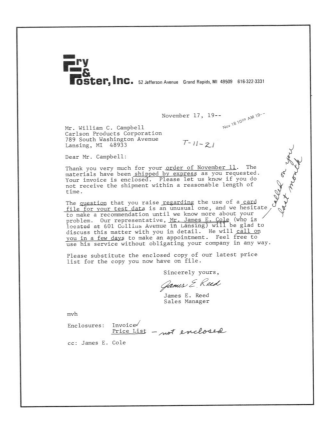

Illus. 7-3 Annotated and date-stamped letter

Attaching Related Materials

Photocopies or carbon copies of previous correspondence, reports, and other related information will be of great assistance to your employer in answering the mail. They may be attached to the incoming mail or placed where your employer can get them easily if needed when dictating the replies.

Organizing Correspondence

attachments:
additional items

When annotating has been completed and all **attachments** have been added, the mail should be placed on your employer's desk or in the incoming mail basket.

The mail should be arranged according to your employer's preference. As a general rule, you should arrange the mail in the order of its importance. The following arrangement is usually satisfactory:

1. Unopened personal and confidential letters
2. Business letters of special importance to your employer
3. Letters containing checks or money orders
4. Other business letters
5. Letters containing orders
6. Letters containing bills, invoices, or other requests for payment
7. Advertisements
8. Newspapers and magazines

Special delivery letters and registered mail are usually delivered before the regular mail. They should be handled promptly upon receipt and brought to your employer's attention quickly. If a special delivery letter or a registered letter should come to your desk along with the regular mail, you should process it immediately and turn it over to your employer without delay.

Illus. 7-4

A secretary checks incoming mail carefully.

Ohio National Life Insurance Company

Photocopying Mail

Very often a letter addressed to an executive should also be read by one or more other executives or assistants. Photocopies of such letters are sent to the proper persons in the organization for immediate action. A photocopy for each person who should see the correspondence should be clipped to the letter and the names of the persons to whom you are suggesting that the photocopies be sent should be listed at the bottom of the original copy. Your employer may want to add to the list or reduce it. Instructions may be written on the photocopies so that your employer's orders will be carried out promptly.

Referring and Routing Mail

devise:
prepare; create

Correspondence is frequently referred to an executive's associates or assistants for an answer. Referral slips simplify this task. If you have none available, you may **devise** and duplicate referral slips that will save both your employer's time and your time in getting information to associates and requesting the necessary action from them. When you refer correspondence, reports, or other business documents to someone else, be sure to keep a record of the transfer in a notebook. Otherwise you may lose track of very important business papers. The record should include the date it was sent, the name of the person to whom it was sent, the subject, the action to be taken, and the date when you expect to follow up if a follow-up should be necessary.

DATE *9/18/77*

TO *Tressa Stratman*

Refer to the attached material and

☐ Please note.
☐ Please note and file.
☑ Please note and return to me.
☐ Please mail to_____
☐ Please note and talk with me
    this a.m._____; p.m._____.
☐ Please answer, sending me a copy.
☐ Please write a reply for my signature.
☐ Please handle.
☐ Please have_____photocopies made
    for_____.
☐ Please sign.
☐ Please let me have your comments.
☐ Please RUSH–immediate action desired.
☐ Please make follow-up for_____

REMARKS:

Signed *Nina Forman*

Illus. 7-5   Referral slip

Albert Martin, Director
Public Relations Department

Date *3/25/77*

ROUTING SLIP

		Date Forwarded
_____	Everyone	_____
_____	Babb, B.	_____
✓	Gryder, H.	*3/25*
_____	Igo, J.	_____
_____	Mundt, K.	_____
✓	Primrose, N.	*3/25*
✓	Roehr, P.	*3/28*
_____	Slaughter, G.	_____
✓	Tucker, C.	*3/28*
_____	Wingfield, M.	_____
✓	*Brown, M.*	*3/28*

Will you please:

_____	Read and keep
_____	Read and pass on
_____	Read and return
✓	Read, pass on, and return

Illus. 7-6   Routing slip

Some correspondence and often important articles in trade magazines are to be read by others. Many firms use either a rubber stamp or a duplicated routing slip with the names of all the departments or executives of the firm to whom the material is to be sent. Either you or your employer should check the names of the persons who are to receive and pass on the material.

Special Memorandums

As you read certain letters, you will notice promises of materials that are being sent under separate cover, which means in another envelope or package. To be sure that you receive them, it will often be desirable for you to keep a record of mail expected in another package. Check at least twice a week to see which items have not been received so that you can follow up on delayed mail. This mail will also have to be referred to the department or the person to whom the original letter was referred, if it was routed or photocopied. One type of record for separate cover mail is illustrated below.

DATE OF ENTRY	ARTICLE	FROM WHOM	DATE SENT	DEPARTMENT	INDIVIDUAL	DATE RECEIVED
9-5	Book	Welch Bros.	9-3		A. Ward	9-6
9-12	Folders	Hill Supply	9-10	Filing		9-14
9-23	Report	Lehman & Cole	9-21	Research		9-25
10-1	Catalog	Tate Mfg. Co.	9-30	Purchasing		10-4
10-3	Tickets	Jack Wylie	10-1		H. Lewis	

Illus. 7-7

Register of mail expected under separate cover. Note that the last item has not arrived yet.

Because of its special importance, you may find it necessary to keep a record of the receipt of mail that is insured, special delivery, or registered. Use a form similar to the one illustrated below.

RECEIVED		FROM WHOM		FOR	KIND OF MAIL RECEIVED
DATE	TIME	NAME	ADDRESS	DEPARTMENT OR INDIVIDUAL	
4-5	3:20pm	J.J. McIntosh	St. Louis, Mo.	Purchasing	Insured
4-6	9:15am	Grove Mfg.	Memphis, TN	Sales	Special Delivery
4-9	10:45am	Mo. P. Williams	Des Moines, Ill	M. Jones	Registered

Illus. 7-8

Register of insured, special delivery, and registered mail

REVIEWING

1. If you were opening incoming mail with an electrically operated letter opener, how would you avoid cutting the contents of the envelopes?
2. What types of mail may be handled by the secretary?

3. A letter is received but the enclosure is missing. What should the secretary do?
4. When is it desirable to attach the envelope to the contents of a piece of mail?
5. How should personal mail be handled and what should be done if you open a personal letter by mistake?
6. Why are letters time stamped upon their receipt?
7. How is annotating helpful to an employer?
8. What is a satisfactory order of importance for most executives' mail?
9. Why is it necessary to keep a record of all transferred records, reports, or documents? What information should be recorded in the notebook?
10. A letter is received in which reference is made to a package coming under separate cover. How can a secretary be reminded to look for the package in a later delivery?

MAKING JUDGMENTS

Your employer, the office manager in a medium size company, has learned that there are many difficulties and problems in handling incoming mail. You have been asked to study the situation and report your findings to the office manager. You have found the following practices used throughout the company:

a. The mail is opened by hand by the receptionist who also handles the switchboard. When the mail is too heavy for her to take care of by herself, she receives help from any of the stenographers in the office who happen not to be busy.

b. Enclosures that are referred to in letters frequently are not with the letters that are distributed to the various executives. The executives are, therefore, uncertain whether the enclosures have been received or whether they have been received and separated from the letters.

c. Often a letter is not answered until sometime after it is received, but the executives do not know whether the delay is in their own offices or whether the letter has not been delivered to them promptly.

d. Before an order is filled, it is handled by the credit department, the sales department, and the order department. In some instances, it goes first to one department and in other instances first to another department, according to where the mail clerk is going first.

e. Sometimes in a letter, reference is made to a package being sent under separate cover. The executive, however, usually never sees the package or knows if it arrived.

After studying your report the office manager asks you for suggestions for eliminating these difficulties. What methods for solving these problems would you suggest?

WORKING WITH OTHERS

You received a special delivery letter for your employer, Mrs. Angela Santos, while she was away at lunch. During her absence you began working on a long and involved project; consequently, you forgot to give her the letter. The next morning as Mrs. Santos was walking by your desk, she noticed the letter.

How should you handle your mistake? Should you just ignore the situation and hope she says nothing to you?

REFRESHING LANGUAGE SKILLS

Semicolons are used to punctuate complex elements in a sentence. Below are three uses of the semicolon:

A. Between independent clauses not joined by a conjunction

Example: Letters marked "personal" are for the person addressed only; they should not be opened by the secretary.

B. Before a conjunction joining two independent clauses when one clause (or both) has internal punctuation

Example: By dating incoming mail, the receiver is reminded of when it arrived; and responsibility for delay can be established.

C. After each independent clause in a series when one (or more) has internal punctuation

Example: The secretary removed the letter from the envelope; he checked the enclosures against the list at the bottom of the letter; and then he placed a paper clip on the letter, the price list, the booklet, and the sample.

Punctuate the sentences below based on the three semicolon rules you have reviewed above.

1. Many letters can be answered by the secretary others should be handled by the executive.
2. After reading the letter Mr. Lacey decided that Mr. Strickland should handle the request but as it turned out Mr. Strickland was out of town until Friday.
3. Advertising materials should be kept on the left orders should be kept on the right correspondence should be kept in the center unopened personal and confidential mail should be handed to your employer immediately checks and other enclosures should be attached to correspondence.

4. In most offices correspondence is stamped orders are stamped invoices are stamped including both copies if they are sent in duplicate new price lists are stamped and brought to the employer's attention advertising material as a rule is not stamped.

5. The secretary placed the annotated correspondence on the executive's desk the executive reviewed it quickly and told the secretary to answer the inquiries as soon as possible.

PERFORMING SECRETARIAL TASKS

1. The mail listed below is expected under separate cover. Record the information on the form in your *Supplies Inventory* or draw a form like that on page 255.

May 1 A letter from Boyd C. Waggoner refers to a mailing list that was sent under separate cover on April 28, to the Advertising Department.

May 1 In his letter dated April 29, David P. Harding stated that he was returning a parcel post package to the Shipping Department.

May 2 In his letter of April 30, Thomas B. Jennings said that he was shipping a catalog to the Purchasing Department.

May 3 In a letter dated May 1, Jack D. Clary stated that he is returning a desk calculator to the Service Department.

May 4 In his letter of May 1, Harry J. Michaels stated that he sent his analysis of our operations systems to Keith McIntire.

May 4 Margaret Russell, in her letter of May 1, said that she shipped 16 reams of 8½ × 11, S-20, green duplicating paper to the Duplicating Department.

May 5 In a letter of May 2, Lee Alberts stated that she returned a rental typewriter to the Rental Department.

May 6 Francis Brooks in his letter of May 2, stated that he sent a book to the Accounting Department.

May 6 In a letter of May 3, Gary T. Campbell stated that he sent pamphlets to the Sales Department.

May 6 A letter from Cynthia McLarty refers to a package of folders sent on May 3 to the Research Department.

May 7 A letter from David P. Boucher refers to an art booklet that was sent under separate cover May 4 to the Advertising Department.

2. The insured, special-delivery, and registered mail listed below has been received by your company. Record the information on the form in your *Supplies Inventory* or draw a form similar to that on page 255.

May 15 At 9:30 a.m. a registered letter was received from Mr. Richard F. Davidson, Phoenix, Arizona. It was referred to the Sales Department.

May 15 At 11:25 a.m. an insured package was received from Ms. Katherine Whitely, Augusta, Maine, for the Advertising Department.

May 16 At 2:15 p.m. a registered letter was received from Mr. Jesse R. Pennington, Memphis, Tennessee, for the Accounting Department.

May 17 At 10:40 a.m. a special-delivery letter was received from Ms. Beverly Anne Hayes, Chicago, Illinois, for the Purchasing Department.

May 17 At 3:15 p.m. a registered letter was received from Mr. Douglas J. Fullerton, Mobile, Alabama, for the Sales Department.

May 18 At 4:00 p.m. a special delivery letter was received from Mr. Kevin E. Sealy, Flint, Michigan, for Larry Fannon.

May 19 At 11:05 a.m. an insured package was received from Mr. Walter D. Kemp, New York, New York, for the Maintenance Department.

May 19 At 1:30 p.m. a registered letter was received from Mr. Alan B. Conwell, Seattle, Washington, for the Sales Department.

Part 2
Handling Outgoing Mail

"Mr. Chun, I have several packages that need to be wrapped and mailed as soon as possible. Please take care of them properly." Mrs. Crim knows that Mr. Chun is well informed about postal requirements, rates, and services. He knows how to wrap each package; and according to the contents, he can decide how each package should be sent.

Outgoing mail may mean one letter to thousands of persons. It may mean first to fourth class and even mixed mail; or it may mean domestic, foreign, and special service mail. Your knowledge and understanding of postal services and effective mail handling can save your employer time and money and can increase the efficiency of the business.

You should be able to select the proper mailing service for all the different types of outgoing mail. A complete listing of postal services with the details for their use can be found in the Postal Service Manual of the United States. Postal services and rates are changed from time to time; therefore, it is important that you have an up-to-date copy of the Postal Service Manual in your office. It may be purchased from the Superintendent of Documents, United States Government Printing Office, Washington, D.C. 20402.

You can speed the mail delivery and reduce the cost of mailing if you use the right mailing service at the right time. A United States Postal Service official states that millions of dollars are wasted each year because of the general lack of knowledge of the various postal services. The official estimates that **extravagance** adds at least 10 percent to the annual cost of all mailing in the United States. You can always get up-to-date postal information free of charge at the Information window of your local post office.

extravagance:
spending much more than necessary

Handling Outgoing Mail

The system of handling outgoing mail, like the system of handling incoming mail, depends upon the size and the type of business in which you are employed. In a small office the secretary usually is responsible for all the details connected with outgoing mail. In a large office the mail is collected from each department several times throughout the day by a messenger or a mail clerk and taken to the mailing department where it is sealed and stacked near the *postage meter,* a machine that automatically prints the amount of postage, the postmark, and the mailing date on the envelope.

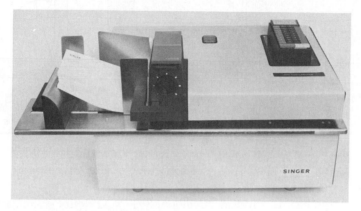

Illus. 7-9

Postage meter

Singer Mailing Equipment Division

Folding and Inserting Letters

Folding a business letter properly is not a difficult task. Care should be taken so that the creases are straight and are made without detracting from the neatness of the letter. A letter should be inserted in an envelope in such a way that it will be in a normal reading position when it is removed from the envelope and unfolded. Paper, 8½" × 11", to be inserted in a small envelope (No. 6, 6½" × 3⅝") is folded and inserted as follows:

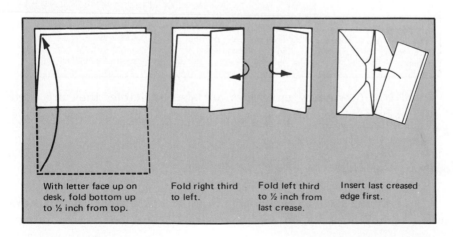

With letter face up on desk, fold bottom up to ½ inch from top.

Fold right third to left.

Fold left third to ½ inch from last crease.

Insert last creased edge first.

Illus. 7-10

Only two folds are necessary if the letter is to be placed in a large envelope (No. 10, 9½″ × 4⅛″):

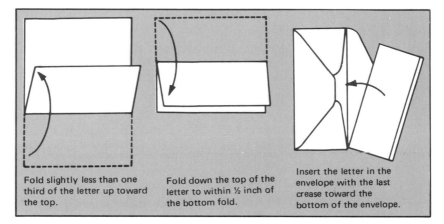

Illus. 7-11

Fold slightly less than one third of the letter up toward the top.

Fold down the top of the letter to within ½ inch of the bottom fold.

Insert the letter in the envelope with the last crease toward the bottom of the envelope.

The enclosures that accompany the letter should be folded with the letter or inserted so that they will come out of the envelope at the same time the letter is removed.

For a large No. 10 window envelope, 8½″ × 11″ letter sheets are folded as shown below:

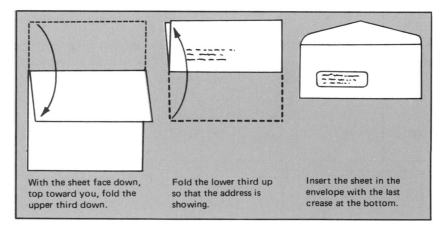

Illus. 7-12

With the sheet face down, top toward you, fold the upper third down.

Fold the lower third up so that the address is showing.

Insert the sheet in the envelope with the last crease at the bottom.

Small No. 6 window envelopes are also available; they are used mostly for bills or statements that are designed to fit with only a single fold.

Sealing Envelopes

If you should have to seal a large number of envelopes without the use of a sealing machine, spread about ten envelopes on a table, address down, flap open, one on top of the other with gummed edges showing. Brush over the gummed edges with a moist sponge or a moistener to soften the glue so that the flaps can be closed quickly and sealed. When sealing, start with the top envelope, the one nearest you, and work down to the first one placed on the table.

Stamps

You may also put postage stamps on rapidly by arranging six to eight envelopes on top of each other, showing just the upper right part of each one. Moisten the strip of stamps with a damp sponge and put on one stamp after the other. You can save time and increase your **efficiency** this way.

efficiency: productivity without waste

Postage stamps may be purchased in sheet, booklet, or coil form. The bound booklets of stamps are preferred for personal and home use; business firms find it better to work with the 100-stamp sheets or the coiled stamps. Coiled stamps are often used in business because they can be quickly placed on envelopes and packages and because they are less likely to be lost or damaged than are individual stamps.

Precanceled Stamps and Envelopes

For an advertising campaign your employer may wish to use precanceled stamps or precanceled stamped envelopes. Their use reduces the time and cost of handling mail. Precanceled stamps and envelopes are purchased from the post office with the cancellation lines already stamped on them. When the sorted mail is returned to the post office, it is not necessary for the letters to go through the canceling machine again. Therefore, the mail is **dispatched** more quickly. Precanceled stamps and envelopes cannot be used for first-class mail.

dispatched: sent

Stamped Envelopes and Cards

Another means of saving your time is through the use of stamped envelopes of different **denominations** which may be purchased in various sizes — singly or in quantity lots. The return address will be printed on them by the post office for a small fee if the envelopes are purchased in quantity lots.

denomination: kind or class

First-class postal cards may be purchased in single or double form. The double form is used when a reply is requested on the attached card.

Spoiled stamped envelopes and cards (if uncanceled) may be exchanged for stamps, stamped envelopes, or postal cards. You may also obtain an exchange on stamps if you buy the wrong denomination.

Metered Mail

The most efficient device you can use to put postage on any class of mail is the postage meter machine. This machine prints the postmark and the proper amount of postage on each piece of mail. The imprint of a fully automatic metering machine may also carry a slogan or a line or two of advertising, such as IT'S SMART TO BE THRIFTY, next to the postmark. Metered mail is neither canceled nor postmarked at the post office; therefore, it is processed and dispatched quickly.

The meter of the postage machine is set at the post office for the amount paid at the time. The meter registers the amount of postage used on each piece of mail, the amount of postage remaining in the meter, and the number of pieces that have passed through the machine. The meter locks when the amount paid for has been used; it is then necessary to take it to the post office again to pay for more postage. Additional postage should be bought before the meter locks. You will find the postage meter very easy to operate, and it will save you a great deal of time.

ZIP Codes

To assure prompt delivery of your mail always use ZIP Codes. Their use increases the speed, accuracy, and quality of *all* mail service. The ZIP Code is a five-digit number that identifies the **destination** of a piece of mail. For instance:

destination: place to which something is sent

9	45	77
Area	Sectional Center or Large City	Local Zone

The 9 identifies one of ten large areas made up of three or more states into which the entire country has been divided. The next two figures, 45, represent the sectional center or large city within that area. And, finally, the 77 represents the local delivery zone within that city or sectional center.

The code should appear on the last line of *both* the envelope address and the return address following the city and state. One or two spaces should be left between the last letter of the state and the first digit of the code. The address should be typed in block form:

> Fisk Division
> The Radcliff Company
> 2350 Washington Avenue
> San Leandro, CA 94577

All Zip Codes can be found in the *National Zip Code Directory*.

Optical Character Reader (OCR)

The post office is installing Optical Character Readers, electronic equipment which will speed up the mail. This equipment can read printed or typewritten addresses and sort letters with speed and accuracy.

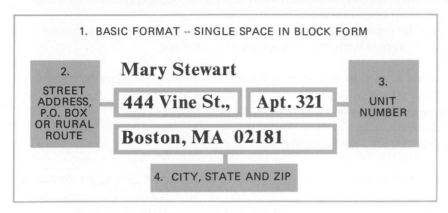

Illus. 7-13

Even if your post office does not have OCR equipment yet, the following rules will help to speed the processing of your outgoing mail.

1. *Basic Format.* The address should be single spaced in block form.
2. *Street Address, P.O. Box,* or *Rural Route.* These should be shown on the line immediately above the City, State, and ZIP Code.
3. *Unit Number.* Mail addressed to occupants of a multi-unit building should include the number of the apartment, room, suite, or other unit. The unit number should appear immediately after the street address on the same line — never above, below, or in front of the street address.
4. *City, State,* and *ZIP Code.* They should appear in that order on the bottom line of the address.

processing: to move toward an end by a series of actions

occupants: those residing therein

Items to Check Before Mailing Letters

Before mailing your outgoing correspondence, check each letter first to be sure that:

1. Any enclosures noted at the bottom of the letter are actually enclosed in the envelope.
2. Numbers, such as order numbers, referred to in the correspondence are correct.
3. Carbon copies for others are prepared for mailing.
4. Your initials appear below your employer's signature on any letter you have signed for your employer.

Then check each envelope to be sure that:

1. The address on the envelope agrees with the inside address of the letter.
2. The ZIP Code is typed on the last line of *both* the envelope address and the return address.
3. Any special notations, such as Registered or Special Delivery have been noted on the envelope.
4. The typed address on a label for a package to be sent separately agrees with the address on the envelope.

Finally, to skip one sorting operation at the post office, separate and identify the *Local* and the *Out-of-Town* mail. Free self-sticking, wrap-around labels are available from most post offices.

Domestic Mail Service

Domestic mail is mail sent within the United States, its territories and possessions, Army-Air Force (APO) and Navy (FPO) post offices, and also mail for delivery to the United Nations, New York City.

Classes of Domestic Mail

Your employer will expect you to know the different kinds of domestic mail most widely used by business firms. The five kinds of domestic mail listed below will be considered separately.

1. First-class mail — letters, postal cards, and postcards
2. Second-class mail — newspapers and periodicals
3. Third-class mail — circulars and other miscellaneous printed matter
4. Fourth-class mail — parcel post
5. Mixed classes of mail

First-Class Mail

First-class mail is usually sealed letters only; however, the following mail must also be sent first class:

1. All matter sealed against postal inspection
2. Postal cards (cards sold by the post office with stamps imprinted on them) and postcards (privately purchased mailing cards on which stamps are put)
3. Business reply cards and envelopes
4. Matter, partly in written form, such as statements of account, checks, punched cards, and filled-in forms
5. Other matter in written form, such as typewritten reports and documents

Second-Class Mail

Certain newspapers and magazines are sent at second-class rates of postage which are lower than third- and fourth-class mail. Authorization to publishers and news agents to mail at bulk second-class rates must be obtained from the Postal Service.

Third-Class Mail

Almost every day you receive in your own home circulars and advertisements that have been sent through the mail at third-class rates. This mail is used for materials not otherwise classified as first- or second-class mail and that weigh less than 16 ounces. The same material in parcels weighing 16 ounces and over in considered fourth-class mail. The following may be sent by third-class mail service:

1. Circulars, books, catalogs, and other printed matter
2. Merchandise samples

Envelopes may be sealed if marked *Third Class* on the address side of the envelope. In the absence of such a marking, sealed envelopes will be subject to first-class mail rates.

Fourth-Class Mail (Parcel Post)

Fourth-class mail is also known as parcel post. It includes merchandise, printed matter, and all other mailable matter not included in first-, second-, or third-class mail that weighs 16 ounces or more. Parcel post rates are determined according to (1) the weight of the parcel and (2) the distance the parcel is being sent. There are limitations on the weight and size of parcel post packages.

Parcel post packages may be sent sealed or unsealed. Unless it is clearly marked *First Class* a sealed package is usually treated as parcel post by the postal sorters regardless of the amount of postage paid.

Mixed Classes of Mail

Sometimes it is better to send two pieces of mail of different classes together as a single mailing to be sure that they both arrive at the same time. A first-class letter may be attached to the outside of a large envelope or parcel of a different class of mail, or it may be enclosed in a large envelope or parcel. When a first-class letter is *attached*, the postage is affixed to each part separately. When a first-class letter is enclosed, its postage is added to the parcel postage and affixed on the outside of the

affixed: fastened; attached in any way

package. The words *First-Class Mail Enclosed* must be written, typed, or stamped below the postage and above the address. A piece of mixed mail is handled and transported by the post office as mail matter of the class in which the bulky portion falls — not as first-class mail.

Mailing Suggestions for Fast Delivery

There are many ways to help the United States Postal Service send your mail rapidly. Here are four suggestions to speed the processing and delivery of your outgoing mail:

1. *Mail early and often.* Mail early in the day, often, and regularly, at 11 a.m. and 4 p.m. for example, to avoid getting your mail caught in the five o'clock rush. Most post offices receive about three-quarters of the day's mail in the late afternoon or early evening.
2. *Check collection times.* If you ordinarily mail from a building lobby or street mail box, check the "Hours of Collection" listing on the box. Collections are made only once a day at some street mail boxes. If you should miss the last daily collection and want your mail to move fast, take it directly to the nearest post office.
3. *Keep Local Mail separate from Out-of-Town Mail.* Use separate labels for *Local Mail* and *Out-of-Town Mail* to make certain that your mail skips one sorting operation at the post office.
4. *Use ZIP Codes in both the mailing address and in the return address.* To assure speedy delivery of your mail, *always use ZIP Codes.* Make sure your addressing is clear, complete, and correct. Check to be sure that you have written the *correct street number* in the mailing address. Remember that all envelopes should carry your return address with your ZIP Code so that undeliverable mail can be returned to you.

International Mail

Mail is now sent to all parts of the world, either by air or surface transportation, in ever-increasing volume. **International** mail is divided into two general categories — postal union mail and parcel post. Postal union mail is further divided into two groups — *LC* mail and *AO* mail. LC mail (letters and cards) consists of letters, letter packages, and postal cards. AO mail (articles, other) includes printed matter, samples of merchandise, matter for the blind, and small packets.

The postage for letters and postal cards mailed to Canada and Mexico is the same as that for the United States. To all other countries the rates are higher and the weights are limited. Overseas parcel post packages

international:
between or among
different nations

must be packed even more carefully than those for delivery within the continental United States. A *customs declaration* form must be attached to each parcel with an accurate and complete description of its contents.

Special Postal Services

The United States Postal Service also provides many special services, such as:

1. Special Delivery
2. Special Handling
3. Registered Mail
4. Certified Mail
5. Insured Mail
6. COD Service
7. Tracing Mail
8. Recalling Mail

Special Delivery

Special delivery provides the fastest handling and delivery service for any kind of mail. Special delivery mail is handled at the post office of destination with the same promptness given to first-class mail and, in addition, is given immediate delivery (within prescribed hours and distances). The fees charged are in addition to the regular postage. They vary according to the weight of the letter or parcel. The mail must be stamped or marked *Special Delivery*.

Special Handling

On payment of a fee in addition to the regular postage, a parcel labeled *Special Handling* will be given the same prompt handling and delivery service as is given to first-class mail. Special handling parcels are delivered the same way that parcel post is ordinarily delivered — on regularly scheduled trips, not special delivery. The fees are lower than special delivery fees. Special handling services may be used only with parcels sent as third- or fourth-class mail.

Registered Mail

Mail is registered to give protection to valuable and important mail. Money, checks, jewelry, stock certificates, and bonds are included in the valuable items frequently sent by registered mail. Important items include contracts, bills of sale, leases, mortgages, deeds, wills, and vital business records. Registration provides insurance, a receipt for the sender, and proof of delivery. Mail may be registered for insurance up to $10,000 if no other insurance is carried. If other insurance is carried, postal insurance liability is limited to a maximum of $1,000. All classes of mail may be registered provided the first-class rate is paid.

Before your mail will be accepted for registration, you must

1. Seal it. Masking tape or transparent tape cannot be used to seal registered mail.
2. Have the complete names and addresses of *both* the sender and the addressee on the mail.
3. Declare the *full* value of the mail to the postal clerk.

You will be given a receipt showing that the post office has accepted the registered mail for transmittal and delivery. For an additional fee you may obtain a *return receipt* to prove that the mail has been delivered.

Certified Mail

If your mail has no value of its own (such as a letter, a bill, or an important notice) and yet you want proof of mailing and delivery, send it by *Certified Mail*. It provides a receipt for the sender and a record of delivery. No insurance coverage is provided for certified mail.

Insured Mail

reimburse:
to pay back

Third- or fourth-class mail may be insured for up to $200 against loss or damage. A receipt is issued for insured mail. It should be kept on file until the insured mail has arrived in satisfactory condition. If an insured parcel is lost or damaged, the post office will **reimburse** you for the value of the merchandise or the amount for which it was insured, whichever is the smaller.

COD Service

Merchandise may be sent to a purchaser COD, that is, *collect on delivery*, if the shipment is based on an order by the buyer or on an agreement between sender and addressee. The seller may obtain COD service by paying a fee in addition to the regular postage. The maximum amount collectible on one package is $300. The total fee varies with the amount to be collected, the weight of the package, and the distance it is to travel.

Tracing Mail

If mail has not been delivered within a reasonable time, you may make a written request to have it traced. The post office will supply you with a form for tracing a piece of mail. Although the post office will cooperate in every possible way, it is almost impossible to trace unregistered, uninsured, or uncertified mail, especially if it does not carry a return address. Consequently, all mail should carry a complete return address and valuable or important mail should be registered, certified, or insured.

Recalling Mail

Once in a great while it may be necessary to recall a piece of mail you have already mailed. This will require prompt action on your part. Go to the post office in your mailing zone to recall a letter mailed to a local address or to the central post office to recall a letter mailed out of town. Fill in Form 1509 (*Sender's Application for Withdrawal of Mail*) and the post office will have the piece of mail returned to you.

Aids for Volume Mailing

There are several mailing aids to business firms for use in advertising campaigns and for announcements of new products and services.

Mailing Lists

Many firms keep lists of their customers, prospective customers, subscribers, clients, or others to whom they address mail repeatedly. A firm may use a number of mailing lists for different purposes — for instance, to advertise a new product, to announce a new service, or to **initiate** a new policy. Special mailing lists of all kinds of prospective buyers, both nationwide and regional, can be purchased. One of your secretarial duties may be to develop the mailing list and keep it up to date.

initiate: begin

Mailing Lists on File Cards

Names and addresses for a mailing list are frequently kept on 5" × 3" cards that are filed in alphabetic order. These cards may be grouped under various classifications, such as doctors, druggists, jewelers, and stationers. The different groupings may be indicated by colored tabs, or the cards for each group may be filed in separate drawers or compartments in the card file.

The cards may also be filed by subject — the subject that the prospective customer has been interested in or may be interested in later.

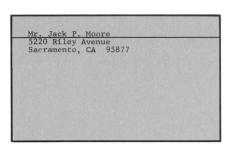

Up-to-Date Mailing Lists

Unless mailing lists are kept up to date, they soon lose much of their usefulness. The names on all mailing lists are constantly changing as newcomers move into the sales area and others move out. Additions, deletions, and corrections of names and addresses should be made whenever the information is received. You learn of many of the necessary changes in addresses when mail is returned because of nondelivery.

The post office will assist you in maintaining an up-to-date mailing list. It will make corrections on a mailing list or correct individual addresses if requested to do so. For a small fee it will also supply the ZIP Codes for an entire mailing list.

Chain Feeding of Envelopes for a Mailing List

The names and addresses on a mailing list are usually typed on the envelopes if the list is used infrequently. A chain feeding method of inserting and addressing the envelopes will save a great deal of time in typing from the list. The four steps in the widely used *front-feed* method follow:

1. Stack the envelopes *face down*, with the flaps toward you, at the side of the typewriter.
2. Address the first envelope; then roll it back (toward you) until a half inch shows above the alignment scale.
3. Insert the next envelope from the front, placing it between the first envelope and the cylinder.
4. Turn the cylinder back to remove the first envelope and to position the second one. Continue the "chain" by feeding all envelopes from the front of the cylinder.
5. The envelopes will stack themselves in order at the back of the cylinder. Remove them after about every sixth envelope is typed.

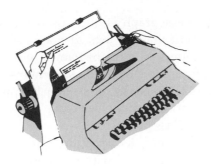

Illus. 7-15

Front-feed method
of chain feeding
envelopes

The steps in the *back-feed* method are:

1. Stack the envelopes *face up* at the left side of the typewriter.
2. Insert the first envelope to typing position; place a second envelope behind the cylinder in the "feed" position.
3. Address the first envelope. As you twirl the first envelope out of the machine with the right hand, feed another envelope in the "feed" position with the left hand.
4. As the first envelope is removed, the second envelope will be moved into typing position. Continue the "chain" by placing a new envelope in the "feed" position each time the addressed envelope is removed.

Illus. 7-16

Back-feed method
of chain feeding
envelopes

Addressing Machines and Addressing Services

You may use an addressing service or, if your office has it, an addressing machine in addressing a large number of envelopes. Because mailing lists are used over and over again, the names and addresses are often stenciled or embossed so that the envelopes can be automatically addressed on an addressing machine. Two widely used styles of addressing machines are the Addressograph, which prints from a metal plate; and the Elliott, which prints from a stencil plate. Also, some businesses are using their computers for addressing large numbers of envelopes.

Metal Plates. The Addressograph is often used for addressing envelopes and cards for permanent mailing lists. It may also be used to print the inside addresses on letters or to print names, addresses, numbers, and other identifying information on bank statements, monthly bills, time cards, paychecks, dividend checks, and other business forms. The plates can be coded so that an automatic selecting device can be used as the letters are addressed. Classification tabs can be attached to the address plates of a particular mailing list, and the automatic selector will then select and print only these plates without changing the order of any of the plates in the file.

Stencil Plates. The stencil address plates used in the Elliott addressing machine can be prepared on a typewriter. When a small attachment is used, the small stencil plates are typed in much the same manner as ordinary stencils. The stencil addressing equipment is not often used to print inside addresses on letters or other material that should give the appearance of being completely typed. The plates are, however, often used for mailing lists with frequently changing addresses.

Computer Addressing. Some large firms use their computers for addressing envelopes and cards. The computer can print the addresses directly on the cards and envelopes, or it can print address labels which have an adhesive backing. When adhesive-backed labels are printed, they are then attached to the front of the envelopes.

REVIEWING

1. What is a postage meter?
2. How is payment made for postage used in a postage meter machine?
3. Why are ZIP Codes now used with all classes of mail?
4. What are the four rules of addressing mail?
5. What are some of the items to be checked in a letter and on the envelope before it is released for outgoing mail?
6. List the five kinds of domestic mail.
7. What kind of mail must be sent at the first-class rate?
8. What are some suggestions to speed up the mail?
9. Which letter would cost more, one to Canada or one to France?
10. What are the differences between *Special Delivery* and *Special Handling*?
11. What are the differences between *Registered Mail* and *Certified Mail*?
12. Once you have mailed a letter, can you ever get it back again? If so, how?

13. What is the purpose of keeping a mailing list?

14. If you are uncertain as to how to mail a package, who can you call for assistance?

MAKING JUDGMENTS

Miss Sealy is a secretary for three doctors in a medical building. Anytime a patient changes his or her address, Miss Sealy makes a note in the margin of the appointment book to save time. During a free moment she transfers the changes of address to the permanent files. After the monthly statements were mailed in June, two were returned to the office stamped "Return to Sender, Address Unknown." Miss Sealy was surprised to see the statements because she thought she had transferred all the changes of address to the permanent file. A quick check in the appointment book showed that she had missed two address changes. How would you improve Miss Sealy's procedure of keeping the mailing list up to date?

WORKING WITH OTHERS

In the office where Charlie works, the mail goes out four times daily — 8:30, 11:30, 3:30, and 5:15. Early Monday morning Charlie received a telephone call from an executive in the branch office. She urgently needed a shipment of typewriter ribbons to fill a customer's order. Charlie assured the executive that he would get the shipment into the 11:30 mail. After getting the ribbons, Charlie told the mail clerk that the package had to go out in the 11:30 mail. Several hours later he checked to see if the package had been mailed. It was still in the mail room and had missed the 3:30 mailing. Should Charlie approach the mail clerk for an explanation and hope that the package would be put in the 5:15 mail, or should he leave the office to mail the package himself?

REFRESHING LANGUAGE SKILLS

1. The following terms were taken from Unit 7, Parts 1 and 2. Write the meaning of each term. Consult the text or a standard dictionary if you are not sure of the definition.

a. computer addressing
b. metered mail
c. LC and AO international mail
d. mailing lists
e. mixed mail

f. OCR
g. precanceled stamps
h. return receipt
i. annotation
j. domestic mail

2. Only one spelling of each of the following words used in mailing is correct. Type the correct spelling of each word:

    a. denominations   denomunations
    b. catagories   categories
    c. cataloges   catalogs
    d. certified   certefied
    e. circulars   circulers
    f. exceding   exceeding
    g. optical   opticle
    h. receipt   reciept
    i. transmited   transmitted
    j. confidential   confedential

PERFORMING SECRETARIAL TASKS

1. Using an 8½" × 11" sheet of paper and an ordinary No. 6 envelope, fold the paper as you would a letter and insert it in the envelope.
2. Using three sheets of 8½" × 11" paper and a large No. 10 envelope, fold the three sheets together and insert them in the envelope.
3. Using an 8½" × 11" sheet of paper and a large No. 10 window envelope fold the sheet and insert it in the envelope. (If you do not have a window envelope, fold the sheet as though it would be inserted in a window envelope.)
4. Using a chain feeding method, address envelopes of either 6½" × 3⅝" (No. 6) or 9½" × 4⅛" (No. 10) for the following names and addresses. If envelopes are not available, type the addresses on slips of paper of approximately one of these sizes. These names and addresses were taken from the classified directory of St. Louis, Missouri.

A-1 Copy-Printing, 36 N. Central Avenue, 63105

Broadway Office Interiors, 2115 Locust Avenue, 63103

Burroughs Business Forms, 8630 Delmar Blvd., 63124

Business Forms and Supply Company, 76 Grasso Plaza, 63123

Business Guidance Corporation, 11960 Westline Industrial Road, 63141

Business Service By Professionals, 9322 Manchester Road, 63119

Clayton Business Service, 1670 South Brentwood Blvd., 63144

Leewood Business Supply Center, 2374 Grissom Drive, 63141

Missouri Envelope Company, 10655 Gateway Blvd., 63132

Moore Business Forms 1015 Locust Avenue, 63101

Officeplus, 7777 Bonhomme Avenue, 63105

Quality Office Outfitters, 8574 St. Charles Rock Road, 63114

Quill and Ink Office Supplies, 3230 Olive Avenue, 63101

Shaw-Walker Office Furniture, 520 Olive Avenue, 63101

Steelcase Office Furniture, 11902 Lackland Road, 63141

Supreme Filing Systems, 705 Olive Avenue, 63101

Tomkins Printing Company, 922 Pine Avenue, 63101

Typographic Studio, 608 North Skinker Blvd., 63130

5. Ask one of the employees at your local post office how much it would cost to mail from your town the following:
   a. Parcel post package weighing two pounds — destination is Tampa, Florida
   b. Registered envelope less than one ounce containing a check for $1,000, return receipt requested — destination is Milwaukee, Wisconsin
   c. First-class package containing typed reports weighing 10 ounces — destination is Ponca City, Oklahoma
   d. First-class letter less than one half ounce — destination is Paris, France

Part 3
Air and Surface Shipping

John Larson was recently employed for the summer in the mail department of Northwood Electronics. When he applied for the job, he was told that he must deliver company mail, file literature requests, handle outgoing volume mail, and operate mailing equipment.

The job has become a challenge. John has learned to perform all his duties well. He had never realized how much mail was involved in a company or how important it was to use systematic procedures when handling mail.

"What's the best way to send the package?" your employer may ask. It may be just a small parcel urgently needed by a customer, or it may be a large package of advertising materials. Your employer may consider the speed of delivery to be of much more importance than the cost. Whatever the case may be, you must be familiar with all the available types of ground and air shipping services.

commodities:
goods bought and sold

Every business firm uses a number of different shipping services to deliver parcels and to distribute large **commodities**. As an alert and intelligent secretary, you should be familiar with the advantages of each service. You may be required to decide how small parcels should be sent. You may be called upon to prepare the necessary forms for express and freight shipments for which trains, planes, trucks, and buses are used. Occasionally you may be asked to prepare the forms for tracing a shipment or for filing a claim for goods damaged in **transit**.

transit:
being delivered

Recent Developments in Shipping

With a great increase in volume, the shipping of goods in the United States and Canada has undergone many rapid changes in the past few years. Trucks have replaced trains for a great deal of shipping across the nation, and shipping by air is becoming widespread.

Improved packaging has also aided the shipping process. Light-weight, theft-proof containers are used in place of heavy wooden crates.

In addition, shipping terminals and airports are equipped with automatic equipment which uses high speed conveyer belts to handle packages of all sizes. Railroad terminal yards are equipped with automatic switching equipment and closed-circuit TV to save time and shipping costs.

Methods of Shipping

Goods may be shipped to various points by railway, truck, bus, planes, or by a combination of two or more of these services. Each of these services has its own advantages: some offer faster delivery; some offer a higher degree of safety; some are less expensive; and some are much more convenient for the shipper, for the receiver, or for both. The values of each of these services should be known to the shipper so that the best and the most suitable shipping service can be selected.

Shipping Guides

Where can you look for the information you and your employer need about shipping? There are several guides which are widely used in business offices and which you will find very helpful in selecting the method that is best for each shipment.

The United States Postal Service Manual gives complete information about all classes of mail.

The Express and Parcel Post Comparative Rate Guide gives a complete list of all express stations and the comparative charges between express and parcel post shipments.

Leonard's Guide gives rates and routings for freight, express, and parcel post.

Parcel Post

Also called fourth-class mail, parcel post is a method of transporting goods that is used most often when small items are to be shipped to widely scattered places. Some details of parcel post service are discussed in connection with the classes of mail in Unit 7, Part 2. Parcel post shipments are handled by the United States Postal Service. The cost of sending a package parcel post depends on the weight of the package and the distance it is to travel.

Air Parcel Post

When speed is important in the delivery of a package, you will probably send the parcel by air. The delivery time can be greatly reduced by using air parcel post. The rates are higher than for ordinary parcel post. Increasingly, air parcel post is being used to carry merchandise to distant and isolated places. This is especially true for Hawaii and Alaska and other areas where delivery by surface travel would require longer times.

Express Mail

Designed to meet the demand of business and industry for fast and reliable delivery, express mail is based upon a network of 58 **metropolitan** areas in the United States and some foreign countries. Anything up to 50 pounds may be sent by express mail. The shipment is insured (at no extra charge) and is guaranteed delivery within 24 hours. This service receives top priority on the airplane, which means express mail is first to be loaded on the plane. There are five options for pick up and delivery; the options are flexible to meet the sender's schedules.

Air Express

You will find air express the swiftest method of commercial transportation. This service includes shipping by air to all parts of the United States and to most foreign countries. Air express shipments receive special pick-up and delivery service. Almost all types of goods, including machine parts, **perishable** foods, printed materials, and flowers, are moved by air express. Small packages or shipments may be placed on regular passenger planes. Large or bulky shipments are usually sent by special air freight cargo planes.

Bus Express

Most bus lines throughout the country offer package express service. This is a particularly useful service when destination points are located where there is no airport and when speed of delivery is important. Many points receive same day delivery — many within a few hours — which may be even faster than air service. Frequent and direct bus trips between the cities and the fact that terminals are usually located in business districts account for the speed of handling and delivery.

United Parcel Service

United Parcel Service is a specialized carrier of small packages that weigh no more than 50 pounds. Its rates are **competitive** with parcel post. The service is provided in all 48 **contiguous** states plus the island of Oahu in Hawaii.

Unit 7 • Using Mail and Shipping Services

Illus. 7-17

Businesses depend on the services of specialized carriers of small packages.

United Parcel Service

Truck Transportation

Another shipping service which your employer may use is truck transportation. The truck is the best type of local transportation available. Arrangements can easily be made with a trucking company to make regular calls at your place of business to pick up and deliver goods. Truck transportation is also available for long-distance hauls. Some long-distance trucking firms offer overnight service to insure prompt delivery.

Railway Freight Service

For shipping bulky articles and goods for which the speed of delivery is less important, railway freight service is often used. Shipping by rail is generally less expensive than shipping by truck or any other method.

Illus. 7-18

Railway freight service, while slower than other methods of shipping, is generally less costly.

Union Pacific Railroad Photo

Packaging

Goods for shipment must be packaged properly if they are to be delivered without damage. It is the responsibility of the shipper to properly package the item for shipment. The item to be shipped, the method of transportation to be used, and the distance to be traveled will be the determining factors in packaging. The decision on a damage claim is often decided on the basis of how well the goods have been packaged.

Marking Goods for Shipment

Whether goods are shipped by freight, express, parcel post, or some other way, it is important to the prompt movement and proper delivery of shipments that the goods be marked correctly. The rules of the carriers require that the shipper mark each package plainly, legibly, and durably. In marking shipments, the following rules should be observed in order to insure the proper delivery of packages:

1. The addressee's name, address, and ZIP Code must be shown.
2. The word *From* should precede the name and address of the shipper. This explanation is of great assistance to both the shipper and the carrier if the shipment gets lost, is unclaimed, or is refused by the addressee.
3. Packages containing articles easily broken should be marked *Fragile* or *Handle with Care*. Packages containing merchandise that is perishable, such as fruit, should be marked *Perishable*.

Illus. 7-19

Packaging goods durably and marking them plainly insures prompt movement of shipments.

Ohio National Life Insurance Company

4. Marking should be done with a brush, stencil, crayon, or rubber stamp. If lettered by hand, a good clear style of lettering should be used. Labels should be prepared on a typewriter and fastened securely to the packages.

Tracing

It may be necessary to trace a shipment if the goods are not delivered within a reasonable time. All carriers in all **modes** of transportation provide tracing services. Information required to trace a shipment includes:

modes: methods

1. Shipper's name and address
2. Name and address of the person to whom the goods were shipped
3. Shipping date
4. Quantity of packages involved
5. Shipping receipt
6. Routing used

Claim for Loss

A claim to the transportation company should be submitted for a total or partial loss if the shipment is not delivered, if it is totally or partially destroyed, or if it is delivered in a damaged condition. Claims for loss are presented by either the shipper or the addressee, depending upon who owns the goods.

REVIEWING

1. Name some of the more recent developments in shipping services.
2. What are four methods of shipping?
3. What shipping guides are commonly used in business offices?
4. What factors determine the cost of parcel post?
5. What are the advantages of express mail?
6. What are the advantages of air express?
7. When might bus express be useful?
8. What are some advantages of shipping by truck?
9. What are some of the rules you should follow in marking goods for shipment?
10. What information is needed to trace a shipment?

MAKING JUDGMENTS

You received a package containing fragile items. When you opened the box, about half of the contents were broken. Whom should you talk with about replacing the broken items? Who should handle the claim if the package was insured?

WORKING WITH OTHERS

Ms. Fay Little, an executive of a large brokerage firm in New York City, asked her new secretary, Miss Barbara Weaver, to photocopy the entire file folder of a client with a large account. The client had moved to Hawaii; so Miss Weaver was also asked to wrap the photocopies and mail them by air parcel post to the manager of the firm's branch in Honolulu.

Two weeks later Ms. Little received a telephone call from the manager of the Honolulu branch. She said that the records had not been received. However, much to her embarrassment, the client had already called but she could not suggest investments because she had no record of the customer's holdings.

Ms. Little then learned that Miss Weaver had delayed mailing the photocopies because she said that she did not have the time to wrap them. Furthermore, she felt that it was not her job as a secretary to wrap and mail packages. When she finally had them ready, she mailed them by ordinary parcel post.

What do you think of Miss Weaver's attitude with regard to the wrapping and mailing of packages? What was wrong with shipping the records by ordinary parcel post? If you were in Ms. Little's place, what would you do?

REFRESHING LANGUAGE SKILLS

Adjectives are used to indicate an increasing or decreasing degree of quality, quantity, or manner. The three degrees of comparison are positive, comparative, and superlative.

Example: *Positive*
light
useful

Comparative
lighter
more (less) useful

Superlative
lightest
most (least) useful

On a separate sheet of paper list the adjectives in the sentences below and indicate which degree of comparison is used.

1. The secretary's work gets better every day.
2. Of all the merchants on Fifth Avenue, Mr. Clay had the prettiest window display.
3. Jane received a fine compliment from her employer because her work was the most efficient in the department.
4. The package was wrapped less securely than it should have been.
5. The typewriter, the books, the calculator, the stove, and the produce had to be crated carefully before shipment to either a close or a far destination.
6. He put it in the largest box available.

Unit 7 • Using Mail and Shipping Services

7. The driver spoke more softly now even though the anger showed on his face.
8. Of the two, Mr. Nance is definitely the more organized executive in that section.
9. The book that I ordered is on the Best Seller list.
10. The building offered much ventilation, more light than, and the most space of any of the warehouses they examined.

PERFORMING SECRETARIAL TASKS

1. Make a study of the following shipping services available in your community and be prepared to report your findings orally to the class and in writing to your teacher:
   a. Express Mail
   b. Bus Express
   c. United Parcel Service
   d. Truck Service
   e. Railway Freight Service
2. What transportation service would you suggest for shipping the following items from your community:
   a. Two swivel office chairs to a branch office 400 miles away.
   b. The 24 volumes of the *Encyclopaedia Britannica* to a relative 230 miles away.
   c. An overhead projector with a case of transparencies to a rural school 70 miles away.
   d. A portable electric typewriter to a temporary field office 100 miles away.
   e. A 500-pound refrigerator to the company's recreation center 45 miles out of town.
3. Mrs. Koehler, the office manager, has become concerned because mailing expenses have increased about 4% in each of the first five months of this year. If costs keep increasing at this rate, mailing expenses would be up 48% at the end of the year. In discussing the problem with you, Mrs. Koehler mentioned:

   a. Employees send packages by air express to Philadelphia which is only 300 miles away, on Thursdays and Fridays. The packages do not arrive until Monday morning. Parcel post mail, at a less expensive rate, will also arrive on Monday morning.
   b. The company is doing more business than last year. There is no way to avoid the additional expense because of this increase in business.

To identify and overcome the problem, she has asked you to list the possible reasons for the increase and some ways to keep the costs down. For ideas, check your textbook, your Post Office Customer Services representative, or office workers you know. Mrs. Koehler suggests that you and she discuss your findings at lunch tomorrow.

IMPROVING SECRETARIAL SKILLS (Optional)

You work in the main office of a large plastics corporation. Every day you are responsible for seeing that certain correspondence is mailed out in time to reach branch offices across the state on certain dates. You have updated the following outgoing mail schedule and are ready to type it in final form. Type the schedule in an attractive form on plain white paper.

OUTGOING MAIL SCHEDULE

Depart Post Office	Destination	Via Flight	Arrive
6:10 AM	Fresno	BL-174	9:50 AM
	Anaheim	~~BL-273 e~~ CA-132	7:55 AM
	Stockton	"	7:45 AM
	Pasadena	"	9:30 ~~9:25~~ AM
	~~San Francisco e~~	~~CA-273 e~~	~~10:25 AM e~~
	Santa Rosa	"	11:05 AM
9:10 AM	Pasadena	~~ST-389~~ BL-180	10:50 AM
	Santa Rosa	CA-283	11:15 ~~11:10~~ AM
	~~San Francisco e~~	~~ST-392 e~~	~~11:55 AM~~
	Fresno	"	11:55 PM
12:55 PM	Stockton	BL-197	2:00 PM
2:30 PM	Fresno	~~CA-234~~ BL-349	2:55 ~~3:35~~ PM
	Anaheim	ST-454	4:40 PM
	Pasadena	"	4:55 PM
	San Francisco	~~"~~ CA-127	5:30 ~~5:00~~ PM
	Stockton	"	5:05 PM
5:15 PM	San Francisco	CA-384	6:40 PM
	Santa Rosa	ST-234	9:05 PM
	Pasadena	~~BL-233~~ CA-128	10:25 ~~10:10~~ PM
	Anaheim	~~BL-224~~ "	11:15 ~~11:21~~ PM
7:30 PM	Anaheim	BL-214	8:40 ~~8:35~~ PM
	Fresno	"	11:30 PM
	Santa Rosa	"	12:00 AM
	Pasadena	CA-441	4:25 ~~4:00~~ AM
8:25 PM	Fresno	~~BL-220~~ ST-211	5:00 AM
	Pasadena	"	6:14 AM
	Stockton	CA-311	7:19 AM

Meeting the Public

Part 1. The Care of Callers
Part 2. Oral Communications

1

The Care of Callers

Mr. Fred Sumners is secretary to Mr. Walter Amos, one of the most popular lawyers in downtown New Orleans. Mr. Amos has many clients, and when he is in his office, there seems to be an endless stream of people to see him. Mr. Sumners has an amazing ability to maintain a calm, peaceful environment for the clients. Mr. Amos feels that Fred has a "sixth sense" for recognizing an emergency that requires special treatment. Mr. Sumners realizes that Mr. Amos is genuinely interested in his clients. He is fully cooperative when it is necessary to rearrange his schedule to accommodate a particularly anxious client with a serious problem. Mr. Sumners makes it a point to learn every client's name quickly. He finds it easy to remember the clients, for he is intensely interested in providing the individual attention that makes his job so pleasant and rewarding.

While much business is transacted by telephone and letter, there continue to be many person-to-person meetings. Executives meet with customers and other business people individually and in groups. They have conferences with other executives and with company employees. In addition, many companies participate in civic activities. Community leaders visit and meet with executives in their offices. Acquaintances and friends may come to the office for business-related reasons or for brief, friendly visits. Members of executives' families may stop by from time to time.

The Responsibilities of the Secretary

While a receptionist is usually the first person callers meet when they arrive at the office, as an executive's secretary you are an official host or hostess. In this role you must be aware of appropriate office behavior. While customs vary from office to office, there are some general practices that are observed in most offices.

First, a secretary is genuinely interested in those who come to the office, which means there is a continuing desire to be helpful. While it is, of course, possible to "learn to act" — how to **feign** an interest in others — such learning is usually shallow and inadequate. What you should seek is the deep, natural desire to behave kindly toward others.

feign: pretend

Second, a secretary is acquainted with the regular callers to the office. This means that a secretary recognizes visitors by being able to call them by name. Since appointments are generally made ahead of time, the secretary has a record of the visitors' names on the calendar and, thus, it is relatively simple to recognize them when they appear.

Third, a secretary makes visitors comfortable by inviting them to hang their coats, to sit down, and to enjoy any publications that are available. Furthermore, the secretary attempts to keep visitors informed of what is happening if there is a delay in an appointment.

Fourth, a secretary **maintains** the schedule the employer prefers and should aid the employer in dealing with visitors. While there is considerable variation among executives as to how visitors are to be taken care of, in general, executives desire a cooperative, friendly, yet businesslike, environment. The procedures discussed on the following pages will aid in achieving such an environment.

maintains: provides for

Scheduling Appointments

In some offices executives will see no one from outside the organization without an appointment. In other offices executives will make no specific appointments but will see people if it is convenient. In still other offices executives reserve part of each day for scheduled appointments and a part for unscheduled appointments.

Some executives prefer to approve every appointment, which means that you must check each request before you can confirm it. It may be more practical, however, for you to make the appointments after you fully understand the time that is available. Generally an executive will discuss weekly plans early on Monday and then review them briefly each morning so that you have up-to-date information on the executive's plans.

You will receive requests for appointments in many different ways. There will be callers who request appointments in person; there will be telephone calls from people wanting appointments; and there will be letters requesting appointments. All such requests should receive immediate attention.

If the appointment is requested in person, after recording it on your calendar, you should record on a small card the details of the appointment so that the caller will have a record of it. When the appointment is requested by telephone, you should be sure to state very clearly the details of the appointment. Also, when an appointment is requested by letter, the return letter should be complete concerning the date, time, and office location. If the person writing is unfamiliar with the general location of the office, it is thoughtful to enclose a map with directions to the office clearly marked.

Maintaining a Calendar

You must be sure to get full details about each caller who is requesting an appointment for the first time. These details aid the executive in knowing the nature of business to be **transacted** at the time of the appointment. Also, if there arises a need to change the date of the appointment or to talk with the person prior to the visit, you will know where to call or write to the individual. Your records on each caller should include full name, address, telephone number, and the organization with which the caller is associated. Also, there must be recorded the date and the exact time of the appointment; the name of the individual with whom the appointment is made, in case you make appointments for more than one executive; and the amount of time to be set aside.

The details of appointments may be noted on an ordinary desk calendar if the number of appointments for each day is limited. If there are many appointments each day, a ruled schedule form is commonly used. The appointment record should include the executive's appointments away from the office. Many executives have their secretaries keep

transacted:
carried out

reminder calendars that list engagements of a personal nature, such as luncheons with friends or medical appointments.

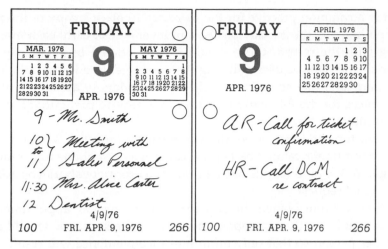

FRIDAY 9 APR. 1976

MAR. 1976
S M T W T F S
1 2 3 4 5 6
7 8 9 10 11 12 13
14 15 16 17 18 19 20
21 22 23 24 25 26 27
28 29 30 31

MAY 1976
S M T W T F S
1
2 3 4 5 6 7 8
9 10 11 12 13 14 15
16 17 18 19 20 21 22
23 24 25 26 27 28 29
30 31

9 - Mr. Smith
10 to 11 } Meeting with Sales Personnel
11:30 Mrs. Alice Carter
12 Dentist
4/9/76
100   FRI. APR. 9, 1976   266

FRIDAY 9 APR. 1976

APRIL 1976
S M T W T F S
1 2 3
4 5 6 7 8 9 10
11 12 13 14 15 16 17
18 19 20 21 22 23 24
25 26 27 28 29 30

AR - Call for ticket confirmation
HR - Call DCM re contract
4/9/76
100   FRI. APR. 9, 1976   266

Illus. 8-2

Calendar pad appointment record

It is common for the executive, as well as the secretary, to maintain a calendar. In such instances, it will be necessary for you to check your employer's calendar frequently to be sure that there are no conflicts with appointments. All appointments which the executive makes should be recorded on your calendar so that you have a complete list of all business and personal engagements. You are also responsible for adding the appointments you have made to the executive's calendar. In this way, the executive is fully aware of what is to take place each day.

APPOINTMENTS
FRIDAY, APRIL 9, 1976

Time	Engagements	Memorandums
9:00	Mr. Smith	HR - Call D.C. Mohr re contract
9:30		
10:00	} Meeting with Sales Personnel	See Jane Kumar for annual sales graph
10:30		
11:00		
11:30	Mrs. Alice Carter	
12:00	Dr. Pardi	

Illus. 8-3

Appointment schedule

Reminding the Employer

It is a common practice for the secretary to place a copy of the record of appointments for the day on the employer's desk early each morning. Along with the record, there should be any related business papers or materials that will be useful during the meetings. In addition, the record for a particular day sometimes includes reminders of appointments and conferences for the following few days that require preliminary work by the executive.

From time to time, appointments must be canceled. When a scheduled appointment cannot be kept, a caller may telephone and request a change. You should handle such a request as courteously as you handled the original request.

There are times when the executive must cancel an appointment. As soon as you know that an appointment cannot be kept, you should notify the other person so that only minimum inconvenience will result. If the executive's future schedule is firm, you may be able to suggest some future dates and times for another appointment which will be convenient for your employer and also for the individual who is requesting the appointment.

tactful:
sensitive

Once in a while an appointment will not be canceled until very near the scheduled time, which means that the caller will arrive at the executive's office only to learn that the appointment is canceled or postponed. In such circumstances you must be very **tactful** and considerate toward the caller. If someone else can assume the absent executive's role, efforts should be made to arrange for that person to talk with the caller. This procedure will often avoid inconvenience to the caller and create goodwill for your firm.

Arranging for Facilities

There are many times when a conference brings together more people than can meet conveniently in the executive's office. In such instances you must be sure there is an appropriate place for the meeting. If there is a conference room in the building where you and your executive work, you will probably have to make arrangements to use it.

Shortly before the time of the meeting, you should check to be sure that the room is open; that the furniture is arranged satisfactorily; that water and glasses are on the table; and that pads, pencils, and other materials that will be needed are in place.

Illus. 8-4

Preparing the conference room is a secretarial responsibility.

Assisting Callers

The people who come to your office are important to your organization. Therefore, your manner must reflect your concern with helping callers. Consider the attitude conveyed by the secretary in the following example:

> Patrick is busy typing a letter when Mr. Mann, who has a 10 a.m. appointment with his employer, enters the office. Mr. Mann is from out of town and wrote for the appointment. The last time he was in the office was about nine months ago. Patrick — preoccupied — looks up and, continuing to type, says,

> Patrick: "Oh, hi, Mr. Mann. Will you see if Mrs. Heinz is free? I'm busy trying to get this letter finished."

> Mr. Mann: (embarrassed by such casual treatment): "Yes, of course. Will I find Mrs. Heinz in her office?"

> Patrick: "I think so. It's the one over there." (He points vaguely to the right.)

What is Patrick's attitude toward callers?
Now let us assume that the call was handled in this manner:

> Patrick is busy typing a letter when Mr. Mann enters the office for his 10 a.m. appointment. He stops typing immediately and graciously greets Mr. Mann:

> Patrick: "Good morning, Mr. Mann. It's good to see you again. Mrs. Heinz is expecting you. Did you have good flight from St. Louis?"

Mr. Mann: "Hello. It's good to see you, Patrick. My flight was fine, and I'm glad to be here again."

Patrick: Please have a seat, and I'll check to see if Mrs. Heinz is free now. It is just a minute before 10."

What impression does Patrick give by his behavior in this instance?

In the second example, the secretary presented a friendly, helpful attitude toward the caller. The caller who was expected, recognized, and treated graciously will have a positive opinion of the organization. The secretary gave his full attention until the caller was guided into the executive's office. Contrast this impression with that which could result from the behavior in the first example. The visitor was not given any hint that he was expected, even though he was called by name which was only a minimum courtesy. The caller could easily have believed that he was unwanted and was interrupting the secretary, since he did not even stop typing — in fact, he continued his work while he motioned him toward the executive's office where the *caller* had to determine if the executive was ready to see him. It is extremely discourteous to let a caller enter an executive's office alone. If the executive is on the telephone or has someone in the office, the caller will be embarrassed at entering unannounced. The secretary's behavior in the first instance was rude and ill-mannered. The caller will remember this office only as being impolite, unfriendly, and disrespectful toward a visitor!

Illus 8-5

Even if busy momentarily, the secretary acknowledges the visitor in a friendly manner.

Ohio National Life Insurance Company

In greeting callers who have appointments you should indicate your knowledge of the appointment and your genuine interest in seeing that the visitor is given assistance.

In greeting a caller who is unfamiliar you should be **hospitable** and helpful. You should determine the purpose of the caller's visit and give assistance by making an appointment or by referring the caller to someone who can be of help. Notice the manner in which Marsha treated this stranger:

Marsha: "Good morning. May I help you?"

Caller: "Yes, I am Paolo Calenz, of the Intercontinental Transportation Services. I would like very much to see Mrs. Kuo about the services we can provide for your international sales meeting next year."

Marsha: "I am sure Mrs. Kuo will be interest in what you have to offer, but, unfortunately, she is in a meeting and has appointments scheduled throughout the day. Would it be convenient for you to come in this Friday or next Tuesday?"

Mr. Calenz: "No, I will be out of town for the next week."

Marsha: "Could you send her a letter with descriptive brochures? As you realize, Mrs. Kuo would be particularly interested in the cost of your services and what you provide."

Mr. Calenz: "Yes, I could write a letter and possibly I could talk with her when I return from London."

Marsha: "Fine. Your letter will receive attention, and Mrs. Kuo will call your office if she wishes further information. I will note on the letter that you were in the office today."

Mr. Calenz: "Thank you very much."

In this instance the secretary knew that Mrs. Kuo was gathering information about travel services that were available and knew that she would want this additional information. The secretary, however, did not reveal any information to Mr. Calenz, which was wise. Secretaries do not reveal the company's business concerns without being told to do so by their employers.

Maintaining a Record of Callers

In some companies a record is kept of all callers. If you have all the information from having recorded it at the time the appointment was made, you may merely confirm the accuracy of the material you have in your card file. If you are talking to a caller without an appointment, you will ask for the information after you have greeted the caller courteously. If the caller has a business card, you may find that it contains all the information you need. You may merely staple the business card to a 5" × 3" card and record below the business card any additional information needed.

If you are in an office where a card file of callers is maintained, you will want to review it from time to time so that it contains only the names of current callers. Notes of dates of appointments and purpose of visits and similar details are sometimes written on the backs of the cards for reference purposes. This card file enables you to recall earlier visits and, therefore, to greet returning callers appropriately.

Handling Difficult Callers

From time to time an unfamiliar caller may be a difficult caller. The difficult caller may refuse to indicate the purpose of the visit, but continues to insist on seeing the executive *immediately*. The caller may speak discourteously and appear angry. It is important that you remain calm in such a situation. You should continue to be helpful as you seek to get information about the purpose of the visit. Generally such a caller responds to kindness and will eventually give you the information you need. The caller may have a good reason for seeing the executive. If the executive is in and available, you may proceed as you would with an unscheduled appointment. If the executive is not available, you might suggest that the caller write a letter explaining the situation to be discussed. It might be appropriate to invite the caller to sit down to write a letter immediately. After such courteous treatment, the caller will leave feeling satisfied about the visit.

Callers who refuse to give their names and remain firm about not revealing the nature of their business should not be admitted to the executive's office. In such situations you must remain courteous but firm!

Handling Delays

Sometimes callers must wait to see the executive. They may arrive too early. The executive may have taken more time than was scheduled for earlier appointments. Emergencies may have arisen. In such cases waiting is unavoidable. You should try to make the delay as pleasant as possible. If you know the length of the delay, you may indicate this to the caller. If you are not certain you may say:

"I'm sorry, but Mr. Leitman is still in a meeting. I am not sure how long the meeting will last, but possibly it will end shortly. Mr. Leitman knows you were expected at eleven and he will not want to keep you waiting."

or

"Mr. Leitman tells me that the meeting should be ended in about ten minutes. He apologizes for this delay and will see you as quickly as possible."

When the executive is ready to see the next caller, you may walk into the office with the caller and say, "Here is Mr. Smith." If the caller is unacquainted with the executive, you will want to introduce the caller in a friendly, gracious manner. Any one of the following is considered a proper introduction:

"Mrs. Ableson, may I present Mr. Cannon?"

"Mrs. Ableson, may I introduce Mr. Cannon? Mrs. Ableson is from International Communications."

"Mr. Cannon, this is Mr. Dawson, of Denon Electronics."

"Mr. Cannon, Mr. Dawson, Vice-President of Denon Electronics."

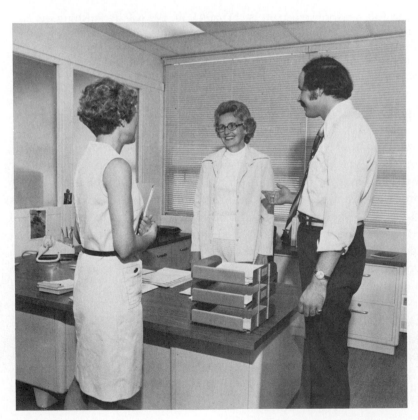

Illus. 8-6

If the caller is unacquainted with the executive, the secretary performs a simple introduction.

Maintaining the Schedule

While you attempt to schedule appointments for the length of time that seems correct, there will be times when the schedule will be disrupted. A caller has a longer, more complicated matter to discuss than had been anticipated; the executive is interrupted with important telephone calls which prolong the conference; callers arrive late; or numerous other situations, many of them unavoidable, require adjustments throughout the day.

Generally executives appreciate the assistance of their secretaries in keeping the schedule. For example, some executives follow a policy of having the secretary inform them of the next appointment about five minutes before the scheduled end of the appointment underway. One secretary to an executive who sees people for many hours most days, uses this procedure which the employer likes:

> Walking quietly to the door of Mr. Falk's office, Mr. Arnett will wait for a slight pause in the conversation and then say, "Mr. Falk, Mr. Nichot, who has an appointment with you in approximately five minutes, has arrived."

> Mr. Falk's response usually is, "Thank you. We will be finishing our discussion very shortly." However, there are times when Mr. Falk will respond, "Mr. Arnett, will you apologize to Mr. Nichot for keeping him waiting, but we must continue this conversation for about fifteen minutes more."

Leaving the Desk

If you find that you must be away while your employer is talking with someone, you should tell a co-worker how long you will be away and where you may be reached. If there is no one else in the area, it may be appropriate to slip a note to the executive stating that your desk is unattended. The executive then will be able to be alert to the arrival of the next appointment or of unexpected persons. Executives often call on their secretaries to get materials that are needed at a conference. If you leave your desk without informing your employer, the result may be an embarrassing and time-consuming search.

REVIEWING

1. What do you believe a secretary should keep in mind as callers are greeted in a business office?
2. In what ways are requests for appointments received?
3. Is it a wise practice to make all appointments tentatively so that you can check with your employer before confirming them? Discuss.

4. Why should a secretary get the telephone number and address of a person for whom a first appointment has been made?
5. Why is it necessary for both the employer and the secretary to maintain calendars of appointments?
6. How should a secretary handle an appointment that had to be canceled after the person was on the way to the office for the appointment?
7. Describe how a secretary should check a conference room prior to a scheduled meeting there.
8. What is the information a secretary might include on the card that is placed in a file of callers?
9. Describe a potentially "difficult" caller and how you would handle such a caller.
10. If a caller arrives early, should the secretary say that the caller is early and will have to wait even longer than if the caller had come on time? Discuss.

MAKING JUDGMENTS

1. Mr. Gary McMann believes that his job is basically to accomplish the important tasks of the office, that is, write letters, transcribe those dictated, maintain the financial records, and handle other related jobs. Taking care of callers seems to him to be an interruption in an otherwise calm period when he can get jobs done. Thus, he has determined that the minimum attention possible to callers is justifiable. He hasn't taken time to get to know regular callers; he looks up only when there is an appropriate break in his work; he lets new callers find the office of his employer. What is your reaction to Mr. McMann's attitude?

2. Miss Beth Banfield believes in following the rules that her employer has established, including the one that she will see people only between 10 and 11:30 in the morning. One afternoon at three o'clock a caller arrived and asked to see Ms. Quall, her employer, briefly. The caller had talked with Ms. Quall two weeks earlier, he told Miss Banfield. Furthermore, the caller indicated that he would be leaving for London later in the day and a short conference would be beneficial for his activities in London. Miss Banfield responded: "I am very sorry, but you see, Ms. Quall is available only between 10 and 11:30. I can arrange for you to see her tomorrow morning if you will postpone your departure to London for a day." What do you think of Miss Banfield's response? If you were in her position, what would you have done?

3. Mr. T. F. Felder, who has an appointment with your employer, arrives at 2:55 for his 3:00 appointment. You greet him pleasantly and tell him that Mr. Saltini, your employer, will be with him in a few minutes. Immediately thereafter, another caller comes to your desk

and says to you that he has a 3:00 appointment with Mr. Saltini. You think: "Two appointments at the same time." What do you do at this moment?

WORKING WITH OTHERS

Miss Shirley G. Andersen enjoys her job as secretary to Mrs. Zimmerman, who is a very hard-working, considerate person. Mrs. Zimmerman is helpful to many colleagues in the firm, so her office is a very popular place. Miss Andersen likes the friendly, informal atmosphere, but she is careful to complete all her work and not take advantage of the freedom given her. She respects her colleagues, all of whom had been very responsible and conscientious about doing their work. However, there is a new assistant to one of the vice-presidents and he, too, has seen that Mrs. Zimmerman is kind and extremely helpful. Increasingly, Miss Andersen finds that the new assistant likes to talk with Mrs. Zimmerman, and he comments that never before has he been in a company with such a friendly atmosphere. Miss Andersen is perplexed, for she sees that this young assistant is insensitive to the limits of friendliness, and is taking far too much of Mrs. Zimmerman's time for unimportant chatter. What do you think Miss Andersen should do?

REFRESHING LANGUAGE SKILLS

For each of the following responses made by a secretary, indicate whether you think the response is appropriate or inappropriate. If inappropriate, rewrite the response so that it is appropriate.

1. Jill: "Good morning. Did you want something, Mr. Salter?"
2. Ralph: "I really don't care how well you know Mr. Fellows. He is a busy person and the thought that you can just come any time you want means that you don't understand how busy he really is. You can write him a letter if you'd like."
3. Kay: "Ms. Willson will see you at 2 this afternoon, Mr. Johnson. Is that a convenient hour for you?"
4. Wanda: "I can make an appointment for you, but only for 15 minutes. I would think that is plenty of time for your purpose."
5. Steve: "Mrs. Ritchie, Mr. Elson has arrived for his 10:30 appointment. Will you be able to see him shortly?"
6. Ruth: Ms. Tarwell, you've been here before, so just make yourself at home; hang up your coat and then look in to see if Mr. Barnes is ready to talk with you."
7. Betty: "Oh, do you have an appointment this morning. I guess I just forgot all about it — it isn't even on my calendar."

8. Marianne: "Mr. Berger, I'm so very sorry, but Mr. Garrison has been unexpectedly called to the factory — just minutes ago, after you had left your office — and he is not at all sure he can get back to the office this afternoon. May I schedule another appointment? Mr. Garrison said he would be happy to call you at home later this evening if you would prefer that he do that."

9. Roger: "Mr. Murray is in a conference on the 14th floor, but he knows about your appointment and I'm sure he will be here within ten minutes. Please, won't you be seated?"

PERFORMING SECRETARIAL TASKS

1. The following appointments are made for your employer, Mr. Howard Perez, executive vice-president, for Wednesday, October 21. The date preceding each item is the date the appointment was made. Record the appointments on the form provided in the *Supplies Inventory*.

October 1   A letter received from Mr. Darrell T. Yost asks if an appointment can be arranged for 10:00 a.m. on the 21st. You are able to confirm the day and hour.

9   One of Mr. Perez's associates, Mr. Kaufman, calls to see if he can meet with some of the staff in Room 314, on Wednesday the 21st, at 9 a.m. The meeting will require a half hour.

14   Mr. Perez asks you to arrange a luncheon meeting at 12 in private dining room B for Ms. Frances Blackwell, Mr. Wells Onderski, and Mr. Edward Rutford, who, along with Mr. Perez, are members of the nominating committee of a metropolitan association of architects. You check with the three to determine if they are free for an hour and a half meeting. They are all free and the meeting is scheduled.

16   Ms. Lange, one of the research associates in the technical division, calls to see if she can talk with Mr. Perez for approximately 15 minutes on the 21st at his convenience in the late afternoon. You schedule an appointment for 4:30.

20   A secretary to Mr. T. W. Williams calls from Pittsburgh to see if Mr. Perez could meet with Mr. Williams late in the afternoon of the next day. Mr. Williams will be in the City and would like to discuss a job on which they are both working. You quickly check with Mr. Perez about a 5:00 appointment and

receive this response: "Of course, I'll be able to see Tom. If it's more convenient, tell him I'll meet him at his hotel." You check with Mr. Williams' secretary who says that Mr. Williams will be able to be at Mr. Perez's office at 4:00.

2. The Great Northwest Bank has its executive offices in downtown Seattle, Washington. Mr. Antonio Bartelli is executive director of foreign operations. The following events occur during the early hours of the afternoon:

   a. At 1:20 Mr. Lin Kawasaki and Mr. Richard Yushida arrive for a 1:30 appointment with Mr. Bartelli, who has not yet returned from lunch. These two callers are from Tokyo, Japan, and they arrived the day before in Seattle. This is their first visit to Seattle, although they have previously been in San Francisco and New York City. They speak English well.
   b. Mr. Bartelli arrives about 1:32.
   c. At 2:30 Mr. Helmut Schneider of the research division calls to see if he can talk with Mr. Bartelli for a few minutes before 4:00. You know that Mr. Bartelli wanted about 1½ hours for the conference with the callers from Tokyo.
   d. At 3:15 you receive a telephone call from Mr. Theodore Wemple, president of a company in Chicago. Mr. Wemple, who has an appointment with Mr. Bartelli at 9 the next morning says to you: "I've arrived in Seattle earlier than anticipated, and I'm wondering if Mr. Bartelli could see me later in the afternoon for about 15 minutes, or possibly have dinner with me."

Consider how you would handle each of these situations. Be prepared to play the role of the secretary or one of the visitors. Also, be prepared to evaluate the manner in which your classmates handle the situations.

Part 2
Oral Communications

Mr. Marco George finds his work pleasurable. His office isn't typical — he is out "in the sticks," as he likes to describe it. He is working as secretary to Mr. Frederic Helpin, director of a housing development about ten miles from the edge of the small community where Mr. George lives. Mr. Helpin has a clear concept of his work; he is responsible for building houses so as to minimize the cutting down of trees and other plant life. Each house fits in a particular site among the trees and hills. Mr. George's office is a small, rustic house, but he has all the conveniences necessary to do his work well. Several model houses are open for inspection, and among Mr. George's responsibilities is the conducting of tours of these houses. He has learned much about houses and their construction and he is able to talk knowledgeably about them with prospective buyers. He enjoys presenting the key features of each house and answering questions.

Talking with others is a common activity in modern life. Talking ranges from informal discussions of work to be done among co-workers to formal presentations before persons within or outside the organization. The speech for modern business is similar to that used in ordinary conversations with acquaintances and the general public. Appropriate speech for the business office is somewhat more formal than that used with family members or close friends. Since such persons know you well, they may understand what you mean without your saying it very clearly. On the other hand, persons who do not know you will appreciate your using precise language so your message is accurately understood.

Non-Verbal Influences

Impressions are based a great deal on non-verbal influences, so they demand some attention. Some non-verbal influences are: appearance, manners, and posture and movement.

Your Appearance

When you talk with others, your appearance may either enhance or detract from what you are saying. Some believe that how a person looks is an important factor in judging what is said. In business offices, there is a general respect for people who wear appropriate clothing that is clean and neat. Of course, what is deemed appropriate varies from one area of the country to another and, sometimes, from company to company. As an office worker, you will want to maintain good taste in your appearance, which means that you want your clothing to be comfortable, yet appropriate for your office.

Your Manners

Accepted ways of behaving in a variety of situations are what we mean by manners. Manners, in much the same way as clothing, change with the times. However, there are certain codes of behavior in the business world.

Poised, calm, self-confident secretaries are much admired. Such secretaries are able to greet callers courteously, introduce strangers with ease, and handle emergencies calmly. While it is possible to learn "how

Illus. 8-7

Careful listening requires patience and attentiveness.

Ohio National Life Insurance Company

to behave" as a courteous secretary, it is far more important to have a deep-seated attitude of helpfulness and interest in your work and in the persons with whom you associate.

One especially important aspect of manners for the office worker is the ability to listen carefully. While a person is talking with you, you should strive to be patient and attentive. Being **indifferent** and preoccupied is not only discourteous, but it often means that you fail to get the complete meaning of what the person is saying to you.

indifferent: not interested

Posture and Movements

How a person walks, stands, sits, uses hand and arm gestures, and uses facial expressions will convey thoughts to listeners. In general, while walking, standing or sitting, you want to convey a general sense of well-being and alertness. Movements of your hands and arms as you talk should be meaningful; that is, they should help to emphasize what you are saying in words. Improper movements, such as playing with a ring on your finger or rolling a pencil on your desk, can be a **distracting** influence as you talk with others.

distracting: pulling attention away from

Your Speech Habits

Your speech habits are an extremely important part of your total personality. Your speech habits reflect *you*. Therefore, you will want to spend some time in understanding how you speak and in eliminating unpleasant speech habits.

Expressing Ideas

Have you ever heard the comment, "I know what I want to say, but I don't know how to say it"? An effective speaker is one who thinks well and who is able to outline mentally what is to be said. If ideas are worth presenting, they deserve attention before they are shared with others.

In a business office it is important that what is said is clearly understood. Misunderstandings cause problems between people. What you say should mean clearly what you intend it to mean. When speaking with someone, have you ever said, "Oh, you didn't understand what I meant . . ."? Making this comment indicates that your thoughts were not clearly expressed.

Ideas should be expressed in such a way that

1. The speaker conveys what is intended to be said.
2. The listener understands what the speaker is saying.
3. The speaker and listener are able to make progress in their conversation.

Voice

A voice that is pleasant is an asset in the business office. A pleasant voice is one that does not distract from the message being spoken; that is, the listener concentrates on *what* is said, not *how* it is said.

Your voice is not separate from the rest of your body. It will reflect the quality of both your physical and mental health. If you are not feeling well, for example, you will generally convey the feeling of discomfort through your voice. On the other hand, if you are in excellent health, your sense of well-being is reflected in your voice. Are you able to determine how happy your friends are by the tone of their voices? Do you know what happens to your voice when you are fatigued?

Become aware of your voice. Does the way you speak need improvement? Do you talk too rapidly? too slowly? too softly? too loudly? Are you happy with the pitch of your voice? Can you speak easily and without straining your voice? These are just some of the questions that you will want to think about as you become aware of your own voice.

When you are tense your voice tends to become higher pitched than is normal for you. It is then strained, and words are produced only with heightened effort. The final effect is not attractive to the listener.

Because of the great amount of speaking a secretary must do during a working day, it is extremely important that you learn to use your voice effectively. The most effective use of your voice will also produce the most pleasing voice for your listeners.

Pronouncing Words

adopt:
accept for use

You should **adopt** the pronunciation of words most readily understood and accepted in the office and community where you work and live. It is sometimes difficult to find an acceptable standard of pronunciation inasmuch as standards differ from place to place. What is acceptable pronunciation in Boston may not be acceptable in Atlanta. Speech authorities say that you should attempt to follow the usage of the educated people of the community. Of course, if you should be working in a community that is in a different part of the country from where you grew up, you will find that people are tolerant of differences they will find in your pronunciation. In fact, to attempt immediately to imitate the speech of a new area is to make your speech sound affected. To say that your speech is *affected* means that you are attempting to speak in an unfamiliar manner. A person from Atlanta who is working in Boston will not be able to assume the pronunciation of the new city without sounding affected. Most people find such assumed speech patterns unattractive.

Enunciation is the precision with which you pronounce each word. It is important that you develop correct enunciation so that you always will be understood. Two of the most common errors in enunciation are running words together and failing to sound all the syllables of a word. *Didya* for *did you, gimme* for *give me, whatchagonna* for *what are you going to, uster* for *used to, lemme* for *let me* are examples. Some other common errors in enunciation are listed below.

	FAULTY	CORRECT
Dropping the sound of *g* in words ending in *ing*	*workin'*	for *working*
	goin'	for *going*
	typin'	for *typing*
Dropping the sound of *r* in words ending in *r*	*fatha*	for *father*
	numba	for *number*
	dolla	for *dollar*
Adding the sound of *r* when it is not called for	*idear*	for *idea*
	rawr	for *raw*
Using the wrong vowel sound	*fur*	for *for*
	fell	for *fill*
	git	for *get*
Substituting one syllable for another	*chimley*	for *chimney*
	punkin	for *pumpkin*
	libery	for *library*
Adding an extra syllable	*athalete*	for *athlete*
	remnant	for *remnant*
	realator	for *realtor*
Misplacing the accent	*genuine'*	for *gen'uine*
	re'search	for *research'*
	formid'able	for *for'midable*

There are many words in the English language that are very similar to at least one other word. Such words must be enunciated clearly if the listener is to grasp the word meant. Words of this nature include:

ascend	attack	statue
assent	attach	stature
		statute
cease	immigration	
seize	emigration	track
		tract
descend	irrelevant	
descent	irreverent	while
		wild
eminent	picture	wile
imminent	pitcher	
		worth
incite	sense	work
insight	since	word

As you know, the dictionary will aid you when you are uncertain of the pronunciation of a word.

Colloquial Words and Expressions

colloquial:
conversational

As you know, the spoken language of a society is constantly changing. There always will be at a given time certain words and expressions that are considered satisfactory for informal communication but are not appropriate for more formal situations, such as communication in the business office. Often these **colloquial** words and expressions lend ease and naturalness to what is said; however, they must be used with care. Seldom are they as appropriate as the accepted words that convey the same meaning. Some examples are:

COLLOQUIAL	PREFERRED
contact for *get in touch with* or *call* or *talk with*	I will *call* (not *contact*) Mr. Jones when I arrive in Chicago tomorrow.
post for *informed*	Be sure to keep me *informed* (not *posted*) of your progress.
Turnout for *attendance*	The *attendance* (not *turnout*) was surprising.
wait on for *wait for*	Will you be able to *wait for* (not *wait on*) Mr. Ray tonight?

Slang

Although colloquialisms are sometimes acceptable, slang is out of place in a business office. Slang is made up of widely used current terms which have a forced meaning such as *to get with it* meaning *to cooperate* or *dig this* meaning *understand this*. Words or expressions of this type are contrary to good language usage.

The wide usage of certain slang words and phrases, such as *cut the mustard* or *to miss the boat*, have caused them to lose some of the undesirable quality that they had in the past; however, their usage in the business office should be very much limited. A vocabulary made up of *gross, lousy, guy*, and other slang is an indication of a very weak English background. It is very difficult to convey ideas clearly with such language.

Discussions and Presentations

In addition to person-to-person communications, there are times when the secretary must engage in group situations. The secretary may be asked, for example, to explain a new procedure to a group of recently hired typists or take a group of visitors on a tour of offices. There are times when a secretary must make a relatively formal presentation on the company's **premises** or away from the office.

premises:
property

Group Participation

Generally there is a specific purpose for a meeting. All members of a group should understand the purpose of meeting and **endeavor** to participate thoughtfully so that the group is able to accomplish its goal.

endeavor: try

> Helene Gallager, the executive secretary to the publisher of a fashion magazine, was asked to participate in a meeting with a consultant from an interior design company who had been hired to plan the renovation of the headquarters' offices. Helene knew the purpose of the meeting ahead of time so she thought about her office as well as other offices and was prepared when she reached the meeting to offer some suggestions. She listened carefully to the comments of the others. When one of the executives commented about the use of color, which was one of her points, she offered her major suggestions.

The role of the chairman, chairperson, moderator, or leader — all these terms are used for the person who guides a discussion — is a special one. The chairperson, first of all, must convey the purpose of the meeting in such a way that all understand it clearly. Secondly, the chairperson encourages active participation of all those present and acknowledges the contribution of each. There are times when the chairperson shifts the attention of the group somewhat if the discussion appears to be moving beyond the particular topic under review.

Presentations

When a secretary is asked to make a presentation, it is important to know what the precise topic is to be, the background of the audience, and how long the presentation is to be. The skills you have developed in your various school activities, including presentations made in classes and club meetings, will be valuable when you are called on to make presentations in your work.

Miss Roberta Simpson is secretary to the Director of Public Affairs. She has been asked to talk with a group of high school students who are visiting the company to see the range of office jobs found in a large manufacturing company. Miss Simpson began her work in this company as a clerk-typist three years earlier, and she has a good understanding of the jobs in the company's various offices. Her employer asked her to plan to talk for approximately 15 minutes. She would talk with the group of 20 students in the company's large conference room. As she thought about her presentation, she realized that some charts showing the general categories and the qualifications for each would be helpful. She knew that her task was to introduce the students to the jobs so that when they visited a range of types of offices and talked with office workers, they would have the background to understand the specific jobs more clearly.

Office workers with the skills necessary to communicate with others will find many opportunities to be helpful in their jobs.

REVIEWING

1. Name an important non-verbal influence on communication.
2. How would you define "appropriate dress" for the business office.
3. How do you show that you are listening attentively?
4. If a person understands what is to be said, but can't say it, what should that person do?
5. How is tenseness indicated in a person's voice?
6. Give an illustration of a poor speech habit.
7. Identify two words that must be enunciated carefully so that they are not confused with each other.
8. Why should you avoid the use of slang in the business office?
9. What responsibilities does a leader of a group assume?
10. What must you know before you can prepare an appropriate presentation?

MAKING JUDGMENTS

1. Willa likes comfortable, casual clothes and does not believe there is any reason why she can not wear such clothes to her office.

Although during the orientation period, an assistant personnel officer had discussed the type of clothing appropriate for the modern, formal offices of the company, Willa decided that she was free to wear what she wanted, so during the second week at her new job she wore an old pair of jeans that she found comfortable. What do you think of Willa's judgment?

2. Harold feels that most people take too long to explain simple, obvious ideas to other people, so he is constantly finishing sentences for others or saying in the middle of another person's words, "Oh, you don't have to go on; I know what you mean, so why waste words?" What do you think of Harold's behavior?

3. David realizes that people in his office are always saying to him: "I'm sorry, but I can't hear what you are saying. Could you talk a little louder?" David doesn't understand why people don't listen to him more carefully; he thinks talking softly — at times just above a whisper — is the only way to keep from interfering with others who are trying to work. What do you think of David's judgment?

WORKING WITH OTHERS

Jack had never given much attention to his speech. He was, in fact, rather lazy about pronouncing words carefully and believed that people seemed to know what he was "tryin' to say" (as he would say it!). At the point of seeking a job, Jack continued to be indifferent to good speech. What do you think of Jack's attitude?

REFRESHING LANGUAGE SKILLS

Homonyms are words that are pronounced alike, but are different in meaning. The pairs of words below include some that are homonyms and some words that are often incorrectly pronounced as though they were homonyms. Those pairs that are not homonyms require careful pronunciation so that the difference in the words is clear to the listener. Use a dictionary to check the pronunciation of each pair of words, as well as the meaning of each word. Then write a sentence using each word correctly. Indicate which pairs are homonyms.

1. affect	6. real
effect	reel
2. expansive	7. residence
expensive	residents
3. precedent	8. sight
president	cite
4. precede	9. than
proceed	then
5. profit	10. their
prophet	there

PERFORMING SECRETARIAL TASKS

1. Errors of pronunciation are commonly made. Listen to the speech of your classmates, as well as the speech of radio and television speakers, making a note of all errors you hear. Then, classify the errors you have heard using the types of errors listed on page 307. Type your listing and be prepared to discuss it in class.
2. Prepare a list of slang words and expressions that you and others in your school use that you believe are out of place in the business office. Be prepared to indicate the standard words that would express the idea of the slang word or expression.
3. For one of the following topics, outline a brief presentation. Type your outline and be prepared to make the presentation to the entire class or to a small group from the class.

   a. The procedure for preparing letters for mailing
   b. Handling the receptionist's desk
   c. Preparing mail for the executive's desk
   d. Procedure for composing letters on your own for the executive's signature

IMPROVING SECRETARIAL SKILLS (Optional)

1. If a tape recorder is available, make a recording of the following:

   a. Read a paragraph from a textbook.
   b. Discuss with one of your classmates the responsibilities that the secretary has when meeting the public.
   c. Explain to a classmate the manner in which callers ought to be treated in a business office.

   Listen to your own voice and write your reactions to it. As you listen, pay attention to your ability to express ideas; your voice; your pronunciation; and your use of colloquial and slang words and phrases.
2. Assume that you are to make a presentation to a group of 8th or 9th graders who are interested in learning about the programs in the high school you attend. You are to talk about the courses offered for students who want the skills and knowledges needed in the modern business office. Assume that you have ten minutes for the presentation. Outline your presentation. Type the outline on plain paper and be prepared to discuss the reasons for the nature of your presentation and the sequence of topics included.

Rapid Communications Services

Part 1. Receiving Calls
Part 2. Placing Calls
Part 3. Special Telephone Equipment
Part 4. Special Communications Services

<h2>Part 1</h2>

Receiving Calls

Miss Madeline Twordman is secretary to the director of merchandising for a large department store in San Francisco. One morning when there was a pause in her work, she found herself wondering what the world would be like without telephones. She thought: "How could we ever get our work done as quickly as we do now — goodness, in just the last hour, I've received calls from Mexico City, London, Boston, and New York City." Telephone conversations make it possible to resolve questions, reconsider plans, and, thus, make decisions that allow work to move ahead.

The telephone is one of the basic means of communications in today's office. Steadily, there have been improvements in telephone service. Indeed, there continue to be **innovations** that add to the effectiveness of the services.

innovations: changes

Using the telephone is likely to be one of your daily tasks. You will probably receive and make calls many times a day. Proper techniques as well as an understanding of the importance of this communications **medium** will be helpful in your work.

medium: means

Telephone Manner

Your interest, your knowledge, and your concern for others are all conveyed when you talk with people on the telephone; yet, all impressions are shaped from your voice and your speech.

Voice

A voice can convey a spirit of interest, alertness, courtesy, and helpfulness over the telephone; or it can reflect an attitude of indifference, impatience, or inattention. It is often true that it is not *what* is said but the *way* it is said that really counts in a telephone conversation. A pleasant voice is much nicer to listen to than one which is loud, harsh, or shrill. You can improve your voice if you think and speak with a smile. Try to think of the caller as a person — not just as an unknown voice — who needs your help. You can have the *voice with a smile* if you talk with callers in a pleasant manner. Here are some suggestions to improve your telephone voice.

1. *Speak clearly*. A normal tone of voice — neither too loud nor too soft — carries best over the telephone.
2. *Use a low-pitched voice*. A low-pitched voice carries better over the telephone and is kinder to your listener's ear. A high-pitched voice tends to become shrill and irritating.
3. *Use voice inflection*. The rise and fall of your voice not only gets your thoughts across but also adds personality to your voice. A **monotonous** voice sounds indifferent.

monotonous:
not varying; without change

Illus. 9-1

The voice with a smile gives the caller a favorable impression.

Courtesy of American Telephone & Telegraph Company

Speech

Speech habits (as you learned in Unit 8) are as important as your voice: a pleasant voice makes you easy to listen to; good speech habits make you easy to understand. You should pronounce words clearly and correctly so that callers understand what you are saying. It is important that callers hear your message correctly.

Below are some suggestions for good telephone speech.

1. *Speak carefully*. Distinct speech is essential, since the listener can neither read your lips nor see your expression. Pronounce each word clearly; don't mumble or slur syllables.

2. *Talk at a proper pace.* A moderate rate of speech is easily understood, but the pace should be related to the ideas you are expressing. You should give some information more slowly: for example, technical information, lists, information the listener is writing down, numbers, names, and foreign or unusual words.

3. *Use emphasis with words.* The stress or emphasis placed on words, or groups of words, may change the meaning of what you are saying.

4. *Consider the listener's comments and questions.* Allow the listener's ideas to be expressed.

Illus. 9-2

Distinct speech is especially important when talking over the telephone.

Vocabulary

Your ideas should be stated simply. Technical, awkward, and unnecessarily lengthy words may confuse the other person and may require an explanation or may even cause a misunderstanding.

offend:
to have a negative
reaction

Avoid language which will offend the listener or create a bad impression of your company. Avoid trite words, phrases and expressions. *Please repeat* sounds better than *huh*.

Courtesy

Courtesy is just as important in telephone conversations as it is in person-to-person conversations. You are courteous if, when you respond to a call:

1. You transfer all your attention to the person calling; you convey no impatience because the ringing telephone is interrupting you.
2. You listen quietly and allow the person to express the purpose of the call.
3. You don't keep a person waiting while you search for information. If you think you need more than one minute to get the information, you should suggest that you will call back.
4. You follow through conscientiously any promises to return a telephone call or provide information.

Incoming Calls

As part of your secretarial duties you will probably answer many of your executive's incoming calls. Other executives prefer to answer their own calls but expect the secretary to handle calls when they are busy or away from their desks.

Answer Promptly

You should answer all incoming calls promptly and pleasantly. In fact, the telephone should be answered on the first ring.

As you reach for the receiver, reach for your notebook. You must be ready to take notes immediately. *You should hold the mouthpiece about an inch from your lips* and speak directly into the telephone in a normal conversational tone of voice.

Identify Yourself

A telephone conversation cannot really begin until the caller knows that the right number has been reached. You should always identify yourself and your firm, office, or department immediately. You should never answer by saying "Hello" or "Yes?" — these greetings add nothing to the identification.

If you answer an outside line, give your firm's name, followed by your name, as in "Northern Construction Company, Jane Meade." If your company has a switchboard, your operator has already identified the company; and you may answer your employer's telephone by saying, "Mr. Keller's office, Jane Meade." When answering an office extension in a department, identify the department and give your name — "Planning Department, Jane Meade."

Screening Calls

There is a practice in some offices of secretaries screening calls. Screening calls is a procedure of determining who is calling and, at times, the purpose of the call. In some instances, much time is saved through screening, for a secretary may be able to immediately transfer the call to the proper person. However, there are instances when it is necessary for the secretary to attempt to determine which calls are important enough to be transferred to the executive. In such instances the secretary determines who is calling and why before any information is given about the **availability** of the executive. Many executives feel that such a practice is not courteous, and their secretaries do not screen in this fashion.

availability:
presence

It is important that you learn the preferences of your employer. If, for example, the executive wants to know who is calling before responding to the ring of the telephone, the secretary should handle a call in this manner:

Secretary: "Good morning. Mrs. Ericson's office. Sally Walker."
Caller: "I'd like to talk with Mrs. Ericson, please."
Secretary: "Yes. May I tell her who is calling?"
Caller: "This is Howard Wolfson of Telton-Taft Manufacturing Company."
Secretary: "Just one moment, Mr. Wolfson, for Mrs. Ericson."

Thoughtful *callers* handle calls in this manner:

Secretary: "Good morning. Mrs. Ericson's office. Sally Walker."
Caller: "Good morning. This is Howard Wolfson of Telton-Taft Manufacturing Company. May I speak with Mrs. Ericson?"
Secretary: "Yes, Mr. Wolfson; one moment for Mrs. Ericson."

Handling Calls when the Executive is Unavailable

There are often times when an executive is not free to talk with telephone callers. At such moments, the secretary should be as courteous and helpful as possible. The secretary may need to say:

"I'm sorry, Mr. Gates is away from his desk and is not expected back until after 11. May I help you? May I take a message?"

or

"I'm sorry, Mr. Gates is talking with a group of visitors at this moment and isn't free. May I help you? May I take a message?"

or

"I'm sorry, Mr. Gates is out of town. He will be back in the office at 3 on Friday afternoon. May I help you? May I take a message?"

Giving Information

Secretaries are generally **cautioned** against conveying information **indiscriminately** to telephone callers. Only that information necessary to handle the call courteously should be communicated to a caller. For example, if an executive has gone to a city to determine the availability of a building site, there may be reasons not to discuss the whereabouts of the executive with callers. To a caller, merely the information that the executive is out of town and the date and time of expected return should be **sufficient**.

Secretaries understand the work of their offices well and are, therefore, able to quickly sense when a caller is just trying to obtain information. In such instances, a quiet but firm **repetition** of a **noncommital** statement should be made. The caller will soon realize that the information wanted will not be gained, and the conversation will end.

cautioned: warned

indiscriminately: without thought

sufficient: adequate

repetition: to say again

noncommital: not stating a position

Talking with the Anonymous Caller

Sometimes callers are **reluctant** to identify themselves, even if asked to do so. At such times, the secretary must maintain calm, and at the same time assume a position of firmness. Here is a conversation with such a caller:

reluctant: hesitant

Secretary: "Good afternoon. Mr. Perry's office. Barry Cardile."
Caller: "Is Mr. Perry in; I want to talk with him."
Secretary: "No, I am sorry. Mr. Perry is out of town. May I help you? May I take a message?"
Caller: "Where is Mr. Perry today. I really need to know."
Secretary: "With whom am I talking, please?"
Caller: "It isn't important who I am; can't you give me a number where I can reach Mr. Perry?"
Secretary: "I am sorry; Mr. Perry is out of town. If you would like to leave a message, I will be happy to see that Mr. Perry receives it when he returns."
Caller: "I don't appreciate your lack of cooperation. Goodbye."

Taking Messages

Messages should be recorded accurately, for an inaccurate detail may make the total message worthless. It is generally a good practice to repeat unfamiliar names — including proper spelling — and the telephone number so that the caller can verify what you have recorded.

It should not be necessary to rewrite the message for the executive. You should record each message fully, in clear handwriting, as you receive it from the caller.

The message, written clearly, should include:

1. The exact time of the call and the date

2. The name of the caller and company (check the spelling of any unusual names)

3. The telephone number, the caller's extension, and area code, if it's a long-distance call (recheck the number)

4. The details of the message

5. The initials of the person who wrote the message

MEMO OF CALL

TO: _Mrs. Werner_

FROM: _Mr. Lang, Capital Savings Bank_

PHONE NO. _606 - 433 - 8331_

☑ Telephoned ☐ Please Phone ☐ Came To See You

☑ Will Call Again ☐ Returned Your Call ☐ Wishes To See You

Message: _Wants you to refer to deposit on 3/15, deposit slip #1222 (slip is attached)_

Date: _3/17_ Time: _11:30_ Received By: _gf_

Illus. 9-3   Memo of call

Transferring Calls

Sometimes you will have to transfer a call to another extension or number. Calls are usually transferred when the caller has reached a wrong extension, when the caller wishes to speak with someone else, or when the caller's request can be handled better by someone else. Tell the caller why the transfer is necessary, and be sure that the call is being transferred to the proper person. In these instances you may say to the caller:

> I am sorry; you have reached the wrong extension. What extension were you calling? . . . I can transfer your call. Just a minute, please.

> or

> I shall be glad to transfer your call to Mr. Reynolds. His extension is 2368. Just a minute, please.

or

Mr. Weinhart has all the information on that matter. May I transfer your call to him?

To transfer a call you should push down and release the receiver button of the telephone *slowly*. This action flashes a signal light on the switchboard which will attract the operator's attention. After the operator answers your signal, you might say, "Please transfer this call to Mr. Reynolds," or, "Please place this call on Extension 2368."

When a call is disconnected, the calling party should place the call again. If your call was long distance, and you placed it, you should dial the Operator (0) and explain that you were disconnected.

Automatic Answering and Recording Set

A telephone answering and recording set will automatically answer the telephone and record a message after business hours or during the regular business hours if there is nobody to answer the telephone. Here is how it works. Before leaving the office for the day, the executive dictates a message to the set, such as:

This is Winston Lunn speaking. You are listening to a recording. When you hear a signal, you may record a message, which I shall listen to on my return to the office tomorrow morning at 9 a.m.

At the first opportunity either the executive or the secretary can listen to the recorded messages.

Telephone Answering Service

With a telephone answering service you know that all your calls will be answered when you are unable to receive them personally. The telephone answering service operator takes your calls for you and relays the messages to you or your business associates. The names of firms that supply telephone answering service are listed in the Yellow Pages.

Terminating Calls

Try to leave a favorable impression by ending each telephone conversation in a friendly, unhurried manner. You should not end a call by hanging up abruptly. As the conversation ends, thank the caller for the call with an appropriate remark such as:

Thank you for calling, Ms. Bailes.

or

Thank you for your message. I'll ask Mr. Bernard to telephone you as soon as he returns.

or

Thank you for the information. I'll give it to Mr. Bernard.

Be sure to say "Good-bye." After the caller has hung up, replace the receiver *gently*.

Personal Telephone Calls

The policy of using a business telephone for personal calls varies from office to office. Some firms permit a limited number of personal calls; others discourage all such calls. Generally brief to-the-point personal calls that are urgent can be tolerated in most offices.

REVIEWING

1. What is the meaning of "telephone manner?"
2. How does one speak "with a smile?"
3. Why should a high-pitched voice be avoided when talking on the telephone?
4. How is indifference conveyed over the telephone?
5. Should technical information be conveyed over the telephone at a slower-than-usual rate of speaking? Why?
6. How can you convey courtesy to a telephone caller?
7. What details are especially important when recording a telephone message?
8. How should you handle a caller who refuses to identify himself or herself?
9. What is the usefulness of the automatic answering and recording devices?
10. What should you do if a long distance call is disconnected?

MAKING JUDGMENTS

1. Ms. Leyton is frequently out of the office because her work involves many tasks in the factory. As a result, her secretary, Mr. Oliver, is constantly getting calls. He decided recently that he was wasting too much time taking messages. When Ms. Leyton is away from her desk now, he says to a caller: "Im sorry, Ms. Leyton is not here. Would you call back after 4 this afternoon? I am too busy to take a message." What do you think of Mr. Oliver's judgment?

2. Mr. Winters realizes that many people use the telephone unwisely, and he thinks his employer, Mr. Jones, is too busy to have so many telephone interruptions. So, he decided to suggest to callers that they write letters. His standard response now is:

"I'm very sorry; Mr. Jones is not available at this moment. Could you write him a letter which I am sure he will read and respond to without delay."

He thinks that within a month there will be fewer calls as people get the hint that they shouldn't be calling. What do you think of Mr. Winters' judgment?

WORKING WITH OTHERS

Peter noted that his employer is regularly out to lunch for about two hours with clients. Peter, on the other hand, takes only an hour for lunch. He realized that one to two o'clock was a great time for his close friends to call him. During this time, many business people all over town are out to lunch, so it would be unlikely that anyone would call to talk to his employer. In other words, no one would know the line was busy! So, Peter suggested regularly to friends: "Why don't you call me between one and two, just any day."

What do you think of Peter's plan?

REFRESHING LANGUAGE SKILLS

Below are three simple rules for helping you correctly add *ing* endings to verbs.

A. An *e* is usually dropped before adding *ing*.

Examples: arrive   arriving
judge   judging

B. Before adding *ing*, *ie* is changed to *y*.

Examples: die   dying
lie   lying

C. When the final syllable contains a long vowel, the *ing* will be preceded by a double consonant. Note, however, that this is not an absolute rule; single consonants are becoming increasingly more common.

Examples: counsel   counseling or counselling
program   programing or programming

On a separate sheet of paper, type the following words using the correct *ing* ending. When in doubt, check a dictionary.

1. advise	11. occupy
2. apply	12. page
3. argue	13. promise
4. change	14. qualify
5. continue	15. recur
6. dictate	16. run
7. get	17. screen
8. imply	18. tie
9. label	19. transfer
10. motivate	20. type

PERFORMING SECRETARIAL TASKS

1. Role play the following situations. If there is recording equipment available, you may want to record the conversations so that you can later listen to your own performance to note what you are doing satisfactorily and what might be improved. While two students are role-playing a situation, the other members of the class should make notes for evaluating the conversations. In evaluating telephone conversations, note especially the "message" of the voice and the words used.

   Situation 1: A Mr. Edmonson, with whom the secretary has not talked prior to this moment, wants to talk with Ms. Wilkes about a special product his company needs. He is calling to make an appointment. Miss Penny is secretary to Ms. Wilkes. When Mr. Edmonson calls, he asks to talk with Ms. Wilkes, who is out of the office.

   Situation 2: A Ms. Grant is calling Mr. Casey to see if he can meet with a group at a local club the following Wednesday for a professional purpose. She feels that she must talk with Mr. Casey directly. Ms. Bird is secretary to Mr. Casey. Mr. Casey is at his desk when the call is received.

   Situation 3: A Mr. Wilson is calling Mrs. Rogers in order to check a detail in a contract his company is negotiating with her company. Mr. Tanner is Mrs. Rogers' secretary. Mrs. Rogers is in, but she is talking with two colleagues and has asked not to be disturbed.

2. The following telephone calls were received on March 5, 19––, while the persons called were out of the office. Prepare a report of each call on a form from the *Supplies Inventory* or draw a form similar to that shown in the illustration on page 320.

a. William C. Adams, of Chicago, called Alfred Rogers at 10:30 a.m. regarding Order R-325-C. Mr. Adams' telephone number is 312-891-3456. He will call again at 2:00.
b. Mrs. James Arthur called Mr. Arthur (her husband) at 12:30 p.m.
c. Mr. James Linden, of Philadelphia, called William Spencer at 11:45. He said that he had received Order 10256 but not received Order 10245, which had been placed a week before Order 10256. His telephone number is 215-922-8230.
d. Earl Kramer called Alfred Rogers at 4:15. He will meet Mr. Rogers at 5:30 at the club.

Placing Calls

Miss Ida Bunner must place many calls in her position as secretary to Miss Elsie Hickey, a vice-president for a management consulting firm. Miss Hickey is often out of town and sends Miss Bunner instructions which involve placing many calls. Miss Bunner realizes she must understand her work thoroughly to handle telephone calls intelligently.

delegated:
assigned to be done

comprehension:
understanding

Secretaries must make calls in order to get information or give information in relation to those tasks that are **delegated** to them. In such instances, they know well the purpose of their calls. However, there are often occasions when secretaries must make calls for their employers. In order to transmit a complete message, the secretary must have all details, as well as a **comprehension** of the total situation. The situation in the following conversation is not a good one:

First Secretary:	"This is Patricia Rollins, Mr. Toney's secretary. May I talk with Mr. James?"
Second Secretary:	"Just one minute."
First Secretary:	"Mr. James, Mr. Toney asked me to call you to tell you that the meeting this afternoon will get underway at 3:00 instead of 2:30. Is this all right with you?"
Mr. James:	"My, yes, but how long will the meeting last? I have a 4:30 meeting back here in my office.
First Secretary:	"I am sorry, but I have no idea how long the meeting will last. Mr. Toney didn't tell me."
Mr. James:	"Is the meeting going to be in the same room as formerly announced?"
First Secretary:	"I guess so. Mr. Toney didn't say anything about the meeting room. . . ."

The secretary should have obtained more details originally. There are times when a busy executive asks a secretary to place a call to someone with whom the executive wishes to talk. In such instances, the secretary must be sure the executive is ready to begin the conversation as soon as the party sought is on the line. It is not courteous to call and then keep the answering party waiting for the executive who requested the call.

Telephone Directories

Telephone directories are valuable references. You should be able to reach them quickly and use them effectively. You may have a personal directory for frequently used telephone numbers, as well as a company Directory, the Telephone Directory (white pages), and the Yellow Pages. If your office makes calls to certain large cities frequently, you may have some out-of-town directories. A secretary for a company vice-president commented:

> I realized we were calling companies in New York City and Philadelphia so often that I decided to get directories for these two cities. I save a lot of time by consulting the directory directly. Of course, in the instances where I use a number frequently, I make a card for my personal telephone directory, which I keep in a nearby file.

Be sure you have the correct number before you place a telephone call. You should consult the appropriate directory, and only if the number is not listed should you call Information. Your local telephone directory will give you details for dialing Information.

Personal Telephone Directory

An up-to-date list of frequently called local and out-of-town telephone numbers will save you and your employer a great deal of telephoning time. Booklets to be used as personal telephone directories can be obtained from most telephone companies. For the small firm or office, an "automatic finder" can be used. By moving the indicator to the correct letter of the alphabet, you can reach the desired page immediately. A large personal listing can be kept more easily on cards in a revolving visible file on your desk.

The Alphabetical Directory

The names of subscribers are listed alphabetically in this directory. Individual names and firm names are easily located, unless the spelling of a name is unusual, and then it is cross-referenced as:

> Brown — See also Braun, Browne
> Kaufman — See also Caufman, Kaufmann
> Rees — See also Reis, Reiss, Riess

For the convenience of their customers or clients, business and professional people often list their home numbers directly below their business listings: for example,

Johnson, L. T. att. 621 Park Ave. 271-3469
Res 4 Ladd Rd...(516) 271-4092

It is often necessary to call government agencies to request information or to get answers to questions which are constantly arising about government regulations. Government agencies are listed under three categories:

Federal agencies under United
States Government ...............................U.S. Government
                                                Interior Dept of
                                                State Dept of

State agencies under state
government..Missouri State of
                                                Employment Service
                                                Highway Dept

County and municipal agencies
under local governments ....Denver City of
                                                Education Board of
                                                Fire Dept
                                                Police Dept

The first few pages of the alphabetical directory contain useful information including instructions for making emergency calls, local and long-distance calls, service calls (repair, assistance, etc.) and special calls (overseas, conference, collect, etc.). In addition, area codes for the United States and Canada, sample rates, and telephone company business office addresses and telephone numbers are listed.

The Yellow Pages

The Yellow Pages are used when you wish to find out quickly where you may obtain a particular product or service. The names, addresses, and telephone numbers of business subscribers are listed alphabetically under the name of the product or service. Many business organizations use advertising space and artistic displays to tell their customers about the organization's operations, including brands carried, hours, and services. Nationally advertised or trademarked products may be listed with the names, addresses, and telephone numbers of most of the local dealers arranged alphabetically under a word or trademark design.

Placing Long-Distance Calls

When you are a secretary, you will frequently be asked to place long-distance calls for your executive. The two most commonly used types of out-of-town calls are *station-to-station* and *person-to-person* calls.

Station-to-Station Calls

A station-to-station call is made to a certain telephone number. Make this type of call if you are willing to talk with anyone who may answer the telephone or if you are fairly certain the person with whom your employer wishes to speak is within easy reach of the telephone.

Person-to-Person Calls

When you wish to speak with a particular person in a large company, place a person-to-person call. A person-to-person call is directed to a specific person, room number, extension number, or department. Make this type of call only if you wish to talk with a particular person or if you are not sure that person is within reach of the telephone. You must have assistance from a telephone operator to place a person-to-person call.

Illus. 9-4

When placing out going calls, a secretary should have a short-hand notebook at hand for recording notes related to the call.

Courtesy of American Telephone & Telegraph Company

Direct Distance Dialing (DDD)

Direct distance dialing is a method of placing all station-to-station calls and some person-to-person calls by using the dial on your telephone. No assistance is needed from the operator in order to complete the call. The front pages of the Telephone Directory provide complete directions for direct distance dialing.

Station-to-Station DDD. In order to use direct distance dialing in making a station-to-station call, in many areas you must first dial the number *1*, which a prefix code that will give you a long-distance line. Next you dial the three-number area code which represents the area of the country you are calling. Area codes are required when calling from one area to another. In those areas of the country where the prefix code is not required, you simply dial the three-digit area code to get a long-distance line. Finally, you dial the seven digits of the particular telephone number you wish to reach. For example, suppose you were in Charleston, West Virginia, and wished to make a call to the Oxford Book Center in Pittsburgh, whose telephone number is 691-5309. You would dial 1-412-691-5309.

> 1 is the prefix code to get a long-distance line.
> 412 is the area code for Pittsburgh.
> 691-5309 is the telephone number of the Oxford Book Center.

Person-to-Person with DDD. In more and more cities it is also possible to use direct distance dialing for person-to-person calls. You must first dial a special prefix code. This special prefix code signals the telephone company's computer that you wish to make a person-to-person call with DDD. You then dial the area code and the particular telephone number. The operator will come on the line and ask for the name of the person you are calling. When that person answers, the operator notes the start of the call. This is required for billing purposes.

Person-to-Person without DDD. If you cannot dial the person-to-person call directly, you dial the operator and ask that the call be placed for you. Place the call with the operator in this order: area code, telephone number, and the name of the person with whom you wish to speak. For example, you should say, "I'm making a personal call to 201-781-2932. I would like to speak with Mr. John Heyez." Remain on the telephone until your call is completed or until you receive a report from the operator. If your call cannot be completed at the time it is placed, try it later.

Overseas Telephone Calls

Underseas cables, satellites, and radio now make it possible to telephone 200 countries and areas overseas. Most calls are operator dialed. To place an overseas call or to obtain additional information, refer to the front pages of the local Telephone Directory. You usually dial ''0 Operator.''

Time Factor

It is important that you be aware of the time differences when placing long distance calls. The United States is divided into four standard time zones: Eastern, Central, Mountain, and Pacific. Each zone is one hour earlier than the zone immediately to the east of it. When it is 3 p.m. Eastern Standard Time, it is 2 p.m. in the Central zone, 1 p.m. in the Mountain zone, and noon in the Pacific zone. This means it is noon in New York when it is 9 a.m. in Los Angeles.

You must also be aware of 17 different time zones when placing calls to other countries. When it is 9 a.m. in Chicago and Mexico City (both are in the same time zone), it is noon in Rio De Janeiro, 2 p.m. in London and Lisbon, 4 p.m. in Athens, and midnight in Tokyo.

Illus. 9-5

Map of telephone area codes and time zones.

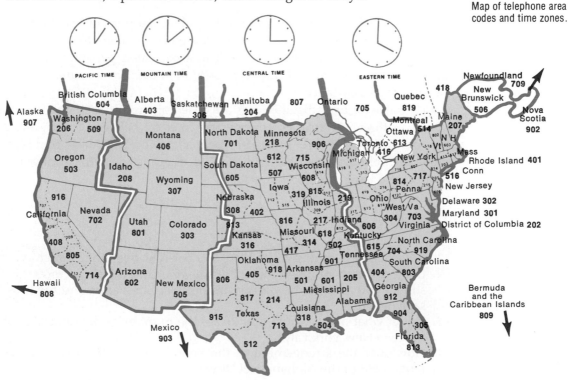

The Cost of Telephone Service

The cost of telephone service is determined by the kinds of equipment the business has and the ways in which the equipment is used.

Cost for Local Calls

Businesses are charged in many different ways for their telephone service. In most communities the business is charged a basic rate for its telephone service, and it then can make as many local calls as it wishes. In a few large cities you are allowed a certain number of calls for a base rate and are charged for each extra call.

Costs for Long-Distance Calls

Charges are made for all out-of-town telephone calls or calls made beyond the local service area. The amount of the charge depends upon the distance, the type of call, the time of day or night that the call is made, and the length of the conversation. As a secretary you should know when it is advisable to make each type of call and the relative costs of the calls.

The cost of a station-to-station call is about 30 percent less than the cost of a person-to-person call because a call can be made to a particular number in much less time than a call to a particular person. Long-distance calls you dial yourself are less costly than calls for which you need the operator's assistance.

The rates for long-distance calls are based on an initial charge for one minute or three minutes. Lower rates are in effect between 5 p.m. and 8 a.m. on weekdays. Lower rates also apply all day on Saturdays, Sundays, and some holidays. You will find the rate schedule in the front pages of your current local telephone directory.

REVIEWING

1. What numbers should you include in a personal telephone directory?
2. If there is no number for a person in the appropriate directory, should you assume the person has no telephone and send the message by letter?
3. Under what name would you locate the number of the central post office in New York City?
4. How does the arrangement of the Yellow Pages differ from the arrangement of the Alphabetical Directory?

5. How does a person-to-person call differ from a station-to-station call?
6. When making a person-to-person call with direct distance dialing, what information will the operator want from you?
7. During what hours in New York are you likely to find offices open in San Francisco?
8. How does the cost of a person-to-person call compare with the cost of a station-to-station call?
9. How many minutes are allowed in the initial cost of a long-distance call?

MAKING JUDGMENTS

1. As soon as Ms. Dannen reached her office at 8:30 one morning, she asked her secretary to call the company's sales manager who was attending a meeting in Los Angeles. The secretary realized that it was only 5:30 in Los Angeles, but she felt that Ms. Dannen must realize this, so she said nothing and placed the call. What do you think of the secretary's judgment?
2. Mrs. Handy asked her secretary to place a call to Chicago for her, and immediately thereafter she walked out of the office. The secretary thought it would take time to get the party in Chicago, so the call was placed, person-to-person. What do you think of the secretary's judgment?

WORKING WITH OTHERS

Miss Thurman is a frugal young woman who is very concerned about the costs of telephone services in her office. She doesn't think so many long distance calls are necessary. As she listened to the conversations she realized that seldom was there any urgency to the matter being discussed and she believed letters would have been satisfactory in most cases. However, she doesn't feel she has any authority to make a comment about the situation.

Then one day, while taking dictation, she was asked the following by her employer: "Are you making long-distance calls to your friends? Here is our long-distance telephone bill from Central Accounting, and I certainly am not using the telephone as much as this bill indicates. This bill shouldn't be so high, I'm sure." What should Miss Thurman say at this time?

REFRESHING LANGUAGE SKILLS

Some of the following words are spelled correctly; others are spelled incorrectly. Type the list, correcting all incorrect words.

1. accummulation
2. alocation
3. amendement
4. appropriate
5. assocciates
6. assurance
7. bankrupcy
8. brusquely
9. colapse
10. convey
11. courteous
12. conversationel
13. dependding
14. dailing
15. economical
16. efficeint
17. equilibruin
18. financial
19. flexable
20. frequently
21. guaranted
22. inflationery
23. improvement
24. monotoneous
25. overseas
26. preferance
27. prequisite
28. procede
29. productivity
30. relatively
31. renewel
32. specific
33. stability
34. techneques
35. temporery
36. transfering
37. unecessery
38. upheaval
39. utelization
40. vocabulery

PERFORMING SECRETARIAL TASKS

1. Assume that you are setting up your personal directory on 3″ × 5″ cards and you want to place at the front of your file a single card with emergency numbers.

   a. Identify the offices you will want on this list.
   b. Locate the numbers.
   c. Type your emergency card.

   (Note: You may assume you are working in an office in the city where you are now a student or in another city for which a telephone directory is available.)

2. If Yellow Pages are available, refer to them to get numbers for the following:

   a. A travel agency that may be able to help plan trips to different countries.
   b. The business office of a local newspaper.
   c. A telephone repair office.
   d. The name of a restaurant that may have a private dining room for a party.
   e. The name of an office supply store.

   Type each of the above on a 3″ × 5″ card. Use a form that is appropriate for frequent use.

Part 3

Special Telephone Equipment

Miss Sheila Wong understands very well the modern telephone equipment used in her company, a large brokerage house that maintains facilities for easy communications across the country. She, along with other secretaries, is regularly introduced to the newest installations so that she has a comprehensive understanding of the services and can, therefore, make proper use of them.

Increasingly, companies are installing telephone systems that allow direct dialing from outside to particular offices as well as direct dialing within the company. Each telephone has a number, which when added to the company prefix, can be dialed from outside.

Example: G. T. Walters & Company   730-2300
           Personnel Office   730-2343

When the company number (730-2300) is dialed, the central switchboard responds. With direct dialing systems, there is generally maintained a central switchboard staff that is much smaller than that required in a non-direct dialing system. The operator in the central office can transfer calls that come in through the main number. It is also possible to dial the personnel office, for example, from outside by dialing 730-2343. A person calling that office from within the company needs to dial 2-3-4-3 only. When someone from within the company wishes to dial a number outside the company, it is necessary to dial for an outside line first, generally 9, and then the full number of the party desired.

Switchboards

Many companies continue to use a private business exchange (PBX) system or switchboard to handle telephone calls. Such a system requires one or more operators who receive calls from outside, place all outgoing calls, and handle calls within offices of the company.

A PBX system has three main functions:

1. To receive incoming calls
2. To place outgoing calls
3. To make calls between offices within the business

Usually companies have special switchboard operators. Sometimes, however, secretaries are asked to fill in at the switchboard at the noon hour or at other times during the day.

Cord Switchboard

Cord switchboards are used in large businesses where many telephone lines are needed. The switchboard operator receives all incoming calls, makes the connection for interoffice calls, and either places outgoing calls or provides the outside line to dial the call.

Cordless Switchboard

There are many kinds of cordless switchboards. Usually companies that do not have a great volume of telephone calls will use a cordless board. A full-time operator is not needed since incoming calls usually can be made to any extension number and employees can place their own outgoing calls. The operator will normally answer only those calls that are of a general nature.

Illus. 9-6.

A cordless switchboard is used by companies that do not handle a great number of telephone calls.

Call Director

The Call Director is a small desk switchboard which permits you to answer many lines from one location. You can also transfer calls and make outside calls. An executive can both make and receive calls without assistance.

Illus. 9-7

In a busy office a Call Director is a time-saver for both secretary and executive.

Courtesy of American Telephone & Telegraph Company

Touch-Tone Telephone

Touch-tone telephones have buttons instead of the rotary dial. Listen for the dial tone; then push the numbered buttons for the telephone number. As each button is pushed you will hear a tone.

Touch-tone calling systems are being installed throughout the country and are available to both home and business users. The advantage of this calling system is the increased speed in dialing. More and more firms also use touch-tone buttons to send data to computers.

Key Telephone

Key telephones have almost completely replaced the two or three individual telephones that were formerly found on the busy executive's desk. A key telephone may have anywhere from one to six keys along the base of the instrument, but the six-key variety is most commonly used.

Arrangement of the Keys

The keys on a six-key telephone should be arranged and labeled in this order:

1. The *hold* key is the key on the left side of the telephone. When it is depressed you will be able to hold a call while you make or answer another call. The first caller is then unable to over-hear your second conversation. The hold key does not remain depressed but returns to normal when you release it. However, if you do not use it before pressing another key to accept a second call, the first call will be cut off.

2. The pick-up keys, Keys 2, 3, 4, 5, and 6, are used to make and receive outside calls. A line will be connected when you de-press the correct key.

Illus. 9-8

A six-key telephone enables a secretary to handle more than one call on a single extension.

Key 1	Key 2	Key 3	Key 4	Key 5	Key 6
Hold	381	382	383	384	385

Operating a Key Telephone

A number of calls can be handled on a push-key telephone at the same time. The steps in the receiving and handling of two incoming calls follow:

1. Depress the *pick-up* key connected with the ringing line before lifting the receiver. (Pick-up keys usually light up when in use.)
2. If a call comes in while you are talking on another line, excuse yourself, depress the *hold* key, then depress the pick-up key connected with the ringing line and answer it.
3. When the second call is completed, return to the first call by depressing the key for that line.

Custom-made arrangements, designed to meet the special needs of a particular office, are found in many offices. For instance, a *signal* key may be used as an internal buzzer to seek the assistance of the secretary.

Speakerphone

You need not pick up the receiver at all when you use the Speakerphone. When a call comes in, you press a button and talk as you would to a visitor in your office. The caller's voice comes from a small loudspeaker on your desk. The volume of the loudspeaker can be adjusted to suit your desire. Your own voice is picked up by a microphone **sensitive** enough to hear your voice anywhere in your office or all the voices in an office conference. You can talk and listen with both hands free to take notes or to look up records. When you want to make a private call, you can pick up the receiver and your Speakerphone automatically becomes a regular telephone again.

sensitive: receiving sounds easily

Automatic Dialing Telephones

There are several automatic dialing telephones commonly used in business offices. Automatic dialing telephones save a great deal of telephoning time, and they eliminate the possibility of dialing a wrong number.

Card Dialer

The Card Dialer uses small plastic cards for numbers you expect to call frequently. They should be coded and placed in the storage area in the unit. To place a call, you insert the proper card in the dial slot, lift the receiver, and when you hear the dial tone, press the start bar. There is no need to dial the number each time you want it.

Illus. 9-9

The Card Dialer is useful for the secretary who places volume calls.

Courtesy of American Telephone & Telegraph Company

Touch-A-Matic

The Touch-A-Matic is a Touch-Tone automatic dialer. It is a combination of a six-button key Touch-Tone telephone and an automatic dialer with a storage for up to 31 telephone numbers.

Illus. 9-10

The Touch-A-Matic tape dialer is another telephone feature that can save valuable executive and secretarial time.

Courtesy of American Telephone & Telegraph Company

Bellboy

The Bell System provides a personal signaling service called the Bellboy. The Bellboy is actually a pocket radio receiver with a 40-mile radius that, by means of a tone signal, alerts the carrier to call the office or home for a message.

> Mrs. Leslie works for a very busy doctor who is often called to the three hospitals in the County. The doctor finds the Bellboy service invaluable. There are times when Mrs. Leslie receives a distressing call about a very ill patient. She is able to signal the physician, who immediately calls her for the message. The physician's schedule can then be changed to go to the site of the emergency.

Mobile Telephone

A mobile telephone provides telephone service in a car or truck. It is possible to receive or place calls in the same way as in an office. This radio telephone service provides a listed number for the car or truck that is part of a nationwide dial network. Sales representatives, doctors, and municipal officials are among the common users of this special telephone service.

REVIEWING

1. What do you believe is a major advantage of a direct dialing system when compared with a private business exchange system?
2. How are calls within a company handled in a direct dialing system?
3. Why is the Touch-Tone telephone considered an improvement to the rotary dial type of telephone?
4. What is the function of the "hold key" on a telephone?
5. What is the usefulness of a Card Dialer?
6. How can a secretary determine if someone is speaking on a line if there are 4 keys on the telephone?
7. What is an advantage of a Speakerphone?
8. What is the key feature of the Touch-A-Matic?
9. What is the usefulness of the Bellboy?
10. What does the mobile telephone provide?

MAKING JUDGMENTS

1. Miss Ellis had a memorandum from Administrative Services inviting her to a presentation and demonstration of new telephone equipment that is to be installed in all the offices, including hers. She thinks: "After all, a telephone is a telephone . . . so what could I learn at the demonstration?" What do you think of her decision not to attend the presentation?
2. Drew was talking with an associate on line 3458 when another line rang. Since he doesn't like to interrupt a conversation, he ignored

the other ring. The associate with whom he was talking heard the ringing and asked: "Drew, don't you want to answer the other line?" Drew said: "Oh, no, if it's an important call, the party can call back later when I'm free." What do you think of Drew's comment?

WORKING WITH OTHERS

Miss Peyton works for a company that has just installed a direct dialing system. The supervisor of telephone services has sent all secretaries a memorandum telling them that cards are available to simplify their notifying regular callers of the new telephone numbers.

Miss Peyton thinks sending cards is an unnecessary task, so she drops the memorandum in her waste basket. She feels that callers will learn that there is a new number when they telephone the office. When they reach the central number, the operator will transfer the call to the appropriate office and also tell each caller what the direct number is.

What do you think of Miss Peyton's decision?

REFRESHING LANGUAGE SKILLS

An adverb, in the same way as an adjective, may be used in comparisons. The positive degree is the simple form in which no comparison is indicated.

Example: Audra reads the mail *rapidly*.

The comparative degree indicates relative positions of two possibilities.

Example: Audra reads the mail *more rapidly* than does Susan.

The superlative degree indicates position relative to more than one other possibility.

Example: Audra reads the mail *most rapidly* of all the correspondence clerks.

On a separate sheet of paper, type the following sentences selecting the appropriate adverb in each instance.

1. The receptionist received the visitor (kindly, more kindly).
2. Gail drives (more slowly, most slowly) than her sister when the streets are wet.
3. Mr. Brown canceled the afternoon's appointments (immediately, most immediately).
4. The flight from Denver arrived in Chicago (sooner, soonest) than was anticipated.
5. Of the three assistants, Sarah viewed the report (more critically, most critically).

6. The sound of the bells resounded (more sharply, sharply) in the nearby courtyard.
7. John listened (attentively, most attentively) to the instructions.
8. This proposal must be considered (critically, most critically) if it is to be an alternative.
9. Pat walked (most rapidly, rapidly) across the plaza when she realized it was already two o'clock.
10. This machine works (fast, faster) than the machine I used last week.

PERFORMING SECRETARIAL TASKS

As a secretary to the managing editor of a small magazine, you have the task of setting up a company directory that will be duplicated on a heavy cardboard in a size appropriate for desk use. You are to type the directory on standard size plain paper in the form that you believe is most useful. Below is a listing of staff, with their titles and telephone extensions.

Norman Krauss, Editor in Chief x5691

Patricia Weaver, Executive Editor x5679

William M. Graves, Managing Editor x5611

John P. Walsh, Art Director x5613

M. Jane Podell, Senior Editor x5651

Joy Flori, Senior Editor x5632

Giovanna Sparci, Senior Editor x5644

Ruth Landman, Senior Editor x5690

Gail Cassel, Associate Editor x5670

Robert S. Stephens, Associate Editor x5678

John M. Hill, Associate Editor x5643

Mortimer S. Allen, Production Editor x5645

Sally T. Fox, Associate Art Director x5622

Lawrence G. Zackman, Assistant Art Director x5688

Jean R. Leeper, Art Assistant x5689

Carol Cohen, Editorial Assistant x5603

William C. Hyde, Editorial Assistant x5647

Davis Roberts, President x5609

John T. Norris, Publisher x5612

David Bowman, Associate Publisher x5673

James W. Rutman, Advertising Sales Director x5637

Marilyn T. Podell, Special Projects Director x5633

4

Special Communications Services

Mr. Gerald Maxon works in a large steel producing company with headquarters in Pittsburgh. However, there are offices of the company in many parts of the world, and it is not uncommon for Gerald, as secretary to one of the executive vice-presidents, to send messages via teletypewriter and telegraph practically every day. He also arranges for conference telephone calls at least twice a month. Gerald finds his job fascinating and thinks the modern means of communication make it possible to maintain a smooth effective tempo in a business office.

Special Long-Distance Calls

There are special long-distance services with which you will want to be familiar. These services include collect calls, credit card calls, conference calls, wide area telephone service, and overseas telephone calls. The front pages of the Telephone Directory will give you instructions for these services.

Collect Calls

If you want the charges reversed — if you want the station or the person you are calling to pay the charges — notify the operator when you place the call. This gives the station or person you are calling an opportunity to accept or refuse the call before the connection is made. The charges may be reversed on both station-to-station and person-to-person calls.

Credit Card Calls

Many business executives have credit cards from the telephone company that allow them to charge long-distance calls. Credit card telephone service is convenient for making long-distance calls when traveling.

If you are asked to place a credit call, you must be sure you have the credit card number. The card number, together with the area code and the telephone number, must be given to the operator who handles your call. The charges for the call will be billed to your executive's account.

Conference Calls

A conference call is a telephone call that enables several persons at different locations to talk to each other at the same time. As many as ten locations can be connected for a conference call. To arrange such a call you should give the operator the names, telephone numbers, and locations of the persons to be connected for the call. Be certain to give the exact time of the scheduled conference.

Wide Area Telephone Service (WATS)

Some of the telephone lines into the company for which you work may be called "WATS" lines, and some phones may be called "WATS" phones. This means that the firm offers its customers, without charge, Wide Area Telephone Service. Customers and potential customers are able to call them without cost. Firms that use this service believe that, if they offer their customers this free service, they will get more business. Many hotel and motel chains use WATS service in order to make it easier for their customers to make room reservations.

The WATS phones or lines are used only for making and receiving station-to-station long-distance calls. To determine whether the company you wish to call offers this service, dial Area Code 800 and then 555-1212. The 800 is the standard area code for all WATS lines, and the 555-1212 is for operator assistance.

Teletypewriter Service

A teletype is a typewriter-like machine which operates on the same principle as a telephone except that the typewritten, rather than the spoken, word is transmitted. Messages typed on the standard typewriter keyboard of a teletypewriter are transmitted and reproduced as they are typed. A message may be reproduced on a single machine or on many machines, depending on the kind of service the business wants.

Teletype equipment is often used for communication between offices of the same firm and between offices of different firms when speed is an important factor and when a written record of the message is desired. There are basically two types of teletype service: teletypewriter exchange service and teletypewriter private line service.

Illus. 9-11

Teletype machines make possible the rapid transmission of written messages.

Courtesy of American Telephone & Telegraph Company

Teletypewriter Exchange Service (TWX)

Teletypewriter exchange service (TWX) operates through a Western Union service. Each subscriber has a teletypewriter number and is furnished with a directory of all teletypewriter subscribers in the United States.

Before sending a message, the teletype operator signals the TWX equipment being called and types the exchange and the number to be reached. After the connection has been made and the called unit is ready to receive, the teletype operator types the message. As the sending operator types the message, the receiving machine instantly copies it. The rates for teletyped messages are much lower than the rates for station-to-station telephone calls.

Teletypewriter Private Line Service (TWPL)

Teletypewriter private line service (TWPL) or leased wire service messages do not go through a central Western Union office. The machines are connected by direct wires. They are used for interoffice communications by firms with a number of branch offices and plants throughout the country.

Data-Phone Service

Data-phone service provides the means for computers to "talk" to computers. Payrolls, inventories, sales figures, and other business data can be transmitted rapidly from one location to another.

Data-phones can handle data prepared on punched cards, paper tape, or magnetic tape. Machine signals from the punched cards or tape are converted into tones that are sent over regular telephone lines. The Data-phone at the receiving offices changes the transmitted tones back into whatever is required: punched cards, paper tape, or magnetic tape.

Data-phone sets are capable of transmitting at speeds of up to 4,500 words per minute. The charge for this service is the same as it would be for a regular long-distance call.

Illus. 9-12

Data-phones transmit large quantities of business data over regular telephone lines.

Courtesy of American Telephone & Telegraph Company

Domestic Telegraph Services

A network of communications services is provided by Western Union for those persons who wish to send messages quickly from one place to another across the United States. Messages can be transmitted to a Western Union office in person or by telephone and from that office it is quickly forwarded to the recipient's town or city.

The Telegram

The telegram is a rapid means of written communication. It can be sent anywhere in the country and is often delivered within a few hours of the time of its transmission. A telegram sent a distance of 1,500 miles will be delivered in less than an hour, while the average business letter requires two to three days for delivery to such a distance.

Selecting the Service

The telegraph company provides two different types of telegrams. Messages are sent and delivered according to the type of telegram used. Some are sent and delivered immediately; others are sent during the night and delivered early during the following morning. The two types are the

1. Full-rate telegram.
2. Overnight telegram.

Full-Rate Telegram. When there is great urgency about the message or when speed in having the message received is important, you will send the full-rate telegram. A full-rate telegram, usually referred to simply as a telegram, is the faster type of telegraph service. The message is sent immediately at any time during the day or night, and, if it is received during business hours, it is telephoned or delivered to the addressee at once. Delivery is made within five hours of receipt of the message. Although it is a more expensive type of service, it is used most frequently by businesses because of the speed with which it is sent and delivered. The basic charge is made for a message of 15 words or less; a small charge is made for each additional word in the message.

Overnight Telegram. An overnight telegram is more economical than a fast full-rate telegram but it is a slower type of telegraph service. It will be accepted by the telegraph office any time up to midnight for delivery the following morning. The basic charge is for a minimum of 100 words. Additional words are charged at the rate of approximately 3 cents a word. It is used mostly for messages of considerable length such as business proposals, progress reports, and detailed instructions.

Preparing a Telegram

You must prepare a telegram carefully if it is to be delivered without delay and if it is to be understood by the one who receives it. The secret of a well-worded telegram is to state your message as clearly and briefly as possible. The suggestions listed below should be kept in mind when preparing a telegram.

Since charges are based on the number of words beyond a minimum, you should secure from your local Western Union office the current basis for charges. You should acquaint yourself with the way in which numbers and special symbols are counted so that you can carefully write your messages to take advantage of the lowest cost available.

The following suggestions will aid you in preparing telegrams:

1. *Use Western Union telegram blanks.* You can obtain pads of telegram blanks free of charge at any Western Union office. However, a telegram may be typed on plain paper.
2. *Type three copies of the telegram.* Ordinarily the original goes to the telegraph company, the second copy to the correspondence file, and the third to the addressee so that the message can be checked to see if it was transmitted correctly.
3. *Type the message with capital and lower case letters.* The message should be double spaced. Do not divide a word at the end of a line.
4. *Indicate whether the message is sent paid, collect, or charge.* If it is to be charged, indicate the account below the heading, CHARGE TO THE ACCOUNT OF.
5. *Indicate the type of service desired.* Type an "X" in the box before Over Night Telegram at the upper right of the blank if you want to send an overnight telegram. Unless the box is checked the message will be sent as a full-rate telegram.
6. *Type the date.*
7. *Type the full name of the addressee.*
8. *Type the complete address and telephone number of the addressee.* Whenever possible give the office number. Spell out such words as *North* and *South*. Do not use suffixes with street numbers (34 not 34th Street).
9. *Write the message clearly and include punctuation.* The use of puncutation marks makes the message clearer. There is no extra charge for them.
10. *Include your address and telephone number.* After the signature type the sender's telephone number, name, and address. This is important if hotel or travel reservations are requested.

Filing a Telegram

A message can be provided to the Western Union office for transmission in any one of the following ways:

1. *Over the Counter*. A prepared message can be taken to a Western Union office or a message can be written at the counter.
2. *Over the Telephone*. A telegram can be filed over the telephone. When a message is telephoned to a Western Union office, care must be taken to be sure that names and unusual words are transmitted accurately. Such words should be spelled out to the operator to avoid confusion.
3. *Tie Line Service*. Tie lines are used when the firm sends and receives a large number of telegrams. A tie line is a system of direct wires between the business and the telegraph company.
4. *Teleprinter Service*. A specially installed printing machine, the teleprinter, permits a secretary to type the message with **simultaneous** recording on a tape or a message form in the telegraph office.

simultaneous:
at the same time

Paying for Service

Telegraph service may be paid for in any one of four ways:

1. *With cash at the time the message is sent*. Cash may be required of an infrequent telegraph user.
2. *Through business charge accounts*. Charge accounts are carried by the telegraph company, particularly for large firms that send many telegrams every business day. These accounts are billed on a monthly basis.
3. *Through telephone subscribers' accounts*. An individual may send a telegram from a telephone or from a Western Union office and have it charged to the individual's telephone bill.
4. *By the person receiving the message*. A message may be sent collect. This means that the receiver of the telegram pays for it upon delivery. To send a telegram collect, type the word *Collect* beneath the heading PD OR COLL. at the top of the blank.

Sending Money

One of the quickest and safest ways for you to send money is to send a telegraphic money order. The amount to be sent is given to the telegraph office together with the name and address of the recipient and any accompanying message. There is a charge for sending the money order and a slight additional charge for any accompanying message. You will be given a receipt for the amount of money sent.

The recipient is notified when the money order arrives. To receive the money, the recipient will have to provide evidence of identity, such as a passport.

Delivering Telegrams

A telegraphic message may be delivered in any one of the following ways:

1. *By messenger*. The message may be delivered in a sealed envelope by a Western Union messenger.
2. *By telephone*. The telephone is often used instead of the messenger for speed and convenience, especially when the addressee is located at a distance from the telegraph office. The Western Union operator will mail a copy of a telephoned message to the addressee upon request at no extra charge.
3. *By teleprinter*. This machine, described under "Filing a Telegram" on page 350, automatically receives and prints the messages.

When the telegraph company fails to deliver a message or makes an error in the transmission of the message, it is liable for damages. The limits of liability are stated on the back of each telegram blank.

liable:
responsible

Using Special Telegram Services

When messages are of a legal nature or of serious concern to both sender and recipient, two additional services are available.

Repeat Back. At the time the message is filed with the telegraph company, you may decide that the message is important enough to need special attention. For example, the message may contain figures, names to be published, or dates. For an additional charge, a message may be repeated back from its destination to the sending office to be checked for possible errors. If errors are discovered, the corrected message is then sent at no additional charge. *Repeat Back* must be typed at the top of the telegraph blank if this additional service is desired.

Report Delivery. Occasionally written evidence of the time of delivery and the address of the person or firm to whom the telegram was delivered is considered necessary. To get this additional information, you must pay the cost of a return telegram and type *Report Delivery* or *Report Delivery and Address* at the top of the telegraph blank. These words of instruction are counted and charged for.

Differences in Time Zones

A branch office in Portland wishes to contact your office in Atlanta. It is 5 p.m. in Portland. It is a long message which will be reported at a branch meeting on the following afternoon. The secretary in Portland wisely sends it as an overnight telegram. You will receive it when you arrive at work the next day. If a telegram is to be sent any great distance east or west, the secretary must be aware of the difference in time between the sending office and the receiving office to decide upon the correct service.

The Mailgram

The Mailgram combines features of a letter and a telegram. This means of communication is available through Western Union, which uses the facilities of the U.S. Postal Service for final delivery.

It is possible to send a mailgram by calling the local Western Union office number, which is a toll-free number, or by Telex or TWX. Each message is routed by wire to the post office nearest the addressee and printed out individually. The Mailgram receives **preferential** treatment and may be delivered the day it is received if the regular mail of that day is not yet delivered. Delivery is guaranteed for the following day in the 48 contiguous states.

preferential: preferred

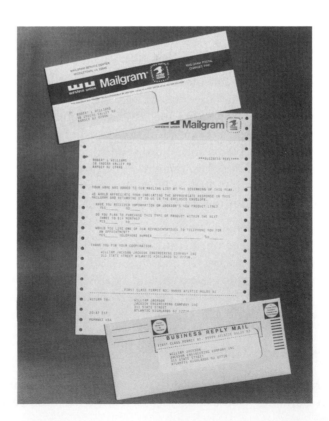

Illus. 9-13

Mailgram

The Mailgram is less expensive than the telegram, yet it provides for speedier delivery than an ordinary letter. It is placed in a distinctive blue and white envelope and is credited with gaining the attention of the recipient more readily than does an ordinary letter. There are special rates for sending the same message to a number of persons.

Mailgrams, in the same way as telegrams, may be sent at any time, day or night, seven days a week.

International Telegraph Service

Many businesses have transactions with foreign companies. International communications are very common. Cablegrams may be sent to foreign countries by means of cables under the seas and by radio.

Kinds of Service

International telegraph service and domestic telegraph service are similar. There are three types of international telegraph service: *Full-Rate* (FR) messages, *Cable Letters* (LT), and *Ship Radiograms.*

Full-Rate Messages (FR). A full-rate message is the fastest and most expensive type of overseas service. It is transmitted and delivered as quickly as possible. It may be written in any language that can be expressed in letters of ordinary type, or it can be written in code. A minimum charge is made for a message of seven words or less.

Cable Letters (LT). A cable letter, or letter telegram, is transmitted during the night and delivered at its destination the following morning. The message must be written in plain language, not code. A minimum charge is made for a message of 22 words or less. The cost is only one half that charged for full-rate messages.

Ship Radiograms. Plain language or code may be used in sending radiograms to and from ships at sea. A minimum charge is made for a message of seven words or less.

Code Messages

Cablegrams and radiograms are more expensive than domestic telegrams. Not only are the rates higher but many more words are counted and charged for. In order to reduce the cost of overseas messages, many firms send their messages in code. One five-letter code word may be used in place of a common phrase that would normally take four or five words. For example, the code word *ODFUD* may be used in place of the statement, "Please cable at once," and only one word would be charged for instead of four.

You count chargeable words for international messages in about the same way that you do for domestic telegrams. The major differences are:

1. Each word in the address is counted and charged for.
2. Code words are counted as five letters to the word.
3. Each punctuation mark is counted as one word.
4. Special symbols, such as ¢, $, and #, must be spelled out because they cannot be transmitted.

Cable Code Addresses

Because each word in the address is counted as a chargeable word, firms that have a great many international messages often use a single code word as the business's cable address. Below are the regular address and the cable code address of Jones Lang Properties in London.

Regular Address	*Cable Code Address*
Jones Lang Properties	Jolpr
43 St. James Street	
London, England U.K.	

There is a small annual charge for registering the cable address with the telegraph company.

Differences in Time

Time differences will determine, in part, the service you choose. If you work in an office that has a heavy volume of overseas communications, be sure you have a chart of the time zones around the world.

REVIEWING

1. How does a collect call differ from a credit card call?
2. Describe a situation where a conference call would be useful.
3. Why do companies use WATS?
4. Describe the nature of teletypewriter services.
5. What does Data-phone service provide?
6. How might you file a telegram?
7. What is the nature of "repeat back" service?
8. How does a Mailgram differ from a letter?
9. What are the basic types of international telegraph service?
10. Why do companies often use a single code as their business cable address?

MAKING JUDGMENTS

1. Mr. Sanders learns that his employer must leave the next day for New York City, and he wants a hotel room in one of the large hotels

there that is part of a chain of hotels. Mr. Sanders wonders what is the best way of making a reservation quickly. What do you think he might do?

2. At the end of the day, Mr. Ruol gives Mr. Pulman a message that he wants sent as quickly as possible to a customer in Boston. Mr. Ruol is in an office in Portland, Oregon. What service would you recommend that Mr. Pulman choose?

WORKING WITH OTHERS

Three secretaries, Bruce, Bette, and Marisa, use the same teletypewriter to transmit messages for their employers. At times there is much activity at the machine, and it is not possible for three secretaries to type messages at the same time. One afternoon, about a half hour before the end of the day, the three arrived at the machine at the same moment. Each felt that his or her message was the most urgent. Finally, Bette said: "This situation is becoming intolerable. My message must get out first; I *must* be first. After all, my employer has the most important position in this office. I think I should always get first place!"

What do you think of Bette's pronouncement? How do you feel the problem of needing to use the machine at the same time might be peacefully resolved?

REFRESHING LANGUAGE SKILLS

A conjunction is a word that connects other words, phrases, or clauses. Conjunctions may be *coordinate* or *subordinate*. In Unit 3, Part 3, coordinate conjunctions were presented. A subordinating conjunction introduces a dependent clause and connects it with the main clause.

Example: *Although* it was late, the secretary stayed to complete the typing of the report.

Type the following sentences and underline the subordinating conjunctions:

1. While the visitor waited, the receptionist telephoned Mr. Taylor's office.
2. There are four clerks here since Ms. Williams said she would need much help.
3. The new machine can be moved to another office if you think it should be.
4. The plans for the meeting were changed since it was clear that the report would not be ready.
5. The dictionary, which Jane is using, belongs to Yvonne.
6. The costs of telephone services are to be allocated to departments as Mr. McCann indicated in this morning's staff meeting.

7. There will be two hours for discussion because there are many questions among the members.
8. The rules that we are to follow will be available in printed form.
9. If you have the March figures, we can compute averages quickly.
10. The group doesn't want to leave before Mr. Wellman finishes his presentation.

PERFORMING SECRETARIAL TASKS

1. Type the dialogue that would take place between you and the operator in the following situations:
   a. Your employer has asked you to place a conference call with John T. Smithers at 202-561-3456 (Washington, D.C.) and Theodore Kreidel at 212-786-5432 (New York City) for 3 o'clock on the following afternoon. You work for Mr. H. I. Isman.
   b. You are asked to place a credit card call for an executive working temporarily in your office. His name is G. R. Toothman and his card number is 567-71891. He wants to call Mr. G. H. Barnes at 412-561-5301 (Pittsburgh)
   c. You are asked to place a collect call for a caller who wants to talk with his home office. He is Mr. F. T. Gordon and he is calling 513-567-5432 (Cincinnati, Ohio) to talk with Mr. H. J. Lawson.
2. Your employer, Mr. E. S. Carson, asks you to send a telegram to Mr. Prentice W. Elsworth telling Mr. Elsworth that he will not be able to see him at 3 on Friday afternoon because his plans have been changed and he won't be getting to Rochester until the following Monday. If Mr. Elsworth is free on Monday afternoon, he should leave a message at the Royal Hotel, indicating the time after 3 when he might meet Mr. Carson. Mr. Elsworth's address is 48 East Race Street, Cincinnati, OH 45202. Prepare the message as clearly and concisely as you can on the blanks provided in the *Supplies Inventory* or on plain paper. Make one carbon copy on a form and one on plain paper.

IMPROVING SECRETARIAL SKILLS (Optional)

1. Visit a local telephone office for a demonstration of the newest equipment available for local business. Note the improvements of such equipment over previous models. After your visit, write a brief report in which you describe the advantages to a company that are to be realized with the use of such equipment.
2. Your employer is concerned that a supply of special letterheads for a forthcoming national conference has not yet been received. He asked you to send a telegram to the firm inquiring about the order. According to your files, your order number was P-4561, and the order was placed six weeks prior to today's date. Delivery was assured for a week ago. On plain paper, prepare the message for the telegram as concisely as possible.

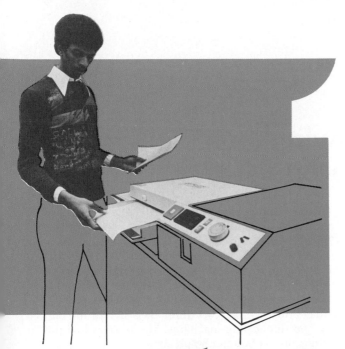

UNIT 10

The Secretary and Reprographics

Part 1. Copying and Reproducing
Part 2. Duplicating

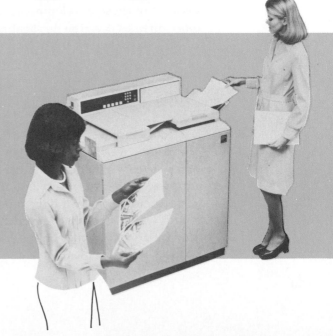

Copying and Reproducing

Last summer Bob Foster worked in the Dietary Department of a university hospital. He passed by a room that was called "Office Services." In this large room there were many different kinds of complicated looking machines. These machines were used to duplicate and copy work for all departments of the hospital. Bob never had the time to find out exactly what the machines were and how they were used.

Yesterday Bob's Office Procedures class started the unit on copying and duplicating machines. The teacher had put up illustrations on the bulletin board similar to the machines that Bob saw in the hospital. Bob is pleased to know that he will now learn all about the machines he saw on his job last summer.

Manufacturers are introducing many new types of duplicating and copying machines. Sometimes these machines are connected to each other so that they are more efficient than if they were used separately. Because of these developments, the word "reprographics" is being used more often to describe duplicating and copying processes.

Copiers

Your employer will often ask you to make copies of business papers. The fastest way to make a copy is by using a copying machine, sometimes called a photocopying machine. Copying machines are used more and more in recent years and are now standard equipment in most offices. Some offices will have more than one copier. There may be a floor model which is used when many copies are needed. In addition, there may be a small model on a desk or table which is more convenient for making several copies quickly.

Features of Copiers

Copiers have the following features:

1. Exact copies of an original can be produced. This can be important when the item to be reproduced is a **complicated** drawing or illustration.

2. They reproduce limited quantities rapidly. It is not necessary to prepare a stencil or a master from the original.

3. They can be used when one or several copies are needed, although combination copier-duplicator equipment will reproduce an unlimited number of copies.

4. They are inexpensive when only a few copies are made from the original.

5. Copiers are easy to operate. You simply set the dial for the number of copies desired and insert the original in the copier. The original is scanned by the machine and copied. The copy of the original then comes out of the machine.

6. Some models prepare transparencies that can be projected on a screen. These may be used by your employer to illustrate important points in a business meeting.

7. Some models prepare offset mats, fluid masters, and stencils which are placed on duplicating machines. Many copies can then be reproduced rapidly.

8. Most copies reproduce only in black. Some copiers will reproduce color but the cost per copy is **considerably** higher.

complicated:
complex, many parts

considerably:
very much

Types of Copiers

Copiers may be the pass-through type or the flatbed type. With the pass-through copier you insert the original in an opening of the copier and rollers pass the original through the copier, ejecting both the original and the copy. With the flat-bed copier, you place the original on a sheet of glass at the top of the copier where it is copied. The flat-bed copier permits you to copy the pages inside a bound book by placing the pages of the book face down on the glass.

Copying machines prepare copies through different processes, but you will probably use the electrostatic and infrared copiers most frequently in the office.

Electrostatic. There are more electrostatic copiers in offices than any other type of copier. Electrostatic copiers produce dark black copy that can look very much like the original. Corrections, if you make them properly on the original, are not **visible** on the copy.

You can make copies at the rate of one a second on some machines. You can also make enlargements or reductions on some models during

visible:
capable of being seen

the copying process. This process is frequently called "Xerox," after the brand name of one of the companies that makes this type of copier.

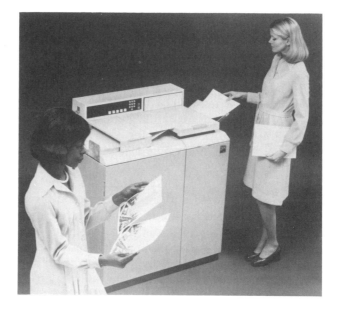

Illus. 10-1

Electrostatic copier

IBM Corporation

Infrared. An infrared copier can make copies in as little as five seconds. With this machine you must use a special paper. The *image* (material to be copied) must contain carbon; for example, lead pencil and print such as in this book. Since ball point pens have no carbon in their ink, images made by them will not reproduce by this process. The infrared copier will not copy all colors, particularly red, blue, and green. You can prepare offset mats and fluid masters on the infrared copier. Sometimes this process is called "Thermofax," after the brand name of a company that makes this type of copier.

Illus. 10-2

Infrared copier

3M Company

Answering Correspondence

Your employer may sometimes use copiers for answering letters, as shown on page 362. Handwritten notations are made on the original letter and it is then copied. The letter is mailed back to the sender, and the copy is placed in the office files. This saves your employer's time since an answer does not have to be dictated. You will not have to type an answer, so your time is saved also. Both the letter and the reply are on one sheet; so filing space is saved.

Since this method of answering letters is somewhat informal, it is used when corresponding with persons who know each other quite well or when the subject of the letter requires an immediate reply.

Collators

Any time you have a duplication job of two pages or more, you must collate it — that is, the pages must be assembled in proper order and fastened into sets. The simplest method of collating is to place the copies of each page in individual stacks on a table, then lift the top page from each stack until a complete set is assembled. This method, however, is both tiring and time-consuming.

Mechanical collating machines are often used in offices where there is a great deal of duplicating and collating. The pages of a duplicated job are stacked in separate compartments of the collator. A rubber-tipped

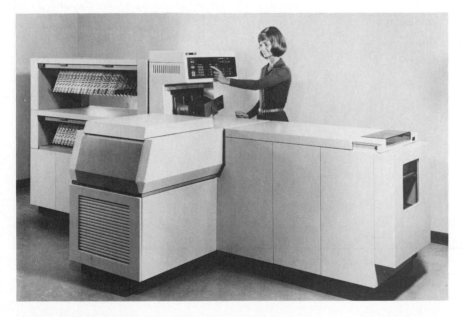

Illus. 10-3

Collator combined with electrostatic copier.

Xerox

metal rod rests on each stack and pushes a page out of each compartment as the foot control is depressed. The pages are gathered in sets and criss-crossed for stapling or binding after each depression of the foot control.

Richardson
ART SUPPLY 1643 DURRETT AVENUE OMAHA, NE 68109

April 20, 19--

Mr. Robert P. Nelson
Hauser Art Center
15 North Park Blvd.
Bismarck, ND 58501

Your Invoice 79822

Dear Bob

Our Receiving Department just informed me that on March 15 we ordered 25 cases of quarter inch paint brushes on our Purchase Order 472566. On March 21 we received your invoice showing that the paint brushes were shipped on March 18.

Sorry Adam, our error; 10 cases placed on back order

We received 15 cases of the paint brushes on March 29. As yet we have not received the other 10 cases. Will you please let me know immediately if the additional paint brushes were placed on back order or if they were shipped separately?

Also, we need about 250 additional advertising sheets on the pastel chalks for distribution to our customers. Bob, will you please let me know by return mail when we can expect this shipment.

Shipping today by separate package

Thanks.

Sincerely

Adam

Adam Tabler
Manager

gh

Illus. 10-4

Copy of letter with notations

Available also are automatic collators that mechanically gather the pages together and bind them into sets. These collators may be attached to some models of copiers.

REVIEWING

1. What is reprographics?
2. What are the features of copiers?
3. What are the advantages of using copiers for answering letters?
4. What should you consider in determining the method of duplicating or copying to use?
5. Define collating.

MAKING JUDGMENTS

1. Your employer has never told you when to make a carbon copy of correspondence and when to type an original and make a copy of it on the copying machine. How do you determine when to use each procedure?
2. Your employer is considering the purchase of a copying machine. What facts can you present to help your employer make the decision as to which type to purchase?

WORKING WITH OTHERS

During the last year, Mr. Bentley, President of Bentley Corporation, was concerned about the huge increase in the number of copies made and the expense of the copying machine. He asked the Administrative Manager, Mr. Mitchell, to find a solution to the problem.

Mr. Mitchell found that employees made more copies than they actually needed, used the copying machine when a duplicator would have been more efficient, and made copies of personal papers.

To overcome the problem, it was decided that everyone, including Mr. Bentley, would bring all work to be copied to you. You would record the date, number of copies, and the person for whom copies were made on a Copy Record sheet. All of the employees, except Mr. Simpson, the vice-president, follow this procedure very well. Mr. Simpson strides past your desk directly to the copying machine and makes his own copies. You notice that sometimes he records the information on the Copy Record sheet and sometimes he does not.

At the end of the month you know that the number of copies on the counter of the machine will not be the same as the number of copies on the Copy Record sheet. What should you do?

REFRESHING LANGUAGE SKILLS

The word *get* is one of the most overworked terms in the English language. In the sentences below, substitute a word that will improve the sentence by eliminating the *get* construction. (Do not rewrite or rephrase the sentence.)

1. *Get* a cup of coffee for me, please.
2. *Get* a reservation for me at the Hilton Hotel in Los Angeles for the night of April 13, late arrival.
3. We ought to *get* a new file cabinet to replace the one in Mr. Jones' office.
4. The Atlanta office *got* the order we sent.
5. The shipment *got* broken when the clerk dropped it on the floor.
6. He *got* control of the company through purchase of the stock.
7. We must *get* to the meeting immediately.
8. He was surprised to learn he had *gotten* the promotion.
9. The Minneapolis office *got* the award for selling the most policies.
10. He *got* the information, but with great difficulty.

PERFORMING SECRETARIAL TASKS

1. Assume that the following material is to be reproduced on an office copier. Type the copy in an attractive style on plain paper. Arrange items in descending order with the largest number of shareholders at the top of the list.

PROFILE OF SHAREHOLDERS

This list shows the types of shareholders who own Investment Fund shares and the amount of their holdings as of June 30, 19--.

Men, 3,972, $39,000,000; Women, 9,672, $114,200,000; Joint Accounts, 9,815, $72,500,000; Custodians for Minors, 2,379, $5,400,000; Individual Fiduciaries, 2,123, $24,300,000; Bank Fiduciaries, 205, $5,600,000; Corporate Retirement Accounts, 430, $7,760,000; Self-Employed Retirement Accounts, 1,152, $7,140,000; Union Welfare Funds, 19, $2,190,000; Municipal and State Welfare Funds, 10, $1,250,000; Charities Including Hospitals and Religious Organizations, 190, $5,300,000; Educational Institutions, 121, $2,200,000; Other, 320, $5,100,000.

Part 2

Duplicating

Miss Sally Ripley works in one of the branch offices of National Real Estate, Inc. Each office prepares a newsletter of its monthly activities for the other offices to read. Miss Ripley is responsible for gathering the articles for the newsletter from the department heads, typing the masters, duplicating, and collating the newsletter. Each newsletter is about ten pages in length, and Miss Ripley must keep one copy for the files.

Recently, the president of NRE sent a memo to all the offices informing them of the increase in paper costs. The employees were told to cut down on their paper usage as much as possible.

To comply with the president's request, Miss Ripley decided to duplicate the newsletter on both sides of the paper; thus, she cut the paper usage in half. Each newsletter now used only five sheets of paper. This also cut down on filing space — only half the space was now needed — and it made the collating much faster.

After seeing Miss Ripley's idea, the other offices soon changed their duplicating procedure, too.

Where there is a need for many copies, duplicating equipment can meet the demand. In many large offices there is a central duplicating department. When you need copies of a business paper, you send detailed instructions to the duplicating department, along with a master or stencil. The central duplicating department then makes the copies. In a small office you may be responsible for the entire procedure. You will have to cut the stencil or master and operate the duplicator. Some duplicators are very simple to operate; others require skilled operators.

Offset Duplicating

If your employer wants a large number of copies of a business paper and the quality of reproduction is very important, the job should be done on an offset duplicator. Copies made on an offset duplicator are of a much finer quality than those made on a stencil or fluid duplicator.

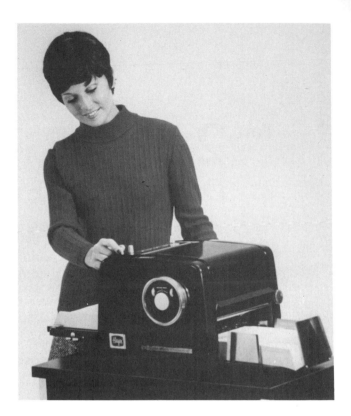

Illus. 10-5

When many copies are needed, the secretary may use a stencil duplicator.

Heyer Inc.

Features of Offset Duplication

Offset duplicating has the following features:

1. Copies of excellent quality are produced. The copy looks like the type on the page of this book.
2. Many thousands of copies can be produced from a master.
3. Cost is moderate for short runs and inexpensive for long runs.
4. Masters are easily prepared, but machine operation is more difficult.
5. Copies can be produced in many colors.
6. Many copies can be produced quickly.
7. Copies can be printed on a variety of weights, sizes, colors, and qualities of paper.
8. Illustrations can be reproduced.

Principles of Offset Duplication

There are three basic methods of preparing masters for use in the offset process.

In the first method, images (typewritten, handwritten, or drawn) are placed directly on the paper master (or "mat") by a special typewriter ribbon, carbon typewriter ribbon, pencil, crayon, or ink. Because of this direct application, the method is called "direct image."

In the second method, an original or layout is prepared on a plain sheet of paper and photographed. The resulting negative is then placed over a **sensitized** master (or "plate") and the plate "exposed."

In the third method, a master is made by **substituting** special offset sensitized master paper for the regular copy paper in some models of copying machines. The original or layout is processed as a regular original would be copied.

The offset process operates on the principle that "grease and water will not mix." The master is placed on the cylinder and comes in contact with rollers that have ink and water on them. Ink **adheres** to grease on the master. Water keeps ink from adhering to other parts of the master.

A reverse-image results when the ink on the master is **deposited** on a large drum of thick rubber called a "blanket." The ink is then transferred from the blanket to the copy paper being fed through the machine when the impression roller presses the copy paper against the rubber blanket.

Types of Offset Duplicators

One of your office tasks will probably be preparing offset masters to be used on one of the three major types of offset duplication models.

Table Model. New table model offset duplicators are easy to operate. The operation has been simplified, and secretaries and other office workers can operate the machine.

Illus. 10-6

Table model offset duplicator

Addressograph Multigraph

Floor Model. These machines are usually in a central duplicating department and are run by skilled operators.

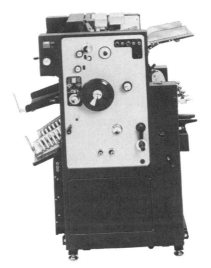

Illus. 10-7

Floor model offset
duplicator

A. B. Dick Company

Continuous Copy Model. With this model, originals are fed into a copier which produces an offset master. The master moves on a belt to a machine that processes the master without being touched by the operator. The master is then automatically attached to the cylinder of the offset duplicator, and many copies can be duplicated very rapidly.

Illus. 10-8

Continuous copy model

Addressograph Multigraph

Preparing Offset Masters

Preparing a paper master with the use of a typewriter or special writing tools is a simple process.

1. *PREPARE TYPEWRITER.* Type faces should be clean and feed rolls and platen free of ink smudges and deposits. You should use typewriter ribbons of carbon plastic, carbon paper, or special grease fabric because they are receptive to the special offset ink. Move the paper bail rollers outside the lined left and right boundary markings on the master to prevent the rollers from smearing the type. Greasy deposits on the master will pick up ink during duplication.
2. *INSERT MASTER.* Insert the master so that the markings on it face you. Guide markings on paper masters include a top edge paper guide, center markings for both 8" and 8 ½" wide paper, and warning numerals for use when nearing the bottom of 11" and 14 " long paper.
3. *TYPE MASTER.* Set the pressure control on an electric typewriter to the lowest position where all characters will print. On a manual typewriter, use an even touch in typing, firm enough to deposit a uniformly dark image. A too heavy touch results in embossing on the **reverse** side of the master. Avoid embossing since the embossed letters may be pressed beyond the reach of the ink roller, resulting in hollow-looking letters.
4. *CORRECTING ERRORS.* A very soft, nongreasy eraser must be used. Special offset erasers produce best results. Erase the image very lightly with a "lifting" motion. It is necessary only to remove the greasy deposit. It is not necessary to remove the ghost image left since this image will not reproduce. The slick finish on the master should not be damaged. Keep the eraser clean by frequently rubbing it on a piece of clean paper.

reverse: opposite

Stencil Duplicating

You are likely to find in an office a stencil or mimeograph duplicator. It is a very dependable and **versatile** machine. You should know how to prepare stencils and how to operate the duplicator.

versatile: able to do many things

Features of Stencil Duplication

The stencil duplicator has the following features:

1. It is used when up to 10,000 copies are needed.
2. Copies are inexpensive for long runs and comparatively expensive for short runs.
3. Compared with the fluid duplicator, copies are of better quality; compared with the offset duplicator, copies are of poorer quality.
4. It is not difficult to cut a stencil or to operate the duplicator.

5. Illustrations can be traced onto the stencil, or manufactured insets may be purchased and used.
6. It can reproduce color.
7. Stencils can be stored and used again when more copies of that item are needed.
8. It prints best on **absorbent**, rough finished paper of any color.

absorbent:
spongelike

Principles of Stencil Duplication

The four elements necessary for the stencil duplication process are stencil, ink, copy paper, and the stencil duplicator. A stencil is prepared by pushing aside the wax coating on the fibrous stencil sheet with a typewriter key or a stylus. This is called *cutting a stencil* or *stencilization*. The stencil sheet is then placed on the stencil duplicator. Duplication occurs when ink flows through the openings made by the typewriter keys and comes in contact with the copy paper being fed through the machine.

By looking at the illustration on page 372, you can see that stencils are designed to aid you in placing properly the material to be duplicated. Following the guidelines and numerals shown will insure attractively positioned copies.

Illus. 10-9

Stencil duplication

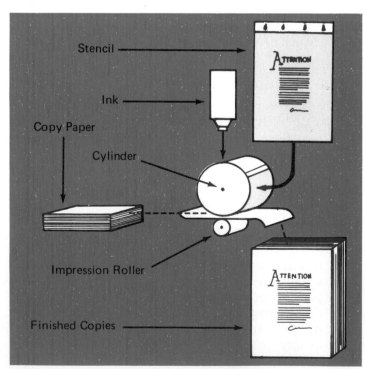

A. B. Dick Company

Preparing a Stencil

These are the steps that you should follow in preparing a stencil:

1. *PREPARE THE GUIDE COPY.* To assure proper positioning on the stencil sheet, you should type the material to be put on the stencil on ordinary typing paper first. (Be sure to use the same size paper that will be used to run off the duplicated copies.) Remember that you must plan to stay within the boundary lines on the stencil sheet. As you gain experience in preparing a stencil, it usually will be unnecessary to prepare a guide copy unless the job is difficult.

2. *PREPARE THE TYPEWRITER.* Shift the ribbon control to "stencil" position. This **disengages** the ribbon and allows the type face to strike the stencil sheet directly. Clean the type. A type face covered with ink deposits from the ribbon can interfere with the "cutting" process. Move the paper bail rollers so that they are just outside the boundary markings on the stencil sheet.

   disengages: disconnects

3. *PREPARE THE STENCIL.* If the stencil has a protective sheet, remove it. Place the guide copy directly beneath the stencil sheet, making sure that the top edge of the guide copy is aligned with the top edge paper guide marking on the stencil sheet. Since you can see through the stencil sheet, it is easy to check the position of the guide copy beneath. Mark the stencil sheet with dots of correction fluid to aid in positioning the material when the stencil sheet is inserted in the typewriter. Remove the guide copy and lay it aside. Place the cellophane film over the stencil sheet and smooth it down. This film helps make the typed copy broader and therefore, bolder. Insert the cushion sheet between the stencil sheet and the backing sheet.

4. *INSERT THE STENCIL IN THE TYPEWRITER.* With the back ing sheet next to the platen, carefully roll the stencil into the typewriter, taking care to avoid wrinkling the stencil sheet. Straighten the stencil in the same manner that you would an ordinary sheet of typing paper. (Disengage the paper release, match top and bottom right corners and top and bottom left corners. Engage the paper release.)

5. *TYPE THE STENCIL.* An electric typewriter automatically gives even pressure needed for typing a stencil. If a manual typewriter is used, however, you will probably obtain better results if you type a little slower than your usual rate. Strike with greater force those letters and special characters that have a large printing surface, such as *M, W, E, A, $, #, &,* and *@* , so that the entire typeface area will cut through the stencil. Strike with less force letters and punctuation marks having

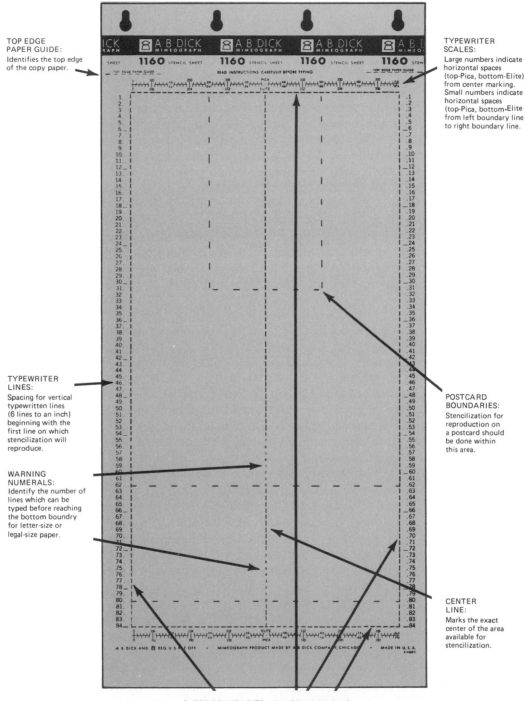

TOP EDGE PAPER GUIDE: Identifies the top edge of the copy paper.

TYPEWRITER SCALES: Large numbers indicate horizontal spaces (top-Pica, bottom-Elite) from center marking. Small numbers indicate horizontal spaces (top-Pica, bottom-Elite from left boundary line to right boundary line.

TYPEWRITER LINES: Spacing for vertical typewritten lines (6 lines to an inch) beginning with the first line on which stencilization will reproduce.

WARNING NUMERALS: Identify the number of lines which can be typed before reaching the bottom boundry for letter-size or legal-size paper.

POSTCARD BOUNDARIES: Stencilization for reproduction on a postcard should be done within this area.

CENTER LINE: Marks the exact center of the area available for stencilization.

OUTER BOUNDARIES: Identify horizontal and vertical area available for stencilization. Nothing typewritten or drawn outside these boundaries will reproduce.

Illus. 10-10
Stencil sheet markings

A. B. Dick Company

Unit 10 • The Secretary and Reprographics

small sharp printing surfaces, such as *c* and *o*, the comma, and the period.

6. *CORRECT ERRORS IMMEDIATELY AFTER THEY ARE MADE.* Lift the paper bail; turn the stencil up several lines so that you may work at the point the typing error occurred. If a film covers the stencil sheet, pull it loose from the top of the stencil assembly and lay it over the front of the typewriter. (The correction must be made on the stencil sheet itself.) Correct the error by lightly rubbing a rounded object such as a paper clip or a glass rod burnisher in a circular motion over the error. This corrects the error by smoothing a small amount of the surrounding stencil coating over the error.

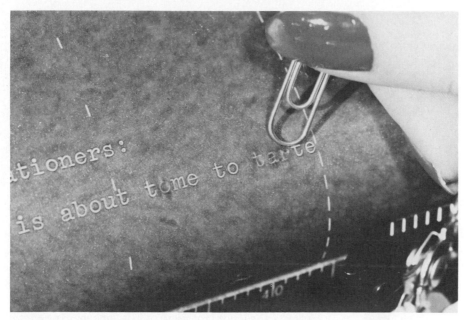

Illus. 10-11

Burnishing to correct an error

A. B. Dick Company

Replace the coating to the area with a single upward stroke for each character from the brush of a bottle of stencil correction fluid, a chemical compound which is about the same as the stencil coating itself. Before applying fluid, be sure to remove the **excess** liquid from the correction brush. Only a thin coating is needed.

excess: extra

Replace the brush quickly; tighten the cap on the bottle. This prevents the fluid from becoming dry and thick. Allow 30 to 60 seconds for the fluid on the correction area to dry.

Roll the stencil back to typing position and then type the correction, using a stroke slightly heavier than normal. A very heavy stroke may cut too deeply into the weakened stencil fiber.

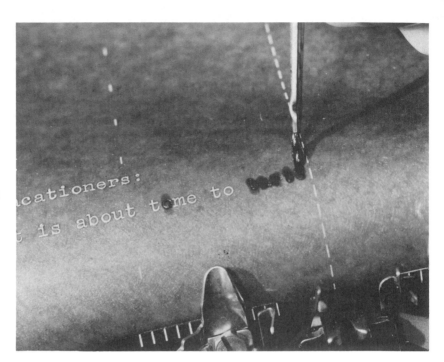

Illus. 10-12

Replace stencil coating with correction fluid.

A. B. Dick Company

7. *PROOFREAD.* Always proofread carefully and make corrections *before* removing the stencil from the typewriter. If you discover an error after the stencil has been removed, you must **realign** the stencil in the typewriter in the same position as when the copy was first typed.

realign:
line up again

Illus. 10-13

A poorly cut stencil

Dear Vacationers:

    It is about time to start planning for
to work Yes the summer recess must end s
letter is to notify you f the preopening

    We have all of you ha e had g d vacat
you will share your experiences wi h us O
seems from the cards we have received that

Illus. 10-14

A correctly cut stencil

Dear Vacationers:

    It is about time to start planning for t
to work. Yes, the summer recess must end so
letter is to notify you of the preopening n

    We hope all of you have had good vacatio
you will share your experiences with us. On
seems from the cards we have received that

A. B. Dick Company

8. *REMOVE THE STENCIL FROM THE TYPEWRITER.* To avoid wrinkling or damaging the stencil sheet, be sure to disengage the paper release before attempting to remove the stencil.

Duplicating

Detailed instructions of operation may be obtained from the manufacturer of the machine. Some machines have step-by-step directions attached to the duplicator. Since these instructions are designed for a particular machine, it is wise to study them carefully before attempting to duplicate copies.

Fluid Duplicating

You will probably find that the fluid duplicating process is the easiest to learn. When many copies are needed but the quality of the copies is not of great importance, you should probably use a fluid duplicator.

Features of Fluid Duplication

Fluid duplicators have the following features:

1. They are used when up to 200 copies are needed; although, with a well-typed master and careful operation of the duplicator, as many as 300 copies can be made from a long-run master.
2. Fluid duplication is probably the least expensive duplicating process for about 10 to 30 copies.
3. It is easy to prepare a master and easy to operate the fluid duplicator.
4. Copies are not as attractive as those produced by most other duplicating methods.
5. Several colors can be duplicated.
6. They print best on smooth-finished, glossy paper of any color.
7. The masters can be saved to be used again.
8. The purple dye from the master soils your hands very easily.
9. Handwriting and artwork can be reproduced easily and quickly.
10. They are used mostly for interoffice communications such as notices of meetings, informal reports, safety rules, and company activities.

Principles of Fluid Duplication

The five elements necessary for fluid duplication are a master sheet, carbon sheet, copy paper, fluid, and the fluid duplicator.

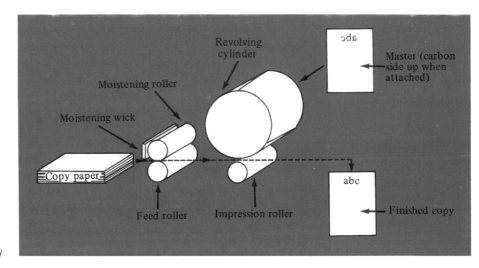

A master sheet is attached over the carbon side of a carbon sheet. Pressure on the face of the master with a typewriter or writing instrument deposits a carbon image on the back of the master sheet in reverse image.

The master sheet is placed on the cylinder of the fluid duplicator. As the cylinder rotates, the master comes in contact with a sheet of copy paper which has been moistened with an alcohol-like fluid as the paper enters the duplicator. The fluid causes of very light coating of carbon to transfer from the master sheet to the copy paper.

Preparing a Master

You will have best results when preparing a typewritten master by following these instructions:

1. *PLAN THE PLACEMENT OF THE COPY ON THE MASTER.* Leave at least one-half inch blank at the top or bottom of the master. This allows space for the master to be clamped onto the cylinder (either end of the master can be attached to the cylinder).
2. *PREPARE THE TYPEWRITER.* Clean the type well, giving extra attention to type faces where ink is likely to **accumulate**, such as *e, a, w, g, o*.

accumulate:
to collect; pile up

3. *INSERT THE SET IN THE TYPEWRITER.* The *set* refers to the sheet of master paper and the sheet of carbon. The open end of the master should be inserted first in the typewriter so that you can make corrections on the master without separating the master sheet from the carbon sheet. As you see it in your typewiter, the white master sheet is nearest you; the carbon is next, carbon side toward you. Be sure to remove the tissue sheet between the master sheet and the carbon sheet before inserting it in the typewriter. If your typewriter does not have a smooth, medium hard platen, place a sheet of heavy paper or **pliant** plastic behind the carbon sheet to serve as a backing sheet.

pliant: flexible; springy

4. *TYPE THE MASTER.* An electric typewriter automatically gives the even pressure needed for typing a master. If a manual typewriter is used, you will probably obtain better results if you type a little slower than your usual rate. The carbon will be deposited on the back of the sheet on which you type, thus making a reverse reading copy.

     Because of the positioning of the materials in the typewriter, typing results in a positive ribbon image on the front of the master sheet which can be proofread.

5. *CORRECT ERRORS.* If corrections are necessary, make them according to the information which follows.

     When you type a master copy, your typing simply puts carbon deposits on the back of the master sheet. When you make an error, you have carbon where you do not want it. Be sure to make the correction on the carbon deposit side of the master sheet.

     To correct an error (as in a misspelled word), you must first eliminate the error. The best procedure for doing this is to lightly scrape off the unwanted carbon deposit with a razor blade or knife, or cover the error with correction tape. After the error has been removed, you are ready to type the correction in its place.

     However, remembering that *fluid carbon paper can be used only once*, and that you have used the carbon at that point where you typed the error, you must provide some new carbon there. So, insert a slip of fresh carbon (cut from the bottom of the carbon sheet or from another carbon sheet) under the master at the point where you must type the correction; after you type the correction, remove the extra carbon slip before going on.

6. *PROOFREAD.* Always proofread and make corrections *before* removing the master from the typewriter.

7. *DISENGAGE THE PAPER RELEASE AND REMOVE THE SET FROM THE TYPEWRITER.* Carefully separate the master sheet from the carbon sheet, and discard the carbon sheet. Cover the carbon side of the master copy with the tissue sheet to protect it until it is attached to the machine for duplicating.

Electronic Stencil or Master Makers

The firm for which you will work may have a machine that will make offset masters, fluid masters, and stencils for you. With these machines, the original copy is wrapped around one cylinder and an offset master, a fluid master, or a stencil is wrapped around another cylinder. When the machine is started, the original copy is exactly reproduced on the master or stencil in a matter of minutes. This process is faster than the manual typing of masters or stencils. Also, it completely eliminates the need for proofreading the master or stencil because an exact copy is produced, whether it is an engineer's drawing, a complicated tabulation, a detailed business form, or an interoffice communication.

Illus. 10-16

Electronic stencil maker

A. B. Dick Company

Selecting a Reprographics Process

Many offices will have a variety of duplicating and copying machines that are used to complete different types of reprographics work. Sometimes you will have to decide which process to use. Most of the time a decision can be made because of your general knowledge of the process as outlined in the following chart:

USING THE PROPER COPYING AND DUPLICATING PROCESS

Process	Used Primarily For
Electrostatic copier	Quick copies; excellent quality; few copies
Infrared copier	Quick copies; few copies; quality not important
Offset duplicator	Many copies; excellent quality
Electrostatic copier/ offset duplicator	Many or few copies; excellent quality
Stencil	Many copies, good quality; moderate cost
Fluid	Low cost

Sometimes it will take more specific information about the reprographic processes to make a decision. You will then analyze the work to be done more precisely and consider the features of each process described on this chart:

FEATURES OF DUPLICATING AND COPYING PROCESSES

Process	Optimum number of copies in relation to cost	Quality of copies	Comparative labor cost to prepare and run	Comparative cost of equipment	Ease of preparing original/ master/ stencil	Ease of operating machine
Electrostatic	1–10 per original	Excellent	Inexpensive	Expensive	Very easy to moderate	Very easy
Infrared	1–10 per original	Fair	Inexpensive	Moderate	Very easy to moderate	Very easy
Electrostatic Copier/Offset Duplicator	10–many thousands	Excellent	Inexpensive	Very expensive	Very easy	Complicated
Offset	10–many thousands	Excellent	Expensive	Expensive	Moderate	Complicated
Fluid	50–300	Fair to poor	Moderate	Inexpensive	Moderate	Easy
Stencil	50–3,000	Good	Moderate	Moderate	Difficult	Moderate

REVIEWING

1. What are the features of offset duplication?
2. Discuss the three methods of preparing masters for the offset.

3. What are some of the features of stencil duplication?
4. Why are guide copies used?
5. Describe how to make corrections on a stencil.
6. Why should you proofread a stencil before you remove it from the typewriter?
7. List four of the most important features of the fluid duplicator.
8. Explain the principles of fluid duplication.
9. Describe how to make a correction on a fluid master.
10. What are the advantages of an electronic stencil or master maker?

MAKING JUDGMENTS

Mr. Patterson, the Office Manager of Brown Manufacturing Company, has asked Mr. Cox to prepare 540 copies of an announcement to be sent to all customers. The important dates and times are to be duplicated with red ink while the rest of the information will be duplicated with black ink. A quarter-page illustration will also be included. Brown Manufacturing Company has fluid, stencil, and offset duplicating equipment. Which duplicating process should Mr. Cox use? Why?

WORKING WITH OTHERS

Dennis works in an office where much duplication is done. Executives who need a master and copies place a rough draft in a basket with instructions on which machine to use and how many copies to make. Any secretary not busy at the moment gets duplication work from the basket and processes it.

Most of the secretaries complain about this duty. They claim that the duplication is too messy; consequently, Dennis does more than his share of the duplication work. How should he handle the situation?

REFRESHING LANGUAGE SKILLS

Type the correct spelling of each of the following words:

1.	accommodate	acommodate	accomodate
2.	accumulate	acumulate	acummulate
3.	recievable	recievible	receivable
4.	receed	recede	resede
5.	annoyance	annoyence	annoiance
6.	cecede	seceed	secede
7.	exceed	excede	exsede
8.	procede	proceed	prosede
9.	responsable	responsible	responseble
10.	comitte	comittee	committee

PERFORMING SECRETARIAL TASKS

The following announcement is to be typed on a stencil, reproduced on a stencil duplicator, and sent to all sales representatives in the company for which you work. Type the stencil. If stencils are not available, type the announcement on plain paper.

June 5, 19--

All Caps → To All Company Sales Representatives:

Because of rising costs, it will be necessary to increase prices on duplicating equipment listed below. Please increase the list

of all
equipment
price by 20% in your copy of the catalog. The new prices are effective on July 1.

Stock Number	Item ——→
S-270	Stencil duplicator
S-120	Stenafax electronic imaging unit
F-470	Fluid duplicator
C-320	Collator, mechanical
O-280	Offset duplicator, table model
O-580	Offset duplicator, floor model
O-341	Offset plate exposure unit

Robert Mathis
Sales Manager

IMPROVING SECRETARIAL SKILLS (Optional)

Your company is considering purchasing a copying machine. Your employer has asked you to prepare a one-page report discussing the advantages of a copying machine and listing any points that should be considered before making such a purchase. Type the report on plain white paper.

UNIT 11

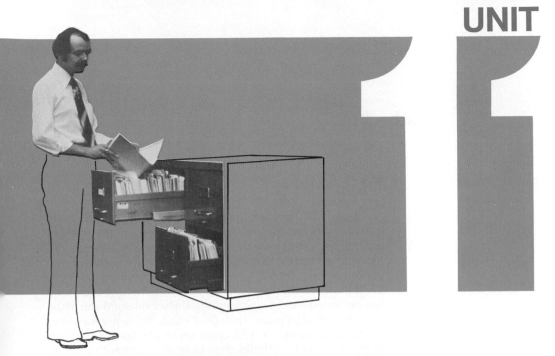

Filing Records

Records Control

As Mr. Ellis and Mr. Spray were having lunch, Mr. Spray told about his embarrassing incident that morning in which a client had called about a loan. After asking his secretary to locate the client's file, Mr. Spray resumed the telephone conversation. When his secretary did not return with the file, he asked what was wrong. It seems that the file could not be found! Mr. Spray apologetically explained the situation and asked to return the client's call. Thirty minutes later the file was found. Mr. Ellis understood Mr. Spray's problem and said, "No one thinks that filing is important until you can't find something. Then it's too late."

Because of one filing error, both the executive and the secretary suffered embarrassment and the possible loss of a client. Most secretaries maintain efficient and orderly filing systems. They know that by following filing rules, they can locate information quickly.

Illus. 11-1

Your employer doesn't expect to have to wait for urgently needed materials that have been filed

Even in our high-speed "computer age," paper work must accompany every business action. A telephone call may require papers to place an order, report on a shipment, or make a payment. The information contained in these papers forms the basis for a variety of decisions and moves the business forward.

All the records which you will file will be important to the continued successful operation of your firm. The records become part of the *memory* of the organization. Not only do the records provide a history of the business, but they also provide a basis for future decisions. In today's business offices, important decisions are based upon available up-to-date information. The risks are too great for an executive's decisions to be based upon guesses or hunches.

The proper care of records is also important to every family. Everyone has records to keep — insurance policies, appliance guarantees, bills, receipts. When personal records are not kept in order, insurance policies soon **lapse** because the **premiums** have not been paid; service cannot be obtained when an appliance breaks down because the guarantee cannot be found; bills become overdue; or an item is charged for twice because the receipt from the first payment cannot be found.

lapse:
discontinue

premium:
amount paid for
insurance

Records Control

Every important record, whether it belongs to the nation's largest business or to its smallest, must be stored where it can be found when needed. The way in which a business keeps track of its records and correspondence is called *records control*. Since business information is created and spread about in so many different ways, a records control program plays an important role in providing the "business intelligence" of any firm for which you may work.

Four main areas with which records control is concerned are:

1. *Files Management* — Developing effective information (or filing) systems, deciding upon the particular type of equipment and supplies needed for each of the systems, and controlling and improving the different systems.
2. *Information Retrieval* — Developing effective and rapid methods of retrieving filed information.
3. *Records Protection* — Deciding what the vital records of a firm are and developing a program for protecting them. (*Vital* records are the important papers of a business that are needed in order to continue operating after a fire or some other disaster.)
4. *Records* **Retention** *and* **Disposition** — Determining which records should be kept, where, and for how long; deciding when and how outdated records should be destroyed.

retention:
keeping

disposition:
disposal

Secretarial Files

As a secretary, you will be responsible for keeping your employer's business records in an orderly fashion. You may be expected to decide which material should be filed, where it should be filed, and how it should be filed. A great deal of mail that is addressed to your employer (advertisements, announcements, and other third-class mail) need not be filed at all. When you are first employed, a brief discussion of the files with your employer should prove helpful in deciding which material should be **discarded** and how the material to be filed should be classified. Most large firms have a records retention schedule which helps classify materials according to their importance. In addition to the regular business files of your office, you may be asked to keep a separate file of your employer's semi-personal correspondence which may include records of civic and professional activities.

discarded:
thrown away

Central Files

Many firms find it economical to maintain a central file of all materials that may be needed by different departments or by the entire organization. It is also possible that a large department within an organization, such as the purchasing department, may centralize its own files.

Because the file clerks in a central file department are well-trained specialists and are properly supervised, faster and better filing service is possible. A central file department eliminates the keeping of duplicate copies of material and makes for more efficient use of filing equipment and filing floor space. The central file department should also serve as an active information file — not just as a place for filing old and unneeded records. As a secretary, you will work with the central file department. You will have to decide which material must be filed in central files and which material should be kept in your own office. You will also have to know how to call for information kept in the central files.

Filing

Filing is a system of arranging and storing business papers in an orderly and efficient manner so that they can be located easily and quickly when they are wanted.

Filing is one of the *most important*, yet one of the most neglected, duties performed by most office workers. Errors in filing may appear to be funny in cartoons, but they are costly and embarrassing in a business office. Your employer doesn't expect to have to wait for filed copies of correspondence or other business papers.

To *find* material efficiently, you must *file* material efficiently. You must follow standard rules and procedures of filing. Not only must you know the rules of filing and apply them but you must also keep your files up to date by setting aside some part of every day to filing. Otherwise you may get so far behind that you will have to search through the files and then rummage through the unfiled material on your desk to produce requested information.

Filing Systems

The most important reason for having a filing system is to locate information quickly. Filing systems should be developed according to the way records are called for, or the way they are used.

Alphabetic Name Files

Since most business records are referred to by the name of a firm, these names determine the type of filing system that will be used. This system of filing, known as an *alphabetic name file*, is the most widely used in business. When you look for a firm name in a telephone directory, you are using this system.

Alphabetic Subject Files

Another filing system found in most business offices is an alphabetic subject file. The Yellow Pages of a telephone directory are arranged in alphabetic subject file order. Under the letter *E* in the Yellow Pages you will find such subject headings as Employment Agencies, Employment Contractors, Employment Counselors, and Employment Service. Most offices have both an alphabetic name file and also an alphabetic subject file. Sometimes these two systems are combined into one file.

Geographic Files

To find the names of customers and prospective customers in the parts of the country in which they are located, some offices maintain geographic files. A geographic file may be set up alphabetically according to the name of a state and then be further subdivided by the sales territories within the state, or by cities, towns, or counties. Many sales offices and magazine publishers use geographic filing systems.

Numeric Files

Since some business papers are identified by number rather than by name, numeric files are frequently used. Life insurance companies file their policies by the policy number. In addition to the main numeric file, an alphabetic file by the names of all policyholders (listing policy numbers as well) is kept on cards or computer tape for fast retrieval.

Chronological Files

Another basic filing system is the chronological file, a file maintained in the order of time according to the year, month, and day. For example, an automobile insurance company would keep a chronological file showing the exact day of the year on which each automobile owner's insurance policy **expires**. This helps the company prepare and mail new policies to owners before their current automobile insurance expires.

To help your employer plan daily activities, you would also use a chronological file. These files are kept for daily appointments, conferences, and other important business engagements. Since it is almost impossible to remember everything that must be done on a given business day, a chronological file should be developed and checked daily so that proper action may be taken at the right time. A desk calendar is one form of chronological filing. Other chronological files of unfinished, **pending**, or follow-up work may be kept in a *tickler file*, a file arranged according to the days of the month.

The Care of Records

For business purposes, records are classified in four general groups: vital, important, useful, and nonessential. All records considered critical to the operation and growth of an organization, such as the financial statements, legal papers, and tax records, are classified as *vital records*. Many business firms that lose their vital records in a fire, flood, or tornado are forced to go out of business. These records should be protected by microfilming them (photographing on a narrow film) and storing the microfilm in a fireproof cabinet, or by photocopying them and filing the copies in another location.

Important records are those which could be replaced, such as personnel records, but only at great expense. These records should also receive protection because of their **confidential** nature. *Useful records*, such as the

expires:
runs out

pending:
undecided

confidential:
secret

records of accounts payable, are those which can be replaced — but with some delay and inconvenience. They should be kept in regular file cabinets.

Non-essential records, such as press releases, are those which soon outlive their usefulness — perhaps some of them should never have been filed in the first place. They should be destroyed to save valuable file space and floor space. Records management experts estimate that approximately 85 percent of all files are never referred to again.

Secretarial Responsibilities

Some of your secretarial time will be taken up by matters related to records control. When you are typing a letter, you are preparing a record (the carbon copy) for the files. When you are reading and deciding what to do with incoming mail, you are preparing materials for filing. The result of almost *all* your secretarial duties will be placed in the files.

To be most effective as an assistant to an executive, you must thoroughly understand business filing and records control procedures.

REVIEWING

1. Why do business firms keep records?
2. Name and describe each of the four main areas of records control and management.
3. What is the purpose of a central filing department?
4. Define the term *filing*.

5. Name five systems of filing.

6. Give an example of each of the following terms: vital record; important record; and useful record.

MAKING JUDGMENTS

Mr. Carson is a secretary for the service manager of an air conditioning company. To avoid filing the documents one at a time, he places them in a tray on his desk. There are very few days when he finds the time to file, so the documents accumulate in the tray day after day. Most of the time, Mr. Carson can remember what is in the tray so he really doesn't worry about filing daily. What do you think of Mr. Carson's daily filing practices?

WORKING WITH OTHERS

Mr. Charles Kelly, a recent high school graduate, accepted his first full-time position as a stenographer in the purchasing department of a very large company. During his first two weeks of work, Mrs. Williams, supervisor of the department, acquainted him with the department's operations. The supervisor also explained the tasks and duties for which Mr. Kelly alone would be responsible.

After introducing Mr. Kelly to his co-workers and giving him an overview of the purchasing department and what it does, Mrs. Williams explained to Mr. Kelly the filing system used in the department. Mr. Kelly was then given several correspondence files to read and prepare for filing. While having lunch with several of the employees in the department, Mr. Kelly commented that he didn't know if he would stay on this job or not. "After all," he said, "I accepted this position to be a stenographer, not a file clerk."

Is Mr. Kelly correct in having doubts about his new position? Could the supervisor have chosen another way of teaching him the basics of his job? How can reading correspondence and preparing it for filing help a new employee?

REFRESHING LANGUAGE SKILLS

On a sheet of paper list the words in Column 1. Then write the number of the correct definition for each word from Column 2. The first one is done for you in the example below.

Example: (a) retrieval   (3) act or process of recovering or finding

Column 1	Column 2
(a) retrieval	(1) a person who engages the professional services of another
(b) manually	(2) arranged by date or by order of occurrence
(c) retention	(3) act or process of recovering or finding
(d) confidential	(4) a maximum measure of content or output
(e) chronological	(5) an orderly collection of papers
(f) file	(6) relating to or involving the hands
(g) document	(7) an official paper that conveys information
(h) capacity	(8) of a secret nature
(i) client	(9) to set down in writing as evidence
(j) record	(10) act of keeping in possession or use

PERFORMING SECRETARIAL TASKS

You have been employed recently by State Bank and Trust, 906 South Main Street, Albany, NY 12210. Because of the many records that must be kept, the bank is quickly running out of filing space, and the current filing system needs updating. Your employer has asked you to be responsible for locating a filing equipment company to obtain information about microfilming equipment and filing efficiency.

Consult the Yellow Pages of your local telephone directory under Filing Equipment, Systems & Supplies, and then compose and type letters to be sent to at least two companies explaining your problem, requesting information, literature, and the assistance of one of their representatives. Use the letterheads in your *Supplies Inventory*, if available, or use plain paper.

Part 2

Filing Rules for Personal Names

During a unit on filing, Mrs. Sands, Vocational Office Education teacher, told the students that in the average company about 1 in 100 documents is misfiled; and each misfile costs about 68 cents. She explained that many factors must be considered when figuring this cost, such as the secretary's time to locate the missing file and the inconvenience to others.

The students were surprised by this information and realized the importance of knowing and applying their filing rules properly. Because the students used filing in some way in their afternoon jobs, one student suggested that they each compile a notebook of the rules of filing learned in class. The notebook would be used as a reference while on the job. The class decided that this would be a very helpful and worthwhile assignment.

A filing system is costly to set up and maintain. Therefore, if the system you use is to be worth this high cost, the information in it must be available when it is needed. This means that business correspondence and other filed materials must be arranged in an exact and established order.

Filing Rules

Every filing method makes use of filing rules. Only if you know the standard rules for filing, and apply them the same way every time, can you find the filed materials quickly when they are needed.

The most widely used method of filing is based on the alphabet; however, because of difficulties involved in deciding how some materials are to be filed, or because of the great volume of materials filed, other filing methods have been developed. These are numeric, geographic, and subject filing.

By following one set of filing rules and recognizing the importance of records control, you will be of great assistance to your employer and play an important role in the successful operation of your office. Since every business, regardless of its size, uses one or more of the alphabetic filing methods, it is important that you learn the rules for alphabetic filing. In certain cases, where more specialized filing procedures are used, you will need on-the-job training to fully understand these methods.

Alphabetic Indexing for Individuals

The first step in filing procedures is *indexing*. When you arrange names for filing purposes, you are indexing. The rules for alphabetic indexing follow.

1. Order of Indexing Units

When you consider the name Walter B. Anderson, each word and each initial or abbreviation is a separate *indexing unit*. Thus, you have three indexing units. The units of an individual's name are considered in this order: (a) last name (surname); (b) first name, initial, or abbreviation; (c) middle name, initial, or abbreviation. Therefore *Anderson* is the first indexing unit, *Walter* is the second, and *B.* is the third. (In the examples below, the names are in alphabetic order.)

Names	INDEX ORDER OF UNITS		
	Unit 1	Unit 2	Unit 3
Walter B. Anderson	Anderson	Walter	B.
Henry David Brown	Brown	Henry	David
Edward J. Cox	Cox	Edward	J.
A. B. Davis	Davis	A.	B.

2. Last Names (Surnames)

When the last names of individuals are different, the alphabetic order is determined by the last names alone. *The letter that determines the order of any two names is the first letter that is different in the two names.* In the following lists the underlined letter in each last name determines the alphabetic order of that name when compared with the preceding name. Note that when one last name (Johns) is the same as the first part of a longer last name (Johnston), the shorter names goes before the longer. This is often called the *nothing before something* rule of filing order.

Last Names	Last Names	Last Names
Hall	Hoffman	Johns
Hill	Hoffmann	Johnston
Hull	Hofmann	Johnstone

3. Last Names Containing Particles or Articles

A last name containing a foreign particle or article (also called prefixes) is considered as one indexing unit. The common prefixes include *D', De, Del, du, Fitz, La, Mac, Mc, O', Van, Von,* and *Von der*. Spacing between the prefix and the rest of the last name, or capitalization of the prefix, makes no difference when indexing.

Names	INDEX ORDER OF UNITS		
	Unit 1	Unit 2	Unit 3
Frances C. D'Arcy	D'Arcy	Frances	C.
Mario L. Del Favero	Del Favero	Mario	L.
Robert J. du Pont	du Pont	Robert	J.
Malcolm Paul MacDonald	MacDonald	Malcolm	Paul
James J. Manning	Manning	James	J.
Helen C. McConnell	McConnell	Helen	C.
Charles H. Mead	Mead	Charles	H.
Mary M. O'Shea	O'Shea	Mary	M.
Henry T. Van Allen	Van Allan	Henry	T.
Carol A. Van Derbeck	Van Derbeck	Carol	A.
Elsie D. von Koch	von Koch	Elsie	D.

4. Compound Last Names

Compound last names such as *Fuller-Smith* and *San Martin* are indexed as two separate units. When the compound name is hyphenated, the hyphen is ignored. In a compound last name such as *St. Claire, St.* is considered to be the first unit (in spelled-out form as *Saint*) and *Claire* the second unit. *St.* is not considered a prefix as in Rule 3 because it is an abbreviation for the word Saint. None of the prefixes under Rule 3 are abbreviations.

INDEX ORDER OF UNITS			
Names	Unit 1	Unit 2	Unit 3
Michael Ross-Harris	Ross(-)	Harris	Michael
Robert J. Ross	Ross	Robert	J.
Allen Ross-Sanders	Ross(-)	Sanders	Allen
George J. Rosse	Rosse	George	J.
Edwin St. Claire	Saint	Claire	Edwin
Gerald St. John	Saint	John	Gerald
John San Martin	San	Martin	John
Marie T. Satone	Satone	Marie	T.
Harold Twigg-Porter	Twigg(-)	Porter	Harold

5. First Names (Given Names)

When the last names are alike, you consider the first names in determining the alphabetic order. When the last names and the first names are both alike, the middle names determine the alphabetic order, as illustrated below.

INDEX ORDER OF UNITS			
Names	Unit 1	Unit 2	Unit 3
William A. Smith	Smith	William	A.
Winifred C. Smith	Smith	Winifred	C.
Walter Clark Thompson	Thompson	Walter	Clark
Walter Crane Thompson	Thompson	Walter	Crane

6. Initials and Abbreviated First or Middle Names

A first initial is considered an indexing unit and goes before all other names that begin with the same letter. An abbreviated first or middle name (*Wm.* for *William*), is usually treated as if it were spelled in full. Nicknames — *Bob* for *Robert*, *Larry* for *Lawrence*, etc. — are indexed as written.

INDEX ORDER OF UNITS			
Names	Unit 1	Unit 2	Unit 3
R. Robert Brogan	Brogan	R.	Robert
Robt. R. Brogan	Brogan	Robert	R.
Robert Richard Brogan	Brogan	Robert	Richard
Sam F. Brogan	Brogan	Sam	F.
Sam'l George Brogan	Brogan	Samuel	George

7. Unusual Names

When you can't decide which part of a name (as in a foreign name) is the last name, the last part of the name as written should be considered the last name. (This type of name is often cross-referenced as explained on page 415.)

INDEX ORDER OF UNITS			
Names	Unit 1	Unit 2	Unit 3
Juan Maria Mallendez	Mallendez	Juan	Maria
Boyd Nelson	Nelson	Boyd	
Arthur Patrick	Patrick	Arthur	
Lee Kuan Yew	Yew	Lee	Kuan
Geza Zsak	Zsak	Geza	

8. Identical Personal Names

When the full names of two or more individuals are exactly the same, the parts of the addresses are used to determine the filing order. The parts of the address are not considered indexing units but *identifying elements*. Identifying elements are another means of determining the alphabetical order when the names are identical.

The order in which the parts of the address are used for determining the alphabetical order is as follows:

    (a) Town or City Name
    (b) State Name
    (c) Street Name
    (d) House Number (in numeric order)

| Names | INDEX ORDER OF UNITS | | | IDENTIFYING ELEMENTS | | | |
	Unit 1	Unit 2	Unit 3	City	State	Street	House Number
Charles G. Grant 145 Beach Street Kingston, IL 60145	Grant	Charles	G.	Kingston	Illinois	Beach	145
Charles G. Grant 204 Pearl Street Kingston, NY 12401	Grant	Charles	G.	Kingston	New York	Pearl	204
Charles G. Grant 177 State Street Kingston, NY 12401	Grant	Charles	G.	Kingston	New York	State	177
Charles G. Grant 350 State Street Kingston, NY 12401	Grant	Charles	G.	Kingston	New York	State	350

9. Seniority in Identical Names

A term indicating **seniority**, such as *Senior* or *Junior*, or *II (Second)* or *III (Third)*, is not considered an indexing unit. The terms are used as identifying elements in determining the alphabetic order for filing purposes. The titles "Junior" (Jr.) and "Senior" (Sr.) are arranged in alphabetical order. The titles "I," "II," and "III" are arranged in numeric order.

seniority: first in age or service

| Names | INDEX ORDER OF UNITS | | IDENTIFYING ELEMENTS |
	Unit 1	Unit 2	Seniority Titles
John Young	Young	John	
John Young, Jr.	Young	John	(Junior)
John Young, Sr.	Young	John	(Senior)
George Zack II	Zack	George	II
George Zack III	Zack	George	III

10. Titles and Degrees

Below are the rules for indexing a personal or professional title (Mayor, Dr., Senator) or a degree (Ph.D., M.D., D.D.).

(a) A personal or professional title or degree is usually not considered in filing, but it is put in parentheses at the end of the name.

(b) When a religious title (Father) or foreign title (King) is followed by a first name only, it is indexed as written.

Names	INDEX ORDER OF UNITS		
	Unit 1	Unit 2	Unit 3
(a) Mayor Alfred G. Brown	Brown	Alfred	G. (Mayor)
Arthur E. Brown, Ph.D	Brown	Arthur	E. (Ph.D)
Raymond C. Ellis, M.D.	Ellis	Raymond	C. (M.D.)
Mme. Jeannine Patou	Patou	Jeannine (Mme.)	
Dr. John J. Ryan	Ryan	John	J. (Dr.)
Lieut. Earl T. Stewart	Stewart	Earl	T. (Lieutenant)
Senator Ralph Williams	Williams	Ralph (Senator)	
(b) Brother Andrew	Brother	Andrew	
Father Henry	Father	Henry	
King George	King	George	
Lady Anabel	Lady	Anabel	
Prince Philip	Prince	Philip	
Princess Margaret	Princess	Margaret	
Sister Mary Martha	Sister	Mary	Martha

11. Names of Married Women

If it is known, the legal name of a married woman should be used rather than her husband's name for filing purposes. When a woman marries, the only part of her husband's name that she legally may assume is his last name. Her legal name then includes either (a) her first name, her maiden last name, and her husband's last name, or (b) her first name, her middle name, and her husband's last name. In other words, a married woman's legal name could be *Mrs. Jane Foster Burke* or *Mrs. Jane Melinda Burke* but not *Mrs. Marvin J. Burke*.

The title *Mrs.* is put in parentheses after the name but *it is not considered in filing*. Her husband's name is given in parentheses below her legal name and is often cross-referenced, as explained on page 416.

	INDEX ORDER OF UNITS		
Names	Unit 1	Unit 2	Unit 3
Mrs. Mary Parker Smith (Mrs. Thomas Smith)	Smith —	Mary	Parker (Mrs.)
Mrs. Herta Marie Zeller Mrs. Theodore Zeller)	Zeller —	Herta	Marie (Mrs.)

REVIEWING

1. Using your own name, illustrate indexing units.
2. What is meant by the *nothing before something* rule?
3. Explain the difference in the filing rules applied to St. John and Von Schmidt.
4. How is an abbreviated name like *Benj.* treated?
5. If two people have the same names (first, middle, and last), what determines the order in which they are filed?
6. Explain identifying elements.
7. How are terms indicating seniority used in determining the order for filing purposes?
8. What is done about the *Dr.* in *Dr. James B. Moulton*?
9. How are religious and foreign titles treated in indexing?
10. Which is the correct legal name: Mrs. Peter G. Bryce or Mrs. Janet Cox Bryce?

MAKING JUDGMENTS

Miss Sanchez, a secretary at a small realty firm, was far behind in her filing. She knew that her employer, Ms. Dunn, would be unhappy if she didn't have all of the filing done by Friday. At 4:15 on Friday, Miss Sanchez realized that she would not be able to finish the filing by herself. In desperation, she called Mr. Carmichael, a stenographer, to help her. Miss Sanchez didn't take time to explain the filing procedure to Mr. Carmichael. She assumed that everybody knew the alphabet. On Monday morning, Ms. Dunn called for the file on Harold De Forrest. Miss Sanchez could not find the file so she asked Mr. Carmichael if he knew where it was. Mr. Carmichael cheerfully replied that he knew exactly where it was. "Look under "F" for Forrest," he said. Miss Sanchez was relieved that she found the file under "F," but was worried about how many more folders were improperly filed. What do you think of Miss Sanchez's decision to have Mr. Carmichael help her. Why?

WORKING WITH OTHERS

Miss Susan Randle is a secretary in a small office. Because she is the only secretary, her files contain such records as personnel information, contracts, and other confidential files. She is often called from her desk to handle other matters. Rather than wait for her return, many of the salespeople in the office get the information they need from her files without her knowledge.

Should her files be open to all employees? If not, how can she correct this situation?

REFRESHING LANGUAGE SKILLS

A good practice is not to use a capital unless a rule exists for its use. Four basic rules of capitalization are:

A. Capitalize the first word of a sentence.
   Example: He asked if we were ready to go.
B. Capitalize the first word of a direct quotation.
   Example: He asked, "Are you ready to go?"
C. Capitalize proper nouns and adjectives.
   Example: Beaumont High School   Mexican music
D. Capitalize the important words of titles
   Example: *A Short History of the English People*

Type the following sentences on a separate sheet of paper using capitalization wherever necessary

1. a condensed version of his new novel will appear in the march issue of the reader's digest.
2. the new york firm had all its vital records on microfilm stored underground at a secret location in altoona, pennsylvania.
3. she asked, "is the albany contract being considered?"
4. when she opened the drawer marked contracts and agreements, she was surprised at the number of files it contained.
5. dean lindsey told his secretary to file the volume entitled an inquiry into the nature of certain nineteenth century pamphlets in the school library.

PERFORMING SECRETARIAL TASKS

In completing the following filing exercise, you will need one hundred 5" x 3" filing cards, or plain paper cut to about that size. (When the dimensions of a card are mentioned, the first number indicates the width of the bottom edge, and the second number indicates the depth. With a 5" by 3" card, the 5" means that the bottom edge is 5 inches wide, and the 3" means that the card is 3 inches in depth. Normally, however, these cards are referred to as 3" by 5" cards.)

(a) Type each of the following names in index form at the upper left side of a card.

(b) Type the number of each name in the upper right corner of the card. (These numbers will aid in checking the answers.)

(c) After the names have been properly indexed and typed, together with their respective numbers, arrange the cards in alphabetic order.

1. Dr. Herman G. Hofmann	35. Rev. Herbert W. Hansen
2. Salvatore L'Abbate	36. Jean Farrell
3. Joan Neuhaus	37. Paul G. Clarke, Jr.
4. Shirley M. Schecter	38. Gina Borsesi
5. Mrs. Adele C. Welsh	39. Thomas L. D. Berg
6. Mrs. Minnie B. Ballau	40. Bette P. Albert, M.D.
7. Ernestine Sanford Black	41. Robert S. Hackett
8. Lloyd C. Carpenter	42. Olga Ellison
9. Thomas F. Corey	43. Mrs. Evelyn E. Clarke
10. David E. Forbes-Watkins	44. Charles W. Borman
11. Harry D. Van Tassell	45. Thomas L. Beckett, Ph.D.
12. Stanley Schechter	46. Norma J. Abrams, D.D.S.
13. Arthur Neuhaus	47. Mrs. Sharon Ennis
14. Hedda M. Kaufmann	48. Edwin C. McDonald, Jr.
15. George A. Heinemann	49. Alfred H. Phillips
16. Vicki Forbes	50. Anthony Y. Szu-Tu
17. Maryalice Corey	51. Julia B. Fee
18. Mrs. Evelyn M. Cannon	52. N. R. Heinneman
19. Sidney J. Bernstein	53. Julia Ann Kaufman
20. Albert Theron Baldwin	54. Kazan Michel
21. Hartzell P. Angell	55. William St. John
22. Mrs. Bessie Berkowitz	56. Seymour C. Ullmann
23. Joseph A. Colombo	57. Patrick Colombo
24. Mrs. Agnes F. Burns	58. George L. Cady
25. John A. Farrell	59. Marvin T. Bernstein
26. Arnold H. Hansen-Sturm	60. Mrs. Lilliam M. Backer
27. Arthur Jacobs	61. David B. Bandler, Jr.
28. Robert L. Michalson	62. Malcolm Carpenter, M.D.
29. Viggo Rambusch	63. Mrs. J. Black
30. W. Anthony Ullman	64. D. Howard Daniels
31. E. Cooper Taylor	65. Maxine Friedman
32. Niccola Rambone	66. Richard D. Hoffman
33. James D. McLean	67. Annette C. LaBelle
34. C. Albert Jacob, Jr.	68. Arabelle J. O'Brien, M.D.

69. Madelyn Russell Segal
70. Harold A. Welch
71. Richard D. Zirker
72. Mrs. Gladys Smythe
73. Jane F. O'Neill
74. R. O. Ennis
75. James A. Gilmartin
76. Thomas M. Ellis
77. Samuel H. Clark
78. Roberta D. Block
79. Edward J. Barrett
80. Albertina V. Marcus
81. Joseph Lloyd Barnett
82. Samuel Clark
83. A. Marvin Gillman, M.D.
84. Leo J. Madden, D.D.S.

85. William M. Smith
86. Gloria Younger
87. Dr. William Bloch
88. A. V. Danielson
89. Harriet A. Humphries
90. Carol Philipps
91. Barbara Ann Barken
92. Wilford R. Young
93. Joseph E. Black
94. Irene T. Siegel
95. James E. Clark, Jr.
96. William J. O'Neil
97. Malcolm MacDonald
98. Harry S. Humphreys
99. Louisa M. Friedmann
100. Henry L. Daniels

Part 3

Filing Rules for Names of Organizations

Because Miss Dolores Rivera was leaving her job at PYCO, Inc., Mr. Singleton hired Mr. Larry Anderson to replace her. One of Miss Rivera's last duties as Mr. Singleton's secretary was to train Mr. Anderson for the responsibilities of the job. Miss Rivera set aside two afternoons to explain the efficient filing system that she had established at the beginning of her job with PYCO. Mr. Anderson was very impressed with the complete and up-to-date system. He began to realize how many companies depended on PYCO for their products. He knew that maintaining this filing system would be a key responsibility and a very satisfying one.

Alphabetic Indexing for Business Firms and Other Organizations

The alphabetic indexing rules presented in Part 2 are also used in filing for business firms and other organizations. Business names, however, can sometimes present special indexing problems. A mastery of the following rules should give you the confidence you need to file materials for other than names of individuals.

12. Business or Firm Names

The following rules determine the indexing of a business or firm name:

(a) As a general rule, the units in a firm name are indexed in the order in which they are written. The word *and* is not considered an indexing unit.

(b) When a firm name includes the full name of a person, the person's last name is considered as the first indexing unit, the first name or initial as the second unit, the middle name or initial as the third; and then the rest of the firm name is considered.

occasionally:
at infrequent times

(c) **Occasionally** a business name contains the name of a person (for example, *Arthur Murray* or *Fanny Farmer*) who is so well known that it would confuse most people if the name were to be transposed. In such cases, the name is indexed as it is popularly known and cross-referenced. (See page 415.)

(d) The name of a hotel or motel is usually indexed in the order in which it is written. However, if the word *Hotel* or *Motel* appears first, it is transposed to allow the most clearly identifying word to become the first indexing unit (for example, *Hotel McKitrick* is indexed as *McKitrick Hotel*).

(e) The names of banks are indexed first by the name of the city in which they are located. (For example, *First National Bank, Cincinnati*, is indexed as *Cincinnati First National Bank*.)

| Names | INDEX ORDER OF UNITS | | | |
	Unit 1	Unit 2	Unit 3	Unit 4
Ames Art Shop	Ames	Art	Shop	
Hotel Ames	Ames	Hotel		
Brown and Son Realty Co.	Brown (and)	Son	Realty	Company
Campbell Soup Company, Inc.	Campbell	Soup	Company	Incorporated
Canton National Bank	Canton	National	Bank	
John Hancock Mutual Life Insurance Co.	John	Hancock	Mutual	Life
John H. Kramer Shoe Repair Shop	Kramer	John	H.	Shoe
Trust Bank, Minneapolis	Minneapolis	Trust	Bank	
Modern Tile Store	Modern	Tile	Store	
Montgomery Ward and Company	Montgomery	Ward (and)	Company	
Motel Morris Gift Shoppe	Morris	Motel	Gift	Shoppe
L. Morrison Moss Supply Co.	Moss	L.	Morrison	Supply
Singer Wallpaper and Paint Company	Singer	Wallpaper (and)	Paint	Company

13. Alphabetic Order

The first units of firm names determine the alphabetic order when those units are different. The second units determine alphabetic order when the first units are alike. The third units determine alphabetic order when the first and second units are alike.

Names	INDEX ORDER OF UNITS			
	Unit 1	Unit 2	Unit 3	Unit 4
Gunn Printing Company	Gunn	Printing	Company	
Gunn Radio Shop	Gunn	Radio	Shop	
Hess Beauty Shoppe	Hess	Beauty	Shoppe	
Mary Hess Beauty Salon	Hess	Mary	Beauty	Salon
Hess Specialty Shop	Hess	Specialty	Shop	
Irwin Shoe Distributors	Irwin	Shoe	Distributors	
Irwin Shoe Mart	Irwin	Shoe	Mart	

14. Articles, Prepositions, and Conjunctions

The articles (*a, an, the*); prepositions (*of, on, for, by*, etc.); and conjunctions (*and, &, or*) are *not* considered as indexing units and should be put in parentheses. However, when a preposition is the first word in a business name (as in *At Home Bakery* or *In Town Motel*), the preposition is treated as the first indexing unit.

Names	INDEX ORDER OF UNITS			
	Unit 1	Unit 2	Unit 3	Unit 4
L. S. Andrews & Co.	Andrews	L.	S. (&)	Company
A Bit of Scotland	Bit (of)	Scotland (A)		
By the Sea Inn	By (the)	Sea	Inn	
First National Bank of Cincinnati	Cincinnati	First	National	Bank (of)
The House of Design	House (of)	Design (The)		
In Between Book Store	In	Between	Book	Store

15. Abbreviations

An abbreviation in a firm name is indexed as if it were spelled in full. Single-letter abbreviations are also indexed as though spelled in full.

Names	INDEX ORDER OF UNITS			
	Unit 1	Unit 2	Unit 3	Unit 4
Amer. Paper Co.	American	Paper	Company	
Ft. Lee Stores, Inc.	Fort	Lee	Stores	Incorporated
Penn Central R.R.	Penn	Central	Railroad	
St. Vincent's Hosp.	Saint	Vincent's	Hospital	
U.S. Rubber Co.	United	States	Rubber	Company
YWCA	Young	Women's	Christian	Association

16. Single Letters

When a firm's name is made up of single letters, each letter is considered as a separate indexing unit. The spacing between the single letters is not considered in indexing. Firm names made up of single letters are filed before words beginning with the same letter because of the *nothing before something* rule.

Names	INDEX ORDER OF UNITS			
	Unit 1	Unit 2	Unit 3	Unit 4
A & A Auto Parts	A (&)	A	Auto	Parts
ABC Printers	A	B	C	Printers
A C Cleaners	A	C	Cleaners	
A–Z Dry Cleaners	A (–)	Z	Dry	Cleaners
Acme Rug Co.	Acme	Rug	Company	
WNBC	W	N	B	C
X-Cel Advertising Service	X (-)	Cel	Advertising	Service

17. Hyphenated Names and Words

(a) Hyphenated firm names are indexed as if they were separate words; thus, they are separate indexing units (for example, *Allis-Chalmers*).

(b) Each part of a hyphenated **coined** word (such as *The Do-It-Yourself Shop*) is considered to be a separate indexing unit.

coined:
made up

(c) A single word written with a hyphen (a word containing a prefix, such as *anti-, co-, inter-, mid-, pan-, trans-, tri-*) is filed as one indexing unit.

| Names | INDEX ORDER OF UNITS | | | |
	Unit 1	Unit 2	Unit 3	Unit 4
(a) McGraw-Edison Company	McGraw(-)	Edison	Company	
Shaw-Walker	Shaw(-)	Walker		
Stokens-Van Buren, Inc.	Stokens(-)	Van Buren	Incorporated	
(b) Bar-B-Q Drive-Inn	Bar(-)	B(-)	Q	Drive(-)
C-Thru Window Company	C(-)	Thru	Window	Company
Econ-O-Me Cleaners	Econ(-)	O(-)	Me	Cleaners
(c) Inter-State Truckers Assoc.	Inter-State	Truckers	Association	
Mid-City Garage	Mid-City	Garage		
Pan-American Insurance Co.	Pan-American	Insurance	Company	

18. Two Words Considered as One

If separate words in a firm's name are often considered or written as one word, these words as a group should be treated as one indexing unit. The use of a hyphen or spacing is of no indexing significance. This rule does away with the separating of similar names in the files. Examples of such words include *airlines, carload, crossroads, downtown, eastside, goodwill, halfway, mainland, railroad, seaboard*, and points of the compass words, such as *northeast, northwest, southeast*, and *southwestern*.

| Names | INDEX ORDER OF UNITS | |
	Unit 1	Unit 2
Down Town Garage	Down Town	Garage
Good Will Agency	Good Will	Agency
The Half-Way Restaurant	Half-Way	Restaurant (The)
Northeastern Airlines	Northeastern	Airlines

19. Titles in Business Names

(a) A title in a *business name* is treated as a separate unit and is indexed in the order in which it is written.

(b) The titles *Mr.* and *Mrs.* are indexed as written *rather than* spelled in full.

Names	INDEX ORDER OF UNITS			
	Unit 1	Unit 2	Unit 3	Unit 4
Dr. Posner Shoe Co., Inc.	Doctor	Posner	Shoe	Company
Madame Adrienne French Cleaners	Madame	Adrienne	French	Cleaners
Mr. Foster's Shops	Mr.	Foster's	Shops	
Sir Michael, Ltd.	Sir	Michael	Limited	

20. Compound Geographic Names

Compound geographic names containing two English words (such as *New York*) are treated as two separate indexing units, but compound names written as one word (such as *Lakewood*) are considered as one indexing unit.

Names	INDEX ORDER OF UNITS			
	Unit 1	Unit 2	Unit 3	Unit 4
Ft. Wayne Finance Co.	Fort	Wayne	Finance	Company
New Jersey Thruway Res't	New	Jersey	Thruway	Restaurant
Newport Knitting Co.	Newport	Knitting	Company	
St. Louis Post Dispatch	Saint	Louis	Post	Dispatch

21. Numbers

A number in a business name is treated as though written in full and is considered one indexing unit (regardless of the length or number of digits). In order to use a smaller number of letters to indicate a number, four-digit numbers are written in hundreds and five-digit numbers are written in thousands. For example, the four-digit number *1,250* would be written *twelve hundred fifty* instead of *one thousand two hundred fifty*. The five-digit number *10,010* would be written *ten thousand ten*.

	INDEX ORDER OF UNITS			
Names	Unit 1	Unit 2	Unit 3	Unit 4
A-1 Envelope Co.	A(-)	One	Envelope	Company
40 Winks Motel	Forty	Winks	Motel	
42nd Street Playhouse	Forty-second	Street	Playhouse	
40,000 Investment Association	Forty Thousand	Investment	Association	
The 400 Cake Shop	Four Hundred	Cake	Shop (The)	
4th Federal Loan Co.	Fourth	Federal	Loan	Company

22. Foreign Names

(a) Each separately written word in a compound foreign name is considered as a separate indexing unit. The words *San* and *Santa* mean *Saint* and are, therefore, indexed separately.

(b) A foreign prefix is combined with the word that follows it and is indexed as one filing unit (as explained in Rule 3, Part 2, page 394).

(c) Unusual foreign names are indexed as written.

	INDEX ORDER OF UNITS			
Names	Unit 1	Unit 2	Unit 3	Unit 4
(a) Mesa Verde Distributors	Mesa	Verde	Distributors	
Puerto Rico Travel Bureau	Puerto	Rico	Travel	Bureau
San Francisco Chronicle	San	Francisco	Chronicle	
Terre Haute City Service	Terre	Haute	City	Service
(b) Du Bois Fence & Garden Co.	Du Bois	Fence (&)	Garden	Company
LaBelle Formal Wear Shops	LaBelle	Formal	Wear	Shops
Las Vegas Convention Bureau	Las Vegas	Convention	Bureau	
Los Angeles Wholesale Institute	Los Angeles	Wholesale	Institute	
(c) Ambulancias Hispano Mexicana	Ambulancias	Hispano	Mexicana	
Iino Kauin Kaisha Imports	Iino	Kauin	Kaisha	Imports
Mohamed Esber, Cia	Mohamed	Esber	Cia	

23. Identical Business Names

(a) Identical names of two or more businesses are arranged in alphabetical order according to the names of the cities in the addresses. The name of the state is disregarded unless the towns have the same name.

(b) If several branches of one business are located in the same city, the names of those branches are arranged alphabetically or numerically by streets. If more than one branch is located on the same street in the same city, the names are arranged according to the numeric order of the building numbers. Names of buildings are not considered unless street names are not given.

| | INDEX ORDER OF UNITS | | | IDENTIFYING ELEMENTS | | | |
Names	Unit 1	Unit 2	Unit 3	City	State	Street	House Number
(a) Office Supplies Company Akron, Ohio	Office	Supplies	Company	Akron	Ohio		
Office Supplies Company Canton, Ohio	Office	Supplies	Company	Canton	Ohio		
Office Supplies Company Lansing, Michigan	Office	Supplies	Company	Lansing	Michigan		
(b) National Food Market 225 Main Street Columbus, Ohio	National	Food	Market	Columbus	Ohio	Main	225
National Food Market 187 Prospect Street Columbus, Ohio	National	Food	Market	Columbus	Ohio	Prospect	187
National Food Market United Building 341 Stone Drive Columbus, Ohio	National	Food	Market	Columbus	Ohio	Stone	341
National Food Market 722 Stone Drive Columbus, Ohio	National	Food	Market	Columbus	Ohio	Stone	722
National Food Market Young Building Columbus, Ohio	National	Food	Market	Columbus	Ohio	Young	

24. Possessives

The *apostrophe s* (*'s*), for the singular possessive, is *not* considered in filing. An *s apostrophe* (*s'*), for the plural possessive, *is* considered as part of the word. Very simply, consider all letters in the indexing unit up to the apostrophe; drop those after it.

Names	INDEX ORDER OF UNITS			
	Unit 1	Unit 2	Unit 3	Unit 4
Brook's Jewelry Store	Brook('s)	Jewelry	Store	
Brooks' Brothers Clothing	Brooks'	Brothers	Clothing	
Paul's Limousine Service	Paul('s)	Limousine	Service	
Pauls' Real Estate Agency	Pauls'	Real	Estate	Agency

25. Churches, Synagogues, and Other Organizations

(a) The name of a church or synagogue is indexed in the order in which it is written unless some other word in the name more clearly identifies the organization.

Names	INDEX ORDER OF UNITS		
	Unit 1	Unit 2	Unit 3
First Baptist Church	Baptist	Church	First
The Chapel at Brown & Vine	Chapel (at)	Brown (&)	Vine (The)
Congregation of Moses	Congregation (of)	Moses	
Trinity Lutheran Church	Lutheran	Church	Trinity
St. Paul's Church	Saint	Paul('s)	Church

(b) The name of a club or any other organization is indexed according to the most clearly identifying unit in its name. For example, the most clearly identifying unit in *The Ancient Order of Mariners* is *Mariners*.

Names	INDEX ORDER OF UNITS		
	Unit 1	Unit 2	Unit 3
Fraternal Order of Eagles	Eagles	Fraternal	Order (of)
Loyal Order of Moose	Moose	Loyal	Order (of)
Retail Store Employees Union	Retail	Store	Employees
Rotary Club	Rotary	Club	

26. Schools

(a) The names of elementary and secondary schools are indexed first according to the name of the city in which the schools are located, and then by the most distinctive word in the name.

Names	INDEX ORDER OF UNITS			
	Unit 1	Unit 2	Unit 3	Unit 4
Indian Prairie School, Kalamazoo, Michigan	Kalamazoo	Indian	Prairie	School
Oakwood Elementary School, Kalamazoo, Michigan	Kalamazoo	Oakwood	Elementary	School
Oakwood Junior High, Kalamazoo, Michigan	Kalamazoo	Oakwood	Junior	High
Pershing School Portage, Michigan	Portage	Pershing	School	

(b) The names of colleges or universities are indexed according to the most clearly identifying word in the name.

Names	INDEX ORDER OF UNITS		
	Unit 1	Unit 2	Unit 3
Albany Business Col.	Albany	Business	College
Indiana Business School	Indiana	Business	School
Iowa State University	Iowa	State	University
University of Iowa	Iowa	University (of)	
Northwestern University	Northwestern	University	
Slippery Rock State College	Slippery	Rock	State
Urbana College	Urbana	College	

27. Newspapers and Magazines

(a) The name of a newspaper is indexed in the order in which it is written unless the city of publication does not appear in its name. In that case, the name of the city is inserted before the name of the newspaper.

	INDEX ORDER OF UNITS			
Names	**Unit 1**	**Unit 2**	**Unit 3**	**Unit 4**
The Canton Herald	Canton	Herald (The)		
The Journal Gazette Ft. Wayne, Indiana	Fort	Wayne	Journal	Gazette (The)
The New York Times	New	York	Times (The)	
The Wall Street Journal, New York, NY	New	York	Wall	Street

(b) The name of a magazine is indexed in the order in which the name is written. (A cross-reference may be made listing the publisher, as described on page 415.)

	INDEX ORDER OF UNITS		
Names	**Unit 1**	**Unit 2**	**Unit 3**
Administrative Management	Administrative	Management	
Harvard Business Review	Harvard	Business	Review
The Office	Office (The)		
Reader's Digest	Reader's	Digest	

28. Federal Government Offices

The names of all federal government agencies and offices are indexed under United States Government. They are indexed as shown at the top of page 414 following the order given below.

(a) United States Government (three indexing units)
(b) Name of the department
(c) Name of the bureau
(d) Name of the division or subdivision
(e) Location of the office
(f) Title of official, if given

District Director
Internal Revenue Service
Indianapolis, Indiana 46204

would be indexed

United States Government
   Treasury (Department of)
   Internal Revenue Service
   Indianapolis
   District Director

(Note: Rule 28 also applies to foreign government offices.)

GOVERNMENT OFFICE	WOULD BE INDEXED
District Director Agricultural Research Service Federal Building Tallahassee, Florida 33602	United States Government 　Agriculture (Department of) 　Agricultural Research Service 　Tallahassee 　District Director
Bureau of International Commerce U.S. Department of Commerce Philadelphia, Pennsylvania 19108	United States Government 　Commerce (Department of) 　International Commerce (Bureau of) 　Philadelphia
Division of Employment Statistics Bureau of Labor Statistics U.S. Department of Labor Cleveland, Ohio 44199	United States Government 　Labor (Department of) 　Labor Statistics (Bureau of) 　Employment Statistics (Division of) 　Cleveland
Customs Service U.S. Department of the Treasury San Francisco, California 94102	United States Government 　Treasury (Department of the) 　Customs Service 　San Francisco
Data Processing Center Veterans Administration St. Paul, Minnesota 55511	United States Government 　Veterans Administration 　Data Processing Center 　St. Paul

29. Other Political Subdivisions

The names of other political subdivisions — state, county, city, or town government — are indexed according to:

(a) Geographic name of the subdivision, such as *New Jersey, State (of); Westchester, County (of);* or *Philadelphia, City (of)*
(b) Name of department, board, or office
(c) Location of the office
(d) Title of the official, if given

Names	INDEX ORDER OF UNITS			
	Unit 1	Unit 2	Unit 3	Unit 4
Police Department 　Alliance, Ohio	Alliance	City (of)	Police	Department
Clinton Co. Park Commission 　Dubuque, Iowa	Clinton	County (of)	Park	Commission
Municipal Public Works Div. 　Lancaster, Pa.	Lancaster	City (of)	Public	Works
State Health Department 　Columbus, Ohio	Ohio	State (of)	Health	Department

30. Subjects

Sometimes it is better to file materials according to subject rather than under the name of the person or business. This is done because the subject may be more important than the name of the person or business. Applications for employment are examples of this type of indexing. The applications are of major importance; the names of the applicants are of secondary importance.

Names	INDEX ORDER OF UNITS			
	Unit 1	Unit 2	Unit 3	Unit 4
C. J. Browning (Advertiser)	Advertisers:	Browning	C.	J.
R. M. Smith (Advertiser)	Advertisers:	Smith	R.	M.
H. L. Kramer (Application)	Applications:	Kramer	H.	L.
Jack Myer (Application)	Applications:	Myer	Jack	
J. Frank Smith (Application)	Applications:	Smith	J.	Frank

Cross-Referencing

What will you do when a letter or other material to be filed could be asked for by more than one name? Examples are firm names that consist of two or more surnames, the names of married women, and the names of magazines. You may look for the name according to an indexing order that is not shown on the piece of correspondence or on the file card. For example, you may remember only the name *Goodman* in the firm name *Bergdorf Goodman*; you may not remember a married woman's legal name — you may remember only that her husband's name is *Thomas Devine*; or you may remember the name of a magazine, *Business Week*, but not the name of the publisher, *McGraw-Hill, Inc.*

In such instances, a cross-reference sheet or card should be filled out and filed under the other title. It should indicate where the material is actually filed. If a photocopying machine is available, it is more efficient to make a photocopy than to fill out a cross-reference sheet. The photocopy should then be filed under the other title.

Although cross-referencing is important for locating filed information quickly, care should be taken in deciding which records really need to be cross-referenced. Too much cross-referencing takes **excessive** time and a lot of space. Too little cross-referencing will cause needless and costly delays in getting important information. A more detailed discussion of cross-referencing is given on page 440.

excessive: too much

Cross-Reference for a Company Known by More than One Name

If the name of a firm is *Rogers-Turner Food Mart*, the original piece of correspondence should be indexed as it is written. You should, however, make a cross-reference card or sheet for the second name in the title. Consequently, if you remember only the second name, *Turner*, you will find on the cross-reference for *Turner* "See Rogers-Turner Food Mart."

Cross-Reference for the Name of a Married Woman

You will file the original piece of correspondence for a married woman under her legal name, that is, her given first name, her maiden last name, and her husband's last name. Her husband's given name might be cross-referenced to find the filed piece of correspondence faster. If the legal name of a married women is *Mrs. Martha Lee Laidly*, this name should be indexed on the original piece of correspondence; and a cross-reference card or sheet based on her husband's name should be prepared.

```
Laidly, Martha Lee (Mrs.)

Mrs. Thomas Q. Laidly
1700 Maple Street
Shaker Heights, OH  44120
```

Illus. 11-3

```
Laidly, Thomas Q. (Mrs.)

See Laidly, Martha Lee (Mrs.)
```

Illus. 11-4

REVIEWING

1. In what order are the units of a business name considered for filing purposes.
2. What is done when units of an individual name are included in a firm name?
3. How are the words *and, of,* and *for* treated in indexing?
4. What rule is used when filing firm names made up of single letters?
5. In a firm name what differences are made in indexing between two words combined with a hyphen and a single word containing a hyphen — for example, Walker-Gordon Mills, Inc., and Mid-Hudson Electric Co.?

6. State simply the rule for indexing possessive words.
7. How would the following be indexed: Federal Reserve Bank, Branch Office, Dallas, Texas?
8. Give examples of subject titles that would be used in preference to the names of the persons or businesses that are concerned.
9. What is a cross-reference card?
10. Give two examples of types of names that are frequently cross-referenced.

MAKING JUDGMENTS

Miss Bradford has been the file clerk for a trucking firm for five years and has become familiar with the names of the regular customers. Wednesday, however, Miss Bradford was sick and at home. Mr. Garvin, her employer, decided to look for a certain file for some customer research he was doing. He remembered a particular Pottery Company that had shipped with them once last year, but had not done so again. Since it had been so long ago, he could not remember the exact name of the pottery company. He was sure the name had a "Hartley" in it somewhere, but when he looked under Hartley in the files, there was no record of a pottery company. Miss Bradford did not have a cross-reference sheet for any of her files, so Mr. Garvin had to wait until Miss Bradford returned to find the file. What do you think of Miss Bradford's decision not to maintain a cross-reference sheet? Why?

WORKING WITH OTHERS

Mrs. Ruth Greene has been with the ABC Printing Company for fifteen years. She developed the filing system for the firm and is now supervisor of the central files. Her filing procedures are used in all the executive offices so that materials sent to the central files can be filed and found quickly.

She has her own ideas about filing rules; for instance, the customer's names beginning with Mac and Mc are placed ahead of all the other names in the M section of the alphabetic filing at the ABC Printing Company.

New employees are confused because the system is so different from the rules of filing they have been taught. They waste much time and energy filing and finding correspondence.

If you were employed as a secretary at the ABC Printing Company, how would you attempt to reconcile the differences between company practice and the filing rules learned in school? Since her system has been in use for 15 years, should you expect Miss Greene to change her filing procedures to fit those taught in school? How would you plan to get along with her?

REFRESHING LANGUAGE SKILLS

On a separate sheet of paper write the plural form of each of the following business words. After you have written the plural forms, check your answers in a dictionary.

1. attorney
2. belief
3. business
4. chief clerk
5. city

6. company
7. delivery
8. prefix
9. salesman
10. secretary

11. series
12. statistic
13. studio
14. trade-in
15. youth

PERFORMING SECRETARIAL TASKS

1. On a separate sheet of paper type each of the following. Underline the first indexing unit and circle the second indexing unit.

(a) R. Harold Dana

(b) The Holden Paper Co.

(c) Hubert Smith-Johnson, Jr.

(d) Woodward & Lothrop Dept. Store

(e) Lois J. McDowell

(f) A to Z Cleaning Service

(g) National Association of Life Underwriters

(h) Trans-Canada Air Lines

(i) Father Francis

(j) North West Wholesale Furriers

(k) Provident Bank & Trust Company of Cleveland

(l) Tommy Tucker's Toys

(m) Mrs. Sally (John) Hanson

(n) Johnson-Hardin Produce Co.

(o) President Walter C. Schott

(p) San Bruno Public Warehouse

(q) Disabled American Veterans

(r) A-1 Window Washers

(s) Attorney Edward K. Wilcox

(t) St. Louis Pharmaceuticals, Inc.

(u) University of Cincinnati

(v) Miss Hall's Preparatory School for Girls

2. Is the order of the names in each of the following pairs correct? Type the pairs of names on a separate sheet of paper. Make any corrections in indexing order that are necessary.

(a) H. M. Jones
   Henry M. Jonas
(b) Carl O'Bannon
   J. B. Obannon
(c) Mrs. Rena Lawson Carter
   Harold Lawson-Carter
(d) Professor Walter Hampton
   Walter Charles Hampton
(e) George Carpenter, II
   George Carpenter, III
(f) Sister Julia
   Julia Sisson
(g) Ernest V. Mellon, Sr.
   Ernest V. Mellon, Jr.
(h) Dr. Frank Tarkington
   Frank D. Tarkington
(i) Francine the Florist
   Francis J. Flanagan
(j) Charlie's Place
   Charlie Porter, Plumbing

3. On a separate sheet of paper, type the order in which the parts of the following titles are considered in indexing.

(a) Board of Education
   Hamilton County, Oregon
(b) Pennsylvania State Department of Highways
(c) Central Trust Company of Delaware
(d) Department of Public Welfare
   City of Minneapolis, Minnesota
(e) Phillips & Woods (Real Estate)
(f) Division of Unemployment Compensation
   Ohio State Employment Service
(g) Oakwood First National Bank
(h) M. Meredith Weatherby (Application for Employment)
(i) The Gerald Gerrard Gun Shop
(j) The War College
   U.S. Department of Defense

4. On a separate sheet of paper, type the following names in correct alphabetic order in each group.

Group 1

(a) H. Duncan McCampbell
(b) Mack Campbell
(c) The Campbell Soup Company
(d) J. C. MacCampbell

Group 2

(a) Martin and Ulberg
(b) Martin C. Ulberg
(c) Martin-Ulberg, Inc.
(d) K. Martin Ulberg, M.D.

Group 3

(a) Rosewood Delicatessen
(b) Olde Rosewood Tea Shoppe
(c) Rose Wood (Mrs.)
(d) Roselawn Public Library

Group 4

(a) Five Corners Car Wash
(b) Five-Corners Creamery
(c) Five O'Clock Shop
(d) 15th Avenue Apartments

Group 5

(a) Williams Ave. Brake Service
(b) William's Coiffures
(c) Williams' Sons (Brokers)
(d) Williamson Heater Company

Group 6

(a) La Maisonette
(b) Lamson & Towers Advertising
(c) Lamps & Lighting, Inc.
(d) Laap Brothers Furniture

Group 7

(a) 2 in 1 Cleaning Service
(b) 22d Street Theater
(c) Twenty-One (Restaurant)
(d) Twosome Dance Club

Group 8

(a) Mrs. J. C. (Barbara) Sands
(b) Santa Barbara Police Dept.
(c) St. Barnaby's Episcopal Church
(d) Barbara St. John

Group 9

(a) Boy Scouts of America
(b) Boy's Scouting Club
(c) Boy and Bike Shop
(d) Boys' and Dads' Day Committee

Group 10

(a) J. & L. Fruit Market
(b) Jones & Laughlin Steel
(c) J. L. Jones, Jr.
(d) J. L. Jones, Sr.

Group 11

(a) Southern Railway
(b) South Boston Beanery
(c) South Western Printing Company
(d) Rachael W. Souther

Group 12

(a) Black's
(b) Blacks'
(c) Blacks' Super Market
(d) S. Black & Son

Group 13

(a) K-P Kitchenware
(b) Kennedy-Porter Fencing
(c) Arthur P. Kennedy
(d) P. Kennedy Arthur

Group 14

(a) St. Joseph's Orphanage
(b) St. Joseph (Missouri) Railroad Depot
(c) San Jose Growers' Assn.
(d) Sanjor Coffee House

5. In completing this exercise you will need 50 5" x 3" file cards or plain paper cut to about that size.

(a) Type each of the following names in index form at the top of a card. Type the number of each name in the upper right corner of the card. (These numbers will aid in checking the answers.) Type the name and address below the indexed name. (See Illustration 11-3 on page 416.)

(b) After the names, numbers, and addresses have been typed, arrange the cards alphabetically.

(c) Save these cards for use in assignments in Unit 12, Parts 1 and 2.

(1) Janitrol Heating Service, 6602 No. Clark St., Chicago, IL 60626.

(2) Kitty's Korner Kitchen, Cooper Bldg., Marietta, OH 45750

(3) Mlle. Jeanette Cecil Sagan, 3 Rue de la Pais, Paris, France

(4) Janitor Supplies & Equipment Co., 9 W. 7th St., Akron, OH 44314

(5) Robert P. Van der Meer, 221 Watervliet St., Detroit, MI 48217

(6) Jerome Labelson, Apt. 3B, 60 Sutton Place, South, New York, NY 10022

(7) Williams & Williams, Tax Consultants, Suite 12, Statler Hotel, Cleveland, OH 44141

(8) Jasper J. Seaman, Chalfonte Hall, Campus Station, Durham, NC 27707

(9) Meyer Lufkin & Son, Commercial Bldg., 9th & Walnut, Omaha, NE 68108

(10) Meyer, E. Jones & Millikin Co., 210 N. State St., Albany, NY 12210

(11) Youman & Garties Mfg. Company, 316 Spring St., N.W., Atlanta, GA 30308

(12) The World-Telegram News, Dallas, TX 78421

(13) Raymond J. Vandermeer, 3920 Alamo Drive, Houston, TX 77007

(14) Mid Way Service Station, Junction State Routes 7 & 9, Osburn, ID 83849

(15) Ringling Bros.-Barnum & Bailey Circus, Winter Headquarters, Sarasota, FL 33580

(16) Greenstone Zion Reform Temple, Cor. Reading & Vine Sts., Greenstone, PA 17227

(17) William's U-Fix-It Shop, 4920 Carthage Rd., Richmond, VA 23223

(18) Seamen's Rest, 60 Front St., New Orleans, LA 70130

(19) Wati Rajhma, Room 2100, United Nations Secretariat, New York, NY 10017

(20) Oberhelman Bros. Flooring, Inc., 420 Vine St., Seattle, WA 98121

(21) P. M. Diners' Clubhouse, 22 Regent St., Louisville, KY 40218

(22) Society for the Sightless, 1404 K St., N.W., Washington, D.C. 20005

(23) J. & K. Seaman Hauling Line, 160 N. First St., Ottumwa, IA 52501

(24) 29th Street Mission, 13 - 29th St., San Francisco, CA 94110

(25) La Belle Dresses, 18 Circle Drive, Rogers, CT 06263

(26) Rosenswig's Dept. Store, 6920 Appletree Rd., Wilmington, DE 19810

(27) R. & L. Benjamin & Company, 14 West Decatur St., Ft. Smith, AR 72901

(28) Mayor Michael O'Berne, City Hall, Baltimore, MD 21202

(29) Midway Seafood House, 3109 Collins Ave., Miami Beach, FL 33839

(30) The Hobby Shop, 1010 Pacific Blvd., Portland, OR 97220

(31) Automatic Food Dispenser Co., 112 High St., Colorado Springs, CO 80904

(32) Automatic Food Dispenser Co., 19th & Ewald Sts., Camden, NJ 08105

(33) Automatic Food Dispenser Co., Camden, OH 45311

(34) Hobby Haven, 730 Pine St., St. Joseph, MO 64504

(35) Lufkin Central Savings Society, 9 So. Main St., Lufkin, TX 75901

(36) Rosen's Fresh Fruit Market, 1403 La Cienega St., Los Angeles, CA 90035

(37) Kitty-Kat Products, Ashport, TN 38003

(38) Long Island Railroad, 69–75 Rockefeller Plaza, New York, NY 10020

(39) Adolph G. Meier Lumber Co., First St. at B. & O. R.R., Columbus, OH 43201

(40) Dr. John W. Barnhart, 22 Medical Arts Bldg., Oak Park, IL 60403

(41) John Barnhart, 635 Capitol Ave., Springfield, IL 62701

(42) Drury Hill Farms, Inc., Box 10, Route 4, Drury, PA 18222

(43) Carthage Mills, Inc., Springvale, GA 31788

(44) Police Department, Drury, PA 18222

(45) P. M. Dinersman Company, 1614 Meridian St., Indianapolis, IN 42625

(46) Branford & Branford Co., Artesia, MS 39736

(47) Branford, Branford and Branford, Attorneys, Union Life Bldg., St. Louis, MO 63155

(48) Olde Seaport Inn, Front and Plum Sts., Alexandria, VA 22313

(49) John L. Barnhart, Sr., 2226 Washington Avenue, Fargo, ND 58102

(50) Ninety and Ninth Apartments, 90th St. at 9th Ave., New York, NY 10024

Part 4

Filing Equipment and Supplies

As Mr. Jackson was searching the files for some information, he noticed how crowded the drawer was. He asked his secretary, "Mr. Crume, must these file drawers be so packed? It's difficult to find anything!"

"I know what you mean, Mr. Jackson, but this is our only filing cabinet. We could certainly use another one."

"Why don't you call some office supply stores, Mr. Crume, and ask their advice on the type of filing equipment best suited for our office. We have sufficient space to add more files. Anything you can do will be appreciated."

Knowing the indexing rules for filing is absolutely necessary. But, unless you have the proper filing equipment and the correct supplies, you will not have an efficient filing system.

Filing Equipment

Good tools are necessary to make your filing system work for you. In large offices filing equipment is usually ordered through the purchasing department, and filing supplies are available from the supply room. However, in a small office you may make recommendations and assist your employer in purchasing equipment and supplies. This will require careful study to make correct decisions. Whether you work in a large office or a small office, you will be more efficient if you are familiar with the kinds of equipment and supplies that you will be using on your job.

Proper storage of records is necessary in all businesses. The *size* of the material to be filed is the first factor to be considered; the *number of items* to be filed each day is second.

Standard filing cabinets are available for storing the two most common sizes of business records: letter size (8½" x 11") and the legal size (8½" x 13" or 8½" x 14"). Other cabinets are designed to **house** card files, visible records, punched cards, computer print-outs, blueprints, and other materials.

house:
store

Vertical Files

The typical pull-out drawer file cabinet — the vertical file — is used in most business offices. Vertical file cabinets are manufactured in two-, three-, four-, and five-drawer units. Two-drawer vertical file cabinets are used beside the desk and contain only the most active records. Three-drawer vertical file cabinets are often referred to as counter-height cabinets. Five-drawer vertical file cabinets are replacing four-drawer units since they occupy the same amount of floor space, but contain an additional drawer.

Office space in the business districts of many large cities is very expensive; so a saving in floor space for filing cabinets can greatly reduce the cost of housing records.

Every business office has correspondence files. Some typical contents of correspondence files include letters, telegrams, teletype messages, purchase orders, invoices, memorandums, reports, and interoffice messages. Reading the correspondence files of any company is the easiest way to learn the nature of its business and the history of its transactions. Active correspondence files are sometimes kept in desk-side, two-drawer files; while files on completed transactions are kept in three-, four-, or five-drawer files in other areas of the office.

Illus. 11-5

Business offices make use of two-drawer, three-drawer, and five-drawer vertical file cabinets.

Ohio National Life Insurance Company

Lateral and Shelf Files

Because of the increasing number of records that must be kept in expensive office space, many organizations are now using lateral and shelf files. The lateral cabinets look like a chest of drawers and are frequently used as area dividers or low partitions. Often the secretary and the executive will have lateral cabinets behind their desks to house the records they refer to constantly such as current correspondence, sales reports, price lists, production reports, trade handbooks, and periodicals of the industry.

In shelf filing, papers are held in folders placed on shelves in an upright position. Some shelf files are built with open shelves (like the shelves for library books); others are equipped with sliding doors to protect the records. Some are equipped with sliding shelves which draw out sidewise, similar in operation to the pull-out drawer in a typical file cabinet.

Units that are seven or eight shelves high provide the maximum amount of filing area for the floor space while keeping the records within reach. While much floor space can be saved by using shelf files, many records management consultants believe that individual records cannot be filed or found as quickly as in vertical files, particularly when sliding doors are used to protect the shelf files. They believe shelf filing is most effective for storing records that are not frequently used.

Illus. 11-6

Shelf files save much floor space.

In addition to the standard filing equipment mentioned here, there is a great deal of specialized filing equipment that is used in microfilming and in the data processing field which is described and illustrated in Part 4 of Unit 12. You will usually be most concerned with vertical files and lateral files since your files should contain only materials that are needed frequently. Shelf files and special files are usually found in the central filing department where less frequently called for materials are stored.

Filing Supplies

Since your secretarial duties will be concerned mostly with alphabetic name and subject files, which are often combined in one system, you should know how to use the tools within a file drawer to their greatest advantage.

Each drawer in a correspondence file contains two different kinds of filing supplies — guides and file folders. The *guides* in an alphabetic correspondence file divide the drawer into alphabetic sections and serve as signposts for quick reference. They also provide support for the folders and their contents.

File folders hold the papers in an upright position in the file drawer. They are made of heavy paper stock and serve as a container to keep papers together.

Guides

Guides are heavy cardboard sheets which are the same size as the folders. Extending over the top of each guide is a tab upon which is marked or printed a notation or title called a *caption*. The caption indicates the alphabetic range of the material filed in folders behind the guide. For example, a guide may carry the caption *A* which would tell the secretary that only material starting with the letter *A* would be found

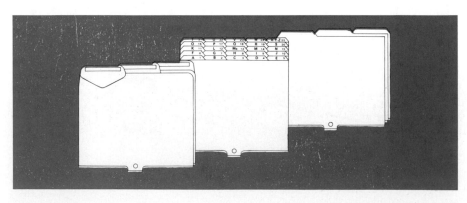

Illus. 11-7

File guides with metal eyelets for projection rods.

between that guide and the next guide. This tab may be part of the guide itself, or it may be an attached metal or plastic tab. Sets of guides may be purchased with printed letters or combinations of letters and numbers that may be used with any standard filing system. Other guide tabs are blank, and the specific captions are made in the user's office.

Guides may be obtained with a small projection that extends below the body of the guide. The projection contains a metal **eyelet** through which a file drawer rod may be run, thus holding the guides in place and preventing the folders from slipping down in the drawer.

Kinds of Guides. Guides are classified as primary or secondary. The *primary guides* indicate the major divisions — alphabetic, numeric, subject, geographic, or chronological — into which the filing system is divided. *Secondary guides* (also called auxiliary or special name guides) are subdivisions of the primary guides and are used to highlight certain types of information, for example, to indicate the placement of special folders (such as those for *Advertising* or *Applications*). They are also used to indicate a section of the file in which many folders with the same first indexing unit are placed. For example, if a file contains many individual folders for the name *Brown* behind the primary guide with the caption *B*, a secondary guide with the caption *Brown* might be placed in the file drawer to aid in finding one of the *Brown* folders.

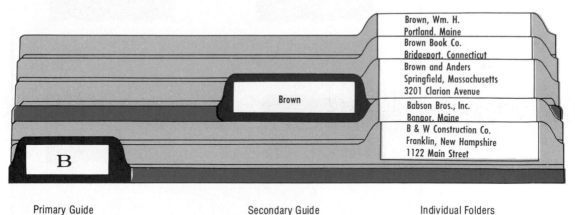

| Primary Guide | Secondary Guide | Individual Folders |

Illus. 11-8

Number of Guides. If individual folders are to be located quickly, not more than ten should be filed behind any one guide. The number of guides, however, will depend on the actual use of the file and the amount of material in each folder. Anywhere from 15 to 25 guides in each file drawer will help in finding and filing in most filing systems.

Folders

A folder is made of a sheet of heavy paper that has been folded once so that the back is about one-half inch higher than the front. Folders are larger than the papers they contain so that they protect them. Two standard folder sizes are *letter size* for papers that are 8½" x 11" and *legal size* for papers that are 8½" x 13" or 8½" x 14".

Folder Cuts. Folders are cut across the top so that the back has a tab that **projects** above the top of the folder. Such tabs bear *captions* that identify the contents of each folder. Tabs vary in width and position. The tabs of a set of folders that are *one-half cut* are half the width of the folder and have only two positions. *One-third cut* folders have three positions, each tab occupying a third of the width of the folder. Another standard tab is *one-fifth cut* which has five positions. Other folders "hang" from a metal frame placed inside the file drawer.

projects:
sticks out

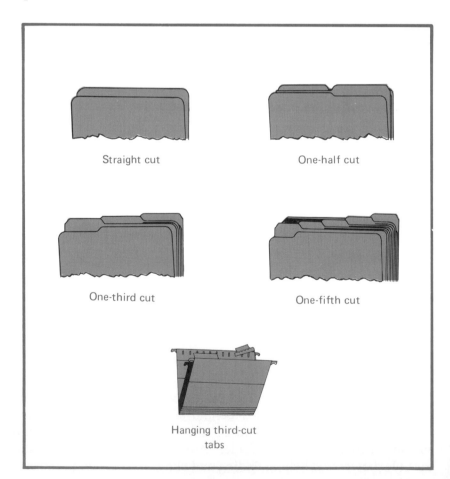

Illus. 11-9

Folder cuts

Straight cut   One-half cut

One-third cut   One-fifth cut

Hanging third-cut
tabs

Miscellaneous Folders. A miscellaneous folder is kept for every alphabetic primary guide. It is called a *miscellaneous* folder because it contains filed material from more than one person or firm. When there are fewer than six pieces of filed material to, from, or about the same person or firm, these documents are placed in a folder bearing the same caption as the primary guide it serves. For example, if the caption on the primary guide is *B*, the caption on the miscellaneous folders will also be *B*.

Individual Folders. When a certain number of pieces of filed material (generally about six) to, from, or about one person or subject have accumulated in the miscellaneous folder, an individual folder for this material is prepared. The caption on the tab of an individual folder identifies the correspondent. Obviously materials will be found faster if they are filed in an individual folder rather than in a miscellaneous folder.

Special Folders. When an organization files a large amount of material that relates to one subject (such as applications for employment), all this related material is placed in a special folder. The caption identifies the subject or the name of the material. A special folder may be prepared to file all identical last names, thus removing them from the miscellaneous folder. For example, all the *Smiths* may be removed from the miscellaneous folder and placed in a special folder, thus permitting material filed under *Smith* to be found faster.

Capacity of Folders. Folders should never become overcrowded. Each separate folder should contain not more than one inch of filed material. Most file folders have *score lines* at the bottom that are used to widen each folder and thereby increase its capacity. When the folder begins to fill up, the first score line is creased; as more pieces of filed material are inserted, the remaining scores are creased.

When a folder can hold no more material it should be subdivided into two or more folders. Subdivisions may be made according to date or by subject:

```
    Jones Company            Jones Company
      January-March            Orders
    Jones Company            Jones Company
      April-June               Receipts
```

A subdivided folder should be properly identified. *Folder 1* or *Folder 2* does not indicate what is in the folder.

Miscellaneous folders should be examined often so that individual and special folders may be prepared to expand the filing system logically.

Labels

There are two principal kinds of labels for filing — folder labels and file drawer labels.

Folder Labels. Folder labels come in a variety of colors. Each company has its own system of identifying file folders by the use of color. The use of color coding in filing is a great help in locating particular files in a matter of seconds and thus helps in keeping costs under control.

The captions on folder labels should be typewritten. It is better if they are typewritten because they can be read more easily.

Consistency in typing captions on labels is important. The captions should always be typed in exact indexing order (*Brown John A* — not *John A. Brown*). Punctuation other than a hyphen or dash is usually omitted. In order to insure uniformity in the files you should type the first letter in the caption at the same point on each label, usually two spaces from the left edge. Type the name on the label so that after the labels have been attached to the folders, the names will appear at the top edge of each tab. For ease in reading, upper and lower case letters should be used. In a subject file, however, the caption of the main subject is sometimes typed in all capital letters to make it stand out. The subdivision file labels are then typed in upper and lower case.

Labels must be kept in good condition and must be replaced when torn or difficult to read. Hard-to-read or torn labels tend to delay the filing and finding of materials.

consistency: following same pattern

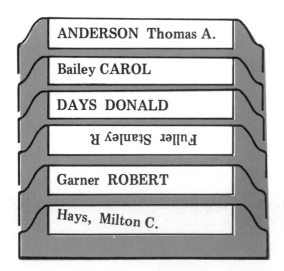 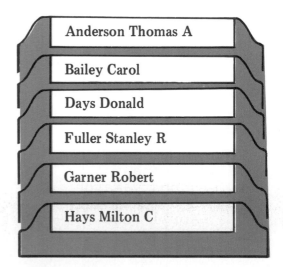

Illus. 11-10 The captions at the left are inconsistent in their punctuation, capitalization, and placement. Captions may be typed in all capital letters or as shown at the right.

Drawer Labels. Drawer labels are used to identify the contents of each file drawer. To locate filed material quickly, the labels must be specific, easily read, and up to date. The information should appear on the drawer as illustrated below.

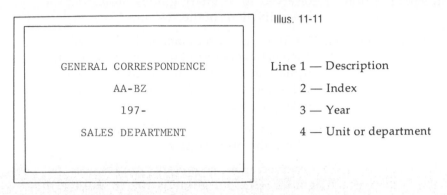

Illus. 11-11

GENERAL CORRESPONDENCE

AA–BZ

197–

SALES DEPARTMENT

Line 1 — Description

2 — Index

3 — Year

4 — Unit or department

When the contents of a cabinet are changed in any way, the drawer label must be corrected immediately.

Positions of Guides and Folders

Since the tabs on guides and folders take up only part of the horizontal edge from which they extend, they may appear in several positions. In any filing system, the tabs in each position should be of the same width. Specific positions should be reserved for each type of guide and

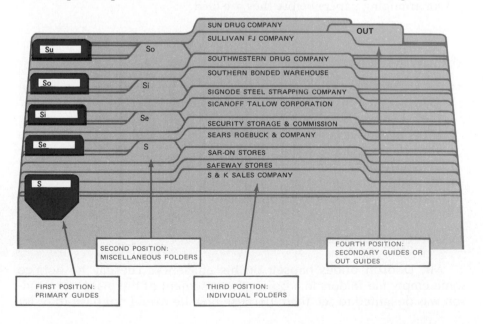

Illus. 11-12

folder. When guide positions are made with regard to the position of the folders, the filing system becomes well organized. An example of this is an alphabetic system in which four filing positions are used.

1. First position: Reserved for primary guides indicating the major divisions of the system.

2. Second position: Reserved for miscellaneous folders. Miscellaneous folders carry the same caption as the primary guides and are placed at the end of each category, *immediately in front of the next primary guide.*

3. Third position: Reserved for individual folders filed directly behind the primary guides.

4. Fourth position: Reserved for secondary guides or out guides. (An out guide is put in the file to indicate that a folder has been borrowed.)

Filing Accessories

accessories:
extra, but not
essential items

In addition to filing cabinets, guides, and folders, there are many accessories that will make your filing job easier. Some of these are a table or desk to be used when arranging material for the files, file boxes or baskets into which material is placed, and a sorter, illustrated on page 443 for arranging papers before they are filed.

REVIEWING

1. Why would a five-drawer vertical file be preferred to a four-drawer file?
2. What is a miscellaneous folder, and where is it placed in relation to the primary guide and the other folders?
3. When should an individual folder be prepared?
4. What information should a drawer label contain?
5. What is the purpose of an out guide?

MAKING JUDGMENTS

Mr. Dodson prides himself on his efficiency. Tuesday he noticed some empty file folders in a box in the basement of the plant. Mr. Dodson was delighted to see them because now he would not have to order more file folders. Using the folders in the basement, he would save money by not having to order more folders and would save time by not having to wait for the order to come in. He brought the folders from the basement upstairs to his office, but noticed that the folders from the basement were thinner and shorter than the folders now in his cabinet. Mr. Dodson didn't think it mattered that much. Thursday, Miss Mayes, Mr. Dodson's employer, asked him to find a file while she was on "hold" with a long distance call. Mr. Dodson searched every file drawer for the folder. He couldn't find it! After Miss Mayes hung up, she came out to see why Mr. Dodson could not find the folder. Just then Mr. Dodson saw that the folder had slipped down underneath several other folders and could not be seen. What do you think of Mr. Dodson's decision to use the folders from the basement even though they were thinner and shorter? Why?

WORKING WITH OTHERS

Scott Thomas has worked in the office of the Top Name Music Company for three months. The company has six employees.

When Scott was hired, Mr. Davidson, the owner of the company, asked him to "be generally in charge of the files." Mr. Davidson explained that while everyone will need to use the files, he is asking Scott to be responsible for such things as "keeping the files neat and making sure that all of the papers are in the proper order." Mr. Davidson said that "all of the employees will help you in this job."

That sounded all right when Mr. Davidson explained the responsibility to Scott, but it's not working out that way. For example, some employees remove folders from the file cabinets and do not return them for several weeks. When employees cannot find a folder in the files, they ask Scott where it is. Also, since the employees know that Scott is responsible for keeping the files neat, some of them will open the file drawer and simply place a folder on top of the other folders instead of inserting it back in its proper place between the other folders.

Scott knows that the files are not neat, and he is sure that Mr. Davidson also knows this, but just doesn't say anything to Scott. Scott hasn't tried to get the other employees to improve their filing habits, because they are all older than Scott.

This situation is beginning to bother Scott, and he is worrying. He knows he is expected to do a good job, but, yet, he doesn't seem to be able to do what is expected of him. What should he do?

REFRESHING LANGUAGE SKILLS

Ten of the following words are misspelled. Type the entire list giving the correct spelling of each.

1. accessories	11. guarentees
2. appostrophie	12. initial
3. asist	13. miscellaneous
4. chronalogical	14. partition
5. consistency	15. possessive
6. correspondance	16. reciepts
7. efficiency	17. refered
8. equitment	18. retrieval
9. facilitate	19. similiar
10. foreign	20. sirname

PERFORMING SECRETARIAL TASKS

List five or more places where your name is on file indicating in each instance just how it is filed. For example, list how your name is filed for Social Security purposes, for school records, for life insurance, for a charge account, for a driver's license, for a public library card, in a telephone directory.

IMPROVING SECRETARIAL SKILLS (Optional)

You work for a national insurance company. Records of policyholders are placed in an alphabetic file and also in a chronological file set up according to the dates the policies are accepted. The names, addresses, and policy dates listed below are for policyholders whose records must be added to each filing system. Type the information on a 5" × 3" card in index form at the upper left corner of the card. Type the number of each in the upper right corner to aid in checking the answers.

For the alphabetical file, type the last name first with the address and policy date underneath. Arrange the cards alphabetically. For the chronological file, type the policy acceptance on the first line with the name and address underneath. Arrange these cards chronologically.

(1) Ms. Adrienne Thurman
5414 Highland Road
Denver, CO 80214
Policy: 11/21/77

(2) Mr. Tom Freeman
253 Garver Heights
Stockton, CA 95201
Policy: 1/26/77

(3) Ms. Cathy Green
34 Melrose Drive
Denver, CO 80202
Policy: 1/29/78

(4) Mr. Glen Caldwell
8254 South Willow Road
Syracuse, NY 13271
Policy: 8/14/77

(5) Mr. John Buckner
6333 Hudson Avenue
Seattle, WA 98112
Policy: 6/12/77

(6) Ms. Mallory Young
8731 First Street
Memphis, TN 38122
Policy: 2/10/78

(7) Mr. Fred Sellers
3212 53rd Street
Little Rock, AR 72214
Policy: 5/18/77

(8) Mr. Curtis Banks
5445 Linden Avenue
Pittsburgh, PA 15221
Policy: 10/2/77

(9) Ms. Linda Meyers
334 Madison Road
Santa Fe, NM 87501
Policy: 9/4/77

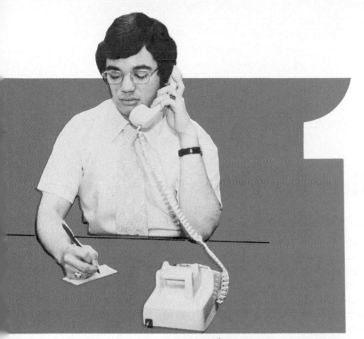

12

The Secretary and Records Management

Part 1
Filing Procedures

Mr. Vincent Morgan began his job as file clerk five years ago under the supervision of Mrs. Rachel Simms. Mrs. Simms emphasized the importance of proper collection, inspection, and cross-referencing of materials to be filed. She also stressed the fact that a good file clerk never falls behind in filing papers.

Mr. Morgan followed these tips in filing and formed good work habits. After several promotions, he has become secretary to Mr. John Ramsey, vice-president of sales. Among his fine qualifications is his experience in filing. Mr. Ramsey has been very impressed by his simple but efficient filing system.

Effective filing procedures begin long before any material is actually placed in the files. If they are properly applied, systematic filing procedures will in the long run save you time which you can use to perform other important office duties. But even more important, well-organized and carefully followed filing practices insure the prompt **retrieval** of filed records.

retrieval:
finding; recovery

Collecting Papers for the Files

The basic reason for having a filing system is so that you or your employer can find desired information when it is needed. Unless materials are filed promptly and properly, this is not possible.

Correspondence and other business papers that are to be filed should be collected in an orderly manner. Materials to be filed should be kept in a special basket or tray which is usually marked *File*.

Several times a day you should gather the materials to be filed from both your desk and your employer's. Occasionally it may be necessary to go through the papers on your employer's desk (with permission, of course) to gather materials that should be filed.

Inspecting

The next step in the filing process is *inspecting* each document that is to be filed. During inspection you should separate those current materials that will go into your or your employer's files from those that will go to the central filing department. In large offices several times a day a messenger collects the papers to be filed in the central files.

During the inspection process you look for a *release mark*, which is your authority to file each letter. This mark indicates that action has been taken on the letter, and it is released for filing. The release mark usually is indicated by your initials or those of your employer. These initials are placed in the upper left corner of the letter.

Since it is assumed that carbon copies are ready to file, they do not bear release marks. Many firms prepare carbon copies on paper with the words F I L E C O P Y printed in large outline letters across the face of the sheet. Frequently colored paper is used for the file copy.

In addition to checking for the release mark, you should examine records for completeness. All correspondence that is clipped together is examined and stapled (if it belongs together) in the upper left corner. The reply is stapled on top of the incoming letter. Paper clips, rubber bands, or straight pins are never placed in the file drawer. Torn papers should be mended at this time.

Indexing

Although every step in the filing process is important, the indexing step is particularly **significant**. *Indexing* is the process of determining how a document is to be filed. An incorrect decision at this time may mean a lost letter. At the very least, it means lost time in locating the letter. It is necessary, therefore, to scan or read each letter carefully to determine the *key name* or *title* (first indexing unit) that best identifies the material.

significant: important

The way materials are requested usually determines the way they should be indexed. An incoming letter could be filed under the name appearing on the letterhead, the name of the person signing the letter, the name of a person or business mentioned in the body of the letter, or the subject of the letter. For example, a letter announcing a new fire-resistant file cabinet would probably be filed under the heading "Office Equipment" in a folder labeled "Filing Cabinets" rather than under the name of the distributor appearing on the letterhead.

Copies of outgoing letters could be filed under the name of the addressee, the name of a person or business mentioned in the letter, or the subject of the letter. If a letter is of a personal nature, it is filed under the name of the person to or by whom it is written, even though the letter may have been written on a company letterhead. If there is any doubt about how a document should be indexed, the person who has released the record for filing should be consulted.

Coding

After the exact indexing order has been chosen, the document is marked or **coded**. A document may be coded in several different ways. The indexing units may be underlined:

Alamo Dry Cleaning Corporation

R. Robert Wilson

or the units may be numbered:

$$1 \quad 2 \quad 3 \quad \quad 4$$
Alamo Dry Cleaning Corporation

$$2 \quad 3 \quad \quad 1$$
R. Robert Wilson

If the name or subject does not appear in the letter, it must be written in, preferably in the upper right corner of the paper. All coding is done with a colored pencil. Coding aids in filing the record each time it is removed from the file as it does not need to be reread.

Cross-Referencing

Although selecting the indexing caption is relatively simple in most cases, there are always some records that might be requested in different ways. For example, your firm might receive a letter from a good customer recommending an applicant for a position. Obviously this letter of recommendation should be filed with other records referring to the applicant and would be filed in the applicant's folder in the "Applications" section. It may be wise, however, to keep a record of the letter in the customer's folder. The name of the applicant, therefore, is underlined on the letter as the primary indexing unit. The customer's name (of secondary importance in this instance) is also underlined and an X placed at the end of the line in the margin to show that a **cross-reference** should be made.

Kipley's Collection Agency
PHONE: 512-321-4122
253 LUDLOW AVENUE
AUSTIN, TX 78714

ALG

19- OCT 1 AM 9:30

October 1, 19--

Mrs. Alice L. Freeman, President
Arden Manufacturing Company
5328 Belview Road
Austin, TX 78702

Dear Mrs. Freeman

Every company has to deal with difficult-to-collect accounts receivables. They are costly in both time and money.

Kipley's has developed a procedure for collecting bad accounts that has helped our clients increase their profits. A brochure and sample copies of letters to collect your accounts are enclosed. Just give us your accounts that are uncollectible and we do the rest!

To reduce the costs of bad accounts and to increase your profits, please call me collect at 512-231-4122 for more information.

Sincerely

Gary P. Lord X
Gary P. Lord
Representative

Enclosures

ag

Illus. 12-1   Letter properly released and coded

CROSS REFERENCE RECORD

Name or Subject   Lord, Gary P.   File No.   L371

Date   October 1, 19--

Remarks   Procedure to collect bad accounts

SEE   Kipley's Collection Agency   File No.   E442
253 Ludlow Avenue
Austin, TX 78714

Authorized by   Marilyn Jarvis   Date   Oct. 1, 19--

File Cross-Reference Record under name or subject listed at top of this sheet, and in proper date order. The document referred to should be filed under Name or Subject listed under "SEE".

Illus. 12-2   Cross-reference for a letter

distinctive:
different

A cross-reference sheet (usually of a **distinctive** color) is prepared with the name and address of the customer, the date of the letter, a brief description of the letter, and the location of the letter following the "SEE." This cross-reference is then placed in the customer's folder, in its proper date sequence with the other papers, as a record of the letter.

Rather than prepare regular cross-reference sheets, many companies prefer using a photocopy of the original. This speeds retrieval since a complete copy of the record is available at each file point. Do not forget, however, to underline and mark an X on each copy, so that you will know in which folder each is to be filed.

Many hard-to-index documents should be cross-referenced in several places, for this is your one opportunity to think of the number of ways by which materials may be requested. Too much cross-referencing requires considerable time as well as filing space; however, too little cross-referencing may delay retrieval.

If a permanent cross-reference is desired, a cross-reference guide is prepared. This is a manila card the same size as a file folder, having a tab in the same position as those used for individual folders. A situation requiring a permanent cross-reference guide might be as follows: The name of a company with which you do a great deal of business is changed. Another folder is prepared for the new name and all material is placed in this folder. The old folder is now replaced with a permanent cross-reference guide with the necessary retrieval information on its tab:

Adams and Smith Manufacturing Co.
See Adams and Jones Manufacturing Co.

If the special cross-reference guide form is not available, use the back half of the folder as a cross-reference guide by cutting off the front flap of the folder at the score line. The cross-reference guide remains in the file as long as the name or subject is still active. (See page 415 for additional information on cross-referencing.)

Sorting

After the records have been coded and the necessary cross-reference sheets prepared, the material is ready to be sorted. *Sorting* is the process of arranging the records in indexing order before placing them in the folders.

Sorting serves two important purposes. First, it saves actual filing time. Since the records are in exact indexing order, you are able to move quickly from drawer to drawer, thus saving time and energy for other

Illus. 12-3

A sorting tray helps to reduce daily filing time.

Yarman & Erbe

important tasks. Second, if documents are requested before they are filed, they can be found quickly.

If the volume of filing is high, special sorting trays or compartments should be used. Sorting trays are equipped with alphabetic, numeric, or geographic guides depending upon the classification system you are using. When you sort materials alphabetically, records beginning with the letter *A* are placed behind an *A* guide; those beginning with *B*, behind a *B* guide, and so on through the alphabet. After the materials have been rough-sorted, they are removed from the sorting tray and placed in exact alphabetic order (fine sorting). If the volume of material is low, this same procedure may be followed on your desk top.

Placing Records in the File

After the records have been fine sorted they are placed in the files. A systematic routine should always be followed:

1. Locate the proper file drawer by examining drawer labels.
2. Scan the primary guides in the drawer to locate the major alphabetic section desired.
3. Check to see if an individual or special folder has been prepared for this material. If so, file the record here.
4. If no individual or special folder is available for this particular record, file the letter in the miscellaneous folder for the section.

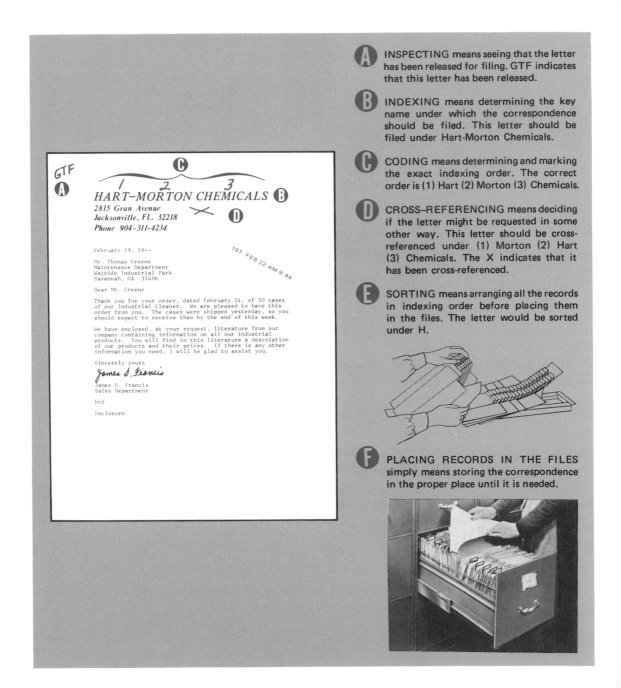

A INSPECTING means seeing that the letter has been released for filing. GTF indicates that this letter has been released.

B INDEXING means determining the key name under which the correspondence should be filed. This letter should be filed under Hart-Morton Chemicals.

C CODING means determining and marking the exact indexing order. The correct order is (1) Hart (2) Morton (3) Chemicals.

D CROSS-REFERENCING means deciding if the letter might be requested in some other way. This letter should be cross-referenced under (1) Morton (2) Hart (3) Chemicals. The X indicates that it has been cross-referenced.

E SORTING means arranging all the records in indexing order before placing them in the files. The letter would be sorted under H.

F PLACING RECORDS IN THE FILES simply means storing the correspondence in the proper place until it is needed.

Illus. 12-4   Basic filing procedure

Arranging Materials in Folders

Letters should always be placed in folders with the front of the letter facing the front of the folder and the top of the letter at the left side.

In *individual* folders, letters are arranged according to date, with the *most recent* record in front. In *miscellaneous* folders, the documents are arranged alphabetically by name; if there are two or more records for the same individual or company, they are arranged according to date, with the most recent record first. In a *special* folder, the records are arranged alphabetically by name and then by date in each group of names.

Filing Efficiency

Twenty filing suggestions recommended by experienced secretaries are given on the following pages.

1. Follow systematic procedures. Well-organized, carefully administered files encourage accurate filing and rapid retrieval. What is more, you will enjoy filing!
2. Don't economize needlessly on file supplies. Good quality supplies hold up through continued hard use; poor quality supplies soon wear out and hinder the efficiency of the system. Choose the right supplies for the right records with a particular system in mind.
3. Set aside a definite time each day for filing. Remember: records belong in the file — not in or on desks.
4. Keep your system simple. If others must use your files, be certain they understand how the system works, but insist that you do all the filing and refiling. Provide a handy place for them to place the materials they have removed from the files. They will be glad to cooperate — and it will guarantee file accuracy.
5. Before refiling any folder that has been removed from the files, quickly examine its contents. You may find a lost document by performing this simple procedure. Always "jog" the contents of a folder before returning it to the file.
6. Constantly analyze your filing system and recommend ways in which it can be improved. Your employer will appreciate any suggestion for an improved information system. Seek the advice of your office supplies dealer. Constantly review the various business publications. They'll keep you informed on the latest products and new developments in the field of records management.
7. Protect the tabs on guides and folders. Always lift a folder or guide by the side — never by the tab. Replace folder labels as soon as they are difficult to read.

8. File the most active records in the most easily reached parts of the file cabinets. Active records belong in the top drawers, less active documents in bottom drawers. This saves both time and energy.

9. Use your filing cabinets only for filing, not for storing office supplies and other items. File only vital records in the special fire-resistant equipment that has been purchased for their protection.

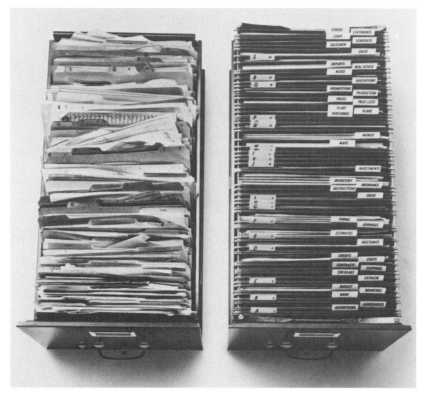

Illus. 12-5

Bulging, messy folders encourage filing errors. Materials in an organized file are found without delay.

Oxford Pentaflex Corporation

10. To avoid accidents, close a file drawer immediately after using it; and open only one drawer at a time.

11. Don't allow folders to bulge. Bulging folders encourage filing errors. When necessary, subdivide individual folders into monthly folders. Expand your system by preparing special and individual folders whenever possible.

12. Don't fill a file drawer to capacity. Leave at least six inches of working space in each file drawer. It speeds up your work and prevents papers from being torn.

13. Mend all torn documents before placing them in a file folder.

14. If smaller than normal sized documents are placed in file folders, glue or tape them to standard size paper. They will be easier to find.

15. If a particular document was difficult to find, cross-reference it when it is finally retrieved. It will save time when it is requested again.
16. Let color help. Use different color labels for different file years or periods. A well-planned color scheme will aid in prompt filing and retrieving.
17. Separate records that must be maintained in the files for long periods of time from those of temporary value.
18. Use the proper filing tools. A rubber finger helps separate documents; a file shelf makes you more efficient at the file; sitting on a file stool conserves your energy.
19. Follow a regular program of removing inactive records from the active files.
20. Be certain to follow, without variation, the office procedures that have been established to protect vital records.

REVIEWING

1. How are letters and other papers gathered together for filing and by whom?
2. What does a release mark mean and how is it recognized?
3. Why is indexing so important?
4. What are the various captions under which incoming letters could be filed?
5. Under what captions may copies of outgoing letters be filed?
6. Under what caption is a personal letter filed?
7. Illustrate two ways of coding.
8. What is cross-referencing?
9. What are two important purposes of sorting?
10. How are letters arranged in *individual* folders? In *miscellaneous* folders? In *special* folders?

MAKING JUDGMENTS

1. You notice that a secretary in another department has neat, orderly files similar to those on the right hand side of page 446. Your files look like those on the left. What should you do to improve the appearance of your files?
2. It is said that cross-referencing can be overdone. Under what circumstances might this be true?

WORKING WITH OTHERS

In the office of the Kruger Packing Company, Mr. W. E. Hedges has received a letter asking for an answer to an earlier letter written by the

Brooks Grocery Store. The unanswered letter was found in the *special* folder of the Brooks Grocery Store. The letter bears the initials *WEH* as a release-for-filing mark, but Mr. Hedges says he does not remember initialing the letter. The initials were actually placed there by mistake by Mr. Hedges' secretary. What should the secretary do in this situation?

REFRESHING LANGUAGE SKILLS

All twenty key words listed below are used in filing. After you have studied the example, type the key word and the word or phrase you believe is *nearest in meaning* to the key word.

Example: facilitate — (a) appreciate (b) depreciate (c) *make easier* (d) negotiate

1. *adhere* — (a) expect (b) hold closely (c) part (d) loosen
2. *appropriate* — (a) approximate (b) apt (c) fitting (d) unsuitable
3. *caption* — (a) finishing stone (b) heading or title (c) rank of captain (d) seizure
4. *comprehensive* — (a) compelling (b) complex (c) extensive (d) limited
5. *consistent* — (a) consonant (b) incompatible (c) incongruous (d) tribunal
6. *conventional* — (a) contrary (b) customary (c) jovial (d) well informed
7. *distinctive* — (a) distasteful (b) sound harsh (c) intemperate (d) individual
8. *document* — (a) a particular principle (b) an established opinion (c) any written item (d) ownership of land
9. *effective* — (a) exhausted of vigor (b) flowing out (c) producing intended results (d) show enthusiasm
10. *identical* — (a) idealistic (b) matching (c) unlike (d) visionary
11. *initial* — (a) beginning (b) concluding (c) inheriting (d) suggesting
12. *legible* — (a) branch of military science (b) multitude (c) valid (d) capable of being read
13. *primary* — (a) humble (b) last (c) main (d) proud
14. *procedure* — (a) a disposition (b) course of action (c) to defer action (d) to progress
15. *propel* — (a) foretell (b) multiply (c) project (d) prove
16. *retention* — (a) silence (b) rejoinder (c) remedy (d) memory
17. *retrieval* — (a) recovery (b) retraction (c) retrenchment (d) retribution
18. *sequence* — (a) separation (b) series (c) seriousness (d) sermon
19. *variation* — (a) deviation (b) sameness (c) truthfulness (d) word for word
20. *vital* — (a) unimportant (b) expendable (c) resounding (d) essential

PERFORMING SECRETARIAL TASKS

1. The following letters pertaining to the application of John A. Dillon are filed in the "Applications" folder of the firm where you work. Indicate the order, from front to back, in which the letters should be placed in this folder.
   (a) Henry & Currier Company's March 8 letter of recommendation
   (b) John A. Dillon's March 12 letter concerning his call on March 15
   (c) Your firm's March 3 letter to Mr. Dillon asking him to come in for an interview
   (d) John A. Dillon's March 18 letter accepting the position
   (e) Your firm's March 5 letter to the Henry & Currier Company asking for information about Mr. John A. Dillon
   (f) Your firm's March 11 letter to Mr. Dillon asking him to come in for a second interview
   (g) Your firm's March 17 letter offering Mr. Dillon a position in the cost accounting department
   (h) John A. Dillon's March 1 letter of application
   (i) Your firm's March 9 letter to Henry & Currier Company thanking them for their cooperation

2. The following letters are filed in the Harvey O. Jackson individual folder. Indicate the order, from front to back, in which the letters should be placed in this folder.
   (a) Harvey O. Jackson's order of April 1
   (b) Your firm's letter of April 8 enclosing the April 6 invoice
   (c) Harvey O. Jackson's letter of April 30 enclosing a check
   (d) A cross-reference sheet dated April 10
   (e) Your firm's letter of May 3 acknowledging the check of April 30
   (f) Your firm's invoice of April 6 for the April 1 order

3. The letters listed below are filed in the "To-Tw" miscellaneous folder. Indicate the order, from front to back in which the letters should be placed in this folder.
   (a) Your firm's letter of September 30 to Arthur Towne, Jr.
   (b) The receipted invoice sent to you on September 21 by Albert Town
   (c) Towne and Lovitt's order of September 2
   (d) Your firm's letter of September 28 to Richard G. Twitchell
   (e) Your firm's invoice of September 6 covering the September 2 order from Towne and Lovitt
   (f) An advertising circular and letter dated September 14 sent to your employer by H. J. Tweed

4. This is a continuation of the alphabetic indexing exercise begun in Unit 11, Part 3.
   (a) Type the following names in index form on 25 file cards. Type the number in the upper right corner and the name and address below the indexed name as you did in Unit 11, Part 3.

(b) Combine these 25 cards in proper filing order with the 50 cards prepared in Unit 11, Part 3.

(c) Save the cards for the Performing Secretarial Tasks assignment in Unit 12, Part 4.

(51) X-Cel Paints & Varnishes, 532 Mill St., Pittsburgh, PA 15221

(52) Theodore C. Haller, 59 E. 10th St., Charleston, WV 25303

(53) Henry R. Elston, II, 660 N. Michigan Ave., Chicago, IL 60611

(54) XYZ Electrical Repair Service, 2d and Main Sts., Lexington, KY 40507

(55) Countess Flora's Dance Academy, Chase Hotel, St. Louis, MO 63166

(56) Mrs. K. D. Ingles (Hazel Parks), 40 Sheridan Dr., Providence, RI 02909

(57) Quick Brothers Florists, 6720 Turkey Run Rd., Nashville, TN 37202

(58) Charles T. Hallam, 4600 Pueblo St., Phoenix, AZ 85041

(59) Hall-Kramer Printing Co., Inc., 7700 S. Wells St., Chicago, IL 60621

(60) R. Nelson Forrester, 377 Desert Drive, Reno, NV 89504

(61) Robert N. Forrest, 781 University Ave., Minneapolis, MN 55413

(62) Sister Julietta, Sacred Heart Academy, Racine, WI 53401

(63) William A. Graves, 239 N. Vineyard Drive, Kenosha, WI 53140

(64) Mrs. Arthur P. Matthews (Helen), 5229 Crest Drive, Cleveland, OH 44121

(65) Town & Country Furniture Co., Town & Country Shop-In, Centerville, IN 47330

(66) U.S. Electrotype Corp., 2101 - 19th St., Long Island City, NY 11105

(67) Prince George Hotel, St. Thomas, Virgin Islands 00801

(68) Les Trois Chats Inn, 48 Henri St., Quebec, Province of Quebec, Canada

(69) 29 Palms Motel, U.S. 60 First St., Twenty-Nine Palms, CA 92277

(70) Venice Yacht Club, 29 Oceanside Drive, Venice, CA 90291

(71) Mr. Morris Book Store, 6th & Pike Sts., Mt. Morris, IL 61054

(72) State Auditor, Columbus, OH 43216

(73) Hire-the-Handicapped Committee, 30 Le Veque Tower, Denver, CO 80201

(74) Hamilton County SPCA, Colerain & Blue Rock Sts., Cincinnati, OH 45223

(75) Port-au-Prince Imports, Inc., 21 Main St., Gulfport, MS 39501

5. The following letter has just come to your office. Properly date, code, and if necessary, cross-reference the letter. (Use the letter provided in the *Supplies Inventory*, or type the letter as shown

below. If cross-referencing is necessary, use the form from the *Supplies Inventory*, if available, or type one similar to that on page 441.)

William Carter co.

815 Lakeland Dr. Kansas City, MO 64151 Area Code 816 891-1129

June 14, 197-

Allis-Bowen Products, Inc.
9621 East Tracy Street
Los Angeles, CA 90028

Attention Mr. B. P. Warren

Ladies and Gentlemen

Thank you for your letter of June 12 in which you inquired about the possibility of our printing for you a booklet giving a short description of your company and an illustrated description of the products that you manufacture.

Before we are able to quote prices on a publication of this kind we need the following information:

1. An estimate of the length of the booklet

2. The approximate number and dimensions of illustrations

3. The size of the page desired

4. The kind and quality of paper and cover stock.

We shall be glad to give you an exact quotation on cost of the booklet as soon as we receive this information.

At the present time we are in a position to give you prompt as well as efficient service. We can assure you of an attractive booklet with suitable type, clear illustrations, and strong binding.

Very truly yours

Earl E. Whitmore
Earl E. Whitmore

ecb

Part **2**

Managing the Records System

Mrs. Pamela Stewart has been with Tempro Corporation for many years as supervisor of the central files. When she first started her job, the filing system was very small and easily controlled. Through the years it has grown into a very large, complex system. Mrs. Stewart has put into effect many aids for controlling the files. One of them is the use of the charge-out system, which provides a record of who has each folder that has been removed from the files. This saves time when it comes to locating it. When workers at Tempro need a certain file, they can be sure that Mrs. Stewart has it or knows where it can be found.

Records are kept because they contain needed information; filing systems are developed in order to retrieve this information promptly and efficiently. Yet if records are often removed from the files without *charging* them to the borrower, the system will soon become useless. It will certainly not be worth the time, effort, and money that have gone into its development and maintenance.

Since the people who borrow records from the files are busy, they may neglect to return these documents to the files. Although every worker should feel responsible for maintaining an effective office information system, it is your responsibility as a secretary to protect the records placed under your control. Therefore, some type of charge-out and follow-up system must be developed to insure the return of borrowed documents to the files.

Charge-Out

There are times when other executives or secretaries will need materials that are stored in your files. When materials are borrowed from your files, you should prepare a form that identifies the records removed. This form (usually 5″ × 3″ or 6″ × 4″) is known as a *requisition* card and has spaces for a full description of the material borrowed, the name and the department of the borrower, the date the material was removed from the file, and the date it is to be returned. The requisition cards may later be used to analyze the activity of the files. A tabulation of the cards will determine how often the files are used and which records are most active.

Charge-Out Forms

In addition to the requisition card, four kinds of forms are commonly used when material is taken from the files. They are *out guides, out folders, carrier folders,* and *substitution cards*.

Out Guides. An out guide is a pressboard guide with the word *OUT* printed on its tab. It is placed in the files when an entire folder is borrowed. There are two forms of out guides. One type is ruled on both sides, and the charge information is written directly on the guide. When the folder is returned, the out guide is removed and the charge information crossed out. The guide is then ready for further use.

The other kind of out guide has a pocket into which a requisition card is placed. This form is preferred since it is faster to use and the charge information is usually more legible.

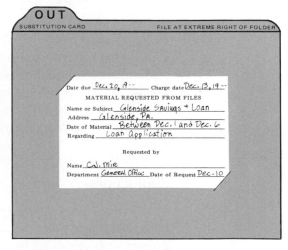

Illus. 12-6 Ruled out guide   Illus. 12-7 Out guide with inset

Out Folders. Some firms prefer using out folders when an entire folder is requested from the files. If additional material reaches the files before the regular folder is returned, it is temporarily filed in the out folder. This material is then filed in the regular folder when it is returned.

Carrier Folder. A carrier folder is useful in reminding the borrower to return records to the files. It is of a different color from the regular folders with the words *RETURN TO FILES* printed on it. The requested material is removed from the regular folder and sent to the borrower in a carrier folder. An out card or guide is placed in the regular folder containing the charge-out information. The regular folder remains in the file to hold any material placed in the file before the carrier folder is returned. A carrier folder saves the regular folder from the wear and tear it would receive when removed from the files.

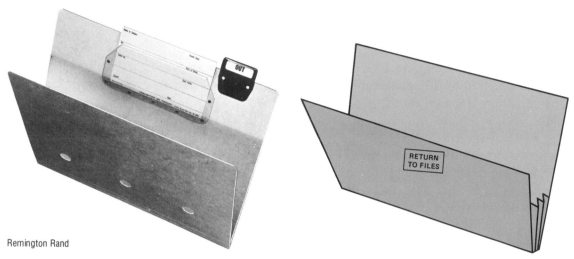

Remington Rand

Illus. 12-8   Out folder   Illus. 12-9   Carrier folder

Substitution Cards. A substitution card is a tabbed card, usually salmon-colored, that is placed in a folder when single documents are borrowed. The word *OUT* is printed on the tab. The charge-out information may be recorded on the card itself or on a requisition form inserted in a pocket of the substitution card. A substitution card is basically the same as an out guide.

Photocopies

To avoid removing important papers from the files, some firms prepare photocopies of a requested record. When this method is used, the document is removed from the files and copied on a copying machine. The original document is then refiled and the photocopy sent to the borrower with instructions to destroy it after use. This method is generally used when single documents are requested rather than an entire folder.

Length of Charge Time

Borrowed materials are used by the borrower immediately and should be returned to the files as soon as possible. The longer records are away from the files, the more difficult it is to get them back; furthermore, they are likely to be lost or discarded. Most firms charge out records for only one week (with weekly extensions, if found necessary). It is best to have short charge-out periods and prompt follow-up of materials that are not returned to the files.

Illus. 12-10

File requests may be made in person, by phone, or through interoffice mail. They should be prepared on a form that fully identifies the records removed from the files.

Follow-Up

How will you remember to give attention to the many matters that require future attention? Since you should not rely on your memory, you will find it necessary to devise a system that will call your attention to these matters at the exact date when action must be taken. A file that is designed for this purpose is called a *follow-up file* and is arranged in **chronological** order. Two common follow-up files are the card tickler file and the dated follow-up folder file.

chronological: arranged by date or time

Card Tickler Files

A card tickler file consists of a set of 12 monthly primary guides and 31 daily secondary guides. Important matters to be followed up are recorded on cards and placed behind the appropriate month and day guides in the file. A card tickler file may be used to follow up records that have been borrowed from the files or to follow up other matters that require attention.

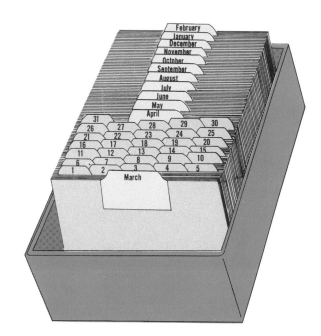

Illus. 12-11

Follow-up file

Dated Follow-Up Folders

This file resembles the card tickler file except that a folder is available for each day of the month. Items that require follow-up are placed in the correct day folder, and the folder is then placed behind the appropriate monthly guide. For example, a folder may contain a photocopy of an incoming letter or an extra carbon of an outgoing letter that requests an answer by a certain day. On that particular day you should check to see if an answer to the letter has been received. If not, follow-up action is taken. By using photocopies and extra carbons for follow-up, the correspondence can be filed in its proper place and the official folder is always complete. This procedure saves a great deal of time.

Transfer

Office files should contain only those records that are needed to operate efficiently. If **inactive** or outdated records are never removed from the files, needed information becomes more and more difficult to **retain** and retrieve. Every organization should adopt a plan of removing inactive documents from the active files by *transferring* these records to a records center.

Removing inactive records from the office files serves three important purposes:

inactive:
needed, but not often used

retain:
keep; store

Unit 12 • The Secretary and Records Management

1. Active records can be filed and retrieved quickly.
2. Expensive office space and file equipment are kept at a minimum.
3. Costs are reduced since transferred records are housed in inexpensive file equipment, usually cardboard transfer cases.

It is important to remember that not every document received in an office should be filed; not every document in the active file should be transferred.

Transferring File Folders

Records that must be kept for long periods of time should be separated from those of temporary value when placing records in transfer cases. Miscellaneous, special, and individual folders are usually transferred from the active to the inactive files when they are no longer needed. Each transferred folder should be stamped *Transfer File* to prevent it from being returned to the active files should it be requested from the records center. Many firms use different colored folder labels to identify different file periods.

The Records Center

A records center is an important part of any transfer program. This center houses documents no longer needed for daily reference. Records may be stored at the center indefinitely or for a temporary period only.

Illus. 12-12

Inactive documents are stored in a records center.

Inactive records are inexpensively maintained in the center, since all the floor space can be utilized (floor to ceiling filing) and inexpensive equipment can be used to house the records.

Documents maintained in the center must be accurately indexed and controlled so that they will be available if requested. Without adequate indexing, protection, and control of these inactive records, all the time and effort spent in the transfer program have been wasted.

Retention

Every organization is faced with the problem of how long to retain its records. Because of the growing volume of paper work, many firms have established *record retention schedules*. Such a schedule identifies the retention value for every type of record created or received by an organization and determines which records must be retained and for how long. Useless records occupy expensive floor space and costly equipment; they hinder the rapid retrieval of needed information.

While certain documents must be retained permanently, most records created and received in the average business organization have a limited period of usefulness. The National Records Management Council estimates that 95 percent of all corporate paper work over a year old is rarely, if ever, referred to again. Record authorities estimate that 40 percent of all stored records can be legally destroyed.

Even though every organization must develop its own retention schedule, factors that affect the retention value of business records include:

1. Legal requirements (federal, state, and local)
2. Office use (those records needed to operate on a daily basis)
3. Historical documents
4. Vital records

A retention schedule can be adopted only after a thorough study of the record requirements of a particular organization. Legal counsel should always be sought. Once a schedule is adopted, it must be continually revised to meet changing conditions and needs.

REVIEWING

1. Why should all materials taken from files be *charged out* to the person taking them.
2. What information is included on a requisition card?
3. What are the two types of out guides? Which is better?
4. What is the difference between an out guide and a substitution card?

5. How is the out folder used?
6. Why are carrier folders used?
7. Describe a card tickler file and tell of its use.
8. What is the difference between a card tickler file and a dated folder file?
9. Why is it less expensive to store inactive records in a records center?
10. What four factors affect the retention schedule of business records.

MAKING JUDGMENTS

Miss Kittle, the receptionist of a large law office, is also supervisor of the legal library. Because of her varied duties, she cannot devote her full time to the library. Files are often misplaced because someone failed to fill out a charge card or a file is several weeks overdue. What suggestions can you recommend for improving this system?

WORKING WITH OTHERS

An important folder is missing from the files. Your employer asks you if you have it or know where it is. After looking around, you say "No." The next day as you are looking through a stack of materials on the table behind your desk, you find the missing folder. What should you do?

REFRESHING LANGUAGE SKILLS

Type the following sentences and insert the correct punctuation.

1. Yes she said Ill take the folder with me
2. What are these Xs for
3. The management of jefferson and company considered the workers grievances three of which were justified but the other problems needed further negotiation
4. Smiths folder was removed early Tuesday morning it should have been returned by Thursday afternoon
5. Mr. green requested that you bring the harden jonas and mitchell folders to the board of directors meeting

PERFORMING SECRETARIAL TASKS

1. Type captions on folder labels for each of the following authors, who contributed articles to a recent issue of *The Office*, a magazine of management, equipment, and automation. (If folder labels are not available, type the names on blank sheets of paper approximately 3½" × 1½".)

George H. Harmon
Aretha L. Ratz
Jord H. Jordan, Jr.
J. A. Mosher
Wesley S. Bagby
Thomas G. Morris
Richard I. Tanaka
Fran Plasha
Brook I. Blackstone
Bernice Goldstein
G. Peter Ignasiak
Clarissa E. Franke
James D. Parker, Jr.
William W. Newell

Jan E. Torrence
Charles A. Agemian
Denise S. Greensmith
Theodore K. Cobb
T. M. Galloway
E. Philip Kron
Patrick R. Gaffney
Carla W. Golgart
John H. Dunham
Roberta E. Bennis
Eleanor H. Morse
K. R. Atkins, Jr.
Donald F. Evans
Walter M. Carlson

Type the name without punctuation on the lower half of the folder label about two spaces from the left edge, as illustrated.

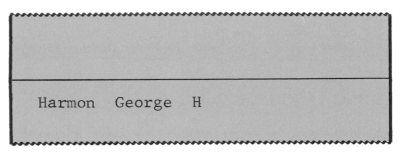

2. After the names in Problem 1 are indexed in alphabetical order type the list on a single sheet of paper. Center the heading, AUTHORS OF THE JANUARY ISSUE, and then type the list in two double-spaced columns.

Part 3

Subject, Numeric, and Geographic Filing

New secretaries hired by Marsh Clothing Distributors, Inc. are required to spend one week in the filing department. The management feels that this acquaints each secretary with the different filing systems used within the company. In addition to the alphabetic system, Marsh uses a numeric system for orders and stock numbers, a subject system for the different types of clothing, and a geographic system for the sales territories.

As a secretary, you will probably be more concerned with alphabetic correspondence filing methods than with subject, numeric, or geographic. To assist your executive properly, however, you may need to understand other filing systems and how they operate. You may be required to request records from a filing department that uses one of the other systems. You may also be required to code correspondence for storage in the central files.

Records must be filed according to how they will be requested — by name, by subject, by number, or by geographic area. When you have correspondence with a customer, you know that it will be filed alphabetically by the company name. All the forecasts on anticipated expenditures for your department for the coming year will be filed by the subject caption *Budgets*, not under *Controller Jamison*. If your executive asks that copies of the sales reports be sent to the managers of each territory, you will make use of a geographic file. In a purchasing department, you will keep a numeric file by the purchase order number.

Subject Filing

Every organization has materials which are important because of their content rather than because of the person to whom or by whom they are written. For these materials a *subject* filing system is necessary. Your secretarial duties should bring you into direct contact with this system of filing. Subjects are arranged in alphabetical order, and related subjects may be grouped together. A folder labeled "Applications" with the subheading "Sales Representatives" is an example. The names of all sales applicants are not easily remembered; therefore, the names are of secondary importance in filing, and letters should be placed in a special subject folder labeled "Applications — Sales Representatives." As long as there are only a few subject folders, they are filed in a regular alphabetic or numeric system along with the other folders.

The following list shows some typical subject filing captions:

Advertising	Finance	Payroll
Applications		Personnel
Associations	Government — Federal	Price Lists
Audit Reports	Government — Municipal	Production
	Government — State	Public Relations
Balance Sheets		
Budgets	Insurance	Real Estate
		Reports
Conferences and	Legal Matters	Research
Conventions		
Contracts	Maps	Sales
Credits and Collections	Methods and Procedures	Speaking Invitations
	Minutes	Statistical Data
Directors' Meetings	Mortgages	
		Taxes — Federal
Employee Benefits	Operating Overhead	Taxes — Municipal
Equipment & Supplies	Operating Policies	Taxes — State

Guides and Folders Used in Subject Filing

In a subject file you will make use of several different types of guides and folders. The main subject titles are used as captions for primary guides. These serve the same purpose as primary guides in an alphabetic file. Secondary guides are used for the subordinate titles that are related to the main subjects on the primary guides behind which they are placed.

There is a miscellaneous folder for each main subject in which all papers relating to that topic are filed. Individual folders are made for subdivisions of the main subject when sufficient papers (usually six or seven) accumulate for the subtopic. Subdivisions may be made by subject, name, or date.

Subject:	*Name:*
Safety	Associations
Accident Prevention	American Bankers Assocation
Accident Reports	American Manufacturers Association

Date Periods:
Production Reports
    January–June, 19––
    July–December, 19––

When individual folders are used in a subject file, they are placed behind the primary or secondary guides that classify the subject matter of the correspondence in those folders. In this way correspondence is doubly identified — by subject, as shown by the guide captions; and by titles, as shown on the folder captions. Main subject and subdivision captions must be shown on each folder tab.

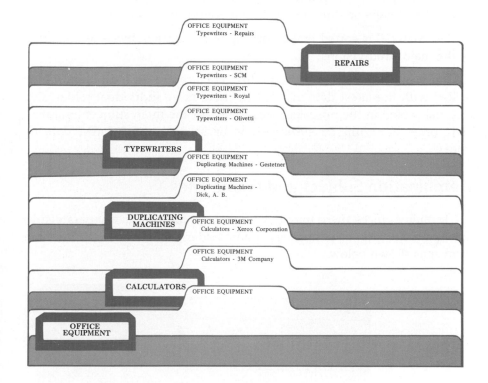

Illus. 12-13

A subject file

Subject Filing Procedures

When filing by subject, there are six basic steps which you should follow.

Inspecting. Each letter should be checked to see that it has been released for filing.

Indexing. The letter must be read carefully to determine under which subject it should be filed. Thorough familiarity with the outline of subjects and their subdivisions is necessary.

Coding. When the subject of a letter has been determined, the caption is written on the letter in the upper right corner or it is underlined if it appears in the letter.

Cross-Referencing. If more than one subject is involved in a letter — a very frequent occurrence — a cross-reference caption is underlined and an X is placed at the end of the line in the margin. An extra carbon copy, a photocopy of the letter, a cross-reference sheet, or a 5" × 3" index card should also be prepared.

Some companies distribute copies of the main subjects of the filing system (and possibly a definition of each) to each department for its use in dictating letters or when requesting materials from the files.

Sorting. Material is sorted first according to the main subjects and second by the main subdivisions.

Placing Material in Folders. Material that is placed in an individual folder is filed with the latest date in front. If there is no individual folder, the material is filed in the miscellaneous folder for the main subject in alphabetic order according to subdivisions or in date order, latest date in front.

Combination Subject and Name Files

In many offices there may not be enough files to have separate subject and name files, so subject and name folders may be filed in the same drawer as shown below.

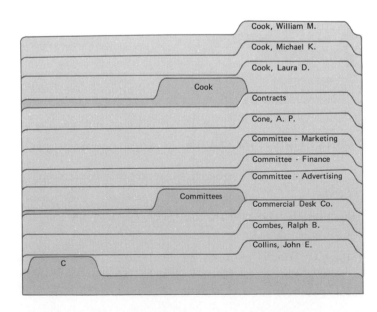

Illus. 12-14

A combined subject and name file

Numeric Filing

With the widespread use of data processing systems for repetitive and statistical operations in many organizations, numbers have become important in identifying many records in today's businesses. In general, only large systems use numeric filing. Records that are frequently identified by number and filed in a numeric sequence are insurance policies, purchase orders, sales orders, contracts, licenses, customers' charge accounts, bank accounts, and credit card accounts. Many large government agencies such as the Social Security Administration, the Veterans Administration, and state motor vehicle bureaus file their records in numerical order.

Illus. 12-15

Business and government agencies with large volumes of records typically use numeric files.

Oxford Pentaflex Corporation

Since it would be impossible to remember the file number of every business paper, an alphabetic card index of the numerically filed material is maintained by name or by subject as a cross-reference. Numeric filing systems are *indirect* in filing and finding because, in many instances, reference must be made to the alphabetic card index before a document is found or coded.

A numeric file usually consists of three parts:

1. The file itself, in which the documents are filed by an assigned number and in which the guides and folders bear numeric captions.
2. An index card control file, in which names or subject titles are arranged alphabetically.
3. An *accession* book or *register*, in which a record of assigned numbers is kept.

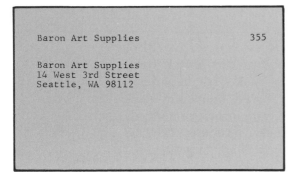

Illus. 12-16   Alphabetic and subject index control cards

Numeric Arrangements

There are several arrangements of numbers that may be used in numeric filing:

1. The numbers may be in consecutive order (consecutive number filing).
2. Certain portions of a long number may be used as the first indexing unit (terminal-digit and/or middle-digit filing).
3. The number may be combined with letters of the alphabet (alpha-numeric filing).

Consecutive Number Filing

In this arrangement documents are filed in strict numeric sequence. The number is written in the upper right corner of the paper, and an alphabetic card is typed as a cross-reference to the assigned number. The papers are filed in numerical sequence in folders, and the card is filed alphabetically in the index. Additional papers related to the same subject are checked against the card index and coded with the same number.

Legal Files. In legal firms a number (for example, 607) is assigned to a client and as additional matters are handled for the same client, they are given a secondary number (607-1 — Will) to separate the new material. An alphabetic cross-reference card is made for each client as well as for each item the legal firm is taking care of for the client. Individual folders are prepared for each and are filed numerically:

607   John W. Rodgers
607-1   Will
607-2   Real Estate Holdings
607-3   Income Tax Records
607-4   Insurance

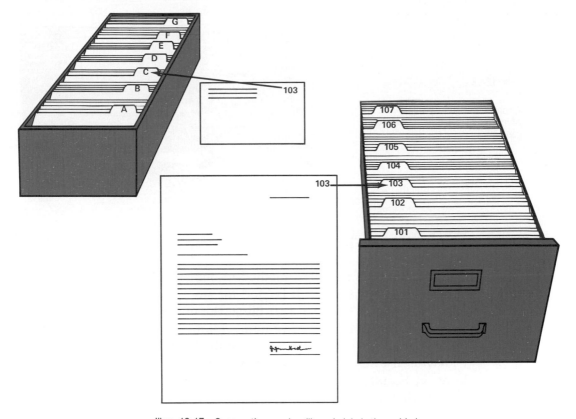

Illus. 12-17   Consecutive number file and alphabetic card index

Project and Job Files. Consecutive numeric filing is used for these two types of records primarily because there are related drawings, blueprints, and artwork connected with the correspondence and such material is controlled more easily through a numbering system. Almost always it is necessary to subdivide the correspondence by subject. Drawings will have secondary numbers for parts of the project or job, and dates for revisions of drawings become an important identifying factor. Numbers are obtained from the accession book. The alphabetical card index is an essential key for locating material by name or subject.

Numeric Correspondence Files. Because it is a slow and indirect method, ordinary correspondence today is seldom filed numerically. The need to keep papers confidential is the primary reason for using this system. Numbers are assigned in consecutive order from the accession book, and individual folders are made for each correspondent. All papers for this correspondent are placed in this folder, with the most recent material in the front. An alphabetic index card is made. Neither the accession book nor the card index is available to unauthorized personnel.

Illus. 12-18

A confidential correspondence file in which numbers and names have been combined.

Shaw-Walker

Terminal-Digit Filing

Terminal-digit filing is a method of numeric filing based on reading numbers from *right to left*. It is ideal for any large numeric file with five or more digits. In terminal-digit filing, the numbers are assigned in the same manner as for consecutive number filing, but the numbers are read in small groups (00–99) beginning with the terminal (or final) group. It is widely used by banks for depositors' savings accounts, mortgages, and loans; by hospitals for medical case records; and by insurance companies for policyholders' applications.

Illus. 12-19

Terminal-digit filing is useful in numeric files with five or more digits.

Shaw-Walker

In the terminal-digit system, the primary division of the files is based on the last two digits of a number, the secondary division upon the next two digits, and the final division upon the first digits. For example, if you were to look up life insurance policy number 225101, you would read the numbers from right to left in pairs of digits instead of from left to right as whole numbers.

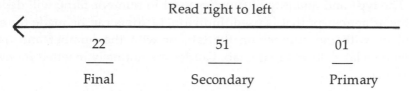

You would first locate the drawer containing those materials or records whose numbers end with 01. Then you would search down the guides in that drawer for the number 51. Lastly, you would file or find the material in proper order behind the number 22. Numbers of fewer than six digits are brought up to that figure by adding zeros to the left of the number.

When even larger numbers are common, they may be broken down for filing in groups of three digits, 000 to 999.

Alpha-Numeric Filing

Banks now identify the checking accounts of their depositors by numbers. In some banks an individual account number is assigned to each depositor according to an *alpha-numeric plan*. This is a method of assigning numbers to accounts in such a way that even with additions and deletions, accounts filed in numeric sequence will also be in alphabetic sequence. Originally the accounts are arranged in exact alphabetic sequence and assigned account numbers with uniform gaps between numbers to allow for additional accounts. This number is printed with a special magnetic ink on a set of blank checks before the checks are given to the depositor. After a check has been drawn, cashed, and returned to the bank, a machine automatically "reads" the number and charges the account of the depositor. The canceled checks are filed daily in front of check size guides, which usually contain the signature card of the depositor, and are accumulated until the time of the month when the statement and canceled checks for the period are returned to the depositor.

There are other alphabetic-numeric filing systems which are highly specialized and are used in large filing departments with special problems that these systems are designed to solve. Your secretarial duties may indirectly bring you into contact with these various filing systems.

Filing personnel who work with alphabetic-numeric systems are given on-the-job training before being assigned to the operation of such systems. On-the-job training is normally necessary because of the differences in the systems.

Guides and Folders Used in Numeric Filing

The type and quantity of supplies used in numeric filing will depend on the arrangement that is used. Individual folders can be made for each number, with the number on the tab, or with the number and name typed on a label affixed to the tab. Guides are normally inserted for every ten folders.

Geographic Filing

prime:
primary; main

If you are using a geographic filing system, geographic location is the prime indexing factor. In the United States, for instance, materials would be arranged alphabetically first by states, then by cities or towns within the states, and finally alphabetically by the names of the correspondents in the cities or towns. A geographic file may also be based upon sales territories, upon cities in a single state, or upon districts or streets for local correspondence.

Typical users of geographic filing systems are publishing houses, mail-order houses, radio and television advertisers, real estate firms, and organizations dealing with a large number of small businesses scattered over a wide area. The personnel in many of these small businesses change frequently; therefore, the name of the individual owner or manager is often less important than the location of the business.

Geographic filing is an indirect method of locating folders for individual correspondents. It is slower to operate since papers must be sorted as many as three times, depending on the geographic arrangement that is selected.

Arrangement of a Geographic File

The primary guides in a geographic filing system bear the names of the largest geographic divisions. The specific arrangement will depend on the needs of the company and the volume of records. For example, a geographic filing system based on states would have each guide tab printed with the name of a state; and all correspondence with people in that state would be filed behind that guide. These state guides are usually arranged alphabetically; thus, Alabama is first, followed by Alaska and the other states in alphabetic order. They would also be arranged by a division of the country into areas, such as "West Coast"; and behind these guides the secondary guides or folders for the states of California, Oregon, and Washington would be filed.

The secondary guides bear the names of the geographic subdivisions. For example, behind each primary state guide there are secondary guides with captions that provide for the alphabetic arrangement of cities and towns within that state.

A geographic file may include several different kinds of folders, such as individual folders, city folders, and state folders. Individual folders in a geographic file are used in the same manner as in an alphabetic file. They differ, however, in their captions, because in a geographic file, the caption on an individual folder includes the name of the city and state, as well as the name of the correspondent. The geographic identification should appear on the top line, the correspondent on the second. This arrangement of the captions aids in the correct placement of the folders behind the appropriate state and city guides.

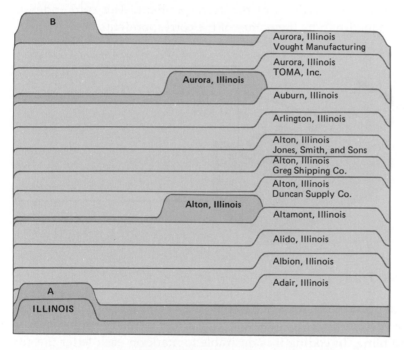

Illus. 12-20

Geographic file

If there is no individual folder for a correspondent, communication from that correspondent is filed in a city folder. If there is not enough correspondence to **warrant** the use of a separate city folder, the communication is placed in a miscellaneous state folder at the back of the appropriate state section of the file.

warrant:
necessitate; justify

For larger cities, several city folders are sometimes necessary. These are assigned alphabetic captions and placed behind a secondary city guide. For example, five Chicago folders might be used, the first for those Chicago correspondents whose names fall into the alphabetic range of A–C; the second, D–H; the third, I–M; the four, N–R; and the fifth, S–Z.

Cross-Reference for Geographic Filing

As in alphabetic filing, there are times when cross-references must be prepared on a letter. The geographic location, the correspondent's name, and other information about the letter are recorded on the form.

Card Index

In geographic filing you must know the name of the city and state in which a person or business firm is located to find a letter referring to that correspondent. Since this information is not always known, it is advantageous to keep a card index with a geographic correspondence file. This is usually a 5" × 3" card file, which includes a card for each correspondent giving the name and address of the correspondent. The card index is arranged alphabetically by the names of the correspondents.

Illus. 12-21

Card index and individual correspondent card

Shaw-Walker

Geographic Filing Procedure

The filing procedure for a geographic file is similar to that for alphabetic filing, except that the state and city are of primary importance in coding and filing. In coding it is desirable to mark on each letter the city and state as well as the name of the correspondent. The location may be circled and the name of the correspondent underlined.

Materials are sorted by geographic units, starting with the key unit for the first sorting and continuing until all the units involved in the filing system have been used. For example, the first sorting might be on the basis of states, the second sorting on the basis of cities or towns, and the final sorting on the basis of correspondents.

Letters are arranged in the folders as follows: (1) in an individual folder by date, (2) in a city folder by the names of the correspondents and then by date, (3) in an alphabetic state folder by the names of cities or towns and then by the names of correspondents according to date. In each case, of course, the most recent letter is placed in front.

Summary of Filing Methods

Each filing method has its advantages and disadvantages. On page 474 is a summary of the outstanding features of the four methods.

There are many types of commercial filing systems. All make generous use of color to code classifications of primary and secondary guides, include individual and miscellaneous folders, and are designed for efficiency and ease of operation.

"Office-Made" Filing System

In many small businesses and separate offices in large businesses, it is not economical to purchase commercial filing systems. You may be asked to devise or reorganize a file system in such circumstances.

A practical, inexpensive system using one-third cut folders would include:

1. First position: primary guide that is also a miscellaneous folder for that letter in the alphabet. The letter of the alphabet is printed on the label.
2. Second position: special guide that is also a miscellaneous folder for that section of the file.
3. Third position: individual folders.

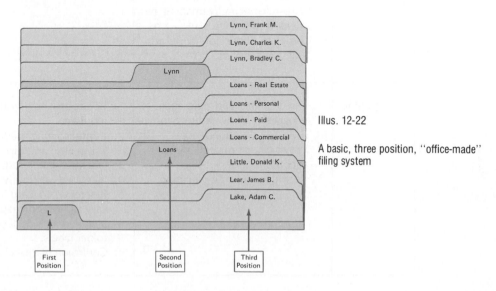

Illus. 12-22

A basic, three position, "office-made" filing system

METHOD	ADVANTAGES	DISADVANTAGES
Alphabetic	1. Direct filing and reference. 2. No index required. 3. Records may be grouped by individual or by company name. 4. Simple arrangement by guides, folders, and colors. 5. Easy to locate miscellaneous records.	1. Possibility of error in filing common names. 2. Related records may be filed in more than one place. 3. Too little or too much cross-referencing.
Subject	1. Records grouped by subject in technical or statistical files. 2. Unlimited expansion.	1. Extensive cross-referencing necessary. 2. Difficulty in classifying records for filing. 3. Difficulty in filing miscellaneous folders. 4. Necessary to use an index to determine subject heading or subdivision.
Numeric	1. Most accurate of all methods. 2. Unlimited expansion. 3. Definite numbers to identify name or subject when requesting files. 4. Uniform system of numbers used in departments of company. 5. Cross-referencing permanent and extensive. 6. Complete index of correspondents and subjects.	1. Requires specialized training. 2. High labor cost. 3. Indirect filing and reference. 4. Miscellaneous records require separate files. 5. Cumbersome index.
Geographic	1. Direct filing and reference for geographic area (indirect for individual correspondence). 2. Provision for miscellaneous records. 3. Records grouped by location.	1. Location as well as name required. 2. Triple sorting necessary — by state, city, and alphabet. 3. Increased labor cost. 4. Increased possibility of error. 5. Reference to card index necessary to find correspondent. 6. Detailed typed descriptions on folder labels. 7. Confusion in miscellaneous files.

REVIEWING

1. Why must a secretary be acquainted with all the basic types of filing systems?
2. When is a subject filing system preferable to other systems?
3. How is a letter coded in a subject file?
4. Name the three parts of a numeric filing system. What is the purpose of each?
5. How is terminal-digit filing read?
6. What is the disadvantage of geographic filing?
7. What kinds of guides and folders are used with a geographic filing system?
8. What is the primary importance in coding and filing of a geographic filing system?
9. With a geographic system, how are materials arranged in an individual folder? in a city folder? in an alphabetic state folder?
10. An "office-made" file system is likely to be used in what type of business?

MAKING JUDGMENTS

Warren has just started working for a newly established insurance company. He has been asked by his employer, Miss Stevens, to help set up a filing system for each sales representative's accounts. Warren decides to set up a geographic file based upon the territories of the sales representatives. He also suggests using color coded folders for each of the sales representatives. What do you think of Warren's decision about color coding?

WORKING WITH OTHERS

A secretary filing under a subject system must read letters and papers carefully since they may contain references to more than one subject. Leonard Nelson, with whom you work, fails to read the material to be filed, and, as a result, there is much misfiling and improper cross-referencing.

Whenever the chief file clerk corrects him, Leonard becomes impatient and tells the chief clerk the system is stupid and does not make sense.

How would you help Leonard to improve his work habits and to understand the importance of proper operation of the filing system?

REFRESHING LANGUAGE SKILLS

The relative pronouns *who* and *whom* are frequently misused. When a relative pronoun is the subject of a subordinate clause, *who* is used. When a relative pronoun is the object of a verb or a preposition, *whom* is used. Type each of the sentences below inserting the correct pronoun.

Examples: Samuel Todd is the player *who* can score the touchdown.
Gretel is the girl *whom* we chose for the job.

1. Sally is the girl _____ knows the system better than anyone.
2. Don't you know _____ called me?
3. _____ do you want to do the job?
4. For _____ are you waiting?
5. To _____ did you wish to speak?
6. The matter of _____ shall pay for the delay is still to be decided.
7. Do you know _____ is going to get the promotion?
8. Was it _____ I thought it was?
9. She is the one _____ should be fired.
10. Have you noticed _____ is always late?

PERFORMING SECRETARIAL TASKS

Type the following twenty business firm names, addresses, and account numbers on 5" × 3" cards. File them three ways: (1) alphabetically, (2) geographically, and (3) numerically.

5001 Cobin & Sons, Washington, D.C. 20013
5004 Connel Manufacturing Co., Seattle, WA 98111
5009 The Cole Manufacturing Co., San Francisco, CA 94101
5006 Crawford, Crawford and Croll, Cincinnati, OH 45201
5003 Cone, Lambert and Ulysses, Chicago, IL 60690
5002 Corn and Frederick, Dallas, TX 75221
5005 Max Collier & Sons, Tallahassee, FL 32302
5007 Conwit Tailors, Gainesville, FL 32601
5008 Cone, Arnold & Co., New York, NY 10001
5010 Cobbs Corporation, Boston, MA 01432
5019 Conklin Company, Erie, PA 16512
5015 Conner Corporation, Cleveland, OH 44101
5016 The Samuel Collins Company, St. Louis, MO 63177
5013 Colton Company, Boise, ID 83707
5012 Conrad & Matthew, Reno, NV 89504
5011 Coyne Corporation, Los Angeles, CA 90053
5014 Craig & Stanton Corporation, San Luis Obispo, CA 93401
5017 Cole & Monford Co., Nashville, TN 73202
5018 Conners Metal Manufacturing, Inc., Cicero, IL 60650
5020 Conover & Sterling, Baton Rouge, LA 70821

4

Special Files, Micrographics, and Information Systems

"Mr. Houghton, will you call Mr. Peterson, with Peterson, Vickers, and Sanford law firm, please."

"Yes, Ms. Rice."

Although Mr. Houghton does not know Mr. Peterson's number, he can easily and quickly find it by using his rotary file. Ms. Rice can always depend on him to either have the requested information or know where it can be found.

In a matter of minutes, Mr. Houghton is able to say, "Mr. Peterson is on the telephone, Ms. Rice."

Card Files

From small to large, practically all offices make use of card files. You may keep a small card file on your desk that contains the names, address, and telephone numbers of people whom you call or write to frequently. Secretaries for doctors and dentists usually have card files containing information about patients; teachers often have a card file for each of their classes; libraries, of course, have card catalogs covering all the books in the library. A card file is needed as a cross-reference in subject, numeric, and geographic filing. Card files are used in almost every department in a business firm; shipping, receiving, purchasing, inventory control, personnel records, payroll, and stock records may be maintained on cards.

Cards used in filing are usually 5" × 3", 6" × 4", or 8" × 5". The size selected usually depends upon the amount of information that is needed on the card. The 5" × 3 " is the most widely used card size.

When typing information on the cards for the files, follow this simple procedure:

1. Type the name in exact indexing order.
2. If the card is not ruled, begin typing on the third line from the top of the card. If the index card is ruled, begin typing above the printed line.
3. Indent two spaces from the left edge of the card file and set a margin.

4. Use upper and lower case letters. They are easier to read.
5. Abbreviations may be used since space is limited.
6. Be **consistent** in spacing, capitalization, punctuation and style.

Vertical Card Files

These are the types of files in which the card stands on edge, usually the width of the card. Thus, a 5″ × 3″ card rests on the 5-inch edge; the 6″ × 4″ card rests on the 6-inch edge; the 8″ × 5″ card rests on the 8-inch edge. There are, however, exceptions to this; some cards are filed according to the depth of the card. The cards may or may not be ruled, depending upon whether they will be typed or handwritten.

Illus. 12-23

A secretary works at a numeric vertical card file

Ohio National Life Insurance Company

Just as guides are needed to divide the file drawer to keep the folders in order, it is also necessary to divide the cards in an alphabetic card file into convenient alphabetic sections with a set of *card guides*. These card guides indicate on projecting tabs the various alphabetic sections into which the file drawer is divided. In some cases special primary and secondary guides are used, and cards will often be color coded.

The notations on the tabs of the guides consist in most cases of letters, such as *Alf, Alli, Alm, Alt, Am, An*; but they may consist of popular surnames such as *Allen, Anderson, Andrews,* as you will notice in the illustration below. They indicate the alphabetic range of the cards filed in each section. The file cards are placed in alphabetic order behind the appropriate guide just as the folders are placed behind the guides in the file drawer.

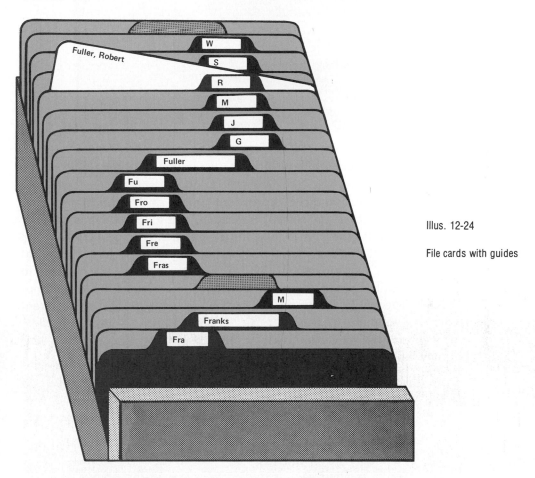

Illus. 12-24

File cards with guides

Visible Card Files

These are files in which a portion of the card is visible at all times, that portion generally showing the name, department, or product to which the card record refers. These cards are generally placed in pockets on horizontal trays, or on vertical sheets, or in files that appear in book form. The total card becomes visible as the overlapping cards are raised to provide a view of the whole card.

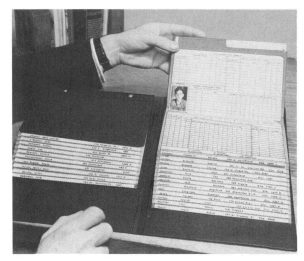

Illus. 12-25

Visible record card
book

Sperry Rand
Corporation

Signals on Visible Records. In addition to cards that are especially printed for use with visible files, small metal or plastic signals are available. These may be placed in various positions on the cards to indicate something important about the record. For example, if a visible file is used for collection records, the signal may indicate that the account is in good standing, or that it is overdue. Some signals may be used to indicate that it is very much overdue or that the firm with the account is no longer to be given credit because of poor standing. These signals are sometimes placed in special positions on the card and frequently are in different colors. For example, blue may indicate a good credit standing, yellow may suggest mildly overdue, orange may mean very much overdue, and red may tell you that no further credit is to be extended.

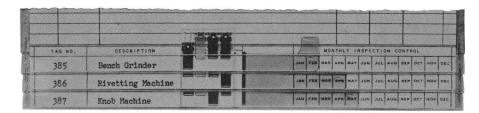

Illus. 12-26

Signals on visible
records

Remington Rand

Reference Visible Systems. These files usually carry only a strip instead of a whole card, the strip containing perhaps a name, address, and telephone number of persons who are called rather often. The strips are usually referred to as visible panels and are generally limited to one or two lines.

Rotary Files

These are cards to be used where quick reference to a large number of cards is needed. Cards used with this type of equipment are punched or cut at the bottom or at the side depending upon the style of wheel. There are small rotary files for desk-top use and also large rotary motorized equipment that is used when a great deal of information must be available for fingertip retrieval.

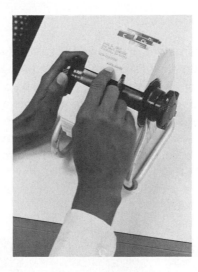

Illus. 12-27

Rotary file

Random Files

In this kind of system, the cards not only have typed or printed information on them, but are also equipped with strips of metal teeth which are attached to the bottom edge of the card. These teeth are cut in relation to magnetic rods that run under the cards. These files are operated by a keyboard, and the depression of certain keys causes one or more cards to be pushed up, thus locating them and making them available quickly. This system has the advantage of allowing one card to be identified under one of several possible captions. It is often found in banks, savings and loan associations, and finance companies where fast reference to a customer's file assures prompt service and goodwill.

Illus. 12-28

At the touch of the keys this file automatically selects the card needed.

Acme Visible Records

Elevator Files

This type of file is power driven and is in a sense a multiple card file with trays arranged on shelves which may be brought to the level of the operator by the use of an elevator or power-driven system. The shelves in this kind of a file operate on the same principle as a ferris wheel at an amusement park. The shelves may be wide enough to take four, five, or more trays of 5″ × 3″ cards; and any single machine may include a large number of shelves. The operator pushes a button to move any particular shelf into position. At that point the operator may work directly on some cards, or may remove a complete tray of cards and turn them over to someone else to work on.

Illus. 12-29

Elevator files

Wheeldex, Inc.

Micrographics

Micrographics includes the entire process of photographically reducing information on paper to some type of film. The word "micrographics" is comparatively new and is sometimes used interchangeably with the more familiar word "microfilm." An 8½ × 11 inch sheet of paper can be reduced 1/24 of its original size in one second.

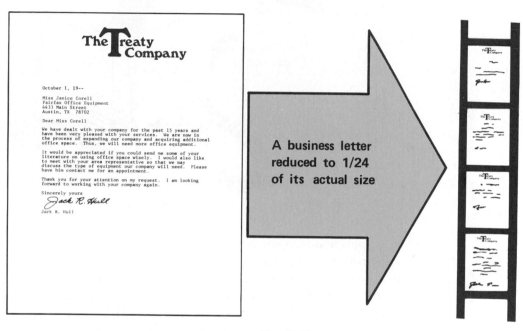

Illus. 12-30

There are several types of micrographics: microfilm, microfiche, aperture card, and computer output microfilm (COM).

Microfilm

The original documents are photographed on a roll of film, similar to motion picture film, which is placed in a 4 × 4 inch cartridge.

The Process. (See Illustration 12-31, p. 484) A roll of microfilm in a **cartridge** is snapped into the camera (1). The original document (for example, a letter) (2) is fed into the machine and photographed instantly. The camera reads out the location of the document on the film (3) and this location is indexed on the outside of the cartridge for future retrieval.

cartridge:
protective case

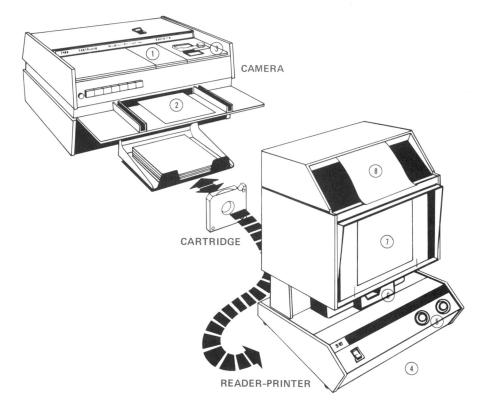

Illus. 12-31

A microfilm filing system

CAMERA

CARTRIDGE

READER–PRINTER

3M Company

When a specific document is to be retrieved, the cartridge is placed on a reader-printer (4). Turning the dial (5) on the front of the machine permits the operator to scan the film. When the reading on the printer (6) matches the location of the document on the index of the cartridge, the document appears on the screen of the reader (7). If hard copy (paper copy similar to that made from a copying machine) is desired, the print button is pressed and the reader-printer produces an exact copy (8) of the picture on the screen.

Advantages. Microfilming has the following advantages:

1. *Space saving.* About 3,000 letter-size documents can be placed on a 100-foot role of microfilm.
2. *Accurate filing.* All of the documents in the cartridge are always in the same **sequence** and cannot be misfiled.
3. *Efficient retrieval.* A letter on a microfilm can be located in a few seconds while the operator is seated at the reader-printer.
4. *Security.* An extra copy of the microfilm can easily be made which can then be stored in a different, protected location.
5. *Duplication.* Documents can be duplicated **inexpensively**. The copies are as good as the originals even though hundreds of copies are made.

sequence:
order

inexpensively:
with very little cost

Microfiche

Microfiche (pronounced *micro feesh*) is a 4" × 6" sheet of microfilm that can contain 98 business documents (8½" × 11") reduced 24 times. Typed information is recorded on the top of the microfiche so that it can be filed and retrieved. Duplicate copies of 4" × 6" film can be made inexpensively. Six microfiche can be mailed in an envelope as first-class mail.

Aperture card

Aperture cards are punched cards that contain a piece of microfilm. The holes in the card make it possible to file and retrieve the cards on a sorter as described in Unit 6, Part 2, page 227.

Computer Output Microfilm

Computer output microfilm (sometimes abbreviated COM) makes it possible to place information stored in a computer directly onto microfilm. Information can be recorded at the rate of 20,000 typewritten lines a minute. This is approximately 20 times faster than the computer can print the same information onto paper.

Electronic Data Processing

Electronic data processing equipment can store more information and retrieve it faster than any other system. Specially trained people handle the equipment for both input and retrieval of data. As a secretary in a data processing department, you would be very much concerned with the equipment and how it is used. As a secretary in any other department, you should be familiar with how the data processing equipment can aid your employer and you. In almost all cases, however, you would need the assistance of the people in the data processing department in order to store or retrieve information.

Tabulating (Punched) Cards

extensive:
broad

With the tremendous increase in the use of electronic data processing equipment, most companies have **extensive** tabulating card files. The tabulating or punched cards are often stored in vertical files. In the drawers of the filing cabinets, the cards are stored in removable trays. Alphabetic, numeric, and alpha-numeric indexing systems are used.

Computer Tapes and Disks

Magnetic tapes and disks can hold more information in less space than can punched cards. The tapes and disks are usually stored in fire- and heat-resistant cabinets or safes.

Some electronic data processing equipment uses punched paper tape to store information. The punched paper tapes themselves are usually placed in specially designed folders that contain pockets for the tape.

Retrieval

Retrieval of information stored in a computer is quite rapid. When you request information from a computer, it may print out the information on a continuous sheet of paper or on specially prepared business forms. It is possible that you may work in a business that has visual display units for retrieving information. With visual display units, the information you request is shown on a television-like screen.

Illus. 12-34

Visual display unit for retrieving information

Courtesy of American Telephone & Telegraph Company

Which Filing System?

If a filing system is to operate effectively, **considerable** time must be given to its development. A good filing system cannot be designed casually. The solution to many records management problems is neither simple nor easy. The development of an effective filing — and finding — system must be based on good planning, careful analysis, clear thinking, and extensive experience.

considerable: much

Here are some factors that should be considered when developing a filing system:

1. *The record requirements of the office.* What kinds of records are retained? How are these records created or received? What is the total volume of records retained each week, month, or year? What about future expansion of the system?
2. *Using the system.* How are the records requested and used? How active are the records? How long must the records be retained in the file?
3. *Storing the records.* What type of classification system should be used? Will a centralized or decentralized file plan be most effective? Where will the inactive records be stored?
4. *Equipment and supplies.* What specific types of equipment and supplies — out of the vast **array** available — would be most appropriate for this system in this office?

array: variety of items

Since every office has different records requirements, a system used in one office is not always suitable for another. Remember that you are storing important information that must be retrieved quickly — you are not merely keeping pieces of paper.

Every filing system should be as simple as possible to use. In addition, the system should be efficient and reliable in providing needed information and should be economical to operate and maintain.

When an office decides to install a new filing system or to change an old one, three methods may be considered. A qualified person in the office may analyze the particular information requirements and develop an "office-made" system, a system may be purchased from a filing equipment and supplies manufacturer, or a records consultant may be engaged to design a tailor-made filing system to meet the company's particular needs.

REVIEWING

1. Why are card files needed?
2. What procedure should be followed for typing information on cards for filing?
3. Why are metal or plastic signals used with visible card records?
4. When are cards filed on rotary files?
5. Give one of the advantages of a random file.
6. Give one of the advantages of an elevator file.
7. What does the term "micrographics" mean?
8. What are the three advantages of duplicating and copying micro-filmed materials?
9. Why are magnetic tapes and disks preferred to punched cards in electronic data processing systems?
10. What are four of the factors to be considered in developing a filing system?

MAKING JUDGMENTS

Miss Estelle Weeks began working for Cliffside Advertising Agency as a file clerk during their busiest period of the year. She soon discovered that many of the materials were misfiled, that proper procedures were not being followed for charging out materials, and that the firm also was in need of some new and more appropriate filing equipment. Miss Weeks decided to do her best under the current circumstances and to talk with her employer as soon as possible about some changes that should be made after the company's business slowed down. Do you think Miss Weeks' decision not to try to make changes at this particular time was a wise one? Why or why not?

WORKING WITH OTHERS

When Kenneth was promoted, he was asked to train Howard as his replacement. Kenneth spent a considerable amount of time teaching Howard the different filing systems used by the department. For several weeks Kenneth has been available to answer Howard's questions. Now, however, Kenneth feels that Howard should be able to manage on his own. How can he encourage Howard to become more independent?

REFRESHING LANGUAGE SKILLS

Type each of the following sentences using the correct form of the word in parentheses.

1. My sister and (I, me) went to the movies last night.
2. The folders fell (off, off of) the table.
3. She types (better, more better) every day.
4. Jane (can hardly, can't hardly) work because her telephone rings so often.
5. The invitation included my friend (too, also).
6. We don't have (no, any) more carbon paper.
7. Please (bring, take) that letter here, and I'll photocopy it.
8. Where do the typists place (there, their) initials on the letters?
9. Resort reservations are not (so, as) expensive this summer as they were last summer.
10. Mary (sure, surely) knew her filing rules.
11. (Try to, Try and) picture a more perfect setting.
12. They work (well, good) together.
13. (Leave, Let) me answer the phone, please.
14. (It don't, It doesn't) matter if you are a bit late.
15. Everyone in our class (has, have) seen the movie on filing, *It Must Be Somewhere.*
16. You were (very, real) thoughtful to call.
17. They (should of, should have) mailed it sooner.
18. We (differ with, differ from) you on the value of such elaborate planning.
19. Act (as if, like) you were interested in the suggestion.
20. Please (lay, lie) down to rest at the end of the day.

PERFORMING SECRETARIAL TASKS

This is the conclusion of the alphabetic indexing exercise begun in Unit 11, Part 3, and continued in Part 1 of this unit.

Prepare your last 25 index cards from the names listed on page 490 and integrate them with the 75 cards you now have from the two previous assignments.

Part 4 • Special Files, Micrographics, and Information Systems

(76) Henry R. Elston, IV, 2728 Germantown Rd., Germantown, PA 19144

(77) Chamber of Commerce, 12th & Olive Sts., Joliet, IL 60433

(78) Chief Engineer, Safety Division, Arkansas State Highway Dept., Ft. Smith, AR 72901

(79) Horace Mann Junior High School, 2500 Euclid Ave., Erie, PA 16511

(80) St. Mark's Episcopal Church, Oakwood, MO 63401

(81) University of New Mexico, Albuquerque, NM 87103

(82) Wm. A. Graves, 1620 N. Vernon Place, Winnetka, IL 60093

(83) Second National Bank, 8th & Race Sts., Spokane, WA 99202

(84) Garden Gate Antiques, 49 W. Elm St., Independence, KS 67301

(85) Security Savings Society, 74 Ohio Ave., Watertown, NY 13601

(86) Vera's Beauty Salon, 29 W. Adams St., Bennington, VT 05201

(87) Jack the Tailor, 536 S. 29th St., Oklahoma City, OK 73129

(88) Downtown Merchants Assn., 1200 Transportation Bldg., Wheeling, WV 26003

(89) Lady Constance Cosmetics, 128 W. 63rd St., New York, NY 10023

(90) Citizens Bank & Trust Co., Manchester, NH 03105

(91) Hartford Water Department, Hartford, CT 06101

(92) U.S. Marshal, Justice Dept., Federal Bldg., Boise, ID 83707

(93) Arnold A. Townley-Jones, 5021 Eastman Blvd., Chicago, IL 60622

(94) Chief Inspector, Food & Drug Administration, Health & Welfare Dept., Post Office Bldg., Butte, MT 59701

(95) United Fine Arts Fund, Terminal Bldg., Dallas, TX 75222

(96) Baldwin-Wallace College, Berea, OH 44017

(97) Harold McArthur & Sons, 4587 Roland Ave., Glendale, CA 91209

(98) MacArthur Sportswear, 688 Jefferson St., Kalamazoo, MI 49007

(99) Bernice L. McAdoo, 3 Alpine Terrace, Trenton, NJ 08610

(100) Perkins-Reynolds Insurance Agency, 200 Nicollet Ave., Minneapolis, MN 55401

IMPROVING SECRETARIAL SKILLS (Optional)

Arrange the following items into an "office-made" filing system. Type them in the proper order on a separate sheet of paper. Indent to show first, second, and third position folders.

1. Sporting Goods Department
2. Dodson, Jane R.
3. Derrick, Lance
4. Departments
5. Music Department
6. Furniture Department
7. Dearing Office Supplies
8. Appliance Department
9. Derryman, Samuel
10. Dodson, Rosemary

The Secretary and Travel Responsibilities

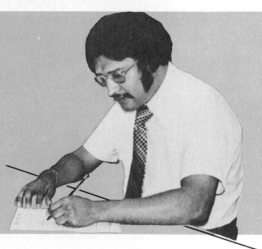

Part 1

Travel Services

Ms. Gilda Stiles, secretary to Ms. Gertrude Welman, handles travel details frequently. Ms. Welman is one of the vice presidents of a large educational foundation, and she spends much time traveling throughout the United States, Canada, and Latin America. Planning for Ms. Welman's trips is a task Ms. Stiles finds very interesting. She has planned so many trips that Ms. Welman now gives her only limited information to initiate the task. Ms. Welman is likely to say: "I have a meeting in Denver at 3 next Thursday, and I should plan to spend the night there." Then, Ms. Stiles goes ahead with flight arrangements and hotel reservations.

Business executives often travel. Some have jobs that require extensive travel, while others travel less frequently. Executives travel to visit offices of their own companies, to see customers, and to attend conferences and other types of meetings held in all parts of the world. As companies increasingly become worldwide in their operations, the need for executives to travel beyond the boundaries of the United States is increasing.

Secretaries perform many important tasks for traveling executives. Not only are secretaries delegated tasks to handle while executives are away, but they are also responsible for many of the details of travel arrangements.

Planning Trips

A trip out of town requires planning. To plan successfully, it is necessary for the secretary to find out from the executive:

1. Places to be visited
2. Length of each visit
3. Desired times of arrival and departure
4. Whether there is a particular hotel or motel where accommodations are to be secured
5. Desired travel services

With such information, the secretary can then seek the assistance of the travel department of the company, if there is one, or a local travel agency, or secure the details through checking with travel companies and hotels directly.

Travel Departments

Many large companies have special travel departments that are able to handle details of trips for individual executives. Generally the secretary serves as an **intermediary** for the executive and the travel department. The secretary may need to fill out a form giving the basic details such as travel time, length of stay, and type of **accommodations**. The form is then forwarded to the travel department. When a **tentative** plan has been outlined, the travel department staff obtains approval before final reservations are made.

intermediary: middle person

accommodations: hotel/motel arrangements

tentative: suggested; open to change

Travel departments in large companies may have a fleet of automobiles as well as several small airplanes that they are able to reserve for individuals and small groups of executives who must travel for the company. Such departments may also maintain hotel accommodations on a regular basis in major cities where executives regularly work for brief periods of time.

Travel Agencies

Some companies use a local travel agency for travel services. The agency may function in much the same manner as the travel department of a company. The staff member of the travel agency who aids the secretary will require the same information needed by a travel department. Once a plan is drawn up, the staff member checks with the secretary, who may need to secure **confirmation** from the executive before reservations are made and tickets purchased.

confirmation: approval

In general, travel agency staffs are knowledgeable about travel to most parts of the world. They also have current references to secure details of schedules, costs, and nature of accommodations. If you work for an executive who uses a travel agency, you will find that the staff of such an organization will be able to give you much useful information. Travel agency fees are paid by the companies whose services it sells to its clients, so your company pays no direct fees for travel agency services.

The Secretary

Very often executives assign details for a trip to their secretaries. In effect, the secretary serves as a travel agent. Sometimes this is necessary as there may not be any travel agencies in the community.

In order to handle travel details, the secretary will want to secure certain references, including up-to-date schedules from airlines and railroads serving the area, references for hotels and motels, and a comprehensive road atlas.

allowances:
amounts of money available for expenses

The secretary also needs to know the company policies relative to travel **allowances**. Generally the policies are in writing, and the secretary should keep a copy at hand so that the reservations and accommodations secured are within the ranges specified in the policies.

Domestic Air Travel

Air travel is common in the United States. Business people often prefer it because of its speed. By air it is possible to visit several cities and return to the home office before the end of a working day.

Illus. 13-1

The fastest way to travel from one city to another is to fly.

American Airlines

inclement:
stormy

Because of the uncertainty of flights during **inclement** weather — especially during the winter in certain parts of the country — it may be necessary for a secretary to make alternative arrangements by railroad or automobile.

Classes of Service

Most airlines provide two classes of service — first class and coach. First-class service is somewhat more expensive than coach service, and provides seats in the smoothest section of the plane, as well as more **elegant** meals than those provided in coach sections.

elegant:
fancy

Unit 13 • The Secretary and Travel Responsibilities

There are a few flights that are first class only; however, most airlines provide both types of service. Small airlines that serve intermediate stops between major cities tend to have only one class of service.

The policies of the company will determine the type of service to be reserved for executives.

Flight Information

Airlines offices in all major American cities are cooperative in providing information when you are arranging details of a trip. You may telephone a local number to secure information on possible flights. However, if you are frequently planning trips that require the services of several airlines, you may find it useful to have a copy of the *Official Airline Guide* at hand so you can determine all the possible flights for a forthcoming trip. Also, airlines publish complete schedules, which they will provide to you without cost. Each schedule clearly indicates the period of time for which it is valid.

Follow these steps in finding and using the information from the *Official Airline Guide*. Refer to the schedule on the following page.

1. Find the name of the city to which your employer is going at the top of the page.
2. After finding the "To" city, look down the listing beneath until you find the city from which your employer is departing.
3. Determine the fare by reading that section. Fares for various classes of service are shown for one-way and for round trips. Coach is indicated by "Y."
4. Determine the flight information by reading across the next section. The information is given in the following order:
   a. Frequency Code (An x followed by a number indicates that the flight will *not* operate on that day — 1 is Monday, 2 is Tuesday, etc. A number by itself indicates that the flight operates only on that day — "6," for instance, would mean that the flight operates only on Saturday.)
   b. Departure time
   c. Arrival time
   d. Airline (EA refers to Eastern Air Lines, NW to Northwest Airlines, UA to United Air Lines, and DL to Delta Air Lines)
   e. Flight number
   f. Classes of service available
   g. Type of aircraft being used
   h. Meal service (if any)
   i. Number of intermediate stops

To **ATLANTA, GA.** **EDT MIA**

From **MIAMI, FLA.**

One-way
Round trip

F	83.33	6.67	90.00	180.00	
S	60.19	4.81	65.00	130.00	
Y	60.19	4.81	65.00	130.00	
FN	60.19	4.81	65.00	130.00	
YN	48.15	3.85	52.00	104.00	
YM	49.00				

SO EX/2 S 16 DAY		98.00
UA EX/5 YL 30 DAY		91.00
EX/2 Y 16 DAY		98.00
EX/ 39 Y MIDWEEK		104.00

a	b	c	d	e	f	g	h	i
	3:25	5:04a	DL	1090	FN/YN			0
	6:05a	8:40a	EA	630	F/Y		*	1
				EA 630 * MEALS			SB/S	
	6:19a	8:50a	EA	320	F/Y	727	B	1
	6:20a	8:44a	EA	270	F/Y	72S	S	1
	7:00a	8:47a	EA	678	F/Y	727	B	0
	7:30a	11:09a	EA	614	F/Y	D9S	S	2
	7:48a	9:27a	DL	940	F/Y	D8S	B	0
	8:20a	11:28a	DL	238	F/Y	72S	S	2
X5	8:35a	11:20a	EA	538	F/Y	72S	S	1
	8:40a	11:25a	EA	330	F/Y	727		1
	8:45a	11:23a	EA	106	F/Y	727	S	1
	8:45a	11:25a	EA	368	F/Y	72S	S/	1
	8:50a	11:20a	EA	348	F/Y	D9S		1
X23	8:55a	11:30a	EA	146	F/Y	72S		1
	9:40a	11:19a	DL	960	F/Y	D8S	S/	0
	9:40a	11:30a	EA	252	F/Y	D9S	S/	0
	10:40a	2:08p	SO	216	S	DC9		3
	12:30p	2:20p	EA	594	F/Y	72S	L	0
	1:30p	3:09p	DL	1122	F/Y	L10	L	0
	1:40p	3:23p	NW	27	F/Y	D10	L	0
	2:28p	4:10p	UA	570	F/Y	727		0
	3:00p	5:39p	EA	998	F/Y	727		1
5	3:30p	5:07p	DL	456	F/Y	72S	S/	0
	3:35p	5:25p	EA	616	F/Y	72S	S/	0
	5:35p	7:14p	DL	1056	F/Y	L10	D	0
6	6:25p	9:40p	EA	672	F/Y	D9S		2
X6	6:55p	9:21p	EA	792	F/Y	DC9		1
	7:59p	9:42p	EA	602	F/Y	727	S/	0
	10:00p	11:37p	EA	452	FN/YN	727		0
	10:00p	11:37p	DL	182	FN/YN	72S		0

Illus. 13-2   A flight schedule from the *Official Airline Guide*

Airline Reservations

Once the executive has decided which flights are most suitable, you must make the flight reservations. Advance reservations are necessary for almost all airline flights. The reservations may be made in person at the airport, at the airline ticket office, or at a travel agency. You may also make airline reservations over the telephone. When you request a reservation either in person or on the telephone, the airline representative will tell you immediately whether your reservation is **confirmed**. A computerized network maintains an up-to-the-minute record of all available seats.

confirmed: firmly established; accepted

Illus. 13-3

Airline tickets can be picked up by the employer at the airlines counter before the flight.

American Airlines

Pickup of Tickets

When you make flight reservations, it is most important for you to know when and where to pick up the tickets. They may be picked up before the flight at the airline ticket office, at the air terminal as your employer checks in, or they may be mailed to either the business or home address of your employer. Air transportation may be paid for in cash or by check, or it may be charged on some credit cards. When tickets are mailed, the airline expects a check in payment within 72 hours after they have been received unless tickets were purchased on credit.

Transportation to the Airport

When helping plan a trip, you must remember to allow enough time for your employer to get to the airport. Airports are usually located away from the center of the city. Sometimes it takes an hour or more to go to the airport. In addition most airlines expect passengers to check in about 30 minutes before flight time.

As you plan the trip, you will need to know whether the executive will go to the airport by private car, taxi, or use the airport ground services. Allowances must be made for this additional travel.

Airport Limousines. Most cities have airport limousines or bus service to take passengers to and from the airport. The limousines usually leave from major downtown hotels, suburban motels, and airline ticket offices. This service is usually much less expensive than taking a taxi. Limousine services operate on a regular schedule, and you should check the schedule with the airlines for your employer when you help plan the trip.

Helicopter Service. Some cities have helicopter service available to carry passengers between the airport and the center of the city, or to suburban areas, and also between airports when there is more than one in a large city. Naturally this is the fastest way to get to the airport. While this service is expensive, it is often less costly than the executive's time spent in traveling 20 to 30 miles in heavy traffic.

Airport Parking. Some executives drive their own cars to the airport and leave them there while out of town. In this case, the secretary needs to know the additional time required for parking a car at the local airport. In most places, long-term parking is some distance from the central terminal. Of course, if the executive is going to be gone for only a day, the car may be parked in the regular parking lots.

Cancellation of Reservations

If, at the last minute, your employer cannot leave as scheduled, you should cancel the reservation immediately. Cancellation is possible at any time up to the time of departure. When a flight reservation is canceled, the unused tickets should be returned to the airline as soon as possible for a refund or credit.

Air Shuttle Flights

The employer who frequently travels between two major cities, may wish to take an air shuttle flight. These are regularly scheduled flights that travel only in a limited area. For example, there are shuttle flights between New York and Boston. There are also shuttle flights between San Francisco and Los Angeles.

To take a shuttle flight, the executive goes to the proper gate at the airport, gets a free boarding pass from a vending machine, fills out the boarding pass, and boards the plane. No advance reservations are necessary. After the plane takes off, the stewardess prepares a ticket and collects the fare, which may be charged by the use of an appropriate credit card. A seat is guaranteed every passenger no matter how many people arrive for a given flight. If one plane is filled, another is brought into service.

Train Travel

Trains are used by business people for relatively short trips and, at times, for overnight travel to more distant places. Amtrak, a national train service, provides a network of trains across the United States. There are some rapid trains between major cities. For example, it is possible to travel from New York to Boston in 4 hours, or from New York to Washington, D.C., in slightly less than 3 hours on Amtrak trains. Daily service from Chicago to Denver allows an executive to leave Chicago at 3:30 in the afternoon and arrive in Denver at 8:30 the following morning.

Train stations tend to be in the center of towns so that the executives who are traveling to the downtown area will find they are nearby when they arrive by train.

Illus. 13-4

Modern passenger train service provides rapid transit between many major cities

Amtrak

Classes of Service

Railroads, like airlines, offer different classes of service. The two classes of train service are coach and first class.

Coach Accommodations. Reservations need not be made for travel in most coach cars. A regular railroad ticket, which may be purchased at the station window, entitles you to a seat in a coach car. You need not get the ticket in advance; however, reservations are necessary for seats on some special trains, such as the *Metroliner.*

First-Class Accommodations. If your employer wants sleeping quarters, more spacious accommodations, or room to do some work while traveling by train, you should make a first-class or Pullman (sleeping car) reservation. Reservations for Pullman accommodations are made at the railroad ticket office. The tickets must be picked up and paid for or charged sometime before the scheduled departure time of the train. First-class accommodations are more expensive than coach accommodations.

Railroad Timetables

Every railroad publishes a timetable. Timetables tell which trains are available, where they go, and when they leave and arrive.

Bus Travel

Business people sometimes take buses to make calls in suburban and outlying districts. In regions where no other kind of public transportation is available for intercity travel, bus transportation is convenient and popular. Buses operate on regular schedules from terminals located in or near the business district. Bus transportation is the least expensive means of travel. Fares on all buses are lower than coach fares on railroads and airlines.

Automobile Travel

There are many times when business people prefer to drive a car to get to their appointments. This is often true for short trips in the local area. Also, an executive who flies into a large city may decide that a rented car provides a faster and more economical way to reach a destination than any other way. This is especially true when there are several stops to make or if some of the appointments are in small towns or outlying areas. By traveling by automobile, an executive does not have to plan appointments according to bus or train schedules.

Rental Services

Rental cars are available at almost every airport and at locations convenient to train stations and/or downtown hotels. Your employer can choose to rent a car at the local branch of the car rental agency or by calling a toll-free reservation number. Simply tell the agency when and where the car is wanted. When your employer arrives at the destination, the car will be waiting.

The cost of a rental car is usually determined by two factors — the length of time the car is used and the number of miles it is driven. The charges can be paid for by cash, check, or credit card.

Automobile Clubs

The employer who travels much of the time by car will probably be a member of one of the automobile clubs, such as the American Automobile Association (AAA). Among the many services offered by these clubs are routing assistance, insurance, emergency repair and towing service, and advice on where to stay and where to eat.

Automobile Routing

Planning the route for a proposed automobile trip is not difficult. If your employer does belong to one of the automobile clubs, the club will furnish the maps needed and mark the best route to take. Several major oil companies also offer this service.

You and your executive can plan the trip yourselves with the use of a current *Road Atlas* which includes maps of each state and usually Canada and Mexico. Be sure that it is up to date, because new highways are constantly being opened in all parts of the world.

International Travel

Trips to other countries by American business people are quite common. When a trip to another country is planned, the details of the trip should be provided well in advance to the travel department or to a travel agency. Enough time must be allowed to make all the necessary reservations. Generally most international travel is done by air. The time differences between the secretary's location and the places where the executive will be traveling should be noted.

Passports

Passports are required for travel in almost all foreign countries except Canada, Mexico, and the Central American countries. The employer who needs a passport must apply for it from the Department of State. The application should be completed at least a month before the passport is needed.

Visas

endorsement: approval in written form

Foreign travelers are required to have visas in order to travel in some countries. A visa is simply an **endorsement** on a passport by a representative of the country granting permission to enter the country for a certain purpose and length of time. If your employer's travel plans include a country that requires a visa, it will be obtained from the foreign consulate located in the United States.

Inoculations

inoculations: means of preventing disease; generally shots

When an executive is planning a trip outside the United States, be sure to check on requirements for **inoculations**. If traveling in rural areas, an executive may want to have the recommended, though not required, inoculations.

Hotel Arrangements

Hotels and/or motels of varying quality are available in all large cities. You will need to know company policy about allowance for hotel accommodations and your employer's preferences before you make reservations. It is then a relatively simply procedure either to call the hotel or motel, if it has an 800 number (toll-free service for reservations), or write a letter in which you indicate precisely the date and time of arrival and the type of accommodations desired.

Selecting a Hotel or Motel

A useful reference for selecting appropriate accommodations is the *Hotel and Motel Red Book*, which is published annually. This book provides a comprehensive listing of hotels and motels throughout the United States by state and city. For each hotel or motel listed, a number of details are provided to help you choose suitable accommodations. Services are provided under two plans: The American Plan and the European plan. Under the American Plan, which is not common in the United States, a room and meals are included in the basic price. However, under the European Plan, the price includes the room only. There will be, therefore, additional costs for meals taken in the hotel's dining room or coffee shop. The *Red Book* also indicates the number of rooms available, the general location of the hotel or motel, whether or not credit cards are accepted, what languages are spoken, and other useful details. Below is an illustration of a page from the *Red Book*.

| GEORGIA | | | | RATES | | Atlanta |
Name / Address / Manager	No. Rms.	Telephone Number	Toll Free or TWX No.	Single	Double	Loca- tion
Squire Inn—Sandy Springs 5750 Roswell Rd NE 30342 T. C. Adderhold, Mgr Credit Cards: AE; BA; CB; DC; MC	100	404- 252-5782		Ⓔ $15	Ⓔ $18–21	E
Squire Inn—South I-75 S 4730 S Expwy 30054 H. C. Aldredge, Owner	125	404- 361-6100		Ⓔ $11	Ⓔ $14–18	A E
Squire Motel—Northeast 2115 Piedmont Rd NE at I-85 30324 H. C. Aldredge, Owner	200	404- 876-4365		Ⓔ $12.50	Ⓔ $16–21	
Stouffer's Atlanta Hotel 590 W Peachtree St NW 30308 Stewart Gully, Mgr Credit Cards: AE; BA; DC; MC Commission to Travel Agents	505	404- 881-6000	800- 323-4455	Ⓔ $27–35	Ⓔ $34–45	D E
TraveLodge at Executive Park 2061 N Druid Hills Rd NE 30329 TraveLodge International, Inc John E. Porter, Gen Mgr Credit Cards: AE; BA; CB; DC; MC Commission to Travel Agents	212	404- 321-4174	800- 255-3050	Ⓔ $20–24	Ⓔ $24–28	E S
TraveLodge—Peachtree 1641 Peachtree St NE 30309 TraveLodge International, Inc Harold Bryant, Mgr Commission to Travel Agents	60	404- 873-5731	800- 255-3.50	Ⓔ $16–18	Ⓔ $20–22	E
ᴮ **White House Inn** 70 Houston St NE 30303 White House Inns, Inc Kalman Held, Gen Mgr Commission to Travel Agents Languages: S F G	219	404- 659-2660 (See also listing p. B-33)		Ⓔ $22–28	Ⓔ $26–35	D
AUGUSTA Richmond Co. / Bush Field 8 mi S of City. Airlines: Delta; Eastern; Piedmont. / Car Rental: Avis, Econo-Car, Hertz, National, Thrifty. / Pop. 59,864						
Augusta Hotel 604 Broad St at 6th 30902 J. J. Jones, Jr, Owner & Mgr	32	404- 724-7638		Ⓔ $9–14	Ⓔ $15–19	D

KEY: **B**—Business Meeting Facilities **C**—Resort or Condominium Ⓢ—Summer Ⓦ—Winter
Ⓐ—Amer. Ⓔ—Eur. **A**—At Airport **D**—Downtown **S**—Suburban **E**—On Expressway
R—Resort Languages: **S**—Spanish **F**—French **G**—German **J**—Japanese

280

Illus. 13-5

Many large hotel and motel chains publish booklets which provide details of their accommodations in various cities across the country. The booklets are provided free of charge upon request.

Making Reservations

After an executive has decided which accommodations will meet the requirements for the forthcoming trip, you may make the reservations by telephone, telegram, or letter, depending on the time available. Most large hotel and motel chains have central reservation offices through which you may make instant reservations by calling a toll-free reservation number. Your request, either by telephone or letter, should include:

1. Type of accommodations desired — single room, double room, or suite
2. Preferred rate
3. The number of persons in the party
4. The date and approximate time of arrival
5. The date and approximate time of departure
6. A request for confirmation, if there is sufficient time

A confirmation, which the hotel or motel sends to you, should be read carefully to be sure the details are all as you specified them. Then, the confirmation should be filed in the travel folder and attached to the itinerary so that the executive will have it at the time of checking in at the hotel or motel.

REVIEWING

1. Is a secretary always responsible for making the detailed arrangements for a business trip? Explain.
2. What basic information must be available before the details of a trip can be planned?
3. What kinds of services do travel departments of large companies provide?
4. Who pays a travel agency for the services provided for its clients?
5. What classes of service are generally provided on airlines?
6. In what reference is a secretary able to secure a comprehensive listing of the flights of all airlines?
7. Do airlines mail tickets to customers?
8. How does an air shuttle flight differ from a regular flight?
9. What is a useful reference for locating hotels and motels in various American cities? What information does this reference contain?
10. What kinds of documents are required for international travel that are not required for travel within the United States?

MAKING JUDGMENTS

1. Mrs. McGowan told her secretary, Mr. Lange, that because of some unexpected problems in the factory, she would not be leaving for Los Angeles the next afternoon. Mrs. McGowan had planned to call for her ticket at the point of checking in for the flight, so Mr. Lange didn't waste time calling to cancel the reservation he had made the day before for Mrs. McGowan. What do you think of Mr. Lange's action?

2. Ms. Ruth Ackers always travels in her own state by bus, because she enjoys seeing the countryside, and bus travel is inexpensive. When the executive for whom she works told her she was to be at the state capitol in Columbus at 3 p.m. the following Wednesday, she called the local bus station and learned that if the executive left on the 9:30 a.m. bus, she would arrive in Columbus at 2:30 p.m. Since she needed to be in the center of the city, there would be plenty of time to walk to her appointment.

   Ms. Ackers left a note on the executive's desk indicating the schedule, and as she did, she thought what a lovely day the executive was going to have riding through the small towns of Ohio. What do you think of her judgment?

WORKING WITH OTHERS

Mr. Vernon Netters works for a busy executive in a large company in Chicago. The company has a central travel department that provides many services for the executives. However, Mr. Netters has found that the office is not cooperative when he calls at the last minute to reserve a car for Ms. Radigan, the executive for whom he works. Often, Ms. Radigan doesn't know until the last minute that she must drive to one of the branches in another section of the state. Mr. Netters has learned that a local rental car service is helpful in such emergencies, so he began calling that office to rent a car for Ms. Radigan. When he told Ms. Radigan that he had changed from their own Travel Department to an outside service, Ms. Radigan approved of his action. However, about a month after he began this practice, he received a call from Central Accounting telling him he had no right to hire a rented car when they had a fleet of cars for executive use. What do you think Mr. Netters should do?

REFRESHING LANGUAGE SKILLS

On a piece of paper type the correct spelling for each of the 20 words that follow and give an appropriate synonym or brief meaning for each word.

Example: routing or routeing
Correct: routing
Meaning: plan for traveling

1. agancy	or	agency
2. alternative	or	alternetive
3. boarding	or	bording
4. conferance	or	conference
5. destination	or	destenation
6. efficeint	or	efficient
7. exceded	or	exceeded
8. flys	or	flies
9. foriegn	or	foreign
10. hellicopter	or	helicopter
11. immediately	or	immadiately
12. itinerery	or	itinerary
13. limousine	or	limosine
14. per dien	or	per diem
15. preference	or	preferance
16. reimbursement	or	reimborsement
17. shuttel	or	shuttle
18. spaceous	or	spacious
19. suberban	or	suburban
20. terminal	or	terminel

PERFORMING SECRETARIAL TASKS

1. Assume that you are a secretary in the town in which you are now a student. You make all the travel arrangements for the executive for whom you work. For each of the following, identify where you would be able to get the needed information in your town. (Note: You are not asked in this problem to actually get the information.)

a. The executive wants to go to the capital city in your state, but doesn't want to drive. Where would you get:

(1) Information about alternative means of transportation?
(2) Times of departures and arrivals?
(3) Cost for each type of service?
(4) Hotels and motels available near the center of town?

b. The executive must fly to London for one week. Where, in your town, would you be able to find:

(1) The nearest air service for London?
(2) Flight hours?
(3) Costs of service?
(4) Hotel accommodations in inner London?

Be prepared to discuss those sources of information you would consult.

2. You are secretary to Ms. Gallagher in the State Department of Education in Harrisburg, Pennsylvania. Ms. Gallagher has asked you to make a reservation for her on a forthcoming trip to Denver. She has a meeting in Denver on Thursday morning at 10 on May 5. She wants to know if there is a flight in the morning, but she thinks that she will want to leave the night before the meeting. What information can you give Ms. Gallagher before you make a reservation? (See excerpt from *Official Airline Guide* below.)

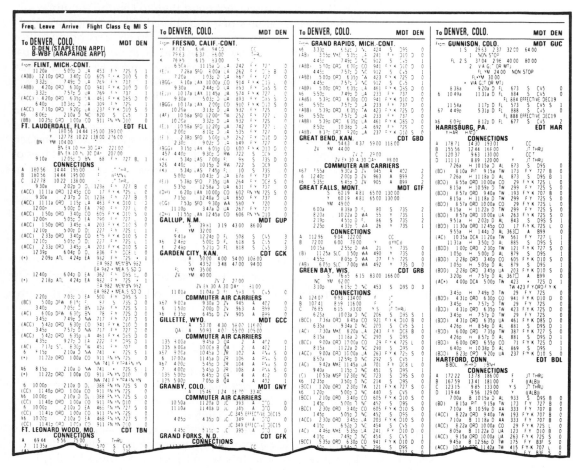

Official Airline Guide

Part 2

The Itinerary and the Expense Report

Mr. Andrew Foote has just learned from Miss Cynthia LaRue, the executive for whom he works, that she must go to Brussels for two weeks and then to London for one week. This is Miss LaRue's first trip abroad. She is a vice president in charge of construction for a rapidly expanding office equipment company. While she is in Brussels, she must make short trips to Paris, Munich, and Milan. Miss LaRue gave Mr. Foote the details, including the days when she will want to travel from Brussels to the other European cities. Mr. Foote has never planned an international trip. Yet, he knows that in New York City there are enough services to provide him with all the information he will need. In fact, during his lunch hour he plans to stop at the travel offices of the four countries Miss LaRue will visit to get additional information about the cities, as well as the countries in general, so that Miss LaRue will have some background knowledge of the places.

Careful plans make travel much more pleasant than it would otherwise be. Executives recognize the value of secretaries who thoughtfully plan their trips. Secretaries maintain **references** to handle such tasks simply and efficiently.

references:
books and booklets that contain useful facts

The secretary of a partner of a large accounting firm spoke of the past year's activities in her office in these words:

The executive for whom I work has just completed a term as president of her national professional organization. As president, she served on an important international committee. So, in addition to her travels to many state meetings around the United States, she was in eight foreign countries in less than twelve months — and I planned all the traveling. I thought it would be interesting to note how much traveling she did, so I kept a record of it (this wasn't part of my official tasks, I assure you!), and I found that she traveled 126,000 miles last year. In planning trips to Mexico City, Paris, London, Munich, as well as several other cities outside the United States, I learned much about international travel right here at my desk.

The Travel Folder

As trips are scheduled, the secretary should set up travel folders. In many instances, an executive makes similar trips year after year at approximately the same time. For example, annual sales meetings may be held at a given time each year; conferences tend to follow similar schedules year after year. As additional details for the trip become available, they can be placed in the appropriate folder so that all related information is in the same place. One secretary to a professor/lecturer commented:

> Professor Richards is often asked to read his poetry or discuss contemporary poetry in American colleges and universities or before literary groups. Each year he accepts about ten such invitations, but before one is accepted I must determine if the trip is feasible; that is, can Professor Richards handle it without missing one of his own classes or seminars here on campus. So, I am often calling an airline to get the schedule for 7 to 9 months in advance in order to determine if a particular date is a possibility. As soon as I write a letter of acceptance, I set up a file folder. Then, about six weeks to two months prior to the scheduled appointment, I make plane or train reservations and hotel reservations. Then, within a month of the appointment, I write to the person handling the program giving that person all the details of Professor Richard's arrival and departure.

The Itinerary

An *itinerary* is a detailed plan of a trip. It is generally prepared by the secretary and serves as a guide to the executive while away from the office. An illustration of part of an itinerary is shown on page 510. It is important that all **relevant** details are listed:

relevant:
related; necessary

1. *Date, time, and place of all departures and arrivals.* While it may be sufficient to merely indicate "airport" as the place of departure in a small town serviced by only one airport, it is inadequate in a large city where there may be several.

   Since there are time changes both within the United States and in foreign countries, time designations must indicate what time zone you are listing. Generally the local time, that is the time at the place of departure, and the time at the place of arrival are used.

2. *Type of transportation.* For airlines, the name of the **carrier** as well as the flight number should be indicated. For railroads, it is possible to use the name of the train, number, or city of destination.

   carrier:
   the airline company

3. *Hotel or motel accommodations.* The name of the hotel or motel should be listed as it appears on the confirmation; also, it is a

```
                    ITINERARY FOR ROBERT MERRILL
                          August 1 - 10, 19--
                 Boston - New York - Baltimore - Pittsburgh


TUESDAY, AUGUST 1 (CINCINNATI TO BOSTON)

3:30 p.m.        Leave Greater Cincinnati Airport on American
                 Airlines flight #515 (ticket in American Airlines
                 envelope).

4:55 p.m.        Arrive Logan Field Airport. Limousine to Sheraton
                 Hotel, downtown (confirmation attached).

8:30 p.m.        Meet Marvin Pearson at Bankers Club Restaurant, 32
                 West 53 Street (reservation in Pearson's name).

WEDNESDAY, AUGUST 2 (BOSTON)

9:00 a.m.        Daily conference with Boston office management at
                 the Boston office (notes for conference in envelope
                 marked "Conference").

THURSDAY, AUGUST 3 (BOSTON TO NEW YORK)

8:00 a.m.        Arrive at Logan Airport for commuter flight to
                 New York. Buy ticket.

9:05 a.m.        Commuter flight leaves for New York.

9:30 a.m.        Arrive at La Guardia. Limousine to New York Hilton
                 at Rockefeller Center (confirmation attached). Check
                 at desk for speech package. Will be mailed August 1.

12:30 p.m.       Convention Registration and luncheon at Rockefeller
                 Center.

4:00 p.m.        Your speech (in briefcase; duplicate in speech
                 package).

7:00 p.m.        Banquet (white tie).

                 Reminder: Talk with George Casey to confirm his
                          appointment with you next week in
                          Cincinnati.

FRIDAY, AUGUST 4 (NEW YORK)

9:00 a.m.        Convention Meetings and luncheon (luncheon ticket
(through the     in envelope marked "Convention").
afternoon)

7:00 p.m.        Dine at Mark Gentile's home, 630 Park Avenue.
                 Also dining with you are John McVay, Dave
                 Draudt, Ann Garrison.
```

Illus. 13-6 A portion of a finished travel itinerary

good idea to give the full address and telephone number as well as expected time of arrival.

4. *Appointments, engagements, special instructions.* The dates, times, and exact addresses for each appointment should be listed. All information needed to handle the business details of the particular appointment should be provided.

Preparation of an Itinerary

Secretaries use varying procedures for preparing the details of an itinerary. Some secretaries set up working papers, which are single sheets for each day of a trip. They make notes indicating special instructions they have received from their employers concerning dates, accommodations, etc. They also have a list of details to be taken care of:

> Airlines
> Helicopter
> Bus
> Car
> Hotel/Motel
> Other

Secretaries who handle many itineraries duplicate travel plan forms to facilitate their work. A form prepared by one secretary is shown on page 512.

Travel arrangements. You will want to be especially careful that your arrangements fit the plans of the executive. The executive should arrive in sufficient time to be at the first appointment on schedule. Generally, if the trip is a long one, there should be several hours between arrival and the first appointment. It is usually not good for an executive to have to leave home during the night or to arrive in a strange town in the middle of the night. Of course, limited service into some towns may require travel during the night hours.

You must also check the time zone differences and note these in your planning. For example, if an executive had to be in New York for an early afternoon meeting and left at 11 a.m. from Denver, it would be unfortunate; at 11 a.m. in Denver, it is already 1 p.m. in New York City. You must also note the time necessary to get from the airport or train station to the location where the executive is expected.

Finally, there are variations in schedules on weekdays and weekends. Be sure the transportation service you seek is available for the day required.

If the travel department or travel agency handles the details, obtain accurate information from them so that you can prepare the itinerary.

TRIP WORKSHEET

PLACE _Boston_

DATE _August 1, 19--_

PURPOSE _Conference with Boston office_

Completed:

Airlines _american_
Helicopter _____
Train _____
Bus _____
Car _____
Hotel/Motel _Sheraton_

Other: _____
_____

TRANSPORTATION:

American Airlines from Greater Cincinnati to Logan Field.
Limousine to Sheraton
Taxi to dinner

ACCOMODATIONS:

Sheraton Hotel, downtown Boston

SPECIAL ARRANGEMENTS:

Dinner with Marvin Pearson at Bankers Club Restaurant

OTHER:

Illus. 13-7   A secretary's travel form

Information obtained by telephone should be verified by repeating it back to the clerk.

Keep in the travel folder all notes of reservations, all tickets, and any accompanying documents as you receive them.

Hotel/Motel arrangements. You may write or telephone for reservations. If there is sufficient time between the time you make a reservation and the date of the expected trip, the hotel or motel will send you a written confirmation of the accommodations reserved. This confirmation should be filed in your trip folder.

Illus. 13-8

After consulting the appropriate resources, the secretary telephones for the executive's plane and hotel reservations.

Final preparation. After you have all the details of the trip, you should prepare a rough draft of the itinerary. If there are some points about which you are not sure, you may want the executive to check what you have done so that you may modify the plans.

modify: change

When all plans are in order, you should prepare a final copy of the itinerary, making as many copies as are needed. Executives like to have an opportunity to review the final itinerary before they leave town so that if they have any questions they can discuss them with the secretary.

Distribution of the Itinerary

You should have handy for quick reference at all times a copy of your employer's itinerary so that important messages and mail can be forwarded. Some companies require that copies of itineraries of key personnel be distributed to others in the organization so that they too are able to get in touch if it becomes necessary. However, it is most important that you be aware of your employer's location at all times so that should an emergency arise, your employer can be reached immediately.

The secretary to the president of a large company discussed her procedures in this manner:

> When Mrs. Blanden goes abroad for the Company, she always visits from six to nine countries and possibly as many as fifteen of our offices. We want all these offices to know her plans in the event they should want to get in touch with her while she is enroute. Therefore, I prepare a standard itinerary which I send to Central Duplicating for copies. We send copies to all offices in the United States so that the managers who want to communicate with Mrs. Blanden about one of the overseas offices on the itinerary will be able to get in touch with her. The itinerary for overseas travel, therefore, is completed about six weeks prior to the scheduled departure from the home office.
>
> I keep a copy at my telephone here at the office and one at my telephone at home. If Mr. Blanden isn't traveling with his wife, he also has a copy.

Travel Funds

The executive whose trip is to be lengthy probably will not want to carry enough cash to pay all the travel expenses because cash is too easily mislaid or stolen. Your employer may prefer to carry a limited amount of cash for minor expenses and to pay all bills with travelers' checks, credit cards, a letter of credit, or a personal check.

Credit Cards

Your employer will want to carry one or more of the nationally recognized credit cards when travelling, such as *Master Charge, BankAmericard, American Express, Carte Blanche,* or *Diners' Club*. They will be accepted at almost all restaurants, hotels, motels, gift shops, florist shops, and car-rental agencies throughout the United States and Canada. Furthermore, the charge slips and itemized statements furnished by the credit card organizations provide a written record that may be used as proof of items listed on an expense account or to justify certain types of income tax business deductions.

Travelers' Checks

Travelers' checks are sold at travel agencies, banks, American Express offices and Western Union offices. The American Express Company travelers' checks are sold in various denominations and cost one dollar per $100. Some banks provide travelers' checks to their depositors at no cost.

The buyer of a travelers' check is required to sign it in the presence of the agent who issues the check. When it is presented for payment, the buyer is required to sign the check again in the presence of the person who cashes it. If the signatures seem to be identical, sufficient identification has been established. Travelers' checks may be cashed at banks, hotels, Express and telegraph offices, and other places where travelers frequently make purchases. Since you cannot sign travelers' checks for your employer, they must be picked up by the employer.

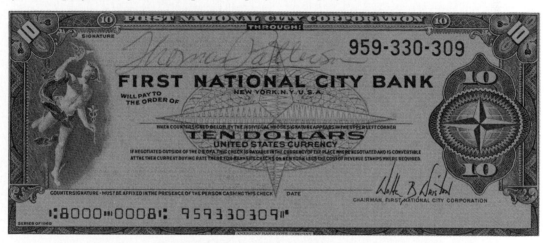

Illus. 13-9 A traveler's check

Travelers' checks have the following advantages:

1. The checks may be cashed easily almost everywhere.
2. The company issuing the check will refund the face value of a lost travelers' check if it has not been signed the second time.
3. The holders of American Express Company travelers' checks may, while they are traveling abroad, use the services of the Express offices in other countries for such things as the receipt of personal mail, radiograms, and cablegrams.

Letters of Credit

On extended business trips or international trips for which a considerable amount of money will be needed, your employer may consider it wise to carry a letter of credit. The cost of exchanging a large amount of money into a letter of credit is considerably less than it would be to change it into travelers' checks.

A letter of credit may be purchased from a bank by depositing the required amount. The letter states that the individual carrying it is entitled to the privilege of getting money from the banks named in the letter of credit up to the amount on deposit in the issuing bank. In using a letter of credit, your employer would apply at one of the named banks; and, after being identified by signature on an identification card on file at the bank, a draft would be drawn against the letter of credit to obtain the money. The bank honoring the draft would endorse the amount on the back of the letter of credit. All endorsements on the back are deducted from the face of the letter of credit to show the exact balance that may still be drawn against it.

Personal Checks

Most hotels, motels, airlines, and railway systems will accept a personal check in payment if the traveler can produce a driver's license or other proper identification. In addition to a signature on the personal check, a driver's license usually lists the motorist's identification number, date of birth, sex, height, and color of eyes.

Cash for International Travel

The executive who is traveling in other countries may want a limited amount of money of the other countries in order to handle small initial expenses, such as tipping, paying for taxi service or airport bus service, and buying newspapers. In large American cities, you may find a company that specializes in the sale of moneys of other countries. Also, large banks have foreign moneys for sale to their customers. It is also possible for the executive to buy foreign money at international airports. However, the executive may like to have this matter taken care of before leaving the home office.

Expense Reports

Part of your responsibility in handling the executive's business trips may be the preparation of a final report of expenses. Business firms expect executives to submit itemized accounts of travel expenses. Some firms advance funds to traveling executives; others reimburse executives after expense reports have been approved. Such items as plane and train

WEEKLY TRAVEL EXPENSE REPORT

Eller-Pierce Industries

	DEPARTURE		RETURN			
	HOUR	PLACE	HOUR	PLACE		
	2:30 □AM ☒PM	HOME □ PLANT ☒	□AM □PM	HOME □ PLANT □		DATES
	(WHICHEVER IS LATER)		(WHICHEVER IS EARLIER)			

NAME				BADGE NUMBER	DEPT. NO.	FROM	TO
Robert Merrill				585	24	8/1/--	8/4/--

EXPENSE ITEMS DATE→	SATURDAY	SUNDAY	MONDAY	TUESDAY 8/1	WEDNESDAY 8/2	THURSDAY 8/3	FRIDAY 8/4	TOTALS
1. ROOM				32 00	32 00	41 00	41 00	146 00
2. MEALS & TIPS				22 50	15 50	3 00	6 50	47 50
3. LAUNDRY						4 50		4 50
4. TIPS				6 00	4 00	3 50	2 50	16 00
5. SUB-TOTAL OR PER DIEM				60 50	51 50	52 00	50 00	214 00
6. RAILROAD								
7. AIRPLANE				138 00		32 00		170 00
8. CAR OR BUS								
9. PERSONAL AUTO								
10. TAXI				3 50	7 00	5 00		15 50
11. PARKING								
12. TOLLS								
13. TEL. & TELEGRAMS								
14.				1 50	4 75	2 50	4 00	12 75
15.								
16.								
TOTALS →				203 50	63 25	91 50	54 00 →	412 25

MILEAGE

FROM: (INDICATE PLACE OF DEPARTURE) Cincinnati	REG. ATTACHMENTS	
	LODGING RECEIPT	□ AMOUNT
TO: (INDICATE DESTINATION) Boston, New York, Baltimore, Pittsburgh	AIRLINE TICKETS	□ DUE RAD
PURPOSE OF TRIP: Invest. Analysts Convention & Branch office visits	RENTAL CAR INV.	□ DUE EMPLOYEE
APPLICABLE CHARGE NO. Executive Travel 24	PARKING-TOLL RECEIPT	□ ADV. REDUCTION
ACCT. NO. 2 6 8 7 - 1 1 9 9 - 9 7 3 2 4	CONFERENCE RECEIPT	□ DATE APPLIED

FOR OFFICE USE ONLY

REMARKS:
Trip continued to Baltimore, Pittsburgh. See accompanying expense report for August 5-7.

RENTAL CAR MILEAGE BREAKDOWN:

I CERTIFY THE ABOVE EXPENDITURES WERE MADE ON BEHALF OF REPUBLIC AVIATION DIVISION	DATE 8/9/--	DEPT. HEAD APPROVAL Joseph J. Cohen	CHECKED BY KEB
SIGNED Robert Merrill		TREASURY APPROVAL Harold R. Mason	

Illus. 13-10   Completed expense report

fares, taxis, tips, meals, and hotel accommodations are considered legitimate travel expenses. Firms differ, however, in their policies regarding such items as laundry and entertainment expenses. Your employer may expect you to check the records and receipts and to assist generally in the preparation of the expense reports.

Federal income tax regulations suggest a daily diary of expenses. In it your employer should itemize all travel and entertainment expenses.

The diary should include the date and amount of expenditures for transportation, lodging (place), meal expenses, entertainment expenses (meal costs, place, and receipt if the meal runs above $25, names of persons entertained and indication of business relationship), and tips and telephone calls (daily totals are sufficient).

Final Preparation for a Trip

Often the time immediately preceding a trip, especially an extensive one, is a busy time for an executive. Therefore, a calm, organized secretary is exceptionally valuable. As a secretary, you can be very helpful by checking to see that the executive is taking all the needed travel documents and business materials.

For traveling purposes, check to see that the executive has:

1. All tickets and reservations for every portion of the trip.
2. Hotel confirmations.
3. Copy of the itinerary.
4. Travel documents for overseas (passport, health record, if required, international driving license, if required).
5. Cash, credit cards, travelers' checks, and if going out of the country, foreign funds.

For handling the business of the trip, check to see that the executive has:

1. All letters, memoranda, speeches, and reports for each phase of the trip.
2. Lists of names and addresses and telephone numbers of persons to be seen.
3. Supplies for working, including pencils, tape, stationery, etc.
4. Equipment, such as dictating machine, pocket calculator.
5. Forms for recording expenses.

Maintaining the Office While the Executive is Away

foresight:
a sense of what is to come

A secretary with **foresight** will look ahead on the calendar to see what is scheduled for the period during which the executive is to be away. It may be necessary to check with the executive about pending matters, so that the secretary has a clear idea of how to proceed during the executive's absence.

Executives generally discuss with their secretaries how matters are to be handled while they are away and what situations should be communicated to them. In some instances, executives establish with their secretaries a schedule of when they will call the office. At such times, the secretary should have at hand a list of urgent matters for which the executive's attention is needed.

Often, the secretary will use a short form letter to inform correspondents that the executive is away and to give the correspondents an idea when a response is likely to be forthcoming. There are some matters that don't require immediate attention, and these are set aside until the executive's return.

The secretary's goal is to maintain the on-going activities of the office in an efficient, effective manner. Matters that will need the attention of the executive are carefully organized. The day before the expected return of the executive, the secretary should plan to organize the executive's desk so that attention can be given to the most pressing matters. Thoughtful secretaries type up a list of the matters they have taken care of and any special comments so that the executive can be brought up to date quickly.

It is reassuring to executives to return to their offices and find that all their work has been carefully organized for them and that all matters delegated to the secretary were taken care of as planned.

REVIEWING

1. What is the usefulness of a folder for each trip an executive is to make?
2. What is an itinerary?
3. Explain the details that should be included in an itinerary.
4. What should the secretary keep in mind when establishing the times for arrivals and departures?
5. What does it mean to verify the details received by telephone from an airlines clerk?
6. How does a travel plan form aid the secretary in organizing information for an itinerary?
7. Why would an executive carry travelers' checks?
8. For what reason would an itinerary be prepared in multiple copies?
9. Why should an executive keep a list of business expenses?
10. What is the nature of the secretary's work while the executive is away?

MAKING JUDGMENTS

1. While making arrangements for his employer to attend a meeting in Houston, Mr. Murray found that the flight to Houston originated in Pittsburgh, a three-hour drive from the office. Plane service between Altoona and Pittsburgh was limited. The best connection would require an hour and a half wait in Pittsburgh. He decided that the executive could easily drive to the Pittsburgh airport and leave her car there. On her return trip, she would reach the Pittsburgh airport about nine in the evening; this would mean that she would be home shortly after midnight, which seemed reasonable to Mr. Murray. What do you think of his judgment? What should he do?

2. Miss Autry had read in several periodicals how simple it is to rent a car at airports by using the services of one of the advertised companies. Therefore, when her employer told her he needed to visit a paper company in a small town south of Asheville and would need to rent a car at the Asheville airport, she made no reservation but merely wrote on the itinerary: "Stop at the Car Rental Service; no advance reservation seems necessary." What do you think of her judgment?

WORKING WITH OTHERS

Miss Hyde is a good secretary who finds the variety of tasks she does very interesting. Her employer, Ms. Johns, is away from her office about 30 percent of the time, and she appreciates the manner in which Miss Hyde keeps the office work on schedule. She knows the work thoroughly.

There are two executives with offices nearby who spend all their time in the home office. They think that Miss Hyde has little to do. Although she seems always to be doing something, they believe she is merely acting busy. As soon as Ms. Johns leaves, they come to her to see if she will help their secretaries, whom they feel are overworked. Miss Hyde graciously tells them that she has been left a great deal of work, and if she finishes it, she will let them know. However, Miss Hyde isn't anxious to be helpful because the two secretaries are not working all day as they should. They generally take an extra half hour for lunch; their 15-minute coffee breaks in the morning and afternoon seldom last less than 45 minutes. Miss Hyde wishes the executives would not constantly seek her assistance.

What do you think Miss Hyde should do?

REFRESHING LANGUAGE SKILLS

The following sentences contain commonly misused terms. On a separate sheet of paper, type each sentence using the correct form in each case.

1. I would not go (except, unless) you go with·me.
2. I think it would be (all right, alright) for you to leave the files at your desk overnight.
3. He (could have, could of) gone if he had known of the meeting before lunch yesterday.
4. We are not sure what the (affect, effect) of this change will mean to our mailroom.
5. He will do it (good, well) this time, we are sure.
6. He went (in, into) the bank.
7. Did you (lay, lie) the paper on the first desk in Room 314?
8. There will be (fewer, less) people at the meeting than anticipated.
9. By this time he (may be, maybe) in his hotel room in Chicago.
10. There was agreement (among, between) the three secretaries who are doing the special job.

PERFORMING SECRETARIAL TASKS

Assume that you have made all the arrangements for a trip for Ms. E. Phelan. The details of the trip are given below. Arrange them for preparation of an itinerary, and type the final itinerary.

May 2	3:45 p.m.	Leave office by taxi for Newark airport
	4:45 p.m.	Leave airport on American Airlines Flight No. 451 for Chicago
	5:10 p.m.	Arrive at O'Hare Airport, Chicago (You have hotel reservation at Blackstone, Michigan Boulevard; expected arrival at 6:30 p.m.)
May 3	9:30 a.m.	Meeting with Mr. Albert Sansome and Mr. Gilbert T. Amendson at T. W. Wendt Company, 1213 Monroe Street, 5th floor; Tel: 571-5690
	12:30 p.m.	Lunch with Mr. Roy Yates and Ms. Sherry Rosen at Fath Corporation, 345 Michigan Avenue; Tel: 561-6000
	4:00 p.m.	Leave downtown Chicago for O'Hare; can get airport bus at Conrad Hilton Hotel or take taxi
	5:10 p.m.	Take Flight 341 on TWA for St. Louis
	6:30 p.m.	Arrival at St. Louis (You have a reservation of Sheraton House; expected there at 8 p.m.; address is 6 Center Street; Tel: 567-2333)
May 4	9:00 a.m.	Meeting with Mr. Arthur F. Summa and Mr. Richard Kahn at 3 Fourth Avenue, Suite 14F; Tel: 456-8900

12:00 Noon	Luncheon meeting with William C. Frank of Frank and Sullivan, 1 Monroe Plaza; Tel: 456-7889
3:00 p.m.	Departure from hotel (by bus from hotel or taxi)
4:10 p.m.	TWA Flight 281 for New York, Newark Airport
7:15 p.m.	Arrival at Newark Airport

IMPROVING SECRETARIAL SKILLS (Optional)

Assume that you are in the process of developing the itinerary you prepared in PERFORMING SECRETARIAL TASKS above. Using the letterheads provided in the *Supplies Inventory*, or plain paper, type letters to the Blackstone Hotel and Sheraton House for reservations for Ms. Phelan, who will be traveling alone and wants a single room.

UNIT

14

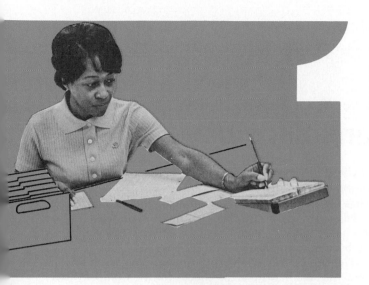

The Secretary and Financial Records

Part 1

Bank Records

As executive secretary to the two owner-managers of the Bishirjian-Cousins Catering Service, Ms. Diana Wetherford has full responsibility for maintaining the records for all financial activities. The two talented home economists, who built a home industry into a small business with a staff of 8 and a beautiful new facility in a growing suburban area of Louisville, rely on Ms. Wetherford for managing the banking matters. Ms. Wetherford signs checks for the Company and maintains all records so that Ms. Bishirjian and Ms. Cousins can review them at any time.

Secretaries have varying responsibilities for banking activities. As with many other duties, the size and type of firm for which you work will determine the extent of your association with banks and the related recordkeeping tasks. For example, if you are employed by a large firm with a central accounting department, your dealings with banks may be limited to handling records for special projects or for travel expenses. On the other hand, if you work in the office of a professional person, such as a lawyer, psychologist, architect, or medical doctor, you may have full responsibility for transactions with banks and may maintain all the banking records for your employer.

Accounts

Business firms of all sizes use the services of commercial banks rather than maintain large sums of money on their own premises. Money deposited in checking accounts is then available for the payment of all types of **obligations** through writing checks. Cash, if used at all, is used for only the smallest transactions.

obligations:
financial duty

Checks facilitate the handling of transactions. Checks can be sent through the mail safely, and a canceled check can be used as a receipt for payment. Furthermore, checks can be transferred from one person to another by merely indorsing them properly. Of course, checks can be deposited in a commercial account either in person or by mail.

Often secretaries handle bank accounts and, therefore, have the responsibility for making deposits, writing checks, keeping account of the checkbook, and **reconciling** bank statements. There are occasions when secretaries are authorized to sign checks and indorse those received for deposit. Handling financial matters must be treated in a confidential manner. Accuracy is also extremely important.

reconciling:
bringing into
balance

Opening a Bank Account

A secretary working for a company that is just getting underway may have the task of securing the forms from a local bank to open a commercial checking account. While banks have varying procedures for opening accounts, many do require some references to know that they will be dealing with a responsible group of people. Generally a new company is able to provide references with no difficulty.

All persons in the organization who will be authorized to sign checks must fill out a *signature card*. The signatures must be written exactly the way they will appear on all checks that are signed by these persons. In most cases only a few persons are authorized to sign checks for a particular organization.

Authorized Signatures of	Brooks, Alison R.	ACCOUNT NUMBER

FOR THE PEOPLE'S SAVINGS BANK, PORTLAND, MAINE — 511-400-24

Below are duly authorized signatures, which you will recognize in the payment of funds or in the transaction of other business on my account. In making this deposit and at all times in doing business with this bank, I specifically agree to all of the terms and conditions printed on the reverse side hereof.

Date *May 26, 19--*

Signature *Alison R. Brooks*

Signature — Telephone No. *799-0624*

Signature *{Alison R. Brooks* — Account

Signature *by William R. Nelson}* — Accepted by *M.C.*

Address — 200 Columbia Street

Business — Singers Department Store

Introduced by — Ralph M. Kennedy

Please honor the above signature on checks against my account or as endorsement on checks or drafts in my favor.

Illus. 14-1 Signature card

Making Deposits

Checks and cash received by an organization are generally deposited in the bank as soon after receipt as possible. In offices where the volume of funds received is great, there may be daily or twice-daily deposits in the bank. In other offices, deposits may be made only once or twice a week. Plan a schedule that assures that large amounts of money — in either checks or cash — are not held in your office overnight.

A deposit slip must be prepared for every deposit. This form is supplied by your bank, and you should keep a stock of the forms in your office so that you can prepare the deposit slip before you go to the bank.

The information needed on a deposit slip includes:

1. Name and address of depositor
2. Date
3. Account number
4. Items to be deposited

Generally checks should be identified on the deposit slip in one of the following ways:

1. By transit number, which appears in fraction form in the upper right-hand corner of the check and is assigned to each bank by the American Bankers Association. An illustration of a check is on page 528.
2. By name, if the bank is a local one.
3. By the city and state of out-of-town banks.

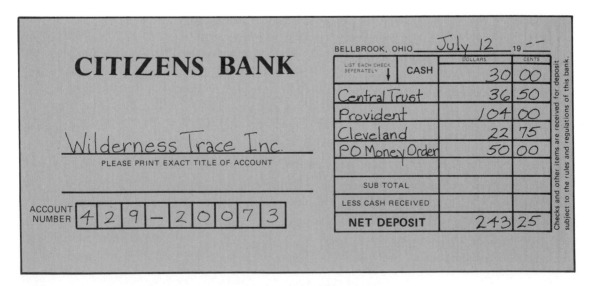

Illus. 14-2 Deposit slip

If, however, you have a large number of checks, you may show the total only on the deposit slip and attach an adding machine tape showing the individual items, as well as the total.

If you must regularly deposit large sums of coins and bills, you should get a supply of wrappers which the bank will provide. Coins and bills should be packaged in designated quantities. It is a general practice to write or stamp the name of the depositing firm on each roll of coins and each package of bills so that if one should be misplaced, it will be credited to the proper account.

Deposits consisting of checks only may be made by mail or in person. If by mail, a deposit will be acknowledged by the bank by a prompt return of a receipt. Deposits that include cash are made in person at a teller's window at the bank where the account is maintained. A teller receives your deposit, checks the items, and immediately provides you with a receipt. This receipt should be filed when you return to your office.

Writing Checks

A check is a written order directing a bank to pay out the money of a depositor; therefore, it should be written with extreme care. The following procedures are generally acceptable.

1. Type checks or write them in ink — never in pencil.
2. Number each check if numbers are not printed on them. Be sure that the number of the check corresponds with that of the check stub.
3. Date the check on the exact date that it is written.
4. Write the name of the payee, the person who is to receive the money, in full. If you are not sure of the correct spelling, try to verify it in the telephone directory or from previous correspondence. Omit titles such as Mr., Mrs., Miss, Ms., Dr., or Prof.
5. Write the amount of the check in large, bold figures next to the printed dollar sign and close enough to prevent the insertion of other figures. In spelling out the amount, start at the extreme left, capitalize the first letter only, and express cents as fractions of one hundred:
   Two hundred fifty-two no/100 ----------------------------Dollars
   Three thousand two hundred forty 75/100 ---------------Dollars
   If you should write a check for less than a dollar, precede the spelled-out amount with the word *Only* and cross out the printed word *Dollars* as:
   Only forty-nine cents -------------------------------------Dollars

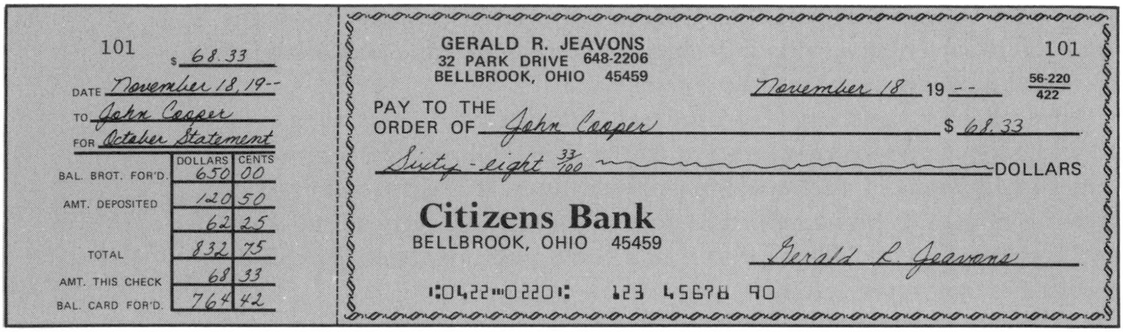
101 $ 68.33
DATE November 18, 19--
TO John Cooper
FOR October Statement

	DOLLARS	CENTS
BAL. BROT. FOR'D.	650	00
AMT. DEPOSITED	120	50
	62	25
TOTAL	832	75
AMT. THIS CHECK	68	33
BAL. CARD FOR'D.	764	42

GERALD R. JEAVONS
32 PARK DRIVE 648-2206
BELLBROOK, OHIO 45459
101
November 18 19 --
56-220
422
PAY TO THE ORDER OF John Cooper $ 68.33
Sixty-eight 33/100 DOLLARS
Citizens Bank
BELLBROOK, OHIO 45459
Gerald R. Jeavons
⑆0422⑉0220⑆ 123 45678 90

Illus. 14-3

Check with stub

6. Fill in all blank spaces before and after the names of the payee and after the written amount with hyphens, periods, or a line.
7. You may wish to write the purpose of the check, such as In Payment of Invoice 1691, at the bottom of the check. Some checks have a special blank line for this purpose.
8. Do not erase on a check. If you should make an error in writing a check, write the word *Void* across the face of both the check and the check stub. Save the voided check and file it in numerical order with the canceled checks when they are returned by the bank.
9. Do not sign blank checks. Anyone can fill them out and cash them.
10. Do not write a check payable to "Cash" unless you are in the bank and plan to present it for bills and coins immediately.
11. Write legibly. An illegible signature creates difficulties at the bank and is no protection against forgery.

Frequently, a firm has a checkwriter, a machine that perforates and inks in the amount into the check paper to prevent **alterations**.

alterations: changes

Maintaining a Record

The form of checks used in an office varies, but there is always some means of maintaining a record of checks written. Some checkbooks contain a stub for each check. Fill in the stub first, recording on it the exact information that will be included on the check itself. Additionally, the stub has a place for the balance brought forward as well as the balance after the amount of the check being written is subtracted.

Indorsing Checks

Indorsements are necessary to make checks *negotiable*, that is, transferable from one person to another. There are several types of indorsements, each of which serves a different purpose and carries a different degree of protection. The most common types of business indorsements are *restrictive*, *full* or *special*, and *blank* indorsements. A knowledge of indorsements will help you safeguard checks.

A *restrictive indorsement* allows you to send an indorsed check safely through the mail. It transfers the ownership for a specific, stated purpose. For example, the following words may be written above the signature of the indorser: *For Deposit Only*. If you indorse a check in this way it can only be deposited in the account for which you have responsibility. Since the check cannot be cashed by anyone else, there is little danger if the check is misplaced, lost, or stolen.

Indorsements are usually written in ink, but restrictive indorsements made with rubber stamps are often used for depositing checks. This type of indorsement is satisfactory because it makes the checks payable only to the account of the depositor and would not benefit anyone who might obtain a rubber stamp and attempt to use it improperly.

An *indorsement in full*, or a *special* indorsement as it is sometimes called, shows the name of the person to whom the check is being transferred. For example, the words *Pay to the order of William T. Rosen* may be written before the indorser's signature. A check indorsed in this way cannot be cashed by anyone without William T. Rosen's signature. Therefore, you may send a check indorsed in this manner through the mail without danger in case of loss.

A *blank indorsement* consists only of a signature across the back of the check. It makes the check payable to anyone who may possess it. You should use this type of indorsement only when you plan to cash or

Illus. 14-4

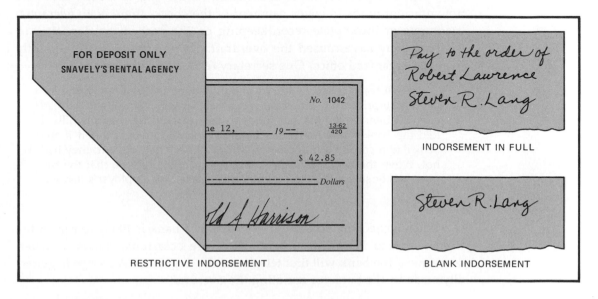

FOR DEPOSIT ONLY
SNAVELY'S RENTAL AGENCY

No. 1042

ne 12,   19 --   13-62⁄420

$ 42.85

----------------------- Dollars

Ld A Harrison

RESTRICTIVE INDORSEMENT

Pay to the order of
Robert Lawrence
Steven R. Lang

INDORSEMENT IN FULL

Steven R. Lang

BLANK INDORSEMENT

deposit a check immediately. It is not the correct indorsement for a check that is being sent through the mail or for a check that could be lost or misplaced because the check can be cashed by anyone who holds it — even if that person has no right to it.

Stopping Payment on Checks

There are times when it is necessary to stop payment on a check. To "stop payment" means to inform the bank on which a check was drawn that it is not to honor that check when it arrives at the bank.

Payment on a check may be stopped for a number of reasons. Among them are: when a check is lost or stolen, when a check was written incorrectly, or when the check was written for goods or services that have been canceled.

Generally it is a good practice to telephone the bank telling them of the check for which payment is to be stopped. The bank will need the following information: the name of the drawer (the one who signed the check), the date of the check, the amount of the check, and the name of the payee. It is also a good practice to follow up the telephone conversation with a letter or form confirming the information that was provided by telephone.

Overdraft

When a depositor writes a check on an account in which there are not sufficient funds to cover payment of the check, there is an *overdraft*. Inaccurate or incomplete recordkeeping on the part of the depositor or the bank may have caused the overdraft. Overdrafts occur infrequently in a well-organized office. One secretary related this experience:

> When I was called by the local bank about an overdraft, I was extremely surprised. My employer was a new lawyer in town, and we had carefully deposited sufficient funds to take care of our monthly bills. I told the banker that there had possibly been an error. I asked if the bank had recorded our deposit of May 30. They checked, and they had not. When the bank called back in an hour, they told me that the deposit had been credited to J. Noble by mistake. My employer's name is J. Nobel.

When a checking account is overdrawn, a bank is likely to return the checks marked *Insufficient Funds*. There are occasions, however, when someone at the bank will first telephone the depositor. A charge is generally made by the bank for handling the overdraft.

Reconciliation of the Bank Statement

A bank statement and the canceled checks that the bank paid out of your firm's account are sent to you periodically, usually once a month.

As shown below, the Statement of Account will list the Statement Period — A; the Beginning Balance — B; Total Deposits — C; Total Checks — D; the Service Charge — E, deducted by the bank for handling the account; and the Ending Balance — F — of the period.

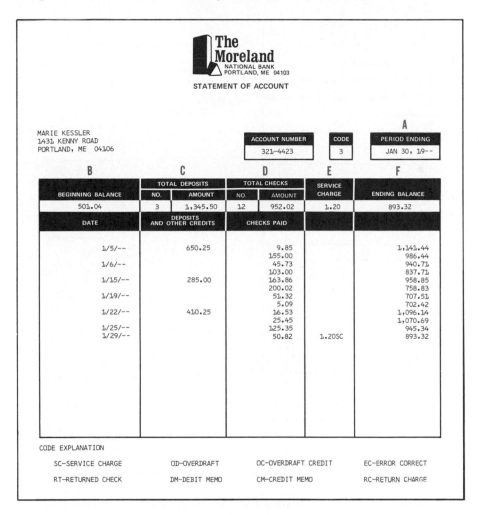

Illus. 14-5 Statement of Account

This banking service permits you to check the accuracy of your checkbook with the bank records and to file the canceled checks as proof of the firm's payments.

MONTH *January* 19 - -

THIS FORM IS PROVIDED TO HELP YOU BALANCE
YOUR BANK STATEMENT

*CHECKS OUTSTANDING - NOT
CHARGED TO ACCOUNT

NO.	$	
143	50	00
144	16	00
147	90	00
TOTAL	$ 156	00

BANK BALANCE $ *893.32*

ADD +

DEPOSITS NOT CREDITED
IN THIS STATEMENT
(IF ANY) $ _____

_____

TOTAL $ *893.32*

SUBTRACT –

CHECKS OUTSTANDING $ *156.00*

BALANCE $ *737.32*

CHECK BOOK BALANCE $ *738.52*

DEDUCT:
SERVICE CHARGE *1.20*

OTHER CHARGES NOT
PREVIOUSLY ENTERED
IN CHECK BOOK _____

ADJUSTED CHECK BOOK BALANCE $ *737.32*

You should compare the final balance on the bank statement with the checkbook balance and account for the difference. This process of accounting for the difference is called *reconciling the bank statement* . For the convenience of their depositors, many banks print a reconciliation form on the back of the monthly statement. The following steps should be taken to reconcile an account:

1. Compare the amount of each canceled check with the amount listed on the bank statement. This step will show any error made by the bank or the depositor in recording a check. Place a check mark beside each verified amount.
2. Arrange the canceled checks in numerical order.
3. Compare the returned checks with the stubs in the checkbook. Place a check mark on the stub of each check that has been returned.
4. Make a list of the outstanding checks — those that have not been paid and returned. Include on the list the number of each outstanding check and the amount.
5. Add the amounts of outstanding checks and deduct the total from the balance shown on the bank statement.
6. Subtract the amount of the service charges listed on the bank statement from the checkbook balance.
7. After the service charge has been deducted from the checkbook balance, the remaining amount should agree with the balance shown on the bank statement after the total of the outstanding checks has been deducted.

Illus. 14-7

A bank statement should be reconciled immediately after it is received, so that the balance is always up to date

You will generally prepare a rough draft of a bank reconciliation in pencil, and if necessary, type a final copy for your records. Bank reconciliations are maintained for at least a year. The form provided on the back of the bank statement is generally a sufficient record, so it may not be necessary to type another copy.

On the next page is an example of a typed reconciliation.

RECONCILIATION OF BANK ACCOUNT

January 30, 19--

Balance as shown on bank statement $893.32
Less checks outstanding:

```
            143...............$50.00
            144............... 16.00
            147............... 90.00          156.00
```
Adjusted Bank Balance $737.32

Balance as shown by check book $738.52
Less January service charge 1.20
Adjusted checkbook balance $737.32

REVIEWING

1. Why do organizations use the services of commercial banks?
2. What are some banking responsibilities that secretaries may be asked to handle?
3. If a secretary is authorized to sign checks for a firm, what records at the bank must be signed? Why?
4. What is the purpose of a deposit slip?
5. When may a check be written to "Cash"?
6. Why must checks be indorsed?
7. Why is a checkwriter used?
8. When might payment be stopped on a check?
9. Why is a bank reconciliation prepared?

MAKING JUDGMENTS

1. Mrs. Wilma Knolles receives large amounts of cash in her office. She puts the cash in a box, and at least twice a week she takes the box to the bank. She feels she should not waste her time counting the money because the bank teller is an expert at counting it and is both quicker and more accurate than she is. What do you think of Mrs. Knolles' judgment?
2. Ms. Celeste Harsh receives many checks in her office, and since they are not negotiable until indorsed, she lets them accumulate in her desk drawer until she feels like walking down to the bank. Then she indorses the checks and goes to the bank. She often has several thousands of dollars of checks before she decides to deposit them. What do you think of Ms. Harsh's procedure?

WORKING WITH OTHERS

Ms. Janice Honcar is secretary to three psychologists who have their own clinic. The three have delegated all check writing to Ms. Honcar. She, therefore, writes and signs checks for all business expenses. An accountant checks the records once each month and handles accounting tasks.

One day a junior member of the staff came to Ms. Honcar's office and asked if he could borrow $100. He knew she wrote his monthly paycheck and he wanted an advance on his salary. He said he really didn't want any one of the three psychologists to know he was asking for money.

What do you think Ms. Honcar should do?

REFRESHING LANGUAGE SKILLS

Three common usages of parentheses are:

A. Around explanatory, nonessential material used within a sentence.
   Example: We are going to stop first at Jack Thomson's (he is a distant cousin of the popular actor, James Thomson).

B. To enclose references, directions, and sources of information.
   Example: There is a decline in the number of cows in Vermont (Department of Agriculture).

C. Around numbers or letters indicating listings or divisions within a sentence.
   Example: There are three reasons for considering this city: (1) it is centrally located; (2) it has a large manpower pool; (3) it has several institutes and colleges where technical training is provided.

Type the following sentences on a separate sheet of paper, inserting parentheses where necessary:

1. Mr. Theodore Stone is an outstanding politician and a talented artist and will be most impressive on the lecture platform.
2. When the visitor made reference to America using the term loosely to mean the United States, he was surprisingly knowledgeable about its customs.
3. Titles and salaries for professional persons see Appendix E vary with the profession.
4. In order to open a checking account it is necessary to fill in an application form provide references sign a signature card.
5. I will telephone him assuming he has a listed number as soon as I reach home tonight.

PERFORMING SECRETARIAL TASKS

1. The checking account balance for T. F. Foxe, an architect, on the first of April was $1,950.45. During the month there were deposits totaling $4,510.50. During the same period checks totaling $2,950.35 were written. On the last day of the month, checks amounting to $895.65 had not yet been cashed. What is the checkbook balance on April 30? What is the bank balance on the same date?

2. Assume you are secretary to a management consultant, Mr. T. W. Caswell, 43 Grand Plaza, Newark, NJ 07142. You have the responsibility of maintaining the banking records, including the writing and signing of checks for business matters (Account No. 321-291-23). If forms are available, write the checks, prepare the deposit slip, and complete the check stubs for handling the following transactions on one afternoon.

   April 2 Balance in checkbook is $2,321.90 (Last check written was No. 671)

   2 Write a check for $350.00 for services rendered by Dr. Richard T. Corr.

   2 Write a check for $132.00 for telephone services, New York Telephone Company.

   2 Write a check for $46.50 to National Maintenance Services.

   2 Write a check for $450 to Simpson Rental Services.

   2 Prepare a deposit slip for the following checks:

Continental	$ 500.00
First National	1,500.00
National City	1,200.00

   If forms are not available, determine the checkbook balance after the transactions.

3. Assume that you are responsible for handling banking tasks for your employer, who is a medical doctor. Among your tasks is the reconciliation of the bank statement each month. Assume that the following checks were written during the month of April:

No. 843	$ 50.45	853	$ 31.49
844	15.25	854	29.45
845	425.00	855	75.60
846	125.34	856	105.43
847	156.75	857	45.00
848	89.90	858	19.50
849	111.20	859	23.45
850	24.50	860	154.19
851	149.00	861	45.67
852	345.30	862	15.32

The checkbook balance after reconciliation on April 1 was $3,210.34. The deposits for the month were: $350.00, $1,325.50, $869.00, $1,140.40 and $890.40.

The bank statement for the month of April showed a balance of $5,936.86. The checks missing were: 858 for 19.50, 860 for 154.19 and 862 for 15.32.

Using the form provided in the *Supplies Inventory* or plain paper, prepare the reconciliation of the bank statement.

Part 2

Making Payments

Among the tasks that Mr. Glen Rogers does monthly is making payments for the variety of goods and services required in the insurance agency office for which he serves as secretary. Mr. Rogers knows that maintaining a good credit standing requires payment of obligations on a regular schedule. He gives priority to the task of preparing payments near the close of each month so that such payments are in the mail on the same date each month.

Paying Monthly Bills

Your office will undoubtedly have a system for checking the accuracy of each bill received for payment. You will want to verify each statement before preparing the check necessary for payment. For example, if a payment reaches its destination later than expected, the statement for the succeeding month may include an amount in arrears. You should determine, in such an instance, whether the preceding month's bill had been paid. When you find that a check had been written for the preceding month, you would subtract the amount shown in arrears and write a check for the difference, representing the expense for the last month only.

arrears:
due but not paid

Your records will also indicate when payment must be made and in what form since there are some firms that do not accept ordinary checks.

Forms for Payments

Some of the various forms that are used in making payments include:

1. ordinary check
2. voucher check
3. certified check
4. bank draft
5. cashier's check
6. postal and American Express money orders.

Ordinary Checks

You learned in the preceding Part how checks are written. For many payments, it is sufficient to write ordinary checks and send them by mail in time for arrival at their destination on the due dates.

Voucher Checks

Voucher checks are checks with vouchers attached which are perforated for detaching easily. The voucher provides details of the check's purpose. As you see below, the invoice number, a description of the goods purchased, the amount, the discount allowed, and the net amount are all included on the voucher. The voucher is detached before the check is deposited. The voucher is verified against the records of the receiving company, and if it is in agreement with that record, the voucher may be discarded or filed.

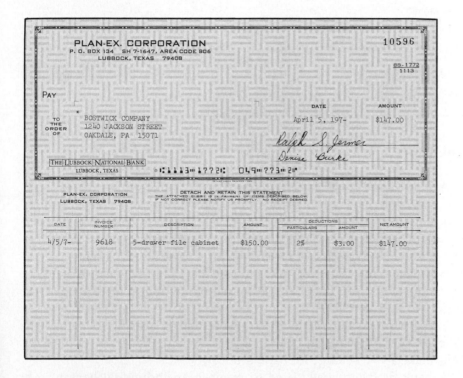

Illus. 14-8

Voucher check

Certified Checks

Certified checks are checks that the bank has confirmed will be paid when presented. You obtain a certified check by presenting an ordinary check to the bank and asking a bank official, usually a cashier, to certify it for you. The official will look at the account on which the check is drawn to see if there are sufficient funds to cover the check. If there are sufficient funds, the official will stamp CERTIFIED on the face of the check you prepared and add his or her signature. Immediately, the account is charged for the amount of the check. From this point on, the bank becomes responsible for payment of the amount indicated on the check. Because the bank now guarantees payment, the check is received by the payee without hesitation, even if the payee doesn't know the drawer. Such a check is deposited the same as an ordinary check.

Certified checks are generally requested when the payee does not know the business reputation of a person or company providing goods or services.

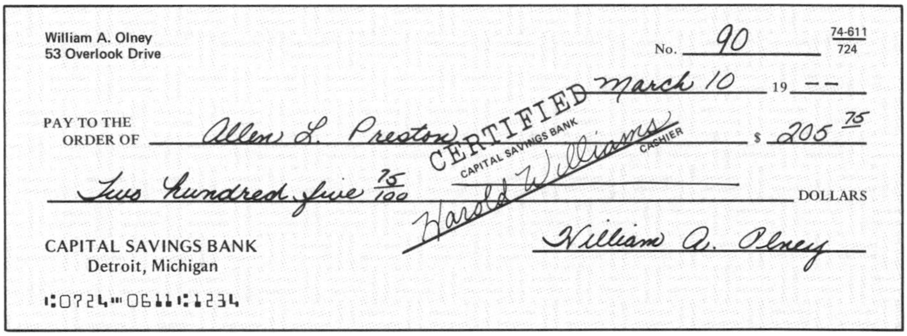
William A. Olney
53 Overlook Drive
No. 90
74-611
724
March 10 19 --
PAY TO THE ORDER OF Allen L. Preston $ 205 75/100
Two hundred five 75/100 DOLLARS
CERTIFIED
CAPITAL SAVINGS BANK
Harold Williams
CASHIER
CAPITAL SAVINGS BANK
Detroit, Michigan
William A. Olney
⑆0724⑈0611⑆1234

Illus. 14-9

Certified check

Bank Draft

A bank draft is an order drawn by one bank on its deposits in another bank to pay a third party. Since this type of draft, like a certified check, has the bank's assurance of payment, it is accepted more freely than an ordinary check. In the illustration, the Southern Trust Bank is the drawer; the First National Bank of Denver, Colorado, the drawee, is the bank that must pay the draft; and the payee is K and S Construction Co. The cashier of the Southern Trust Bank, Barbara J. Jones, merely signs for the drawer.

You may purchase a bank draft by presenting cash or your employer's check to a bank. The cashier will make out the draft. Ordinarily banks make a small charge for bank drafts.

remit: send

A bank draft is usually used to **remit** to an individual or firm in a distant city who might not care to accept an ordinary check from a person or firm unknown to them. Although bank drafts and certified checks should be passed with equal confidence, business firms prefer bank drafts.

No. 5111

SOUTHERN TRUST BANK

23-322 / 1020

September 15 19 --

PAY TO THE ORDER OF _K and S Construction Co._ $ 1247 55

The sum of $1247 and 55 cts

_____ DOLLARS

THE FIRST NATIONAL BANK
Denver, Colorado

Barbara J. Jones

CASHIER

⑈1020⑈0322⑈1234

Cashier's Check

Another type of cash payment you or your employer might use is the cashier's check. A cashier's check is written by a bank on its own funds. It serves somewhat the same purpose as a bank draft. It differs in that it is drawn by the cashier on funds in the cashier's own bank, whereas a bank draft is drawn upon deposits in another bank. When you wish to pay a person who may be unaware of your credit standing or to cash a check in a distant city, where you are not known and your personal check might be questioned, you could use a cashier's check.

You need not be a depositor in a bank to purchase a cashier's check. You may give the cashier your employer's check or cash to cover the amount of the cashier's check. The cashier will then write a check for the specific amount, payable to the person whom you **designate**. A small charge is usually made by the bank for issuing a cashier's check.

designate:
specify

Postal and American Express Money Orders

Postal money orders or American Express money orders are documents that are exchangeable for the sums indicated when they are presented at the proper offices. When payment must be made by a person who does not have a checking account, the postal or American Express money order provides a safe, secure way of sending money.

Domestic postal money orders may be purchased at all post offices, branches, and stations in the United States and its possessions; international postal money orders at many of them. Express money orders may be purchased at any American Express Company or at many banks.

If you are sending an international money order, you must fill out a printed application form. None is required for a domestic money order or an American Express money order. When you purchase a domestic money order, you are required to enter on the appropriate lines the name of the payee, your own name, and your address.

Postal money orders are limited to $300, but two or more may be purchased to make up any desired amount.

To cash a postal money order, take it to a money order office within thirty days after issue; after that time, the orders will be paid only at the office designated on the order.

You may cash American Express money orders either at American Express offices or at banks. They are good indefinitely.

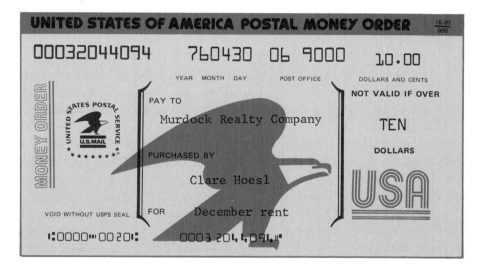

Illus. 14-11

Domestic postal money order

REVIEWING

1. How does an ordinary check differ from a voucher check?
2. Who writes a certified check?
3. For what reason may a person be asked to make payment with a certified check?
4. Who is responsible for the payment of a certified check that is deposited?
5. How does a bank draft differ from a certified check?
6. How does a cashier's check differ from a certified check?
7. Where does one buy a postal money order?
8. Where may you cash a postal money order?
9. Where may you cash an American Express money order?
10. When might a person use a postal money order to make a payment?

MAKING JUDGMENTS

1. Although there was a note on the statement indicating that payment was to be made by certified check, Miss Westfield knew that her company's check was "as good as gold," so she merely wrote an ordinary check and sent it along with a copy of the statement and no explanation. What do you think of Miss Westfield's judgment?
2. Jason received a voucher check for services rendered; he glanced at the details indicated on the voucher, and they seemed accurate to him, so he detached the voucher, threw it away, and filed the check for deposit in the bank the next day. What do you think of Jason's procedure?

WORKING WITH OTHERS

Art works for a very busy lawyer who expects him to handle all payments. One day he tells him that a check for $350 must be sent to a Mr. Stanley T. Arnett in Chicago, who had done some work for him. He said nothing further. When Art began the task of writing the check, he began to wonder why his employer had made a point of asking him to send out a check to Mr. Arnett. He ordinarily wrote checks as he received the statements for work done. He has nothing indicating that a check is to go to Mr. Arnett, except the employer's word. He ponders the matter for a few moments and then decided that a special type of check must be needed in this instance. His employer was busy writing a brief, and he felt that he shouldn't bother him; yet, he was hesitant about what he should do. Finally, he decided to write a check to Mr. Arnett and have it certified at the bank.

What do you think of the manner in which Art handled this task?

REFRESHING LANGUAGE SKILLS

The dash indicates a sudden change in the thought or the structure of a sentence. Dashes should not be overused because such overuse tends to be distracting and may fail to communicate clearly the thoughts of the writer. The dash is used:

A. To show a sudden break in thought

Example: I think this is wise — you were so kind to think of it — and there is no reason for postponing its implementation.

B. To substitute for commas when emphasis is important

Example: The new computer — and only the new computer — will assure us of a smooth system for completing this type of analysis.

C. To introduce a word or statement that summarizes a series

   Example: Secretaries, typists, clerks — all were eager to hear the plans for the new offices.

D. To give special emphasis to an appositive

   Example: I want to see Miss Winters — our hard-working, cooperative mailroom supervisor.

Type the following sentences on a separate sheet of paper, inserting dashes where needed.

1. This reference book how fortunate we are to have three copies is possibly your best source for the appropriate titles for government officials.
2. Learning to handle the mail a key task in this office requires understanding the purpose of each procedure and the schedule.
3. Charlotte Gertrude's beautiful sister was always gracious to her foreign-born cousin who worked in the family's firm.
4. Checks, money orders, bank drafts all provide means of making payments safely.
5. The Personal Banking Department made by far the largest contribution to the corporation's overall profits some 12 million dollars underscoring the importance of continued growth in our business.

PERFORMING SECRETARIAL TASKS

1. For each of the following situations, indicate the type of payment you would use and explain your reasons for the choice:

   a. You need to pay the regular monthly rent for the offices in which your employer does business.
   b. You must send $300 for a staff member to use for expenses while traveling in a new territory.
   c. You must forward a check with a first order for printing supplies from a company that doesn't know your employer.

2. You have received a voucher check from a customer. When you check the details, you note that the customer has made an error in computing the discount of 2 percent. The check is written for $458.40; however, the amount should have been $482.30. You must write the letter explaining the error. Write what you believe would be an appropriate letter. The customer's name and address are: Mr. William Randall, Westhall Manufacturing Company, 1214 Bonway Drive, Decatur, GA 30032. Use a letterhead from the *Supplies Inventory* or plain paper. Make one carbon copy.

Part 3
Income Tax Recordkeeping

Mr. Leroy Talmadge works as secretary to a management consultant who has his own business. His business is virtually a one-person operation; however, he does much traveling in his work, and must maintain complete and accurate records for the accountant who prepares his annual income tax forms. Mr. Talmadge has developed a plan to assure that he has all the business expenses for his employer. He maintains a careful calendar of the employer's travels and is able to check his records against the calendar to verify the completeness of the expense records.

Keeping tax records accurately and carefully is very important to businesses as well as to individuals. Making an error in recording your employer's income or forgetting to keep a record of a deductible expense can make a considerable difference in the amount your employer must pay the United States Government.

Records Needed for Taxes

Your tax duties as a secretary will vary depending upon the firm for which you work. Some firms have the Accounting Department keep all tax records and you, as a secretary, will have very few tax duties. Other firms, however, may require you to perform a variety of duties involving your employer's tax records. Some of these duties may be:

1. *Keeping records of deductible items.* The federal and state tax laws are constantly changing the guidelines on which items are deductible and which are not. Any expenses connected with business matters should be kept in complete detail since they may be deductible.
2. *Keeping records of taxable income.* Many kinds of incomes are taxable. For example, such things as rents from property and interest must be reported as income on your employer's tax report. You should have a general knowledge of what should be reported so that you can keep adequate records.

3. *Organizing records.* The records that you keep for your employer on deductible items and taxable incomes should be well organized so that they can be referred to easily and quickly. A file folder should be established each year for income tax materials. All records and supporting documents should be put in this folder, so that all data will be in one convenient place.

4. *Making sure your employer does not miss a deadline.* Some firms make periodic payments throughout the year on their income taxes. If this is the case, you should make sure these payments are made on time and that records are kept for each payment.

consultant:
one who advises

5. *Providing information to tax consultant if needed.* Some records may not be entirely clear to the tax consultant. You should be informed enough about your employer's tax records so that you can answer the questions for the tax consultant. If you cannot answer a question, contact your employer immediately.

Tax Information Helpful to the Secretary

In order to understand the significance of the records that you must maintain for tax purposes, you will want to know the current regulations on taxable income. Generally the following types of income are considered taxable:

honoraria:
payments made for speeches or special presentations

1. *Wages and salaries.* The total amount received from wages, salaries, fees, tips, commissions, honoraria and similar items are considered taxable income. The records should show the gross amount, that is, the amount before any deductions are made. Bonuses, awards, and prizes are also considered to be taxable income.

2. *Dividends.* Generally dividends on stock when paid in cash are taxable. However, some dividends may be partially or wholly exempt from taxation. It is best to keep a complete record of all dividends.

3. *Interest.* Most interest payments are taxable. Interest on state and municipal bonds and some United States Government bonds is not taxable.

4. *Rents from properties.* Rent from all properties owned is taxable. The owner, however, is allowed to deduct expenses for maintaining the property, including services and repairs.

5. *Profits from sale or exchange of real estate.* Profits from the sale of real estate are usually taxable, however, this, too, will vary depending on the circumstances. It is best to keep detailed records of all transactions involving property in the tax folder.

6. *Royalties.* Royalties usually include income from books, patents, and inventions. This income is taxable, but deductions are allowed for any expenses incurred in producing the item that provides the royalty.

In addition, you will want to know the general types of allowable expenses. As noted earlier, you should keep a record of all business expenses so that the accountant who prepares the final income tax forms will be able to review such expenses and decide whether they are deductible. On page 548 is a type of record that might be maintained to help you in keeping expenses organized.

You may find it efficient to prepare a form that you use regularly to report expenses. The form could then be filed in an income tax file folder. An illustration of such a form is shown below. Your employer should provide you with all receipts collected in the course of spending money for the business. Receipts attached to the expense summary forms simplify recordkeeping as well as reviewing the records later when the tax forms are being prepared.

DEDUCTIBLE EXPENSE

DATE: January 13, 19--

ITEM: Luncheon

EXPLANATION: Lunch at the Townhouse with Joe Morrow and Ted Rowe from Jackson & Jackson Company. Possible new customer.

TOTAL COST: $15.35

You may be responsible for typing and mailing your employer's income tax forms. You will want to check the accuracy of your typewriting and the completeness of the report. Often accompanying schedules are needed to provide a more complete report of expenses incurred during the taxable year. It is important that a tax return be received by the deadline date, so you will want to be sure you mail it in sufficient time to meet such a deadline date.

Sources for Information

If you are in a large American city, you will find an office of the Federal Internal Revenue Office where it is possible to secure tax forms as well as basic, up-to-date information on tax regulations. If you are in a small town, you may write to the Washington headquarters, or to a regional office nearer your town. The Washington office address is:

Internal Revenue Service
Washington, D.C. 20225

Income Tax Record

	Income				Date	Explanation	Deductible Expenses				
Salary	Dividends	Interest	Rents & Royalties	Misc.			Contributions	Interest	Taxes	Medical & Dental	Misc.
	35 00				Jan. 3	Acme Mfg. Co. - dividend					
			75 00		5	Q. C. Larson - rent					
					8	Merchants Bank - interest on mortgage		52 50			
					10	Dr. Thomas Wales - dental work				36 00	
				600 00	11	Profit on sale of Benton Corp. stock					
					14	Salem County - real estate taxes			52 50		
300 00					15	Salary					
					16	Sam's Auto Repairs - repairs from accident					139 75
		10 00			18	F. M. West - interest on loan					
					22	Red Cross - donation	25 00				
					23	Salem County - personal property tax			15 00		
	11 25				24	George & Co. - dividend					
					25	Queen Optical Co. - eyeglasses				30 00	
					28	Southern Publishing Co. - professional books					7 50
300 00					31	Salary					
					31	Christ Church - donations for month	20 00				
600 00	46 25	10 00	75 00	600 00	31	Totals	45 00	52 50	67 50	66 00	147 25

Illus. 14-12   Income tax record

INCOME TAX CHECKLIST

When keeping income tax records for your employer, check the following list of common deductible and nondeductible items.

	DEDUCTIBLE	NON-DEDUCTIBLE
Automobile expenses (car used only for pleasure) —		
Gasoline taxes..	x	
Interest on automobile loans..........................	x	
License fees..		x
Ordinary upkeep and operating expenses......................		x
Burglary losses over $100, if not covered by insurance	x	
Casualty losses over $100, if not covered by insurance (fire, flood, windstorm, lightning, earthquake, etc.)...............	x	
Charitable contributions to approved institutions.................	x	
Dues, social clubs for personal use		x
Fees paid to employment agencies.....................................	x	
FICA taxes withheld by employer.......................................		x
Fines for violation of laws and regulations...........................		x
Funeral expenses..		x
Gifts to relatives and other individuals................................		x
Income taxes imposed by city or state	x	
Interest paid on personal loans...	x	
Life insurance premiums		x
Medical expenses over 3% of adjusted gross income, if not covered by insurance (including the cost of artificial limbs, artificial teeth, eye glasses, hearing aids, dental fees, hospital expenses)	x	
Property taxes, real and personal	x	
Residence for personal use —		
Improvements		x
Insurance...		x
Interest on mortgage loan..	x	
Rent paid		x
Repairs		x
Taxes..	x	
Sales taxes, state and local	x	
Traveling expenses attending professional meetings..............	x	
Traveling expenses to and from place of business or employment		x
Uniforms for personal use including cost and upkeep, if not adaptable for general use (nurses, police, athletes, fire fighters)	x	
Union dues	x	

REVIEWING

1. Why should a record of all business expenses incurred be kept?
2. Have tax laws been consistent over the years?
3. Is income earned from property rented taxable?
4. Is income earned from savings accounts taxable?
5. What types of income does the Internal Revenue Service identify as "wages and salaries"?
6. What are royalties? Are royalties taxable?
7. What kind of record might a secretary find helpful in keeping a record of expenses?
8. What information is generally needed for each deductible expense?
9. Are receipts for expenses necessary if you keep a note of the actual expense at the time it is incurred?
10. Are there deadline dates for submitting tax reports to the Federal Government?

MAKING JUDGMENTS

1. Mr. Todd Turner works for a very busy executive who does much traveling. The executive finds she has no time to keep records of expenses. After trying to find out what her expenses were on a number of trips, Todd decided it was too difficult and he would not try again. Now, he merely notes on his calendar where the executive has gone, how long she was gone, and any other details he has such as method of travel and hotel reservations. When it is time for the accountant to do the tax return for the executive, Todd plans to give the executive a sheet with all the dates she traveled on it and ask her to make a listing of her expenses. What do you think of Todd's plan?
2. Jim's employer asked him to get another set of income tax forms for him. The set received through the mail had been misplaced. Jim's employer does his own tax return since he knows the procedures thoroughly. Jim wonders where he can get another set of income tax forms. What would you suggest to him?

WORKING WITH OTHERS

Every year the accountant seems to wait until the last days to complete the tax report for Mr. Stanford, who is Mr. Timons' employer. Generally Mr. Timons is called on to type the final schedules and mail the return. On this occasion, however, when the accountant calls Mr. Timons, she finds that he is very busy with special work because the national convention of one of Mr. Stanford's professional associations is being held now in the City. He just hasn't had time to type the schedules even though he knows there is a penalty if the return is not received by the deadline. What do you think Mr. Timons should say to the accountant?

REFRESHING LANGUAGE SKILLS

On a separate sheet of paper, type the following sentences capitalizing the words that need to be capitalized and adding the necessary punctuation marks.

1. some 2,300 members and their families opened the three days of sessions and social activities with a reception sunday, october 13 in the grand ballroom of the olympic hotel in seattle, washington.
2. the new president was born in the state of montana but lived in denver colorado for most of his childhood.
3. mr. wallace c petersen president of western industries incorporated, will preside at the annual awards dinner of the local chapter of the national management association.
4. the board of directors approved a shift in next year's meeting from st. louis to omaha and selected st. louis for the meeting of the following year.
5. at a session discussing "the public crisis in accounting legislation," cpas were urged to become active in their state societies.

PERFORMING SECRETARIAL TASKS

1. Using the forms provided in the *Supplies Inventory* or forms similar to the one on page 547, prepare expense deduction sheets given the following information:

   a. Visited a client, Dr. T. W. Jacobs in Oakdale; 89 miles round trip; used my car. Took client to lunch $13.45. Tuesday, the 17th of April.
   b. Bought some special forms in town for the report we must prepare. April 20. $5.65.
   c. Trip to Washington to talk with prospective client, National Investments Associates. Air fare $134.50; taxi service $9.45; meals $19.85; telephone calls $4.50; parking of car at airport $3.50; miles to and from airport 31; miscellaneous $3.50, April 23.

2. As secretary to Ms. Statler, a consultant in office systems, you have accumulated the items listed below. Record in the Income Tax Record the items that belong there. If a copy of the Record is not available, use a form similar to the one on page 548.

April	4	Received dividend — R. T. Gage and Co.	$ 12.50
	4	Contributed to Community Charity	$ 50.00
	5	Purchased two new books on computer systems for the office	$ 21.49
	7	Gave a contribution to child on street	$ 1.00
	7	Received dividend — T. W. WEST Corporation	$ 24.45
	7	Paid Dr. R. W. Stone for medical checkup	$110.50
	11	Took taxi to meeting of City Planning Board; served as volunteer	$ 7.65
	11	Sent check to Church Society	$ 25.00
	11	Bought ticket for a professional luncheon	$ 12.50
	14	Bought ticket for an opera performance	$ 11.50

Part 4

Other Financial Records

Mr. Douglas Simmons is secretary to a project manager for a large construction company. One of his key responsibilities is maintaining an up-to-date record of expenditures. His employer has a budget for an apartment house under construction, and because of unforeseen increases in some costs, he strives to keep a very close watch on all expenditures. He appreciates the care with which Mr. Simmons maintains the budget records.

Business executives in their efforts to get the most value for their **expenditures** maintain a variety of records. How many activities you will have in the general area of financial recordkeeping will depend on the size and nature of the organization for which you work. Some of the more common tasks that secretaries assume are discussed briefly in this Part.

expenditures:
payments made

Budgets

There are times when a secretary must maintain the records related to a particular budget. A *budget* is a detailed estimate of expected expenses. Budgets are generally drawn for a year, either the calendar year or the fiscal year. While a fiscal year may begin any time during the calendar year, July 1 is a very common beginning date.

fiscal year:
a 12-month period used as accounting period

Preparing a Preliminary Budget

A secretary may have the responsibility of collecting information for the employer when a new budget must be prepared. Former budgets and records attached to them are valuable sources of information for a new budget. If a budget represents new activity for the company, the secretary may secure figures from a variety of sources that provide the goods and services necessary for the forthcoming activities.

The secretary may have the task of typing the final budget plan and **accompanying** report.

accompanying:
going with

Maintaining a Budget

allocation:
amount specified

anticipated:
expected

The secretary may be given the task of maintaining the budget, which means keeping an account of the expenses assigned to each of the budget items. The **allocation** for each of the items represents **anticipated** expenditures for the fiscal period. While there may be possibilities for transferring funds from one item to another or securing additional funds, there is a basic responsibility to keep expenditures within the amounts allocated.

If a new budget follows closely the style of a previous budget, the secretary merely continues with the system of recordkeeping earlier designed. If the secretary must manage a budget for new expenditures, it is necessary to establish a set of records. You should try to create as simple a system of records as is adequate for the task. Often a loose leaf notebook is used with each item in the budget given a separate sheet. An index at the front of the notebook makes it easy to find a particular item quickly. A common practice is to list the budget allocation at the top of the page and as expenditures are made, they are subtracted from the allocation. The last figures on the page represents the amount still available. This means that it is possible for the secretary to determine readily the **status** of a particular item, or the total budget, if necessary.

status:
current position

requisitioning:
requesting approval
for

A system of **requisitioning** is necessary to purchase goods and services under a budget. The secretary may be responsible for preparing such requisitions, but generally they must be approved by the executive. At the time the requisition is sent to the office responsible for purchasing goods and services, the secretary should record the transaction in the budget records and file a copy of the requisition form. If the cost of the item desired is not known, the secretary must await a copy of the purchase order before it can be recorded in the records. The purchase order is placed with the requisition form, and together they should be placed in a file of "Goods and Services in Transit." When the order is received, the secretary must check the invoice or statement of goods shipped with the original requisition and purchase order to be sure that the total order was received and the computations are accurate.

One secretary who is responsible for a large travel budget made the following comments:

> We have a travel budget for promoting a new product. Mr. Gray, who is responsible for the budget, must approve all plans. For example, any member of the staff who wants to travel to another city must submit a requisition for the total expenses as well as a plan of the activities. Mr. Gray then reviews and either approves or rejects. I keep a record of all requisitions approved in my project files. Only when actual expenses are submitted to me do I subtract them from the remaining balances in

the budget. I prepare forms for payment, which must go to Central Accounting, which in turn sends me a statement when the payment has been made.

In most large organizations, the central accounting department will, from time to time, send statements of the transactions which relate to all items in a particular budget. This financial record provides the secretary with the official figures which can be checked against the accounts maintained in the particular office. If there are discrepancies, their source must be discovered by the secretary. If the error is in the office records, the records are revised. If the error is not there, the secretary should talk with the accounting office personnel to discover the source of the error.

discrepancies: differences

Payrolls

Most payrolls are handled in central accounting offices and increasingly by computers. However, there are still small offices that use manual systems, particularly those offices which have ten or fewer employees. In such instances, it is common for the secretary to have responsibility for maintaining some of the payroll records.

Original Records

To handle the task of managing a payroll, you will need an original record showing the basis for payments and the schedule of payments. An appointment letter authorizing you to make payments to an employee is necessary along with an Income Tax Deduction Form, commonly referred to as the W-4 Form. The W-4 form, which is illustrated below must be signed by the person to whom payments are to be made.

Form **W-4** (Rev. Dec. 1975) Department of the Treasury Internal Revenue Service	**Employee's Withholding Allowance Certificate** (This certificate is for income tax withholding purposes only; it will remain in effect until you change it.)
Type or print your full name John Quist	Your social security number 202-54-7747
Home address (Number and street or rural route) 1899 Blind Brook Drive	Marital status [X] Single [ ] Married
City or town, State and ZIP code Houston, Texas 77079	(If married but legally separated, or spouse is a nonresident alien, check the single block.)

1 Total number of allowances you are claiming 1

2 Additional amount, if any, you want deducted from each pay (if your employer agrees) . . . . $

I certify that to the best of my knowledge and belief, the number of withholding allowances claimed on this certificate does not exceed the number to which I am entitled.

Signature ▶ *John Quist*   Date ▶ March 15 , 19 --

Illus. 14-13

Employees withholding allowance certificate (Form W-4)

Work Records

There are two basic records that the secretary must maintain in order to know what to pay employees. These are:

Illus. 14-14

Payroll register

1. Payroll Register — lists each individual's name, the gross wages for the period, deductions, and net wages.

						THE WAKEFIELD PUBLISHING COMPANY						
PAYROLL REGISTER									DATE November 5, 19--			
EMPLOYEE		Allow.	Marital Status	Gross Earnings	DEDUCTIONS						Total Deductions	Net Earnings
No.	Name				Federal With. Tax	F.I.C.A.	Group Insurance	Hosp.	Bonds			
9	BROCK, PERRI	1	S	78 00	6 30	4 56	1 60	1 75			14 21	63 79
13	FRANKS, CHRISTINE	1	S	90 00	8 60	5 27	1 60	1 75			17 22	72 78
35	GANGL, ALAN R.	4	M	162 92	10 40	9 53	4 10	2 25	5 50		31 78	131 14
11	GATES, STEPHAN M.	1	S	90 00	8 60	5 27	1 60	1 75			17 22	72 78
32	HEIDT, CAROL A.	2	M	150 39	14 20	8 80	2 85	2 25			28 10	122 29
26	JUNG, MAY	3	M	104 00	1 90	6 08	2 85	2 25	3 00		16 08	87 92
24	WERNER, CHARLES	2	M	101 00	4 30	5 91	2 85	1 75			14 81	86 19

2. Cumulative Individual Earnings Record — indicates name, address, number of exemptions, and basis for payment for each person on the payroll. This record will be used for preparing reports for individual tax payments to the Federal

Illus. 14-15

Employees earnings record

			EMPLOYEE'S EARNINGS RECORD									
	Gates		Stephen		M.				289-54-3802			
	LAST NAME		**FIRST**		**MIDDLE**				**SOC. SEC. NO.**			
Week	Period Ending	Earnings	Deductions						Net Pay		Taxable Earnings Accumulated	
			Fed. With. Tax	F.I.C.A.	Group Ins.	Hosp.	Other	Total	Amount			
	Total First Three Quarters	3537 60	340 80	206 95	62 40	68 25		678 40	2859 20	3537 60		
1	10/8	90 00	11 00	5 27	1 60	1 75		19 62	70 38	3627 60		
2	10/15	90 00	11 00	5 27	1 60	1 75		19 62	70 38	3717 60		
3	10/22	83 50	9 50	4 88	1 60	1 75		17 73	65 77	3801 10		
4	10/29	90 00	11 00	5 27	1 60	1 75		19 62	70 38	3891 10		
5	11/5	90 00	11 00	5 27	1 60	1 75		19 62	70 38	3981 10		
6												

Government and to the State when there is a state income tax. Also, reports required quarterly for Social Security and Income Withholding taxes are prepared with the information available in this record.

Many stationery stores sell appropriate forms for these records.

Petty Cash Fund

Many firms have a special fund called a *petty cash fund* from which they pay small expenses. The petty cash fund can be used to buy stamps, to pay COD charges, to pay for inexpensive office supplies, or any other small expense items. Since most of the records on petty cash are handwritten, it is important that they be written so that you, as well as your employer, can read them easily.

Illus. 14-16

The receiver of a petty cash payment signs a receipt for the amount.

The fund is generally handled by one person, often a secretary or a receptionist. The nature of expenses to be handled from the fund determines the amount maintained. Funds ranging from $10 to $100 are common. The money in the fund is generally maintained in a metal cashbox in the desk of the person handling it and placed in a safe at night.

Establishing the Fund

To establish a petty cash fund:

1. A check is written payable to Petty Cash for the amount to be placed in the fund.
2. The check is signed by an authorized person and cashed at the firm's bank.
3. The money is placed in the petty cash box.

Each time that you make a payment from the petty cash fund, you should make out a receipt for the amount and have it signed by the person receiving the money. The receipts should be numbered consecutively. Each should show the date, to whom the payment is to be made, and the purpose of the payment. The signed receipts should be kept in the petty cash box. At all times the cash on hand plus the total amount of the receipts should equal the original amount placed in the fund. A receipt is important because it serves as **verification** of the use of the money.

verification:
proof

Illus. 14-17

Petty cash
receipt

```
                        Pearson & Smith
                      PETTY CASH RECEIPT
    No. 422                        Date April 1        19--
    Received of Pearson & Smith              $ 1.05
    One  05/100                                    Dollars
    For Postage due
    Account Charged: Miscellaneous Signed H. R. Burke
```

Replenishing the Fund

Additional cash must be placed in the fund whenever the amount of cash is insufficient to pay for expected expenses. To replenish the fund, follow this procedure:

1. Add all receipts and count the cash in the petty cash box.
2. "Prove" the petty cash fund by adding the amount of cash on hand to the total of all petty cash receipts. The sum should equal the amount originally set aside for the fund. An illustration of a proof follows:

   Total of petty cash receipts .... $ 97.95
   Petty cash on hand..   2.05
   Total.. $100.00

3. Prepare a summary report of petty cash expenditures and attach the receipts for them.

```
               SUMMARY REPORT OF PETTY CASH

                     May 5 to 31, 19--


Balance on hand, May 5 . . . . . . . . . . . . . $100.00

Expenditures:

     Office Supplies . . . . . . . . . . . $ 6.50
     Postal Service  . . . . . . . . . . .  13.00
     Transportation  . . . . . . . . . . .  12.10
     Messenger Services  . . . . . . . . .   9.50
     Miscellaneous . . . . . . . . . . . .  46.85

Total expenditures  . . . . . . . . . . . . . . .  87.95

Balance on hand, May 31 . . . . . . . . . . . . . $ 12.05
```

4. Write a check payable to "Petty Cash" for the total amount of the receipts shown in the summary report ($87.95 in the illustration above).
5. Submit the summary report and the attached receipts to your employer with the check payable to the petty cash fund.
6. After your employer has signed the check, cash it and place the money in the petty cash box, thus replenishing the fund.

Sometimes a more permanent record is made of the petty cash fund in a petty cash book as illustrated on page 560.

Continuing Need for Records

As organizations learn more about budgeting as a means of determining more precisely costs of operation, there is increased financial recordkeeping for all employees, including secretaries. As you are asked to keep such records, you should strive to develop a system that is simple yet assures accurate information. One secretary described his experience with a new recordkeeping task:

> The director of foods advertising in our agency, Mr. F. Y. Dilworth, for whom I work, talked about the need for a better picture of the costs of doing jobs for each customer. He felt that if we knew the time spent by each staff member who worked on a particular job, we would have a better basis for establishing fair fees.
> Together we determined rates for the hourly work of the members of the staff. I was to keep these rates confidential. Then, I had the task of designing a simple form and instructions for its use. Mr. Dilworth

Date	Explanation	Receipts	Pay-ments	Distribution of Payments				
				Office Supplies	Postal	Trans-portation	Mes-senger	Miscel-laneous
May 5	Balance	100 00						
6	Cleaning supplies		5 90					5 90
7	Window washer		12 50					12 50
8	Delivery of contract		4 50				4 50	
18	Taxi		2 20			2 20		
19	Develop photographs		16 00					16 00
20	Immediate delivery of sale		5 00				5 00	
20	Taxi		5 30			5 30		
21	Postage stamps		13 00		13 00			
22	Miscellaneous office supplies		6 50	6 50				
23	Taxi		4 60			4 60		
25	Miscellaneous art supplies		12 45					12 45
31	Totals	100 00	87 95	6 50	13 00	12 10	9 50	46 85
31	Balance		12 05					
		100 00	100 00					
31	Balance	12 05						
31	Check No. 456	87 95						

Illus. 14-18   Petty cash book

held a staff meeting at which he discussed the reason for maintaining such records. I distributed a tentative design for the form and the instructions for using it. I then asked for suggestions. After getting some good suggestions, we revised the form and had a supply printed.

The system is working satisfactorily, and I find the information extremely interesting.

REVIEWING

1. What is a budget?
2. What are some activities that secretaries handle in relation to preparing a budget?
3. What does each item in a budget represent?
4. What kind of check does a secretary make when the central accounting office forwards a statement of status of the budget?
5. What are the necessary original records for establishing the name of an employee on a payroll?
6. What information is found in a payroll register?
7. What information is maintained in a cumulative individual earnings record?
8. Describe briefly the nature of a petty cash fund.

9. For what purpose is a receipt important for each payment made from a petty cash fund?
10. When is the petty cash fund replenished?

MAKING JUDGMENTS

1. One of Pamela's responsibilities is to keep track of the expenditures for a new budget in her department. She believed that no one would be concerned about that budget until near the end of the fiscal year, which would be June 30. Since June is generally a quiet month, Pamela decided that the best way to handle items related to the budget would be to put them in a file folder as she got them. Then, in June, she could organize the papers and determine what transactions were related to each item in the budget. What do you think of Pamela's decision?
2. Larry works in a small office with three other persons. They know each other well and they trust each other. Although Larry was given responsibility for taking care of the petty cash fund, he decided that it was unnecessary for the transactions to be handled through him. Therefore, he told the others to use the fund when they needed to make payments, but to remember the purpose of each payment. At the end of the month, he would ask them about expenditures when he found that the balance of cash on hand didn't equal the receipts in the folder. What do you think of Larry's procedure?

WORKING WITH OTHERS

Raymond is responsible for maintaining the budget records for a research project in a nuclear physics center. The accounting office sends him monthly computer statements about the status of each account in the budget. When he checked the May computer statement, he found that three balances were different from his. He knows that he has maintained his records carefully and, therefore, there cannot be errors in his accounts. Obviously, the computer hasn't functioned properly or someone in the accounting office introduced figures incorrectly into the computer.

Without checking his work, Raymond writes a memorandum to the clerk in the accounting office who is responsible for the statement in which he says: "I've just received the May statement for our Project Budget No. 5671 and I note that you have made three errors, for three of your balances don't agree with mine. These are . . ."

How would you evaluate the manner in which Raymond handled the errors he discovered?

REFRESHING LANGUAGE SKILLS

On a separate sheet of paper write the plurals of the following words:

agency	index
analysis	leaf
basis	library
belief	money
best seller	ourself
boundary	phenomenon
brother-in-law	photocopy
cargo	proof
child	roof
clinic	shelf
criterion	syllabus
curriculum	thesis
datum	two-year-old
formula	university
gentleman	vacancy

PERFORMING SECRETARIAL TASKS

1. The following transactions pertain to the petty cash fund maintained by the Jones Drug Company during the months of September and October.

Sept.　1 Check No. 175 for $25 was cashed to establish the petty cash fund.

　　　　3 Paid Bill Smith $6 for cleaning the store and office.

　　　13 Paid the Lake Supply Company 95 cents for miscellaneous office supplies.

　　　17 Paid Johnny Stone 75 cents for delivering merchandise.

　　　24 Paid $3 for postage stamps.

　　　29 Paid the Stevens Hardware Company 50 cents for a duplicate key for the office.

　　　30 Check No. 221 for $11.20 was cashed to replenish the petty cash fund.

Oct.　 4 Paid the Howsam Stationery Company $1.15 for miscellaneous office supplies.

　　　10 Paid Bill Smith $6 for cleaning the store and office.

　　　17 Paid Central High School $5 for advertisement in school paper.

　　　22 Paid the Jackson Paper Company 85 cents for miscellaneous office supplies.

29 Paid Marion Dillinger $6.75 for repainting store sign.

31 Check No. 256 for $19.75 was cashed to replenish the petty cash fund.

Record the receipts and expenditures in the petty cash book from the *Supplies Inventory* or on a form like the one shown on page 560. Write a receipt for each of the payments made using the receipt forms from the Supplies Inventory if available.

2. You have been given the following handwritten budget for the forthcoming year. Type it on plain paper in good form.

J. W. M. Corporation

Budget Request July 1, 19-- to June 30, 19--

Dept'l Operating Request

	Request Dept. Head
Salaries	22,500 –
Consulting	3,500 –
Travel, Conferences, & Meetings	1,500 –
Communications	1,000 –
Postage	1,500 –
Printing	1,000 –
Books & Publications	500 –
Memberships	250 –
Advertising	750 –
General Supplies	1,200 –
Repairs	650 –
Rental – Premises	1,500 –
Rental – Equipment	500 –

IMPROVING SECRETARIAL SKILLS (Optional)

Mr. Roland S. Emberman, secretary to Mrs. Theresa Walsh, handles all banking activities in their small office. On May 3, when he received the customary monthly bank statement, Mr. Emberman found that a service charge of $4 was listed. However, he knew that there should be no service charges if an average daily balance of $500 was maintained in the account. He checked all the balances on the statement. None was below $500. Therefore, he knew that there should have been no service charge for the month's transactions. On plain paper, type a letter to City Bank, 400 Main Street, Jackson, OH 45230, explaining the situation and asking for a correction.

You and Secretarial Work

Part 1. **Opportunities**
Part 2. **Employment Application Papers**
Part 3. **The Personal Interview**
Part 4. **Secretarial Positions in Specialized Fields**
Part 5. **Promotional Prospects**

Part 1
Opportunities

Karen, Bill, Jane, Sally, and Randy were sitting in the school cafeteria after lunch talking about the future. The school year was ending — and so were their four years of high school. They had been together in an office procedures course for the full year, and on many occasions, they had discussed their new skills and knowledge. From time to time they talked about their ideas of an "ideal job." They knew their teachers had provided them with realistic, long-term experiences. They felt confident there would be opportunities for them. They also realized that they might have choices to make. They had studied together and had many common interests; but they also had differences which they felt should be explored as they considered opportunities for work.

The Job Market

What jobs are available in the modern business community? Is there a need for office workers? While automation has transferred many tasks from the desk of an office worker to a machine, there continues to be great demand for office workers of all types. Beginners with limited or no experience find jobs available to them. Beginners do not become executive secretaries immediately upon graduation from high school. However, there are many instances where high school graduates who do superior work in their beginning jobs are quickly moved into positions of greater responsibility. Businesses are eager to use all the talents and skills of their workers, and their efforts to reward new employees who show special interest in their work result in many promotional opportunities for good workers.

The types of positions that beginners generally fill are typist, clerk-typist, transcribing machine operator, junior stenographer, receptionist, and office machine operator.

Organizational Types

Organizations are classified in a number of ways. A classification based on the nature of activity carried on in the organization is given below.

You will want to consider the type of organization in which you would like to work.

ORGANIZATIONS CLASSIFIED BY ACTIVITIES

Organization	Activity
Manufacturing	Producers of household appliances, glass products, pianos, carpeting, textiles, electronics, automobiles
Mining	Coal, copper, silver
Construction	Housing, mobile homes, offices, hospitals and bridges.
Transportation and Public Utilities	Trucking, airlines, railroads, bus lines, electricity, gas, telephone
Trade	Wholesale, central retailing chain, department store, grocery store, specialty store
Finance, Insurance, and Real Estate	Commercial banks, savings banks, security dealers and brokers, insurance companies, real estate brokers
Health Services	Hospitals, clinics, doctor's office, dentist's office
Community Agencies	YMCA, YWCA, Red Cross, 4-H, Boy Scouts, Girl Scouts
Religious	Church mission services of coordinated groups of churches
Communications	Periodicals, newspaper, book publishing, radio, television, films
Government	City government, state government, federal government
Education	Preschool centers, elementary schools, secondary schools, community colleges, colleges, universities, research centers
Professional	Law offices, counseling services, consultant services, architects' offices, theatre services.

Eileen was fond of cooking; in fact, she was very skillful in the kitchen. At the same time, she liked office work and wanted a full-time job in an office. She explored job possibilities in New York City and, fortunately, found an office job in a magazine company that published several home magazines. She was assigned to the office of the director of food services.

Peter was constantly building hi-fi equipment and found such equipment fascinating. He knew much about the components available, and his friends sought his judgment when they were planning to buy such equipment. He also wanted to do office work. He applied for an office job in a large store that sold all types of equipment. He was a general clerk in the office of the buyer of stereo equipment. His employer found Peter's knowledge of equipment extremely valuable. Peter even worked at times on the selling floor. He found that the buyer was grateful for his assistance, so his job became more and more what he liked to do — an interesting combination of office work and involvement with equipment.

Size of Organization

Organizations range all the way from small ones where an individual works alone with an office assistant to giant ones where there are thousands of employees located in a large office complex. What size do you prefer? You will want to give attention to this question. Some office workers like to be a part of a large company that is fully organized with specific rules and policies about job tasks, promotional possibilities, and salary **scales**. Others, however, choose to work in very small, informal surroundings where everyone is fully acquainted with everyone else in the organization and promotional opportunities are limited.

scales:
range of wages paid

When Stewart thinks about the job he wants when he graduates from high school, he knows that he wants to be in a large company. He feels he could learn so much more in a large company. There would be many people with whom to talk, and it would be relatively easy to have many friends. He thinks a large company would be up to date and would always be introducing new ways of work. He feels that if he works diligently in a large company, he will have many opportunities to be promoted to more responsible positions.

Illus. 15-1

In large organizations job tasks and promotional opportunities are well-defined.

Clyde is of a different nature. He likes to know everyone around, and he thinks a small place would be so much nicer than a large one. In fact, Clyde is hoping to get a job in the county seat, which is just ten miles from his home. He knows many people in the area, and to work in one of the county offices means that he will be associating with people whom he knows. Clyde likes the informal manner of the people in his county, and at this point, he isn't worrying about promotional opportunities.

Illus. 15-2

In smaller organizations the working environment is frequently more informal and job duties are often more diverse

Location

Where do you want to work? Your choice is wide! There are jobs in downtown centers of large metropolitan areas, in suburban communities, in small villages. Jobs are available in places as different as Portland, Maine, and Miami Beach, Florida, or London, England, and Lima, Peru. Some beginning office workers expect to **commute** from their homes when they are working; others plan to **relocate** so that they may live near the place of their work.

commute:
to travel back and forth

relocate:
to find a new place in which to live

Laura commutes daily from her suburban home into the financial district of Chicago, where she is working as a stenographer. She drives to work with two friends who also work in the financial district. She says that she enjoys the trip in and back and finds the financial district an exciting, alive place in which to spend her working days.

Bernie, who lives in a small village near the eastern tip of Long Island in New York, chose to work in a lawyer's office which is within walking distance of his home. He says he loves walking to where he must be each day.

Becoming Acquainted with Job Opportunities

There are many ways for you to become acquainted with job opportunities in the community where you seek employment. Use as many as necessary to aid you in securing a position that is best for you.

Placement Office in Your School

Many secondary schools have placement offices as a part of the counseling services provided students. Possibly you used such a service for securing a part-time position or a summer position. Plan to talk with a placement counselor about job opportunities that match your interests and skills. Once a placement counselor knows of your interests, you will undoubtedly receive notices of positions that are available. You should follow through immediately on each job lead and report as requested to the placement office. Many companies seek employees through school placement offices, and you may find that this source is sufficient to secure a position.

Employment Agencies

In many communities there are both private and public employment agencies that will provide aid to you in your efforts to find a position. Private employment agencies are sometimes specialized; so you will want to be sure that you are inquiring at one that does place office personnel. Private employment agencies earn their income from fees which are paid either by the individual who secures a position through services provided by the agency or by the company that hires the new employee. The fee is a percentage of salary, generally based on a year's salary.

Public employment agencies provide a service without fee. Such agencies are supported through public funds. You may register at a public employment agency for aid in seeking a position. In large cities public agencies are specialized; so you will want to be sure that you visit the department that handles office vacancies.

Classified Advertisements

Many companies as well as employment agencies use the classified section of newspapers to announce vacancies. While many of the advertisements identify the company or agency seeking personnel for positions, some are listed as blind advertisements. A *blind advertisement* is one that lists only a box number so that the identity of the company seeking an employee is not revealed. Blind advertisements are used so that some preliminary **screening** can be done on the basis of a written letter and data sheet that are submitted by interested applicants.

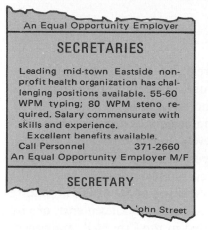

An Equal Opportunity Employer

SECRETARIES

Leading mid-town Eastside non-profit health organization has challenging positions available. 55-60 WPM typing; 80 WPM steno required. Salary commensurate with skills and experience.
Excellent benefits available.
Call Personnel   371-2660
An Equal Opportunity Employer M/F

SECRETARY

'ohn Street

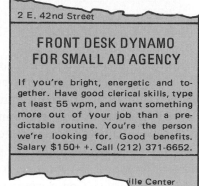

2 E. 42nd Street

FRONT DESK DYNAMO FOR SMALL AD AGENCY

If you're bright, energetic and to-gether. Have good clerical skills, type at least 55 wpm, and want something more out of your job than a pre-dictable routine. You're the person we're looking for. Good benefits. Salary $150+ +. Call (212) 371-6652.

...lle Center

Illus. 15-3

Blind advertisements for secretarial positions

Direct Inquiry to Organization

Some people learn about office positions through relatives and friends who are employed in companies that are seeking new employees. If you are informed of an opening through such a source, your relative or friend may make the initial inquiry to the personnel department and arrange an interview for you. You will be expected to visit the company and indicate to the personnel officer who made the suggestion to you.

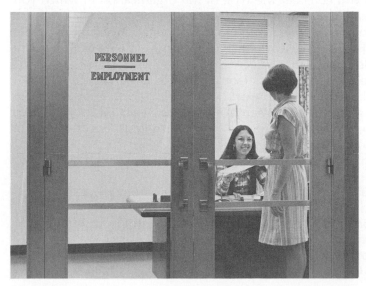

Illus. 15-4

A company forms its first impression of you in its personnel office.

Ohio National Life Insurance Company

If there is a company in which you have special interest, it is proper to write a letter of inquiry and to indicate your skills and the type of position you are seeking. If you are writing to a company that often hires beginning workers, your chances of being granted an interview are very good.

Civil Service Announcements

Many positions in government require that candidates take examinations and, therefore, there are general public announcements about the dates of such examinations. If you are interested in employment in government, you will want to note the announcements that are posted in public buildings and that appear in newspapers. Announcements for federal positions are often displayed in post offices and in regional civil service offices throughout the country. You can also write directly to the United States Civil Service Commission, Washington, D.C. 20415, asking for information on forthcoming examinations. Announcements of city civil service examinations are usually posted in the City Hall; announcements of county and state examinations, in the County Courthouse or principal county building. Also, you can consult your local telephone directory to find the Civil Service Commission office in your city and request information directly from that office.

REVIEWING

1. What are some office positions that are open to high school graduates without experience?
2. Why would you consider the type of the organization in which you might find employment?
3. Tom is a good carpenter; he enjoys working in his father's home workshop. He wants to work in an office. In what type of firm might Tom consider employment?
4. For what reasons might a person choose a large company rather than a small one in which to work?
5. Even if there are a great many office jobs available in your own home town, is there any reason why you might consider jobs in other locations?
6. What are the placement services provided by your high school? by government agencies in your area?
7. How do public employment agencies differ from private employment agencies?
8. What section of the newspaper contains notices of job openings?
9. What information is missing in a *blind* advertisement?
10. How can you learn about examinations for civil service positions in the Federal Government?

MAKING JUDGMENTS

1. Marcella would like to work in the large city about 25 miles from her home town, a small rural community. She goes to a consolidated school, and although she has had excellent instruction, she is hesitant about her ability to meet the requirements for jobs in the city. She wonders, therefore, if it would be more realistic to find a job in her own home town. What do you think of Marcella's judgment?
2. Aaron, while reading the classified section of a local newspaper in a large American city, saw an advertisement for a position as a beginning office worker that sounded very interesting. When he noted that it was necessary to send a letter and personal data sheet to a box number at newspaper office, he decided that he wasn't interested in communicating with an unknown company. What do you think of Aaron's judgment?

WORKING WITH OTHERS

Andy's father is an executive in the only big firm in the small town where Andy and his family live. This large firm is a producer of all types of household linens — towels, sheets, bedspreads, etc. They need many office workers in their various departments. Andy's father is highly respected in his company, and when the personnel director happened to meet Andy on Main Street one afternoon and learned that he was soon to graduate from high school, he said: "Andy, we have many good job openings for high school graduates with good business skills. Why don't you come by to see us one afternoon next week? We would like to have you work for us."

Andy does want to work in an office, but he wonders if he should work in the same company where his father is employed. What do you think Andy should say to the personnel director?

REFRESHING LANGUAGE SKILLS

Some of the words in the following list are incorrect. Type the list correcting those that are not correct.

1. achievement	11. conseling
2. objectivly	12. comunications
3. coordinated	13. utilites
4. specialty	14. suburrban
5. recomendations	15. personnel
6. municipal	16. comute
7. federel	17. diversified
8. specilized	18. religous
9. metropolitan	19. suroundings
10. candidetes	20. prelimenary

PERFORMING SECRETARIAL TASKS

1. Job opportunities vary from community to community. Your own community may be in need of many office workers or it may need few or virtually none. Review the job situation in your community and type answers to the following questions:

   a. What is the actual job situation in your community?
   b. If there are limited job opportunities in your community, where are communities where you might seek employment?
   c. What are possible places where you can learn of job vacancies in your community or in nearby communities if local opportunities are limited?

2. From the newspapers read in your community, clip the advertisements for secretarial and related office positions that have appeared in the past week which you are qualified to fill. Be ready to discuss these job opportunities in class indicating why you believe you are able to meet the job requirements.

3. Write an advertisement for an office position that you would find fully satisfactory. In your advertisement indicate the factors that you believe are important in the position which you would like to have.

Part 2
Employment Application Papers

George's high school counselor had given him the details of the job opportunities in a large insurance company and had arranged an appointment for him. When George arrived at the Employment Office, he was given an application form to fill in. George had with him a copy of his personal data sheet with details that he needed for the application form. He read each item carefully and then wrote the answer in his best handwriting.

The Personal Data Sheet

Before you apply for a job, you will want to prepare a personal data sheet. The personal data sheet tells a potential employer who you are and what you are trained to do.

Its Purpose

A prospective employer needs to become acquainted with you in very little time. A personal data sheet is helpful in achieving this purpose. A personal data sheet outlines in clear form the important facts about your background that will be of value in determining whether you are a good candidate for a position.

Its Content

Generally personal data sheets are divided into the following parts:

Personal information
Education
Extracurricular activities
Experience
References

Personal Information. The personal information includes your name, home address, telephone number, your age (date of birth), your height, your weight, your marital status, and your physical condition (a general statement is sufficient).

Education. Under education you will give the complete name of your high school, plus the curriculum that you studied or the major courses taken, and the secretarial skills that you have developed. You will want to add any scholastic awards that you received while in high school.

Extracurricular Activities. Extra class activities are of interest to prospective employers; so you will want to list all your organizational activities while you were a student and those activities in the community in which you continue to be active. Any offices that you held in a class or club should also be listed. This section of your personal data sheet reflects your special interests, your ability to work with other people, and your leadership qualities.

Experience. Experience at work, even though limited, should be listed. Begin with your most recent experience and list the jobs you have held for more than a few weeks. Give the job title first, then the name of the firm or organization, and the dates of your employment. If you have had little or no work experience for which you were paid, you will want to list all volunteer jobs that you have held in the community.

evaluating:
judging; determining
qualities

References. In **evaluating** candidates, prospective employers review references. You will want to list as references persons who know you well enough to judge you on the traits and attitudes that employers are concerned about. Generally it is a good idea to give at least one name for each of the following:

1. Experience — the recommendation of your present employer or a former employer or supervisor to indicate the quality of your work and your ability to get along with people with whom you work.
2. Scholarship — the recommendation of a former teacher is valuable to indicate your scholastic accomplishments and your potential ability to perform on a job.
3. Character — the recommendation of a person who has known you for several years and can comment on your integrity, loyalty, and reliability is useful. Clergy, business people, and other professionals are appropriate references. You should not list relatives or neighbors. You should telephone or write notes to persons you wish to list as references. It is courteous to request approval before listing a person's name.

Its Appearance

Your personal data sheet should be organized logically and typewritten carefully. It is permissible to use duplicated copies, for data sheets. You will want to send only attractive copies to prospective employers, and you will want to be sure to proofread your copy so that no uncorrected errors remain on the copy.

Letter of Application

A short letter indicating your interest in a position should accompany your personal data sheet. A letter of application is a direct, concise letter in which you state clearly the position in which you are interested. If you are not certain if the company to which you are applying has a vacancy for the type of job in which you are interested, then your letter of application is also a letter of inquiry.

Below are guides to follow in writing your letter of application:

1. Be certain to include your full address above the date of your letter.
2. Address the letter appropriately: If you are responding to a classified advertisement that provides a return box only, you should use the address given and the salutation should be *Ladies and Gentlemen.*

   If you have learned about a position through your high school placement office or through a friend, you will be given the name of the firm and perhaps the name of the person in charge of employment. If a person's name is given, address your letter in this manner:

   ```
   Mr. Thomas L. Leeper, Personnel Manager
   The Azzaro Corporation
   3689 Wilson Street
   Atlanta, GA   30315
   ```

   The salutation should be *Dear Mr. Leeper:*
3. State your interest in the first paragraph:

   ```
   The stenographic position which you adver-
   tised in The Atlanta Times on Monday, June
   3, is of interest to me.
   ```
   or

   ```
   Miss Cathie Royer, the Placement Counselor
   at Greenville High School, has suggested
   that I apply for the stenographic position
   which is available in your firm.
   ```

2309 Vernon Avenue
Joliet, IL 60431
June 16, 19--

Mr. Frederick C. Moore
Personnel Director
Constitution Life Insurance Company
209 West Fourth Street
Joliet, IL 60432

Dear Mr. Moore

Miss Dorothy Fowler, one of your employees who attended Central
High School with me, told me that there will be an opening in
your stenographic pool on July 1. I should like to apply for
the position. As I have indicated on the enclosed personal data
sheet, my secretarial qualifications meet the high standards of
your company.

I graduated in the upper fourth of my high school class. During
the fall term I plan to take courses in business and finance in
the evening division of Joliet Community College. My application
for admission has already been approved.

During the past two summers I have had experience as a clerk-
typist with the Metropolitan Life Insurance Company, as listed
on the data sheet. The office manager, Mr. Arthur T. Sweeney,
has given me permission to list his name as one of my business
references.

I enjoyed my work with the Metropolitan Life Insurance Company,
and I should like to continue in the life insurance field. May
I expect to be called for an interview? My telephone number
is 555-2368.

Sincerely yours

Margaret Jean Collins

(Miss) Margaret Jean Collins

Enclosure

Illus. 15-5 Letter of application

P E R S O N A L   D A T A   S H E E T

NAME: Margaret Jean Collins   HEIGHT: 5'6"
ADDRESS: 2309 Vernon Avenue   WEIGHT: 116 pounds
                 Joliet, IL 60431
TELEPHONE: Area Code 815 555-2368   MARITAL STATUS: Single
AGE: 18 years   PHYSICAL CONDITION: Excellent

EDUCATION

  Graduated from Central High School, Joliet, Illinois, on June 13,
  19--, after completing the Secretarial Studies program.
  Admitted to the Evening Division of Joliet Community College for
  the fall semester of 19--.

  Secretarial Skills:
    Typewriting rate--60 words a minute
    Shorthand dictation rate--120 words a minute
    Transcription rate--35 words a minute
  Awards and Certificates:
    Central High School Student Service Award
    Alphabetic Filing Certificate
    Dictaphone Transcription Proficiency Certificate
  Office Machines Operated:
    Transcribing machine, Mimeograph, Offset duplicator,
    Printing calculator, Call Director

EXTRACURRICULAR ACTIVITIES

  Treasurer of the Secretarial Service Club
  Secretary of the Central High School Chapter of the Future
    Business Leaders of America
  Reporter for Spot Light, school newspaper

EXPERIENCE

  Clerk-typist in the office of the Metropolitan Life Insurance
    Company in Joliet, Illinois, for the last two summers
  Part-time secretary for the Placement Director during senior
    year at Central High School

REFERENCES

  Mr. Arthur T. Sweeney, Office Manager, Metropolitan Life
    Insurance Company, 236 Main Street, Joliet, IL 60634,
    Telephone 555-2200
  Miss Helen C. Harris, Chairman, Secretarial Studies Department,
    Central High School, Joliet, IL 60433, Telephone 555-1715
  Dr. August W. Brustat, Pastor, Trinity Church, 23 Crane Road,
    Joliet, IL 60432, Telephone 555-8230

Illus. 15-6 Personal data sheet

4. In the second paragraph, you will want to refer to your personal data sheet which is enclosed. This paragraph should highlight the main points of your education and experience. You might write:

```
As you will note from the enclosed data
sheet, I will graduate from Central
High School in June.  While in high school
I successfully completed several business
courses, including typewriting, shorthand,
secretarial procedures, and bookkeeping.
I have also held two summer jobs where I
have had opportunities to use my business
skills and abilities.  During the last two
years I have been a volunteer secretary in
the high school and have worked for a num-
ber of school administrators and teachers.
```

5. In the final paragraph of your application letter, you will want to indicate your interest in a personal interview as well as the times when you are available:

```
I would be happy to visit your office for
the stenographic position which you seek
to fill.  I complete my school day at three
each afternoon and would be free to come to
your office any afternoon after that time.
```

6. The complimentary close may be a simple *Sincerely yours* or *Yours very truly*, depending upon your salutation (see pages 98–99). Be sure to sign your name and indicate the enclosure.

If you apply for a job through an agency, you will generally go to the firm for an interview. No letter of application will be necessary. In such a case, you will find it helpful to have a copy of your personal data sheet with you, for the details on it will be useful in filling in an application form.

The Application Blank

Most companies request that job applicants complete an application blank. Some companies will send you the application blank, and you are to have the form completed when you appear for the employment interview. Other firms will wait until you appear for the interview before requesting that you complete the form.

APPLICATION FOR EMPLOYMENT

WITH

Booth, Marcus, and Murdock Associates

(Applicants should complete in their own handwriting using pencil or pen)

GENERAL INFORMATION

Name Wright, Valerie Rose	Date July 1, 19—
Street Address 3466 Border Lane	Phone Number 794-5544
City Shreveport Zip 77109 State LA	Social Security Number 567-84-0897

In Case of an Emergency Notify Mrs. John A. Wright	Address 3466 Border Lane	Phone Number 794-5544

Date of Birth May 28, 19—	Type work desired Clerk-typist

Any defects in sight, hearing, or speech? No	How much time have you lost through illness in the past two years? 1 day	Nature of illness Cold

Give names of any members in our organization with whom you are acquainted Harry Robinson

Are you related to any of these people? No	If so, to whom? —

Who referred you to us for employment? Stratford Business School

Have you ever served in the United States Armed Forces? No	Rank and branch of service —
Are you now employed? Yes	If so, where? Uranus Corporation

EDUCATION

High School attended South High School	City & State Shreveport, LA	Year Graduated 19—
Business School attended Stratford Business School	City & State Shreveport, LA	Number of months attended One year
College or University attended —	City & State —	Year Graduated — Degree —

Business subjects studied while in school	HIGH SCHOOL Typing, Office Practice
	BUSINESS COLLEGE Typing, Purchasing Procedures, Office Procedures
	COLLEGE

Are you studying now? Yes	If so what? Accounting		Where? LSU, Shreveport Branch
Other special training		System of shorthand studied Century 21	

In the space to the right indicate your present speed in shorthand and typing, if you have these skills. Place an (X) after the office machines you can operate.	Shorthand		Typing 60 words/min.	Transcribing Machine	
	Billing Machine	X	Bookkeeping Machine	Duplicating Machine	X
	Addressograph		Calculator	X	PBX Board	
	Adding Machine	X	Key Punch	Other	
	Posting Machine		IBM Tabulator		

Illus. 15-7

Page 1 — Application blank

EXPERIENCE AND REFERENCES

Business Experience & References (Show last position first)

	From	To	Period Yrs.	Period Mos.	Name of Company	City & State	Person to whom you reported
1	7/—	Now	2		Uranus Corporation	Shreveport, LA	Thomas Adams
2							
3							
4							

Business Experience and References (Continued)

	GIVE TITLE AND NATURE OF YOUR WORK	Monthly Earnings	Why did you leave?
1	Stenographic and General Clerical Duties	$420	Am seeking work with more responsibility and higher potential earnings.
2			
3			
4			

Character References: Do not refer to previous employers or relatives.

NAME	ADDRESS	OCCUPATION
Mrs. C. C. Clark	3470 Poplar St., Shreveport	Purchasing Agent
Mr. Donald Calhoun	South High School, Shreveport	Teacher, business subjects
Miss Mary Wagner	1312 Pearl St., Shreveport	Owner of clothing store

By signing this application I affirm that all statements made herein are true to the best of my knowledge. If employed by the company, I agree to consider my salary a confidential matter and to refrain from discussing it with other employees.

Valerie Rose Wright

Signature of Applicant

APPLICANTS SHOULD NOT WRITE BELOW THIS LINE

Interviewed by:	Date of interview	Date applicant available for work	E G F P
Remarks:			

Date Employed	Clock Number	Department	Classification
Enrolled in Group Insurance		Enrolled in Pension Plan	Blue Cross — Blue Shield Coverage ☐ Ind. ☐ Fam. ☐ Surg.
Date Employment Terminated	Reason		Consider for Re-employment

Illus. 15-8

Page 2 — Application blank

Purpose

Companies have developed standard forms for the information they need so that the processing of a new employee can be taken care of easily and quickly.

Interviewers read an applicant's information carefully. In fact, the applicant is evaluated on the basis of the application blank in many instances. Interviewers note the completeness of the form, the neatness of the handwriting (or typewriting), and the extent to which the answers are related to the questions asked.

Cautions in Filling in the Application Blank

When you are asked to fill in an application blank, you should first read the instructions carefully. Sit at a table or desk so that you will be able to write easily. If you are asked to type the form, insert a scrap sheet of paper in the typewriter and practice a few lines of typewriting so that you become familiar with the machine before you begin to fill in your form. Start at the beginning of the form, filling in each item that applies to you. Note if you are to write your last name first or your first name first, *before* you begin to write your name. For each item that does not apply, draw a short line in the space provided for the answer or write in *NA* (not applicable).

Illus. 15-9

Proofread your application form for accuracy and completeness before returning it to the personnel officer.

Ohio National Life Insurance Company

After you have completed filling in all the spaces for which you can supply answers, go back to the beginning and read what you have written to be sure it is accurate and complete before returning it.

Testing

In many companies applicants for positions are asked to take tests along with filling in application blanks. The tests provide additional evidence for the interviewer to use in determining the skill and ability of potential employees.

You should be prepared to take tests when you apply in person for a position. Many applicants find it helpful to carry with them a shorthand pad, pen, pencil, and eraser.

While the specific tests that companies use vary considerably, there are some commonly used tests for office workers. Performance tests in typewriting and stenography are frequently given. The typewriting tests may be simply copying tests that are timed, or they may be job-like tests that require the applicant to set up material appropriately and to make carbon copies and corrections. Companies are interested not only in the rate of typewriting but in the skill of applicants in handling jobs such as the typing of letters and tabulated material. The stenographic test is used to determine the skill of an applicant in preparing a mailable transcript in a reasonable period of time.

Illus. 15-10

Stenographic and secretarial applicants are usually asked to take a typewriting performance test.

Ohio National Life Insurance Company

In addition to performance tests, some companies administer general aptitude tests, clerical aptitude tests, and general information tests. Most of these tests are relatively short and are similar to the types of tests you have taken as a student in school. You should feel confident that you are prepared for the tests.

Physical Examination

productive:
achieve at high level

A physical examination is also required by many companies. Good health is important if workers are to be fully **productive** on their jobs. Companies, therefore, have established health standards which applicants must meet if they are to be employed. Furthermore, many companies provide health insurance for workers, and such coverage requires evidence of good health of the worker at the time of employment.

REVIEWING

1. In general, what should the personal data sheet convey to a prospective employer?
2. What information about your education should you include on your personal data sheet?
3. Why might a prospective employer find your extracurricular activities of interest?
4. Who is most likely to know your business skills and understandings and, thus, serve as a reference for you?
5. Does every copy of your personal data sheet need to be an original copy?
6. Is it satisfactory to address someone merely as Mr. Gallager?
7. In writing an application letter, why should you specify the position for which you are applying?
8. What types of tests may an applicant for an office job be asked to take?
9. How do you indicate on an application form that a question doesn't apply to you?
10. Why is a health examination sometimes required for employment?

MAKING JUDGMENTS

1. Zachary knew that the persons whom he had listed as references would be happy to write letters for him, so he just didn't take time to ask them if he might list their names. What do you think of Zachary's judgment?
2. Joyce wanted a job in a large company in a major American city about 60 miles from her home town. She, therefore, prepared a personal data sheet and a short letter and made duplicate copies on

a stencil duplicating machine. These she will send to a dozen firms. Her letter was addressed: *To the Personnel Director*. She didn't use an inside address. In her first paragraph she said: "I would like very much to work in one of your offices. Do you have an office job for a person who is soon to graduate from high school?" What do you think of Joyce's procedures?

WORKING WITH OTHERS

When Stanley applied for a position as clerk-typist in a large manufacturing company in his home town, he was asked to take a typewriting test. The woman responsible for administering the test told Stanley to choose a typewriting station and she would return soon with the copy for the test. Stanley looked at the three typewriters available and realized that he had never used a typewriter of the makes represented. "Oh," he thought, "what do I do now? I don't know these machines; I can't possibly take a typing test. What should I do? Is it all right if I ask the woman giving the test to help me?"

What do you think Stanley should do?

REFRESHING LANGUAGE SKILLS

Three important uses of the colon are:

A. To introduce a long or formal *direct* quotation
   Example: As Thoreau said: I left the woods for as good a reason as I went there. Perhaps it seemed to me that I had several more lives to live, and could not spare any more time for that one.

B. To introduce a number of examples or a formal list of any sort which contains a *summarizing* word
   Example: There will be four groups: artists, musicians, dancers, and actors.

C. To introduce an independent sentence or clause when the second gives an illustration of a general statement in the first
   Example: The young man realized his obligation: To return to the office immediately and talk with the executive responsible for the job.

Type the following sentences inserting colons where appropriate.

1. In order to be prepared for transcription you must have adequate supplies stationery, second sheets, carbon, eraser, and a pencil.
2. All the details have been confirmed the group will leave from the Central Station at 8:00 in the morning and arrive in Washington about four hours later.

3. Sir Thomas Browne said I could never divide myself from any man upon the difference of an opinion, or be angry with his judgment for not agreeing with me in that from which perhaps within a few days I should dissent myself.
4. Her original contention was justified that in time those who study, prepare their assignments, and apply themselves to their classes will receive good grades and be ready to accept positions in business offices.
5. Every detail indicated that Mary was interrupted at her work and intended to return to it the open stamp pad on her desk, the unfinished letter in her typewriter, the shorthand notebook lying open, the pen ready for use.

PERFORMING SECRETARIAL TASKS

1. Develop a rough draft of a personal data sheet. Review your draft carefully. Then type a final copy with one carbon copy.
2. If an application form is available, complete it carefully in ink. If a form is not available, type a copy of the form on pages 580 and 581 and fill in the required information in ink. Evaluate the neatness and the legibility of your handwriting. Identify the improvement you believe your handwriting requires.
3. Type a letter of application in response to a local newspaper advertisement. Give only the facts related to your experience, education, and other qualifications. Include all your qualifications in the body of the letter of application; that is, do not use a separate data sheet. Attach the advertisement to your letter. Submit your letter to your instructor for suggestions for improvement.

Part 3

The Personal Interview

Margaret had an interview for 9 a.m. in a company in the center of the large city where she lived. She knew where the company was, for she had been in the neighborhood before. Even so, she allowed an extra twenty minutes for getting there, because she didn't want to be late. She had with her a copy of her personal data sheet and basic supplies for taking a stenographic test. She, of course, went alone for her interview.

The Purpose of an Interview

Companies differ in many ways. Each has its own manner of conducting business, its own policies that direct the relationships among employees, and between employees and the outside world. Companies also have various benefits for their workers. Because of these differences, each company is careful in choosing its employees; for it wants them to be able to fill the job qualifications specified for specific positions. Companies, therefore, talk with prospective employees as a way of determining who will be best suited to their **environment**. As a prospective employee, you also want to be sure the company meets your desires as the place in which you will want to work. Thus, the interview provides a means for this two-way exchange of understanding.

environment: surroundings of the organization

Topics Discussed in an Interview

You can expect the interviewer to give you the following types of information:

1. A description of the position (or positions) for which you have applied or for which the interviewer believes your education and experience fit you
2. Information regarding the number of hours that you will work each day, the number of days that you will work each week, and other responsibilities that you will assume

3. The salary and other benefits that are provided employees including such items as coffee breaks, vacation, holidays, hospitalization, pension plans, tuition payment plans
4. The future opportunities in the company for those who are successful in their work

As a candidate for a position, you should not hesitate to ask questions about any of these topics if the interviewer should fail to discuss them adequately. Your **primary** attention, of course, is on the basic job requirements and the degree to which you are qualified to meet them. Interviewers are not favorably impressed with beginning workers who are primarily interested in salary, fringe benefits, and promotional opportunities. Such an attitude leaves the impression that the beginner is more concerned with the material rewards of a position and not the position itself.

Other questions that come to mind while you are talking with the interviewer may be asked. For example, you may be planning to drive to work and will wish to know if a parking lot is provided.

primary: main

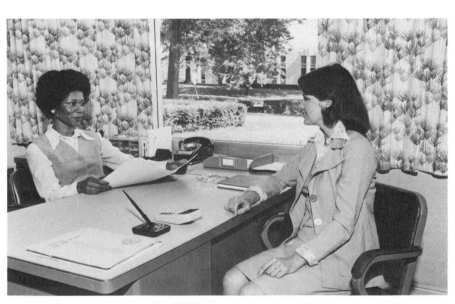

Illus. 15-11

The interview is your opportunity to evaluate the company for which you may be working.

Ohio National Life Insurance Company

Try to behave as naturally as possible during the interview giving attention to *learning about the job*. Any question that is related to that subject is appropriate for you to ask. Don't think of the interview as an oral test of your ability to assume a job. The interview provides **mutual** information. Remember that *you were asked* to come for an interview. This realization should give you sufficient confidence to handle the situation comfortably.

mutual: shared in common

The Interviewer's Evaluation

During the interview, the interviewer is developing an impression of you as a member of the organization. When you come to the end of the interview, the interviewer may be prepared to offer you a position or to indicate to you when you will hear from the company. Policies differ in regard to hiring procedures. In some companies, for instance, all invitations to join the organization are mailed to prospective workers. Decisions are not made in the presence of an applicant. In such companies, the interviewer will write a report or fill in a form that gives a full evaluation of each candidate who has applied for a position. Among the considerations of interviewers are these:

Appearance

As soon as a prospective candidate steps into the office of the interviewer, the first impression is formed. How appropriately is the applicant **attired**? How neatly? Does the applicant have poise? Is the applicant alert? Does the applicant walk with ease?

attired: dressed

Voice and Language Usage

Some interviewers have a special interest in the voice of a prospective employee. Is the applicant's voice pleasant? Does it indicate an interest in what is being discussed? Does the applicant speak clearly and thoughtfully?

Temperament

While interviewers understand that the interview is not a natural situation and that applicants may not be at ease, they attempt to determine the underlying **temperament** of each candidate. If ill at ease in the situation, is the applicant likely to handle emergencies on the job with calmness and confidence?

temperament: disposition, character

Knowledge and Skills

While the personal data sheet and the application blank indicate educational background and skills developed, the interviewer will try to learn how thorough the preparation is. Does the applicant have a good comprehension of business as well as the world in general? Will the applicant be able to work through problems? Does the applicant possess the technical skills needed for the job?

Mental Attitude

Generally interviewers are favorably impressed by young workers who are willing to learn and who seem to be actively participating in life and reflecting on their own lives. Some of the questions the interviewer wants answered are: Is this applicant open-minded and tolerant? likely to be willing to make changes in the work? likely to become fully involved?

Objectivity

An ability to view a situation clearly and without undue influence because of your personal feelings is considered valuable in an office. An interviewer will seek to answer the questions: Is the applicant objective? able to make the use of facts in a logical way and view them impartially without regard to own personal interests?

Self-Confidence

What is the applicant's self-concept? This is a key question to interviewers. They hope to find applicants with sufficient self-confidence and self-reliance to take initiative and responsibility on their jobs. However, they are not favorably impressed with applicants who *think they know everything and are right at all times*, for such individuals are not likely to realize when they are going beyond the bounds of initiative and responsibility set for positions.

Effectiveness with People

isolated:
set apart

As you have learned through your studies, business is not an **isolated** activity. It requires the cooperative efforts of many who can work well together. The interviewer will be particularly interested in assessing how well you are *likely* to get along with co-workers as well as with customers and other visitors to the office.

Job Interest

Interviewers are looking for workers who will be keenly interested in doing the job for which they have applied and are willing to remain with the company for a reasonable period of time. The interviewer will ask questions that will give clues as to how you view your future.

Adaptability

Interviewers, as they think about an applicant in a particular position, also look to the future and try to determine how the applicant will fit into the organization over a period of time. Is this applicant one who is willing to learn new skills and accept new assignments? Has the applicant approached studies and extracurricular activities eager to increase knowledge? Is the applicant able to determine what is needed in a given situation? Companies find workers who can *measure up to new demands* extremely valuable in carrying out the many tasks that must be completed each day.

The Conclusion of the Interview

At the end of the interview, the interviewer will generally thank you for having come in and will indicate to you what the next step is. If the interviewer fails to give you details as to how you are to follow up or when you are to do so, it is proper to ask about the matter. For example, you may say, "Mr. Stout, will I hear from you or should I call?"

Before you leave the office, be sure that you clearly understand whether the company will inform you only if you are successful, or whether the company will write to all applicants.

When you have a clear idea of what is to occur next, thank the interviewer in a very brief, sincere manner, and leave the office. A slow, reluctant departure will not leave a favorable impression.

The Follow-Up

It is always appropriate to write a brief letter thanking an interviewer for a pleasant, informative interview. Such a letter should be written as soon as possible following the interview.

Any correspondence or telephone call from a company that has interviewed you should be acknowledged. If you take a position with one company but receive invitations from other companies that have interviewed you, you should write to each company expressing your appreciation and stating that you have accepted another position.

You must also write to the company that offers you a position to inform them that you accept the position. Letters following up job interviews may be brief, but they should be courteous and complete.

REVIEWING

1. Why do you believe a company includes an interview in its procedures for determining who should be hired for office positions?
2. What kind of information should you expect the interviewer to give you about the job for which you are applying?
3. What kind of information should you expect the interviewer to give you about the company?
4. What should you be thinking of as the interviewer tells you about the job?
5. On what grounds does an interviewer evaluate you as a potential employee?
6. Why does an interviewer want to determine your effectiveness with people?
7. Why would an interviewer be interested in your adaptability?
8. Should you expect an interviewer to tell you whether you will be offered a position at the end of the interview?
9. What are possible procedures following an interview on the part of the interviewer?
10. For what reason might you write a letter to an interviewer after you have had an interview?

MAKING JUDGMENTS

1. Rosella was surprised that the interviewer did not tell her what the specific job duties were in the position for which she was applying. As she thought about it, she decided that maybe what you did on the job wasn't so important, so she didn't ask any questions about the duties. What do you think of Rosella's judgment?
2. While Earl was talking with the interviewer about an office position, the interviewer asked: "Would you tell me something about your preparation for an office job?" Earl said: "Well, as you can see on my application form, I have taken almost all the general business courses that are offered in our high school and have all the skills needed for an office job." What do you think of Earl's response?

REFRESHING LANGUAGE SKILLS

Colloquialisms are words or phrases generally acceptable in informal speech, but are not considered appropriate for standard business communications or formal writing.

On a separate sheet of paper, type each sentence listed below replacing the *underlined* word or phrase with a word or phrase that is considered standard.

1. I am sorry that Mr. Toth isn't here; he has been *held up* in traffic.
2. When Ms. Oldman hears that, she'll be happy for that is *right down her alley*.

3. You need not worry; Mr. Jones will be *on the dot*.
4. He is a *top-notch guy*, there is no question about it.
5. The conference room is in *apple-pie order*.
6. Her employer will not *stand for* any personal telephone calls at the office.
7. Will Sally *take a try* at the dictating machine?
8. He will want to order *lots* of boxes of duplicating paper.
9. What do you *calculate* will be the topic for the meeting next month?
10. He has *got to* complete that job before he goes out to lunch today.

WORKING WITH OTHERS

As Toni sat in the reception area waiting for her appointment with an interviewer, she observed the various office workers coming and going in the area. She listened to the conversations the workers had with the receptionist. While she talked with the interviewer, she observed the interviewer and thought about the questions she was asking her. At the end of the interview, the interviewer offered Toni a position.

Toni, while pleased to be offered a job, didn't feel that she wanted to make a commitment at this moment. There were some points of hesitation in her mind. She wasn't sure she would like to work in the environment. The friendliness didn't seem genuine to her; she wondered if she, a rather timid, but serious person, would be happy with the kinds of office workers she observed.

What should Toni have done?

PERFORMING SECRETARIAL TASKS

1. Assume that you are responsible for evaluating a prospective office worker on the basis of the following factors: appearance, voice and language usage, temperament, knowledge and skills, mental attitude, objectivity, self-confidence, effectiveness with people, job interest, and adaptability. For each topic, identify what you believe would be the most important observations or most useful data. You should have at least two for each topic. Type your suggestions in an attractive format. Be prepared to discuss your suggestions in class. Notice the variety of suggestions made by your classmates. The class may want to select the best suggestions for each topic.
2. Here are three questions that an interviewer of many beginning office workers in a large company commonly asks. For each, type a short response. Be prepared to discuss your responses in class.

   a. As you think about the business subjects you have studied, which one (or ones) have given you the most useful understanding of the business office?
   b. How do you evaluate your own typewriting skill at this moment?
   c. Why do you believe you would find an office job enjoyable?

Part **4**

Secretarial Positions in Specialized Fields

Francine realized that job opportunities for secretaries included working in specialized areas. She had heard about legal secretaries, medical secretaries, and school secretaries. She wondered if she should investigate what these types of jobs were like and what educational background was necessary.

Many specialists are employed in modern business. Those who assist such specialists require an understanding of the work of the office beyond that of generally trained staff. While secretarial workers continue to master technical vocabulary on the job and learn the technical duties required, there is more and more training provided such workers. Technical institutes, community colleges, and business schools offer specialized education. In addition, some companies provide their own training for employees interested in preparing for specialized jobs.

As you think ahead, you may want to consider additional education on either a part-time or full-time basis so that you may enter a specialized field. On the following pages, some specialized positions are discussed. However, there are others for which the preparation is not as organized, but for which you could design your own program of studies. For example, if you wanted to be a secretary in a hotel or the headquarters offices of a large hotel or motel chain, you might enroll in some of the courses offered in hotel management in a local community college.

The Legal Secretary

instruments:
formal legal documents

litigation:
legal proceedings

integrity:
following closely a code of behavior

To qualify as a legal secretary, you must have a high degree of skill in shorthand and transcription. You must have a knowledge and understanding of legal procedures, legal **instruments**, court functions, and **litigation** procedures. You must possess the administrative ability to keep an attorney's office functioning smoothly. You must have the **integrity** to maintain the professional relationships of the law office in working with the lawyer's clients, the courts, and the public.

A posthigh school program of one or two years, offered in a junior college, community college, or private business school, will provide you with the necessary background and skills for this specialized field.

Job Opportunities

General office experience is often a requirement for the person who wants to work as a legal secretary. In a large legal firm, for example, your first job may be that of typist or stenographer. In doing the tasks associated with either of these positions, you will have an opportunity to become acquainted with legal procedures and vocabulary.

Persons with legal secretarial skills are in general demand because there are increasing needs for staff in legal-related offices in government at all levels, in private corporations, as well as in professional offices of attorneys.

Illus. 15-12

Legal transcription requires a high degree of accuracy.

Specific Duties

Unlike the general secretary, who deals with a limited number of customers and callers, as a legal secretary you will constantly deal with all your employer's clients and potential clients. Your attitude in working with them will have a direct bearing upon your employer's effectiveness in counseling them. You must remember that you should always follow the legal code of ethics — everything you know about a client, a case, or a written document is confidential information. You will be required to maintain a reminder system: diaries, card tickler files, and follow-up files. You will be expected to have the ability to code and file legal papers and related correspondence in clients' folders and to find them without delay when they are called for.

You should understand legal **terminology** thoroughly; otherwise, the dictation will seem complex and meaningless and the transcription extremely difficult. You will be asked to set up and type legal instruments such as bills of sale, deeds, leases, and wills. You may be expected to type affidavits, bills of particulars, and other court papers, and to keep a progress record of court matters.

The legal field has become so broad that you may find employment in one of its many subdivisions, and your work in the office may be completely involved in the legal procedures and legal documents of a special phase of law, such as corporation law, tax law, insurance law, patent law, international law, or criminal law.

For a more extensive study of the specific duties of a legal secretary, review the *Legal Secretary's Complete Handbook*.[1] It offers guidance for most law office tasks, from preparing a brief to taking question-and-answer testimony. Examine the *Handbook for the Legal Secretary*[2] if you are interested in legal dictation. The handbook contains material written in shorthand for reading practice with a word-counted key for dictation practice. It was written to serve three groups: (1) the legal secretarial student, (2) the general secretary whose goal is a legal secretarial position, and (3) the legal secretary who would like a better background in law and law office procedure.

The Medical Secretary

The basic qualification for a medical secretary is the ability to take and transcribe medical dictation efficiently combined with a complete mastery of the medical secretarial practices and procedures followed in a doctor's office or in a hospital. A dedication to the profession of medicine is the greatest single qualification you must possess if you are to become an efficient medical secretary. The demands and adjustments of the position are unusual. The medical assistance required of you would depend

---

[1] Besse Mae Miller, *Legal Secretary's Complete Handbook* (2nd ed.; Englewood Cliffs, N.J.: Prentice-Hall, Inc., 1970).
[2] Louis Leslie and Kenneth Coffin, *Handbook for the Legal Secretary* (Diamond Jubilee edition; New York City: McGraw-Hill Book Company, 1968).

entirely upon the office in which you work. One doctor may expect considerable assistance from you in dealing with his office patients; another, none at all. You may be required to work at odd hours because doctors and hospitals have schedules that differ from those in business offices.

A two-year medical secretarial program, usually offered at the community college level, will provide you with the necessary background and skills. The technical courses offered in the program include medical dictation and transcription; medical terminology; anatomy; the operation of medical equipment, such as the cardiograph and the audiometer; medical office procedures; accounting for the doctor's office; and a work-study course which would give you some actual working experience in a doctor's office and/or a hospital.

Job Opportunities

There is an increasing demand for trained medical secretaries. Most of them find employment in the offices of physicians or in large hospitals and clinics. However, nursing homes, insurance companies, public health departments, firms that manufacture and distribute medical supplies, and medical research and medical publishing companies all offer opportunities to the secretary who has specialized in the medical field.

Unlike other areas of secretarial work, the medical secretary is a beginning position. The salary you would receive without experience is about equal to that of a beginning secretary in the average business office. If you are employed in a doctor's office, your salary will probably

Illus. 15-13

Job opportunities for medical secretaries in health services are numerous.

Courtesy of American Telephone & Telegraph Company

constant:
not changing

commensurate:
equal in measurement

remain **constant** after a few years. In hospitals, laboratories, medical associations, and other large medical institutions, however, you would have opportunities for advancement to managerial and administrative posts with **commensurate** increases in salary.

Specific Duties

In addition to your secretarial work, you will perform most of the following duties if you are employed as a medical secretary:

1. Receive patients, salespeople, and all other callers
2. Receive and place telephone calls
3. Make and schedule patients' appointments
4. Keep files — patients' files, general files, personal files, card tickler files, and follow-up files
5. Maintain case histories
6. Keep financial records — the doctor's checkbook, daily record of collections, patients' accounts, cashbook, and general ledger
7. Send out statements to patients
8. Collect fees
9. Write collection letters and letters about appointments and referrals, insurance, fees, supplies, and equipment for the medical office
10. Fill out forms for insurance companies

If you are to act as the doctor's secretary and medical assistant, you may have to perform the following additional tasks:

1. Prepare patients for medical examinations
2. Care for medical and surgical instruments
3. Set up laboratory equipment
4. Make laboratory tests and operate medical equipment

For a detailed presentation of the specific duties of a medical secretary, read the *Medical Secretary's Guide*.[3] Medical dictation and transcription are covered in the *Medical Secretary*.[4]

The Technical Secretary

A technical secretary serves as an assistant to an engineer, scientist, or architect. To qualify as a technical secretary, you must have a thorough

[3]Elaine F. Kabbes, *Medical Secretary's Guide* (Englewood Cliffs, N.J.: Prentice-Hall, Inc., 1967).
[4]Kathleen Root and E. E. Byers, *Medical Secretary* (3d ed.; New York City: McGraw-Hill Book Company, 1967).

knowledge and understanding of the technical language in the field of your interest. This you will gain gradually with advanced training and on-the-job experience.

Job Opportunities

Our technologically oriented society has increasing demands for all types of workers who understand technical terminology and processes. You will find opportunities in electronics industries, in aerospace industries, communications centers, construction firms, and architectural businesses.

Generally some office experience is helpful in securing a position in this specialization. If work as a technical secretary is appealing to you, you may find it valuable to gain experience as a typist or stenographer in a firm involved in some aspect of technology.

Specific Duties

Your ability to take technical dictation easily and to transcribe it accurately will depend to a large extent upon your technical vocabulary.

Illus. 15-14

This technical secretary works in a communications center

Courtesy of American Telephone & Telegraph Company

To increase your vocabulary, prepare a list of the technical words that occur frequently in your employer's dictation. Look up or devise a shorthand outline for each of them so that you can write them without hesitation during the dictation. Consult a technical dictionary every time you add to the list so that you will know the exact technical meaning and the correct **syllabication** and spelling of each word.

syllabication: division of words by syllables

Numbers and fractions are typed more often in technical correspondence than in general business correspondence. You will also be required to type equations and mathematical formulas as you prepare tables, graphs, and reports. To make the typing of this technical material easier, your typewriter probably will be equipped with additional keys at the right of the standard keyboard that permit you to type special symbols.

You probably will use a numeric system in filing and cataloging engineering materials. When numbers are assigned to drawings and prints, they are usually filed in a terminal-digit system. Original drawings may be filed flat, rolled, or vertically. Prints are usually folded and filed in vertical files or in open shelf files.

For a more extensive review of the duties of an engineering secretary, examine *The Engineering Secretary's Complete Handbook*[5] by Laird. It covers secretarial duties in an engineering office from assisting with drafting to acting as administrative assistant to a chief engineer.

The Educational Secretary

Secretaries are needed in all types of educational institutions. To qualify as an educational secretary you must possess the secretarial skills and knowledges required of all other competent secretaries, and, most important of all, a genuine liking for students. You must have the ability to work with the students and all the other people whom you will meet daily — parents, co-workers on the administrative staff, teachers, and the administrators of the educational institution or system.

It is possible to qualify as an educational secretary in a small school system with a high school diploma; this, however, is the exception rather than the general rule. Many large public school systems require a minimum of 30 college credits with additional in-service courses to be completed during your **probationary** period of employment. Included in the 30 college credits are specific course requirements covering the general principles of educational psychology, the role of the school in the community, and the proper processing of school records and accounts.

probationary: trial

[5]Eleanor S. Laird, *The Engineering Secretary's Complete Handbook* (2d ed.; Englewood Cliffs, N. J.: Prentice-Hall, Inc., 1967).

Job Opportunities

Openings for educational secretaries are not limited to schools and colleges. You may find a position with your local board of education, with a state or federal department of education, or with one of the many educational associations.

Illus. 15-15

Openings for educational secretaries are found at universities, in public school systems, and with educational associations.

Specific Duties

Your duties as an educational secretary would vary with the size and type of educational organization in which you find employment. In an elementary or a secondary school, you might be called upon to register new and transfer pupils, to meet parents and other callers, to keep teachers' attendance records, to order supplies, and to handle the correspondence of the school administrators. Your secretarial duties in a college would be limited to a specific department or to an administrative office, such as the office of the president, the registrar's office, the business office, or the office of the dean of students. With an educational association, you would probably be required to deal extensively with communications — membership campaigns, the preparation and distribution of the organization's publications, and the correspondence of the officers of the association. For a more complete description of the duties of an educational secretary, review the *School Secretary's Handbook*.[6]

As an educational secretary you may qualify for membership in the National Association of Educational Secretaries, a department of the National Education Association. The Association conducts workshops and publishes manuals, handbooks, and a magazine, *The National Educational Secretary*, all designed to improve the professional status and efficiency of educational secretaries.

Opportunities for Federal Employment

Since government is one of the largest fields of employment in the United States, you may be interested in knowing about the secretarial opportunities it offers. Almost half the employees of the federal government are office workers.

After you have successfully completed a four-year high school course, you may qualify for a secretarial civil service position without any previous business experience.

Civil Service Tests

Performance tests are given for all branches of civil service for office positions requiring such measurable skills as typewriting, shorthand, transcription, and office machine operation. A minimum typing rate of from 40 to 50 net words a minute on copy material is usually required for initial employment as a typist. Shorthand dictation is generally given at rates ranging from 80 to 100 words a minute. The notes must be transcribed on a typewriter within a reasonable time at a transcription standard set by the examining board.

Under certain circumstances arrangements may be made with some schools for teachers to issue a certificate (on a Civil Service Commission form) attesting to the required degree of proficiency in typing or stenography. The certificate must show that the applicant, not more than six months previous to the filing of the certificate, demonstrated the required proficiency to a teacher of typing or stenography in a public, parochial, or private four-year high school, or an accredited institution such as a business school, community college, or college. The typing or stenographic portion of the written tests will not be required of applicants who present a certificate.

[6]John Allan Smith, *School Secretary's Handbook* (Englewood Cliffs, N.J.: Prentice-Hall, Inc., 1972).

Written tests designed to measure intelligence, aptitudes, and general information possessed by the candidates are administered by the Civil Service Commission. Short answer questions, which can be scored by machine, are used in preference to essay questions. They are presented in a number of forms — multiple choice questions, true-false statements, and the matching of related facts.

Qualifications Requirements

To qualify for stenographer and typist a candidate must:

1. Pass a general written test measuring verbal abilities and clerical aptitude.
2. Demonstrate proficiency in typing, and, if you are applying for stenographer, proficiency in shorthand.
3. Meet the experience and education requirements described below for the grade level for which you are applying:

POSITION	EXPERIENCE AND EDUCATION REQUIREMENTS
Stenographer, GS-2	No experience or education required.
Typist, GS-2 Stenographer, GS-3	a. Successful completion of a 4-year high school course; or b. Six months of appropriate experience.
Typist, GS-3 Stenographer, GS-4	a. Successful completion of 1 academic year of substantially full-time study in a resident school above the high school level; or b. One year of appropriate experience.
Typist, GS-4 Stenographer, GS-5	a. Successful completion of 2 academic years of substantially full-time study in a resident school above the high school level; or b. Two years of appropriate experience; or c. One year of education as described in "a" above *plus* 1 year of appropriate experience.

General Requirements

In addition to educational and experience requirements, there are some general requirements you will have to meet.

Age. There is no maximum age limit for federal civil service employment. The usual minimum age limit is 18, but for the majority of jobs high school graduates may apply at 16. When an examination has a different minimum, the announcement will say so.

Citizenship. Examinations are open only to citizens or to people who owe permanent allegiance to the United States.

Physical Condition. You must be physically able to perform the duties of the position, and you must be emotionally and mentally stable. This does not mean that a physical handicap will disqualify an applicant so long as the applicant can do the work efficiently without being a hazard.

Selection

When an agency wants to hire a new employee, the appointment officer of the agency asks the Civil Service Commission for the names of the persons who are eligible. The Commission then sends the agency the names of the top three persons on the eligibility list. The officer makes a selection from the three. In deciding which candidate to appoint, the officer may ask all three to come in for personal interviews. The names of those who are not selected are retained on the list for future consideration.

Overseas Opportunities

United States citizens are employed in countries around the world. Clerical and secretarial personnel are often needed. General requirements for such positions include:

1. *Age* — You must be at least 21 years of age.
2. *Marital Status* — For most clerical and secretarial positions abroad, agencies prefer single persons without dependents.
3. *Citizenship* — You must have been an American citizen for at least five years.
4. *Worldwide* — You must be available for assignment to any one of the more than 300 American embassies, legations, or consulates maintained in more than 100 countries throughout the world.
5. *Duration of Employment* — You must remain at your post abroad for at least three years before becoming eligible for transportation back to the United States at government expense.
6. *Physical Condition* — You must pass a physical examination comparable to United States military standards.
7. *Education* — You must be a high school graduate, or you must pass the General Educational Development Examination.

8. *Tests* — You must qualify on aptitude, spelling, typing, and shorthand tests. Stenotyping and Speedwriting are acceptable.
9. *Background Investigation* — You are subject to a background investigation which may require from four to six months to complete.

Recruiting is handled through those agencies which use overseas personnel. Details of job opportunities can be obtained by contacting:

Recruitment Branch
Employment Division
U.S. Department of State
Washington, D.C. 20520

or

Recruitment and Examining Division
United States Information Agency
1776 Pennsylvania Avenue
Washington, D.C. 20547

Opportunities for State and Municipal Employment

There are secretarial positions available in state government offices for qualified high school and college graduates. There are many opportunities in state government for high school graduates who have had no work experience.

State Civil Service

While working conditions in state civil service vary slightly from state to state, the following prevail in most states:

1. State employees work a five-day week ranging from 35 to 40 hours in state office buildings that are noted for their modern, air-conditioned facilities.
2. The states maintain a salary schedule for the different job classifications that is in keeping with the prevailing rates of pay for comparable jobs in private industry and in federal and municipal civil service systems.
3. Promotions to higher positions in state government are generally filled from within the state civil service. As a rule, only the highest posts (policy-making and administrative positions or positions requiring highly specialized technical training and experience) are filled from outside the state civil service system. Most states maintain a wide variety of training programs

designed to increase employee efficiency and to prepare employees for advancement within the system.

4. State employees usually receive a four-week paid vacation and pay for ten or eleven legal holidays each year, which is more than the average number granted to employees in private industry and in federal civil service.

5. Most state employees are members of a retirement system and are permitted to retire at half pay after 35 years of service. The tendency is to reduce the retirement age — at least one state has an optional plan of retirement at age 55.

Illus. 15-16

Portion of a bulletin seeking applicants for Ohio state government employment

SCOPE OF EXAMINATIONS: The examinations for Clerk Typists will consist of two parts: a written test and a typing test. The examinations for Clerk Stenographers will consist of three parts -- a written test, a test of dictation and transcription, and a typing test. Applicants must obtain a score of at least 65 percent on each part of the examination and make a final average grade of 70 percent or more to place on the eligible list.

All Clerk Typists and Clerk Stenographers must be able to type at a rate of 40 net words per minute. The Clerk Stenographers must be able to take dictation at the following rates: Grade I, 80 words per minute; Grade II, 85 words per minute; and Grade III, 90 words per minute.

The written examination will consist of items dealing with Spelling, English Usage, Filing, Office Procedure, Arithmetic, Word Definition, and Syllabication.

Special Note: Applicants for the Clerk Typist I or Clerk Stenographer I examination who attain a final average grade of 80 percent or more will be placed on the Grade II eligible list, unless they indicate a preference to be placed on the Grade I list only.

NATURE OF WORK AND QUALIFICATIONS

24-1011 Clerk Typist I -- This is simple and routine clerical work involving full-time or substantial part-time typing.
Qualifications: No experience required.

24-1012 Clerk Typist II -- This is advanced clerical work involving varied and occasionally complex work methods and related typing duties.
Qualifications: One year of clerical experience which included some typing.

24-1013 Clerk Typist III -- This is supervisory clerical work or independent clerical work of comparable difficulty requiring highly skilled typing ability.
Qualifications: Two years of clerical experience which included some typing.

24-1021 Clerk Stenographer I -- This is routine stenographic and clerical work in taking and transcribing dictation and in performing related general office duties.
Qualifications: No experience required.

24-1022 Clerk Stenographer II -- This is advanced stenographic and clerical work which includes taking and transcribing dictation and involves occasionally complex work methods and problems.
Qualifications: One year of clerical experience which included some stenographic work.

24-1023 Clerk Stenographer III -- This is responsible secretarial work or stenographic work of a supervisory or technical nature.
Qualifications: Two years of clerical experience which included some stenographic work.

NOTE: Business school training or college training with course work in secretarial practices or business education may be substituted for an equal amount of experience for any of these examinations, to a maximum of one year. College training in other fields may be substituted on the basis of one year of college for six months of the required experience.

Municipal Civil Service

The number of municipal civil service employees in a city or town varies with the size of the municipality, ranging from fewer than one hundred employees in small communities to over a quarter of a million in some large cities. Employment policies vary with the size of the municipalities. Large municipalities tend to follow closely the civil service policies and practices of their respective states. Municipal salaries and working conditions for office workers compare favorably with those offered by private industry in the same regions of the United States and Canada.

REVIEWING

1. What must a secretarial worker know about a specialized field in order to handle the secretarial tasks competently?
2. In what ways may a person become qualified for a specialized field?
3. What are some of the key tasks of legal secretaries?
4. What are some of the key tasks of medical secretaries?
5. In what kinds of offices do educational secretaries work?
6. What types of tests, performance and written, are included in federal civil service examinations?
7. Where do foreign service secretaries work?
8. List five requirements of a foreign service secretary.
9. What are working conditions like in state civil service positions?
10. What are two advantages of municipal civil service employment?

MAKING JUDGMENTS

1. Lynn felt that a legal office would be a very exciting place in which to work because she always enjoyed the television series that showed lawyers at work on unusual cases. What do you think of Lynn's basis for making a judgment about a job in a legal office.
2. While reading the bulletin board in his high school, Gordon noticed that there was to be a civil service examination the next month in a downtown center. He noted the skill requirements and he realized that he met them. However, he didn't know if he wanted to give up part of his weekend just to take the examination, so he didn't register for the examination. What do you think of Gordon's judgment?

WORKING WITH OTHERS

Tim was a beginning worker in a large insurance company. One day he attended an orientation session, along with other beginning workers, at which time educational opportunities were outlined. He learned that he could attend classes in the company to prepare for advancement to specialized work in the legal or medical departments of the company. Also, there were tuition grants for workers who wanted to study in the local community college or university. He wondered if he should take advantage of such opportunities, since he was very happy in his present job. He felt he would enjoy his present job for a long time and would not be interested in promotional opportunities. There didn't seem to be any reason to go to classes.

What do you think of Tim's attitude and his hesitance about further opportunity?

REFRESHING LANGUAGE SKILLS

The following terms are commonly used in business communications. For each word compose a sentence to show your understanding of the term in business.

1. analysis (noun)
2. capacity (noun)
3. collate (verb)
4. identified (verb)
5. maximum (adjective)
6. notation (noun)
7. participate (verb)
8. replenishment (noun)
9. reservation (noun)
10. specific (adjective)

PERFORMING SECRETARIAL TASKS

Select one of the specialized positions discussed in this Part or identify another in which you might have an interest.

a. List the job opportunities in the specialized areas in your own community or in a community in which you might work.
b. List the most important specialized skills a person should develop for the specialization.
c. List the educational possibilities that are open in your community or in the community where you might work which would prepare you for the specialized position in which you are interested.

Part 5

Promotional Prospects

Miss Elaine Washington began working in an office when she graduated from high school. She had been promoted several times, and each time she liked her new job very much. In fact, she always felt she could stay in it for the rest of her life! In each new job she learned the tasks thoroughly and also increased her understanding of the company. In addition, she studied regularly at a local community college.

She was within two courses of completing an Associate Degree program when she was called to the Personnel Office to talk about becoming an Administrative Assistant. Although she liked her present job very much, she was also challenged by the prospects of new tasks and increased responsibility.

The Secretarial Ladder

The ranking of secretarial positions is based on the rank of executive positions. For example, a secretary to the president of a company has a higher rank than a secretary to the director of the advertising department. Secretarial positions are not subdivided into the same number of levels from company to company. In some companies there may be only two to three levels of secretarial positions, while in other companies there may be as many as a dozen levels. Regardless of the number of levels, in general, the positions range from junior secretary to executive secretary or administrative assistant. Secretaries may move up the secretarial ladder in two ways. When executives are promoted, their secretaries may receive promotions, too. In such situations the secretaries have the qualifications to handle the more responsible tasks of the executives. Secretaries are also promoted independently of their employers if positions should become available, and the personnel officer feels that a particular secretary is ready for a more responsible position.

Preparation for Higher Level Responsibility

While on-the-job experience is one of the key ways of learning about a company and how the tasks are handled in the company, secretaries who move ahead in their companies often combine this on-the-job experience with further educational studies and professional activities. Personnel officers are favorably impressed with the efforts of their staff to increase their knowledge and improve their skills. Secretaries who wish to move ahead often attend local community or four-year colleges during the evening hours to take courses in business administration and secretarial studies. Some secretaries work toward college degrees and thus increase their general educational background as well as their professional knowledge. The general education courses which provide a broad understanding of society are of value in one's work life, too. Many companies encourage further education by providing a tuition-payment plan to any employee who attends evening classes. As a beginning worker, you will want to inquire about the educational benefits provided in the company where you accept a position.

Illus. 15-17

With on-the-job experience and specialized training, many secretaries move into positions of greater responsibility.

International Business Machines Corporation

Secretarial Associations

Secretaries are organized into a variety of associations in the United States. The largest organization of secretaries is the National Secretaries Association, International. This organization invites secretaries with a specific amount of experience to join local chapters and to participate in a wide range of professional activities. This organization through its Institute for Certifying Secretaries sponsors a professional examination for all secretaries who meet work experience and educational requirements. This examination leads to the title of Certified Professional Secretary. The examination is a two-day, 12-hour examination given once each spring in many centers throughout the United States and Canada. The content is based upon an analysis of secretarial work and includes personal adjustment and human relations, business law, business administration, secretarial accounting, secretarial skills and procedures.

You may want to consider joining an organization of secretaries when you meet the requirements for membership. Such an organization provides a means of becoming acquainted with people who are engaged in the same type of work that you are, and association with them broadens your understanding and awareness of your field of work. Personal friendships also develop. Furthermore, organizations of professional workers generally engage in projects and activities that provide services to the community and to the membership. Many, for example, plan workshops and conferences that help the members to keep up to date about secretarial work and the business world.

Beyond a Secretarial Assignment

Secretarial activities provide background experience from which to move into other types of positions in many organizations. There are former secretaries in all types of executive positions. Here are just a few instances:

1. A former secretary is head of the modern art department in a large, international auction center.
2. A former secretary has established her own secretarial service center with a staff of 20 in a conference center in a large American city.
3. A former secretary is vice-president in charge of personnel for a large international firm of consulting engineers.
4. A former secretary is a partner in a small interior decorating company.
5. A former secretary is vice-president for industrial sales for a large manufacturing company.

Companies frequently review their personnel talent and attempt to assign people to positions where they will be most productive for the organization. Many skills that competent secretaries possess are also valuable in other situations. However, secretarial skills alone are not sufficient for promotion to management positions. In fact, secretaries who wish to be considered for management positions will have to develop a far more comprehensive understanding of business than is required for a secretarial assignment.

Administrative Management

One field into which secretaries are sometimes promoted is the field of administrative management. Administrative management refers to a wide range of positions from the supervisor of a small transcribing center to a vice-president responsible for administrative services. In general, the duties and responsibilities of administrative management include the following:

1. Maintaining sufficient office services
2. Maintaining communication facilities
3. Assessing facilities and equipment
4. Organizing the flow of paper work
5. Supervising and evaluating office personnel
6. Managing the office

Maintaining Sufficient Office Services

Considerations in this area include determining how much clerical and secretarial assistance is required in each of the offices of the company and making recommendations to the personnel department about in-company training programs.

Maintaining Communication Facilities

Heads of mail services and of telephone services are administrative managers. Such persons are responsible for overseeing the functions of these departments to assure smooth, effective communications within the organization as well as with outside individuals.

Assessing Facilities and Equipment

With the increasing numbers of innovations in the ways in which office work is handled, administrative managers spend much of their time looking at new equipment and facilities and determining what changes should be made in their own organizations.

As companies expand, their need for office services generally increases; and administrative managers must determine what facilities are needed and make appropriate selections. They ultimately organize and furnish such new facilities.

Organizing the Flow of Paper Work

Modern companies process a great amount of paper during each working day. This processing can become complex if there is no one person overseeing the total function. Administrative managers are responsible for this function. Generally **periodic** studies are made to check on the **adequacy** of the procedures followed and to make recommendations for change. Paper work must be coordinated among many departments. This means there must be central management. Preparation of manuals that outline procedures in handling office tasks and correspondence is the responsibility of administrative managers.

periodic:
from time to time

adequacy:
sufficiency

Supervising and Evaluating Office Personnel

How productive are our typists? What is the extent of the tasks that one stenographer can handle? How well is each file clerk meeting the standards set for the tasks completed? These are some of the questions that are of concern to administrative managers. Further, administrative managers, ranging from supervisors of small staffs of clerical workers to a vice-president who oversees all aspects of administrative functions, are concerned with maintaining high morale among the staff and motivating personnel to greater levels of productivity. Administrative managers participate in determining salaries for various positions and in assessing fringe benefits.

Managing the Office

In many offices secretaries serve as managers. Secretaries generally supervise much of their own time through planning, organizing, and completing the tasks to be done. Furthermore, they may, to some extent, organize the work of their employers by providing them with information that they will need and directing their attention to matters that require supervision. In some offices secretaries have supervision of typists, stenographers, and other office personnel. Through such activities secretaries are, to some degree, administrative managers. Those who are especially skillful in planning and executing tasks — in other words, those who get the job done — are likely candidates for promotion to management positions. Along with their first-hand experience, secretaries should become acquainted with the professional aspects of management and with its technical aspects, such as data processing procedures, office space planning, evaluative techniques for office tasks — all of which must be based on a thorough knowledge of the company's operations and its competitive place in industry. Studying on one's own, through special workshops and seminars in the company or in the local community, and through a college or university are ways of developing the background needed for promotional opportunities. Keeping informed of industry trends by reading trade journals and financial newspapers and magazines is also a valuable practice.

Illus. 15-18

The administrative manager coordinates multiple office procedures and insures the smooth operation of an entire work unit.

Your Future

The pattern of one's career is extremely difficult to predict in a society where an individual has both freedom of choice and many opportunities. With basic education in secretarial skills and procedures, you are prepared to enter many types of organizations. As you become acquainted with the nature of tasks from experience inside an organization, you will want to **reassess** your career objectives and make plans for further study that will prepare you to meet newly formulated goals.

reassess:
to think through again

Opportunities abound. If you combine your wishes with determined effort and sincere commitment, your achievements will bring you personal satisfaction and at the same time contribute to the organization with which you are associated. You must understand your own inner wishes thoroughly, assess them honestly, weigh alternatives both creatively and realistically, and then establish what you must do in order to achieve your goals.

REVIEWING

1. How do secretarial ranks differ from company to company?
2. Is on-the-job preparation likely to be sufficient for entry into management? Discuss.
3. For what reasons would a secretary join a professional organization?
4. Is it realistic for a secretary to believe non-secretarial positions may be among promotional opportunities? Discuss.
5. What are the main concerns of administrative managers?
6. Why are administrative managers concerned about new equipment and facilities?
7. For what purpose are office personnel evaluated?
8. In what ways is a secretary a manager?
9. Is it wise to design the pattern of your career while you are in high school?
10. What must a secretary consider in order to take advantage of work opportunities?

MAKING JUDGMENTS

1. Greg was a conscientious high school student; he studied regularly and performed well on examinations. The teachers in the Business Department agreed that he was a young man with promise. He began working in a local bank shortly after graduation and in two years was a secretary to one of the directors. The officers felt he could move into a management position. The president talked with him about further education in the fields of banking and management. In fact, the bank would pay the costs of such education. Greg told the president that he liked his job and didn't think he would like to become a manager. He said he was interested in being a good secretary, but he was devoting his out-of-work hours to a small theatrical group in the community. He said he loved reading plays and working with this experimental group. At this point in his life, he didn't want to think about becoming "an important person" in the banking community. What do you think of Greg's judgment?
2. Paula felt that the best way to get ahead in business was to enter as a secretary. She really wasn't basically interested in secretarial work; she wanted to be an editor and, possibly, a writer. She applied for a

job as a junior secretary in a publishing company. She got the job and she did her work with minimum attention for her mind was on the editor's position. What do you think of Paula's attitude?

WORKING WITH OTHERS

Mr. Ernest Wilson was considered to be an excellent secretary, and he had confidence in his skills and ability to get work done. He had been promoted rapidly and in less than three years was an executive secretary. One day his employer told him that she had hired an assistant because her work responsibilities had increased and she could not handle all of them by herself. The assistant, Miss Paulson, had recently graduated from a local college with a B.S. degree in general management. Mr. Wilson was stunned by the news. He thought he should have been considered for the position.

Discuss Mr. Wilson's reaction.

REFRESHING LANGUAGE SKILLS

The following sentences are based on the important rules of punctuation which have been presented in the Language Usage sections of this book. On a separate sheet of paper type each sentence and punctuate it correctly.

1. An interviewer considers a variety of factors when interviewing a candidate among them are basic skills ability to talk easily temperament and job interest.
2. Many companies administer performance tests as well as general aptitude tests to all applicants who seem promising.
3. When the applicant reached the receptionist desk the receptionist said Good morning may I help you.
4. There are posthigh school educational institutions where office workers are able to study a wide variety of subjects and to work toward degrees.
5. On the job training is of course a good way to improve ones understanding of a job and at the same time gain a comprehensive view of the company.
6. She had only a slight knowledge of data processing but her new employer said that with on-the-job training and outside class study she would become efficient.
7. She was greeting an applicant for the position when the telephone call came in however the applicant waited while she located the file for the personnel manager.
8. He asked her to bring the numeric the geographic and the subject files.

9. What would a telegram cost as compared with a long-distance call he asked.
10. A secretary will prepare an itinerary make hotel and transportation reservations balance a petty cash fund and make a bank deposit attend a meeting take the notes and type a report and then say this was a quiet day maybe tomorrow will be more exciting.

PERFORMING SECRETARIAL TASKS

Write an essay in which you discuss your ambitions for the next three years. Consider such questions as: Where do you want to work? Are you likely to be interested in further study? If so, in what fields? Are you likely to be interested in further formal education in a college or university? For what purpose? If interested, what do you think, at this point, you would want to study?

IMPROVING SECRETARIAL SKILLS (Optional)

1. Design a guide for an interviewer of office workers. Include those areas which should be discussed fully with a prospective employee.
2. You have been introduced to many aspects of work in the office while studying in high school. You have now had sufficient preparation to fulfill the beginning requirements of a number of office jobs. At the same time, you have had the opportunity to judge yourself — your strengths, your weaknesses. You have also given consideration to your particular interests and to the types of organizations in which you might be able to combine your special office skills and your interests. Write a brief essay in which you identify the types of organizations in which you might be able to combine your special strengths, your skills, and your interests. Consider, also, your weaknesses, and describe briefly what you might do to overcome them in the next year or two in the position you choose.

Travel Tours International

An Orientation

The units in this textbook provide information and exercises to assist you in understanding the key tasks of secretaries. You have already seen that many secretarial tasks are interrelated because you have regularly used knowledge acquired in earlier units as you proceeded through the book. Office tasks aren't done in isolation. To handle incoming mail properly, for example, you must know how to use the files to secure correspondence related to the letters received. Indeed, the secretary combines in each assignment many skills and understandings.

The Simulated Office Activities provided in the *Supplies Inventory* will give you a clearer understanding of how office tasks are interrelated. They will also provide you with an opportunity to plan your work, to make decisions, and to follow the instructions of an employer in a realistic setting. Each of the four Simulated Office Activities will require from two or three hours to complete. All are performed in the same office. Your goal is to complete the assignments just as if you were actually employed in the office and responsible to your employer for your own work. Your teacher may assign one Simulated Office Activity at a time, after completing a block of units in the textbook, or all four Simulated Office Activities at the same time, as a major project at the end of the course.

You will find that you have had experience with all the tasks you are asked to complete. However, you will have to make decisions that go beyond just completing a single assignment. For example, one of your primary decisions will be to determine the order in which you will do a number of tasks based on the importance of each task. You will also have to make decisions about how to arrange materials and what supplies to use. Your decisions in each case will be guided by your knowledge of office procedures.

Your Secretarial Position

You are employed as a secretary to the director of tour development in the office of Travel Tours International, with headquarters at 500 Gateway Boulevard, St. Louis, MO 69881. This large company provides a wide range of travel and tour services. It has branch offices in major cities throughout the United States. There are also affiliated offices in Europe, South America, Australia, and Asia.

Mr. Martin Fitzgerald, the director of tour development, for whom you are working, has major responsibility for analyzing developments in the travel business including the current interests of travelers. His department provides standard popular tours such as the three-week tour of the great cities of Europe and the South Pacific cruise. New tours are continually being organized to attract potential tourists. As you handle various secretarial tasks, you will become acquainted with Mr. Fitzgerald's interesting activities.

Supplies

Many of the supplies you will need for the four Simulated Office Activities are provided in your *Supplies Inventory*. Others are easily obtained supplies which you will furnish yourself.

Supplies Provided

The following supplies are included in the *Supplies Inventory:*

Simulated Office Activity I:
8 Travel Tours International letterheads
2 interoffice memo forms

Simulated Office Activity II:
No *Supplies Inventory* supplies needed.

Simulated Office Activity III:
9 "Memo of Call" forms
4 telegram blanks
2 Travel Tours International letterheads

Simulated Office Activity IV:
3 Travel Tours International letterheads
2 Travel Tours International expense report forms
2 blank checks

Additional Supplies

You will have to furnish the following supplies:

Simulated Office Activity I:
- 1 sheet plain paper
- 9 sheets onionskin paper
- 8 No. 10 envelopes
- 2 sheets carbon paper
- 1 folder labeled "For Your Action"
- 1 folder labeled "To Be Filed"

Simulated Office Activity II:
- 4 sheets plain paper
- 2 sheets onionskin paper
- 20 5" × 3" cards
- 1 sheet carbon paper
- 1 folder labeled "For Your Action"
- 1 folder labeled "To Be Filed"

Simulated Office Activity III:
- 2 sheets plain paper
- 5 sheets onionskin paper
- 2 sheets carbon paper
- 2 No. 10 envelopes
- 1 folder labeled "For Your Action"
- 1 folder labeled "To Be Filed"

Simulated Office Activity IV:
- 5 sheets plain paper
- 8 sheets onionskin paper
- 2 sheets carbon paper
- 3 No. 10 envelopes
- 1 folder labeled "For Your Action"
- 1 folder labeled "To Be Filed"

Each page of supplies in the *Supplies Inventory* is marked with the Simulated Office Activity for which it is to be used. All supplies that are alike, however — for example, all letterheads — are grouped together in the Simulated Office Activities supplies section of the *Supplies Inventory*. You will have to decide on the type of supply you will need to complete each assignment. Make sure it relates to the Simulated Office Activity you are working on and remove it from the *Supplies Inventory*.

General Procedures

Each of the four Simulated Office Activities takes place on one day in the office. At the beginning of each day, you are given a number of business papers by Mr. Fitzgerald with which to work in completing your assignments. These papers may be incoming letters to which you are to respond, memos which you are to type, forms which you are to complete in ordering supplies, or other types of business papers. These business papers are found in the *Supplies Inventory* and are labeled to match the Simulated Office Activity you are working on. There may also be some dictation from your teacher which you will transcribe.

Each Simulated Office Activity includes realistic instructions. However, this does not mean that all instructions will be complete. You are to assume that any instructions not provided should be considered standard instructions which you understand from your study of the textbook.

To make the experience as realistic as possible, approach the activities just as you would your work at the beginning of a regular day on a real job. Follow these basic procedures:

1. Locate the business papers for the Simulated Office Activity you are to complete. Remember that the papers are labeled to match the Activity. Remove the business papers from the workbook, separating them at the perforation marks.
2. Read each business paper carefully, including all handwritten instructions. You will have to decide which jobs to complete first, second, third, etc., based on the importance of the job and on how soon you are told it is due. After reading each paper carefully, decide the order in which you will complete the jobs and sort the papers into three stacks as follows:
   A. *RUSH*. All items which must be completed immediately or which affect Mr. Fitzgerald's appointments or schedule for that day; all items that must be completed so that further action can be taken by someone else in the immediate future; all items which must be sent out in the morning mail, all telephone calls and telegrams.
   B. *ASAP (As Soon As Possible)*. All items which must be done today but which do not require immediate attention; items marked "take care of today," or "needed by end of today."
   C. *AYC (At Your Convenience)*. All other items which do not require *RUSH* or *ASAP* handling. These are routine assignments which are done when all other tasks are completed, or items on which action need not be taken until some time in the future.

3. After sorting the papers by priority, complete the Summary Form which you removed from the *Supplies Inventory* along with the business papers. Indicate in the appropriate blanks on the form which business papers you placed in each priority category by writing the circled job number that appears on each business paper. Later, when you have finished all the jobs in the Simulated Office Activity, you will attach the Summary Form to the completed jobs and submit them to your teacher for evaluation.

4. After filling in the Summary Form, place the business papers in one stack, with the *RUSH* items on top and the *AYC* items on the bottom. You are now ready to start the tasks beginning with the *RUSH* items.

5. Before processing a paper, read it a second time. Look at the circled job number on the business paper and find this job number in the list of instructions for the Simulated Office Activity on which you are working. Read the instructions carefully. Some of the instructions for a task may be given on the business paper itself. If all the instructions are not given, you must decide how to proceed based on what you have learned in your study of the textbook. Unless you are directed otherwise, refer to the textbook anytime you need to review specific procedures.

6. Secure the supplies you need to complete the job from the *Supplies Inventory* and from those you furnished. For each job make a carbon copy on onionskin paper unless you are instructed otherwise.

7. Use letterheads and prepare envelopes for all letters typed. Mr. Fitzgerald prefers the modified block style letter with open punctuation and paragraph indentions. His name and title are typed as:

    Martin Fitzgerald
    Director — Tour Development

8. After you finish a job, check it carefully. The responsible secretary strives to present the employer with work that is error-free and that can be sent immediately to the recipient. After you have completed and checked the job, type your name at the top unless you are directed otherwise by your teacher. Attach the business paper relating to each job to the back of the original you typed and place them in the "For Your Action" folder. Place the carbon copy of the completed job in the "To Be Filed" folder.

9. When you have completed all the jobs in a Simulated Office Activity, do the following:

    a. Remove the completed jobs from the "For Your Action" folder.
    b. Arrange the jobs in the order in which you completed them.
    c. Attach the Summary Form you completed earlier to the finished jobs.

d. Put the completed jobs and the Summary Form back into the "For Your Action" folder and then give the folder to your teacher for evaluation.

After your work has been checked, the folder will be returned to you for use in the next Simulated Office Activity. (You may place the completed assignments returned to you by your teacher in another folder if you desire.)

You are now ready to begin work on the Simulated Office Activities. Good luck!

Grammar

Grammar is important in speaking and writing. Knowing the rules of grammar is necessary if you are to carry out your responsibilities confidently.

Grammar is the study of the words of a language, but particularly the study of the relationship of those words to one another. Words are subdivided into nine classifications that are known as parts of speech.

I. Nouns	VI. Adverbs
II. Pronouns	VII. Prepositions
III. Adjectives	VIII. Conjunctions
IV. Articles	IX. Interjections
V. Verbs	

I. Nouns

A noun is a word that names

A. A person (Winston Churchill)
B. A place (Palm Beach)
C. A thing (cake)
D. A quality (happiness)
E. An action (dancing)
F. An idea (love)

Proper Noun. A proper noun names a particular being or thing. It is always capitalized.

Thomas Edison, California, Statute of Liberty

Common Noun. A common noun names any member of a class of beings or things.

woman (women), light (lights), flower (flowers)

Collective Noun. A collective noun is a common noun that names a group.

company, committee, family, group, team

II. Pronouns

A pronoun is a word that is used instead of and that refers to a noun.

Pronoun	used instead of	Noun
he		John
she		Marilyn
they		jury

Personal Pronouns and Their Antecedents. A personal pronoun is a pronoun that shows by its form whether it represents the

A. Speaker (first person)
B. Person spoken to (second person)
C. Person spoken of (third person)

An antecedent is a noun that is referred to by a pronoun. (In all examples below, the antecedent is shown by one underline and the pronoun by two underlines.)

The singer took his stereo onto the plane.

His (the pronoun) refers to *singer* (the noun). *Singer* is therefore the antecedent of *his*.

The pronoun must be in agreement with its antecedent in person, number, and gender. There are several types of antecedents that require particular attention.

1. When two or more singular antecedents of a pronoun are connected by *and*, the pronoun must be plural.

    The clerk and the mail boy received their checks.

    If, however, the antecedents are merely different names for the same person or thing, the pronoun must be singular.

    The well-known businessman and public servant has received his award.

2. When two or more singular antecedents of a pronoun are connected by *or* or *nor*, the pronoun must be singular.

    Either Joyce or Linda must bring her notebook.

    If one of the antecedents is plural, it should be placed last, and the pronoun should be plural.

    Neither the general manager nor his assistants realized that they had so little time.

3. If the antecedent of a pronoun is a collective noun that expresses unity, the pronoun must be singular.

    The committee quickly reached its decision.

If the collective noun refers to the individuals or parts that make up a group, however, the pronoun of which it is the antecedent must be plural.

The class brought their own lunches.

4. The number of an antecedent is not changed when it is followed by such connectives as *in addition to* and *as well as*.

The boy, as well as his brothers, did his duty.

5. Since there is no third person, singular number, common gender pronoun, the masculine he, his, or him is generally used when the antecedent requires such a pronoun.

Each office worker must do his best.

The issue of deciding whether to use a feminine or masculine pronoun is sometimes avoided by using a plural pronoun.

All office workers must do their best.

When it is especially important to be accurate, both masculine and feminine pronouns may be used.

Every employee should be careful about his or her personal appearance.

Relative Pronouns. A relative pronoun is one that joins a subordinate clause to its antecedent. *Who, which, what,* and *that* are the relative pronouns.

Secretaries *who* know grammar are valuable.

The relative pronoun *who* joins its antecedent *secretaries* to the subordinate clause *know grammar*.

Some compound relative pronouns are *whoever, whichever,* and *whatever*; they differ from regular relative pronouns in that they contain their antecedents.

Relative pronouns present two problems:

1. Using the correct relative pronoun with reference to persons and things — for example, *who* refers to persons and, sometimes, to highly trained animals; *which* refers to animals or things; *that* refers to persons, animals, or things.

2. Using correct case form.

Who and *whoever* are in the nominative case and are used when a relative pronoun is the subject of a subordinate clause.

Mr. Johnson is a man *who* can do the job.

Whose is in the possessive case and is used to show ownership.

> *Whose* hat is this?

Whom and *whomever* are in the objective case and are used when a relative pronoun is the object of a verb or preposition.

> Grace is the girl *whom* we are addressing.

The Pronoun after *Be*. The same case may be used after the verb *be* in any of its forms *(am, are, is, was, were, be, being, have been)* as appears before it. This is usually the nominative case. When the object of a transitive verb, however, precedes the infinitive *to be*, the objective case must follow it.

> It was *she* (not *her*).
> If I were *he* (not *him*).
> Did you expect those children to be *them* (not *they*)?

III. Adjectives

An adjective is a word that is used to modify a noun or a pronoun. There are two types of adjectives:

A. A *descriptive* adjective names some quality of or describes the person or object expressed by the noun or pronoun that it modifies.

> *pretty* girl, *handsome* child, *white* dress

B. A *definitive* adjective points out or expresses the number or quantity of the object named by the noun or referred to by the pronoun.

> *eight* people, *this* book, *that* desk, *ten* pages

Proper Adjectives. Proper adjectives are those derived from proper nouns, and they are always capitalized.

> *French* language, *American* interests

Comparison of Adjectives. Comparison is the expression of an adjective to indicate an increasing or decreasing degree of quality, quantity, or manner. There are three degrees of comparison:

1. The *positive degree* is expressed by the simple form of the adjective.

> light, pretty

2. The *comparative degree* is used to compare two objects. The comparative degree of almost all adjectives of *one* syllable, and

Grammar

of a few of two syllables, is formed by the addition of *r* or *er* to the simple form.

lighter, prettier

The comparative degree of most adjectives of *two* or more syllables is formed by the placing of *more* or *less* before the simple form of the adjective.

more beautiful, *less* useful

3. The *superlative degree* is used to compare *three* or more objects. The superlative degree of most adjectives of one syllable, and some of two syllables, is formed by the addition of *est* to the simple form.

lightest, prettiest

The superlative degree of most adjectives of two or more syllables is formed by the placing of *most* or *least* before the simple form of the adjective.

most satisfactory, *least* attractive

Some adjectives are compared irregularly. The following are a few:

Positive	*Comparative*	*Superlative*
good	better	best
much	more	most
little	less	least
bad	worse	worst

IV. Articles

The, *a*, and *an* are articles.

A. *The* is a *definite* article because it refers to a particular person or thing in a class.

The manager read *the* application.

B. *A* and *an* are *indefinite* articles because they refer to persons or things in general. *An* is used before nouns that start with a vowel sound.

a person, *an* application, *an* honor

V. Verbs

A verb is a word that shows action or state of being of the subject. There are two classifications of verbs:

A. A *transitive verb* is one that requires an object to complete its meaning. The object may be a noun or a pronoun and it *must* be in the objective case. The object is used to complete the meaning of the verb.

To determine the object of a transitive verb, ask *What?* or *Whom?* after the verb.

He *reported* the accident (Reported what? the accident).

B. An *intransitive verb* does *not* require an object to complete its meaning.

The light *shines*. The boy *ran*.

Many verbs may be used both as transitive and intransitive verbs. For example, in the sentence, "The boy ran," *ran* is an intransitive verb requiring no object.

The verb *ran* may, however, be used as a transitive verb: for example, The boy *ran* a race. Here *race* is the object of the verb *ran*, and the verb becomes transitive.

Some verbs, however, may be used correctly only as intransitive verbs. *Sit*, *lie*, and *rise* are examples of verbs that are always intransitive verbs since they permit no object; while *set*, *lay*, and *raise* are examples of verbs that are always transitive because they require an object to complete their meaning.

Voice of Verbs. Voice indicates whether the subject of the verb is (1) the doer of the action or (2) the receiver of the action that is expressed by the verb.

A verb in the *active voice* identifies the subject as the doer of the action.

The new stenographer *typed* the letter.

A verb in the *passive voice* identifies the subject as the receiver of the action.

The letter *was typed* by the new stenographer.

Any transitive verb may be used in either the active or the passive voice.

In the independent clauses of a compound sentence or in a series of related statements, verbs of the same voice should be used. This is known as *parallel construction*.

(Wrong) The letter *was dictated* by the executive and the secretary *transcribed* it.

(Right) The executive *dictated* the letter and the secretary *transcribed* it.

Tense. Tense expresses the time of the action of a verb. There are three primary tenses:

1. The *present tense* of a verb is used to denote the present time. It is used in expressing a general truth or that which is customary. The present tense is also used to describe in a more vivid way what took place in past time. This is known as the *historical present*.

> George Washington *crosses* the Delaware and immediately *attacks* Trenton.

2. The *past tense* indicates past time.

> We *shipped* your order yesterday.

3. The *future tense* indicates that which will take place in the future. The future tense is expressed by the use of *shall* or *will* with the present form of the verb.

> I *shall go* early. You *will arrive* on time.
> She *will come* in at eight o'clock.

Frequent errors are made in the use of *will* and *shall*. The future tense may be used to express simple futurity or to express determination or promise. Simple futurity is denoted by the use of *shall* with the first person, and *will* with the second and the third persons.

> I *shall be* happy to see you when you arrive.
> He *will be* home early.

If determination or promise is to be expressed, the rule for futurity is reversed. Use *will* with a first person subject, *shall* with a second or third person subject.

> I *will be* there without fail.
> You *shall* certainly *go*.
> They *shall return* tomorrow.

In asking questions, use *shall* when the subject is in the first person (I, we).

> *Shall* we go?

When the subject is in the second or third person, either *shall* or *will* may be used, depending upon which form is expected in the answer.

> *Will* you write the letter? (Answer expected: I *will* write the letter.)
> *Shall* you miss your friends when you move? (Answer expected: I *shall* miss my friends.)

In addition to the primary tenses, there are three verb phrases, known as the perfect tenses, that represent completed action or being.

1. The *present perfect* tense denotes an action or an event completed at the present time. It is formed by the placing of *have* or *has* before the perfect participle.

I *have read* several chapters.
He *has studied* his French.

2. The *past perfect* tense indicates an action or an event completed at or before a stated past time. It is formed by the placing of *had* before the perfect participle.

They *had completed* the picture by the time dinner was served.
I *had assumed* you would come by plane before we received your letter.

3. The *future perfect* tense indicates that an action or an event will be completed at or before a stated future time. It is formed by the placing of *shall have* or *will have* before the perfect participle.

I *shall have gone* before you arrive.
He *will have arrived* home before you can get there.

Whether *shall have* or *will have* is used depends upon the basic rules for the use of *shall* or *will*.

Mood. Mood is that property of a verb that indicates the manner in which the action or state of being is expressed.

1. The *indicative mood* is used in asserting something as a fact or in asking a question.

She reads well.
Where is the book?

2. The *imperative mood* is used in expressing a command, a request, or an entreaty.

Bring me my coat, please.
Sit up!

3. The *subjunctive mood* is used in expressing a doubt, a wish, or a condition contrary to reality.

(a) A condition contrary to *present* reality is expressed with *were*, not *was*.

(Wrong) If I *was* tall, I could reach the book.
          If Ann *was* going, you could go along.
(Right)   If I *were* tall, I could reach the book.
          If Ann *were* going, you could go along.

(b) A condition contrary to *past* reality is expressed by *had been*.

If the plane *had been* on time, this might not have happened.

Agreement of Verb and Subject. A verb must agree with its subject in person and number. The verb *to be* has person and number forms: *I am, you are, he is, we are, you are,* and *they are; I was, you were, he was, we were, you were,* and *they were.* Other verbs have only one expression for all number and person forms.

When the subject is in the third person, singular number, a verb or an auxiliary (helping verb) in the present or the present perfect tense must end in *s.*

> Mr. White *dictates* very slowly.
> Miss Stewart *has* been his secretary for a long time.

A very common error is the use of a singular verb with a plural subject, or a plural verb with a singular subject.

1. When the verb and the subject are separate in the sentence, the verb must agree with its subject. A common error is to make the verb agree with the word near it rather than with the real subject.

   > (Wrong) The *activity* of the board at its weekly meetings *are* always interesting.
   > (Right) The *activity* of the board at its weekly meetings *is* always interesting.

2. If the subject is plural in form but singular in meaning, a singular verb is required.

   > The news *has* been good.

3. Two or more singular subjects connected by *or* or *nor* require a singular verb.

   > Neither Kurt nor Bill *is* at the office.

4. When two or more subjects connected by *or* or *nor* differ in number, the plural subject is placed nearest the verb and the verb made plural.

   > Neither the vice-president nor the executives have that bulletin.

   When two or more subjects connected by *or* or *nor* differ in person, the verb must agree with the subject that is nearest to it.

   > Either you or I *am* at fault.

   It is frequently better to rephrase the sentence so as to use a verb with each subject.

   > Either you *are* at fault or I *am.*

5. Two or more singular subjects connected by *and* require a plural verb.

The typewriter and the adding machine *are* both in need of repair.

6. When the subjects connected by *and* refer to the same person, a singular verb must be used.

   The great novelist and playwright *is* on his way home.

7. When the subjects connected by *and* represent one idea or are closely connected in thought, a singular verb should be used.

   Ice cream and cake *is* a popular dessert.

8. When either or both subjects connected by *and* are preceded by *each, every, many a*, etc., a singular verb is required.

   Each stock clerk and supervisor *is* expected to work late on the inventory.

9. When one of two subjects is in the positive and the other in the negative, the verb agrees with the one in the positive.

   The teacher, and not the students, *is* planning to attend.

10. The number of a subject is not affected by words connected to it by *as well as, and also, in addition to*, etc.

    Mother, as well as the rest of the family, *is* expecting to go.

11. When a collective noun expresses unity, a singular verb is used.

    The jury *is* asking that a point be clarified.

Contractions. Contractions may be used in informal communications.

In writing contractions, remember that *don't* the contraction of *do not*, is plural and is used with plural nouns and the pronouns *I, we, you,* and *they. Doesn't*, the contraction of *does not*, is singular and is used with singular nouns and the pronouns *he, she,* and *it*.

   It *doesn't* bother them much, but I *don't* like it.

Infinitives. An infinitive is expressed by placing the word *to* before a verb: *to be, to walk, to talk, to cry*. The infinitive may be used:

1. As a subject.

   To run takes energy.

2. As an adjective.

   The place *to go* is Colorado.

3. As a predicate noun.

   To jog is *to exercise*.

4. As a direct object.

> Mary likes *to sing*.

5. As an adverb.

> Jack waited *to leave* with me.

Participles. A participle is a verb form used as an adjective and having the double function of verb and adjective. There are three forms of the participle:

1. The *present participle* is formed by the addition of *ing* to the simple form of the verb. It expresses action as being in progress, usually at the same time as some other action. It is used as an adjective and at the same time retains some of the properties of a verb.

> The clerk *counting* the money is new here.

In this sentence *counting* is an adjective modifying the noun *clerk*; it also has the property of a verb in that it takes the object *money*.

2. The *past participle* expresses action prior to that of the governing verb. It is used as an adjective and is usually formed by the addition of *d* or *ed* to the present tense of the verb.

> The machine *used* by the secretary was defective.
> The teacher, *interrupted* by the students, did not complete her grading.

3. The *perfect participle* is formed by the combination of *being*, *having*, or *having been* with some other participle.

> *Having written* the letters, she was free to go.

In the preceding sentence the perfect participle *having written* modifies the subject of the sentence *she*.

A common error is that of putting at the beginning of a sentence a participial phrase that does not modify the subject. This is referred to as *dangling* participle.

> (Wrong) Having completed the statement, it was time to file the letters.
> (Right) Having completed the statement, she found it was time to file the letters.

VI. Adverbs

An adverb is a word used to modify a verb, an adjective, or another adverb.

A. An adverb modifies a verb by answering the questions *how? when?* or *where?*

> She walked *lightly*.
> He arrived *early*.
> The report is *here*.

B. An adverb modifies adjectives and other adverbs by expressing degree *(how much? how little?)* or by answering the question *in what manner?*

> The clerk will file *more* often.
> She spoke *less* clearly than before.
> He was mechanically precise.
> Julia was painfully aware of the problem.

Comparison of Adverbs. Like adjectives, adverbs are compared to show degree.

1. A few adverbs are compared by the addition of *er* or *est* to the positive form of the adverb.

   > *soon, sooner, soonest; slow, slower, slowest*

2. Some adverbs are compared irregularly.

   > *well, better, best*

3. Most adverbs, however, are compared by the use of *more* or *most* and *less* or *least* with the simple (positive) form of the adverb.

   > *more* brightly, *most* often; *less* lightly, *least* likely

Placing the Adverb. Ordinarily an adverb follows the verb it modifies, but it may precede it. It should be placed where its meaning is most clearly shown. *Only, merely,* and *also,* which are sometimes adverbs and sometimes adjectives, give the most trouble in placing, since they may convey very different meanings in different positions in a sentence.

> *Only* I saw him.   I saw *only* him.
> I *only* saw him.   I saw him *only*.

Other Rules for Adverbs. There are a few errors frequently made in the use of adverbs.

1. *Very* or *too* should generally not be used to modify participles directly.

   > (Wrong) Her work was very improved.
   > (Right)   Her work was very much improved.

2. *Too,* which is an adverb that means *also* or *more than enough,* should be spelled correctly and not confused with *to* or *two.*

   > By *two* o'clock she had *too* much work *to* do.

3. *Well* is usually an adverb. In speaking of health, however, *well* is used as an adjective. Be careful not to use *good* as an adverb in place of *well*.

> (Wrong) He does his work *good*.
> I don't feel very *good*.
> (Right) He does his work *well*.
> I don't feel very *well*.

4. *Very* is an adverb of degree, while *real* is an adjective of quality. Do not use *real* in place of *very*.

> (Wrong) He had a *real* beautiful office.
> (Right) He had a *very* beautiful office.

5. Adverbs of manner, those ending in *ly*, are frequently confused with adjectives derived from the same root. Adverbs of manner modify verbs that express action.

> She sings *sweetly*. (Adverb)
> Her singing is *sweet*. (Adjective)

6. *Not* is an adverb used to express negation; it should not be used in combination with other negatives.

> (Wrong) The clerk will *not* wait for *nobody*.
> (Right) The clerk will *not* wait for *anybody*.
> (Right) The clerk will wait for *nobody*.

VII. Prepositions

A preposition connects a noun or a pronoun with some other element of the sentence and shows the relationship between them. The noun or pronoun that follows the preposition is its object.

There are two kinds of prepositions:

A. Simple — *to, for, at, through of*
B. Compound — *into, in spite of, instead of, in regard to, on account of, because of, according to, out of, as to*.

Prepositional Phrases. A group of words made up of a preposition and its object, together with any words used to modify the object, is called a *prepositional phrase*. The object of a preposition may be determined by asking *whom* or *what* after the preposition; what the prepositional phrase modifies may be determined by asking *what* or *who* before the preposition.

Prepositional phrases, like adjectives and adverbs, should be placed as close as possible to the words they modify to make the sentence as clear as possible.

Choice of Prepositions. Many errors are made in the use of prepositions because some words demand certain prepositions; for example *angry with* is used in reference to persons, and *angry at* is used in reference to things, animals, or situations. Some of the most common situations in which prepositions are misused are given below.

1. *Into* should be used after a verb that indicates the motion of a person or a thing from one place to another. *In* is used after a verb expressing the idea of rest or, in some cases, motion within a certain place

   The girl went *into* the classroom.
   The clerk is *in* the filing department.

2. *Between* should be used only in reference to two persons or objects. *Among* should be used when referring to three or more persons or objects.

   The two boys divided the work *between* them.
   Gifts were distributed *among* the children.

3. Do not use unnecessary prepositions.

   (Wrong) The wastebasket is *in under* the desk. Where is it *at*?
   (Right) The wastebasket is *under* the desk. Where is it?

4. Do not omit prepositions that are needed to make sentences grammatically correct. Avoid telegraphic style in letters.

   (Wrong) Mr. Finley will arrive North Station 11:00 Sunday.
   (Right) Mr. Finley will arrive at the North Station at 11:00 a.m. Sunday.

VIII. Conjunctions

A conjunction is a word used to connect words, phrases, or clauses. There are three kinds of conjunctions:

A. A *coordinate conjunction* connects words or clauses of the same grammatical relation or construction, neither being dependent upon the other for its meaning.

   You *and* I are elected.
   Their father is out of town, *and* their sister is on a vacation.

B. A *subordinate conjunction* connects a subordinate clause with some word in the principal clause upon which it is dependent for its meaning.

   The man left hurriedly *since* he was late.

C. *Correlative conjunctions* are conjunctions that are used in pairs, the first introducing and the second connecting the elements. They must be placed just before the elements that they introduce or connect.

(Wrong) I will *either* meet you in Boston *or* Washington.
I will meet you *either* in Boston *or* Washington.
(Right) I will meet you in *either* Boston *or* Washington.
I will meet you *either* in Boston *or* in Washington.

Or should only be used with *either*, *nor* with *neither*. They are used in reference to two things only.

(Wrong) *Either* Bob, Jack, *or* Don will pitch today's game.
Neither the superintendent, the principal, *nor* the teachers agreed with him.
Neither Jack *or* Don will pitch today's game.

(Right) Bob, Jack, *or* Don will pitch today's game.
The superintendent, the principal, *and* the teachers disagreed with him.
None of them — the superintendent, the principal, the teachers — agreed with him.
Neither Jack *nor* Don will pitch today's game.

Some cautions concerning the use of conjunctions follow.

1. Conjunctions should not be used in place of some other part of speech.

(Wrong) Seldom *or* ever should such an example be used.
You should try *and* improve your speech.
(Right) Seldom *if* ever should such an example be used.
You should try *to* improve your speech.

2. A clause, which is a part of a sentence containing a subject and a predicate, having meaning in itself, is connected to the other parts of the sentence by either a conjunction or a relative pronoun. A phrase, which contains no verb and has no meaning by itself, is introduced by a preposition, participle, or infinitive, but not by a conjunction.

The project cannot be completed *without* your help.
(*Without* is a preposition introducing a phrase.)
The project cannot be completed *unless* you help us.
(*Unless* is a conjunction introducing a clause.)

3. *Except* and *without* are prepositions and should not be used in place of *unless*, which is a conjunction.

(Wrong) You will not master shorthand *except* you concentrate.
(Right) You will not master shorthand *unless* you concentrate.

4. *Like* is not a conjunction and should never be used in place of the conjunction *as*.

(Wrong) She walks *like* you do.
(Right)　　She walks *as* you do.

IX. Interjections

Interjections are exclamatory words or phrases used in a sentence for emphasis or to indicate feeling. They have no grammatical connection with the rest of the sentence, and are set off by a comma or an exclamation mark.

Oh, so you saw it?
Ouch! that hurt.

Grammar Reference Books. Although many questions concerning grammar can be answered by using a good dictionary, you should have available a standard reference book on English grammar.

In Appendix H you will find a list of recommended books. A ready reference on grammar will help you produce better letters and reports for your employer.

Appendix **B**
Punctuation

Punctuation is used to make more forceful and to indicate more clearly the relationship of written thoughts. Punctuation is the written substitute for the changes in voice, the pauses, and the gestures that are used in oral expression.

The excessive use of punctuation marks is not good form. The importance of using punctuation accurately, however, is illustrated daily by the serious errors that may be found in office correspondence.

You will be responsible for the correct punctuation of business letters and reports. Although you are not expected to be an authority on punctuation, you should be familiar with the most important rules.

General guidelines for spacing after punctuation marks are:

1. One space is left after punctuation marks within a sentence with the exception of the colon.
2. Two spaces are left after colons and all punctuation marks at the ends of sentences.
3. No spaces are left between two marks of punctuation when they are used together.

Rules for punctuation are given alphabetically in this appendix.

Apostrophe (')

The apostrophe is used

1. To form possessives. There are several rules that govern the formation of the possessive case of words, depending on the final letter or syllable of the word and whether the word is singular or plural. There are no spaces before or after an apostrophe that is part of a word. A few important rules to follow are listed below.

    (a) The possessive of singular and plural common and proper nouns not ending with the *s* or *z* sound (excepting *ce*) is usually formed by the addition of an apostrophe and *s* to the singular form.

secretary's letter	men's coats
Shaw's plays	Lawrence's mail

(b) The possessive of a singular noun ending in *s* is formed by adding an apostrophe and *s* if the *s* is to be pronounced as an extra syllable. If not, add only the apostrophe.

waitress's	politeness'
class's	species'

(c) The possessive of plural common nouns ending in *s* is formed by the addition of only an apostrophe.

boys' shirts	players' uniforms
committee's reports	

(d) The possessive of a one-syllable proper noun ending in an *s* or *z* sound is generally formed by the addition of an apostrophe and *s*, although in newspapers addition of only the apostrophe is frequently seen.

Burns's poems	Marx's ideas
Liz's book	

(e) The possessive of proper nouns of more than one syllable ending in an *s* or *z* sound (excepting *ce*) is formed by the addition of an apostrophe only.

Essex' papers	Adams' chronicle
Burroughs' house	

(f) The possessive of a compound noun is formed by the addition of an apostrophe or an apostrophe and *s* [according to Rules (a), (b), (c) and (d)] to its final syllable.

mother-in-law's visit
City of Detroit's council
letter carrier's route
passers-by's expressions

(g) The possessive of a series of names connected by a conjunction showing joint ownership is indicated by an apostrophe or an apostrophe and *s* to the last name.

Simon and Walter's garage
Adams and Anderson's firm

(h) If joint ownership does not exist in a series of names, the possessive case is formed by the addition of an apostrophe or apostrophe and *s* to each proper name in the series.

Macy's and Hayne's stores
Jack's, Joe's, and Bill's gloves

(i) The possessive of abbreviated words is formed by adding an apostrophe and *s* to the last letter of the abbreviation.

YMCA's membership
the X's function
the Mr.'s position in the heading
the OK's presence

(j) The apostrophe is never used to form the possessive of pronouns.

his   yours
hers

2. To show the omission of letters (in a contraction) or the omission of figures.

don't (for *do not*)   Class of '78 (for *1978*)
it's (for *it is*)

3. To form the plurals of figures, letters, signs, and words.

If you have no 6's, use 9's turned upside down.
Her *v*'s and *u*'s and *T*'s and *F*'s are too much alike.
The +'s and −'s denote whether the sentences were correct or not.
There were too many *and*'s and *the*'s in the essay.

4. To form the past tense of arbitrarily coined verbs; it is followed by a *d*.

She OK'd the copy.
He X'd out three lines.

Asterisk (*)

The asterisk is sometimes used instead of a raised number to refer to a footnote.

Mr. Martin used the reports* as a reference.
_____
*The reports are from the Mackenzie Case.

Brackets [ ]

Brackets are used

1. To enclose a correction, an addition, or a comment which a writer inserts in matter he is quoting.

"In 1942 [a typographical error for 1492] Columbus discovered America."

2. To enclose the term *sic*, Latin for *thus*, to show that a misspelling or some other error appeared in the original and is not an error by the one quoting.

In applying for the job he wrote, "I am very good in athletics [*sic*], and I can teach mathmatics [*sic*]."

3. When it is necessary to place a parenthesis within another parenthesis; but in general, such complicated usages should be avoided.

> At 3:30 p.m. (the time agreed upon at the conference [see John Coleman's letter of April 9]) the announcement of the new salary agreement was made to the news media.

Colon (:)

The colon is used

1. To introduce formally a word, a list, a statement, or a question; a series of statements or questions; or a long quotation.

> The book had many good points: it contained an interesting story; it contained humor; it was well illustrated.

2. Between hours and minutes whenever they are expressed in figures.

> 8:30 a.m.   1:45 p.m.

3. After salutations in some styles of business letters:

> Dear Sir: Ladies and Gentlemen:
> Dear Mrs. Jones:

Comma (,)

The comma is the most frequently used form of punctuation; therefore, errors in its use are frequent. The comma is used

1. To set off a subordinate clause preceding a main clause.

> When the bell rings, you may leave.

2. To set off a nonrestrictive phrase or subordinate clause. (A phrase or a clause is nonrestrictive if the main clause in the sentence expresses a complete thought when the nonrestrictive phrase or clause is omitted.)

> My doctor, who is now on vacation, will prepare the report next week.

3. To separate long coordinate clauses that are joined by the conjunctions *and, but, for, neither, nor,* and *or.* The comma precedes the conjunction.

> He worked far into the night, for the deadline was noon the next day.

4. To set off phrases or expressions at the beginning of a sentence when they are loosely connected with the rest of the sentence.

Nevertheless, we feel the way you do about it.

5. To separate words, phrases, or clauses in a series. Most writers include a comma before the last item in the series.

The group now has no meeting place, no supplies, and no money.
They told us when they heard it, where they heard it, and from whom they heard it.

6. To separate two or more adjectives if they both precede or follow the noun they modify, provided each adjective alone modifies the noun. If an adjective modifies a combination of a noun and another adjective, however, no comma is used between the two adjectives.

An old, shaggy, forlorn-looking dog came limping out to greet us.
Happy young people come here frequently.

7. To set off words and phrases used in apposition.

My cousin, the doctor in the family, has a practice in Syracuse.

8. To set off parenthetical words, clauses, or phrases.

Tomorrow, on the other hand, business will be much better.

9. To set off words in direct address.

Children, we must get ready for the party.

10. To set off the words *yes* and *no* when used in sentences.

Yes, you may go now.
Frankly, no, I don't care.

11. To set off the name of a state when it is used with a city.

They lived in Denver, Colorado, for many years.

12. To separate the day of the month from the year and to set off the year when used with the month.

The project must be completed by August 20, 1978, at the latest.

13. To set off a mild interjection.

Ah, he surely enjoyed that story.

14. To set off a participial expression used as an adjective.

Smiling pleasantly, she entered the office.

15. To separate unrelated numbers.

    In 1960, 25 new students enrolled.

16. To divide a number of four or more digits into groups of three, counting from right to left. Do not space after the comma.

    1,567,039

17. To set off phrases that denote residence or position.

    Professor William Smith, of Harvard, will speak.

18. To indicate the omission of a word or words readily understood from the context.

    In June the book sales amounted to $523; in July, to $781.

19. Before a short, informal, direct quotation.

    The employer asked, "Have you transcribed those letters?"

Dash (—)

The dash is formed in typewriting by the striking of two hyphens without a space preceding or following them. The dash is used

1. To indicate a change in the sense or construction of a sentence.

    Hemingway, Wolfe, Green — these are my favorites.

2. Instead of a comma to emphasize or to guard against confusing the reader.

    The laborer is worthy of his hire — if his labor is.
    If — and only if — we go, the day will be complete.

3. To precede a reference.

    No, the heart that has truly loved never forgets. — Moore.

Diagonal (/)

The diagonal is used

1. Between two words with no spaces around it. The diagonal indicates that either or both of the words may be used in the sentence.

    You may write the report and/or prepare a notebook.

2. Between two numbers with no spaces around it to express a fraction.

    The height is 2/3 of the width.

Ellipsis (. . .)

The ellipsis is used

1. To show that words have been omitted from the beginning or middle of a sentence. An ellipsis is three periods, each separated by one space. There is one blank space before the first period and one after the last period.

   Original statement: Mary typed and proofread the report.
   Mary . . . proofread the report.

2. To show that a statement is unfinished or dies away. A period is placed at the end of the sentence after an ellipsis.

   Mary typed and proofread . . . .

Exclamation Point (!)

The exclamation point, like the period, represents a full stop. It is used at the end of a thought expressing strong emotion or command. The thought may be represented by a complete sentence, a phrase, or a word.

   Aha! We caught you this time!

Hyphen (-)

The hyphen is used

1. To divide a word between syllables at the end of a line.

   The traffic near my sister's apartment was heavy yesterday afternoon.

2. To show compound words

   She has a new wash-and-wear blouse.

Parentheses ( )

Parentheses are used

1. To enclose figures or letters that mark a series of enumerated elements.

   She wanted three things: (1) a promotion, (2) a salary increase, and (3) more responsibility.

2. To enclose figures verifying a number which is written in words.

   twenty (20) dollars
   twenty dollars ($20)

3. To enclose material that is indirectly related to the main thought of a sentence.

> We shall postpone (at least for the present) a decision.

4. To enclose matter introduced as an explanation.

> The answer (see page 200) is puzzling.

The rules covering the use of other marks of punctuation with parentheses are:

1. If needed in the sentence, a comma or dash that normally precedes a parenthetic element is transferred to follow the closing parenthesis.

> He sent a belated, though clever (and somewhat personal), greeting card.

2. Punctuation at the end of a parenthetic expression *precedes* the parenthesis if it applies to the parenthetic material only; it *follows* the parenthesis if it applies to the sentence as a whole.

> When she heard him (he shouted, "Who goes there?"), she was surprised.
> (See the discussion on page 78.)
> This experiment has interesting results (see Table I).

Period (.)

The period is used

1. After complete declarative or imperative sentences.

> Today we shall study the use of the period.

2. After initials in a name.

> H. L. Andrews

3. Within an abbreviation. Do not space after these periods.

> a.m., e.g., i.e.

4. After most abbreviations:

> pres., lb., et al.

The following are some exceptions:

> (a) Mme (Madame), Mlle (Mademoiselle)
> (b) IOU, c/o, OK, SOS, A1
> (c) Chemical symbols: H_2O, Zn, Pb
> (d) Office and agencies of the federal government: SEC, FBI, FCC

5. In decimal numbers, and between dollars and cents when expressed in figures, and after the abbreviations *s,* and *d,* for shilling and pence. Do not space after a period that is used as a decimal point.

> 3.45, $16.13, 13s., 7d.

Question Mark (?)

The question mark is used

1. After a direct question, but not after an indirect question.

> Are you ready?
> He asked what caused the fire.

It is not necessary to use a question mark after a polite request.

> Will you please let us know your decision at once.

2. To indicate uncertainty.

> The applicant was born in 1952(?).

3. After each question in a series if special emphasis is desired. When it is used in this way, it takes the place of the comma; and each element begins with a small letter.

> Where is my pen? my notebook? my file?

Quotation Marks (" ")

Quotation marks are used

1. To enclose direct quotations. Single quotation marks are used to enclose a quotation within a quotation.

> The director said, "I hope you are familar with this play."
> She said, "Unkind as it may be, I can't help saying 'I told you so' to her."

2. To enclose the titles of articles, lectures, reports, etc., and the titles of subdivisions of publications (that is, the titles of parts, chapters, etc.). The titles of books and magazines are not enclosed in quotation marks, but underscored or typed in all capital letters.

> She thought the chapter "Producing Mailable Transcripts" was helpful.

3. To enclose unusual, peculiar, or slang terms.

> Her "five o'clocks" were famous.
> When they saw us, they "flipped."

4. To enclose words used in some special sense, or words to which attention is directed in order to make a meaning clear.

> He said "yes," not "guess."
> The term "title by possession" is often used.

5. To enclose the titles of short poems, songs, and television and radio shows.

> "Fog" (poem)
> "Yesterday" (song)
> "All in the Family" (TV show)
> "David Brinkley's Journal" (radio show)

6. When consecutive paragraphs of the same work are quoted, at the beginning of each paragraph but at the end of only the last paragraph.

Quoted Matter. When quoted matter appears within a letter, an article, or a report, it is advisable that it be indicated as a quotation. This may be done in three ways:

1. The material may be indented from the regular margins on the left and right.
2. It may be underscored throughout.
3. It may be enclosed in quotation marks.

Sometimes the quoted matter is both indented and enclosed in quotation marks. The practice of using quotation marks is the most widely used.

A long quotation is single-spaced, even though the rest of the copy is double-spaced.

Quotation Marks with Other Marks of Punctuation. At the end of quoted material, a quotation mark and another mark of punctuation are often used together. The rules governing the order of these marks are not entirely logical; but since they are well established and generally accepted, you should follow them.

1. A period or a comma should precede the quotation mark even though it may not be a part of the quotation.

> "I saw you," he said, "when you left."

2. A semicolon or colon should follow the closing quotation mark, even when it is a part of the quotation.

> Mary, Ruth, and John visited that "house of antiques"; and the "antiques" were really unusual.
> There is this to say about his "mission": it is fictitious.

3. Other marks of punctuation should precede the closing quotation mark if they apply to the quotation only, and should

follow the mark if they apply to the sentence as a whole and not just to the quotation.

> She asked, "Will you go?"
> Did you read the article "Better Sales Letters"?

Semicolon (;)

The semicolon is used

1. In a compound sentence between closely related clauses that are not joined by a conjunction.

   > That is good taste; it suggests discretion.

2. In a compound sentence if either clause contains subclauses or long phrases requiring commas.

   > Since the weather was rainy and windy, she grew cold; but she continued on her journey.

3. Before such words and abbreviations as *e.g., i.e., viz., for example, namely,* and *to wit* when they introduce a long list of items. A comma precedes the list.

   > Some pairs of words are bothersome to students; for example, affect and effect, loose and lose, sit and set.

4. Between elements in a listing when there are commas within the elements.

   > James Craig, Newport High; William Parker, Forest Hills High; and Ken Caldwell, Jefferson High were the winners.

5. Before connectives when such words introduce sentences, principal clauses, or an abrupt change in thought. (The comma follows the connective when used in this manner only if the connective is to be emphasized.) Some of these connectives are *accordingly, consequently, hence, however, in fact, moreover, nevertheless, therefore, thus, whereas, yet*.

   > It is February; therefore, we have many holidays.

Underscore (Italics)

A typist can emphasize an important word, phrase, or sentence in typewritten material several ways. The kind of copy and the purpose for which it is being typed determine to some extent the emphasis that should be indicated.

In typewriting, underscoring takes the place of printed italics and is the method most often used to give prominence to a word or group of words. Emphasis is also achieved by typing in red in the midst of copy typed in black or blue, and by making characters darker by typing over them several times.

In addition to emphasizing a word or words, the underscore (italics) should be used

1. To refer to a word or letter taken out of its context.

   Always dot your i's, and cross your t's.
   Do not write and and the slantwise across the line.

2. To designate a foreign word not yet anglicized.

   Her faux pas was noticeable.

3. To indicate titles of plays, motion pictures, musical compositions, paintings, art objects, books, pamphlets, newspapers, and magazines. (Parts of these, such as chapters in a book or article in a magazine or newspaper, are designated by quotation marks.)

   Have you seen My Fair Lady?
   El Greco's View of Toledo was on display at the museum.
   We also saw Rodin's The Thinker.
   She found Unit 8, "Meeting the Public," in Secretarial Office Procedures very helpful.
   The Wall Street Journal contains a regular feature entitled "Washington Wire."

4. To designate the names of ships, airplanes, and spacecraft.

   U.S.N.S. Nautilus
   Lindbergh's Spirit of St. Louis
   Apollo 15

Appendix C

Word Choice and Spelling

The secretary cannot afford to be indifferent to words, but must constantly be concerned with their spelling, their meaning, and their appropriateness. Continuous vigilance is necessary to insure that misspelled words and words that do not convey precisely the meaning intended do not slip by in proofreading copy. A secretary who does not choose and use words carefully soon becomes guilty of poor communication skills.

A dictionary is a regularly used reference by the alert secretary. Become acquainted with your dictionary. Learn to understand all abbreviations that are used. Your dictionary will dispel uncertainties about proper spelling and meanings of words.

Good Usage

To convey messages precisely, it is important that you use words that conform to current good usage. *Colloquialisms*, which are words and phrases that are acceptable in informal conversations and sometimes in letters, are not considered good usage in formal business correspondence. *Provincialisms*, which are terms that are used informally in particular areas of the country, are also to be avoided in formal communications. *Archaic* and *obsolete* words, which are words that were once standard, are no longer in fashion and should be avoided.

Below is a list of *colloquialisms* that should be avoided in business communications.

Incorrect in Formal Writing	*Correct in Formal Writing*
all-round (adj.)	generally serviceable
around	about, nearly
back of, in back of	behind, at the back of
bit	a short time, a little while
calculate	think, plan, expect
cute	clever, amusing
enthuse	enthusiastic
get hold of	to learn, to master
have got to	must, have to

Incorrect in Formal Writing	*Correct in Formal Writing*
lots of, a great deal of	many, much
most	almost, nearly
not a one	not one
off of	off
over with	finished, done
quite some time	a long time
show up	arrive
stand for	allow, stand

Some *provincialisms* which may fail to convey meaning when used outside a local area, and which should be avoided, are shown below.

Use	*Rather than*
declare, maintain	allow
raise	rear
short distance	piece
think, suppose, guess	reckon
want to come in	want in
you	you all
intend to	is fixing to

Words That Are Pronounced Alike

Words that are pronounced alike but differ in meaning are called *homonyms*. These words are often confusing and require close attention to the meaning of the sentence so that the correct word is used.

Some examples of homonyms are:

aid, aide	hoard, horde
aisle, isle	incite, insight
allowed, aloud	knew, new
altar, alter	lead, led
bare, bear	plain, plane
base, bass	right, write
berth, birth	role, roll
brake, break	stationary, stationery
creak, creek	through, threw
fair, fare	ware, wear, where

Words That Are Not Pronounced Alike

Many words that are very close in spelling are *not* pronounced alike. These words are frequently confused in use simply because they look alike when written or sound similar to the ear. Words of this type are listed below. Can you distinguish the meaning and pronunciation of each?

accept, except
adapt, adept, adopt
addition, edition
affect, effect
all ways, always
allusion, illusion
ascent, assent

content, contest
costume, custom
council, counsel
formerly, formally
local, locale
personal, personnel
test, text

Compound Words

In the regular routine of daily business, one class of words that gives considerable trouble is made up of compound words. Compound words fall into three groups: hyphenated compounds, single-word compounds, and two-word compounds.

There are a few rules that will assist you in becoming familar with certain groups of compound words that use the hyphen.

1. A hyphen is always used in a compound number.

   twenty-one, fifty-eight

2. A hyphen is used between the numerator and the denominator of a fraction written in words except when one of the elements already contains a hyphen. A fraction used as a noun requires no hyphen.

   four-fifths share   forty-one hundredths
   two-thirds interest   forty one-hundredths

   one half of the total
   two fifths of the class

3. A hyphen is used between two or more words when the words serve as a single adjective *before* a noun. In applying this rule you must be careful that the words are not a series of independent adjectives. The exception to the rule is that proper nouns made up of two or more words are not hyphenated when used as adjectives.

   a well-liked boy, *but* a boy well liked
   a fresh-water fish, *but* a fish from fresh water
   a New England dinner, a New Jersey product
   a large black horse; a deep, clear pool

4. Groups of three or more words used as a single word are usually hyphenated.

   four-in-hand, well-to-do, sister-in-law, up-to-date

5. A hyphen is used after a prefix

   (a) when the prefix is joined to a proper noun

   pro-English, anti-American

(b) to prevent confusion between some verbs and compounds

re-form (meaning to form again)
re-sign (meaning to sign again)

(c) to prevent an awkward piling up of consonants

bell-like, well-loved

(d) to separate double vowels that might be mispronounced as one sound

de-emphasize, re-ink

When *any, every, no,* and *some* are combined with other words, the compound is a single word: *anything, everyone, nowhere, somehow.* Sometimes, however, the parts of the compound expression are written as separate words: *no one, every one.*

Compound words change form. Some become single-word compounds through constant use; at some time in the past most were hyphenated compounds. The following compound words occur frequently.

Hyphenated Compounds

by-line	do-it-yourself
by-product	self-confidence
cross-reference	vice-president

Single-Word Compounds

billboard	network
bondholder	nevertheless
bookkeeper	northeast
bylaws	notwithstanding
checkbook	outgoing
guesswork	overdue
handwriting	overhead
headline	payday
headquarters	payroll
henceforth	policyholder
hereafter	postcard
laborsaving	postmarked
letterhead	takeoff
meantime	trademark
middlemen	viewpoint

Two-Word Compounds

account book	income tax
bank note	parcel post
card index	price list
cash account	trade union
civil service	vice versa

Plural Forms of Nouns

Some nouns exist in only the plural form (*annals, news, thanks*), and other nouns are the same in both the singular and the plural forms (*deer, corps, chassis*). Still other nouns are irregular in form (*man, men; child, children; foot, feet*). Generally speaking, however, the plural of a noun is formed by adding *s* to the singular form.

The following rules are helpful in the formation of plural nouns.

1. Form the plurals of nouns ending with *y* preceded by a consonant by dropping the *y* and adding *ies*. When the *y* is preceded by a vowel, add *s* only.

   lady, ladies   alley, alleys
   salary, salaries   tally, tallies
   story, stories   turkey, turkeys

2. Form the plural of a hyphenated compound noun by changing the principal word of the compound from singular to plural. The principal word of a compound is not always the last word.

   sisters-in-law, cross-purposes, passers-by

3. Form the plural of a single-word compound by adding *s* to the end of the word.

   cupfuls, viewpoints, headquarters

4. The plurals of some words of foreign origin are formed in accordance with the rules of the language from which they are derived.

   axis, axes   datum, data
   alumnus, alumni   alumna, alumnae

5. A few words of foreign origin have both foreign and English plural forms. In some cases, one form is preferred over the other (*strata* instead of *stratums*); while in other cases both forms are considered equally acceptable (*indexes* and *indices*, *memorandums* and *memoranda*). Consult a dictionary for the preferred usage of plural words of foreign origin.

6. Two persons bearing the same name and title may be referred to in the following manner: *The Messrs. Haviland, The Misses McKenzie, The Doctors Butler*, or *The Mr. Havilands, The Miss McKenzies, The Doctor Butlers*. In formal and business language, the plural form of the title is preferred.

7. The plural of a letter, a noun-coinage, or of a word as a word is formed by the addition of an apostrophe and *s*.

   p's and *q*'s   Her *I-don't-care*'s were . . .
   the *and*'s   too many *that*'s

8. The plurals of proper nouns that have more than one syllable and end with an "s" or "z" sound, are formed by adding just an apostrophe.

> The Curtises' home . . .
> The Mullins' dog . . .

9. The plurals of nouns ending in *o* vary individually; some take *s* and others *es*.

> motto, mottoes   piano, pianos
> potato, potatoes   folio, folios

Word Division

Frequently a word must be divided at the end of a line in order to keep the right margin even. Words should be divided only between syllables. In case of doubt, consult a dictionary. The following rules apply to typewritten copy.

1. When a final consonant preceded by a single vowel is doubled before addition of a suffix, divide the word between the two consonants (*prefer-ring, program-ming*).

2. A single-letter syllable at the beginning or the end of a word should not be separated from the remainder of the word (*above* not *a-bove*).

3. A two-letter syllable at the end of a word should not be separated from the rest of the word (*calmly* not *calm-ly*).

4. A syllable that does not contain a vowel should not be separated from the rest of the word (*coundn't* not *could-n't*).

5. Hyphenated words should be divided only at the hyphens (*follow-up* not *fol-low-up*).

6. A four-letter word should not be divided; it is seldom permissible to divide five- or six-letter words (*into* not *in-to*), (*camel* not *cam-el*), (*never* not *nev-er*).

7. When a word containing three or more syllables is to be divided at a one-letter syllable, the one-letter syllable should be written on the first line rather than on the second line (*maga-zine* not *mag-azine*).

8. When a word is to be divided at a point where two vowels that are pronounced separately come together, these vowels should be divided into separate syllables (*continu-ation* not *continua-tion*).

9. Compound words are preferably divided between the elements of the compound (*turn-over* not *turno-ver*).

Word Choice and Spelling   657

10. Proper names should not be divided; and titles, initials, or degrees should not be separated from names (*President* not *Pres-ident*).

11. Avoid dividing words at the end of more than two successive lines, at the end of a page, or at the end of the last complete line of a paragraph.

12. Avoid awkward or misleading divisions that may cause difficulty in reading (*carry-ing* not *car-rying*).

13. When the single-letter syllable *a*, *i*, or *u* is followed by *ble*, *bly*, *cle*, or *cal*, do not separate the single-letter syllable and the suffix (*agree-able* not *agreea-ble*).

14. Avoid the division of figures and abbreviations, the parts of an address or date. If it is necessary to separate an address, keep together the number and street name, the city and ZIP Code.

| 2143 Market | *not* | 2143 |
| Street | | Market Street |

In separating a date, leave the day with the month.

| March 3, | *not* | March |
| 19–– | | 3, 19–– |

Spelling

Learning to spell correctly requires becoming so familiar with words that you use again and again that you are able to spell them without giving special thought to them. It also means that you should continue to question how you have spelled a word until you are *absolutely* sure of its accuracy. A dictionary will be an important aid in determining whether what you guessed as the right spelling is indeed right. If you find that certain words cause you difficulty frequently, you should make a list of them and take some time to study them so that in the future you will have no uncertainty about them.

Below are some spelling rules that will guide you in determining the correct spelling of many words.

1. To spell words containing *ei* or *ie* pronounced like *ee*, use *ie* after any letter except *c*.

belief	grievance
chief	lien
expedient	relieve
field	reprieve
frieze	siege

Use *ei* after *c*.

ceiling	perceive
conceive	receipt
deceive	

Exceptions:

either	seize
neither	leisure

2. A final *e* is usually dropped before a suffix beginning with a vowel, unless doing so would change the pronounciation or meaning of the word.

bride, bridal	hope, hoping
force, forcible	manage, managing
college, collegiate	subdue, subduing

Exceptions:

dye, dyeing
change, changeable
courage, courageous

3. The final *e* is usually retained before a suffix beginning with a consonant.

lone, lonely	hate, hateful
move, movement	pale, paleness

Exceptions:

judge, judgment	argue, argument

4. Before the suffix *ing*, *ie* is changed to *y*.

die, dying	lie, lying

5. A final double consonant is retained before a suffix.

will, willful	odd, oddly
ebb, ebbing	

6. Usually the final consonant is doubled in words of one syllable, or words ending in a single consonant preceded by a single vowel with the accent on the last syllable, before a suffix beginning with a vowel.

occur, occurred	refer, referring
begin, beginning	plan, planned

Exceptions:

fix, fixed	refer, reference

7. The final *y* preceded by a consonant is usually changed to *i* before a suffix not beginning with *i*.

worry, worried   happy, happiness

Exceptions:

shy, shyness   beauty, beauteous

8. The final *y* preceded by a vowel is usually retained before any suffix or the letter *s*.

annoy, annoyance   buy, buyer
delay, delayed   pay, payable
journey, journeys   attorney, attorneys

9. The final *l* is always single in words ending in *ful*.

careful   hopeful
doubtful   regretful

10. Only one word ends in *sede* — *supersede*; only three words end in *ceed* — *exceed, proceed, succeed*; all other words having this sound end in *cede* — *concede, intercede, precede, secede*.

11. When *i* and *e* come together in the same syllable, generally *i* is used before *e*.

Commonly Used Business Words That Are Often Misspelled

accept	definite	immediately	quantity
accommodate	description	its	questionnaire
across	develop		
affect	difference	judgment	really
all right	disappoint	lose	receive
already			recommend
among	eligible	necessary	reference
analysis	embarrass	noticeable	referred
appearance	endeavor	occasion	
arrangement	equipped	occurred	separate
	especially	opportunity	similar
	except	original	stationery
beginning	existence		
benefited	experience	paid	their
business	explanation	pamphlet	too
		personnel	
canceled (cancelled)	foreign	possession	undoubtedly
coming	fourth	practically	using
committee		preferred	
confident	government	principal	volume
conscientious	grammar	privilege	
convenience		probably	whether
criticism	height	proceed	writing

Appendix D
Abbreviations

Abbreviations are abridged contractions. They provide a means of conserving the space required for words and phrases. With the extensive use of computers and related equipment, the need for using abbreviations has grown. The use of abbreviations is guided by custom and equipment restrictions. A general rule that continues to be followed is that abbreviations are used sparingly in correspondence. Abbreviations are common, however, in the typing of forms, such as invoices and statements, where space is limited.

Abbreviations of Proper Names

For proper names these are generally accepted rules.

1. A person's family name should never be abbreviated. Given names may be represented by initials, but it is desirable for others to conform to a person's own style or signature. For example, if a person signs his name *Henry F. Grimm*, it is good form for others to write his name that way, rather than *H. R. Grimm*. As a general rule, given names such as *Charles* or *William* should not be abbreviated to *Chas.* or *Wm.*, unless the person uses the abbreviation so consistently that it is obviously the spelling preferred.

2. Names of cities, with the exception of those containing the word *Saint (St.)*, should not be abbreviated.

3. Names of states and territories should be spelled out, except in lists, tabular matter, footnotes, bibliographies, and indexes. In such cases the standard abbreviations listed below should be used. The United States Postal Service has authorized the two-letter all-capital abbreviations listed on the next page for use *only* with ZIP CODES.

Abbreviations in the Body of a Letter

The shortening of words in the body of a letter can convey a lack of care and time in presenting an attractive, thoughtful message. One should not write: The advt. can be supplied for your dept. @ 50¢ per p.

Abbreviations

State or Territory	Standard Abbreviation	ZIP Code Abbreviation	State or Territory	Standard Abbreviation	ZIP Code Abbreviation
Alabama	Ala.	AL	Missouri	Mo.	MO
Alaska	*	AK	Montana	Mont.	MT
Arizona	Ariz.	AZ	Nebraska	Nebr.	NE
Arkansas	Ark.	AR	Nevada	Nev.	NV
California	Calif.	CA	New Hampshire	N.H.	NH
Canal Zone	C.Z.	CZ	New Jersey	N.J.	NJ
Colorado	Colo.	CO	New Mexico	N.Mex.	NM
Connecticut	Conn.	CT	New York	N.Y.	NY
Delaware	Del.	DE	North Carolina	N.C.	NC
District of Columbia	D.C.	DC	North Dakota	N.Dak.	ND
Florida	Fla.	FL	Ohio	*	OH
Georgia	Ga.	GA	Oklahoma	Okla.	OK
Guam	*	GU	Oregon	Oreg.	OR
Hawaii	*	HI	Pennsylvania	Pa.	PA
Idaho	*	ID	Puerto Rico	P.R.	PR
Illinois	Ill.	IL	Rhode Island	R.I.	RI
Indiana	Ind.	IN	South Carolina	S.C.	SC
Iowa	*	IA	South Dakota	S.Dak.	SD
Kansas	Kans.	KS	Tennessee	Tenn.	TN
Kentucky	Ky.	KY	Texas	Tex.	TX
Louisiana	La.	LA	Utah	*	UT
Maine	*	ME	Vermont	Vt.	VT
Maryland	Md.	MD	Virginia	Va.	VA
Massachusetts	Mass.	MA	Virgin Islands	V.I.	VI
Michigan	Mich.	MI	Washington	Wash.	WA
Minnesota	Minn.	MN	West Virginia	W.Va.	WV
Mississippi	Miss.	MS	Wisconsin	Wis.	WI
			Wyoming	Wyo.	WY

*No standard abbreviation

It would be better to write: The advertisement can be supplied for your department at the rate of 50 cents per page.

Abbreviations may be used in the body of a letter when they have become commonly recognized symbols, such as SEC, FTC, CIO, and YMCA. A letter should be understood rather than made to follow a single practice. If, therefore, a letter is written to someone who may not understand an abbreviation, it is better to spell it out in the first sentence of its use so that the reader understands the term when it appears thereafter in abbreviated form. For example, the complete term *Securities and Exchange Commission* may be used first; then, in subsequent references, the abbreviation SEC may be used if the document is not a formal one.

Frequently used abbreviations are listed in the dictionary. Each field of work has developed specialized abbreviations, and secretaries learn these when they begin work in a new office.

Periods in Abbreviations

Periods are dropped from an abbreviation when it is commonly recognized and does not require the periods for clarity. NBC, SEC, and FTC, for example, are written without periods and without spaces between the letters. The omission of a period in some abbreviations, however, might be confusing. For example, without the periods, *in.* for *inch* might be mistaken for the preposition; *a.m.* for *morning* might be confused with the verb form. If, in order to avoid confusion, periods are used with an abbreviation, such as *a.m.*, they should be used in *p.m.* in order to maintain a consistent style.

Abbreviations with Numbers

The abbreviations *st, d,* and *th* should not follow a date when the date comes after the month.

> He leaves for London on August 21.

The abbreviations *st, d,* and *th* should follow the date when the date is given before the month. Do not use a period after the abbreviation *st, d,* and *th*.

> He was planning to leave on the 21st of August.
> Mr. Smith went to Los Angeles on the 3d of July.

In enumerations, it is better to write *first, second, third* rather than *1st, 2d, 3d*.

Diagonal Lines in Abbreviations

The use of the diagonal signifies the omission of such words as *per, of, to, upon*. In abbreviated forms that include a diagonal the period is not usually used, as in *B/L*. The period is sometimes retained, however, in three- or four-word combinations, as *lb./sq. ft*.

Plurals of Abbreviations

The plural form of most abbreviations is made by adding *s* to the singular form, but many abbreviations have only one form for both singular and plural. Several single-letter abbreviations are made plural by doubling the letter.

> chgs., lbs.
> ft., in., oz., deg., cwt.
> pp. (pages), ll. (lines)

Plurals of capitalized abbreviations may be formed simply by adding a small *s*. Apostrophe and *s* may be added to form the plurals of abbreviations composed of letters (capital and small), signs, and symbols. There is no single rule, however, that completely governs all cases that may arise.

YMCAs, a.m.s, IOU's, P's, Q's, 6's, FOB's, OK's, #s

Coined Verbs

Often an abbreviation is used as a verb in informal correspondence. To make the necessary change, an apostrophe may be added with *d*, *s*, or *ing* according to the use of the abbreviation.

OK'd

Possessives of Abbreviations

Generally the singular possessive is formed by adding the apostrophe and *s*, as in *Jr.'s, RR's, Sr.'s, SOS's.*

The plural possessive is formed by adding an apostrophe to abbreviations whose plural forms end in *s*, as in *Jrs.', Drs.'*.

Appendix E

Titles, Capitalization, and Numbers

Titles

The use of titles is governed by customs that are accepted by the people of a given society. A secretary should learn the correct titles of the persons with whom she or he associates. There is one principle for the use of titles in oral communication that should always be remembered: *Never use a title alone.* For example, a person who holds a Ph.D. should never be addressed as just *Doctor.* The proper address is *Doctor Jones.* Current practice governing the use of titles in writing follows.

Birthright Titles. The title of *Mr., Ms., Mrs.,* or *Miss* is customary for adults who have no other title.

Mr. is used before the name of a man who has no other title. *Messrs.,* the abbreviation of *Messieurs* (French for gentlemen), is the plural of *Mr.*

Ms. is used before the name of a woman when her marital status is unknown or when the person has shown a preference for *Ms.* as a term of address.

Mrs. is a title used by many married women and widows. A married woman may prefer to be addressed by her husband's name, as in *Mrs. John Brown,* or by her Christian name, as in *Mrs. Helen Brown.* A widow, likewise, may use her deceased husband's name or her own name, whichever she prefers. When *Mrs.* is applied to two or more married women, the title *Mesdames,* or its abbreviation, *Mmes.,* is used, as in *Mmes. Clark, Wright* and *Grant.*

Miss is frequently used before the name of an unmarried woman or girl. *Misses* is the plural of *Miss,* as in the *Misses Alice Henderson* and *Dorothy Jones.*

Doctor. *Dr.* is the title of a person who holds any of the various doctors' degrees. It is usually abbreviated. When two doctors are being addressed, the word *Doctors* or the abbreviation *Drs.* may be used.

Reverend. This title is properly carried by a minister, priest, or rector. The abbreviation *Rev.* is commonly used, although it is considered better usage to write the word in full. More than one Reverend may be addressed as *Reverend Messrs.* or the repetition of the word *Reverend* before each name.

Abbreviated Titles Following Personal Names. *Senior* and *Junior*, terms used to distinguish a father and son of exactly the same name, are written after the name as the abbreviations *Sr.* and *Jr.* The abbreviation is capitalized, followed by a period, and is usually separated from the name by a comma. *Second* and *Third*, which distinguish members of the same family or close relatives whose names are identical, are indicated by the abbreviations *2d* and *3d*, or by the Roman numerals, *II* and *III*. The former style is now more common. Note that these abbreviations are not followed by a period, but they may be separated from the name by a comma.

The abbreviation *Esq.* is used after a gentleman's name in England but is rarely seen in this country. When it is used, the title *Mr.* is omitted.

Double Titles. A person's name may be written with two titles, one before the name and one after, only if the two titles distinguish the person in different ways. Different abbreviations which stand for the same title should not be used together. For example, it is correct to say Rev. H. C. Samuel, Ph.D., but not Dr. H.C. Samuel, Ph.D.

Mr., Ms., Mrs., Miss, and Dr. are dropped whenever another title is used. Thus, you would write Megan Mountain, M.A., never Ms. Megan Mountain, M.A.

Titles in Addresses and Salutations. Except for *Mr., Ms., Mrs.* and *Dr.*, all titles used in the address and salutations of letters are better written in full. Abbreviations, however, are not uncommon. Whenever you are in doubt, type the title in full. No one will be offended by seeing his or her title in full.

The correct titles and salutations to be used for federal and state officials, members of religious organizations, school officials, and individuals are given in Appendix F.

Capitalization

A good dictionary is the best source for determining proper capitalization. A person who must refer to the dictionary for the most elementary information of this type, however, wastes much time. Therefore, a working knowledge of the principles of capitalization adds to the secretary's efficiency and effectiveness.

One of the purposes of capitalization is to designate the names or titles of specific things, positions, or persons. Overuse of capitalization, however, tends to detract from the effectiveness of the writing.

The most common rules of capitalization are:

1. Every sentence begins with a capital letter.
2. The pronoun *I* and the interjection *O* are always capitalized.

3. The salutation and the first word of the complimentary close of a letter begin with capitals.
4. The days of the week, holidays, and the months of the year are capitalized.
5. All important words in the titles of the main agencies of a government begin with capital letters.
6. Direct quotations begin with a capital letter.

Business Titles and Positions. Titles are capitalized when they immediately precede or follow individual names and are directly related to them, or when they refer to specific persons.

> President W. L. Matthews will speak.
> Mr. R. Hubert McGraw, Jr., Vice-President, Investors Corporation
> Mrs. Samamtha Jones is Executive Secretary and Treasurer of Hammett Co.

Business titles are not capitalized when they do not refer to specific persons.

> Three men have been president of this company.
> A treasurer will be elected at the meeting tomorrow.

Geographic Names. Names of countries, cities, rivers, bays, mountains, islands, commonly recognized names given to regions of countries, and sections of cities are capitalized.

> Ohio River, Pacific Ocean, Union County, Harlem, the Great Plains, the Mississippi Valley

A geographic term such as *river, ocean, county, city*, and *street* that is not a part of the name but is used before the name, or a geographic term that is used in the plural, should not be capitalized.

> the river Danube
> county of Hamilton
> the city of San Diego
> the Atlantic and Pacific Oceans
> at the corner of Grant and Lee streets

Points of the compass designating specific geographic sections of the country are capitalized.

> the South, the Midwest, and the Northwest

Points of the compass used to indicate direction are not capitalized.

> South Dakota is south of North Dakota.
> The wind is coming from the west.

A noun that refers to the inhabitants of a particular part of the country is capitalized.

> Westerners, a Southerner, a New Englander

Proper names denoting political divisions are always capitalized.

British Empire, Ward 13, Platt Township, the Papal States

Words before Figures. With the exception of *page, line*, and *verse*, words used in connection with figures in typewritten references are usually capitalized. It is important that one rule be followed consistently. If the word *figure* is capitalized when followed by a number in one place, it should be capitalized in all other places in the text.

Chapter XV	line 3
Figure 8	page iii

Individual Names. All units in the full name of an individual are capitalized, except some surname prefixes such as *von, du, van*, and *je*, which are capitalized or left lower case according to the practice of the individual. When a part of a surname begins a sentence or when a surname is not preceded by a given name within a sentence, however, it is always capitalized.

Vincent van Gogh *but* Van Gogh
George Louis du Maurier *but* Du Maurier

Hyphenated Words. In general, there are three rules that govern the capitalization of the parts of a hyphenated word.

1. If both parts of a hyphenated word would ordinarily be capitalized when written alone, then both parts should be capitalized in the hyphenated word.

   Senate-House debate
   Spanish-American War

2. In a heading or title, it is permissible to capitalize the parts of a compound word to conform to a general style.

   Forty-Second Street   Mid-January Sale

3. In straight text material, the way in which a word is used determines the part of the compound that should be capitalized.

Thirty-first Street	anti-Nazi
mid-January	pro-British
treasurer-elect	French-speaking
ex-president	pre-Pueblo

Headings and Titles of Articles and Reports. Only the first word and important words in headings or titles — nouns, pronouns, verbs, adverbs, and adjectives — are capitalized. Short, unimportant words are not capitalized. Examples of such words are the conjunctions *and, but*, and *or*; the articles *a, an*, and *the*; and the prepositions *of, in, to*, and *but*.

If the word needs to be stressed, however, it may be capitalized. Frequently long prepositions such as *between, after, before*, and *among* are capitalized.

Numbers

Numbers can be written as figures or as words. Although figures are used almost exclusively in business forms, both figures and words are used in letters and other types of transcripts that are written in sentence and paragraph form. If there are two or more ways in which an amount can be expressed, it is usually written in the way that requires the fewest words. A number such as 1,300 is written as *thirteen hundred* rather than *one thousand three hundred*. The following rules specify proper practice in writing numbers.

Numbers at the Beginning of a Sentence. A number that begins a sentence should be spelled out, even though other numbers are expressed in figures in the same sentence. It is wise, therefore, to avoid beginning a sentence with a large number that is cumbersome in words.

Amounts of Money. Amounts of money, except in legal documents, should be written in figures. Amounts less than one dollar are written in figures with the word *cents* following. In writing even sums of money, the decimal and ciphers are omitted.

> We enclose our check for $21.75.
> He paid 22 cents for the paper.
> He will pay $125 for the painting.

Cardinal Numbers. Numbers from one to ten are spelled out unless such numbers are used with others above ten. In business, figures are commonly used for all numbers except those which begin a sentence.

> We have 50 employees
> There will be eight in the group
> We have 8 secretaries in our group of 295 employees.

Dates. Except in legal or formal writing, the day of the month and the year are usually written in figures. When a date appears in the body of a letter, the year is customarily omitted if it is the same as that which appears in the date line. It is necessary to use *st, d,* or *th* in dates only when the day is written before or is separated from the month.

> the 3d of June
> in July, either the 3d or 4th

Streets. It is good form to use words for street numbers that are ten or less; figures should be used for street numbers above ten. When the name of the street is a number that is written in figures, it is separated from the number of the building by a dash. If the street name is preceded by one of the words *South, North, East,* or *West,* that word should not be abbreviated.

Tenth Street
72 — 125 Street   72 Fifth Avenue
19 West 115 Street   173rd Street

Time of Day. The abbreviations *p.m.* and *a.m.* should be written in small letters and should be used only with figures. The hour is spelled in full when *o'clock* is used. Do not use *p.m.* or *a.m.* to designate noon or midnight.

School starts at 8:30 a.m.
He will leave the office at four o'clock.
12 midnight, 12 noon

Measurements. Practically all measurements are written in figures.

Size 7½ AA Shoe   12-gal. bottle

Fractions and Decimals. Common fractions appearing alone are spelled out in ordinary reading matter. Mixed numbers are written as figures. Decimals are always expressed in figures.

Miscellaneous Usage. Sessions of Congress and the identifying numbers of various military bodies, political divisions, and dynasties are always written in words.

the Thirty-sixth Congress   Sixteenth Infantry
Thirteenth Ward

The result of a ballot is written in figures.

The count was 34 in favor of the motion, 36 against it.

Page, chapter, section, and footnote numbers are always written in figures.

pp. 45–67   Section 7
[2]Hawley, J.   Chapter 9

When two numbers immediately follow each other, it is better that the smaller one be spelled out and the larger one be expressed in figures.

125 two-cent stamps   Five 100-dollar bills

Unrelated groups of figures that come together should be separated by commas. Hundreds should be divided from thousands by a comma except in dates, policy numbers, street numbers, and telephone numbers.

In 1970, 417,296 gallons were sold.
The policy number is 73288.

Appendix F

Special Forms of Address, Salutations, and Complimentary Closings

Appendix F lists the correct forms of address with appropriate salutations and complimentary closings for the following special groups:

United States Government officials
Diplomatic representatives
State and local government officials
Members of religious organizations
School officials
Individuals

The correct forms of address for envelopes and letters are shown at the left. Open punctuation is used in addresses. The appropriate salutations and complimentary closings are given in the order of decreasing formality.

United States Government Officials

Address	Salutation	Complimentary Closing

The President of the United States

The President The White House Washington, DC 20500	Sir, Madam Mr. President Madam President Dear Mr. President Dear Madam President	Respectfully yours Very truly yours

The Vice-President of the United States

The Vice-President United States Senate Washington, DC 20510	Sir, Madam Dear Sir, Dear Madam Mr. Vice-president Madam Vice-president Dear Mr. Vice-president Dear Madam Vice-president	Respectfully yours Very truly yours Sincerely yours

The Chief Justice of the United States

The Chief Justice The Supreme Court of the United States Washington, DC 20543	Sir, Madam Mr. Chief Justice Madam Chief Justice Dear Mr. Chief Justice Dear Madam Chief Justice	Respectfully yours Very truly yours Sincerely yours

Associate Justice of the Supreme Court

Mr. Justice (Name)
Ms., Mrs., Miss Justice (Name)
The Supreme Court of the
   United States
Washington, DC 20543

Sir, Madam
Mr. Justice, Madam Justice
Dear Mr. Justice
Dear Madam Justice

Very truly yours
Sincerely yours

The Speaker of the House

The Honorable (Name)
Speaker of the House of
   Representatives
Washington, DC 20515

Sir, Madam
Dear Sir, Dear Madam
Dear Mr. Speaker
Dear Madam Speaker

Very truly yours
Sincerely yours

Member of the Cabinet

The Honorable (Name)
Secretary of (Office)
Washington, DC 20515

Sir, Madam
Dear Sir, Dear Madam
Dear Mr. Secretary
Dear Madam Secretary

Very truly yours
Sincerely yours

Senator

The Honorable (Name)
The United States Senate
Washington, DC 20520

Sir, Madam
Dear Sir, Dear Madam
Dear Senator
Dear Senator (Name)

Very truly yours
Sincerely yours

Representative

The Honorable (Name)
The House of Representatives
Washington, DC 20515

Sir, Madam
Dear Sir, Dear Madam
Dear Representative (Name)
Dear Congressman (Name)
Dear Congresswoman (Name)

Very truly yours
Sincerely yours

Head of a Government Bureau

The Honorable (Name), Chairperson
Commission of Fine Arts
Interior Building
18th and C Streets, N.W.
Washington, DC 20240

Sir, Madam
Dear Sir, Dear Madam
Dear Commissioner
Dear Mr. (name)
Dear Ms., Mrs., Miss (Name)

Very truly yours
Sincerely yours

Diplomatic Representatives

American Ambassador

The Honorable (Name)
American Ambassador
(Foreign City, Country)

Sir, Madam
Dear Mr. Ambassador
Dear Madam Ambassador
Dear Ambassador (Name)

Very truly yours
Sincerely yours

American Minister

The Honorable (Name)
American Minister
London, England

Sir, Madam
Dear Mr. Minister
Dear Madam Minister
Dear Mr. (Name)
Dear Ms., Mrs., Miss (Name)

Very truly yours
Sincerely yours

American Consul General, Chargé d'Affaires, Consul or Vice Consul

(Name), Esq. (male only)
Ms., Mrs., Miss (Name)
United States Embassy
Bonn, West Germany

Sir, Madam
Dear Mr. (Name)
Dear Ms., Mrs., Miss (Name)

Very truly yours
Sincerely yours

Secretary-General of the United Nations

His or Her Excellency (Name)
Secretary-General of the United
   Nations
New York, NY 10017

Your Excellency
Sir, Madam
Mr. Secretary-General
Madam Secretary-General

Very truly yours
Sincerely yours

United States Representative to the United Nations

His or Her Excellency (Name)
Ambassador Extraordinary and
   Plenipotentiary Permanent
   Representative to the United
   Nations
New York, NY 10017

Your Excellency
Sir, Madam
Dear Mr. Ambassador
Dear Madam Ambassador

Very truly yours
Sincerely yours

Ambassador to the United States

His or Her Excellency (Name)
Canadian Ambassador to the
   United States
1746 Massachusetts Avenue, N.W.
Washington, DC 20036

Your Excellency
Sir, Madam
Dear Mr. Ambassador
Dear Madam Ambassador

Very truly yours
Sincerely yours

State and Local Government Officials

His or Her Excellency, the
   Governor of New York
The Executive Chamber, Capitol
Albany, NY 12224

Governor
Sir, Madam
Dear Governor
Dear Governor (Name)

Respectfully yours
Very truly yours
Sincerely yours

Attorney General

The Honorable (Name)
Attorney General of Connecticut
State Capitol
Hartford, CT 06115

Sir, Madam
Dear Mr. Attorney General
Dear Madam Attorney General
Dear Mr. (Name)
Dear Ms., Mrs., Miss (Name)

Very truly yours
Sincerely yours

State Senator

The Honorable (Name)
State Capitol Building
Trenton, NJ 08625

Sir, Madam
Dear Sir, Dear Madam
Dear Senator (Name)

Very truly yours
Sincerely yours

State Representative

The Honorable (Name)
The State Assembly
Albany, NY 1224

Sir, Madam
Dear Sir, Dear Madam
Dear Representative (Name)
Dear Mr. (Name)
Dear Ms., Mrs., Miss (Name)

Very truly yours
Sincerely yours

Mayor

The Honorable (Name)
Mayor of the City of Chicago
City Hall
Chicago, IL 60602

Sir, Madam
Dear Sir, Dear Madam
Dear Mr. Mayor
Dear Madam Mayor
Dear Mayor (Name)

Very truly yours
Sincerely yours

School Officials

President of a University or College

(Name), President
Teachers College
Columbia University
525 West 120th Street
New York, NY 10027

Dear Sir, Dear Madam
Dear President (Name)
Dear Dr. (Name)

Very truly yours
Sincerely yours

Dean of a College

(Name), Dean
School of Education
New York University
Washington Square East
New York, NY 10003

Dear Sir, Dear Madam
Dear Dean (Name)
Dear Dr. (Name)

Very truly yours
Sincerely yours

Professor of a College or University

(Name)
Professor of Business Administration
Indiana University
Bloomington, IN 47401

Dear Sir, Dear Madam
Dear Professor (Name)
Dear Dr. (Name)

Very truly yours
Sincerely yours

Superintendent of Schools

Superintendent (Name)
Tupper Lake Central Schools
Tupper Lake, NY 12986

Dear Sir, Dear Madam
Dear Superintendent (Name)
Dear Mr. (Name)
Dear Ms., Mrs., Miss (Name)

Very truly yours
Sincerely yours

Principal of a School

(Name, Principal
Alexander Hamilton High School
Elizabeth, NJ 07202

Dear Sir, Dear Madam
Dear Mr. (Name)
Dear Ms., Mrs., Miss (Name)

Very truly yours
Sincerely yours

Individuals

One (Man)

Mr. (Name)
65 South Water Street
Chicago, IL 60601

Dear Mr. (Name)

Sincerely yours

One (Woman)

Ms. (Name)
2606 Kanuga Road
Hendersonville, NC 28739

Dear Ms., Mrs., Miss (Name)

Sincerely yours

Two (Women)

Ms. (Name) and Ms. (Name)
Mmes. (Name) and (Name)
Misses (Name) and (Name)

Ladies

Very truly yours

Three (Men)

Mssrs. (Name, (Name), and (Name)

Gentlemen

Very truly yours

Physician

(Name), M.D. or Dr. (Name)
274 Main Street
Springfield, MA 01105

Dear Dr. (Name)

Very truly yours
Sincerely yours

Attorney

Mr. (Name)
Ms., Mrs., Miss (Name)
Attorney at Law
One Pondfield Road
Bronxville, NY 10708

Dear Mr. (Name)
Dear Mr., Mrs., Miss (Name)

Very truly yours
Sincerely yours

Appendix G

Systems of Measurement

There are two commonly used methods of measurement. One, the *English*, or *imperial*, system, is used in the United States; the other is the *metric* system which is used in most parts of the world. In the English system the units used for measuring lengths are inches, feet, yards, and miles. The basic measuring unit for distance in the metric system is the meter. The metric system is a decimal system, which means that you can convert from one measuring unit to another merely by moving a decimal point. For example: 10 decimeters = 1 meter. By moving the decimal point one place to the left, you have converted decimeters into meters.

Lengths

English System	Metric System	Equivalencies
12 inches = 1 foot	10 millimeters = 1 centimeter	1 inch = 2.540 centimeters
3 feet = 1 yard	10 centimeters = 1 decimeter	1 foot = 30.48 centimeters
5,280 feet = 1 mile	10 decimeters = 1 meter	39.37 inches = 1 meter
	10 meters = 1 decameter	1 mile = 1.609 kilometers
	10 decameters = 1 hectometer	
	10 hectometers = 1 kilometer	

Weights

English System	Metric System	Equivalencies
16 ounces = 1 pound	10 milligrams = 1 centigram	1 ounce = 28.35 grams
100 pounds = 1 hundredweight	10 centigrams = 1 decigram	1 pound = 453.6 grams
2,000 pounds = 1 ton	10 decigrams = 1 gram	1 ton = 907.2 kilograms
	10 grams = 1 decagram	
	10 decagrams = 1 hectogram	
	10 hectrograms = 1 kilogram	

Dry and Liquid Measures

English System	Metric System	Equivalencies
Dry Measure:	Dry and Liquid Measure:	Dry Measure:
2 pints = 1 quart	10 milliliters = centiliter	1 pint = 0.550 liters
8 quarts = 1 peck	10 centiliters = 1 deciliter	1 quart = 1.101 liters
4 pecks = 1 bushel	10 deciliters = 1 liter	1 peck = 8.809 liters
	10 liters = 1 decaliter	1 bushel = 35.238 liters
Liquid Measure:	10 decaliters = 1 hectoliter	Liquid Measure:
2 pints = 1 quart	10 hectoliters = 1 kiloliter	1 pint = 0.473 liters
4 quarts = 1 gallon		1 quart = 0.946 liters
		1 gallon = 3.785 liters

H

Reference Books

Every secretary should have at least three reference books available for immediate use: a desk-size dictionary, a secretarial handbook, and a telephone directory.

Dictionaries

If you are to carry out your secretarial assignments efficiently and accurately, you should have a modern desk-size dictionary at your desk. You will find it indispensable in verifying the spelling, syllabication, and proper usage of words as you transcribe your employer's dictation. It contains not only the pronunciation and derivation of words but also the meaning of foreign expressions and standard abbreviations, the names of places and notable people, and other essential information.

If a desk-size dictionary is not readily available, you should invest in a paperback pocket-size one. Pocket dictionaries generally contain definitions; guides to correct spelling and pronunciation; lists of synonyms and antonyms; commonly used abbreviations, foreign words and phrases; and population figures for the United States and Canada.

Secretarial Handbooks

The secretary's handbook is a compact, thoroughly indexed reference book. It includes a wide range of secretarial procedures. It is an authoritative source of information on such topics as proper grammatical construction, plural and possessive forms, pronunciation and punctuation, and the correct writing of numbers in letters and reports. It can be a great help in deciding, for example, where to place the *subject line* in a business letter, whether to place the apostrophe before or after the letter *s* in *women's salaries*, and when to capitalize directions in geographic areas such as on the *East Coast* or in *western Montana*.

Some popular secretarial handbooks are:

Doris, Lillian, and Bessie May Miller. *Complete Secretary's Handbook*, 3d ed. Englewood Cliffs, N.J.: Prentice-Hall, Inc., 1970.

House, Clifford R., and Apollonia M. Koehele. *Reference Manual for Office Personnel*, 5th ed. Cincinnati: South-Western Publishing Co., 1970.

Hutchinson, Lois Irene. *Standard Handbook for Secretaries*, 8th ed. New York City: McGraw-Hill, Inc., 1969.

Telephone Directories

The most frequently consulted reference book in any office is the telephone directory. It is used not only to find the telephone numbers of listed subscribers but also to verify the spelling of their names and the correctness of their addresses. The Yellow Pages, or classified section of a telephone directory, may also serve as a buyer's guide because the names, addresses, and telephone numbers of business subscribers are listed under their product or service.

A small booklet supplied by the telephone company, designed for use as a personal telephone directory, can save considerable telephoning time. On alphabetically arranged pages it provides spaces for writing the names, addresses, area codes, and telephone numbers of frequently called local and out-of-town telephones.

Writing References

The content and format of all types of business communications can be improved if appropriate reference books are consulted.

Business Communications. A recommended reference book for the writing of business letters and other communications of a business nature is:

Wolf, Morris P., and Robert R. Aurner. *Effective Communication in Business*, 6th ed. Cincinnati: South-Western Publishing Co., 1974.

Business Reports. Manuals and style books are available to serve as references on how to present papers and reports. Two widely used manuals and a style book are listed below.

A Manual of Style. The University of Chicago. 12th ed., rev. Chicago: University of Chicago Press, 1969.

United States Government Printing Office Style Manual, rev. ed. Washington: U.S. Government Printing Office, 1973.

Perrin, Porter G. *Writer's Guide and Index to English*, 5th ed., Glenview, Illinois: Scott, Foresman and Company, 1972.

Business Speeches. A wide variety of reference books may be consulted to provide the prospective speaker or master of ceremonies at a business function with words, phrases, ideas, and quotations that will enhance and enliven a presentation. Some of these follow.

Bartlett, John. *Familiar Quotations*, 14th ed. Secaucus, N.J.: Citadel Press, 1971.

Fernald, James C. *Funk & Wagnalls Standard Handbook of Synonyms, Antonyms, and Prepositions*, rev. ed. New York City: Wilfred Funk, Inc., 1947.

Stevenson, Burton E. *Home Book of Quotations*, rev. ed. New York City: Dodd, Mead & Company, 1967.

Roget's Thesaurus of English Words and Phrases. New York City: World Pub., 1970.

Webster's New Dictionary of Synonyms. Springfield, Mass.: G & C. Merriam Company, 1973.

Specific References

Reference books in all fields from many different sources, ranging from the *American Library Association Catalog* to the *Zweng Aviation Dictionary*, are listed and annotated in a single volume, the *Guide to Reference Books*. To determine what, if any, reference books are available on a specific subject, the secretary should first consult this guide:

Winchell, Constance M. *Guide to Reference Books*, 8th ed. Chicago: American Library Association, 1967.

Specific information on business and related subjects may be obtained from many reference books. The information includes statistics on all major industries, directories of all large corporations, biographies of notable people, and factual information on a wide variety of business topics. The examples that follow are arranged alphabetically by subjects.

Accounting The standard handbook in which leading authorities cover the major divisions of accounting is:

Wixon, Rufus, *et. al. Accountants' Handbook*, 5th ed. New York City: The Ronald Press Company, 1970.

Almanacs. Published annually, there are four widely used and comprehensive American almanacs of miscellaneous information.

Information Please Almanac. New York City: Simon & Schuster, Inc.

New York Times Encyclopedic Almanac. New York City: Book and Educational Division, The New York Times Company.

Reader's Digest Almanac and Yearbook. Pleasantville, New York: The Reader's Digest Association, Inc.

World Almanac and Book of Facts. New York City: Doubleday & Company, Inc.

Banks. The Bankers Blue Book, one of the leading bank directories published semiannually with monthly supplements, is:

Rand-McNally Bankers Directory. Chicago: Rand-McNally & Company.

Biographical Information. Revised and reissued every two years, the best known and generally the most useful biographical dictionary, with full biographical sketches of approximately 73,000 notable living American men and women, is:

Who's Who in America. Chicago: Marquis-Who's Who, Inc.

Books. A complete list of all available books, new and old, including hardcovers, paperbacks, trade books, textbooks, and juvenile books is published annually with full ordering information in the following volumes:

Books in Print. Authors, Vol. I, New York City: R. R. Bowker Company.
Books in Print. Titles and Publishers, Vol. II, New York City: R. R. Bowker Company.
Subject Guide to Books in Print. A to J, Vol. I, New York City: R. R. Bowker Company.
Subject Guide to Books in Print. K to Z, Vol. II, New York City: R. R. Bowker Company.

A world list of books in the English language is published annually with monthly supplements in the following:

Cumulative Book Index. New York City: The H. W. Wilson Company.

Business Libraries. A reference book that should be consulted to be sure that the business library is used efficiently and that no available source of business information has been overlooked is:

Johnson, H. Webster. *How to Use the Business Library*, 4th ed. Cincinnati: South-Western Publishing Co., 1972.

City Directories. City directories are compiled, published, and sold commercially for most of the cities of the United States and Canada. Each directory contains the names, the addresses, and the occupations of all individuals residing in a community. It usually contains a street directory and a map of the city.

City Officials. A directory of city officials is usually published annually for each large city. The *City of New York Official Directory*, for example, lists all branches of the city government, the courts, and the state and federal government agencies with offices in New York City. It contains an index of the names of all executives listed in the directory.

> *The City of New York Official Directory.* Room 2213 Municipal Building, New York, NY 10007.

Colleges. A widely used college guide gives the entrance requirements, accreditation, and other factual information about more than 2,800 American colleges and universities. The guide also contains related information about junior colleges, community colleges, and technical institutes.

> Lovejoy, Clarence I. *Lovejoy's College Guide*, 12th ed. New York: Simon and Schuster, Inc., 1974.

A comparative guide to American colleges analyzes every accredited four-year college in the United States. It provides a basis for college selection with data on admission requirements, academic opportunities offered by the institution, special programs, faculty qualifications, and enrollment figures.

> Cass, James, and Max Birnbaum. *Comparative Guide to American Colleges*, 7th ed. New York City: Harper and Row, Publishers, 1975.

Junior Colleges. Information about the recognized, nonprofit junior colleges in the United States, the Canal Zone, and Puerto Rico is published by the American Council on Education. Information for each college includes: admission and graduate requirements, enrollment, curricula offered, calendar, staff, student aid, graduates, foreign students, library, publications, finances, buildings and grounds, history, control, and administrative officers.

> Gleazer, Edmund J. Jr. (ed.). *American Junior Colleges*, 8th ed. Washington: American Council on Education, 1971.

Congress. A directory containing the names, addresses, and brief biographies of all congressmen and chief executives of the federal government is issued annually. In it are also listed the members of all congressional committees, the executives of all departments and agencies of the federal government, and all diplomatic representatives.

> *Congressional Directory.* Superintendent of Documents, U.S. Government Printing Office. Washington, D.C. 20402.

Corporations. A complete national directory of executive personnel in approximately 28,000 companies engaged in all branches of business and industry is published in *Poor's Register of Corporations, Directors, and Executives.* Each company listing includes the names and addresses of all officers, directors, and other executive personnel; the number of employees and the approximate annual sales; and all products and services of the company in order of their importance.

The register is sold commercially and is not available in most public and high school libraries.

> *Standard and Poor's Register of Corporations, Directors, and Executives*. Standard & Poor's Corporation. New York, NY 10014.

Credit Ratings. Credit ratings and credit reports are distributed for retail, wholesale, and manufacturing companies. While the reports are not available to the general public, they may be obtained by annual subscription.

> *Dun & Bradstreet Ratings and Reports*. Dun & Bradstreet, Inc. New York, NY 10007.

Encyclopedias. Encyclopedias provide authoritative information on a great number of subjects in concise and convenient form. Because no other single reference book can offer so extensive a survey of universal knowledge, it is often wise to start an inquiry with an encyclopedia. Two encyclopedias are:

> *Encyclopedia Britannica* (30 volumes). 15th ed. Chicago: Encyclopedia Britannica, Inc., 1974.
> *Encyclopedia Americana* (30 volumes). New York: Grolier Incorporated, 1975.

A compact single-volume general encyclopedia available for instant reference with concise articles on places, persons, and subjects is published in hardcover and paper editions.

> *Columbia Viking Desk Encyclopedia*, 3d ed. New York: The Viking Press, Inc., 1968.

Etiquette. Business and social etiquette is covered in a number of books on etiquette but the two most prominent authors are:

> Post, Elizabeth L. *Emily Post's Etiquette*, 12th ed. New York: Funk & Wagnalls, Inc., 1968.
> Vanderbilt, Amy. *Amy Vanderbilt's Etiquette*. Garden City, New York: Doubleday & Company, Inc., 1972

Geographic Information. Atlases and gazetteers are reference sources for all kinds of geographical information. An atlas is a book of maps with supporting geographical, statistical and population figures for each area. Such a book may be an atlas of the world, of a country, of a state, of a county, or of a city. Two of the atlases frequently used in business offices are given on the following page.

Rand McNally New Cosmopolitan World Atlas, rev. ed. Chicago: Rand McNally & Company, 1975.

Hammond's Contemporary World Atlas New Census Edition: Garden City, New York: Doubleday & Company, Inc., 1971.

A gazetteer is a geographical dictionary giving, in alphabetic order, the names and descriptions of towns, villages, cities, rivers, mountains, and countries with pronunciations and related historical and geographical information. One of the most comprehensive gazetteers with information about all important places in the world and all incorporated cities, towns, and villages in the United States and Canada with populations of 1,500 or more is:

Webster's New Geographical Dictionary, rev. ed. Springfield, Mass.: G. & C. Merriam Company, 1972.

Law. A three-volume law directory, published annually, with a complete list of the lawyers in the United States and Canada given in Volumes I and II and digests of the laws of the states in the United States and the provinces of Canada in Volume III is available.

Martindale-Hubbell Law Directory. Summit, N.J.: Martindale-Hubbell, Inc.

Magazine Articles. Articles in a selected number of periodicals are indexed according to author, title, and subject. They are listed in an annual publication with monthly supplements that are available in all public libraries.

Readers' Guide to Periodical Literature. New York: The H. W. Wilson Company.

Manufacturers. A list of almost all American manufacturers with a classification of their products, trade names, and brands is published annually by the Thomas Publishing Company.

Thomas Register. New York: Thomas Publishing Company.

Medicine. A register of legally qualified physicians of the United States and Canada with related medical biographies and a list of approved medical schools and hospitals is published every two years.

American Medical Directory. Chicago: American Medical Association.

Newspaper Articles. All items and reports printed in the *New York Times* are briefly summarized, indexed, and cross-referenced by subject and name. They are listed alphabetically with the date, page, and column of publication.

New York Times Index. New York: The New York Times
Company.

Postal Information. A complete listing of the postal services in the United States with detailed regulations and procedures covering these services, together with up-to-date postal rates, is given in the following publication:

Postal Service Manual. Superintendent of Documents, U.S. Government Printing Office. Washington, DC 20402.

A directory of ZIP Codes for the entire United States is available:

The National ZIP Code Directory. Superintendent of Documents, U.S. Government Printing Office. Washington, DC 20402.

Shipping Information. Shipments are frequently made by means other than parcel post — by rail, truck, bus, ship, and, more frequently, by air express. A complete shipper's guide containing rates and routings for parcel post, express, and freight shipments is published in separate editions for different parts of the country. This guide also includes information concerning Canadian and foreign parcel post.

Leonard's Guide. New York: G. R. Leonard & Company, Inc.

A complete list of all post offices, railroad stations, shipping lines, and freight receiving stations is published.

Bullinger's Postal Shipper's Guide for the United States, Canada, and Newfoundland. Bullinger's Guides, Inc., Westwood, New Jersey.

Travel Information. Travel information is available in many forms of guide books, bulletins, and directories.

Guides. Ratings for approximately 20,000 accommodations and restaurants in the United States are published in the paperback editions of the *Mobil Travel Guides* by Simon & Schuster, Inc., New York City. The guides also list the outstanding historical, educational, and scenic points of interest throughout the country. Regional guide books are revised and reprinted annually for California and the West, the Great Lakes Area, the Middle Atlantic States, the Northwest and Great Plains States, the Northeastern States, the Southeastern States, and the Southwest and South Central Area.

Bulletins. Travel bulletins may be obtained from all travel agencies. Two of the better known agencies with offices in all the principal cities of the world are *Thomas Cook & Son* and the *American Express Company*.

Directories. The most frequently consulted directory which annually lists hotels and motels approved by the American Hotel Association with their respective rates, accommodations, and plans of operation is:

Hotel & Motel Red Book. New York : American Hotel Association Directory Corporation.

Overseas Guides. Overseas airlines have guides that contain travel information. A popular guide is:

Fodor's Europe, 1976. New York: David McKay Co., Inc.

Separate editions of Fodor's guides are published for other continents, principal countries, and cities of the world.

Index

envelopes:
addressing, 103
business reply, 114
chain feeding, 272–273
interoffice, 114
precanceled, 263
sealing, 262
stamped, 263
standard sizes, 113
items to check before mailing, 266
window, 113
equipment:
at secretarial work station, 31
word processing, 58
erasing:
basic procedure, 59
in legal documents, 187
on offset master, 369
exclamation point, 646
executives:
appointment policies, 289–290
dictating styles, 42–43
expense reports, 516, 517
expenses:
deductible and non-deductible, 549
expense report forms, 547
express mail, 280
Express and Parcel Post Comparative Rate Guide, 279

F

federal employment:
age requirement, 603
citizenship requirement, 604
civil service tests for, 602
overseas opportunities, 604
physical condition for, 604
qualifications for stenographer and typist, 603
files:
card, of callers, 296
card, 477
central, 386
elevator, 482
lateral, 427
managed by secretary, 386
random, 481
rotary, 481
shelf, 427
tickler, 34, 388, 455
vertical, 426
visible card, 479
filing equipment, *see* files, filing supplies
filing guides, 428–429, 442
filing procedures:
arranging materials in folders, 345
basic steps, illustrated, 444
coding, 440
coded letter, illustrated, 441
collecting papers, 438
cross-referencing, 440, 442, 464
efficiency in, 386, 445

filing, defined, 386
indexing, 439
inspecting, 439
placing records in files, 443
release mark, 439
sorting, 442
filing rules, *see* alphabetic indexing for individuals, alphabetic indexing for business firms and other organizations
filing supplies:
accessories, 434, 447
drawer labels, 433
folder labels, 432
folders, 430–432, 445, 453, 456
guides, 428–429, 442
filing systems:
alphabetic name, 387
alphabetic subject, 387
chronological, 388
combination subject and name, 464
geographic, 387, 470–472, 474
how to design, 487
microfilming, 386, 483
numeric, 388
"office-made", 473
tab positions for guides and folders, 433–434
tickler, 388
see also alphabetic indexing for business firms and other organizations, alphabetic indexing for individuals
financial records:
budget, 533
increasing need for, 559
payroll, 55
petty cash fund, 557
see also banking transactions, payments, income tax record-keeping
financial statements:
balance sheet, 174
checking accuracy of, 175
guidelines for typing, 176–177
income statement, 174
proofreading, 180
first-class mail, 266
fiscal year, 174, 553
flow chart, 217, 219
flow chart symbols, 217–218
fluid duplication:
correcting errors in master, 377
features of, 375
preparing master for, 376–378
principles of, 376
folder, travel, 509
folder labels, 432
folders:
arranging materials in, 445
capacity of, 431
captions on, 432
carrier, 453
dated follow-up, 456
hanging, 430
individual, 431, 445
legal size, 430
letter size, 430

miscellaneous, 431, 445
out, 453
special, 431, 445
straight cut, 430
tab widths and positions, 430
follow-up:
card tickler file, 455
dated follow-up folder, 456
follow-up letter:
after interview, 591
in business correspondence, 136
footnotes in a report, 152, 165
form letters:
defined, 140
to prospective customers, 141
requesting reference, 142
forms, *see* business forms
fourth-class mail (parcel post), 267
fourth-class mail, for shipping, 279
full-keyboard listing machine, 225
full-rate telegram, 348

G

geographic files:
defined, 387
advantages and disadvantages, 470, 474
captions for, 471
card index used with, 472
cross-referencing, 472
guides and folders used in, 470–472
procedures, 472
uses of, 470
geographic names, capitalization of, 667
government:
forms of address for officials, 671–674
jobs, *see* federal employment
grammar, 624–639
grammar reference books, 639
graphs:
circle, illustrated, 181
line, illustrated, 181
greeting callers, 288–289
guide sheets for reports, 155
guides:
captions on, 428
cross-reference, permanent, 442
number per drawer, 429
primary, 429
secondary, 429

H

Handbook for the Legal Secretary, 596
handbooks, secretarial, 678
handwriting, neatness in, 24
hard copy, defined, 484
headings in a report:
division, 164
main, 160